메가스터디 N제

영어영역 어법·어휘

222제

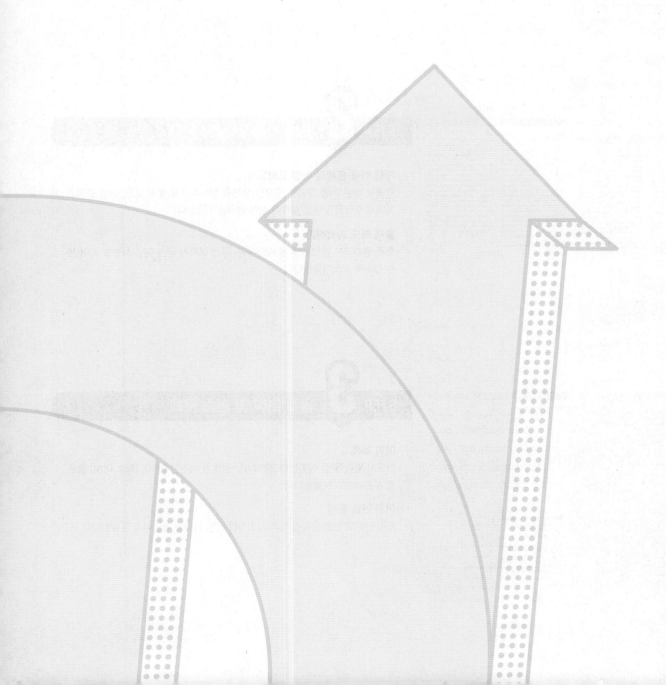

구성과 특징 STRUCTURE

☑ 본 교재는 수능 영어영역에 출제되는 어법과 어휘 유형을 완벽히 대비하기 위한 교재임과 동시에, 모든 영어 독해의 기본인 어법 · 어휘 실력 자체를 탄탄히 갖추도록 해주는 교재입니다. 다양한 기출 및 기출 응용 문제, 예상 문제로 체계적 학습을 하도록 합니다.

STEP 1 어법 개념 학습 및 확인 문제

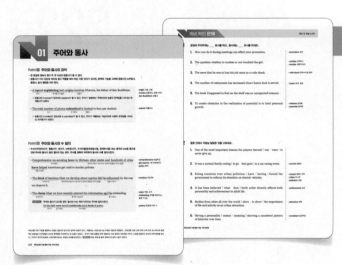

어법 개념 설명
최근 수능에서 자주 출제되고 있는 어법 개념을 크게 9가지로 분류하였으며, 각각을 더욱 세분화된 개념으로 학습합니다.

개념 확인 문제
문장 단위의 확인 문제를 통해 배운 어법 개념을 점검해 봅니다.

STEP 2 개념 적용 및 실전 문제

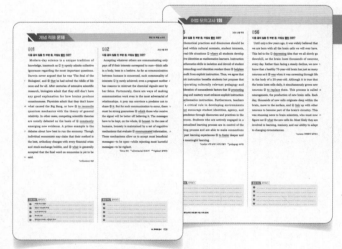

개념 적용 문제와 어법 모의고사
앞에서 배운 어법 개념을 적용한 문제를 집중적으로 풀어 보고, 어법 모의고사에서 종합적인 어법 실력과 실전 감각을 기릅니다.

출제 의도 파악하기
자주 출제되는 어법 사항을 파악하여, 각 선택지가 묻는 어법 사항을 적어 볼 수 있도록 구성하였습니다.

STEP 3 필수 어휘 및 연습 문제

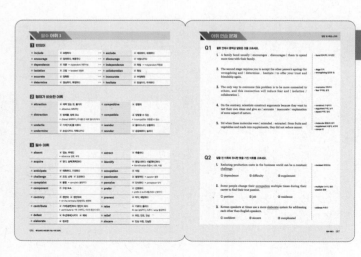

어휘 목록
반드시 알아야 할 어휘들을 [반의어], [형태가 비슷한 어휘], [필수 어휘] 등으로 분류해 제시하였습니다.

어휘 연습 문제
문장 단위의 연습 문제를 통해 기초적인 어휘 실력을 확인하고 점검합니다.

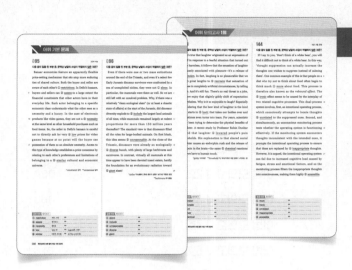

STEP **4** 어휘 기본 및 실전 문제

어휘 기본 문제와 어휘 모의고사

앞에서 배운 어휘를 포함한 다양한 어휘로 구성된 문제를 풀어 보고, 어휘 모의고사에서 어휘 실력을 탄탄히 쌓고 실전 감각을 기릅니다.

출제 어휘 확인하기

출제된 밑줄 또는 네모 어휘의 뜻을 써 보고 반의어도 함께 암기할 수 있도록 구성하였습니다.

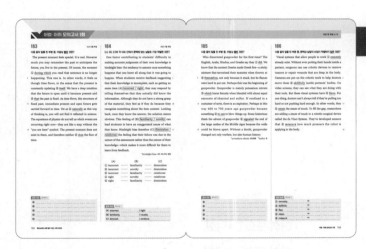

STEP **5** 어법 · 어휘 모의고사

어법과 어휘를 모두 학습한 후, 실전 감각을 익힐 수 있도록 8문항으로 구성한 모의고사 5회분을 제공합니다.

친절하고 자세한 해설

모든 문제에 전문해석, 정답풀이, 오답풀이, 구문풀이와 어휘풀이까지 친절하고 자세한 해설을 제공합니다.

 미니 단어장

메가스터디 N제
영어 어법·어휘
단어장

222제

들고 다니면서 외울 수 있도록
전체 문항의 중요 어휘들만 모아
별책의 미니단어장으로 구성하였습니다.

차례 CONTENTS

N I 어법

| 필수 개념

학습 내용	학습일	맞은 문항 수
01 주어와 동사	월 일	/ 6문항
02 동사의 활용	월 일	/ 6문항
03 to부정사와 동명사	월 일	/ 6문항
04 분사	월 일	/ 6문항
05 명사와 대명사	월 일	/ 6문항
06 형용사와 부사	월 일	/ 6문항
07 관계사	월 일	/ 6문항
08 전치사와 접속사	월 일	/ 6문항
09 병렬구조 및 특수구문	월 일	/ 6문항

| 어법 모의고사

학습 내용	학습일	맞은 문항 수
어법 모의고사 1회	월 일	/ 8문항
어법 모의고사 2회	월 일	/ 8문항
어법 모의고사 3회	월 일	/ 8문항
어법 모의고사 4회	월 일	/ 8문항
어법 모의고사 5회	월 일	/ 8문항

01 주어와 동사

Point 1 주어와 동사의 파악

– 한 문장에 접속사 없이 두 개 이상의 본동사가 올 수 없다.
– 본동사가 이미 있는데 의미상 동사 역할을 해야 하는 다른 단어가 있다면, 문맥과 기능을 고려해 준동사인 to부정사, 동명사, 분사 형태로 써야 한다.

- A legend **explaining** tea's origins involves Dharma, the father of Zen Buddhism.
  주어 / 현재분사구(능동) / 본동사

  ➡ 본동사인 involves가 있으므로 explains가 될 수 없고, 수식을 받는 주어가 '설명하는' 주체이므로 능동의 관계임을 나타내는 현재분사가 쓰였다.

- The total number of photos **submitted** is limited to four per student.
  주어 / 과거분사 / 본동사

  ➡ 본동사인 is limited가 있으므로 is submitted가 될 수 없고, 수식을 받는 주어가 '제출되는' 대상이므로 수동의 관계임을 나타내는 과거분사가 쓰였다.

- **origin** 기원, 근원
- **involve** 포함하다, 관련시키다
- **Zen Buddhism** 선불교

- **submit** 제출하다

Point 2 주어와 동사의 수 일치

– 수식어구(전치사구, 형용사구, 분사구, to부정사구), 수식어절(관계대명사절, 관계부사절) 또는 동격의 that절 등으로 인해 주어와 동사가 멀리 떨어져 있는 경우, 주어를 정확히 파악하여 동사의 수를 일치시킨다.

- Comprehensive no-smoking **laws** in thirteen other states and hundreds of cities
  주어(복수) / 전치사구(주어-동사의 수 일치에 영향을 미치지 않음)

  have helped Americans get used to similar policies.
  본동사(복수)

- **comprehensive** 포괄적인
- **get used to** ~에 익숙해지다
- **policy** 정책

- The **kind** of intuition [that we develop about marine life] **is** influenced by the way
  주어(단수) / 관계대명사절(주어-동사의 수 일치에 영향을 미치지 않음) / 본동사(단수)

  we observe it.

- **intuition** 직관(력)

- The **claim** [that we have recently entered the information age] **is** misleading.
  주어(단수) / 동격의 that절 / 동사(단수)

  어법 Plus 주어와 동사가 도치된 경우, 동사의 수는 뒤에 이어지는 주어에 일치시킨다.

  On the desk **were** several **notebooks** and **a book** of poetry.
  부사구 / 동사(복수) / 주어(복수)

- **claim** 주장, 요구
- **misleading** 오해를 일으키는, 잘못 이끄는

- **poetry** (장르로서의) 시

Point 1 차의 기원을 설명하는 전설은 선불교의 창시자인 달마와 관련이 있다. / 제출되는 사진의 총 수는 학생당 4장으로 제한된다. **Point 2** 다른 13개 주와 수백 개의 도시에서의 포괄적인 금연법은 미국인들이 비슷한 정책들에 익숙해지는 데 도움이 되었다. / 우리가 해양 생물에 관해 계발하는 이런 종류의 직관력은 우리가 그것을 관찰하는 방식에 의해 영향을 받는다. / 우리가 최근에 정보화 시대에 들어섰다는 주장은 오해를 일으킨다. **어법 Plus** 책상 위에 몇 권의 공책과 한 권의 시집이 있었다.

⊘ 출제 Point

1. 주어와 동사를 찾는다.
2. 본동사의 형태가 적절한지 파악한다.
3. 주어와 본동사의 수 일치를 확인한다.

– 동명사(구), to부정사(구), 명사절(that절, whether절, 의문사절)이 주어로 쓰인 경우, 하나의 개념으로 보아 단수로 취급하고 단수형 동사를 쓴다.

- **Building** new golf courses **is** the fastest kind of land development in the world.
  주어(동명사구 = 단수)　　　　　　　동사(단수)

  • **land development** 토지 개발

- **Whether** an animal can feel anything **❶**[resembling the loneliness **❷**{humans
  주어(접속사 Whether가 이끄는 명사절 = 단수)

  • **resemble** 닮다, 비슷하다

  feel}] **is** hard to say.
  동사(단수)

  어법 Plus　❶ anything을 수식하는 현재분사구
  　　　　　❷ the loneliness를 수식하는 목적격 관계대명사절(앞에 관계대명사 that 생략)

Point ❸ 선행사와 주격 관계대명사절 동사의 수 일치

– 주격 관계대명사절의 동사는 선행사에 수를 일치시킨다.

- Many people face **barriers** in their environment [that **prevent** healthy life
  선행사(복수)　　　　　　　　　　　　　　주격 관계대명사절의 동사(복수)

  • **face** 마주하다, 직면하다
  • **barrier** 장벽

  styles].

Point ❹ 형식상의 주어 - 내용상의 주어

– 길이가 긴 to부정사구 또는 that절을 주어로 쓸 경우, 보통 형식상의 주어인 it을 앞에 쓰고 내용상의 주어를 뒤에 쓴다.

- The words [you speak to someone] may have the potential to make or break that
  주어　　　목적격 관계대명사절(that 생략)　　동사

  • **potential** 가능성

  person, so **it** is important **to choose** words carefully.
  형식상의 주어　　　　　　내용상의 주어(to부정사구)

- **It** is highly desirable **that** you learn how to write effective memos.
  형식상의 주어　　　　　　　　　내용상의 주어(that절)

  • **highly** 매우
  • **desirable** 바람직한
  • **effective** 효과적인

새로운 골프장을 짓는 것이 세상에서 가장 빠른 토지 개발 방법이다. / 인간이 느끼는 외로움과 유사한 어떤 것을 동물이 느낄 수 있는지는 말하기 어렵다. **Point ❸** 많은 사람들은 자신의 환경에서 건강에 좋은 생활 방식을 가로막는 장벽을 마주한다. **Point ❹** 여러분이 누군가에게 하는 말이 그 사람을 성공하게 하거나 실패하게 할 가능성을 지닐 수도 있으므로 말을 신중하게 선택하는 것이 중요하다. / 효과적인 메모를 작성하는 법을 배우는 것은 매우 바람직하다.

Q1 문장의 주어부에는 ____ 표시를 하고, 동사에는 ____ 표시를 하세요.

1. How you do it during meetings can affect your promotion.

- **promotion** 승진

2. The question whether to confess or not troubled the girl.

- **confess** 고백하다
- **trouble** 괴롭게 하다

3. The news that he was to lose his job came as a rude shock.

- **rude shock** 갑작스러운 충격

4. The number of restaurants has increased where fusion food is served.

- **fusion** 퓨전, 융합

5. The book I happened to find on the shelf was an unexpected treasure.

6. To create obstacles to the realization of potential is to limit personal growth.

- **obstacle** 장애물
- **potential** 잠재력

Q2 괄호 안에서 어법상 알맞은 것을 고르세요.

1. One of the most important lessons the players learned [was / were] to never give up.

2. It was a normal family outing [to go / that goes] to a car racing event.

- **normal** 보통의

3. Rising concerns over urban pollution [have / having] forced the government to refocus its attention on electric vehicles.

- **concern** 염려, 우려
- **urban** 도시의
- **pollution** 오염

4. It has been believed [what / that] birth order directly affects both personality and achievement in adult life.

- **achievement** 성취

5. Studies from cities all over the world [show / to show] the importance of life and activity as an urban attraction.

- **attraction** 매력

6. Having a personality [means / meaning] showing a consistent pattern of behavior over time.

- **consistent** 일관적인

001

다음 글의 밑줄 친 부분 중, 어법상 틀린 것은?

Modern-day science is a unique tradition of knowledge, inasmuch as ① it openly admits collective ignorance regarding the most important questions. Darwin never argued that he was 'The Seal of the Biologists', and ② that he had solved the riddle of life once and for all. After centuries of extensive scientific research, biologists admit that they still don't have any good explanation for how brains produce consciousness. Physicists admit that they don't know what caused the Big Bang, or how ③ to reconcile quantum mechanics with the theory of general relativity. In other cases, competing scientific theories are noisily debated on the basis of ④ constantly emerging new evidence. A prime example is the debates about how best to run the economy. Though individual economists may claim that their method is the best, orthodoxy changes with every financial crisis and stock-exchange bubble, and ⑤ what is generally accepted that the final word on economics is yet to be said.

*orthodoxy 정설

002

2022 9월 모평

다음 글의 밑줄 친 부분 중, 어법상 틀린 것은?

Accepting whatever others are communicating only pays off if their interests correspond to ours—think cells in a body, bees in a beehive. As far as communication between humans is concerned, such commonality of interests ① is rarely achieved; even a pregnant mother has reasons to mistrust the chemical signals sent by her fetus. Fortunately, there are ways of making communication work even in the most adversarial of relationships. A prey can convince a predator not to chase ② it. But for such communication to occur, there must be strong guarantees ③ which those who receive the signal will be better off believing it. The messages have to be kept, on the whole, ④ honest. In the case of humans, honesty is maintained by a set of cognitive mechanisms that evaluate ⑤ communicated information. These mechanisms allow us to accept most beneficial messages—to be open—while rejecting most harmful messages—to be vigilant.

*fetus 태아 **adversarial 반대자의 ***vigilant 경계하는

출제 의도 파악하기

① 대명사의 수 일치

② 접속사 that의 쓰임

③ to부정사의 쓰임

④ 부사의 쓰임

⑤ 형식상의 주어와 내용상의 주어

출제 의도 파악하기

①

②

③

④

⑤

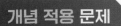

003

다음 글의 밑줄 친 부분 중, 어법상 <u>틀린</u> 것은?

In some countries there is a trend towards shorter workweeks, more flexible working practices, and earlier retirement. But combined with this the age distribution ① <u>being</u> gradually changing in the countries that enjoy
5 much of the increase in disposable income. The populations of these countries are getting older and, indeed, in many countries the reproduction rate is insufficient ② <u>to maintain</u> the population levels. Italy's population, for example, ③ <u>is forecast</u> to decline by
10 30% by 2050. This older population has more leisure time as it reaches retirement and is ④ <u>generally</u> fitter and more active than previous generations. These features, combined with greater ⑤ <u>accumulated</u> wealth, allow for more tourism and other leisure
15 activities. Some of this is quite localized in terms of traveling to eat out or to some local recreational site such as a sports club.

004

2024 9월 모평

다음 글의 밑줄 친 부분 중, 어법상 <u>틀린</u> 것은?

Viewing the stress response as a resource can transform the physiology of fear into the biology of courage. It can turn a threat into a challenge and can help you ① <u>do</u> your best under pressure. Even when the stress doesn't feel helpful—as in the case of anxiety— 5 welcoming it can transform ② <u>it</u> into something that is helpful: more energy, more confidence, and a greater willingness to take action. You can apply this strategy in your own life anytime you notice signs of stress. When you feel your heart beating or your breath 10 quickening, ③ <u>realizing</u> that it is your body's way of trying to give you more energy. If you notice tension in your body, remind yourself ④ <u>that</u> the stress response gives you access to your strength. Sweaty palms? Remember what it felt like ⑤ <u>to go</u> on your first date— 15 palms sweat when you're close to something you want.

*physiology 생리 기능

출제 의도 파악하기
❶ ⟶
❷ ⟶
❸ ⟶
❹ ⟶
❺ ⟶

출제 의도 파악하기
❶ ⟶
❷ ⟶
❸ ⟶
❹ ⟶
❺ ⟶

005

다음 글의 밑줄 친 부분 중, 어법상 틀린 것은?

The industry is composed of different individuals who each perform specific tasks or labour within some or other institution such as an organization. The fact that major or small differences exist between individuals and between the various jobs that they do, ① form the basis of the efficient functioning of such organizations or institutions. It is also closely linked to the function of personnel management as such because it is the explicit task of the personnel department ② to prevent the occurrence of "square pegs in round holes". In other words, a personnel manager must be mindful of individual differences and have sufficient knowledge of the differences between people in order to make sure ③ that every individual or employee is suited to and happy in his/her job. This task becomes extremely complicated when different institutions ④ are taken into consideration. Similar types of individuals may well perform ⑤ similarly doing the same tasks but their performance would differ within different institutions or working groups.

*square pegs in round holes 부적임자

006

다음 글의 밑줄 친 부분 중, 어법상 틀린 것은?

Consider *The Wizard of Oz* as a psychological study of motivation. Dorothy and her three friends work hard to get to the Emerald City, overcoming barriers, persisting against all adversaries. They do so because they expect the Wizard to give ① them what they are missing. Instead, the wonderful (and wise) Wizard makes them aware that they, not he, always had the power ② to fulfill their wishes. For Dorothy, *home* is not a place but a feeling of security, of comfort with people she loves; it is wherever her heart is. The courage the Lion wants, the intelligence the Scarecrow longs for, and the emotions the Tin Man dreams of ③ being attributes they already possess. They need to think about these attributes not as internal conditions but as positive ways ④ in which they are already relating to others. After all, didn't they demonstrate those qualities on the journey to Oz, a journey ⑤ motivated by little more than an *expectation*, an idea about the future likelihood of getting something they wanted?

*adversary 적(상대)

출제 의도 파악하기

❶
❷
❸
❹
❺

출제 의도 파악하기

❶
❷
❸
❹
❺

02 동사의 활용

Point 1 능동태와 수동태

- 주어가 동작의 주체일 때는 능동태로 나타내고, 주어가 동작의 대상일 때는 수동태(be p.p.)로 나타낸다.
- 자동사는 목적어를 취하지 않으므로 수동태로 쓸 수 없다.

- Special radar systems **are being installed** at major airports to detect
  be being p.p.(현재진행형 + 수동태)
  unpredictable thunderstorms.

- install 설치하다
- detect 탐지하다
- unpredictable 예기치 못한
- thunderstorm 폭풍우

- 능동태인 「지각동사/사역동사 + 목적어 + 목적격보어(원형부정사)」 구조가 수동태로 전환되면 목적격보어로 쓰인 원형부정사를 to부정사로 바꿔 써야 한다.

- [능동태] I saw her **get** into a large and very expensive-looking car.
  지각동사   목적격보어(원형부정사)

  → [수동태] She was seen **to get** into a large and very expensive-looking car by me.
  지각동사   to부정사로 바뀜

- get into ~에 타다

- 「동사 + 명사 + 전치사」 또는 「동사 + 전치사/부사」로 이루어진 구동사의 수동태 어순에 주의한다.

- [능동태] The resourceful team **took advantage of** the opportunity.
  동사 + 명사 + 전치사

  → [수동태] The opportunity **was taken advantage of** by the resourceful team.

- resourceful 수완이 뛰어난
- take advantage of ~을 활용하다

어법 Plus take care of ~을 돌보다 / make use of ~을 이용하다
come up with ~을 생각해 내다 / get along with ~와 잘 지내다
refer to ~ as ... ~을 …라고 부르다 / watch out for ~을 주의하다

Point 2 조동사

- 「may/must/cannot have p.p.」는 과거의 일에 대한 추측이나 확신을 나타내며 「should[ought to] have p.p.」는 과거의 일에 대한 후회나 유감을 나타낸다.

- I **should have got** a better price for the car but I'm not a very good businessman.
  should have p.p.: ~했어야 하는데 (하지 못했다)

어법 Plus should have p.p. ~했어야 하는데 (하지 못했다) / must have p.p. ~했음에 틀림없다
would have p.p. ~했을 것이다 / cannot have p.p. ~했을 리가 없다
may[might] have p.p. ~했을지도 모른다

Point 1 예기치 못한 폭풍우를 탐지하기 위해 특수 레이더 시스템이 주요 공항에 설치되고 있다. / 나는 그녀가 크고 매우 비싸 보이는 자동차에 타는 것을 보았다. / 수완이 뛰어난 팀이 기회를 활용했다. **Point 2** 그 차에 대해 값을 더 잘 받았어야 하지만 나는 별로 훌륭한 사업가가 못 된다.

– 조동사가 쓰인 문장이 수동태로 전환되면 「조동사 + be p.p.」 형태가 된다.

• The decision **should be made** by the current committee before the deadline.
　　　　　　　　조동사 + be p.p.

• committee 위원회

Point 3 주장, 요구, 명령, 제안 동사의 목적어로 쓰인 that절의 동사

– 주장(insist), 요구(require, demand), 명령(order), 제안(suggest, propose)을 나타내는 동사의 목적어로 쓰인 that절
에 당위성이 나타나 있을 경우, that절의 동사는 「(should) + 동사원형」 형태로 쓴다.

• They **insist** [that a female lawyer **represent** the female defendant].
　　　　　동사(주장)　　　　　that절 주어　　　that절 동사(동사원형)

➡ insist의 목적어 역할을 하는 that절의 주어가 3인칭 단수이지만 당위성이 나타나 있으므로 that절 동사로 should가 생략
된 represent가 쓰였다. (represents ✕)

어법 Plus　당위성이 없을 경우에 that절 동사는 that절 주어에 맞춰 쓴다.
The study suggests that the food is nutritious.
　　　　　　동사(시사하다: 당위 ✕)　　　be(✕)

• insist 주장하다, 고집하다
• represent 변호하다, 대표하다
• defendant 피고인, 피고측

• nutritious 영양가가 높은

Point 4 대동사

– 일반동사가 쓰인 동사(구)가 반복될 때 대동사를 쓸 수 있으며, do동사를 사용한다.

• They **rode their bicycles to school together** that morning, as they usually **did**.
　　　　일반동사(ride-rode-ridden)가 쓰인 동사구　　　　　　　　　　대동사(= rode ~ together)

• ride 타다

– be동사나 조동사가 쓰인 동사(구)가 반복될 때 be동사와 조동사 뒤에 반복되는 부분을 생략할 수 있다.

• The team **was exhausted after the game**, but their spirits **were not**.
　　　　　be동사가 쓰인 동사구　　　　　　　　　　　　　(exhausted after the game)

• exhausted 지친, 기진맥진한
• spirit 정신

• I **would gladly run for class president** if I **could**.
　　　　조동사가 쓰인 동사구　　　　　　　　(run for the class president)

• run for ~에 입후보하다

현재 위원회는 마감일 전에 결정을 내려야 한다. **Point 3** 그들은 여성 변호사가 그 여성 피고인을 대변해야 한다고 주장한다. / 어법 Plus 그 연구는 그 식품이 영양가가 풍부하다는 것을 시
사한다. **Point 4** 그날 아침 그들은 평소에 그랬던 것처럼 자전거를 타고 함께 등교했다. / 경기 후 팀은 지쳐 있었지만 그들의 정신은 그렇지 않았다. / 만약 할 수 있다면 나는 반장 선거에 기
꺼이 출마할 것이다.

개념 확인 문제

Q1 괄호 안에서 어법상 알맞은 것을 고르세요.

1. I regret having paid little attention to him. In other words, I [paid / should have paid] more attention to him.

• pay attention 주의를 기울이다

2. Tara insisted that I [try / tried] on her glasses. So I put them on, and the world turned into fuzzy shapes.

• fuzzy 흐릿한

3. Being the brightest member of my class, I [asked / was asked] to recite a rather lengthy poem for a school event.

• recite 암송하다, 낭독하다
• lengthy (길이가) 긴
• poem 시

4. Emily's belongings suggested that she [be / was] a physician.

• belongings 소지품
• physician 내과의사

5. The government was made [cancelled / to cancel] the plan because of public opinion.

• cancel 취소하다
• public opinion 여론

Q2 밑줄 친 부분을 어법상 알맞게 고쳐 쓰세요.

1. Henry's father was a house painter. In his lifetime, he <u>must paint</u> hundreds of houses, inside and out.

➡ _____

2. The brain activity of volunteers will be <u>monitoring</u> as they read classical works.

➡ _____

• volunteer 지원자, 자원자
• monitor 추적 관찰하다, 감시하다

3. The project <u>was to as referred</u> a groundbreaking achievement in the industry.

➡ _____

• groundbreaking 획기적인

4. A child who has been repeatedly <u>criticizing</u> for poor performance on math may learn to dodge difficult math problems in order to avoid further punishment.

➡ _____

• dodge (이리저리) 피하다, 면하다
• punishment 처벌

007

2023 9월 모평

다음 글의 밑줄 친 부분 중, 어법상 틀린 것은?

Recognizing ethical issues is the most important step in understanding business ethics. An ethical issue is an identifiable problem, situation, or opportunity that requires a person to choose from among several actions that may ① be evaluated as right or wrong, ethical or unethical. ② Learn how to choose from alternatives and make a decision requires not only good personal values, but also knowledge competence in the business area of concern. Employees also need to know when to rely on their organizations' policies and codes of ethics or ③ have discussions with co-workers or managers on appropriate conduct. Ethical decision making is not always easy because there are always gray areas ④ that create dilemmas, no matter how decisions are made. For instance, should an employee report on a co-worker engaging in time theft? Should a salesperson leave out facts about a product's poor safety record in his presentation to a customer? Such questions require the decision maker to evaluate the ethics of his or her choice and decide ⑤ whether to ask for guidance.

008

다음 글의 밑줄 친 부분 중, 어법상 틀린 것은?

Anytime people or groups appear to be cruel to one another, the popular, inadequate view is that it is an example of "survival of the fittest." Many people wrongly assume that, in society as well as in nature, ① to be strong and aggressive is the only condition for survival. In fact, however, evolution requires creatures to show a whole range of different behaviors, not just cruelty, in order to ② successfully ensure their survival. Many animals, including our nearest relatives such as chimpanzees and bonobos, rely on each other for survival, ③ which means that caring and sympathetic behavior is one of the key factors in their evolution. For example, in Tai National Park, Ivory Coast, chimpanzees have been seen ④ take care of group mates wounded by leopards by carefully removing blood and dirt and waving away flies that gather near the wounds. They protect their injured mates, and travel slowly if they cannot keep up. All of this makes perfect sense given ⑤ that chimpanzees live in groups, like wolves, dolphins and humans.

*bonobo 보노보(침팬지의 일종)

출제 의도 파악하기
1 ....
2 ....
3 ....
4 ....
5 ....

출제 의도 파악하기
1 ....
2 ....
3 ....
4 ....
5 ....

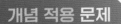

009

2022 6월 모평

다음 글의 밑줄 친 부분 중, 어법상 **틀린** 것은?

Most historians of science point to the need for a reliable calendar to regulate agricultural activity as the motivation for learning about what we now call astronomy, the study of stars and planets. Early
5 astronomy provided information about when to plant crops and gave humans ① their first formal method of recording the passage of time. Stonehenge, the 4,000-year-old ring of stones in southern Britain, ② is perhaps the best-known monument to the discovery of
10 regularity and predictability in the world we inhabit. The great markers of Stonehenge point to the spots on the horizon ③ where the sun rises at the solstices and equinoxes—the dates we still use to mark the beginnings of the seasons. The stones may even have
15 ④ been used to predict eclipses. The existence of Stonehenge, built by people without writing, bears silent testimony both to the regularity of nature and to the ability of the human mind to see behind immediate appearances and ⑤ discovers deeper meanings in
20 events.

*monument 기념비 **eclipse (해·달의) 식(蝕)
***testimony 증언

010

다음 글의 밑줄 친 부분 중, 어법상 **틀린** 것은?

I have emphasized how the country has to act together, cooperatively, if the country's problems are to be solved. Government is the formal institution ① through which we act together, collectively, to solve the nation's problems. Inevitably, individuals will differ 5 in their views of ② what should be done. That's one of the reasons that collective action is so difficult. There needs to be compromise, and compromise has to be based on trust: one group gives in today, in the understanding that another ③ is in another year. 10 There must be trust ④ that all will be treated fairly, and if matters turn out differently from how the proponents of a measure claim it will, there will be change to accommodate the unexpected circumstances. But it's easier to act together if the interests and 15 perspectives of the members of a group are at least loosely ⑤ aligned; if everyone is, as it were, in the same boat.

출제 의도 파악하기
❶
❷
❸
❹
❺

출제 의도 파악하기
❶
❷
❸
❹
❺

011
2023 수능 응용

다음 글의 밑줄 친 부분 중, 어법상 틀린 것은?

Different parts of the brain's visual system ① get information on a need-to-know basis. Cells that help your hand muscles reach out to an object need to know the size and location of the object, but they don't need to know about color. They need to know a little about shape, but not in great detail. Cells that help you recognize people's faces need to be ② extremely sensitive to details of shape, but they can pay less attention to location. It is natural to assume that anyone who sees an object ③ seeing everything about it—the shape, color, location, and movement. However, one part of your brain sees its shape, another sees color, another detects location, and another perceives movement. Consequently, after localized brain damage, it is possible to see certain aspects of an object and not others. Centuries ago, people found it difficult to imagine ④ how someone could see an object without seeing what color it is. Even today, you might find it surprising to learn about people who see an object without seeing where it is, or see it without seeing whether it is ⑤ moving.

012
2021 9월 모평

다음 글의 밑줄 친 부분 중, 어법상 틀린 것은?

Competitive activities can be more than just performance showcases ① which the best is recognized and the rest are overlooked. The provision of timely, constructive feedback to participants on performance ② is an asset that some competitions and contests offer. In a sense, all competitions give feedback. For many, this is restricted to information about whether the participant is an award- or prizewinner. The provision of that type of feedback can be interpreted as shifting the emphasis to demonstrating superior performance but not ③ necessarily excellence. The best competitions promote excellence, not just winning or "beating" others. The emphasis on superiority is what we typically see as ④ fostering a detrimental effect of competition. Performance feedback requires that the program go beyond the "win, place, or show" level of feedback. Information about performance can be very helpful, not only to the participant who does not win or place but also to those who ⑤ do.

*foster 조장하다 **detrimental 유해한

출제 의도 파악하기

❶ ....

❷ ....

❸ ....

❹ ....

❺ ....

출제 의도 파악하기

❶ ....

❷ ....

❸ ....

❹ ....

❺ ....

03 to부정사와 동명사

Point 1 to부정사의 용법

- to부정사는 명사적 용법(주어, 목적어, 보어 역할), 형용사적 용법(명사(구) 수식), 부사적 용법(목적, 결과, 조건 등의 의미)으로 쓰인다.

- My aspiration is **to become** a famous pianist.
  보어(명사적 용법)

- One way **to make** a pursuer work harder is to zigzag.
  명사구 수식(형용사적 용법)

- I took a day's vacation **to escape** the workplace stresses.
  목적(부사적 용법)

- **aspiration** 포부, 야망
- **pursuer** 추격자
- **workplace** 직장

Point 2 목적어로서의 to부정사와 동명사

- 목적어로 to부정사를 취하는 동사에는 want, decide, hope, promise, choose, refuse, expect, plan 등이 있다.

- I cannot accept your offer because I **have decided to pursue** another opportunity.
  목적어(to부정사)

- **pursue** 추구하다

- 목적어로 동명사를 취하는 동사에는 enjoy, avoid, stop, mind, finish, quit, deny, give up, consider, postpone 등이 있다.

- The refugees left their home to **avoid getting** bombed.
  목적어(동명사)

- **refugee** 난민, 피난민
- **bomb** 폭격하다

  어법 Plus 목적어로 to부정사와 동명사를 모두 취하지만 그 의미가 달라지는 동사에는 remember, forget, regret 등이 있다.

Point 3 목적격보어로서의 to부정사

- 목적격보어로 to부정사를 취하는 동사에는 want, expect, allow, ask, enable, cause, encourage, advise, force 등이 있다.

- The survey questions **allowed** the dentists **to recommend** more than one brand.
  목적격보어(to부정사)

- **survey** 설문(조사)

Point 1 나의 포부는 유명한 피아니스트가 되는 것이다. / 추격자를 더 힘들게 만드는 한 가지 방법은 지그재그로 움직이는 것이다. / 나는 직장에서의 스트레스에서 벗어나기 위해 하루 휴가를 냈다. **Point 2** 저는 다른 기회를 추구하기로 결정해서 귀하의 제안을 받아들일 수 없습니다. / 난민들은 폭격당하는 것을 피하기 위해 자신들의 고향을 떠났다. **Point 3** 그 설문 문항은 치과의사들이 한 가지 이상의 브랜드를 추천하는 것을 허용했다.

✅ 출제 Point

1. 앞에 형식상의 주어[목적어] it이 있는지 확인한다.
2. 목적격보어로 to부정사를 취하는 동사가 있는지 확인한다.
3. 전치사의 목적어 자리에 동명사가 제대로 쓰였는지 확인한다.

Point 4 전치사와 동명사

– 동명사는 문장에서 주어, 목적어, 보어 역할을 하며, 전치사의 목적어로는 명사(구) 또는 동명사(구)가 온다.

- **Being** honest at all times is not always easy.
  주어(동명사구)

- He devoted all his time **to studying** physics.
  전치사   전치사 to의 목적어(동명사구)

  • **devote** 바치다, 전념하다

Point 5 내용상의 주어[목적어] 자리에 오는 to부정사구

– 주어 또는 목적어가 to부정사구로 길 경우, it을 형식상의 주어[목적어]로 두고 내용상의 주어[목적어]는 뒤로 보낸다.

- I found **it** hard **to say** it in words.
  형식상의 목적어   내용상의 목적어(to부정사구)

Point 6 to부정사와 동명사의 의미상 주어

– to부정사의 의미상 주어는 「for + 목적격」으로 나타내고, 동명사의 의미상 주어는 소유격 및 목적격으로 나타낸다.

- The slope is too steep **for them** to try.
  의미상 주어   to부정사

  • **slope** 경사(면)
  • **steep** 가파른

- I was disappointed about **his** being so rude to me.
  의미상 주어   동명사

  • **rude** 무례한

Point 7 to부정사와 동명사의 시제

– to부정사와 동명사가 나타내는 시제가 본동사의 시제보다 앞설 경우, 각각 「to have p.p.」와 「having p.p.」 형태로 쓴다.

- She appeared **to have spent** some time in Japan.
  본동사(과거)   to have p.p.(spend가 나타내는 시제가 appeared보다 앞섬)

- I apologize sincerely for not **having presented** myself at the meeting yesterday.
  본동사(현재)   having p.p.(present가 나타내는 시제가 apologize보다 앞섬)

  • **present oneself** 참석하다

Point 4 항상 정직한 것이 늘 쉬운 것은 아니다. / 그는 자신의 모든 시간을 물리학을 공부하는 데 바쳤다. **Point 5** 나는 그것을 말로 하는 것이 어렵다는 것을 깨달았다. **Point 6** 그 경사는 그들이 시도하기에는 너무 가파르다. / 나는 그가 나에게 그렇게 무례한 것에 대해 실망했다. **Point 7** 그녀는 한동안 일본에서 지냈던 것으로 보였다. / 제가 어제 회의에 참석하지 못한 것에 대해 진심으로 사과드립니다.

Q1 괄호 안에서 어법상 알맞은 것을 고르세요.

1. 【 Give / Giving 】 people the latitude and flexibility to use their judgment and apply their talents rapidly accelerates progress.

- **latitude** 자유; 위도
- **flexibility** 융통성, 유연성
- **apply** 적용하다
- **accelerate** 가속화하다

2. More important is the huge increase in parental concern about their children 【 are / being 】 on a winning team.

- **parental** 부모의
- **concern** 염려, 우려

3. This church, about which little is known, is believed by some to 【 be built / have been built 】 already at the end of the fifteenth century.

4. When it comes to 【 play / playing 】 this guitar he is second to none.

- **second to none** 제일인, 누구에게도 뒤지지 않는

5. Taylor advised me 【 stopping / to stop 】 thinking of carrying out such a plan.

- **advise** 충고하다
- **carry out** ~을 수행[실행]하다

Q2 밑줄 친 부분을 어법상 알맞게 고쳐 쓰세요.

1. We make it easy for teachers <u>participate</u> in CPR training at a time to suit your school's schedule.

   ➡ _____

2. Each participant should set a goal for donation by <u>to choose</u> only one of the following courses.

   ➡ _____

- **donation** 기부

3. One objection to <u>keep</u> kids home is that they won't learn to get along with other kids.

   ➡ _____

- **objection** 반대
- **get along with** ~와 어울려 지내다

4. One of the facts is that dinosaurs' body temperatures had to be higher than the air <u>hatching</u> eggs.

   ➡ _____

- **body temperature** 체온
- **hatch** (알을) 부화하다

013

다음 글의 밑줄 친 부분 중, 어법상 틀린 것은?

People sometimes do try to paint themselves in a positive light. ① Whether they are pretending to have seen the space baby on a fictitious television show, to have heard of nonexistent people, or to have been busy to make themselves appear more important, people are going to try to mess with how you think of them. In addition, some people are more prone to this behavior than others, ② pretending to be important. Narcissists even manage to convince ③ themselves that their excuses are true. However, hope is at hand. You can pay attention to the signs—such as the discrepancy between easy-to-fake identity claims and difficult-to-fake behavioral residue—④ which someone is trying to fool you. In addition, research indicates people typically don't want to portray themselves in a false light. They may exaggerate a bit, but there's not much room for exaggeration, and it is very difficult ⑤ to pull off major deceptions.

*residue 잔여물

014

2024 수능

다음 글의 밑줄 친 부분 중, 어법상 틀린 것은?

A number of studies provide substantial evidence of an innate human disposition to respond differentially to social stimuli. From birth, infants will orient preferentially towards the human face and voice, ① seeming to know that such stimuli are particularly meaningful for them. Moreover, they register this connection actively, imitating a variety of facial gestures that are presented to them—tongue protrusions, lip tightenings, mouth openings. They will even try to match gestures ② which they have some difficulty, experimenting with their own faces until they succeed. When they ③ do succeed, they show pleasure by a brightening of their eyes; when they fail, they show distress. In other words, they not only have an innate capacity for matching their own kinaesthetically experienced bodily movements with ④ those of others that are visually perceived; they have an innate drive to do so. That is, they seem to have an innate drive to imitate others whom they judge ⑤ to be 'like me'.

*innate 타고난 **disposition 성향
***kinaesthetically 운동감각적으로

출제 의도 파악하기

❶
❷
❸
❹
❺

출제 의도 파악하기

❶
❷
❸
❹
❺

015

다음 글의 밑줄 친 부분 중, 어법상 <u>틀린</u> 것은?

Public companies are legally overseen by boards of directors, ① <u>who</u> are formally elected by shareholders. In smaller companies, these formalities map onto reality—a small group of shareholders effectively control board elections, and, through ② <u>them</u>, the companies. This is the way corporate law and governance were designed ③ <u>to function</u>. But in the largest public companies, shareholders have long been so numerous—no one person owns more than 1 percent of a company's shares—④ <u>what</u> contested elections of directors are rare. Because board members are typically independent and serve part-time, they have limited ability to direct managers. While boards grew in power at the end of the twentieth century, they still impose only mild constraints on executives. As a result, large public companies for most of the twentieth century ⑤ <u>were</u> controlled not by their owners but by their executives. This fact was first highlighted in a 1932 book by Adolf Berle and Gardiner Means, *The Modern Corporation and Private Property*.

*corporate governance 기업지배구조(기업 경영의 통제 시스템)

016

다음 글의 밑줄 친 부분 중, 어법상 <u>틀린</u> 것은?

To begin with a psychological reason, the knowledge of another's personal affairs can tempt the possessor of this information ① <u>to repeat</u> it as gossip because as unrevealed information it remains socially inactive. Only when the information is repeated can its possessor ② <u>turn</u> the fact that he knows something into something socially valuable like social recognition, prestige, and notoriety. As long as he keeps his information to ③ <u>himself</u>, he may feel superior to those who do not know it. But knowing and not telling does not give him that feeling of "superiority that, so to say, latently contained in the secret, fully ④ <u>actualizing</u> itself only at the moment of disclosure." This is the main motive for gossiping about well-known figures and superiors. The gossip producer assumes that some of the "fame" of the subject of gossip, as ⑤ <u>whose</u> "friend" he presents himself, will rub off on him.

*prestige 명성 **notoriety 악명 ***latently 잠재적으로

출제 의도 파악하기
❶
❷
❸
❹
❺

출제 의도 파악하기
❶
❷
❸
❹
❺

017

다음 글의 밑줄 친 부분 중, 어법상 틀린 것은?

Rational behavior, that is, behavior resulting from conscious thought and decision and not from an unthinking emotional response, ① tends to be goal-directed. It is purposeful, ② intended to accomplish something. That "something" has to do with satisfying some need. Human needs—for example, for survival, security, affection, esteem, or accomplishment—are universal. What is not universal ③ being the value we place on various means for satisfying our needs. One kind of cultural difference is well-known to all of us—food. I may place more value on chicken soup ④ to satisfy my hunger, whereas you may prefer shark fin soup or cream soup. Other, culture-based differences in values are of more interest to us here. For example, self-actualization, a need, may be satisfied in one culture by amassing wealth, praise, or other forms of individual recognition, whereas in another it may mean a sense of making a worthy contribution to ⑤ advancing the processes in one's work-group.

*amass 축적하다

018

다음 글의 밑줄 친 부분 중, 어법상 틀린 것은?

When examining the archaeological record of human culture, one has to consider that it is vastly incomplete. Many aspects of human culture have ① what archaeologists describe as low archaeological visibility, meaning they are difficult to identify archaeologically. Archaeologists tend to focus on tangible (or material) aspects of culture: things that can be handled and photographed, such as tools, food, and structures. Reconstructing intangible aspects of culture is more difficult, requiring ② that one draw more inferences from the tangible. It is relatively easy, for example, for archaeologists ③ to identify and draw inferences about technology and diet from stone tools and food remains. Using the same kinds of physical remains to draw inferences about social systems and what people were thinking about ④ are more difficult. Archaeologists do it, but there are necessarily more inferences involved in getting from physical remains recognized as trash to ⑤ making interpretations about belief systems.

*archaeological 고고학의

04 분사

Point ❶ 명사를 수식하는 분사

– 분사는 명사(구)를 앞이나 뒤에서 수식하며, 수식받는 명사(구)와 분사의 의미 관계가 능동이면 현재분사를, 수동이면 과거분사를 쓴다.

- The square was empty except for a black cat **staring** at me with a scary, sharp look.
  명사구   현재분사(능동)

  ➡ a black cat이 '응시하는' 주체이므로 능동을 나타내는 현재분사가 쓰였다.

- She was staying at home because of a **broken** leg.
  과거분사(수동)   명사

  ➡ a leg가 '부러진' 대상이므로 수동을 나타내는 과거분사가 쓰였다.

- **square** 광장
- **empty** 텅 빈, 비어 있는
- **stare** 응시하다
- **scary** 무서운

Point ❷ 목적격보어로서의 분사

– 분사는 지각동사와 5형식 동사의 목적격보어로 쓰일 수 있으며, 목적어와의 의미 관계가 능동이면 현재분사를, 수동이면 과거분사를 쓴다.

- I saw Tom **looking** into a show window.
  목적격보어(현재분사: 능동)

  ➡ Tom(목적어)이 '보는' 주체이므로 목적격보어로 현재분사가 쓰였다.

- He kept his car **parked** there without permission.
  목적격보어(과거분사: 수동)

  ➡ his car(목적어)가 '주차된' 대상이므로 목적격보어로 과거분사가 쓰였다.

- **permission** 허가

Point ❸ 감정동사의 분사형

– 감정동사의 의미상 주어가 감정을 유발하는 것이면 현재분사를, 감정을 느끼는 것이면 과거분사를 쓴다.

- Bad lighting can increase stress on your eyes. Fluorescent lighting can also be **tiring**.
  의미상 주어(피로감을 유발함)   감정동사의 현재분사

- When Angela was young, she was always **disappointed** about her performance
  의미상 주어(실망감을 느낌)   감정동사의 과거분사

  despite her efforts.

- **fluorescent lighting** 형광등
- **performance** 성과

  > **어법 Plus**   감정동사에는 amaze, confuse, depress, disappoint, embarrass, excite, frustrate, interest, surprise, tire 등이 있다.

Point ❶ 광장은 무섭고 날카로운 표정으로 나를 응시하는 검은 고양이를 제외하고는 텅 비어 있었다. / 그녀는 다리 골절 때문에 집에 머물러 있던 중이었다. **Point ❷** 나는 Tom이 상품 진열창을 들여다보고 있는 것을 보았다. / 그는 허가 없이 자신의 차를 그곳에 계속 주차해 두었다. **Point ❸** 나쁜 조명은 여러분의 눈에 스트레스를 증가시킬 수 있다. 형광등 또한 피로감을 일으킬 수 있다. / Angela가 어렸을 때 그녀는 자신의 노력에도 불구하고 자신의 성과에 항상 실망했다.

Point ④ 분사구문

– 분사구문은 분사가 이끄는 부사구를 의미하며, 때, 이유, 원인, 결과, 조건, 양보, 부대상황(동시상황) 등을 나타낸다.

- **Turning** to the left, you'll find the hospital on your right.
  <u>현재분사 Turning이 이끄는 분사구문</u>

  ➡ 의미상 주어인 you가 '도는' 주체이므로 현재분사가 이끌고 있다.

- **Pressed** for time, she had no idea how to finish the paper.
  <u>과거분사 Pressed가 이끄는 분사구문</u>

  ➡ 의미상 주어인 she가 '압박받는' 대상이므로 과거분사가 이끌고 있다.

• **press** 압박을 가하다
• **paper** 논문, 문서

– 분사구문은 앞에 접속사가 생략된 형태이지만, 의미를 명확히 하기 위해 접속사를 그대로 쓸 수도 있으며, 수동의 분사구문은 앞에 being이나 having been이 생략된 것으로 볼 수 있다.

- **Compared** with the Republic of Korea, Israel spent a lower percentage of GDP on
  <u>접속사 생략 + 과거분사가 이끄는 분사구문</u>

  education.

  ➡ Being compared with ~에서 Being을 생략한 것으로 볼 수 있다. (접속사를 생략하지 않은 When compared with ~도 가능)

– 분사구문의 의미상 주어가 주절의 주어와 다를 경우, 분사구문의 의미상 주어를 표기해 준다.

- **The electricity** having gone out, we had to light a candle.
  <u>분사구문의 의미상 주어</u> <u>분사구문</u> <u>주절의 주어</u>

  ➡ having gone이 이끄는 분사구문의 의미상 주어와 주절의 주어가 일치하지 않으므로, 분사구문의 의미상 주어를 생략하고 Having gone out으로만 쓸 수는 없다.

• **electricity** 전기

Point ⑤ 「with+명사(구)+분사」 구문

– 부대상황(동시상황)을 나타내는 「with + 명사(구) + 분사」 구문은 '~가 …한[된] 채로'의 의미를 나타낸다.

- She was looking at the stars **with her arms folded**.
  <u>명사구</u> <u>과거분사(수동)</u>

  ➡ 명사구 her arms가 '끼는' 동작의 대상이므로 수동을 나타내는 과거분사가 쓰였다.

• **fold (one's arms)**
  (팔짱을) 끼다

Point ④ 왼쪽으로 돌면 오른쪽에서 그 병원을 찾을 수 있을 거예요. / 시간적 압박을 받고 그녀는 논문을 어떻게 끝마쳐야 할지 몰랐다. / 대한민국과 비교할 때 이스라엘은 GDP의 더 낮은 비율(에 해당하는 돈)을 교육에 썼다. / 전기가 나갔기 때문에 우리는 촛불을 켜야만 했다. **Point ⑤** 그녀는 팔짱을 낀 채 별을 바라보고 있었다.

개념 확인 문제

Q1 괄호 안에서 어법상 알맞은 것을 고르세요.

1. There were more cats 〖 living / lived 〗 in Egypt during the time of the pharaohs than in any other place in the world.

2. I felt quite 〖 depressing / depressed 〗 at the thought of the hard work ahead of me.

• depress 낙담시키다

3. 〖 Amazing / Amazed 〗 at all the attention being paid to her, I asked if she worked with the airline.

4. 〖 Situating / Situated 〗 at an elevation of 1,350m, the city of Katmandu enjoys a warm climate year-round that makes living here pleasant.

• situate 위치를 정하다, 위치하게 하다
• elevation 고도

5. With you 〖 watching / watched 〗 me, I couldn't concentrate on what I was studying.

• concentrate 집중하다

Q2 밑줄 친 부분이 어법상 맞으면 괄호 안에 ○ 표시를, 틀리면 X 표시를 하고 맞게 고쳐 쓰세요.

1. If schools only provide knowledge, they may destroy creativity, just <u>producing</u> ordinary people.

➡ (   ) : _____

• creativity 창의력
• ordinary 평범한

2. Teflon, an extremely slippery synthetic substance <u>employing</u> as a coating on cooking utensils, was invented in 1938.

➡ (   ) : _____

• extremely 매우, 극히
• slippery 미끄러운
• synthetic 합성의
• employ 사용하다, 고용하다
• utensil 조리기구, 식기

3. <u>The sun having risen</u>, we started for the village.

➡ (   ) : _____

4. That was the advice of Francis Galton in a book <u>calling</u> *The Art of Travel*.

➡ (   ) : _____

019

다음 글의 밑줄 친 부분 중, 어법상 틀린 것은?

The various shapes ① into which a vine can be trained give us another way of controlling the effect of heat on the ripening of the grapes. The arrangement of the leaves forms what is known as the canopy of the vine. The manipulation of this canopy, or canopy management, ② is particularly important in marginal climates, where the different styles of training can be used to either maximise or minimise the effect of the sun's rays. In vineyards such as Châteauneuf-du-Pape the effect of the sun is deliberately emphasised by training the vines in the bush style, with short stems, so that the producing parts of the vine are close to the ground. This traps the maximum warmth from the sun's rays, both ③ directly and from the reflected heat from the *galets* or 'pudding stones'. This effect continues into the night, when the stones act as gigantic storage heaters, ④ enveloping the vines with warm air. In hot climates where a lighter, crisper wine might be desired, the vines are trained high, with their upper branches ⑤ forming into a pergola. In this formation the grapes hang down underneath the leaves and remain in the comparative cool of the shade.

*train (식물을 바라는 모양으로) 가꾸다

**canopy 캐노피(나뭇가지가 지붕 모양으로 우거진 것)

***pergola 퍼걸러(아치형 구조물)

020

2020 수능

다음 글의 밑줄 친 부분 중, 어법상 틀린 것은?

Speculations about the meaning and purpose of prehistoric art ① rely heavily on analogies drawn with modern-day hunter-gatherer societies. Such primitive societies, ② as Steven Mithen emphasizes in *The Prehistory of the Modern Mind*, tend to view man and beast, animal and plant, organic and inorganic spheres, as participants in an integrated, animated totality. The dual expressions of this tendency are *anthropomorphism* (the practice of regarding animals as humans) and *totemism* (the practice of regarding humans as animals), both of ③ which spread through the visual art and the mythology of primitive cultures. Thus the natural world is conceptualized in terms of human social relations. When considered in this light, the visual preoccupation of early humans with the nonhuman creatures ④ inhabited their world becomes profoundly meaningful. Among hunter-gatherers, animals are not only good to eat, they are also *good to think about*, as Claude Lévi-Strauss has observed. In the practice of totemism, he has suggested, an unlettered humanity "broods upon ⑤ itself and its place in nature."

*speculation 고찰 **analogy 유사점

***brood 곰곰이 생각하다

출제 의도 파악하기
❶
❷
❸
❹
❺

출제 의도 파악하기
❶
❷
❸
❹
❺

021

2023 4월 학평

다음 글의 밑줄 친 부분 중, 어법상 틀린 것은?

Providing feedback to students is a critical task of teachers. General psychology has shown that knowledge of results is necessary for improving a skill. Advanced musicians are able to self-critique their performances, but developing music students ① rely on teachers to supply evaluative feedback. The most constructive feedback is that ② which expresses the discrepancies between a student's performance of a piece of music and an optimal version. Expert teachers give more detailed feedback than general appraisals, and music educators generally recognize that more specific teacher feedback facilitates student performance improvement. Researchers also have explored ③ whether the feedback of effective teachers is more often positively or negatively expressed, that is, constituting praise or criticism. One might intuitively think that positive comments are more ④ motivated to students and, as a result, are more associated with effective teaching. The research, however, paints a slightly different picture. Although positive feedback is ⑤ likely more helpful with younger learners and in one-on-one instruction, more advanced music students seem to accept and benefit from greater levels of criticism in lessons.

022

다음 글의 밑줄 친 부분 중, 어법상 틀린 것은?

Photosynthesis is a chemical process ① in which green plants, using energy from sunlight, produce carbohydrates from carbon dioxide and water. The process takes place in the plant cells using chlorophyll, a green pigment ② capable of converting light energy into a latent form of energy which then will be stored and used when needed. In these plants, water is absorbed through the roots and transferred to the leaves by the xylem, and carbon dioxide ③ being obtained from air through the stomata in the leaves and dispersed to chlorophyll. However, some plants, such as Indian pipe ④ lack this chlorophyll. Therefore, they secure their carbohydrates from organic material, while a few bacteria manufacture their own carbohydrates with hydrogen and energy obtained from inorganic compounds in a process ⑤ called chemosynthesis.

*chlorophyll 엽록소 **xylem 물관부 ***stomata 숨문. 기공(氣孔)
****chemosynthesis 화학 합성

출제 의도 파악하기

❶ ....
❷ ....
❸ ....
❹ ....
❺ ....

출제 의도 파악하기

❶ ....
❷ ....
❸ ....
❹ ....
❺ ....

023

2021 10월 학평

다음 글의 밑줄 친 부분 중, 어법상 틀린 것은?

According to its dictionary definition, an anthem is both a song of loyalty, often to a country, and a piece of 'sacred music', definitions that are both applicable in sporting contexts. This genre is dominated, although
5 not exclusively, by football and has produced a number of examples ① where popular songs become synonymous with the club and are enthusiastically adopted by the fans. More than this they are often spontaneous expressions of loyalty and identity and,
10 according to Desmond Morris, have 'reached the level of something ② approached a local art form'. A strong element of the appeal of such sports songs ③ is that they feature 'memorable and easily sung choruses in which fans can participate'. This is a vital part of the
15 team's performance ④ as it makes the fans' presence more tangible. This form of popular culture can be said ⑤ to display pleasure and emotional excess in contrast to the dominant culture which tends to maintain 'respectable aesthetic distance and control'.

*synonymous 밀접한 연관을 갖는 **tangible 확실한

024

다음 글의 밑줄 친 부분 중, 어법상 틀린 것은?

If there were no people in Africa, the continent would undergo some key changes. Once, North African cattle were wild. But after thousands of years with humans, they've been selected for a gut like an oversized fermentation vat ① to eat huge amounts of food during 5 the day, because they can't graze at night. So now they're not very quick. ② Left on their own, they'd be rather vulnerable prime beef. Cattle now account for more than half the live weight of African savanna ecosystems. Without Maasai spears to protect 10 ③ themselves, they would provide a feast for lions and hyenas. Once cows were gone, there would be more than double the feed for everything else. A million and a half wildebeest can take out grass just as ④ effectively as cattle. Then, the world would see much tighter 15 interaction between them and elephants. They would play the role the Maasai refer to when they say ⑤ that "cattle grow trees, elephants grow grass."

*gut 창자 **fermentation vat 발효통
***wildebeest 누(영양의 일종)

출제 의도 파악하기
❶
❷
❸
❹
❺

출제 의도 파악하기
❶
❷
❸
❹
❺

05 명사와 대명사

Point 1 집합적 물질명사 및 추상명사

– 집합적 물질명사와 추상명사는 복수형으로 쓰지 않으며, 앞에 부정관사 a(n)를 쓰지 않는다.

- The house is 18th century and contains much **furniture** of the period.
  집합적 물질명사(furnitures ×)

  ➡ 셀 수 없는 명사로 취급하여 앞에 many가 아닌 much가 쓰였다.

  어법 Plus 대표적인 집합적 물질명사
  furniture(가구), clothing(의류), jewelry(보석류), equipment(장비류), baggage(화물류),
  luggage(화물류), machinery(기계류), poetry(시, 운문) 등

- Hailey is a girl of very high **intelligence**.
  추상명사(a very high intelligence ×)

  ➡ intelligence를 수식하는 very high 앞에 부정관사가 쓰이지 않았다.

  어법 Plus 추상명사는 가치, 감정, 성격, 특성, 개념, 아이디어, 상태 등 실질적인 형태가 없는 명사를 뜻한다.

- **period** 시대, 시기

- **intelligence** 지능, 지성

Point 2 지시대명사 that

– 지시대명사는 앞에 나온 명사의 반복을 피하기 위한 것으로, 단수 명사를 가리키면 that을 쓰고 복수 명사를 가리키면 those를 쓴다.

- Our product is more durable than **that** of our competitors.
  단수 명사   단수 대명사(product를 대신함)

- Salaries here are higher than **those** in my country.
  복수 명사   복수 대명사(salaries를 대신함)

- **durable** 내구성 있는
- **competitor** 경쟁자, 경쟁사

- **salary** 급료, 봉급

Point 3 재귀대명사

– 재귀대명사는 인칭대명사의 소유격이나 목적격에 -self(단수) 또는 -selves(복수)를 붙인 것으로, 목적어가 동사의 의미상 주어와 동일한 대상이면 목적어로 재귀대명사를 쓴다.

- People consistently overestimate their ability to control **themselves**.
  control의 의미상 주어   재귀대명사(= People)

  어법 Plus 재귀대명사는 단순 강조를 위해 쓰이기도 하며, 이때의 재귀대명사는 생략 가능하다. (강조 용법)
  Brian (himself) is responsible for the security system.
         생략 가능

- **consistently** 지속적으로
- **overestimate** 과대평가하다

- **responsible for** ~에 대해 책임
  이 있다
- **security system** 보안 시스템

Point 1 그 집은 18세기 것으로 그 시대의 가구를 많이 갖고 있다. / Hailey는 매우 높은 지능을 가진 소녀이다. **Point 2** 우리 제품은 우리 경쟁사의 그것(제품)보다 더 내구성이 있다. / 여기의 급료는 우리나라의 그것(급료)보다 높다. **Point 3** 사람들은 자기 자신을 통제할 수 있는 능력을 지속적으로 과대평가한다. / **어법 Plus** Brian (그 자신)이 그 보안 시스템의 책임을 맡고 있다.

Point 4 부정대명사

– 불특정한 사람이나 사물 또는 수량을 언급하는 것으로, one, another, some, others, the other, the others 등의 쓰임을 알아둔다.

- Each of its ears is a different size, and **one** is higher than **the other**.
  (여럿 중) 불특정한 한 개　　　　　　　　one을 제외한 나머지

→ 여럿 중 불특정한 하나가 one이고, 나머지는 the other(단수)로 썼으므로 전체가 총 두 개임을 알 수 있다.

어법 Plus 부정대명사의 의미
one(하나), both(둘 다), either(둘 중 하나), neither(둘 다 아님)
another(또 다른 하나), the other(나머지 하나), the others(복수인 나머지 모두)
some(불특정한 일부), others(불특정한 복수)

Point 5 대명사의 수 일치

– 대명사가 무엇을 가리키는지 정확한 해석을 통해 파악하여 그것이 가리키는 대상에 수를 일치시켜야 한다.

- Plants can't change location or extend **their** reproductive range without help.
  대명사가 가리키는 명사　　　　　　　　　복수 대명사(= Plants)

- The percentage of parents who browsed shelves is the same as **that** of parents who
  대명사가 가리키는 명사구　　　　　　　　　　　　　　단수 대명사(= The percentage)

  borrowed print books.

- **extend** 확장하다
- **reproductive** 생식의, 번식의
- **range** 범위

- **browse** 둘러보다, 훑어보다
- **shelves** 서가(shelf의 복수형)

Point 6 소유대명사와 이중소유격

– 소유대명사는 「소유격 + 명사」의 의미를 나타내며, 이중소유격은 「한정사 + 명사 + of + 소유대명사」의 형태로 쓴다.

- No part of my body touched any part of **hers**.
  = her body

→ 여기서 소유대명사 hers는 my body에 대응하는 her body를 의미한다.

- **A friend of mine** from college lives in Washington.
  a + 명사 + of + 소유대명사

→ 소유격을 a(n), the, this, some 등의 한정사와 함께 써서 의미를 나타내고자 할 경우, 소유격과 한정사를 바로 이어서 쓸 수 없다. (my a friend×)

Point 4 그것의 양쪽 귀는 크기가 다르며 하나가 다른 하나보다 더 높이 있다. **Point 5** 식물들은 위치를 바꾸거나 도움 없이 그것들의 번식 범위를 확장할 수 없다. / 서가를 둘러본 부모의 비율은 인쇄된 책을 빌린 부모의 비율과 같다. **Point 6** 내 몸의 어떤 부분도 그녀의 몸의 어떤 부분에 닿지 않았다. / 대학 때의 내 친구 한 명이 워싱턴에 산다.

Q1 괄호 안에서 어법상 알맞은 것을 고르세요.

1. The results of Experiment A are more reliable than 〔 that / those 〕 of Experiment B.

• **experiment** 실험
• **reliable** 신뢰할 만한

2. In spite of 〔 its / their 〕 close location to these countries, however, Korea has remained free of the deadly disease.

• **in spite of** ~에도 불구하고
• **location** 위치, 장소
• **deadly** 치명적인

3. The first thing I notice upon entering this garden is that the ankle-high grass is greener than 〔 that / those 〕 on the other side of the fence.

• **ankle-high** 발목 높이의

4. The sea lions were friendly to those humans they knew and even enjoyed being with 〔 them / themselves 〕.

5. I have two personal computers; one is a desktop, and 〔 the other / another 〕 is a laptop.

Q2 밑줄 친 부분이 어법상 맞으면 괄호 안에 ○ 표시를, 틀리면 X 표시를 하고 맞게 고쳐 쓰세요.

1. Promise <u>yourself</u> that no matter how much work you have, you will always relax during one full evening.

➡ (　　　　) : _____

2. The percentage of people who mostly watch news videos on news sites in France is higher than <u>those</u> in Germany.

➡ (　　　　) : _____

3. A helpful way of coping with strong negative feelings is to take <u>it</u> for what they are.

• **cope with** ~에 대처하다
• **negative** 부정적인

➡ (　　　　) : _____

4. Musical sounds can be distinguished from <u>that</u> of nature by the fact that they involve the use of fixed pitches.

• **distinguish** 구별하다, 구분하다
• **involve** 수반하다, 포함하다
• **pitch** (음의) 높이

➡ (　　　　) : _____

정답 및 해설 p.018

025

2023 3월 학평

다음 글의 밑줄 친 부분 중, 어법상 틀린 것은?

From the 8th to the 12th century CE, while Europe suffered the perhaps overdramatically named Dark Ages, science on planet Earth could be found almost ① exclusively in the Islamic world. This science was not exactly like our science today, but it was surely antecedent to ② it and was nonetheless an activity aimed at knowing about the world. Muslim rulers granted scientific institutions tremendous resources, such as libraries, observatories, and hospitals. Great schools in all the cities ③ covering the Arabic Near East and Northern Africa (and even into Spain) trained generations of scholars. Almost every word in the modern scientific lexicon that begins with the prefix "al" ④ owes its origins to Islamic science—algorithm, alchemy, alcohol, alkali, algebra. And then, just over 400 years after it started, it ground to an apparent halt, and it would be a few hundred years, give or take, before ⑤ that we would today unmistakably recognize as science appeared in Europe—with Galileo, Kepler, and, a bit later, Newton.

*antecedent 선행하는 **lexicon 어휘 (목록)

***give or take 대략

026

다음 글의 밑줄 친 부분 중, 어법상 틀린 것은?

I was in line with my son James at the store when his cell phone rang. He proceeded ① to carry on a conversation while the cashier rang up his purchase. After we left, I told James it was rude to talk on his phone while he was being waited on. When he said, "Everyone does it," I knew it was a good time to ② discuss cell phone manners. I said people tend to talk loudly on their phones, disturbing others and turning private conversations into public ③ one. James said he hadn't thought about it that way. He agreed to put his phone on vibrate when we're out and to return calls later. My son can't imagine ④ what it was like growing up without cell phones. But I'm trying to help him ⑤ understand that just because we have them, we don't need to use them all the time—and that good manners still apply.

출제 의도 파악하기

❶ ....
❷ ....
❸ ....
❹ ....
❺ ....

출제 의도 파악하기

❶ ....
❷ ....
❸ ....
❹ ....
❺ ....

027

다음 글의 밑줄 친 부분 중, 어법상 틀린 것은?

A question often put to a behaviorist is whether animals have color vision. All species of domestic animals have been shown to possess color vision ① in that they will make discriminations based on color. However, color probably is not as relevant to these animals as it ② is to birds, fish, and primates. For example, teaching cats to discriminate between colors ③ is very difficult, although they learn other visual discriminations with ease and have two types of cones that absorb green and blue. Nevertheless, cats, dogs, horses, cattle, pigs, goats, and sheep can all make discriminations based on color alone. Color vision in domestic animals is not identical to ④ those in humans. In the most ⑤ carefully conducted studies, dogs appear to see the world not in shades of gray but rather in shades of violet, blue, and yellow.

*color vision 색각(빛깔을 알아차리는 감각)

028

2023 수능

다음 글의 밑줄 친 부분 중, 어법상 틀린 것은?

Trends constantly suggest new opportunities for individuals to restage themselves, representing occasions for change. To understand how trends can ultimately give individuals power and freedom, one must first discuss fashion's importance as a basis for change. The most common explanation offered by my informants as to why fashion is so appealing is ① that it constitutes a kind of theatrical costumery. Clothes are part of how people present ② them to the world, and fashion locates them in the present, relative to what is happening in society and to fashion's own history. As a form of expression, fashion contains a host of ambiguities, enabling individuals to recreate the meanings ③ associated with specific pieces of clothing. Fashion is among the simplest and cheapest methods of self-expression: clothes can be ④ inexpensively purchased while making it easy to convey notions of wealth, intellectual stature, relaxation or environmental consciousness, even if none of these is true. Fashion can also strengthen agency in various ways, ⑤ opening up space for action.

*stature 능력

출제 의도 **파악하기**

❶ ....
❷ ....
❸ ....
❹ ....
❺ ....

출제 의도 **파악하기**

❶ ....
❷ ....
❸ ....
❹ ....
❺ ....

029

다음 글의 밑줄 친 부분 중, 어법상 틀린 것은?

The picture people have of the art world ① depends on the artists they happen to know. Successful artists send a general message that they are in fact totally well-informed about the matters at hand. Their success
5 can ② be viewed as the result of their hard work and dedication. They perpetuate the belief that before their success, it was personal satisfaction that kept ③ themselves going as compensation for their low incomes. Failed artists, however, send out a different
10 signal, but, strangely enough, they stick to the same myths. These 'losers' cannot avoid ④ exhibiting their bitterness, but they seldom blame the art world for their failure. They never conclude ⑤ that maybe there are just too many artists. Instead, they blame themselves
15 for a lack of dedication.

030

다음 글의 밑줄 친 부분 중, 어법상 틀린 것은?

The modern adult human brain weighs only 1/50 of the total body weight but uses up to 1/5 of the total energy needs. The brain's running costs are about eight to ten times as high, per unit mass, as ① those of the body's muscles. And around 3/4 of that energy 5 is expended on neurons, the ② specialized brain cells that communicate in vast networks to generate our thoughts and behaviours. An individual neuron ③ sends a signal in the brain uses as much energy as a leg muscle cell running a marathon. Of course, we 10 use more energy overall when we are running, but we are not always on the move, whereas our brains never switch off. Even though the brain is metabolically greedy, it still outclasses any desktop computer both in terms of the calculations it can perform and the 15 efficiency ④ at which it does this. We may have built computers that can beat our top Grand Master chess players, but we are still far away from designing one that is capable of recognizing and picking up one of the chess pieces as ⑤ easily as a typical three-year-old 20 child can.

출제 의도 파악하기

❶ ....
❷ ....
❸ ....
❹ ....
❺ ....

출제 의도 파악하기

❶ ....
❷ ....
❸ ....
❹ ....
❺ ....

06 형용사와 부사

Point 1 형용사와 부사의 수식

– 형용사는 명사(구)를 수식하며(한정 용법), 부사는 명사를 제외한 동사, 형용사, 부사, 문장 전체를 수식한다.

- As **some** researchers found, that does not **necessarily** make things safer.
  형용사 → 명사   부사 → 동사

  어법 Plus 형용사는 –thing, –one, –body, –where 등으로 끝나는 명사나 대명사를 뒤에서 수식한다.
  There is **nothing** more **important** than your health.
  대명사 ↲ 형용사

- **Unfortunately**, **few** scientists are **truly** objective.
  부사(문장 수식)   형용사 → 명사   부사 → 형용사

- **necessarily** 반드시

- **unfortunately** 안타깝게도
- **objective** 객관적인

Point 2 형용사의 보어 역할

– 형용사는 문장에서 주격보어와 목적격보어로 쓰일 수 있으며(서술 용법), 부사는 보어로 쓰일 수 없다.

- As you are well **aware**, a great tragedy took place in our city last week.
  주어   형용사(주격보어)

  ➡ As가 이끄는 부사절에서 형용사 aware는 주어인 you를 서술하는 주격보어이다.

  어법 Plus 서술 용법으로만 쓰이는 대표적인 형용사
  awake, alike, alone, alive, aware, asleep, afraid 등은 명사(구)를 수식할 수 없고, 보어로만 쓰인다.

- When people expect to see someone again, they are more likely to find that person
  목적어

  attractive, regardless of the individual's behavior.
  형용사(목적격보어)

  ➡ 주절에서 형용사 attractive는 to find의 목적어인 that person을 서술하는 목적격보어이며, 부사인 attractively가 올 수 없다. 부사처럼 해석되더라도, 보어 자리에는 반드시 형용사만 올 수 있다.

- **aware** 알고 있는
- **tragedy** 비극
- **take place** 발생하다, 일어나다

- **attractive** 매력적인
- **regardless of** ~와 관계없이

Point 3 수량형용사

– many, a few, few는 셀 수 있는 명사를 수식하여 수를, much, a little, little은 셀 수 없는 명사를 수식하여 양을 나타낸다.

- The police have very **few** clues to the murderer's identity.
  ↳ 셀 수 있는 명사

- Too **little** anxiety or too **much** anxiety can cause a problem.
  ↳ 셀 수 없는 명사   ↳ 셀 수 없는 명사

- **clue** 단서
- **murderer** 살인자
- **identity** 신원, 정체성

- **anxiety** 불안(감)

Point 1 일부 연구자들이 발견했듯, 그것이 반드시 상황을 더 안전하게 만들어 주지는 않는다. / 어법 Plus 여러분의 건강보다 더 중요한 것은 아무것도 없다. / 안타깝게도, 진정으로 객관적인 과학자는 거의 없다. **Point 2** 여러분도 잘 알고 있듯, 지난주에 우리 도시에서 커다란 비극이 일어났다. / 사람들은 누군가를 다시 만날 것을 기대할 때, 그 개인의 행동과 관계없이, 그 사람이 매력적이라고 생각할 가능성이 더 높다. **Point 3** 살인자의 신원에 대해 경찰이 가진 단서는 거의 없다. / 불안감이 너무 적거나 너무 많으면 문제를 일으킬 수 있다.

✅ 출제 Point

1. 형용사[부사]가 수식하는 대상을 파악한다.
2. 보어 자리인지 형용사 보어를 수식하는 부사 자리인지 확인한다.
3. 비교구문에서 형용사[부사]의 원급[비교급]이 해야 할 역할을 파악한다.

Point 4 -ly가 붙으면 의미가 달라지는 부사

– 형용사와 부사의 형태가 같은 단어인 경우, -ly가 붙으면 그 의미가 달라지는 부사가 있다.

• The helicopter is flying **high** over the city. ➡ '높게'의 의미

• The bidding for the contract was **highly** competitive. ➡ '매우'의 의미

> **어법 Plus** -ly가 붙으면 의미가 달라지는 대표적인 부사
> high(높게, 높이) – highly(매우) / most(가장) – mostly(대부분) / late(늦게) – lately(최근에) /
> near(가까이에) – nearly(거의) / short(짧게, 간단히) – shortly(곧, 즉시) /
> hard(열심히) – hardly(거의 ~ 않다)

• **bidding** 입찰 (경쟁), 경매
• **contract** 계약(서)
• **competitive** 경쟁이 치열한

Point 5 원급 비교구문

– 형용사와 부사의 원급을 활용한 다양한 비교구문이 있다.

• I was trying to be **as steady as** I could, but I was shaking.
　　　as + 형용사/부사의 원급 + as: …만큼 ~한[하게]

• Make your plans ten **times as great as** you first planned.
　　　배수사 + as + 형용사/부사의 원급 + as: …보다 –배 ~한[하게]

• **steady** 침착한, 안정된, 꾸준한

Point 6 비교급 비교구문

– 형용사와 부사의 비교급을 활용한 다양한 비교구문이 있다.

• **The higher** the price (is), **the more reliable** the product (is).
　　the + 비교급 ~, the + 비교급 …: ~하면 할수록 더욱 …하다

➡ 「the + 비교급 ~, the + 비교급 …」 구문에서 동사는 생략되는 경우가 많다.

• James is **taller than any other student** in his class.
　　비교급 + than any other + 단수 명사: 다른 어떤 …보다도 더 ~한(최상급을 의미)

> **어법 Plus** 비교급 강조 부사: much, still, even, far, a lot은 비교급 앞에 쓰여 '훨씬 ~'의 의미를 나타낸다.

• **reliable** 신뢰할 만한

Point 4 헬리콥터가 시내 상공을 높이 날고 있다. / 그 계약의 입찰 경쟁이 매우 치열했다.　**Point 5** 나는 내가 할 수 있는 한 침착하려고 노력하고 있었지만 떨고 있었다. / 여러분이 처음에 계획했던 것보다 열 배 크게 여러분의 계획을 세워라.　**Point 6** 가격이 높으면 높을수록 제품은 더욱 신뢰할 만하다. / James는 그의 학급에서 다른 어떤 학생보다도 더 크다. (= James가 그의 학급에서 가장 크다.)

개념 확인 문제

Q1 괄호 안에서 어법상 알맞은 것을 고르세요.

1. Overconfidence can leave students with mistaken impressions that they are 〔 full / fully 〕 prepared for tests and no longer need to study.

- **overconfidence** 지나친 자신감
- **impression** 인상, 느낌

2. Her apparent indifference made him even more 〔 nervous / nervously 〕.

- **apparent** 명백한, 분명한
- **indifference** 무관심
- **nervous** 불안한, 초조한

3. Be as 〔 specific / specifically 〕 as possible when you plan your career.

4. It was 〔 unfortunate / unfortunately 〕 that the patient got worse day by day.

5. Falling in love is 〔 like / alike 〕 being wrapped in a magical cloud.

- **wrap** 감싸다

Q2 밑줄 친 부분이 어법상 맞으면 괄호 안에 ○ 표시를, 틀리면 X 표시를 하고 맞게 고쳐 쓰세요.

1. Surrounded by cheering friends, she enjoyed her victory <u>fully</u> of joy.

→ ( ) : _____

- **cheering** 환호하는, 응원하는

2. One of the hallmarks of evaluating the quality of a black tea is by assessing how <u>tight</u> the leaves are rolled.

→ ( ) : _____

- **hallmark** 특징
- **evaluate** 평가하다
- **assess** 평가하다

3. An individual should not always make himself or herself <u>readily</u> available to the person they are targeting for a longer-term relationship.

→ ( ) : _____

- **available** 이용 가능한
- **long-term** 장기간의

4. The number 799 feels <u>significant</u> less than 800 because we see the former as 7-something and the latter as 8-something.

→ ( ) : _____

- **significant** 상당한, 현저한
- **the former** 전자, 앞에 나온[언급된] 것
- **the latter** 후자, 뒤에 나온[언급된] 것

031

(A), (B), (C)의 각 네모 안에서 어법에 맞는 표현으로 가장 적절한 것은?

One point to consider for a speaker is the motivation of the audience in being there, since this can make a big difference to how (A) successful / successfully your speech may or may not be. Many people attend a
5 public speaking event out of personal or business interest, and are eager to hear the information being shared. However, sometimes people attend events because they are required to (B) be / do so rather than because they want to. For example, an employee may
10 be required to attend a conference on behalf of his company, or a student may be required to attend as a credit requirement for a course of study. In these situations, these members of your audience are less likely to be enthusiastic about the speech you are going
15 to give. If you are not cognizant of these people, your confidence may be severely compromised when you find that they are not responding to (C) that / what you feel is a good and valuable discussion.

*cognizant 인식하는, 깨달은

	(A)		(B)		(C)
①	successful	………	be	………	that
②	successful	………	do	………	what
③	successful	………	do	………	that
④	successfully	………	be	………	that
⑤	successfully	………	be	………	what

032

다음 글의 밑줄 친 부분 중, 어법상 틀린 것은?

The actual problems with monopolies are caused by statism, not capitalism. Under a statist social system, taxes, subsidies, tariffs, and regulations often serve to protect existing large players in the marketplace. Those players often use crony tactics to retain or expand 5 the protections: a new tariff preventing foreign competition, a subsidy making it harder for new players ① to compete with them, or a regulatory measure that a large company has the resources to comply with. Under a capitalist social system, on the 10 other hand, the government has no say in how ② dominantly a company may become in its industry or how companies take over and merge with one another. Furthermore, a capitalist society doesn't have rights-violating taxes, tariffs, subsidies, or regulations 15 ③ favoring anybody nor does it have antitrust laws. Under capitalism, dominance can only be achieved by becoming really good at ④ what you're doing. And to maintain dominance, you have to continue to stay ahead of the competition, which sees your dominance 20 and profits as a sign ⑤ that there is money to be made by others as well.

*statism 국가 통제주의 **crony 정실(사사로운 정에 이끌리는 일)

***antitrust law 독점 금지법

출제 의도 파악하기
❶
❷
❸
❹
❺

출제 의도 파악하기
(A)
(B)
(C)

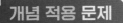

033

다음 글의 밑줄 친 부분 중, 어법상 틀린 것은?

　We tend to experience patterns of dissonance and consonance in terms of tension and relaxation. We feel tension and relaxation ① ourselves in response to the degrees of tension among the intervals, and we also tend to objectify tension and relaxation as features of the music. We easily sense a similarity between the behavior of music and our activity, ② for we notice recurrent tensions, followed by partial or complete resolutions of those tensions in music. These resemble our own patterns of exertion and relaxation. For example, we follow moments of exertion with moments of relaxation. These may be temporary or they may be ③ relatively enduring. We should note, however, that a sense of relative tension among intervals depends upon the hierarchical organization of pitches within a scale, which may not be immediately obvious to the listener who is unfamiliar with the system ④ which the scale is constructed. Also, we should note that what ⑤ counts as consonance, although based on frequency ratios that are simple, is relative to a musical system.

*dissonance 불협화음　**consonance 화음, 조화된 음

034

다음 글의 밑줄 친 부분 중, 어법상 틀린 것은?

　The world's first complex writing form, Sumerian cuneiform, followed an evolutionary path, moving around 3500 BCE from pictographic to ideographic representations, from the depiction of objects to ① that of abstract notions. Sumerian cuneiform was a linear writing system, its symbols usually ② set in columns, read from top to bottom and from left to right. This regimentation was a form of abstraction: the world is not a linear place, and objects do not organize ③ themselves horizontally or vertically in real life. Early rock paintings, thought to have been created for ritual purposes, were possibly shaped and organized ④ to follow the walls of the cave, or the desires of the painters, who may have organized them symbolically, or artistically, or even randomly. Yet after cuneiform, virtually every form of script that has emerged has been set out in rows with a clear beginning and endpoint. So ⑤ uniformly is this expectation, indeed, that the odd exception is noteworthy, and generally established for a specific purpose.

*cuneiform 쐐기 문자　**regimentation 조직화

출제 의도 파악하기

① _____
② _____
③ _____
④ _____
⑤ _____

출제 의도 파악하기

① _____
② _____
③ _____
④ _____
⑤ _____

035

다음 글의 밑줄 친 부분 중, 어법상 틀린 것은?

Anger is normal emotion. Anger is neither good nor bad, and no judgment need be attached to it. Some people believe that a problem arises if a person becomes angry. This idea is not true. To pass judgment on anger and condemn those who admit to becoming angry ① is the equivalent of robbing people of their humanness. Sadness gives a reference point that makes happiness more ② appreciated. Tension can be better understood when compared with relaxation. It is about time we stopped making value judgments about anger. You could be furious right now, but no one would know it unless you demonstrated some behavior associated with the anger. The belief that anger is bad is so strongly ingrained ③ that people will sometimes deny its existence even when it is spilling out all over the place. We have all heard someone with a red face ④ expel angry words, and then say, "I am not angry!" The blame that anger has received has made it even more ⑤ resistantly to examination.

*ingrained 깊이 몸에 밴

036

2020 4월 학평

다음 글의 밑줄 친 부분 중, 어법상 틀린 것은?

Mental representation is the mental imagery of things that are not actually present to the senses. In general, mental representations can help us learn. Some of the best evidence for this ① comes from the field of musical performance. Several researchers have examined ② what differentiates the best musicians from lesser ones, and one of the major differences lies in the quality of the mental representations the best ones create. When ③ practicing a new piece, advanced musicians have a very detailed mental representation of the music they use to guide their practice and, ultimately, their performance of a piece. In particular, they use their mental representations to provide their own feedback so that they know how ④ closely they are to getting the piece right and what they need to do differently to improve. The beginners and intermediate students may have crude representations of the music ⑤ that allow them to tell, for instance, when they hit a wrong note, but they must rely on feedback from their teachers to identify the more subtle mistakes and weaknesses.

*crude 투박한

N 07 관계사

Point 1 관계대명사의 격

- 선행사가 사람일 때: 관계대명사 who(주격), whose(소유격), who(m)(목적격)을 쓴다.
- 선행사가 사람이 아닐 때: which(주격, 목적격), whose(소유격)를 쓴다.

- This is the brand-new smartphone [**which** I want to buy].
  선행사(사람 ×)   관계대명사(목적격)

- Every day I jog along the river [**whose** banks are painted blue].
  선행사   관계대명사(소유격)

  어법 Plus that은 소유격을 제외한 모든 관계사를 대신해 쓸 수 있으며, 목적격 관계대명사 that, which, whom
  은 생략 가능하다.

- brand-new 최신의

- bank 강둑

Point 2 전치사 + 관계대명사

- 「전치사 + 관계대명사」 뒤에는 완전한 구조의 절이 오며, 문장 내에서의 기능과 의미에 따라 다양한 전치사가 온다.

- This is the hotel [**in which** we are going to stay for two days].
  선행사   전치사 + 관계대명사(= where)

- Infants are able to quickly learn any language [**to which** they are exposed].
  선행사   전치사 + 관계대명사

  ➡ they are exposed **to** any language ~의 의미이므로 전치사 to가 쓰였다.

  어법 Plus 선행사 또는 관계부사 중 하나를 생략할 수 있는 경우
  the reason why / the place where / the time when
  (단, 선행사 the way와 관계부사 how는 절대 같이 쓰지 않는다.)

- infant 유아
- expose 접하게 하다, 경험하게
  하다

Point 3 관계대명사의 계속적 용법

- 관계대명사의 계속적 용법은 관계대명사가 콤마(,) 뒤에서 선행사를 부연 설명하는 형태이다.

- Standard English allows access to certain economic opportunities, [**which** is the
  선행사   관계대명사(계속적 용법)

  primary reason for teaching it].

  ➡ which가 콤마(,) 뒤에서 앞 절 전체의 내용을 부연 설명하고 있으며, and it ~의 의미로 볼 수 있다.

- standard 표준의
- access to ~로의 접근
- primary 주된, 주요한

Point 1 이것은 내가 사고 싶어 하는 최신 스마트폰이다. / 매일 나는 둑이 파란색으로 칠해진 강을 따라 조깅한다. **Point 2** 이곳이 우리가 이틀간 머물려고 하는 호텔이다. / 유아들은 그들
이 접하게 되는 어떤 언어든지 빠르게 습득할 수 있다. **Point 3** 표준 영어는 어떤 경제적인 기회에 접근할 수 있게 해 주는데, 그것이 표준 영어를 가르치는 주된 이유이다.

Point 4 관계대명사 what

– 관계대명사 what은 선행사를 포함하며 명사절을 이끄는데, 선행사를 포함한다는 점에서 다른 관계대명사들과 다르고, 뒤에 불완전한 절이 이어진다는 점에서 접속사 that과 다르다.

- Trade will not occur unless both parties want [**what** the other party has to offer].
  선행사 포함　　　　　명사절(want의 목적어)

  - **trade** 거래, 무역
  - **party** 당사자, 측

  어법 Plus 접속사 that 뒤에는 완전한 구조의 절이 이어진다.
  The true champion recognizes that excellence flows most smoothly from simplicity.
  　　　　　　　접속사　주어　　동사

  - **excellence** 탁월함, 우수함
  - **smoothly** 부드럽게

Point 5 관계대명사와 관계부사

– 관계대명사 뒤에는 불완전한 구조의 절이 오고, 관계부사 뒤에는 완전한 구조의 절이 온다.

- The stories [**that** he told us] were not interesting.
  선행사　　관계대명사　　불완전한 구조(told의 직접목적어가 빠져 있음)

- She worked as a lawyer until 1889, [**when** she decided to devote herself to writing].
  　　　　　　　　　　선행사　관계부사　　　　　　완전한 구조

  - **devote oneself to**
    ~에 전념[헌신]하다

Point 6 복합관계대명사와 복합관계부사

– 복합관계대명사 whoever, whichever, whatever는 선행사를 포함하며 명사절 또는 양보의 부사절을 이끈다.

- They said we could invite [**whoever** would enjoy the party].
  명사절을 이끔

- [**Whatever** happens], please don't let me forget to ring Jack.
  양보의 부사절을 이끔

  - **ring** 전화를 걸다

– 복합관계부사 whenever, wherever, however는 선행사를 포함하며 시간 및 장소 또는 양보의 부사절을 이끈다.

- [**Wherever** you go], you'll never find a place like home.
  장소의 부사절을 이끔

- [**However** much you may remember the past], you live in the present.
  양보의 부사절을 이끔

  - **present** 현재

Point 4 양쪽 모두가 상대방이 제공하는 것을 원하지 않으면 거래는 일어나지 않을 것이다. / 어법 Plus 진정한 챔피언은 탁월함이란 단순함에서부터 가장 부드럽게 흘러나온다는 것을 인식한다. Point 5 그가 우리에게 말해 준 이야기들은 흥미롭지 않았다. / 그녀는 1889년까지 변호사로 일했는데, 그때 그녀는 글쓰기에 전념하기로 결심했다. Point 6 그들은 파티를 즐길 것 같은 사람은 누구든지 우리가 초대할 수 있다고 말했다. / 무슨 일이 생기더라도 제가 Jack에게 전화할 것을 잊지 않도록 해 주세요. / 여러분이 어디를 가더라도 집과 같은 곳은 결코 찾을 수 없을 것이다. / 여러분이 아무리 많이 과거를 기억하더라도, 여러분은 현재에 살고 있다.

Q1 괄호 안에서 어법상 알맞은 것을 고르세요.

1. Anniversaries and Valentine's Day are special events [when / that] need beautiful, carefully selected flowers.

• **anniversary** 기념일

2. Consult the dictionary whenever you come to a word [that / what] you don't know.

• **consult** 참조하다, 상담을 구하다

3. As she lived in a small house, [where / which] she could not practice without disturbing the rest of the family, she usually practiced her high notes outside.

• **disturb** 방해하다

4. Many believe we will eventually reach a point [which / at which] conflict with the finite nature of resources is inevitable.

• **eventually** 마침내, 결국
• **conflict** 갈등, 충돌
• **finite** 유한한, 정해진
• **inevitable** 불가피한

5. The building is surrounded by air, [what / which] applies friction to the falling marble and slows it down.

• **apply** 가하다, 적용하다
• **friction** 마찰(력)
• **marble** 구슬

Q2 밑줄 친 부분이 어법상 맞으면 괄호 안에 ○ 표시를, 틀리면 X 표시를 하고 맞게 고쳐 쓰세요.

1. From plants come chemical compounds <u>what</u> nourish and heal and delight the senses.

➡ (   ) : _____

• **chemical** 화학적인; 화학물질
• **compound** 합성물
• **nourish** 영양분을 공급하다

2. You see the world as one big contest, <u>which</u> everyone is competing against everybody else.

➡ (   ) : _____

• **compete** 경쟁하다

3. Blue lights are more attractive and calming than the yellow and white lights <u>that</u> illuminate much of the city at night.

➡ (   ) : _____

• **attractive** 매력적인
• **illuminate** 비추다

4. You want to send the message that <u>which</u> the speaker is saying is important to you.

➡ (   ) : _____

037

다음 글의 밑줄 친 부분 중, 어법상 **틀린** 것은?

The nineteenth century marked a time of change for the way food was served. Before the 1850s, nearly all the dishes of the meal ① were placed on the table at the outset. Guests would arrive to find the food waiting. They would help themselves to ② whatever was nearby and ask for other dishes to be passed or call a servant over to fetch one for them. This style of dining was known as *service à la française* (French service), but now a new practice came in known as *service à la russe* (Russian service), ③ in which food was delivered to the table in courses. A lot of people hated the new practice because it meant everyone had to eat everything in the same order and at the same pace. If one person was slow, it held up the next course for everyone else, and meant ④ that food lost heat. Dinners now sometimes dragged on for hours, ⑤ put a severe strain on nearly everyone's bladders.

*bladder 방광

038

2023 6월 모평

다음 글의 밑줄 친 부분 중, 어법상 **틀린** 것은?

Ecosystems differ in composition and extent. They can be defined as ranging from the communities and interactions of organisms in your mouth or ① those in the canopy of a rain forest to all those in Earth's oceans. The processes ② governing them differ in complexity and speed. There are systems that turn over in minutes, and there are others ③ which rhythmic time extends to hundreds of years. Some ecosystems are extensive ('biomes', such as the African savanna); some cover regions (river basins); many involve clusters of villages (micro-watersheds); others are confined to the level of a single village (the village pond). In each example there is an element of indivisibility. Divide an ecosystem into parts by creating barriers, and the sum of the productivity of the parts will typically be found to be lower than the productivity of the whole, other things ④ being equal. The mobility of biological populations is a reason. Safe passages, for example, enable migratory species ⑤ to survive.

*canopy 덮개 **basin 유역

039

다음 글의 밑줄 친 부분 중, 어법상 틀린 것은?

Until recently, most studies that have argued for a causal connection between population growth and tropical deforestation have not provided detailed, empirical accounts about ① <u>how</u> population growth has spurred land clearing. This weakness has been ② <u>addressed</u> in several different ways during the past 10 years. A study of forest cover change in Costa Rica during the 1970s and 1980s demonstrated a positive association between concentrations of landless peasants and the destruction of nearby forests. Variations in household composition also ③ <u>influence</u> land-clearing rates. Clearing primary rain forest from the land is physically taxing work ④ <u>in which</u> only young people at the peak of their physical powers will routinely undertake. For this reason, only households and communities that have an abundance of young workers will clear much land. If emigration or declines in birth rates reduce the number of young workers in a household, the likelihood of forest clearing on the household's land also ⑤ <u>declines</u>.

*forest cover 숲 분포율(특정 식물이 지상에 퍼져 있는 비율)

040

2023 7월 학평

다음 글의 밑줄 친 부분 중, 어법상 틀린 것은?

The intelligence of monkeys pales in comparison with that of our closest relatives, the great apes: orangutans, gorillas, chimpanzees, and bonobos, whose brains are twice as ① <u>large</u> relative to their body weight. Most primatologists believe the apes acquired their larger brains to help them communicate with and ② <u>manipulate</u> their peers. And they certainly do exhibit complex social interactions within their group; they seem capable of feeling empathy, have a self-image, and exhibit a degree of consciousness as they can recognize ③ <u>themselves</u> in a mirror. But this "social hypothesis" does not explain why it was the great apes that became so clever, rather than monkeys or a group of terrestrial mammals. Nor does it explain why orangutans, who seldom encounter their neighbors, ④ <u>being</u> so intelligent. It seems likely that some other factor must have been in play ⑤ <u>that</u> caused apes to become more intelligent in the first place, and which could subsequently have enabled some members of the group to develop high-level sociality.

*primatologist 영장류 동물학자 **terrestrial 육상의

❶ ....
❷ ....
❸ ....
❹ ....
❺ ....

❶ ....
❷ ....
❸ ....
❹ ....
❺ ....

041

다음 글의 밑줄 친 부분 중, 어법상 틀린 것은?

　As a very general rule (the exceptions are plenty), the humanities, social sciences, and natural sciences are fundamentally geared more toward your ① achieving intellectual growth and development. The primary focus of these "liberal arts" fields ② is not on your gaining a job in a directly related field upon graduation. On the other hand, fields such as business administration, education, engineering, architecture, nursing, pharmacy, journalism, social welfare, and allied health are ③ generally more career-oriented fields. These areas of study are often more payable in the form of a directly related job after graduation. This does not mean you will not be able to find employment if you decide to major in the liberal arts; nor ④ does it imply that you cannot gain intellectual growth and development by majoring in more career-oriented fields. Rather, it calls your attention to majors ⑤ what have historically tended to be more career-oriented.

*allied health 보건 (관련)

042

다음 글의 밑줄 친 부분 중, 어법상 틀린 것은?

　A classic positive-sum game in economic life is the trading of surpluses. If a farmer has more grain than he can eat, and a herder has more milk than he can drink, both of them come out ahead if they trade some wheat for some milk. As they say, everybody wins. Of course, an exchange at a single moment in time only ① pays when there is a division of labor. There would be no point in one farmer giving a bushel of wheat to another farmer and ② receiving a bushel of wheat in return. A fundamental insight of modern economics is that the key to the creation of wealth is a division of labor, ③ in which specialists learn to produce a commodity with increasing cost-effectiveness and have the means to exchange their specialized products efficiently. One infrastructure that allows efficient exchange is transportation, which makes it possible for producers ④ to trade their surpluses even when they are separated by distance. Another is money, interest, and middlemen, which ⑤ allows producers to exchange many kinds of surpluses with many other producers at many points in time.

출제 의도 파악하기
❶ ....
❷ ....
❸ ....
❹ ....
❺ ....

출제 의도 파악하기
❶ ....
❷ ....
❸ ....
❹ ....
❺ ....

전치사와 접속사

Point 1 전치사와 접속사의 구분

– 전치사 다음에는 명사 상당어구가 오고, 접속사 다음에는 주어와 동사를 갖춘 절이 온다.

- Food plays a large part **in** how much you enjoy the outdoors.
  전치사   명사절(의문사절)

  - **play a part** 역할을 하다
  - **outdoors** 야외 (활동)

- **When** we praise kids **for** their ability, kids become more cautious.
  접속사   절   전치사   명사구

  - **praise** 칭찬하다
  - **cautious** 신중한, 조심하는

Point 2 비슷한 의미의 전치사와 접속사

– 이유, 양보, 기간 표현 등을 나타내는 의미가 비슷한 다양한 전치사와 접속사가 있다.

- **Despite** the protective packaging, the dishes were broken.
  전치사(~에도 불구하고)   명사구

  - **packaging** 포장

- **Although** he had only entered the contest for fun, he won the first prize.
  접속사(비록 ~임에도 불구하고)   절

  - **win a prize** 상을 받다

어법 Plus 비슷한 의미의 전치사와 접속사

의미	전치사	접속사
[이유] ~ 때문에	because of, due to, owing to	because, as, since, now that
[양보] ~에도 불구하고	despite, in spite of	although, though, even though
[기간] ~ 동안	during, for	while

Point 3 전치사 to

– 전치사 to 뒤에는 명사(구) 및 동명사(구)가 오며, 전치사 to가 쓰이는 다양한 관용어구가 있다.

- I would certainly get used **to** teaching these girls.
  전치사   명사구 「get used to ~에 익숙해지다」

  - **certainly** 틀림없이

어법 Plus 전치사 to가 쓰이는 주요 관용어구
look forward to ~을 기대하다 / be used to ~에 익숙하다 / be devoted to ~에 전념하다 /
contribute to ~에 기여하다, ~의 원인이 되다 / be accustomed to ~에 익숙하다 /
object to ~에 반대하다 / in contrast to ~와 반대로 / the key to ~의 열쇠[핵심ㆍ비결]

Point 1 음식은 여러분이 야외 활동을 얼마만큼 즐기는지에 있어 큰 역할을 한다. / 우리가 아이들의 능력에 대해 그들을 칭찬할 때 아이들은 더 조심하게 된다. **Point 2** 보호 포장에도 불구하고 접시이 깨졌다. / 그는 그 시합에 그저 재미 삼아 참가했음에도 1등 상을 탔다. **Point 3** 나는 이 소녀들을 가르치는 데에 틀림없이 익숙해질 것이다.

⊘ 출제 Point

1. 전치사 뒤에 명사 상당어구가, 접속사 뒤에 절이 이어지는지 확인한다.
2. 명사절 접속사 that과 if, whether의 쓰임을 구분한다.
3. 문맥상 알맞은 의미의 부사절 접속사가 쓰였는지 확인한다.

Point ④ 명사절 접속사

– 문장에서 주어, 보어, 목적어 역할을 하는 명사절을 이끄는 접속사에는 whether, that, if가 있으며, if절은 주어 자리에 쓰이지 않는다.

- [**Whether** those women are American or Iranian] does not matter.
  접속사   명사절(주어)

  • **matter** 중요하다

- I asked him [**if** he would lend her his car].
  접속사   명사절(직접목적어)

– 접속사 that은 일부 명사 뒤에서 그 내용을 구체적으로 보여 주는 동격의 명사절을 이끌기도 한다.

- The fact [**that** he had not graduated from university] is hard to believe.
  접속사   동격 명사절(= The fact)

  • **graduate from** ~을 졸업하다

Point ⑤ 「so ~ that ...」 구문에 쓰이는 접속사 that

– 원인 – 결과를 나타내는 「so + 형용사/부사 + that ...」 구문과 「such a(n) + 명사 + that ...」 구문에 접속사 that이 쓰인다.

- The math problem is <u>so</u> difficult **that** I can't solve it.
  so + 형용사 + that(접속사)

  • **solve** 해결하다, 풀다

- She is <u>such a considerate girl</u> **that** everyone likes her.
  such + a + 명사 + that(접속사)

  어법 Plus 「so that ~ 」 구문은 목적 및 결과를 나타낸다.
  Fry the onion under low heat so that it becomes soft.
  목적(~하도록)

Point ⑥ 상관접속사

– 상관접속사로 연결된 대상들은 문법적으로 대등한 병렬구조를 이룬다.

- I have **neither** the time **nor** the patience to listen to his complaints.
  상관접속사   └ 병렬구조 ┘   「neither A nor B(A도 아니고 B도 아닌)」

  • **patience** 인내(심)
  • **complaint** 불평, 불만

  어법 Plus 주요 상관접속사
  both A and B A와 B 둘 다 / A as well as B B뿐만 아니라 A도
  not only A but (also) B A뿐만 아니라 B도 / not A but B A가 아니라 B /
  either A or B A 또는 B 중 하나 / neither A nor B A도 아니고 B도 아닌

Point ④ 그 여성들이 미국인인지 또는 이란인인지는 중요하지 않다. / 나는 그가 그녀에게 자기 차를 빌려줄 것인지를 물어보았다. / 그가 대학을 졸업하지 않았다는 사실은 믿기 힘들다.
Point ⑤ 그 수학 문제는 너무 어려워서 나는 그것을 풀 수가 없다. / 그녀는 매우 사려 깊은 소녀여서 모두가 그녀를 좋아한다. / 어법 Plus 양파가 부드러워지도록 그것을 약한 불에 튀겨라.
Point ⑥ 나는 그의 불평을 들어줄 시간도 없고 인내심도 없다.

개념 확인 문제

Q1 괄호 안에서 어법상 알맞은 것을 고르세요.

1. I strongly object to [be / being] charged a fee for using my credit card.

- **charge** 부과하다
- **fee** 수수료, 요금

2. We study philosophy [because / because of] the mental skills it helps to develop.

- **philosophy** 철학
- **mental** 정신적인

3. [Despite / Although] a person's good look may get our attention, it is not an impression that necessarily lasts.

- **last** 지속되다

4. Even in today's tech-savvy world, answering phone calls [during / while] a conversation is disrespectful.

- **tech-savvy** 기술에 정통한
- **disrespectful** 무례한

5. All of a sudden, we must face the possibility [of / that] our ability to be creative is not unrivaled.

- **unrivaled** 경쟁할 상대가 없는

Q2 밑줄 친 부분이 어법상 맞으면 괄호 안에 ○ 표시를, 틀리면 X 표시를 하고 맞게 고쳐 쓰세요.

1. Try on both shoes, <u>as</u> most people have one foot that is slightly larger than the other.

➡ ( ) : _____

- **slightly** 약간

2. All products can be classified as either consumer goods <u>nor</u> producer goods.

➡ ( ) : _____

- **classify** 분류하다
- **goods** 상품

3. One day, he sat on a park bench wondering <u>while</u> anything could save his company from bankruptcy.

➡ ( ) : _____

- **bankruptcy** 파산

4. To argue that knowledge is not progressing <u>because</u> the African or Middle Eastern conflicts misses the point.

➡ ( ) : _____

- **argue** 주장하다
- **progress** 진보하다
- **conflict** 갈등, 충돌

043

2022 10월 학평

다음 글의 밑줄 친 부분 중, 어법상 틀린 것은?

　The idea that leaders *inherently* possess certain physical, intellectual, or personality traits that distinguish them from nonleaders ① was the foundational belief of the trait-based approach to leadership. This approach dominated leadership research from the late 1800s until the mid-1940s and has experienced a resurgence of interest in the last couple of decades. Early trait theorists believed that some individuals are born with the traits that allow ② them to become great leaders. Thus, early research in this area often presented the widely stated argument ③ that "leaders are born, not made." Also, some of the earliest leadership studies were grounded in what ④ referred to as the "great man" theory because researchers at the time focused on identifying traits of highly visible leaders in history who were typically male and associated with the aristocracy or political or military leadership. In more recent history, numerous authors have acknowledged that there are many enduring qualities, ⑤ whether innate or learned, that contribute to leadership potential. These traits include such things as *drive, self-confidence, cognitive ability, conscientiousness, determination, intelligence,* and *integrity*.

*resurgence 되살아남　**aristocracy 귀족

044

다음 글의 밑줄 친 부분 중, 어법상 틀린 것은?

　Flowers inspired the first artists, writers, photographers, and scientists, just as they ① do today on street corners, in florist shops and farmers' markets, in books, paintings, sculptures, and commercial advertising. They moved online with ease. Arguably, ② because of the sustaining role they undoubtedly played in the lives of our hominid ancestors, we might not be here if there was no fondness for flowers. Once captivated by them, I observed nature's infinite palette of garden blooms and wildflowers near my boyhood home. The honey bees I kept ③ visiting flowers for their rewards of nectar and pollen. The bees fed upon the pollen and ④ converted the nectar into delicious, golden, thick honey I drizzled atop slices of hot toast at breakfast. As a child, finding and observing bees of all kinds on wildflowers became my passion and quest across California's wildlands. The bees showed me the way ⑤ leading to a lifelong dedication to flowering plants.

*hominid 사람, 인간

출제 의도 파악하기
❶
❷
❸
❹
❺

출제 의도 파악하기
❶
❷
❸
❹
❺

045

다음 글의 밑줄 친 부분 중, 어법상 틀린 것은?

People from more individualistic cultural contexts tend to be motivated to maintain self-focused agency or control ① as these serve as the basis of one's self-worth. With this form of agency comes the belief that individual successes ② depending primarily on one's own abilities and actions, and thus, whether by influencing the environment or trying to accept one's circumstances, the use of control ultimately centers on the individual. The independent self may be more ③ driven to cope by appealing to a sense of agency or control. However, people from more interdependent cultural contexts tend to be less focused on issues of individual success and agency and more motivated towards group goals and harmony. Research has shown ④ that East Asians prefer to receive, but not seek, more social support rather than seek personal control in certain cases. Therefore, people ⑤ who hold a more interdependent self-construal may prefer to cope in a way that promotes harmony in relationships.

*self-construal 자기 구성

046

다음 글의 밑줄 친 부분 중, 어법상 틀린 것은?

When people think about the wonders of high technology, ① what comes to mind is global communication satellites and giant-size telescopes that can spy on the distant galaxies of the universe. But recent advances in technology have also enabled us to turn the scientific eye on ourselves, to inner recesses of the human brain never ② previously seen. ③ Designed to provide visual images of the live human brain, without our ever having to lift a scalpel, this new technology uses computers to combine thousands of still "snapshots" into models of the brain in action. There are several basic types of imaging techniques, one of which is the computerized tomography (CT) scan. In this technique, X-ray beams are passed through the head at 1-degree intervals over a 180-degree arc, and a computer is used to ④ converting this information into an image that depicts a horizontal slice of the brain. This technique takes advantage of the fact ⑤ that when a highly focused beam of X-rays is passed through the body, the beam is affected by the relative density of the tissue through which it passes.

*recesses 깊숙한 곳   **scalpel 수술용 칼

047

다음 글의 밑줄 친 부분 중, 어법상 <u>틀린</u> 것은?

You turn on a lamp's switch but you get no light. Do you immediately declare that the lamp's switch is broken or that the lamp's wiring has shorted out? No, that would be GULPing. If the lamp has been in perfect working order up to now, those reasons are not very ① <u>likely</u>. But you do know that lamp cords often get pulled out of their outlets, so you would check that first. If that's not the problem, you would check ② <u>whether</u> the outlet is supplying electricity (perhaps a circuit breaker tripped), so you plug a different appliance into the outlet to test it. If the outlet is not the culprit, there's yet another common cause—a ③ <u>blown</u> light bulb—so you would check that. By this point in your troubleshooting, 99.9 percent of the time you ④ <u>will have solved</u> the problem—in minimal time at no expense (except for a new bulb). ⑤ <u>Have</u> you GULPed, you would be halfway to the home center to hand over big bucks for a new lamp.

*gulp 곧이곧대로 생각하다 **culprit 원인
***buck (미국·호주·뉴질랜드의) 달러

048

다음 글의 밑줄 친 부분 중, 어법상 <u>틀린</u> 것은?

Humans are so averse to feeling that they're being cheated ① <u>that</u> they often respond in ways that seemingly make little sense. Behavioral economists—the economists who actually study ② <u>what</u> people do as opposed to the kind who simply assume the human mind works like a calculator—have shown again and again that people reject unfair offers even if ③ <u>it</u> costs them money to do so. The typical experiment uses a task called the ultimatum game. It's pretty straightforward. One person in a pair is given some money—say $10. She then has the opportunity to offer some amount of it to her partner. The partner only has two options. He can take what's offered or ④ <u>refused</u> to take anything. There's no room for negotiation; that's why it's called the ultimatum game. What typically happens? Many people offer an equal split to the partner, ⑤ <u>leaving</u> both individuals happy and willing to trust each other in the future.

*averse to ~을 싫어하는 **ultimatum 최후통첩

出제 의도 파악하기
❶ ....
❷ ....
❸ ....
❹ ....
❺ ....

出제 의도 파악하기
❶ ....
❷ ....
❸ ....
❹ ....
❺ ....

Point ❶ 병렬구조

– 등위접속사, 상관접속사, 비교구문 등을 통해 병렬구조로 연결된 요소들은 어법적으로 대등해야 한다.

- The restaurant serves **cheap** but **excellent** food.
  형용사　　　　　형용사
  등위접속사

- **Riding a bicycle** is more difficult than **driving a car**.
  동명사구　　　　　비교구문　　　　　동명사구

  어법 Plus 반복되는 어구는 지시대명사 that 또는 those로 대신할 수 있다.
  The salaries of professors are lower than those of lawyers.
  　　　　　　　　　　　　　　　　　　= the salaries

- **cheap** 저렴한

- **ride a bicycle** 자전거를 타다

- **salary** 급료
- **professor** 교수

Point ❷ 도치

– 부정어(구), 장소[위치, 방향]의 부사(구), only가 이끄는 부사구, 보어가 문두에 올 때, 주어와 (조)동사가 도치된다.

- **No longer** can managers stick their heads in the sand.
  부정어구　조동사　주어　동사원형

- **Down the street** walks a boy with red hair.
  방향 부사구　　　동사　　　주어

- **Only** for the love of his family does he do such hard work.
  　　only가 이끄는 부사구　　　조동사 주어 동사원형

- **Gone** are the days when you can find a job easily after graduation.
  보어　be동사　주어

- **stick one's head in the sand** 외면하다, 잠자코 있다

- **graduation** 졸업

Point ❸ 강조구문

– 주어, 목적어, 부사(구)는 「It is[was] + 강조 대상 + that ....」 구문으로 강조할 수 있다.
– 일반동사는 「조동사 do + 동사원형」 형태로 강조할 수 있다.

- **It was** Brian **that** broke the window.
  It was　강조 대상　that

- He is generally reserved, but if he **does** talk, he always talks to the point.
  　　　　　　　　　조동사 do(3인칭) 동사원형

- **reserved** 말수가 적은

Point ❶ 그 식당은 저렴하지만 훌륭한 음식이 나온다. / 자전거를 타는 것이 자동차를 운전하는 것보다 더 어렵다. / **어법 Plus** 교수의 급료는 변호사의 급료보다 더 낮다. **Point ❷** 관리자들은 더 이상 현실을 외면할 수 없다. / 빨간 머리의 한 소년이 거리를 걸어 내려온다. / 단지 가족에 대한 사랑 때문에 그는 그렇게 힘든 일을 한다. / 졸업 후에 쉽게 직장을 구할 수 있는 날들은 사라졌다. **Point ❸** 유리창을 깬 것은 바로 Brian이었다. / 그는 보통 말수가 적지만, 말을 하게 되면 항상 요점만 말한다.

☑ 출제 Point

1. 등위[상관]접속사로 연결된 요소들이 병렬구조를 이루는지 확인한다.
2. 도치된 주어와 동사를 파악하고 수가 일치하는지 확인한다.
3. 강조구문에서 주어와 동사를 정확히 파악한다.

Point ④ 생략

– 시간, 양보, 조건 부사절의 주어가 주절의 주어와 같을 때, 부사절에서 「주어 + be동사」를 생략할 수 있다.
– 앞뒤 문맥상 의미가 분명한 어구를 생략할 수 있다.

- [When (**you are**) in Rome], do as the Romans do.
  생략 가능

➡ 명령문이므로 주절의 주어는 you이다.

- You might wish her to sing, but I don't think she will (**sing**).
  생략 가능

Point ⑤ 의문사절(간접의문문)의 어순

– 의문문이 문장 내에서 주어, 보어, 목적어 역할을 하는 의문사절의 경우 「의문사 + 주어 + 동사」의 어순이 된다.
– 의문사가 의문사절 주어로 쓰일 경우 「의문사 + 동사」의 어순이 된다.

- I asked a clerk [**where** the books about music are located].
  의문사   주어   동사

➡ 의문사절이 직접목적어로 쓰였다.

- Do you know [**what** caused the train accident]?
  의문사(주어)   동사

- clerk 점원
- locate 위치시키다

Point ⑥ 「타동사 + 부사」의 목적어 어순

– 목적어가 명사일 때는 「타동사 + 부사 + 명사(목적어)」 또는 「타동사 + 명사(목적어) + 부사」 어순이다.
– 목적어가 대명사일 때는 반드시 「타동사 + 대명사(목적어) + 부사」 어순이어야 한다.

- Turn off your cell phones before the movie begins.
  타동사 부사   명사구(목적어)

➡ Turn your cell phones off (○)

- This novel is so interesting that I can't put **it** down.
  타동사   부사
  대명사(목적어)

➡ put down it (×)

- novel 소설

Point ④ 로마에서는 로마인들이 하는 대로 하라. / 너는 그녀가 노래하기를 원할지 모르지만, 나는 그녀가 할(노래할) 것이라고 생각하지 않는다. **Point ⑤** 나는 점원에게 음악에 관한 책들이 어디에 위치해 있는지를 물었다. / 무엇이 열차 사고를 일으켰는지 아시나요? **Point ⑥** 영화가 시작하기 전에 휴대전화를 꺼 주세요. / 이 소설은 매우 흥미로워서 나는 그것을 내려놓을 수가 없다.

개념 확인 문제

Q1 괄호 안에서 어법상 알맞은 것을 고르세요.

1. Not only [he was / was he] a noted author, but also a gifted speaker.

- **noted** 유명한
- **author** 저자, 작가
- **gifted** 재능 있는

2. I made my bed, straightened the room, [dusting / dusted] the floor and did whatever else came to my mind.

- **straighten** 정리하다, 바로 잡다
- **dust** 먼지를 털다

3. Children are much more resistant to giving something to someone else than to [help / helping] them.

- **resistant** 저항적인

4. One of the most active areas of medical research today aims at making drugs that block or [prevent / preventing] pyrogen production.

- **aim** 목표로 하다, 겨냥하다
- **block** 차단하다, 막다
- **prevent** 예방하다, 막다
- **pyrogen** 발열원

5. I've bought the Christmas decorations and I'm going to [put them up / put up them] before the party on Saturday.

Q2 밑줄 친 부분이 어법상 맞으면 괄호 안에 ○ 표시를, 틀리면 X 표시를 하고 맞게 고쳐 쓰세요.

1. Assigning students to independently read, think about, and then <u>writing</u> about a complex text is not enough.

- **assign** 과제를 주다
- **independently** 독립적으로

➡ (　　　) : _____

2. Everything does <u>happening</u> for a reason—which is to say that events have causes, and the cause always comes before the event.

➡ (　　　) : _____

3. Right in front of his eyes <u>were</u> rows of delicious-looking chocolate bars waiting to be touched.

➡ (　　　) : _____

4. Keep working on one habit long enough, and not only does it become easier, but so <u>does</u> other things as well.

➡ (　　　) : _____

049

2022 3월 학평

다음 글의 밑줄 친 부분 중, 어법상 틀린 것은?

We don't know what ancient Greek music sounded like, because there are no examples of it in written or notated form, nor ① has it survived in oral tradition. Much of it was probably improvised anyway, within certain rules and conventions. So we are forced largely to guess at its basis from the accounts of writers such as Plato and Aristotle, who were generally more concerned with writing about music as a philosophical and ethical exercise ② as with providing a technical primer on its practice. It seems Greek music was predominantly a vocal form, ③ consisting of sung verse accompanied by instruments such as the lyre or the plucked kithara (the root of 'guitar'). In fact, Plato considered music in which the lyre and flute played alone and not as the accompaniment of dance or song ④ to be 'exceedingly coarse and tasteless'. The melodies seem to have had a very limited pitch range, since the instruments ⑤ generally span only an octave, from one E (as we'd now define it) to the next.

*primer 입문서 **lyre 수금(竪琴) ***coarse 조잡한

050

다음 글의 밑줄 친 부분 중, 어법상 틀린 것은?

The Second World War was to have a major impact on the identity of managers. The management of organizations became a key aspect of winning a war that depended as much on the ability to organize the manufacture and transport of supplies ① as on the ability to direct military confrontations. During the war, therefore, governments found ② it necessary to take seriously the techniques of management and administration. In the USA the government turned to the business schools to address the difficulties of administering a war economy, including the tasks of collecting statistics and other information and ③ develop techniques for coordinated decision making across many different organizations. This led to the development of techniques such as linear programming and systems analysis, ④ which led later to computer simulations, network analysis, and cost-accounting systems. There was progress in statistics and statistical sampling, as well as in survey methods and focus groups, under the pressures of assuring the quality of armaments. Engineers developed the theory of systems ⑤ to provide forms of self-regulating control.

*obliterate 없애다, 지우다

출제 의도 파악하기

❶ ....
❷ ....
❸ ....
❹ ....
❺ ....

출제 의도 파악하기

❶ ....
❷ ....
❸ ....
❹ ....
❺ ....

051

다음 글의 밑줄 친 부분 중, 어법상 **틀린** 것은?

 In training a dog, we must take all things into consideration before we punish the dog and ① <u>look</u> upon it with disappointment or disgust. Only by repetition ② <u>does</u> a dog know what is right or wrong
5 when very tiny. It learns this from experience—from the angry tone of the voice of the owner, or the jerk on a leash, or having its privileges ③ <u>take</u> away when naughty. In other words, its mind cannot reason what is right or wrong. But whatever the punishment, it is
10 not effective ④ <u>unless</u> the owner understands the natural reaction of the dog to the treatment it is receiving or is about to receive. The key to changing a dog's behavior lies in the owner's mind, not in the dog's. There are no bad dogs, only inexperienced
15 owners who do not notice that their dogs do have a potential inclination ⑤ <u>to love</u>, honor, and obey them.

*jerk 갑작스러운 잡아당김

052

2020 3월 학평

다음 글의 밑줄 친 부분 중, 어법상 **틀린** 것은?

 When children are young, much of the work is demonstrating to them that they ① <u>do</u> have control. One wise friend of ours who was a parent educator for twenty years ② <u>advises</u> giving calendars to preschool-
5 age children and writing down all the important events in their life, in part because it helps children understand the passage of time better, and how their days will unfold. We can't overstate the importance of the calendar tool in helping kids feel in control of their
10 day. Have them ③ <u>cross</u> off days of the week as you come to them. Spend time going over the schedule for the day, giving them choice in that schedule wherever ④ <u>possible</u>. This communication expresses respect— they see that they are not just a tagalong to your day
15 and your plans, and they understand what is going to happen, when, and why. As they get older, children will then start to write in important things for themselves, ⑤ <u>it</u> further helps them develop their sense of control.

출제 의도 파악하기

❶
❷
❸
❹
❺

출제 의도 파악하기

❶
❷
❸
❹
❺

053

다음 글의 밑줄 친 부분 중, 어법상 <u>틀린</u> 것은?

Critical to crime rates in any culture ① <u>is</u> the parenting and child-care philosophies and methods. Most street crimes, such as burglaries and robberies, in all societies occur among adolescents and young
5 adults. In some societies, parents are seen as ② <u>primarily</u> responsible for their children, but all citizens share that responsibility. In other societies the child is treated as chattel—the property of the parents. The first type of society assures that parents receive
10 preparation for infant care and ③ <u>provides</u> support for parents in caring for their children. In the second type, no such support system exists. In these societies, nothing is ④ <u>required</u> to be a parent—no knowledge, no skills, no income—and the parent is on his or her
15 own in caring for the child. It is not difficult to determine ⑤ <u>which</u> system is more likely to produce a law-abiding young adult.

*chattel 소유물. 동산 **law-abiding 법을 잘 지키는

054

다음 글의 밑줄 친 부분 중, 어법상 <u>틀린</u> 것은?

Informal networks enhance people's ability to cope with difficulties and disasters. Sharing scarce resources during times of hardship is common among communities ① <u>living</u> in poverty or harsh environments, and can be crucial to the survival of 5 some community members. Studies of communities hit by catastrophe, such as a landslide, heatwave or long strike action, ② <u>suggest</u> that those with strong social networks are more likely to recover than those where networks are obliterated or non-existent. In Sri 10 Lanka in the immediate aftermath of the tsunami in 2004, local networks mobilised ③ <u>to provide</u> assistance to those affected on the coast. These indigenous efforts were soon overwhelmed by the influx of well-meaning foreign aid agencies, some of ④ <u>their</u> activities have 15 been criticised as undermining the capacities of surviving communities. Similarly, in the months after Hurricane Katrina caused widespread flooding in New Orleans, it was the informal neighbourhood associations ⑤ <u>that</u> were most effective in helping 20 communities to rebuild their shattered lives, rather than state agencies or non-governmental organizations.

*obliterate 없애다, 지우다

출제 의도 파악하기

❶ ....
❷ ....
❸ ....
❹ ....
❺ ....

출제 의도 파악하기

❶ ....
❷ ....
❸ ....
❹ ....
❺ ....

055

2020 10월 학평

다음 글의 밑줄 친 부분 중, 어법상 틀린 것은?

Mathematical practices and discourses should be situated within cultural contexts, student interests, and real-life situations ① where all students develop positive identities as mathematics learners. Instruction in mathematics skills in isolation and devoid of student understandings and identities renders them ② helpless to benefit from explicit instruction. Thus, we agree that explicit instruction benefits students but propose that incorporating culturally relevant pedagogy and consideration of nonacademic factors that ③ promoting learning and mastery must enhance explicit instruction in mathematics instruction. Furthermore, teachers play a critical role in developing environments ④ that encourage student identities, agency, and independence through discourses and practices in the classroom. Students who are actively engaged in a contextualized learning process are in control of the learning process and are able to make connections with past learning experiences ⑤ to foster deeper and more meaningful learning.

*render (어떤 상태가 되게) 만들다   **pedagogy 교수법

056

다음 글의 밑줄 친 부분 중, 어법상 틀린 것은?

Until only a few years ago, it was widely believed that we are born with all the brain cells we will ever have. This led to the ① depressing idea that we all slowly go downhill, as the brain loses thousands of neurons every day. Rather than facing a steady decline, we now know that a healthy 75-year-old brain has just as many neurons as it ② was when it was careening through life in the body of a 25-year-old. Although it is true that the brain loses cells daily, it simultaneously grows new neurons ③ to replace them. This process is called neurogenesis, the production of new brain cells. Each day, thousands of new cells originate deep within the brain, move to the surface, and ④ link up with other neurons to become part of the brain's circuitry. This was stunning news to brain scientists, who must now figure out ⑤ what the new cells do. Most likely they are involved in learning, memory, and our ability to adapt to changing circumstances.

*careen (위태롭게) 질주하다

출제 의도 파악하기
❶ ....
❷ ....
❸ ....
❹ ....
❺ ....

출제 의도 파악하기
❶ ....
❷ ....
❸ ....
❹ ....
❺ ....

057

다음 글의 밑줄 친 부분 중, 어법상 틀린 것은?

The Internet allows information to flow more ① freely than ever before. We can communicate and share ideas in unprecedented ways. These developments are revolutionizing our self-expression and enhancing our freedom. But there's a problem. We're heading toward a world ② where an extensive trail of information fragments about us will be forever preserved on the Internet, displayed instantly in a search result. We will be forced to live with a detailed record ③ beginning with childhood that will stay with us for life wherever we go, searchable and accessible from anywhere in the world. This data can often be of dubious reliability; it can be false; or it can be true but deeply ④ humiliated. It may be increasingly difficult to have a fresh start or a second chance. We might find ⑤ it harder to engage in self-exploration if every false step and foolish act is preserved forever in a permanent record.

*dubious 의심스러운

058

다음 글의 밑줄 친 부분 중, 어법상 틀린 것은?

All occupied buildings require a supply of fresh air, and this can be achieved by natural convection in most parts of the world, depending on diurnal and seasonal variations in climate. The use of natural convection to remove internal heat gains is dependent on the external air temperature ① being lower than that required internally. In northern Europe the external air temperature is generally below the desired internal temperature, so natural convection can ② be used during the day to remove unwanted heat through much of the year. In southern Europe the external air temperature in summer may be low enough ③ to bring into the building during the day and at night, depending on the building's use and construction characteristics. However, when the external air temperature is above the desired internal air temperature, ④ which implies that (in non-domestic buildings) the air supplied must be pre-cooled either naturally or mechanically, and that ventilators must be controlled appropriately. While generally ⑤ applicable, the perception of thermal comfort will be influenced by internal surface temperatures and the thermal capacitance of the interior.

*convection (열·전기의) 대류 **diurnal 하루 동안의
***capacitance (축적된) 용량

059

2021 수능

다음 글의 밑줄 친 부분 중, 어법상 틀린 것은?

Regulations covering scientific experiments on human subjects are strict. Subjects must give their informed, written consent, and experimenters must submit their proposed experiments to thorough examination by overseeing bodies. Scientists who experiment on themselves can, functionally if not legally, avoid the restrictions ① associated with experimenting on other people. They can also sidestep most of the ethical issues involved: nobody, presumably, is more aware of an experiment's potential hazards than the scientist who devised ② it. Nonetheless, experimenting on oneself remains ③ deeply problematic. One obvious drawback is the danger involved; knowing that it exists ④ does nothing to reduce it. A less obvious drawback is the limited range of data that the experiment can generate. Human anatomy and physiology vary, in small but significant ways, according to gender, age, lifestyle, and other factors. Experimental results derived from a single subject are, therefore, of limited value; there is no way to know ⑤ what the subject's responses are typical or atypical of the response of humans as a group.

*consent 동의   **anatomy (해부학적) 구조
***physiology 생리적 현상

060

다음 글의 밑줄 친 부분 중, 어법상 틀린 것은?

A difference in the concept of justice lies in various societies' ideas of ① what laws are. In the West, people consider "laws" quite ② differently from "customs." There is also a great contrast between "sins" and "crimes." In many non-Western cultures, however, there is little separation of customs, laws and religious beliefs; in other cultures, these three may be quite separate from one another, but still very much different from ③ those in the West. For these reasons, an action may be considered a crime in one country but ④ be socially acceptable in others. For instance, although a thief is viewed as a criminal in much of the world, in a small village where there is considerable sharing of objects, the word "thief" may have little meaning. Someone who has taken something without ⑤ asking is simply considered an impolite person.

출제 의도 파악하기

❶ ....
❷ ....
❸ ....
❹ ....
❺ ....

출제 의도 파악하기

❶ ....
❷ ....
❸ ....
❹ ....
❺ ....

061

2022 7월 학평

다음 글의 밑줄 친 부분 중, 어법상 틀린 것은?

The spider chart, also called a radar chart, is a form of line graph. It helps the researcher to represent their data in a chart ① that shows the relative size of a response on one scale for interrelated variables. Like the bar chart, the data needs to have one scale which is common to all variables. The spider chart is drawn with the variables spanning the chart, ② creating a spider web. An example of this is seen in a research study looking at self-reported confidence in year 7 students across a range of subjects ③ have taught in their first term in secondary school. The researcher takes the responses from a sample group and ④ calculates the mean to plot on the spider chart. The spider chart allows the researcher to easily compare and contrast the confidence level in different subjects for the sample group. The chart, like the pie chart, can then be broken down for different groups of students within the study ⑤ to elicit further analysis of findings.

062

다음 글의 밑줄 친 부분 중, 어법상 틀린 것은?

Excessive positivity expresses itself as an excess of stimuli, information, and impulses. It radically changes the structure and economy of attention. Perception becomes fragmented and scattered. Moreover, the mounting burden of work makes it necessary ① to adopt particular dispositions toward time and attention; this in turn affects the structure of attention and cognition. The attitude toward time and environment ② knows as "multitasking" does not represent civilizational progress. Human beings in the late-modern society of work and information are not the only ③ ones capable of multitasking. Multitasking is commonplace among wild animals. It is an attentive technique ④ indispensable for survival in the wilderness. For example, an animal busy with eating must hold rivals away from its prey. It must constantly be on the lookout, lest it ⑤ be eaten while eating. At the same time, it must guard its young and keep an eye on its sexual partner. In the wild, the animal is forced to divide its attention between various activities.

출제 의도 파악하기
❶ ....
❷ ....
❸ ....
❹ ....
❺ ....

출제 의도 파악하기
❶ ....
❷ ....
❸ ....
❹ ....
❺ ....

063

다음 글의 밑줄 친 부분 중, 어법상 <u>틀린</u> 것은?

Animal groups vary in size from two magpies sitting on a branch to plagues of millions of locusts ① <u>crossing</u> the desert. Not only ② <u>do</u> the sizes of groups vary between species, but they can change dramatically within species. In some cases, a change in group size depends on changes in the environment. For example, locust outbreaks are thought to originate ③ <u>where</u> resources are patchily distributed, causing locusts to move towards these limited resources. In other cases, individuals in similar environments ④ <u>are found</u> in very different-sized groups. Fishermen are used to such intrinsic variation in fish school size. Some days a net contains three fish, while the next day it contains tens of thousands. Human settlements also show similar variety in size, from tiny villages to massive cities, with differences in size ⑤ <u>arise</u> without large differences in the environments in which they were originally founded.

*patchily 군데군데, 드문드문

064

다음 글의 밑줄 친 부분 중, 어법상 <u>틀린</u> 것은?

Not all organisms are able to find sufficient food to survive, so starvation is a kind of disvalue often found in nature. It also is part of the process of selection ① <u>by which</u> biological evolution functions. Starvation helps filter out those less fit to survive, those less resourceful in finding food for ② <u>themselves</u> and their young. In some circumstances, it may pave the way for genetic variants ③ <u>to take</u> hold in the population of a species and eventually allow the emergence of a new species in place of the old one. Thus starvation is a disvalue that can help make ④ <u>possible</u> the good of greater diversity. Starvation can be of practical or instrumental value, even as it is an intrinsic disvalue. ⑤ <u>What</u> some organisms must starve in nature is deeply regrettable and sad. The statement remains implacably true, even though starvation also may sometimes subserve ends that are good.

*implacably 확고히 **subserve 공헌하다

출제 의도 파악하기
❶ ....
❷ ....
❸ ....
❹ ....
❺ ....

출제 의도 파악하기
❶ ....
❷ ....
❸ ....
❹ ....
❺ ....

065

다음 글의 밑줄 친 부분 중, 어법상 틀린 것은?

Social insurance is a relatively modern idea, arising in clear form in the nineteenth century. The idea of social insurance is similar to ① that of public assistance in that both involve a relationship between a government and its citizens. The funds for public assistance and for social insurance ② come from taxes paid by the citizens to the government, and the funds are paid out by the government to recipients. A very fundamental difference, however, is that the recipients of social insurance are receiving benefits ③ that have been earned by work, either their own work, or work by someone else on their behalf. The amounts of the benefits ④ to be paid under various social insurance programs are, in theory, predictable obligations of the government. Thus a person who is, say, age thirty-five, can write to the Social Security Administration and find out the amount of monthly retirement income he or she can ⑤ be counted on upon retirement at age sixty-two or sixty-five or seventy.

066

다음 글의 밑줄 친 부분 중, 어법상 틀린 것은?

A famous experiment in social psychology that involved kids, an adult, and an inflatable Bobo doll ① was conducted almost half a century ago by Stanford University psychologist Albert Bandura. Bandura and his research team wanted to find out ② whether kids can learn aggressive behavior by watching adults. Video cameras and two-way mirrors were set up, and kids were sent into the room, ③ where they found an adult and a large plastic blown-up doll (the kind that bounces back to you after you knock it down) named Bobo. There they watched the adult aggressively knocking Bobo around, as well as sometimes verbally ④ abused the doll. A short while later, the kids were allowed to play with Bobo. It probably comes as little surprise ⑤ that the kids not only copied the adult— excitedly knocking and smacking Bobo—but also developed their own creative forms of aggression toward the doll.

067

2019 3월 학평

다음 글의 밑줄 친 부분 중, 어법상 틀린 것은?

Baylor University researchers investigated ① underline{whether} different types of writing could ease people into sleep. To find out, they had 57 young adults spend five minutes before bed ② underline{writing} either a to-do list for the

5 days ahead or a list of tasks they'd finished over the past few days. The results confirm that not all pre-sleep writing is created equally. Those who made to-do lists before bed ③ underline{were} able to fall asleep nine minutes faster than those who wrote about past events. The

10 quality of the lists mattered, too; the more tasks and the more ④ underline{specific} the to-do lists were, the faster the writers fell asleep. The study authors figure that writing down future tasks ⑤ underline{unloading} the thoughts so you can stop turning them over in your mind. You're telling

15 your brain that the task will get done—just not right now.

068

다음 글의 밑줄 친 부분 중, 어법상 틀린 것은?

A glance at some of history's greatest discoveries and inventions ① underline{demonstrates} the power of the outsider. Michael Ventris was a professional architect who, in his spare time, deciphered Linear B, Europe's earliest writing, a language that had caused classicists ② underline{to be} 5 at a loss for centuries. Ventris succeeded not despite his lack of expertise in the classics but because of it. He wasn't burdened by bad knowledge. Nor ③ underline{was} Luis Alvarez. A nuclear physicist by training, he, not a paleontologist, determined that a huge asteroid 10 striking the earth ④ underline{leading} to the extinction of the dinosaurs. The paleontologists were fixated on explanations ⑤ underline{relating} to something that happened on the earth: climate change or perhaps competition for food with early mammals. Alvarez looked skyward 15 for answers, and that is where he found one.

*decipher 해독하다 **paleontologist 고생물학자

***fixated 집착하는

출제 의도 파악하기

❶ ....
❷ ....
❸ ....
❹ ....
❺ ....

출제 의도 파악하기

❶ ....
❷ ....
❸ ....
❹ ....
❺ ....

069

다음 글의 밑줄 친 부분 중, 어법상 틀린 것은?

So many lives have been wasted because millions have believed that the rich were lucky and the poor were underprivileged. Leaders of all colors and ethnic backgrounds have wrestled power away from the weak, ① exploiting this lie for their own benefit, pitting race against race, brother against sister, and class against class. Encouraged to seek handouts, the underclass and downtrodden ② are kept in spiritual darkness because they do not know where to tap. Their reaction to life is much like ③ that of someone who said, "Why try? The rich get richer and the poor get poorer." They live far beneath their power as persons and their possibilities as inhabitants of our great planet. As the great philosophers pondered and speculated upon society, they became deeply convinced that ④ it is our natural destiny to grow, to develop, to succeed, to prosper, and to find our portion of happiness. In a nation ⑤ which opportunity abounds, each of us is commissioned to find within our lives a personal realization of the very best that exists—including personal wealth.

*pit 경쟁시키다 **handout (가난한 사람에게) 주는 것[돈]

070

다음 글의 밑줄 친 부분 중, 어법상 틀린 것은?

It is clear that Big Data has numerous potential applications. However, there is a certain skepticism regarding how meaningful they are. The common question in this respect is ① whether Big Data really offers significant progress. Let's go through the following example in order to answer that question. eCall is a system through which a car itself, without human intervention, ② alerting the emergency services when an accident occurs. It communicates its location and opens an audio connection between the car and the emergency services. A car manufacturer based on Germany has already taken the decision ③ to include this system in all new cars sold in the Netherlands. Moreover, the EU has made this system ④ mandatory for all new cars sold from 31 March 2018. It claims that the policy will save more than 2,500 human lives annually. The mandatory installation will help rescue workers make better use of the period known as the 'golden hour' after a traffic accident, ⑤ in which rapid and appropriate action means the difference between life and death.

출제 의도 파악하기

①
②
③
④
⑤

출제 의도 파악하기

①
②
③
④
⑤

071

2021 7월 학평

다음 글의 밑줄 친 부분 중, 어법상 틀린 것은?

The idea that people ① selectively expose themselves to news content has been around for a long time, but it is even more important today with the fragmentation of audiences and the proliferation of choices. Selective exposure is a psychological concept that says people seek out information that conforms to their existing belief systems and ② avoid information that challenges those beliefs. In the past when there were few sources of news, people could either expose themselves to mainstream news—where they would likely see beliefs ③ expressed counter to their own—or they could avoid news altogether. Now with so many types of news constantly available to a full range of niche audiences, people can easily find a source of news ④ that consistently confirms their own personal set of beliefs. This leads to the possibility of creating many different small groups of people with each strongly ⑤ believes they are correct and everyone else is wrong about how the world works.

*fragmentation 분열 **proliferation 급증 ***niche 틈새

072

다음 글의 밑줄 친 부분 중, 어법상 틀린 것은?

One interesting illustrative example of the interaction of culture and natural selection can be seen in the ways that human populations have adapted to ① surviving at high altitudes. Cross-cultural comparisons, comparing people who live at high altitudes to low altitude populations, reveal ② that high altitude may have been a source of natural selection in some human populations. Around the world, groups of humans have colonized and survived in mountainous regions. For example, humans seem ③ to have arrived in the Tibetan plateau in the Himalayan mountains around 25,000 years ago. Much later, around 10,000 years ago, humans also colonized the Andes mountains of South America. Without a doubt, ④ culturally transmitted information has been crucial in the success of these populations at high altitude. The cultural innovations that help humans cope with such environments ⑤ including construction of warm and insulated clothing and shelter, domestication of local animal species such as yaks in the Himalayas, and use of the coca leaf to mitigate the effects of altitude sickness in the Andes.

*plateau 고원 **mitigate 완화하다

출제 의도 파악하기

❶ ....
❷ ....
❸ ....
❹ ....
❺ ....

출제 의도 파악하기

❶ ....
❷ ....
❸ ....
❹ ....
❺ ....

073

2022 수능

다음 글의 밑줄 친 부분 중, 어법상 틀린 것은?

Like whole individuals, cells have a life span. During their life cycle (cell cycle), cell size, shape, and metabolic activities can change dramatically. A cell is "born" as a twin when its mother cell divides, ① producing two daughter cells. Each daughter cell is smaller than the mother cell, and except for unusual cases, each grows until it becomes as large as the mother cell ② was. During this time, the cell absorbs water, sugars, amino acids, and other nutrients and assembles them into new, living protoplasm. After the cell has grown to the proper size, its metabolism shifts as it either prepares to divide or matures and ③ differentiates into a specialized cell. Both growth and development require a complex and dynamic set of interactions involving all cell parts. ④ What cell metabolism and structure should be complex would not be surprising, but actually, they are rather simple and logical. Even the most complex cell has only a small number of parts, each ⑤ responsible for a distinct, well-defined aspect of cell life.

*metabolic 물질대사의 **protoplasm 원형질

074

다음 글의 밑줄 친 부분 중, 어법상 틀린 것은?

Humans have never been alone on the Earth. Their lives—culture, technology, and art—have been immeasurably enriched because they learned to watch, listen to, and imitate the other animals ① that shared the land and sea with them. Steven Lonsdale argued in a book filled with examples from every part of the world ② where dance owes its origin and elaboration to human imitation of the varied movements of mammals, reptiles, fish, birds, etc. Our species, from earliest times down through history, ③ gained more from the others than a few crafts. The human species and human culture evolved through natural selection that took place because humans during their history as a species ④ were part of biotic communities where their interactions with other kinds of animals and plants decided whether or not they survived and reproduced. One of the greatest mistakes made by humans today is to think about ⑤ themselves as existing and acting without reference to other forms of life. No species exists in complete isolation; every one relates to others in a living system.

075

2020 7월 학평

다음 글의 밑줄 친 부분 중, 어법상 <u>틀린</u> 것은?

Metacognition simply means "thinking about thinking," and it is one of the main distinctions between the human brain and that of other species. Our ability to stand high on a ladder above our normal
5 thinking processes and ① <u>evaluate</u> why we are thinking as we are thinking is an evolutionary marvel. We have this ability ② <u>because</u> the most recently developed part of the human brain—the prefrontal cortex— enables self-reflective, abstract thought. We can think
10 about ourselves as if we are not part of ③ <u>ourselves</u>. Research on primate behavior indicates that even our closest cousins, the chimpanzees, ④ <u>lacking</u> this ability (although they possess some self-reflective abilities, like being able to identify themselves in a mirror
15 instead of thinking the reflection is another chimp). The ability is a double-edged sword, because while it allows us to evaluate why we are thinking ⑤ <u>what</u> we are thinking, it also puts us in touch with difficult existential questions that can easily become
20 obsessions.

076

다음 글의 밑줄 친 부분 중, 어법상 <u>틀린</u> 것은?

Abraham Lincoln wrote the Gettysburg Address in 1863 on a train travelling from Washington, DC to Pennsylvania so he would have something to say to commemorate ① <u>what</u> was then and still remains the bloodiest battle in American history. Nowadays, 5
American schoolchildren memorize and recite Lincoln's short speech ② <u>to get</u> a better sense of the man and his times. Printed words on a page ③ <u>communicate</u> some of the meaning and power of his message. But if you want to feel the full strength of 10
Lincoln's words, ④ <u>reciting</u> the speech out loud. Only then ⑤ <u>will you</u> feel the effect of his words and his delivery on the crowd gathered that day in 1863. Had Lincoln's address been printed in a few newspapers and not declaimed to an audience, I doubt American 15
schoolchildren would be memorizing and reciting it each year.

출제 의도 파악하기
❶ ....
❷ ....
❸ ....
❹ ....
❺ ....

출제 의도 파악하기
❶ ....
❷ ....
❸ ....
❹ ....
❺ ....

077

다음 글의 밑줄 친 부분 중, 어법상 틀린 것은?

Philosophy is in some sense like mathematics because it relies more on logic—one of the specialties in many philosophy departments—than on empirical data, which can be falsified or distorted. In principle a philosopher can discuss anything. Philosophy is not a field with methodological preferences in the usual sense of standard ways of gathering and analysing data, but ① one with a strong emphasis on ways of thinking systematically and clearly. Language plays a particularly important role in philosophic works because language is the primary tool for ② expressing ideas. Some languages adapt better to levels of abstraction. In German, for example, it is easy to turn a verb into an abstract noun, which makes German philosophers such as Immanuel Kant ③ difficult to translate. Ethics is the part of philosophy ④ where most often appears in discussions of integrity issues and often appears in the deliberations of other disciplines. Professional philosophers sometimes despair at ⑤ how untrained philosophers use concepts from their field, but it is also in some sense a sign of its importance.

078

다음 글의 밑줄 친 부분 중, 어법상 틀린 것은?

A seed knows how to wait. Most seeds wait for at least a year before starting to grow. ① What exactly each seed is waiting for is known only to that seed. A seed is alive while it waits. Neither the seed nor the old oak ② is growing; they are both just waiting. Their waiting differs, however, in that the seed is waiting to flourish while the tree is only waiting to die. When you go into a forest, you probably tend to look up at the plants that have grown so much taller than you ever could. You probably don't look down, where just beneath your single footprint ③ sits hundreds of seeds, each one alive and waiting. They hope against hope for an opportunity that will probably never come. When you are in the forest, for every tree that you see, there are at least a hundred more trees waiting in the soil, alive and ④ fervently wishing to be. Each beginning is the end of a waiting. We are each given exactly one chance to be. Each of us is both impossible and inevitable. Every replete tree was first a seed ⑤ that waited.

*fervently 열심히, 열렬하게 **replete 풍부한, 가득한

출제 의도 파악하기

❶ ....
❷ ....
❸ ....
❹ ....
❺ ....

출제 의도 파악하기

❶ ....
❷ ....
❸ ....
❹ ....
❺ ....

079

2021 3월 학평

다음 글의 밑줄 친 부분 중, 어법상 틀린 것은?

The formats and frequencies of traditional trade encompass a spectrum. At the simplest level ① are the occasional trips made by individual !Kung and Dani to visit their individual trading partners in other bands or villages. ② Suggestive of our open-air markets and flea markets were the occasional markets at which Sio villagers living on the coast of northeast New Guinea met New Guineans from inland villages. Up to a few dozen people from each side ③ sat down in rows facing each other. An inlander pushed forward a net bag containing between 10 and 35 pounds of taro and sweet potatoes, and the Sio villager sitting opposite responded by offering a number of pots and coconuts ④ judging equivalent in value to the bag of food. Trobriand Island canoe traders conducted similar markets on the islands ⑤ that they visited, exchanging utilitarian goods (food, pots, and bowls) by barter, at the same time as they and their individual trade partners gave each other reciprocated gifts of luxury items (shell necklaces and armbands).

*taro (식물) 타로토란   **reciprocate 답례하다

080

다음 글의 밑줄 친 부분 중, 어법상 틀린 것은?

Failure, or a fear of impending failure, amplifies the concern with appearing competent. If you want others to think you are smart, failing an exam will be a very noxious experience for you—① one that may lead you to reach into your self-promotional bag of tricks. In one experiment, students informed that they had performed poorly on a test of social sensitivity ② were especially likely to present themselves afterward as well adjusted. In comparison, students who had succeeded on the test ③ engaging in a more modest self-presentation; because their social competence was validated by the test, they could focus instead on being liked. The desire ④ to appear competent may be particularly strong in pressure-filled, competitive circumstances. Ironically, such circumstances also increase the chance ⑤ that a performer will "choke," or perform well below potential.

*impending 임박한   **noxious 유해한

출제 의도 파악하기
❶ _____
❷ _____
❸ _____
❹ _____
❺ _____

출제 의도 파악하기
❶ _____
❷ _____
❸ _____
❹ _____
❺ _____

081

다음 글의 밑줄 친 부분 중, 어법상 틀린 것은?

Intelligent devices have made great progress in the control of automobiles, airplanes, and ships. They make sense for machines with fixed tasks. They work well in the world of computer agents, ① where they need only some intelligence and an image to display on the screen; real, physical bodies are not needed. They are successful in games and entertainment, controlling dolls, robotic pets, and characters in computer games. In these environments, not only ② are occasional misunderstandings and failures not matter, but they can add to the fun. In the world of entertainment, a well-executed failure can be even more ③ satisfying than success. Tools that rely on statistical inference ④ are also widely popular and successful. Some online stores recommend books, movies, music, or even kitchen appliances by finding products that people similar to you in taste seem to like and then ⑤ recommending those items to you. The system works reasonably well.

082

다음 글의 밑줄 친 부분 중, 어법상 틀린 것은?

Official definitions of sport ① have important implications. When a definition emphasizes rules, competition, and high performance, many people will be excluded from participation or ② avoid other physical activities that are defined as "second class." For example, when a 12-year-old is cut from an exclusive club soccer team, she may not want to play in the local league because she sees ③ it as "recreational activity" rather than a real sport. This can create a situation in which most people are physically inactive at the same time that a small number of people perform at relatively high levels for large numbers of fans—a situation ④ where negatively impacts health and increases health-care costs in a society or community. When sport is defined to include a wide range of physical activities that ⑤ are played for pleasure and integrated into local expressions of social life, physical activity rates will be high and overall health benefits are likely.

출제 의도 파악하기

❶ ....
❷ ....
❸ ....
❹ ....
❺ ....

출제 의도 파악하기

❶ ....
❷ ....
❸ ....
❹ ....
❺ ....

083

2019 수능

다음 글의 밑줄 친 부분 중, 어법상 **틀린** 것은?

"Monumental" is a word that comes very close to ① expressing the basic characteristic of Egyptian art. Never before and never since has the quality of monumentality been achieved as fully as it ② did in Egypt. The reason for this is not the external size and massiveness of their works, although the Egyptians admittedly achieved some amazing things in this respect. Many modern structures exceed ③ those of Egypt in terms of purely physical size. But massiveness has nothing to do with monumentality. An Egyptian sculpture no bigger than a person's hand is more monumental than that gigantic pile of stones ④ that constitutes the war memorial in Leipzig, for instance. Monumentality is not a matter of external weight, but of "inner weight." This inner weight is the quality which Egyptian art possesses to such a degree that everything in it seems to be made of primeval stone, like a mountain range, even if it is only a few inches across or ⑤ carved in wood.

*gigantic 거대한   **primeval 원시 시대의

084

다음 글의 밑줄 친 부분 중, 어법상 **틀린** 것은?

Heating cabbages and their friends has two different effects. Initially the temperature rise within the tissue ① speeds the enzyme activity and flavor generation, with maximum activity at around 60°C. If the enzymes are quickly inactivated by putting the vegetables into boiling water, then many of the flavor molecules will be left ② unharmed. This is often desirable: cooking some mustard leaves quickly, for example, minimizes their hot flavors but ③ preserving the pleasant bitterness. Boiling in water pulls flavor molecules out into the water, and produces a milder flavor than does frying or steaming. However, if the cooking period is prolonged, then the heat gradually transforms the flavor molecules. Eventually the compounds that are mainly responsible for the strong smell of overcooked cabbage ④ are formed. Prolonged cooking makes members of the onion family ⑤ sweet, but the cabbage family gets unpleasant.

출제 의도 파악하기

❶ _____
❷ _____
❸ _____
❹ _____
❺ _____

출제 의도 파악하기

❶ _____
❷ _____
❸ _____
❹ _____
❺ _____

085

다음 글의 밑줄 친 부분 중, 어법상 틀린 것은?

Except for ancient Greece, ① where artists were highly respected and known for their unique talents and styles, before the Renaissance the public was seldom aware of who or what kind of people artists were. Moreover, of the artists ② that names were known, very few were women. It was not until the 20th century ③ that a large number of female artists were recognized and their works were duly appreciated in every area of the arts. It is well-known that the Brontë sisters, talented poets and novelists in the early 19th century, ④ published their first collection of poems under male pen names. The social, educational, and economic conditions that enable women to create works of art ⑤ hardly existed in the past.

086

다음 글의 밑줄 친 부분 중, 어법상 틀린 것은?

We must ask ourselves what it is ① that a true leader has an abundance of. A leader may have superior knowledge or an abundance of energy, but I argue that the one asset that sets a genuine leader apart from a cheap imitation ② being power. True leaders have power. This is not the power of position or wealth or title. It is more the power of influence, ③ which can only be granted by those who choose to be followers. And because a true leader has this power, ④ it is his or her responsibility to share it, in other words, to empower the followers. And, ironically, you cannot empower people unless they have granted you the power to do so. This is the secret to motivating people. You give them back ⑤ what they have given you, and the result is synergistic. It is simply sharing the abundance of power that you have earned by being their servant rather than their master.

*synergistic 상승적인

❶
❷
❸
❹
❺

❶
❷
❸
❹
❺

087

2019 7월 학평

다음 글의 밑줄 친 부분 중, 어법상 틀린 것은?

The idea that hypnosis can put the brain into a special state, ① in which the powers of memory are dramatically greater than normal, reflects a belief in a form of easily unlocked potential. But it is false. People under
5 hypnosis generate more "memories" than they ② do in a normal state, but these recollections are as likely to be false as true. Hypnosis leads them to come up with more information, but not necessarily more accurate information. In fact, it might actually be people's
10 beliefs in the power of hypnosis that ③ leads them to recall more things: If people believe that they should have better memory under hypnosis, they will try harder to retrieve more memories when hypnotized. Unfortunately, there's no way to know ④ whether the
15 memories hypnotized people retrieve are true or not— unless of course we know exactly what the person should be able to remember. But if we ⑤ knew that, then we'd have no need to use hypnosis in the first place!

*hypnosis 최면

088

다음 글의 밑줄 친 부분 중, 어법상 틀린 것은?

Men and women's assumptions to what is interesting ① are different. It seems natural to women to tell and hear about what happened today, who turned up at the bus stop, who called and what she said, not because these details are important in themselves but because 5 the telling of them proves involvement that you care about each other and ② that you have a best friend. ③ Knowing you will be able to tell these things later makes you feel less alone as you go along the lone path of a day. Since it is not natural to men to use talk in 10 this way, they focus on the inherent insignificance of the details. What they find worth telling ④ being facts about such topics as sports, politics, history, or how things work. Women often perceive the telling of facts as lecturing, ⑤ which seems to carry a metamessage of 15 condescension: I'm the teacher, you're the student. I'm knowledgeable, you're ignorant.

*metamessage 초메시지(대화에서 숨은 의미)
**condescension 생색내는 듯한 태도

출제 의도 파악하기
❶ ....
❷ ....
❸ ....
❹ ....
❺ ....

출제 의도 파악하기
❶ ....
❷ ....
❸ ....
❹ ....
❺ ....

089

다음 글의 밑줄 친 부분 중, 어법상 틀린 것은?

During the first centuries CE, the Romans built waterwheels ① underline wherever there were streams or aqueducts furnishing water power. The one at Barbegal in southern France, ② built in 310 CE, used 16 overshot wheels in a row. Water flowed over one wheel, turning it, then over the next wheel, and so on. It was capable of grinding three tons of grain an hour, enough to feed 80,000 people. In other words, it was an establishment of the kind ③ that would not be seen again in that part of the world until the Industrial Revolution of the eighteenth century. The age of the great Eurasian empires marked a radical departure from the more conservative river valley civilizations that preceded ④ them. Before about 1500 BCE, there had been a rough balance between the river valley civilizations and the Neolithic farmers and herdsmen who inhabited the surrounding regions. After 1500 BCE, however, three technological innovations—iron, domesticated horses, and wheeled vehicles — ⑤ upsetting this equilibrium, leading to an era of prolonged warfare that spread over much of Eurasia and North Africa.

*CE 서력기원 (= Common Era) **aqueduct 송수로[교]

090

다음 글의 밑줄 친 부분 중, 어법상 틀린 것은?

It might sound pretty straightforward to ask which hospital in a community provides the best care. But hospitals can ① be rated on any of a bewildering variety of considerations, including inpatient volume, staffing levels, costs of treatment, and specialty practices. Well, we could keep it simple and just look at death rates, as some experts ② do. Of all the things we'd like to see ③ to happen during a hospital stay, avoiding death is usually at the top of the list. But death rates don't simply depend on the quality of treatment rendered by a hospital; they can also depend on how sick or old or poor the population served by the hospital is, the extent ④ to which a hospital takes on more difficult cases, the hospital's ability to administer cutting-edge and higher-risk treatments, and even a hospital's tendency to discharge patients prematurely so that more of them will die elsewhere. The U.S. Centers for Medicare and Medicaid Services attempts to adjust its published hospital death rates for many of these factors, but that doesn't fix the problem—most hospitals simply end up with fairly similar rates, ⑤ making the list of little use.

*bewildering 갈피를 못 잡게 하는

출제 의도 파악하기

❶ ....
❷ ....
❸ ....
❹ ....
❺ ....

출제 의도 파악하기

❶ ....
❷ ....
❸ ....
❹ ....
❺ ....

091

2018 수능

다음 글의 밑줄 친 부분 중, 어법상 틀린 것은?

Psychologists who study giving behavior ① have noticed that some people give substantial amounts to one or two charities, while others give small amounts to many charities. Those who donate to one or two charities seek evidence about what the charity is doing and ② what it is really having a positive impact. If the evidence indicates that the charity is really helping others, they make a substantial donation. Those who give small amounts to many charities are not so interested in whether what they are ③ doing helps others—psychologists call them warm glow givers. Knowing that they are giving makes ④ them feel good, regardless of the impact of their donation. In many cases the donation is so small—$10 or less—that if they stopped ⑤ to think, they would realize that the cost of processing the donation is likely to exceed any benefit it brings to the charity.

092

다음 글의 밑줄 친 부분 중, 어법상 틀린 것은?

Youngsters learn moral behavior not only through verbal explanations, rewards, and punishments but also by observing ① how other people behave. They imitate their parents and peers, and they model themselves after their heroes. Because coaches are often highly admired and very important in the child's life, they are especially likely to serve as models. Without realizing ② it, coaches can behave in ways that teach either morality or immorality. For example, by trying to get a "competitive edge" by stretching the rules, coaches can easily give children the impression that cheating is not really wrong unless it ③ is detected. When coaches bend the rules in order to obtain a victory, children may conclude ④ that the end justifies the means. Likewise, coaches who display hostility toward officials and contempt for the other team ⑤ communicating the notion that such behaviors are appropriate and desirable.

출제 의도 파악하기
1
2
3
4
5

출제 의도 파악하기
1
2
3
4
5

093

다음 글의 밑줄 친 부분 중, 어법상 틀린 것은?

If you've ever collected anything—stamps, bugs, baseball cards, teapots—you may have a natural inclination toward being a museum curator. Especially if you're the type of person ① who keeps a first edition comic sealed in an airtight plastic bag and records notes on its history and value. This kind of passion and concern with detail ② drives most curators. Behind the baseball museum ③ to be someone who really loves the sport and all the stats. The craft museum is curated by someone who lives for handcrafted treasures. ④ Fueled by their passion, museum curators maintain and build collections for private citizens, nonprofit organizations, governments, businesses, associations, and colleges. Most organize art collections, but museums also house artifacts ⑤ pertaining to natural history, American history, rock and roll, glass, fashion, or items you'd never guess.

094

다음 글의 밑줄 친 부분 중, 어법상 틀린 것은?

Our knowledge of the many types of memory organizations points out that rephrasing information in our words ① is critical to encoding and retrieval. Unlike computer disks, we can't afford endless searches through random lists of information. Human memory is built around organizing related information together, ② grouping meaningful units for easier retrieval. Judging from its importance in memory research, ③ takes the time to organize the information you are attempting to learn is key to accomplishing this goal. One trick is to spend time after each class ④ rewriting your notes, organizing clusters of information in hierarchies and related lists. This also helps to point out any missing connections between concepts and prepares you to ask questions at the next class session. You can't rely on your processing during the frantic note taking in lectures to lead to a thoughtful organization ⑤ that suits your learning.

*retrieval 회수, 복구 **frantic 미친 듯한, 정신없이 서두르는

출제 의도 파악하기

① ....
② ....
③ ....
④ ....
⑤ ....

출제 의도 파악하기

① ....
② ....
③ ....
④ ....
⑤ ....

❶ 주어와 동사

01 ignorance   *n* _____

02 extensive   *a* _____

03 convince   *v* _____

04 evaluate   *v* _____

05 flexible   *a* _____

06 accumulate   *v* _____

07 confidence   *n* _____

08 access   *n* _____

09 효율적인   *a* _____

10 explicit   *a* _____

11 persist   *v* _____

12 fulfill   *v* _____

❷ 동사의 활용

01 ethical   *a* _____

02 competence   *n* _____

03 inadequate   *a* _____

04 sympathetic   *a* _____

05 규제하다   *v* _____

06 immediate   *a* _____

07 accommodate   *v* _____

08 align   *v* _____

09 consequently   *ad* _____

10 aspect   *n* _____

11 constructive   *a* _____

12 restrict   *v* _____

❸ to부정사와 동명사

01 portray   *v* _____

02 exaggerate   *v* _____

03 register   *v* _____

04 distress   *n* _____

05 constraint   *n* _____

06 impose   *v* _____

07 psychological   *a* _____

08 동기, 이유   *n* _____

09 rational   *a* _____

10 contribution   *n* _____

11 identify   *v* _____

12 inference   *n* _____

13 intangible   *a* _____

04 분사

01 marginal   *a* _____

02 comparative   *a* _____

03 primitive   *a* _____

04 emphasize   *v* _____

05 최적의   *a* _____

06 facilitate   *v* _____

07 disperse   *v* _____

08 secure   *v* _____

09 dominate   *v* _____

10 spontaneous   *a* _____

11 undergo   *v* _____

12 vulnerable   *a* _____

05 명사와 대명사

01 주다, 수여하다   *v* _____

02 apparent   *a* _____

03 disturb   *v* _____

04 vibrate   *n* _____

05 discrimination   *n* _____

06 identical   *a* _____

07 constitute   *v* _____

08 convey   *v* _____

09 compensation   *n* _____

10 exhibit   *v* _____

11 specialize   *v* _____

12 efficiency   *n* _____

06 형용사와 부사

01 enthusiastic   *a* _____

02 compromise   *v* _____

03 retain   *v* _____

04 merge   *v* _____

05 temporary   *a* _____

06 enduring   *a* _____

07 추상적인   *a* _____

08 emerge   *v* _____

09 attach   *v* _____

10 equivalent   *n* _____

11 intermediate   *a* _____

12 subtle   *a* _____

13 interval   *n* _____

07 관계사

01 fetch   *v* _____

02 strain   *n* _____

03 turn over   _____

04 migratory   *a* _____

05 concentration   *n* _____

06 undertake   *v* _____

07 manipulate   *v* _____

08 subsequently   *ad* _____

09 primary   *a* _____

10 암시하다   *v* _____

11 surplus   *n* _____

12 commodity   *v* _____

08 전치사와 접속사

01 possess   *v* _____

02 contribute to   _____

03 inspire   *v* _____

04 무한한   *a* _____

05 convert   *v* _____

06 motivate   *v* _____

07 cope   *v* _____

08 horizontal   *a* _____

09 density   *n* _____

10 declare   *v* _____

11 pull out   _____

12 reject   *v* _____

09 병렬구조 및 특수구문

01 convention   *n* _____

02 exceedingly   *ad* _____

03 address   *v* _____

04 coordinate   *v* _____

05 privilege   *n* _____

06 notice   *v* _____

07 demonstrate   *v* _____

08 overstate   *v* _____

09 중요한, 결정적인   *a* _____

10 adolescent   *n* _____

11 harsh   *a* _____

12 overwhelm   *v* _____

13 indigenous   *a* _____

01 어법 모의고사

01 devoid of _____

02 decline *n* _____

03 replace *v* _____

04 engage in _____

05 permanent *a* _____

06 variation *n* _____

07 perception *n* _____

08 제출하다 *v* _____

09 involved *a* _____

10 considerable *a* _____

11 analysis *n* _____

12 variable *n* _____

13 stimulus *n* _____

14 attentive *a* _____

15 incorporate *v* _____

02 어법 모의고사

01 distribute *v* _____

02 intrinsic *a* _____

03 sufficient *a* _____

04 disvalue *n* _____

05 obligation *n* _____

06 aggressive *a* _____

07 abuse *v* _____

08 investigate *v* _____

09 specific *a* _____

10 expertise *n* _____

11 멸종 *n* _____

12 prosper *v* _____

13 intervention *n* _____

14 policy *n* _____

15 alert *v* _____

03 어법 모의고사

01 existing *a* _____

02 confirm *v* _____

03 transmit *v* _____

04 shelter *n* _____

05 흡수하다 *v* _____

06 distinct *a* _____

07 evolve *v* _____

08	isolation	*n*	
09	reflective	*a*	
10	obsession	*n*	
11	flourish	*v*	
12	empirical	*a*	
13	distort	*v*	
14	translate	*v*	
15	recite	*v*	

04 어법 모의고사

01	occasional	*a*	
02	suggestive	*a*	
03	competent	*a*	
04	validate	*v*	
05	progress	*n*	
06	reasonably	*ad*	
07	exclude	*v*	
08	inactive	*a*	
09	overall	*a*	
10	characteristic	*n*	
11	외적인	*a*	

12	prolong	*v*	
13	superior	*a*	
14	genuine	*a*	
15	empower	*v*	

05 어법 모의고사

01	normal	*a*	
02	retrieve	*v*	
03	inherent	*a*	
04	conservative	*a*	
05	precede	*v*	
06	inhabit	*v*	
07	straightforward	*a*	
08	adjust	*v*	
09	process	*v*	
10	exceed	*v*	
11	detect	*v*	
12	conclude	*v*	
13	정당화하다	*v*	
14	artifact	*n*	
15	accomplish	*v*	

N Ⅱ 어휘

| 필수 어휘

학습 내용	학습일		맞은 문항 수
필수 어휘 1	월	일	/ 6문항
필수 어휘 2	월	일	/ 6문항
필수 어휘 3	월	일	/ 6문항
필수 어휘 4	월	일	/ 6문항
필수 어휘 5	월	일	/ 6문항
필수 어휘 6	월	일	/ 6문항
필수 어휘 7	월	일	/ 6문항
필수 어휘 8	월	일	/ 6문항

| 어휘 모의고사

학습 내용	학습일		맞은 문항 수
어휘 모의고사 1회	월	일	/ 8문항
어휘 모의고사 2회	월	일	/ 8문항
어휘 모의고사 3회	월	일	/ 8문항
어휘 모의고사 4회	월	일	/ 8문항
어휘 모의고사 5회	월	일	/ 8문항

필수 어휘 1

1 반의어

□ **include**	*v* 포함하다	↔	□ **exclude**	*v* 제외하다, 배제하다
□ **encourage**	*v* 장려하다, 북돋우다	↔	□ **discourage**	*v* 낙담시키다
□ **dependence**	*n* 의존 ▶ dependent 의존하는	↔	□ **independence**	*n* 독립 ▶ independent 독립된
□ **isolation**	*n* 고립 ▶ isolated 고립된	↔	□ **collaboration**	*n* 협업
□ **accurate**	*a* 정확한	↔	□ **inaccurate**	*a* 부정확한
□ **determine**	*v* 결심하다, 확정하다	↔	□ **hesitate**	*v* 망설이다, 주저하다

2 형태가 비슷한 어휘

□ **attraction**	*n* 매력 있는 것, 볼거리 ▶ attractive 매력적인	□ **competitive**	*a* 경쟁의
□ **distraction**	*n* 방해물, 방해 요소 ▶ distract 방해하다, 주의를 딴 데로 돌리게 하다	□ **compatible**	*a* 양립할 수 있는 ▶ incompatible 양립할 수 없는
□ **underlie**	*v* 기저[기초]를 이루다	□ **wander**	*v* 돌아다니다, 방황하다
□ **undermine**	*v* 손상시키다, 약화시키다	□ **wonder**	*v* 궁금해하다, 놀라다

3 필수 어휘

□ **absent**	*a* 없는, 부재인 ▶ absence 없음, 부재	□ **extract**	*v* 추출하다
□ **acquire**	*v* 얻다, 습득[획득]하다	□ **identify**	*v* 동일시하다; 식별[확인]하다 ▶ identification 동일시, 신분, 식별
□ **anticipate**	*v* 예측하다, 기대하다	□ **occupation**	*n* 직업
□ **challenge**	*n* 도전, 난제 *v* 도전하다	□ **passionate**	*a* 열정적인 ▶ passion 열정
□ **complaint**	*n* 불평 ▶ complain 불평하다	□ **perceive**	*v* 인식하다 ▶ perception 인식
□ **component**	*n* 구성 요소	□ **prefer**	*v* 선호하다 ▶ prefer *A* to *B A*를 *B*보다 선호하다
□ **contrary**	*n* 정반대 *a* 정반대의 ▶ on the contrary (정)반대로, 반면에	□ **prevent**	*v* 막다, 예방하다
□ **contribute**	*v* 기여[공헌]하다; 원인이 되다 ▶ contribute to ~에 기여하다, ~의 원인이 되다	□ **raise**	*v* 기르다; 올리다 ※ rise 상승하다, 오르다 / arise 발생하다
□ **defeat**	*v* 무산[패배]시키다 *n* 패배	□ **relief**	*n* 위안, 안도, 안심
□ **elaborate**	*a* 정교한	□ **sincere**	*a* 진심 어린, 진실한

Q1 괄호 안에서 문맥상 알맞은 것을 고르세요.

1. A family bond usually 【 encourages / discourages 】 them to spend more time with their family.

- **bond** 결속(력), 유대(감)

2. The second stage requires you to accept the other person's apology for wrongdoing and 【 determine / hesitate 】 to offer your trust and friendship again.

- **stage** 단계
- **wrongdoing** 잘못한 일

3. The only way to overcome this problem is to be more connected to others, and this connection will reduce fear and 【 isolation / collaboration 】.

- **overcome** 극복하다
- **fear** 두려움, 공포

4. On the contrary, scientists construct arguments because they want to test their own ideas and give an 【 accurate / inaccurate 】 explanation of some aspect of nature.

- **construct** 구성하다
- **argument** 주장, 논거
- **aspect** 측면, 양상

5. Yet when these molecules were 【 extended / extracted 】 from fruits and vegetables and made into supplements, they did not reduce cancer.

- **molecule** (물질의) 분자
- **supplement** 보충제, 보조제
- **cancer** 암

Q2 밑줄 친 어휘와 유사한 뜻을 가진 어휘를 고르세요.

1. Reducing production costs in the business world can be a constant <u>challenge</u>.

- **constant** 끊임없는

① dependence   ② difficulty   ③ supplement

2. Some people change their <u>occupation</u> multiple times during their career to find their true passion.

- **multiple** 다수의, 많은
- **passion** 열정

① pastime   ② job   ③ residence

3. Korean speakers at times use a more <u>elaborate</u> system for addressing each other than English speakers.

- **address** 부르다

① confident   ② sincere   ③ complicated

095

2024 수능

다음 글의 밑줄 친 부분 중, 문맥상 낱말의 쓰임이 적절하지 <u>않은</u> 것은?

　　Bazaar economies feature an apparently flexible price-setting mechanism that sits atop more enduring ties of shared culture. Both the buyer and seller are aware of each other's ① <u>restrictions</u>. In Delhi's bazaars, buyers and sellers can ② <u>assess</u> to a large extent the financial constraints that other actors have in their everyday life. Each actor belonging to a specific economic class understands what the other sees as a necessity and a luxury. In the case of electronic products like video games, they are not a ③ <u>necessity</u> at the same level as other household purchases such as food items. So, the seller in Delhi's bazaars is careful not to directly ask for very ④ <u>low</u> prices for video games because at no point will the buyer see possession of them as an absolute necessity. Access to this type of knowledge establishes a price consensus by relating to each other's preferences and limitations of belonging to a ⑤ <u>similar</u> cultural and economic universe.

*constraint 압박　**consensus 일치

096

다음 글의 밑줄 친 부분 중, 문맥상 낱말의 쓰임이 적절하지 <u>않은</u> 것은?

　　Even if there were one or two mass extinctions around the end of the Triassic, and even if a select few Early Jurassic dinosaur survivors were confronted by a sea of unexploited niches, they were not ① <u>alone</u>. In particular, the mammals were there as well. So we are still left with an unsolved problem. Why, if there was a relatively "clean ecological slate" (or at least a chaotic state of affairs) at the start of the Jurassic, did dinosaur diversity explode to ② <u>include</u> the largest land animals of all time, while mammals remained largely at rodent proportions for more than 150 million years thereafter? The standard view is that dinosaurs filled all the roles for large-bodied animals. On first blush, this idea seems ③ <u>unreasonable</u>. At the close of the Triassic, dinosaurs were already an ecologically ④ <u>diverse</u> bunch, with plenty of large herbivores and carnivores. In contrast, virtually all mammals at this time appear to have been devoted insect eaters, hardly the foundation for an evolutionary radiation toward ⑤ <u>giant</u> sizes!

*niche 적소(適所), (특정 종류의 생물이 살기에) 적합한 환경

**herbivore 초식동물

출제 어휘 확인하기		
① restriction	제한, 제약	↔
② assess	평가하다	↔
③ necessity	필수품	↔
④ low	낮은, 싼	↔ high(높은, 비싼)
⑤ similar	비슷한, 유사한	↔ different(다른)

출제 어휘 확인하기	
① alone	↔
② include	↔
③ unreasonable	↔
④ diverse	↔
⑤ giant	↔

097

다음 글의 밑줄 친 부분 중, 문맥상 낱말의 쓰임이 적절하지 <u>않은</u> 것은?

Imagine if we were suddenly deprived of most or all of the daily occupations and the expectations of future happenings. This is the situation that most residents in care homes have to face. For some with severe disabilities or frailty it may be a ① <u>relief</u> after struggling to cope at home to receive personal care and no longer have the worry of cooking and housework. But the danger is that providing excessive care leads to total ② <u>dependence</u>, which may not be entirely necessary. ③ <u>Reducing</u> the retention of any ability to perform personal care, making choices in selecting clothes and food, and finding ways of overcoming physical problems, help to maintain independence. There needs to be a more integrated approach to care. Activity methods can be ④ <u>incorporated</u> in the basic personal and clinical care system. The provision of activities of any kind should not be regarded as an 'extra', 'a treat' or 'a change': they should be made a vital ⑤ <u>component</u> of the whole caring process.

출제 어휘 확인하기		
① relief	↔	
② dependence	↔	
③ reduce	↔	
④ incorporate	↔	
⑤ component	↔	

098

다음 글의 밑줄 친 부분 중, 문맥상 낱말의 쓰임이 적절하지 <u>않은</u> 것은?

Why is the value of *place* so important? From a historical perspective, until the 1700s textile production was a hand process using the fibers available within a ① <u>particular</u> geographic region, for example, cotton, wool, silk, and flax. Trade among regions ② <u>increased</u> the availability of these fibers and associated textiles made from the fibers. The First Industrial Revolution and subsequent technological advancements in manufactured fibers ③ <u>added</u> to the fact that fibers and textiles were no longer "place-bound." Fashion companies created and consumers could acquire textiles and products made from textiles with little or no connection to where, how, or by whom the products were made. This ④ <u>countered</u> a disconnect between consumers and the products they use on a daily basis, a loss of understanding and appreciation in the skills and resources necessary to create these products, and an associated disregard for the human and natural resources necessary for the products' creation. Therefore, renewing a value on *place* ⑤ <u>reconnects</u> the company and the consumer with the people, geography, and culture of a particular location.

*textile 직물

출제 어휘 확인하기		
① particular	↔	
② increase	↔	
③ add	↔	
④ counter	↔	
⑤ reconnect	↔	

099

(A), (B), (C)의 각 네모 안에서 문맥에 맞는 낱말로 가장 적절한 것은?

Among the strongest influences on food choices are ethnic heritage and regional cuisines. People tend to (A) prefer / exclude the foods they grew up eating. Every country, and in fact every region of a country, has its own typical foods and ways of combining them into meals. These cuisines reflect a (B) common / unique combination of local ingredients and cooking styles. Chowder in New England is made with clams, but in the Florida Keys conch is the featured ingredient. The Pacific Northwest is as famous for its marionberry pie as Georgia is for its peach cobbler. Philadelphia has its cheese steaks and New Orleans has its oyster po'boys. The "American diet" includes many ethnic foods and regional styles, all adding (C) simplicity / variety to the diet.

*conch 고둥

	(A)	(B)	(C)
①	prefer	common	simplicity
②	prefer	unique	simplicity
③	prefer	unique	variety
④	exclude	common	simplicity
⑤	exclude	unique	variety

출제 어휘 확인하기

(A)	prefer	/ exclude
(B)	common	/ unique
(C)	simplicity	/ variety

100

밑줄 친 (a)~(e) 중에서 문맥상 낱말의 쓰임이 적절하지 <u>않은</u> 것은?

Praise is essential to the growth of a healthy brain. The brain grows by forming new networks of interconnected neurons, which are the basic elements in the brain's communication system. Certain hormones provide essential fuel for (a) building new brain circuits. The most important of these hormones in early brain development are oxytocin, sometimes referred to as "the bonding hormone," and the endorphin compounds that release naturally occurring chemicals that give us a high. When a parent's face (b) conveys praise with the message, "I want to see who you are, and I admire you," the infant's brain is awash with both oxytocin and endorphins. These pleasure-giving hormones encourage the friendly, steady gaze that promotes intimacy and understanding between parent and child, and which provides (c) additional brain fuel.

As a neuromodulator, a chemical that affects how the brain functions, oxytocin influences our judgments. With moderate to high levels of oxytocin flowing in our brain, we are more (d) likely to trust others and more resilient to disappointment or betrayal. Moreover, children for whom praise is commonplace show greater accomplishment at the age of three years and again at the age of ten years while children (e) tired of everyday praise show blunted responses in brain networks, particularly those associated with learning and motivation. Praise is an essential building block of the healthy brain and we never outgrow our need for it.

*neuromodulator 신경조절물질 **blunted 둔화된

① (a)   ② (b)   ③ (c)   ④ (d)   ⑤ (e)

출제 어휘 확인하기

①	build	↔
②	convey	↔
③	additional	↔
④	likely	↔
⑤	tired	↔

필수 어휘 2

1 반의어

increase	v 증가하다, 증가시키다	↔	decrease	v 감소하다, 감소시키다
positive	a 긍정적인	↔	negative	a 부정적인
active	a 적극적인, 능동적인	↔	passive	a 소극적인, 수동적인
sufficient	a 충분한 (= adequate)	↔	insufficient	a 불충분한, 부족한 (= deficient)
observance	n 준수 ▶ observe 준수하다; 관찰하다	↔	violation	n 위반 ▶ violate 위반하다 ※ violence 폭력
expansion	n 확장, 확대 ▶ expand 확장[확대]하다	↔	contraction	n 수축, 축소 ▶ contract 수축하다; 계약(서)

2 형태가 비슷한 어휘

consume	v 섭취하다, 먹다 ▶ consumption 소비, 섭취	inhibit	v 억제하다
presume	v 가정하다, 추정하다	exhibit	v 전시하다, 내보이다 ▶ exhibition 전시(회)
indication	n 징후, 표시 ▶ indicate 나타내다, 가리키다	objection	n 반대 ▶ object 반대하다
dedication	n 헌신, 전념 ▶ be dedicated to ~에 헌신하다, ~에 전념하다	objective	n 목적, 목표 a 객관적인

3 필수 어휘

annual	a 연례의, 매년의 ▶ annually 매년, 해마다	launch	v 출시하다, 착수시키다
consent	v 동의하다	moral	a 도덕적인 ▶ morality 도덕성
contribution	n 공헌	obstacle	n 장애물
definite	a 분명한, 확실한 ▶ definitely 분명히, 확실히	promising	a 유망한
disturb	v 방해하다 ▶ disturbance 방해	resistant	a 내성이 있는
diversity	n 다양성 ▶ diverse 다양한	self-esteem	n 자존감
empty	a 공허한, 텅 빈	submit	v 굴복하다, 복종하다; 제출하다
existence	n 존재	susceptible	a 취약한, 영향받기 쉬운
influential	a 영향력 있는 ▶ influence 영향	vulnerable	a 취약한 ▶ vulnerability 취약성
investigate	v 조사하다 ▶ investigation 조사, 연구	worsen	v 악화시키다

Q1 괄호 안에서 문맥상 알맞은 것을 고르세요.

1. The plant [expansion / contraction] will allow for a significant increase in production capability.

- significant 상당한
- capability 능력, 수용력

2. We expect all players to show complete [observance / violation] of the rules of the game.

- complete 철저한, 완전한

3. Your eyes may get tired because of the extra effort it takes to focus if the light is [adequate / insufficient].

- extra 추가의, 여분의

4. She had sung and danced with her friends in the festival, part of a sensational performance. After that, she had become more confident and [active / passive].

- sensational 멋진, 선풍적인
- confident 자신감 있는

5. With a [negative / positive] perspective and persistence, you will get through and find a way through all obstacles.

- perspective 관점, 시각
- persistence 끈기

Q2 밑줄 친 어휘와 유사한 뜻을 가진 어휘를 고르세요.

1. The developers had to <u>submit</u> to the fact that their project was not promising.

① yield　　　② ignore　　　③ appeal

- promising 유망한

2. The government <u>launched</u> a new program to promote renewable energy and reduce carbon emissions.

① dismissed　　　② started　　　③ reviewed

- renewable 재생 가능한
- carbon 탄소
- emission 배출

3. The professor argued that the <u>existence</u> of extraterrestrial life beyond our planet was real.

① process　　　② presence　　　③ significance

- extraterrestrial 외계의

101

2023 수능

다음 글의 밑줄 친 부분 중, 문맥상 낱말의 쓰임이 적절하지 않은 것은?

Everywhere we turn we hear about almighty "cyberspace"! The hype promises that we will leave our boring lives, put on goggles and body suits, and enter some metallic, three-dimensional, multimedia otherworld. When the Industrial Revolution arrived with its great innovation, the motor, we didn't leave our world to go to some ① remote motorspace! On the contrary, we brought the motors into our lives, as automobiles, refrigerators, drill presses, and pencil sharpeners. This ② absorption has been so complete that we refer to all these tools with names that declare their usage, not their "motorness." These innovations led to a major socioeconomic movement precisely because they entered and ③ affected profoundly our everyday lives. People have not changed fundamentally in thousands of years. Technology changes constantly. It's the one that must ④ adapt to us. That's exactly what will happen with information technology and its devices under human-centric computing. The longer we continue to believe that computers will take us to a magical new world, the longer we will ⑤ maintain their natural fusion with our lives, the hallmark of every major movement that aspires to be called a socioeconomic revolution.

*hype 과대광고   **hallmark 특징

102

다음 글의 밑줄 친 부분 중, 문맥상 낱말의 쓰임이 적절하지 않은 것은?

That you might find yourself at times in a situation in which you see no clear alternatives does not mean, objectively considered, that there are no clear alternatives. It simply means that you do not see them. Don't project your ① subjective state of uncertainty upon the world at large and claim objective status for it. To be in a state of uncertainty concerning the truth is neither a pleasant nor a desirable state to be in, and we should always be striving to get out of such states as ② soon as possible. However, consider this: You may, right now, be uncertain about a particular matter, but that experience is only possible because you have known the ③ opposite experience, the experience of being certain about something. Therefore you know that certainty is an ④ unreal possibility. If certainty is possible at all, then it is possible, eventually, with regard to the matter about which you are now uncertain. There is nothing to preclude, theoretically, your one day ⑤ overcoming the uncertainty about a particular matter you are now experiencing.

출제 어휘 확인하기

① remote	↔	
② absorption	↔	
③ affect	↔	
④ adapt	↔	
⑤ maintain	↔	

출제 어휘 확인하기

① subjective	↔	
② soon	↔	
③ opposite	↔	
④ unreal	↔	
⑤ overcome	↔	

103

다음 글의 밑줄 친 부분 중, 문맥상 낱말의 쓰임이 적절하지 <u>않은</u> 것은?

Scientists have to consider ① <u>moral</u> factors before undertaking a new problem. This is particularly true in applied research, whose effects are more easily predictable. Since few applied scientists are ② <u>independent</u> agents, serious personal dilemmas can arise when a scientist believes that the work he is doing for an industrial firm has either no social usefulness or actually harmful consequences. Frequently the ③ <u>difficulty</u> arises from the fact that work done by him is exaggerated or applied in directions never intended. Often this is done by the advertising departments of his employer's firm. It is the right and duty of scientists to protest against these ④ <u>misuses</u> of their work, and most of them will do so, even at the risk of losing their jobs. In this regard they are supported by the great majority of their colleagues, who in fact look down upon those who ⑤ <u>forbid</u> their names or their work to be improperly exploited.

출제 어휘 | 확인하기

① moral   ↔
② independent   ↔
③ difficulty   ↔
④ misuse   ↔
⑤ forbid   ↔

104

2024 6월 모평

(A), (B), (C)의 각 네모 안에서 문맥에 맞는 낱말로 가장 적절한 것은?

To the extent that an agent relies on the prior knowledge of its designer rather than on its own percepts, we say that the agent lacks autonomy. A rational agent should be autonomous—it should learn what it can to (A) compensate / prepare for partial or incorrect prior knowledge. For example, a vacuum-cleaning agent that learns to foresee where and when additional dirt will appear will do better than one that does not. As a practical matter, one seldom requires complete autonomy from the start: when the agent has had little or no experience, it would have to act (B) purposefully / randomly unless the designer gave some assistance. So, just as evolution provides animals with enough built-in reflexes to survive long enough to learn for themselves, it would be reasonable to provide an artificial intelligent agent with some initial knowledge as well as an ability to learn. After sufficient experience of its environment, the behavior of a rational agent can become effectively (C) independent / protective of its prior knowledge. Hence, the incorporation of learning allows one to design a single rational agent that will succeed in a vast variety of environments.

	(A)		(B)		(C)
①	compensate	⋯⋯	randomly	⋯⋯	protective
②	compensate	⋯⋯	purposefully	⋯⋯	protective
③	prepare	⋯⋯	randomly	⋯⋯	protective
④	compensate	⋯⋯	randomly	⋯⋯	independent
⑤	prepare	⋯⋯	purposefully	⋯⋯	independent

출제 어휘 | 확인하기

(A) compensate   / prepare
(B) purposefully   / randomly
(C) independent   / protective

105

다음 글의 밑줄 친 부분 중, 문맥상 낱말의 쓰임이 적절하지 <u>않은</u> 것은?

The laws of chemistry are the same everywhere. The laws of motion are universal. The laws of relativity physics are not relative. The laws of probability are not probable. If the light on the scientist's desk ① <u>fails</u> to go on when he turns the switch, he doesn't change the laws of electrodynamics; he changes the light bulb, or he goes to Niagara Falls to see if the water has stopped running. The lamp going on is not a high probability. It's something that must ② <u>happen</u> each and every time. Every scientific law at least implies a cause. Galileo's law of falling bodies, for instance, although certainly a summary of the data, also implies the ③ <u>existence</u> of gravity as the cause of falling bodies. Indeed, in order to use the law we must know the gravitational constant for the attracting body. Only then can we derive ④ <u>definite</u> results from the formula. To sum up, without ⑤ <u>uncertainty</u> there could be no science of any kind.

*gravitational constant 중력 상수

출제 어휘 확인하기	
① fail	↔
② happen	↔
③ existence	↔
④ definite	↔
⑤ uncertainty	↔

106

밑줄 친 (a)~(e) 중에서 문맥상 낱말의 쓰임이 적절하지 <u>않은</u> 것은?

Car crashes are the result of a temporary imbalance between an individual's performance and the demands of the system in which he or she is functioning. They can be prevented by alterations in either, but most effectively by focusing on the system as a whole, and not on its user alone. A crash can occur when the victim was in fact performing quite well in absolute terms but the demands of the system (a) <u>exceeded</u> the current performance level of the user. In many areas of public health we understand this very well. We know that drinking water should be purified at its source; it is (b) <u>reasonable</u> to expect everyone to boil his water before drinking it. Those societies, which depend upon individuals to purify their own drinking water, suffer from much higher rates of communicable diseases than those which purify water at the source. Ironically, it is quite common to create a product or environment that is likely to cause injury, warn the user to be careful, and then (c) <u>blame</u> the user if a mishap occurs. We would never tolerate a person who introduced cholera germs in a city water supply and then asked every citizen to boil the water before drinking it, using the argument that those who knowingly don't do so would be (d) <u>responsible</u> for getting sick. Nevertheless, this is the kind of argument we all too often use when dealing with matters concerning road safety. We put in place (e) <u>hazardous</u> roads, vehicles and driving rules and then expect road users to be safe by behaving in some ideal manner.

*mishap 불행한 일

① (a)　　② (b)　　③ (c)　　④ (d)　　⑤ (e)

출제 어휘 확인하기	
① exceed	↔
② reasonable	↔
③ blame	↔
④ responsible	↔
⑤ hazardous	↔

필수 어휘 3

1 반의어

□ available	a 이용 가능한, 구할 수 있는	↔	□ unavailable	a 이용할 수 없는, 구할 수 없는
□ supply	n 공급 v 공급하다	↔	□ demand	n 수요 v 요구하다 ▸ demanding 부담을 주는, 요구가 많은
□ aware	a 인식하는 ▸ awareness 인식 ▸ be aware of ~을 알다	↔	□ unaware	a 인식하지 못하는
□ proper	a 적절한, 바람직한 ▸ properly 적절하게	↔	□ improper	a 부적절한
□ concrete	a 구체적인	↔	□ abstract	a 추상적인
□ scarcity	n 부족 ▸ scarce 부족한, 드문	↔	□ abundance	n 풍부 ▸ abundant 풍부한

2 형태가 비슷한 어휘

□ respective	a 각자의, 각각의 ▸ respectively 각각	□ confidence	n 자신감
□ respectful	a 존중하는, 예의바른 ▸ respect 존중하다	□ conference	n 회의
□ assumption	n 가정, 전제 ▸ assume 추정하다	□ transformation	n 변화
□ absorption	n 흡수; 열중 ▸ absorb 흡수하다	□ transmission	n 전달, 전송

3 필수 어휘

□ appropriate	a 적절한, 적합한 ▸ appropriately 적절[적합]하게	□ explode	v 폭발시키다, 분출하다 ▸ explosive 폭발의 ▸ explosion 폭발
□ bias	n 편향, 선입견 ▸ biased 편향된	□ familiar	a 익숙한, 친숙한 ▸ familiarity 익숙함, 친숙함
□ complicated	a 복잡한	□ identical	a 똑같은, 동일한
□ conform	v 순응하다, 복종하다 ▸ conformity 순응, 복종	□ neglect	v 무시하다, 간과하다
□ contradict	v 모순되다 ▸ contradiction 모순	□ obvious	a 명확한, 분명한 ▸ obviously 분명히
□ cultivate	v 함양하다, 양성하다	□ organize	v 정리[정돈]하다, 조직하다
□ demonstrate	v 보여 주다, 예증하다 ▸ demonstration 예증, 실증	□ problematic	a 문제가 되는
□ deny	v 부정하다, 부인하다 ▸ denial 부정, 부인	□ prospect	n 전망, 예상
□ evaluate	v 평가하다 ▸ evaluation 평가	□ reflect	v 반사하다, 반영하다 ▸ reflection 반사, 반영; 심사숙고
□ exclusive	a 독점적인	□ utilize	v 활용하다

Q1 괄호 안에서 문맥상 알맞은 것을 고르세요.

1. Lack of inventory and an unexpected drop in production led to a(n) 【 abundance / scarcity 】 of the item in major population centers.

• **inventory** 재고(품)
• **drop** 감소

2. Neither prosecutor nor defender is obliged to consider anything that weakens their 【 respectful / respective 】 cases.

• **prosecutor** 검찰관, 검사
• **be obliged to** *do* 어쩔 수 없이 ~하게 되다

3. They think he killed his wife, but they have no 【 abstract / concrete 】 evidence.

4. The certification procedure was far more 【 complicated / simplistic 】 than it needed to be. There were too many unnecessary documents.

• **certification** 확인, 보증
• **procedure** 절차
• **document** 서류, 문서

5. Probably the biggest roadblock to play for adults is the worry that they will look silly, 【 proper / improper 】, or dumb if they allow themselves to truly play.

• **roadblock** 장애물
• **silly** 어리석은
• **dumb** 우둔한, 바보 같은

Q2 밑줄 친 어휘와 유사한 뜻을 가진 어휘를 고르세요.

1. The chef will <u>demonstrate</u> the art of fruit carving in a live cooking show.

• **carving** 조각(술)

① organize   ② demand   ③ exhibit

2. We need to consider the long-term <u>prospect</u> of this investment before committing.

• **long-term** 장기적인
• **investment** 투자
• **commit** 약속하다

① outlook   ② opinion   ③ potential

3. To become a better writer, you need to <u>cultivate</u> your creativity and imagination.

• **creativity** 창의력
• **imagination** 상상력

① improve   ② evaluate   ③ diversify

107

다음 글의 밑줄 친 부분 중, 문맥상 낱말의 쓰임이 적절하지 <u>않은</u> 것은?

Going beyond very simple algorithms, some AI-based tools hold out the promise of supporting better causal and probabilistic reasoning in complex domains. Humans have a natural ability to ① <u>build</u> causal models of the world—that is, to explain *why* things happen—that AI systems still largely lack. For example, while a doctor can explain to a patient why a treatment works, referring to the changes it ② <u>causes</u> in the body, a modern machine-learning system could only tell you that patients who are given this treatment tend, on average, to get better. However, human reasoning is still notoriously ③ <u>prone</u> to confusion and error when causal questions become sufficiently complex, such as when it comes to assessing the impact of policy interventions across society. In these cases, supporting human reasoning with more structured AI-based tools may be ④ <u>helpful</u>. Researchers have been exploring the use of Bayesian Networks—an AI technology that can be used to map out the causal relationships between events, and to represent degrees of uncertainty around different areas—for decision support, such as to enable more accurate risk assessment. These may be particularly useful for assessing the threat of novel or rare threats, where ⑤ <u>sufficient</u> historical data is available, such as the risk of terrorist attacks and new ecological disasters.

*notoriously 악명 높게도

출제 어휘 확인하기	
① build	↔
② cause	↔
③ prone	↔
④ helpful	↔
⑤ sufficient	↔

108

다음 글의 밑줄 친 부분 중, 문맥상 낱말의 쓰임이 적절하지 <u>않은</u> 것은?

Although the wonders of modern technology have provided people with opportunities beyond the wildest dreams of our ancestors, the good, as usual, is weakened by a downside. One of those downsides is that anyone who so chooses can pick up the virtual megaphone that is the Internet and put in their two cents on any of an infinite number of topics, regardless of their ① <u>qualifications</u>. After all, on the Internet, there are no regulations ② <u>preventing</u> a kindergarten teacher from offering medical advice or a physician from suggesting ways to safely make structural changes to your home. As a result, misinformation gets disseminated as information, and it is not always easy to ③ <u>differentiate</u> the two. This can be particularly frustrating for scientists, who spend their lives learning how to understand the intricacies of the world around them, only to have their work summarily ④ <u>challenged</u> by people whose experience with the topic can be measured in minutes. This frustration is then ⑤ <u>diminished</u> by the fact that, to the general public, both the scientist and the challenger are awarded equal credibility.

*put in one's two cents 의견을 말하다
**disseminate 퍼뜨리다 ***intricacy 복잡성

출제 어휘 확인하기	
① qualification	↔
② prevent	↔
③ differentiate	↔
④ challenge	↔
⑤ diminish	↔

109

(A), (B), (C)의 각 네모 안에서 문맥에 맞는 낱말로 가장 적절한 것은?

Our conventional view of creativity focuses on and depicts a talented individual puzzling over problems and generating creative ideas and insights. We think the environment plays a (A) huge / small role.
⁵ However, Yale professor Jonathan Feinstein disputes this. In his book, *The Nature of Creative Development*, Feinstein argues that creativity flows from the individual's engagement with the world. Creativity is born from the experiences and elements people
¹⁰ encounter in the environment. This view seems to (B) contradict / parallel the business research. Michael Porter's book, *The Competitive Advantage of Nation*, was a landmark in studies of internationally competitive industries. It showed that the environment
¹⁵ plays a crucial role in determining which businesses are created. For example, the United States has many characteristics that make it an excellent environment for commercializing medical innovations. In fact, so (C) gloomy / positive is the environment for these
²⁰ businesses that many foreign entrepreneurs have come to the United States to start their medical product companies.

(A)	(B)	(C)
① huge	········ contradict	········ gloomy
② huge	········ parallel	········ positive
③ small	········ contradict	········ gloomy
④ small	········ parallel	········ gloomy
⑤ small	········ parallel	········ positive

출제 어휘 확인하기	
(A) huge	/ small
(B) contradict	/ parallel
(C) gloomy	/ positive

110

다음 글의 밑줄 친 부분 중, 문맥상 낱말의 쓰임이 적절하지 <u>않은</u> 것은?

A technology changes the entire environment it operates in. It changes the way we ① <u>perceive</u> the world. It changes the way we understand ourselves. A person born into a print culture would likely think of himself as a book. Perhaps he would refer to himself as ⁵ "an open book" when giving an interview. But a person born into an industrialized culture would likely think of himself as a machine, consuming food as ② <u>fuel</u> to keep the machine running. Such changes to our ③ <u>self-understanding</u> are often impossible to undo. What's ¹⁰ more, we are often oblivious to this kind of systemic change. The generation that spans these technological transformations may recognize that such changes are happening, but those who are born into them are ④ <u>sensible</u> to them. A mother and father may ¹⁵ ⑤ <u>anticipate</u> some of the changes that will come to their family when they buy their first computer, but their children are born into a computer family. They never know life any other way.

*oblivious 의식하지 못하는

출제 어휘 확인하기	
① perceive	↔
② fuel	↔
③ self-understanding	↔
④ sensible	↔
⑤ anticipate	↔

111

다음 글의 밑줄 친 부분 중, 문맥상 낱말의 쓰임이 적절하지 <u>않은</u> 것은?

Many approaches to dealing with demands at work view stress as an inherently toxic experience that should be avoided at all costs, and do not recognize how stress might be used to ① <u>facilitate</u> personal growth, professional development, and higher levels of performance. In addition, researchers have shown a ② <u>preoccupation</u> with burnout as a central outcome of stressful work, without examining other possible responses to tough working conditions. Employees are often viewed as passive recipients of stressful conditions, rather than as active constructors of their work environment who are capable of proactively ③ <u>addressing</u> many of the demands they encounter. We argue that a hyper-concern with the negative effects of stress at work has ④ <u>increased</u> an understanding of how stress can be used for growth. Completely ⑤ <u>eliminating</u> work demands could have negative effects on employees developing to their full potential.

112

2024 9월 모평

밑줄 친 (a)~(e) 중에서 문맥상 낱말의 쓰임이 적절하지 <u>않은</u> 것은?

One reason we think we forget most of what we learned in school is that we underestimate what we actually remember. Other times, we know we remember something, but we don't recognize that we learned it in school. Knowing where and when you learned something is usually called *context information*, and context is handled by (a) <u>different</u> memory processes than memory for the content. Thus, it's quite possible to retain content without remembering the context.

For example, if someone mentions a movie and you think to yourself that you heard it was terrible but can't remember (b) <u>where</u> you heard that, you're recalling the content, but you've lost the context. Context information is frequently (c) <u>easier</u> to forget than content, and it's the source of a variety of memory illusions. For instance, people are (d) <u>unconvinced</u> by a persuasive argument if it's written by someone who is not very credible (e.g., someone with a clear financial interest in the topic). But in time, readers' attitudes, on average, change in the direction of the persuasive argument. Why? Because readers are likely to remember the content of the argument but forget the source—someone who is not credible. If remembering the source of knowledge is difficult, you can see how it would be (e) <u>challenging</u> to conclude you don't remember much from school.

*illusion 착각

① (a) ② (b) ③ (c) ④ (d) ⑤ (e)

출제 어휘 확인하기	
① facilitate	↔
② preoccupation	↔
③ address	↔
④ increase	↔
⑤ eliminate	↔

출제 어휘 확인하기	
① different	↔
② where	↔
③ easier	↔
④ unconvinced	↔
⑤ challenging	↔

필수 어휘 4

1 반의어

allow	*v* 허용하다	↔	forbid	*v* 금지하다
	▶ allow A to *do* A가 ~하도록 허용하다			▶ forbid A to *do* A가 ~하는 것을 금지하다
certain	*a* 확실한, 확신하는	↔	uncertain	*a* 불확실한, 확신하지 못하는
	▶ certainty 확실성, 확신			▶ uncertainty 불확실성, 반신반의
internal	*a* 내적인	↔	external	*a* 외적인
horizontal	*a* 수평의	↔	vertical	*a* 수직의
superior	*a* 우월한, 우수한	↔	inferior	*a* 열등한
simplicity	*n* 단순함, 단순성	↔	variety	*n* 다양성 ▶ a variety of 다양한

2 형태가 비슷한 어휘

emit	*v* 방출하다, 내뿜다	irrigate	*v* 물을 대다, 관개하다
	▶ emission 방출, 배출, 배기가스		
omit	*v* 누락시키다, 빠뜨리다	irritate	*v* 자극하다, 짜증나게 하다
personal	*a* 개인의	status	*n* 지위, 신분
personnel	*n* (직장의) 총인원	statue	*n* 상, 조각상

3 필수 어휘

abuse	*n* 학대; 남용	extend	*v* 연장하다
address	*v* 해결하다 *n* 주소	facilitate	*v* 촉진하다
assign	*v* 할당하다, 배정하다 ▶ assignment 과제	globalize	*v* 세계화하다 ▶ globe 세계, 지구
association	*n* 조합, 협회 ▶ associate 결합[관련]시키다	obsessive	*a* 강박적인 ▶ obsession 강박, 사로잡힘
barrier	*n* 장벽, 장애물	particular	*a* 특정한 ▶ particularly 특히
benefit	*v* 혜택을 주다 *n* 혜택, 이득 ▶ beneficial 이로운, 유익한	preserve	*v* 보존[보전]하다 ▶ preservation 보존, 보전
differentiate	*v* 차별화하다	remain	*v* (~한 채로) 남다
eliminate	*v* 없애다	sacrifice	*v* 희생시키다, 희생하다
evoke	*v* 불러일으키다	security	*n* 안정성 ▶ secure 안정된, 안전한; 확보하다
exceed	*v* 초과하다	visualize	*v* 머릿속에 그리다, 시각화하다 ▶ visual 시각의, 시각적인

어휘 연습 문제

Q1 괄호 안에서 문맥상 알맞은 것을 고르세요.

1. Floors are [vertical / horizontal] and walls are [vertical / horizontal].

2. People sometimes make downward social comparisons—comparing themselves to [superior / inferior] or worse-off others—to feel better about themselves.

- **downward** 아래로 향하는
- **worse-off** 생활이 더 어려운

3. Keeping the sweat away is good because the salt in sweat [irritates / irrigates] the eyes, making them sting a little.

- **sweat** 땀
- **sting** 따갑다

4. More often, an entire habitat does not completely disappear but instead is reduced gradually until only small patches [lack / remain].

- **habitat** 서식지
- **patch** 작은 땅

5. The great climatic change the lake underwent and continued evaporation, [depressing / exceeding] the inflow of fresh water, reduced the lake to one-twentieth of its former size.

- **climatic** 기후의
- **undergo** 겪다
- **evaporation** 증발

Q2 밑줄 친 어휘와 유사한 뜻을 가진 어휘를 고르세요.

1. Money is nothing more than a means to an end. Yet so often we confuse means with ends, and <u>sacrifice</u> happiness (end) for money (means).

   ① abandon   ② promote   ③ mistake

2. Difficulties arise when we do not think of people and machines as collaborative systems, but <u>assign</u> whatever tasks can be automated to the machines and leave the rest to people.

- **collaborative** 협업하는
- **automate** 자동화하다

   ① limit   ② allocate   ③ complicate

3. Once racial and ethnic segregation is <u>eliminated</u> and people come together, they must learn to live, work, and play with each other despite diverse experiences and cultural perspectives.

- **racial** 인종의
- **ethnic** 민족의
- **segregation** 분리, 차별 (정책)
- **diverse** 다양한
- **perspective** 시각, 관점

   ① ignored   ② removed   ③ reinforced

113

2022 수능

다음 글의 밑줄 친 부분 중, 문맥상 낱말의 쓰임이 적절하지 <u>않은</u> 것은?

It has been suggested that "organic" methods, defined as those in which only natural products can be used as inputs, would be less damaging to the biosphere. Large-scale adoption of "organic" farming methods, however, would ① <u>reduce</u> yields and increase production costs for many major crops. Inorganic nitrogen supplies are ② <u>essential</u> for maintaining moderate to high levels of productivity for many of the non-leguminous crop species, because organic supplies of nitrogenous materials often are either limited or more expensive than inorganic nitrogen fertilizers. In addition, there are ③ <u>benefits</u> to the extensive use of either manure or legumes as "green manure" crops. In many cases, weed control can be very difficult or require much hand labor if chemicals cannot be used, and ④ <u>fewer</u> people are willing to do this work as societies become wealthier. Some methods used in "organic" farming, however, such as the sensible use of crop rotations and specific combinations of cropping and livestock enterprises, can make important ⑤ <u>contributions</u> to the sustainability of rural ecosystems.

*nitrogen fertilizer 질소 비료   **manure 거름
***legume 콩과(科) 식물

114

2021 10월 학평 응용

다음 글의 밑줄 친 부분 중, 문맥상 낱말의 쓰임이 적절하지 <u>않은</u> 것은?

If the nature of a thing is such that when removed from the environment in which it naturally occurs it alters radically, you will not glean an ① <u>accurate</u> account of it by examining it within laboratory conditions. If you are only accustomed to seeing it operate within such an ② <u>artificial</u> arena, you may not even recognize it when it is functioning in its normal context. Indeed, if you ever spot it in that environment you may think it is something else. Similarly, if you believe that leadership only takes the form of heroic men metaphorically charging in on white horses to save the day, you may ③ <u>respect</u> the many acts which contribute to their ability to be there. You may fail to see the importance of the grooms who care for the horses, the messengers who bring attention to the crisis or the role played by those ④ <u>cheering</u> from the sidelines. You may miss the fact that without troops supporting them, any claims to leading on the part of these heroes would be rather ⑤ <u>hollow</u>.

*glean 찾아내다

115

(A), (B), (C)의 각 네모 안에서 문맥에 맞는 낱말로 가장 적절한 것은?

The point of doing scientific research is to become part of the ongoing discourse—the never-ending round of questions and responses that makes it possible to understand the world around us. Research results that you keep locked up in your own file cabinet are essentially (A) worthless / worthwhile . Sometimes ethical constraints preclude the sharing of research because they might harm your informants or somehow (B) inflame / soothe public opinion, but for the most part it is a good thing to get the word out to one's scientific peers and even to audiences beyond academe. At first, your audience may be no larger than your instructor or other students in your class. But at some point you may be ready to publish your results, either in the form of a conference paper, a journal article, or a posting on a suitable Web site. You may also want to contribute your findings to a social agency interested in furthering goals, (C) utilizing / neglecting your findings to help their cause.

	(A)	(B)	(C)
①	worthless	inflame	utilizing
②	worthless	inflame	neglecting
③	worthless	soothe	utilizing
④	worthwhile	soothe	neglecting
⑤	worthwhile	inflame	utilizing

출제 어휘 확인하기	
(A) worthless	/ worthwhile
(B) inflame	/ soothe
(C) utilize	/ neglect

116

다음 글의 밑줄 친 부분 중, 문맥상 낱말의 쓰임이 적절하지 않은 것은?

Because each of us can choose our own perceptions, no one can ① force us to feel any particular emotion—we always have the choice as to how we respond to any situation. If we choose to be an emotional sponge by absorbing the negativity and dwelling on the hurt, we are ② allowing someone else to have power over us. On the other hand, if we choose to learn from the situation which has caused us grief by forgiving and moving forward with greater wisdom and insight, we are truly claiming ③ responsibility for our own feelings. This frees us to make a conscious choice to let go. "Letting go" does not mean we forget the entire experience. It means releasing the emotional knot of pain that has tied us to people whom we have not ④ forgiven. This can hardly be considered a ⑤ benefit, since the only thing we are letting go of is our internal bitterness and the hatred which has bonded us to the very people with whom we are angry.

출제 어휘 확인하기	
① force	↔
② allow	↔
③ responsibility	↔
④ forgive	↔
⑤ benefit	↔

117

다음 글의 밑줄 친 부분 중, 문맥상 낱말의 쓰임이 적절하지 <u>않은</u> 것은?

Consumers sometimes purchase certain things just because it is a good deal. In practice, however, such a "good deal", despite being ① <u>profitable</u> from an economic point of view, often is a bad decision from a subjective perspective, that is, the preferences and needs of the person making the purchase. Thaler gives a funny anecdote illustrating such a beneficial decision from an economic point of view but an ② <u>unfavourable</u> choice from the point of view of a given person. He describes his friend who wanted to buy a drape to throw over her sofa. In one store, she found a ③ <u>discounted</u> drape in three different sizes, which originally cost $200, $250, and $350, respectively, and now each cost $150 in the promotion. She bought the largest drape and was very happy with her "smart" buy (biggest discount). From an economic point of view, her choice really was the best as she had ④ <u>spent</u> the largest amount of money. However, from the angle of subjective ⑤ <u>utility</u>, she chose the worst option because the largest drape was far too big for her sofa and trailed along the floor.

정답 및 해설 p.072

118

밑줄 친 (a)~(e) 중에서 문맥상 낱말의 쓰임이 적절하지 <u>않은</u> 것은?

Climate change experts and environmental humanists alike agree that the climate crisis is, at its core, a crisis of the imagination and much of the popular imagination is shaped by fiction. In his 2016 book *The Great Derangement*, anthropologist and novelist Amitav Ghosh takes on this relationship between imagination and environmental management, arguing that humans have failed to respond to climate change at least in part because fiction (a) <u>fails</u> to believably represent it. Ghosh explains that climate change is largely absent from contemporary fiction because the cyclones, floods, and other catastrophes it brings to mind simply seem too "improbable" to belong in stories about everyday life. But climate change does not only reveal itself as a series of (b) <u>extraordinary</u> events. In fact, as environmentalists and ecocritics from Rachel Carson to Rob Nixon have pointed out, environmental change can be "imperceptible"; it proceeds (c) <u>rapidly</u>, only occasionally producing "explosive and spectacular" events. Most climate change impacts cannot be observed day-to-day, but they become (d) <u>visible</u> when we are confronted with their accumulated impacts.

Climate change evades our imagination because it poses significant representational challenges. It cannot be observed in "human time," which is why documentary filmmaker Jeff Orlowski, who tracks climate change effects on glaciers and coral reefs, uses "before and after" photographs taken several months apart in the same place to (e) <u>highlight</u> changes that occurred gradually.

*anthropologist 인류학자 **catastrophe 큰 재해 ***evade 피하다

① (a) 　② (b) 　③ (c) 　④ (d) 　⑤ (e)

출제 어휘 | 확인하기

①	profitable	↔	
②	unfavourable	↔	
③	discounted	↔	
④	spend	↔	
⑤	utility	↔	

출제 어휘 | 확인하기

①	fail	↔	
②	extraordinary	↔	
③	rapidly	↔	
④	visible	↔	
⑤	highlight	↔	

필수 어휘 5

1 반의어

objective	*a* 객관적인	↔	subjective	*a* 주관적인
willing	*a* 기꺼이 ~하는	↔	reluctant	*a* 꺼리는 ▶ reluctance 꺼림, 망설임
obligatory	*a* 의무의 ▶ obligation 의무	↔	optional	*a* 선택의 ▶ option 선택 (사항)
tangible	*a* 실체가 있는, 유형의	↔	intangible	*a* 실체가 없는, 무형의
stabilize	*v* 안정되다 ▶ stability 안정성	↔	fluctuate	*v* 변동하다, 오르내리다 ▶ fluctuation 변동, 오르내림
ordinary	*a* 평범한, 보통의	↔	extraordinary	*a* 특별한, 뛰어난

2 형태가 비슷한 어휘

adapt	*v* 적응하다 ▶ adaptation 적응	conduct	*v* 행동하다, 지휘하다
adopt	*v* 채택하다; 양자로 삼다 ▶ adoption 채택; 입양	deduct	*v* 빼다, 공제하다
contribute	*v* 기여하다 ▶ contribution 기여, 공헌	prospective	*a* 장래의, 유망한
distribute	*v* 나누어주다, 분배[배부]하다 ▶ distribution 분배, 분포	perspective	*n* 관점; 전망; 원근법

3 필수 어휘

abandon	*v* 포기하다, 버리다	original	*a* 독창적인 ▶ originality 독창성
afford	*v* 제공하다 ▶ afford to *do* ~할 (시간적·경제적) 여유가 있다	overwhelm	*v* 압도하다 ▶ overwhelming 압도하는
circulate	*v* 유포하다, 순환시키다 ▶ circulation 유포, 순환	pose	*v* (문제·의문 등을) 제기하다
drawback	*n* 단점, 결점	pressure	*n* 압박, 압력
ethical	*a* 윤리적인 ▶ ethics 윤리(학)	promotion	*n* 승진; 홍보 ▶ promote 승진시키다; 홍보하다
flaw	*n* 단점, 결점, 결함 ▶ flawed 결점 있는	prosper	*v* 번성하다, 번창하다 ▶ prosperity 번영, 번성, 번창
force	*v* 강요하다 *n* 힘	responsibility	*n* 책임 ▶ responsible for ~의 책임을 맡은, ~에 책임이 있는
foresee	*v* 예측하다 ▶ unforeseen 예측하지 못한	reinforce	*v* 강화하다 ▶ reinforcement 강화
interference	*n* 간섭, 방해 ▶ interfere 간섭[방해]하다	retain	*v* 보유하다
measure	*v* 측정하다	seize	*v* 포착하다, 붙잡다

Q1 괄호 안에서 문맥상 알맞은 것을 고르세요.

1. It is [obligatory / optional] to remove your shoes before entering a Korean traditional room.

• **traditional** 전통적인

2. Fortunately, John received [pressures / promotions]. He became the manager of a branch in New South Wales. Finally he became the head of the company for all of Australia.

• **branch** 지점, 지부

3. Without financial backing, the plotters were forced to [abandon / overwhelm] their plan.

• **backing** 도움, 후원
• **plotter** 음모자, 계획자

4. Such assets are known as [tangible / intangible] assets in contrast to the physical ones.

• **asset** 자산
• **physical** 물리적인

5. Financial markets have become more variable and authorities seem to have lost control over them. As a result, interest rates and exchange rates now [fluctuate / stabilize] more rapidly than at any time.

• **variable** 변하기 쉬운, 변동의
• **authority** 당국
• **interest rate** 금리
• **exchange rate** 환율

Q2 밑줄 친 어휘와 유사한 뜻을 가진 어휘를 고르세요.

1. One obvious <u>drawback</u> of experimenting on oneself is the limited range of data that the experiment can generate.

① benefit ② procedure ③ disadvantage

• **obvious** 명백한
• **experiment** 실험(하다)
• **generate** 초래하다, 가져오다

2. Ask a friend to cup his hand, palm face up, and close his eyes. Place a small <u>ordinary</u> object in his palm—a ring, an eraser, anything will do— and ask him to identify it without moving any part of his hand.

① normal ② original ③ useful

• **identify** 식별하다

3. The pattern only changed when someone had the courage to report what was actually <u>measured</u> instead of what was expected.

① gauged ② guessed ③ documented

• **instead of** ~ 대신에
• **expect** 기대하다

119

2023 9월 모평 응용

다음 글의 밑줄 친 부분 중, 문맥상 낱말의 쓰임이 적절하지 않은 것은?

Not only musicians and psychologists, but also committed music enthusiasts and experts often voice the opinion that the beauty of music lies in an expressive deviation from the exactly ① defined score. Concert performances become interesting and gain in attraction from the fact that they go far beyond the information printed in the score. In his early studies on musical performance, Carl Seashore discovered that musicians only ② rarely play two equal notes in exactly the same way. Within the same metric structure, there is a wide potential of variations in tempo, volume, tonal quality and intonation. Such variation is based on the composition but diverges from it ③ individually. We generally call this 'expressivity'. This explains why we do not lose interest when we hear different artists perform the same piece of music. It also explains why it is ④ worthless for following generations to repeat the same repertoire. New, inspiring interpretations help us to expand our understanding, which serves to ⑤ enrich and animate the music scene.

*deviation 벗어남

출제 어휘 확인하기

① defined	↔	
② rarely	↔	
③ individually	↔	
④ worthless	↔	
⑤ enrich	↔	

120

2023 6월 모평

다음 글의 밑줄 친 부분 중, 문맥상 낱말의 쓰임이 적절하지 않은 것은?

In recent years urban transport professionals globally have largely acquiesced to the view that automobile demand in cities needs to be managed rather than accommodated. Rising incomes inevitably lead to increases in motorization. Even without the imperative of climate change, the physical constraints of densely inhabited cities and the corresponding demands of accessibility, mobility, safety, air pollution, and urban livability all ① limit the option of expanding road networks purely to accommodate this rising demand. As a result, as cities develop and their residents become more prosperous, ② persuading people to choose *not* to use cars becomes an increasingly key focus of city managers and planners. Improving the quality of ③ alternative options, such as walking, cycling, and public transport, is a central element of this strategy. However, the most direct approach to ④ accommodating automobile demand is making motorized travel more expensive or restricting it with administrative rules. The contribution of motorized travel to climate change ⑤ reinforces this imperative.

*acquiesce 따르다 **imperative 불가피한 것
***constraint 압박

출제 어휘 확인하기

① limit	↔	
② persuade	↔	
③ alternative	↔	
④ accommodate	↔	
⑤ reinforce	↔	

121

다음 글의 밑줄 친 부분 중, 문맥상 낱말의 쓰임이 적절하지 <u>않은</u> 것은?

Fundamentally, among animals, fighting is not sought nor valued for its own sake; it is resorted to rather as an unwelcome necessity, a means of defending their interests. Above all, aggressive behavior of animals largely results from the ① <u>scarcity</u> of resources such as food and shelter. As a given animal population increases, the competition for available food, mates, and territory ② <u>rises</u>. Animals engage in aggressive behavior to ③ <u>intensify</u> these growing tensions by eliminating competitors, either by forcing weaker members of the population to relocate or by killing them outright. In contrast, as the population density ④ <u>decreases</u>, the need for aggressive behavior does too. Animal species that seldom compete for food or shelter, either due to an ⑤ <u>abundance</u> of resources or to a small population density, rarely exhibit aggressive tendencies.

122

(A), (B), (C)의 각 네모 안에서 문맥에 맞는 낱말로 가장 적절한 것은?

The most difficult and sensitive decisions in end of life care are often those around starting, or stopping, potentially life-prolonging treatments such as cardiopulmonary resuscitation (CPR), artificial nutrition and hydration and mechanical ventilation. These treatments have many potential (A) benefits / drawbacks including extending the lives of patients who otherwise might die from their underlying condition. But in some circumstances they may only prolong the dying process or cause the patient unnecessary distress. The benefits, burdens and risks of these treatments are not always well understood and concerns can (B) arise / subside about over- or under-treatment, particularly where there is uncertainty about the clinical effect of a treatment on the individual patient, or about how the benefits and burdens for that patient are being assessed. Doctors and others involved in the decision-making process may also be (C) clear / unclear about what is legally and ethically permissible, especially in relation to decisions to stop a potentially life-prolonging treatment.

*cardiopulmonary resuscitation 심폐소생술(CPR)

	(A)	(B)	(C)
①	benefits	arise	clear
②	benefits	subside	clear
③	benefits	arise	unclear
④	drawbacks	arise	clear
⑤	drawbacks	subside	unclear

출제 어휘 확인하기

① scarcity	↔	
② rise	↔	
③ intensify	↔	
④ decrease	↔	
⑤ abundance	↔	

출제 어휘 확인하기

(A) benefit	/ drawback
(B) arise	/ subside
(C) clear	/ unclear

123

다음 글의 밑줄 친 부분 중, 문맥상 낱말의 쓰임이 적절하지 <u>않은</u> 것은?

Ideally, when people interact with one another, their behavior ① <u>corresponds</u> to the particular roles they are playing. The socially determined behaviors expected of a person performing a role are called role expectations. For example, doctors are expected to treat their patients with skill and care. Parents are expected to provide emotional and physical security for their children. Police officers are expected to ② <u>uphold</u> the law. In reality, people's actual role behavior does not always ③ <u>match</u> the behavior expected by society. Some doctors do not give their patients the best possible care. Some parents mistreat their children. Occasionally, this problem arises because role behaviors considered proper by a certain segment of society can be seen as ④ <u>inappropriate</u> by society as a whole. This role conflict also occurs when we are asked to perform multiple roles that ⑤ <u>complement</u> one another.

출제 어휘 **확인하기**	
① correspond	↔
② uphold	↔
③ match	↔
④ inappropriate	↔
⑤ complement	↔

124

2024 수능

밑줄 친 (a)~(e) 중에서 문맥상 낱말의 쓰임이 적절하지 <u>않은</u> 것은?

One way to avoid contributing to overhyping a story would be to say nothing. However, that is not a realistic option for scientists who feel a strong sense of responsibility to inform the public and policymakers and/or to offer suggestions. Speaking with members of the media has (a) <u>advantages</u> in getting a message out and perhaps receiving favorable recognition, but it runs the risk of misinterpretations, the need for repeated clarifications, and entanglement in never-ending controversy. Hence, the decision of whether to speak with the media tends to be highly individualized. Decades ago, it was (b) <u>unusual</u> for Earth scientists to have results that were of interest to the media, and consequently few media contacts were expected or encouraged. In the 1970s, the few scientists who spoke frequently with the media were often (c) <u>criticized</u> by their fellow scientists for having done so. The situation now is quite different, as many scientists feel a responsibility to speak out because of the importance of global warming and related issues, and many reporters share these feelings. In addition, many scientists are finding that they (d) <u>enjoy</u> the media attention and the public recognition that comes with it. At the same time, other scientists continue to resist speaking with reporters, thereby preserving more time for their science and (e) <u>running</u> the risk of being misquoted and the other unpleasantries associated with media coverage.

*overhype 과대광고하다 **entanglement 얽힘

① (a)   ② (b)   ③ (c)   ④ (d)   ⑤ (e)

출제 어휘 **확인하기**	
① advantage	↔
② unusual	↔
③ criticize	↔
④ enjoy	↔
⑤ run	↔

필수 어휘 6

1 반의어

□ **effective**	*a* 효과적인, 유능한	↔	□ **ineffective**	*a* 효과적이지 않은, 무능한
□ **natural**	*a* 자연적인	↔	□ **artificial**	*a* 인공적인, 인위적인
□ **satisfactory**	*a* 만족스러운 ▶ satisfy 만족시키다	↔	□ **unsatisfactory**	*a* 불만족스러운
□ **stable**	*a* 안정적인 ▶ stability 안정(성)	↔	□ **unstable**	*a* 불안정한 ▶ instability 불안정(성)
□ **favorable**	*a* 우호적인, 유리한 ▶ favor 호의 (↔ unfavorable 호의적이지 않은, 불리한)	↔	□ **hostile**	*a* 적대적인 ▶ hostility 적개심, 적의
□ **explicit**	*a* 명백한, 명시적인	↔	□ **implicit**	*a* 암묵적인

2 형태가 비슷한 어휘

□ **elaborate**	*v* 상세히 말하다 *a* 공들인, 정교한	□ **infection**	*n* 감염 ▶ infect 감염시키다
□ **collaborate**	*v* 협업하다, 합작하다 ▶ collaboration 합작품; 협업	□ **inspection**	*n* 검사 ▶ inspect 검사하다
□ **convict**	*v* 유죄를 선고하다 *n* 죄수, 기결수 ▶ conviction 유죄 선고[판결]	□ **simulate**	*v* 흉내 내다; 모의실험하다 ▶ simulation 시뮬레이션, 모의실험
□ **convince**	*v* 확신시키다, 납득시키다 ▶ convincing 설득력 있는	□ **stimulate**	*v* 자극하다 ▶ stimulation 자극

3 필수 어휘

□ **academic**	*a* 학업적인, 학문의	□ **outcome**	*n* 결과
□ **appreciation**	*n* 인정; 감상; 감사 ▶ appreciate (가치를) 인정하다; 감사하다	□ **permanent**	*a* 영속적인, 영구적인 ▶ permanence 영속성
□ **characteristic**	*n* 특징, 특성	□ **property**	*n* 재산, 자산; 특성
□ **collective**	*a* 집단적인	□ **respect**	*n* 존중 *v* 존중하다
□ **disconnected**	*a* 단절된	□ **skilled**	*a* 숙련된, 노련한 ▶ skillful 솜씨 있는
□ **disposal**	*n* 처리, 처분 ▶ dispose 처분하다, 폐기하다	□ **temporary**	*a* 일시적인
□ **disregard**	*v* 무시하다, 고려하지 않다	□ **transform**	*v* 변형시키다
□ **illusion**	*n* 착각, 환상	□ **trigger**	*n* 계기, 촉발제 *v* 촉발하다
□ **impair**	*v* 손상을 주다	□ **utility**	*n* 효용(성), 유용(성)
□ **indispensable**	*a* 필수 불가결한	□ **value**	*v* 가치를 인정하다 *n* 가치

Q1 괄호 안에서 문맥상 알맞은 것을 고르세요.

1. The courts will [convict / convince] people who have purposely spread HIV, the AIDS virus, imposing harsh sentences on them.

- **court** 법정, 법원
- **impose** 부과하다
- **sentence** 형벌, 선고

2. Measures should be taken to reduce the likelihood of bacterial [infection / inspection].

- **measure** 조치
- **likelihood** 가능성
- **bacterial** 박테리아의

3. Can you [collaborate / elaborate] on your knowledge of computer viruses in detail?

- **in detail** 상세히, 자세히

4. Separating what's important from what's not important is prioritizing. [Skilled / Ineffective] coaches fail to put the big tasks first.

- **prioritize** 우선순위를 결정하다

5. That's just a [temporary / permanent] measure, not the fundamental solution for the conflict.

- **solution** 해결책

Q2 밑줄 친 어휘와 유사한 뜻을 가진 어휘를 고르세요.

1. Radioactive waste <u>disposal</u> has become one of the key environmental battlegrounds over which the future of nuclear power has been fought.

① removal   ② generation   ③ preservation

- **radioactive** 방사능의
- **battleground** 전쟁터
- **nuclear power** 원자력

2. Science is an <u>indispensable</u> source of information for the contemporary writer. It is, furthermore, a necessary part of his highly technological environment.

① endless   ② essential   ③ independent

- **contemporary** 현대의, 동시대의
- **furthermore** 게다가

3. Small changes in the sensory <u>properties</u> of foods are sufficient to increase food intake.

① features   ② evaluations   ③ components

- **sufficient** 충분한
- **intake** 섭취

125

2021 수능

다음 글의 밑줄 친 부분 중, 문맥상 낱말의 쓰임이 적절하지 <u>않은</u> 것은?

　How the bandwagon effect occurs is demonstrated by the history of measurements of the speed of light. Because this speed is the basis of the theory of relativity, it's one of the most frequently and carefully measured ① <u>quantities</u> in science. As far as we know, the speed hasn't changed over time. However, from 1870 to 1900, all the experiments found speeds that were too high. Then, from 1900 to 1950, the ② <u>opposite</u> happened—all the experiments found speeds that were too low! This kind of error, where results are always on one side of the real value, is called "bias." It probably happened because over time, experimenters subconsciously adjusted their results to ③ <u>match</u> what they expected to find. If a result fit what they expected, they kept it. If a result didn't fit, they threw it out. They weren't being intentionally dishonest, just ④ <u>influenced</u> by the conventional wisdom. The pattern only changed when someone ⑤ <u>lacked</u> the courage to report what was actually measured instead of what was expected.

*bandwagon effect 편승 효과

출제 어휘 확인하기

① quantity	↔	
② opposite	↔	
③ match	↔	
④ influence	↔	
⑤ lack	↔	

126

다음 글의 밑줄 친 부분 중, 문맥상 낱말의 쓰임이 적절하지 <u>않은</u> 것은?

　One characteristic of a trusting organization is a leadership team that practices ① <u>respect</u> for persons and the values of the organization. The leaders and managers of the organization must work as a team. The CEO's job is to make sure that there is evenhandedness and ② <u>fairness</u> throughout the organization. In other words, the CEO maintains balance within the organization while facilitating its growth and development. While profits and products might be ③ <u>outcomes</u> for the organization, money is not a good motivator for members. Studies have shown that what employees miss is ④ <u>appreciation</u>. People need to be ⑤ <u>devalued</u> for their talents and what they contribute to the organization. Organizational members at all levels must practice personal recognition with intangible and tangible rewards tied to performance. Trust, self-esteem, and loyalty are the rewards for the organization.

출제 어휘 확인하기

① respect	↔	
② fairness	↔	
③ outcome	↔	
④ appreciation	↔	
⑤ devalue	↔	

127

다음 글의 밑줄 친 부분 중, 문맥상 낱말의 쓰임이 적절하지 <u>않은</u> 것은?

Some people say that parents and children should be "friends." They say this kind of relationship provides a comfortable atmosphere for children, so they will grow less stressed and have a more ① positive character. As a matter of fact, many mothers and fathers try to be a friend to their children. However, a friends-like relationship is somewhat "dangerous." Parenting is not a popularity contest. ② Challenging authority is a normal part of child development. Setting rules and enforcing them teaches the child that he or she is ③ equal in worth but not equal in authority. Then the child feels safe and secure and can be a kid again. Believe it or not, it's ④ frightening for children to realize they are in charge of the situation. When parents back down from rules they set, children become ⑤ relieved and out of control. They don't trust their parents to protect them. Parents should follow these tips to avoid this situation.

128

(A), (B), (C)의 각 네모 안에서 문맥에 맞는 낱말로 가장 적절한 것은?

The concept of bringing people together in groups, tribes, or organizations is based on the fundamental premise that human being can do more (A) collectively / individually than they can in isolation. Hundreds of years ago, people banded together for the sake of sharing food and shelter and keeping their family safe. The basic assumption was that the association gained by joining a group would (B) benefit / impair individuals and their loved ones. This is why I was taken aback by research Gallup conducted on this topic. When workers across the United States were asked whether their lives were better off because of the organization they worked for, a mere 12 percent claimed that their lives were significantly better. The vast majority of employees felt that their company was a (C) barrier / trigger to their overall health and well-being.

	(A)		(B)		(C)
①	collectively	⋯⋯	benefit	⋯⋯	barrier
②	collectively	⋯⋯	benefit	⋯⋯	trigger
③	collectively	⋯⋯	impair	⋯⋯	barrier
④	individually	⋯⋯	impair	⋯⋯	trigger
⑤	individually	⋯⋯	benefit	⋯⋯	barrier

129

다음 글의 밑줄 친 부분 중, 문맥상 낱말의 쓰임이 적절하지 <u>않은</u> 것은?

Individual men may be moral in the sense that they are able to consider interests other than their own in determining problems of conduct, and are capable of ① preferring the advantages of others to their own.
5 They are endowed by nature with a measure of sympathy and consideration for their kind, the breadth of which may be ② extended by an astute social pedagogy. Their rational faculty prompts them to a sense of justice which educational discipline may
10 ③ refine and rid of egoistic elements. But all these achievements are more difficult for human societies and social groups. The ④ superiority of the morality of groups to that of individuals is due in part to the difficulty of establishing a rational social force which is
15 powerful enough to cope with the natural impulses by which society achieves its cohesion; but in part it is merely the ⑤ revelation of a collective egoism, compounded of the egoistic impulses of individuals, which achieve a cumulative effect when they are united
20 in a common impulse.

*astute 빈틈없는 **pedagogy 교육(학)
***cumulative 누적하는, 가중의

130

밑줄 친 (a)~(e) 중에서 문맥상 낱말의 쓰임이 적절하지 <u>않은</u> 것은?

Once an event is noticed, an onlooker must decide if it is truly an emergency. Emergencies are not always clearly (a) <u>labeled</u> as such; "smoke" pouring into a waiting room may be caused by fire, or it may merely indicate a leak in a steam pipe. Screams in the street 5 may signal an attack or a family quarrel. A man lying in a doorway may be having a coronary—or he may simply be sleeping off a drunk.

A person trying to interpret a situation often looks at those around him to see how he should react. If 10 everyone else is calm and indifferent, he will tend to remain so; if everyone else is reacting strongly, he is likely to become alert. This tendency is not merely blind conformity; ordinarily we derive much valuable information about new situations from how others 15 around us behave. It's a (b) <u>rare</u> traveler who, in picking a roadside restaurant, chooses to stop at one where no other cars appear in the parking lot.

But occasionally the reactions of others provide (c) <u>accurate</u> information. The studied nonchalance of 20 patients in a dentist's waiting room is a poor indication of their inner anxiety. It is considered embarrassing to "lose your cool" in public. In a potentially acute situation, then, everyone present will appear more (d) <u>unconcerned</u> than he is in fact. A crowd can thus 25 force (e) <u>inaction</u> on its members by implying, through its passivity, that an event is not an emergency. Any individual in such a crowd fears that he may appear a fool if he behaves as though it were.

*coronary 관상 동맥증 **nonchalance 무관심, 냉담

① (a)　　② (b)　　③ (c)　　④ (d)　　⑤ (e)

1 반의어

□ rise	v 증가하다, 상승하다 n 상승	↔	□ decline	v 감소하다 n 감소	
□ admit	v 인정하다 ▸ admission 인정	↔	□ deny	v 부정하다	
□ reveal	v 드러내다, 보여 주다	↔	□ disguise	v 숨기다, 위장하다 (= conceal 감추다, 숨기다)	
□ aware	a 알고 있는 (↔ unaware 모르는) ▸ be aware of ~을 알다	↔	□ ignorant	a 모르는, 무지한 ▸ ignorance 무지(함)	
□ familiarity	n 친숙함, 익숙함	↔	□ novelty	n 새로움, 참신함 ▸ novel 새로운, 참신한; 소설	
□ affluence	n 풍요, 풍족 ▸ affluent 풍족한, 풍요로운	↔	□ poverty	n 빈곤, 가난	

2 형태가 비슷한 어휘

□ banish	v 추방하다	□ compliment	v 칭찬하다
□ vanish	v 사라지다	□ complement	v 보충하다 ▸ complementary 상호 보완적인
□ acquire	v 얻다, 획득[습득]하다 ▸ acquisition 습득, 획득	□ proceed	v 나아가다, 전진하다
□ inquire	v 문의하다, 조사하다 ▸ inquiry 문의, 조사	□ precede	v 선행하다, 앞서다 ▸ precedent 앞서는, 선례의

3 필수 어휘

□ advance	v 나아가다, 전진하다 n 진전, 발전	□ opposite	n 반대 a (정)반대의
□ cling	v 집착하다 ▸ cling to ~에 집착하다	□ overestimate	v 과대평가하다
□ concern	v 관련되다 n 우려; 관심	□ relieve	v 완화시키다, 경감하다, 덜다
□ conventional	a 기존의, 관례적인 ▸ convention 전통, 관례; 집회	□ sensible	a 인지하는, 분별 있는
□ influence	v 영향을 주다 n 영향	□ solitary	a 혼자의, 무리를 이루지 않는
□ inherent	a 내재된, 고유의 ▸ inherently 본질적으로, 내재적으로	□ suspicious	a 의심스러워하는 ▸ suspicion 의심, 혐의
□ insecure	a 불안한, 확신이 안 가는	□ tie	n 유대(감) v 묶다, 잇다
□ intellect	n 지성, 지능	□ universal	a 보편적인 ▸ universality 보편성
□ mutual	a 서로의, 상호의	□ vain	a 헛된 ▸ in vain 헛되이
□ offend	v 불쾌하게 하다 ▸ offensive 불쾌한	□ verbal	a 말의, 언어적인

어휘 연습 문제

Q1 괄호 안에서 문맥상 알맞은 것을 고르세요.

1. She [complimented / complemented] the nine-year-old boy on his good manners.

- **manners** 예의범절

2. The king [banished / vanished] the murderer from the land.

- **murderer** 살인자

3. The good news is that it's never too late to start building up muscle strength, regardless of your age. Ideally, though, it's best to start in your mid-forties when muscle mass starts to [decline / rise] significantly.

- **ideally** 이상적으로
- **significantly** 상당히, 크게

4. You have to challenge the [complementary / conventional] ways of doing things and search for opportunities to innovate.

- **challenge** 이의를 제기하다, 도전하다
- **innovate** 혁신하다

5. To say that we need to curb anger and our negative thoughts and emotions does not necessarily mean that we should [admit / deny] our feelings.

- **curb** 억제하다
- **anger** 화, 분노

Q2 밑줄 친 어휘와 유사한 뜻을 가진 어휘를 고르세요.

1. You can't have a democracy if you can't talk with your neighbors about matters of <u>mutual</u> interest or concern.

① exclusive   ② reciprocal   ③ legitimate

- **democracy** 민주주의
- **interest** 관심, 흥미, 이익
- **concern** 우려, 관심

2. Try to brush aside the stuff that <u>offends</u> you to really try to hear what they are saying you can do better next time.

① displeases   ② transforms   ③ distracts

- **brush aside** ~을 제쳐놓다

3. Food unites as well as distinguishes eaters because what and how one eats forms much of one's emotional <u>tie</u> to a group identity.

① tendency   ② bond   ③ burden

- **unite** 결속하다
- **distinguish** 구분하다
- **identity** 정체성

131

다음 글의 밑줄 친 부분 중, 문맥상 낱말의 쓰임이 적절하지 <u>않은</u> 것은?

Over the last 150 years the corporation has risen from relative obscurity to become the world's dominant economic institution. Today, corporations ① <u>govern</u> our lives. They determine what we eat, what we watch, what we wear, where we work, and what we do. We are ② <u>inescapably</u> surrounded by their culture and ideology. And, like the church and the monarchy in other times, they posture as infallible and omnipotent, ③ <u>concealing</u> themselves in imposing buildings and arrogant displays. Increasingly, corporations ④ <u>dictate</u> the decisions of their overseers in government and control domains of society once firmly embedded within the public sphere. The corporation's dramatic ⑤ <u>development</u> to dominance is one of the remarkable events of modern history.

*infallible 절대 옳은

132

다음 글의 밑줄 친 부분 중, 문맥상 낱말의 쓰임이 적절하지 <u>않은</u> 것은?

Sport can trigger an emotional response in its consumers of the kind rarely brought forth by other products. Imagine bank customers buying memorabilia to show loyalty to their bank, or consumers ① <u>identifying</u> so strongly with their car insurance company that they get a tattoo with its logo. We know that some sport followers are so ② <u>passionate</u> about players, teams and the sport itself that their interest borders on obsession. This addiction provides the emotional glue that binds fans to teams, and maintains loyalty even in the face of on-field ③ <u>failure</u>. While most managers can only dream of having customers that are as passionate about their products as sport fans, the emotion triggered by sport can also have a negative impact. Sport's emotional intensity can mean that organisations have strong attachments to the past through nostalgia and club tradition. As a result, they may ④ <u>increase</u> efficiency, productivity and the need to respond quickly to changing market conditions. For example, a proposal to change club colours in order to project a more attractive image may be ⑤ <u>defeated</u> because it breaks a link with tradition.

*memorabilia 기념품 **obsession 집착

출제 어휘 확인하기	
① govern	↔
② inescapably	↔
③ conceal	↔
④ dictate	↔
⑤ development	↔

출제 어휘 확인하기	
① identify	↔
② passionate	↔
③ failure	↔
④ increase	↔
⑤ defeat	↔

133

다음 글의 밑줄 친 부분 중, 문맥상 낱말의 쓰임이 적절하지 <u>않은</u> 것은?

The key features of interpersonal and intergroup relations in the tribal world were cooperation, reciprocity, complementary opposition, and overlapping networks. People performed most daily domestic routines as ① <u>cooperative</u> tasks within corporate groups. Economic activities were shared and products were distributed on the basis of reciprocity between individuals and households, on the assumption that this would be fair because effort and returns would ② <u>balance</u> out over the long run. The assumption of fairness was ③ <u>realistic</u> in these small societies where everyone knew everyone else, and everyone's possessions and activities were on constant public display. Social categories such as male and female, or group A and group B, were treated as connected sets, and the different parts were culturally understood to be two ④ <u>interdependent</u> halves of a larger whole, such that one half could not exist without the other. Membership in social groups also frequently overlapped, forming cross-cutting networks that made it ⑤ <u>easy</u> for aspiring leaders to organize competing alliances.

134

다음 글의 밑줄 친 부분 중, 문맥상 낱말의 쓰임이 적절하지 <u>않은</u> 것은?

The three great American ① <u>vices</u> seem to be efficiency, punctuality and the desire for achievement and success. They are the things that make the Americans so unhappy and so nervous. They steal from them their inalienable right of loafing and ② <u>cheat</u> them of many good, idle and beautiful afternoon. One must start out with a belief that there are no catastrophes in this world, and that besides the noble art of getting things done, there is nobler art of leaving things ③ <u>undone</u>. On the whole, if one answers letters promptly, the result is about as good or as bad as if he had never answered them at all. If you keep them in your drawer for three months; reading them three months afterwards, one might realize how utterly ④ <u>futile</u> and what a waste of time it would have been to answer them all. In this sense, I can understand Thoreau's ⑤ <u>praise</u> for the American who always goes to the post office.

*punctuality 시간 엄수 **loaf (일을) 빈둥거리면서 하다

출제 어휘 확인하기		
① cooperative	↔	
② balance	↔	
③ realistic	↔	
④ interdependent	↔	
⑤ easy	↔	

출제 어휘 확인하기		
① vice	↔	
② cheat	↔	
③ undone	↔	
④ futile	↔	
⑤ praise	↔	

135

(A), (B), (C)의 각 네모 안에서 문맥에 맞는 낱말로 가장 적절한 것은?

Current trends show that population growth is greatest in several economically developing countries. Not only is malnutrition already a significant issue in many of these places, but many of them also include significant tropical areas which may be more negatively affected by climate change processes. Alternatively, increased levels of atmospheric CO_2 and an associated increase in nitrogen fixation could (A) disturb / help to increase biomass productivity and contribute to a higher rate of new soil formation. Climate change processes are likely to generate changes in water supply and demand. Dry regions may be particularly (B) resistant / susceptible to drought that follows the plow as warmer temperatures, water evaporation, and land use techniques combine. Increased rates of urbanization and uneven population increase may (C) prevent / worsen water stress in some places. Likewise, warmer temperatures are likely to contribute to thriving pest populations and a negative impact on agricultural productivity.

*nitrogen fixation 질소 고정   **biomass 생물량, 생물 자원
***plow (쟁기로) 땅을 가는 것, 쟁기

	(A)	(B)	(C)
①	disturb	resistant	prevent
②	disturb	susceptible	worsen
③	help	susceptible	prevent
④	help	resistant	prevent
⑤	help	susceptible	worsen

출제 어휘 | 확인하기

(A) disturb	/ help
(B) resistant	/ susceptible
(C) prevent	/ worsen

136

2023 수능

밑줄 친 (a)~(e) 중에서 문맥상 낱말의 쓰임이 적절하지 <u>않은</u> 것은?

There is evidence that even very simple algorithms can outperform expert judgement on simple prediction problems. For example, algorithms have proved more (a) <u>accurate</u> than humans in predicting whether a prisoner released on parole will go on to commit another crime, or in predicting whether a potential candidate will perform well in a job in future. In over 100 studies across many different domains, half of all cases show simple formulas make (b) <u>better</u> significant predictions than human experts, and the remainder (except a very small handful), show a tie between the two. When there are a lot of different factors involved and a situation is very uncertain, simple formulas can win out by focusing on the most important factors and being consistent, while human judgement is too easily influenced by particularly salient and perhaps (c) <u>irrelevant</u> considerations. A similar idea is supported by further evidence that 'checklists' can improve the quality of expert decisions in a range of domains by ensuring that important steps or considerations aren't missed when people are feeling (d) <u>relaxed</u>. For example, treating patients in intensive care can require hundreds of small actions per day, and one small error could cost a life. Using checklists to ensure that no crucial steps are missed has proved to be remarkably (e) <u>effective</u> in a range of medical contexts, from preventing live infections to reducing pneumonia.

*parole 가석방   **salient 두드러진   ***pneumonia 폐렴

① (a)　　② (b)　　③ (c)　　④ (d)　　⑤ (e)

출제 어휘 | 확인하기

① accurate	↔
② better	↔
③ irrelevant	↔
④ relaxed	↔
⑤ effective	↔

필수 어휘 8

1 반의어

□ resistant	*a* 저항적인	↔	□ susceptible	*a* 영향을 받기 쉬운
□ majority	*n* 대다수	↔	□ minority	*n* 소수 (집단)
□ relevant	*a* 적절한, 관련 있는	↔	□ irrelevant	*a* 부적절한, 관련 없는
□ consistent	*a* 일치하는, 일관적인	↔	□ inconsistent	*a* 일치하지 않는, 일관적이지 않은
□ induce	*v* 유도하다, 귀납하다	↔	□ deduce	*v* 추론하다, 연역하다

2 주요 다의어

□ cast	*n* 배역; 거푸집; 깁스 *v* 던지다; (빛을) 발하다, (그림자를) 드리우다; 배역을 맡기다; 투표하다 ▶ cast a vote 투표하다	□ account	*n* 설명, 이야기; 계좌, 계정 *v* 설명하다; (비율 등을) 차지하다 ▶ account for ~을 설명하다; (비율)을 차지하다
□ ground	*n* 땅, 지면; 근거, 이유; 입장 *v* 근거[기초]를 두다	□ spot	*n* 장소, 지점; 반점, 얼룩; 발진 *v* 발견하다, 알아채다; 얼룩지게 하다
□ charge	*v* 청구하다; (일·책임 등을) 맡기다; 충전하다; 기소하다 *n* 요금; 책임; 비난, 혐의; 기소, 고발	□ commit	*v* (잘못·범죄 등을) 저지르다, 범하다; 약속하다; 충실하다, 전념하다; 위임하다 ▶ commitment 약속; 전념, 헌신

3 필수 어휘

□ accessible	*a* 접근할 수 있는, 이용할 수 있는	□ illustrate	*v* 실증하다, 예증하다
□ compress	*v* 압축하다	□ intensify	*v* 강화시키다
□ conceal	*v* 숨기다, 감추다	□ mental	*a* 정신의
□ concentrate	*v* 집중시키다, 응집시키다 ▶ concentration 집중, 응집; 농도	□ nourish	*v* 기르다, 영양분을 주다 ▶ nourishment 영양(물)
□ consciously	*ad* 의식적으로	□ outdated	*a* 구식의 ※ up-to-date 최신의
□ correspond	*v* 부합하다, 일치하다 ▶ correspondence 부합, 일치; 서신 교환	□ recall	*v* 기억해 내다; (불량 제품을) 회수하다 *n* 상기; 회수
□ desirable	*a* 바람직한	□ similarity	*n* 유사점, 닮은 점
□ dictate	*v* 좌우하다; 지시하다	□ unique	*a* 고유한, 독특한
□ diminish	*v* 줄이다, 축소하다	□ victim	*n* 희생자, 피해자
□ govern	*v* 지배하다 ▶ government 정부	□ vital	*a* 매우 중요한, 필수적인

Q1 괄호 안에서 문맥상 알맞은 것을 고르세요.

1. [Majorities / Minorities] tend not to have much power or status and may even be dismissed as troublemakers, extremists or simply 'weirdos'.

- dismiss 일축하다, 무시하다
- extremist 극단주의자
- weirdo 별난 사람

2. Amnesia most often results from a brain injury that leaves the [suspect / victim] unable to form new memories, but with most memories of the past intact.

- amnesia 기억 상실(증)
- injury 부상, 손상
- intact 손상되지 않은, 완전한

3. Have you ever met someone while you were experiencing significant emotional, psychological, or physical stress? You likely exhibited behaviors that are [consistent / inconsistent] with how you usually act. Meeting someone when you are extremely stressed can create an inaccurate impression of you.

- significant 상당한
- psychological 정신[심리]적인
- exhibit 보이다

4. Sometimes, after punishment has been administered a few times, it needn't be continued, because the mere threat of punishment is enough to [induce / deduce] the desired behavior.

- punishment 처벌
- administer (타격 등을) 가하다

5. Other deep-rooted cultural characteristics of races and racial subgroups are much more difficult to change. These are the cultural patterns that are so [resistant / susceptible] to alteration that they have the appearance of being inherent.

- characteristic 특징
- subgroup 하위 집단
- alteration 변화
- inherent 선천적인, 내재된

Q2 밑줄 친 어휘와 유사한 뜻을 가진 어휘를 고르세요.

1. Once the Internet made music easily <u>accessible</u>, availability of new music became democratized, which meant critics no longer had unique access.

① adaptable ② distributable ③ attainable

- availability 이용 가능성
- democratize 대중화하다
- critic 비평가
- no longer 더 이상 ~ 아니다

2. In other words, the destiny of a community depends on how well it <u>nourishes</u> its members.

① socializes ② unites ③ nurtures

- destiny 운명

3. Likewise, understanding how climate has changed over millions of years is <u>vital</u> to properly assess current global warming trends.

① crucial ② trivial ③ improper

- assess 평가하다
- global warming 지구 온난화

137

2021 6월 모평

다음 글의 밑줄 친 부분 중, 문맥상 낱말의 쓰임이 적절하지 <u>않은</u> 것은?

Chunking is vital for cognition of music. If we had to encode it in our brains note by note, we'd ① <u>struggle</u> to make sense of anything more complex than the simplest children's songs. Of course, most accomplished musicians can play compositions containing many thousands of notes entirely from ② <u>memory</u>, without a note out of place. But this seemingly awesome accomplishment of recall is made ③ <u>improbable</u> by remembering the musical *process*, not the individual notes as such. If you ask a pianist to start a Mozart sonata from bar forty-one, she'll probably have to ④ <u>mentally</u> replay the music from the start until reaching that bar—the score is not simply laid out in her mind, to be read from any random point. It's rather like describing how you drive to work: you don't simply recite the names of roads as an abstract list, but have to construct your route by mentally retracing it. When musicians make a mistake during rehearsal, they wind back to the ⑤ <u>start</u> of a musical phrase ('let's take it from the second verse') before restarting.

*chunking 덩어리로 나누기   **bar (악보의) 마디

138

다음 글의 밑줄 친 부분 중, 문맥상 낱말의 쓰임이 적절하지 <u>않은</u> 것은?

The social and cultural limits to band size are constants, and they define a constant optimum population size, but the size of band territories ① <u>varies</u> widely in response to the natural environmental productivity of local ecosystems. Very rich natural environments make possible small, high-density territories and ② <u>reduce</u> band mobility, because no one wants to walk further than necessary for food. The ③ <u>advantage</u> of a forager production system is that nature does the work of reproducing and maintaining the food supply. Solar energy purifies and recycles the water supply. The trade-off for nature's services is that under extreme desert or arctic conditions band territories must become very large, and bands become highly ④ <u>immobile</u>. In desert environments, where water determines biological productivity, the relationship between rainfall and band density is so ⑤ <u>predictable</u> that it can be described mathematically.

*forager 수렵채집인

출제 어휘 확인하기

① struggle   ↔

② memory   ↔

③ improbable   ↔

④ mentally   ↔

⑤ start   ↔

출제 어휘 확인하기

① vary   ↔

② reduce   ↔

③ advantage   ↔

④ immobile   ↔

⑤ predictable   ↔

139

다음 글의 밑줄 친 부분 중, 문맥상 낱말의 쓰임이 적절하지 <u>않은</u> 것은?

There is good evidence to suggest that the current obesity crisis is caused, in part, not by what we eat (though this is of course vital, too) but by the degree to which our food has been processed before we eat it. It is sometimes referred to as the "calorie delusion." In 2003, scientists at Kyushu University in Japan fed one group of rats hard food pellets and another group softer pellets. In every other respect the pellets were ① identical: same nutrients, same calories. After twenty-two weeks, the rats on the soft-food diet had become obese, showing that ② texture is an important factor in weight gain. Further studies involving pythons (eating ground cooked steak, versus intact raw steak) ③ confirmed these findings. When we eat chewier, less processed foods, it takes us more energy to digest them, so the number of calories our body receives is ④ more. You will get more energy from a ⑤ slow-cooked apple purée than a crunchy raw apple, even if the calories are identical.

*pellet 알갱이 **python 비단뱀

출제 어휘 확인하기	
① identical	↔
② texture	↔
③ confirm	↔
④ more	↔
⑤ slow-cooked	↔

140

다음 글의 밑줄 친 부분 중, 문맥상 낱말의 쓰임이 적절하지 <u>않은</u> 것은?

The history of human interaction with insects goes back to the beginning of civilization. Insects, at an estimated number of 10 quintillion, outnumber and outweigh every form of multicellular life form on earth. Their confrontation with humans is inevitable as humans exploit the planet for food, shelter and resources. Moreover, ① encounters in places such as urban areas or cities are more serious, as many of the insects involved are known to injure or disable human lives and damage property, as well as sharing human resources. Thus, it is not uncommon for the majority of people to make efforts to ② minimize their interaction with the insect world. Homes are sealed, sprayed and kept clean; bodies are bathed, hair shampooed, clothing washed in order to ③ distance humans from insects as much as possible. Culturally, these activities have shaped human life so much that, in some societies, discussing insects in public has become a ④ routine. From the perspective of urban living, the majority of people mistakenly consider insects to be merely a ⑤ nuisance. It is also imperative to mention that insects have literally plagued humanity with death and destruction in the past.

*quintillion 100경

출제 어휘 확인하기	
① encounter	↔
② minimize	↔
③ distance	↔
④ routine	↔
⑤ nuisance	↔

141

(A), (B), (C)의 각 네모 안에서 문맥에 맞는 낱말로 가장 적절한 것은?

In interpreting an argument, we should make every effort to be fair to the arguer. We should not (A) follow / worsen the argument by adding material that would make it less credible, or deleting material that would make it more credible. We should attempt to keep our standardized version reasonably close to the exact words used. Otherwise we will begin to construct a new argument of our own, as opposed to understanding the argument put to us by another person. Sometimes it is suggested that we go further in the direction of charitable interpretation, interpreting a speech or a written passage so as to render it as plausible and reasonable as possible. Such (B) generous / stubborn interpretive charity has been claimed to be the fairest thing to the speaker or author. But there are some risks here. If we do too much to improve someone else's speaking or writing, we may read in too many ideas of our own and move too far away from the original words and thoughts. Charity can lead us away from (C) accuracy / universality if it is taken too far.

	(A)	(B)	(C)
①	follow	generous	accuracy
②	follow	stubborn	universality
③	worsen	generous	accuracy
④	worsen	generous	universality
⑤	worsen	stubborn	accuracy

출제 어휘 확인하기

(A) follow	/ worsen
(B) generous	/ stubborn
(C) accuracy	/ universality

142

밑줄 친 (a)~(e) 중에서 문맥상 낱말의 쓰임이 적절하지 않은 것은?

Many negotiators assume that all negotiations involve a fixed pie. Negotiators often approach integrative negotiation opportunities as zero-sum situations or win-lose exchanges. Those who believe in the mythical fixed pie assume that parties' interests stand in opposition, with no possibility for integrative settlements and mutually beneficial trade-offs, so they (a) suppress efforts to search for them. In a hiring negotiation, a job applicant who assumes that salary is the only issue may insist on $75,000 when the employer is offering $70,000. Only when the two parties discuss the possibilities further do they discover that moving expenses and starting date can also be negotiated, which may (b) block resolution of the salary issue.

The tendency to see negotiation in fixed-pie terms (c) varies depending on how people view the nature of a given conflict situation. This was shown in a clever experiment by Harinck, de Dreu, and Van Vianen involving a simulated negotiation between prosecutors and defense lawyers over jail sentences. Some participants were told to view their goals in terms of personal gain (e.g., arranging a particular jail sentence will help your career), others were told to view their goals in terms of effectiveness (a particular sentence is most likely to prevent recidivism), and still others were told to focus on values (a particular jail sentence is fair and just). Negotiators focusing on personal gain were most likely to come under the influence of fixed-pie beliefs and approach the situation (d) competitively. Negotiators focusing on values were least likely to see the problem in fixed-pie terms and more inclined to approach the situation cooperatively. Stressful conditions such as time constraints contribute to this common misperception, which in turn may lead to (e) less integrative agreements.

*prosecutor 검사 **recidivism 상습적 범행

① (a)   ② (b)   ③ (c)   ④ (d)   ⑤ (e)

출제 어휘 확인하기

① suppress	② block
③ vary	④ competitively
⑤ less	

143

다음 글의 밑줄 친 부분 중, 문맥상 낱말의 쓰임이 적절하지 <u>않은</u> 것은?

If it's true that laughter originated as an expression of relief in response to a fearful situation that turned out to be harmless, it follows that the sensation of laughter is closely associated with pleasure—it's a release of ① <u>tension</u>. In fact, laughing is so pleasurable that we go to great lengths to ② <u>recreate</u> that sensation of release in completely artificial circumstances, by telling jokes. And it's still fun. There's no real threat in a joke, but we enjoy that slightly giddy shift of expectation nonetheless. Why is it so enjoyable to laugh? Especially considering that the best kind of laughter is the kind that starts to ③ <u>hurt</u>; that takes our bodies over and sometimes even turns into tears. For years, scientists have been trying to determine the physical benefits of laughter. A recent study by Professor Robin Dunbar found that laughter ④ <u>lowered</u> people's pain thresholds. His explanation is that shared social laughter causes an endorphin rush and the release of oxytocin in the brain—the same ⑤ <u>chemical</u> reactions that we have to human touch.

*giddy 어지러운 **threshold 역, 역치(자극에 대한 반응이 시작되는 점)

출제 어휘 ▶확인하기

① tension	↔
② recreate	↔
③ hurt	↔
④ lower	↔
⑤ chemical	↔

144

다음 글의 밑줄 친 부분 중, 문맥상 낱말의 쓰임이 적절하지 <u>않은</u> 것은?

If I say to you, 'Don't think of a white bear', you will find it difficult not to think of a white bear. In this way, 'thought suppression can actually increase the thoughts one wishes to suppress instead of calming them'. One common example of this is that people on a diet who try not to think about food often begin to think much ① <u>more</u> about food. This process is therefore also known as the *rebound effect*. The ② <u>ironic</u> effect seems to be caused by the interplay of two related cognitive processes. This dual-process system involves, first, an intentional operating process, which consciously attempts to locate thoughts ③ <u>unrelated</u> to the suppressed ones. Second, and simultaneously, an unconscious monitoring process tests whether the operating system is functioning effectively. If the monitoring system encounters thoughts inconsistent with the intended ones, it prompts the intentional operating process to ensure that these are replaced by ④ <u>inappropriate</u> thoughts. However, it is argued, the intentional operating system can fail due to increased cognitive load caused by fatigue, stress and emotional factors, and so the monitoring process filters the inappropriate thoughts into consciousness, making them highly ⑤ <u>accessible</u>.

출제 어휘 ▶확인하기

① more	↔
② ironic	↔
③ unrelated	↔
④ inappropriate	↔
⑤ accessible	↔

145

(A), (B), (C)의 각 네모 안에서 문맥에 맞는 낱말로 가장 적절한 것은?

We spend so much time consumed by our regrets about the past and the stressors of the present that we give little thought to our hopes for the future. Yes, (A) blessings / obstacles are thrown in our way in the form of illness, difficult relationships, financial hardships, and so on, but we ultimately are the captains of our own ship. Where would you like yours to take you? If you are caught up in the silliness of attaining external objects, like designer clothes, to make you feel like something, try changing your focus. Forget about (B) empty / promising pursuits and turn your energies toward creating a story for yourself. If you want to feel good about yourself, having clothing, food, stuff, and companionship is often not enough; setting a clear life goal and trying to attain it is where the (C) self-esteem / vanity comes from. You may never achieve your goal, but your experiences along the way—the efforts, the challenges, the reconsiderations, the changes of direction, the growth—are where you find your value.

	(A)		(B)		(C)
①	blessings	·········	empty	·········	vanity
②	blessings	·········	promising	·········	self-esteem
③	obstacles	·········	empty	·········	self-esteem
④	obstacles	·········	empty	·········	vanity
⑤	obstacles	·········	promising	·········	vanity

출제 어휘 확인하기

(A) blessing	/ obstacle
(B) empty	/ promising
(C) self-esteem	/ vanity

146

다음 글의 밑줄 친 부분 중, 문맥상 낱말의 쓰임이 적절하지 않은 것은?

The challenge we face in understanding others is that each of us has spent a lifetime developing our own frame of reference. We live within that ① mental set most of the time every day. Our minds are ② jam-packed with our own experiences, opinions, biases, issues, feelings, values, agendas, and so forth. When someone presents his or her idea, our own notions about that subject are likely to be ③ activated. Instead of focusing our mental energy on understanding the other person's position, our thoughts are apt to be dominated by our own mindset—thus ④ coloring our reception of what we take in. Furthermore, our frame of reference has become such a part of us that much of the time we are ⑤ aware of its influence. So taking in the speaker's message can be more of a challenge than is commonly realized.

출제 어휘 확인하기

① mental	↔
② jam-packed	↔
③ activate	↔
④ color	↔
⑤ aware	↔

147

2020 7월 학평

다음 글의 밑줄 친 부분 중, 문맥상 낱말의 쓰임이 적절하지 <u>않은</u> 것은?

At a time when concerns about overpopulation and famine were reaching their highest peak, Garrett Hardin did not blame these problems on human ① <u>ignorance</u>—a failure to take note of dwindling per capita food supplies, for example. Instead, his explanation focused on the discrepancy between the ② <u>interests</u> of individual households and those of society as a whole. To understand excessive reproduction as a tragedy of the commons, bear in mind that a typical household stands to gain from bringing another child into the world—in terms of the net contributions he or she makes to ③ <u>household</u> earnings, for example. But while parents can be counted on to assess how the well-being of their household is affected by additional offspring, they ④ <u>overvalue</u> other impacts of population growth, such as diminished per capita food supplies for other people. In other words, the costs of reproduction are largely ⑤ <u>shared</u>, rather than being shouldered entirely by individual households. As a result, reproduction is excessive.

*dwindling 줄어드는

148

다음 글의 밑줄 친 부분 중, 문맥상 낱말의 쓰임이 적절하지 <u>않은</u> 것은?

The columnist Thomas Friedman declared, "The world is flat," by which he claimed that thanks to the Internet, global competitors have equal opportunities regardless of their location. Despite Friedman's famous ① <u>assertion</u>, the world is not yet flat, and location still matters a great deal in many industries. If human geography didn't matter, then there would be little income disparity across countries for similar tasks that can be done ② <u>remotely</u>. If location didn't matter, then computer programmers, legal document reviewers, certified accountants, and even radiologists would earn about the ③ <u>same</u>, whether they worked in America or in India. Yet there are vast differences in incomes around the world. Jobs that can easily be outsourced to lower-income countries tend to pay less domestically and be less ④ <u>unstable</u>. Also, jobs that are ⑤ <u>subject</u> to domestic competition from low-skilled immigrant labor usually pay low wages.

*disparity 격차   **radiologist 방사선 전문의

출제 어휘 확인하기	
① ignorance	↔
② interest	↔
③ household	↔
④ overvalue	↔
⑤ share	↔

출제 어휘 확인하기	
① assertion	↔
② remotely	↔
③ same	↔
④ unstable	↔
⑤ subject	↔

149

다음 글의 밑줄 친 부분 중, 문맥상 낱말의 쓰임이 적절하지 <u>않은</u> 것은?

One of the distinctive features of European history compared to that of Eurasia's three other zones of dense sedentary civilization—Southeast Asia, India, and China—concerns imperial unity. In both Southeast Asia and China, imperial unification on a ① <u>massive</u> scale was achieved early in their histories, and thereafter became the norm, with only relatively brief relapses. Even in India, empires that encompassed most of the subcontinent ② <u>alternated</u> with periods of fragmentation. By contrast, Europe was never united by force from within, nor was it conquered from outside. Rome, the only arguable ③ <u>exception</u>, was a Mediterranean, rather than a European, empire and incorporated only southern Europe. Moreover, while enduring for centuries and being highly influential, it ④ <u>lasted</u> for only a fraction of European history. All other attempts at imperial unification—the Carolingian, Ottonian, Habsburgian, and Napoleonic —were geographically even more ⑤ <u>extensive</u> and short-lived.

*sedentary 정착한 **relapse 재발생

150

밑줄 친 (a)~(e) 중에서 문맥상 낱말의 쓰임이 적절하지 <u>않은</u> 것은?

For quite some time, science educators believed that "hands-on" activities were the answer to children's understanding through their participation in science-related activities. Many teachers believed that students merely engaging in activities and (a) <u>manipulating</u> objects would organize the information to be gained and the knowledge to be understood into concept comprehension. Educators began to notice that the pendulum had swung too far to the "hands-on" component of inquiry as they realized that the knowledge was not (b) <u>inherent</u> in the materials themselves, but in the thought and metacognition about what students had done in the activity. We now know that "hands-on" is a dangerous phrase when speaking about learning science. The (c) <u>missing</u> ingredient is the "minds-on" part of the instructional experience. (d) <u>Uncertainty</u> about the knowledge intended in any activity comes from each student's re-creation of concepts—and discussing, thinking, arguing, listening, and evaluating one's own preconceptions after the activities, under the leadership of a thoughtful teacher, can bring this about. After all, a food fight is a hands-on activity, but about all you would learn was something about the aerodynamics of flying mashed potatoes! Our view of what students need to build their knowledge and theories about the natural world (e) <u>extends</u> far beyond a "hands-on activity." While it is important for students to use and interact with materials in science class, the learning comes from the sense-making of students' "hands-on" experiences.

*pendulum 추(錘) **metacognition 초(超)인지

***aerodynamics 공기 역학

① (a)　　② (b)　　③ (c)　　④ (d)　　⑤ (e)

출제 어휘	확인하기	
① massive	↔	
② alternate	↔	
③ exception	↔	
④ last	↔	
⑤ extensive	↔	

출제 어휘	확인하기	
① manipulate	↔	
② inherent	↔	
③ missing	↔	
④ uncertainty	↔	
⑤ extend	↔	

151

다음 글의 밑줄 친 부분 중, 문맥상 낱말의 쓰임이 적절하지 <u>않은</u> 것은?

We currently inhabit a world in which we are exposed to infinitely more information than we can store. For example, we only remember a ① <u>fraction</u> of the names and faces we encounter. Evolutionarily speaking, it is
5 no secret that the human brain did not evolve to store the names of a large number of people. The ability to recognize individuals of a social group is an ability shared by many of our mammalian contemporaries; yet we appear to be ② <u>unique</u> in our ability to use
10 names. Furthermore, early in human evolution the total number of different people any one individual encountered was probably fairly low. Even assuming that 250,000 years ago our ancestors gave each other names, it seems ③ <u>likely</u> they were exposed to more
15 than a few hundred different people. Eventually, agriculture and other technological innovations fostered the ④ <u>emergence</u> of villages and cities. Today, further technological advances including photography, TV, the Internet and its social networking have
20 ⑤ <u>ensured</u> that the number of people we are exposed to is likely orders of magnitude higher than the number of people our distant ancestors would have encountered.

*orders of magnitude 상당히, 많이

152

2022 9월 모평 응용

다음 글의 밑줄 친 부분 중, 문맥상 낱말의 쓰임이 적절하지 <u>않은</u> 것은?

Enabling animals to operate in the presence of harmless stimuli is an almost universal function of learning. Most animals innately ① <u>avoid</u> objects they have not previously encountered. Unfamiliar objects may be dangerous; treating them with caution has 5 survival value. If persisted in, however, such careful behavior could interfere with feeding and other necessary activities to the extent that the benefit of caution would be lost. A turtle that ② <u>withdraws</u> into its shell at every puff of wind or whenever a cloud casts 10 a shadow would never win races, not even with a lazy rabbit. To overcome this problem, almost all animals ③ <u>habituate</u> to safe stimuli that occur frequently. Confronted by a strange object, an inexperienced animal may freeze or attempt to hide, but if nothing 15 unpleasant happens, sooner or later it will ④ <u>continue</u> its activity. The possibility also exists that an unfamiliar object may be useful, so if it poses no immediate threat, a closer inspection may be ⑤ <u>worthless</u>.

*innately 선천적으로

출제 어휘 확인하기		
① fraction	↔	
② unique	↔	
③ likely	↔	
④ emergence	↔	
⑤ ensure	↔	

출제 어휘 확인하기		
① avoid	↔	
② withdraw	↔	
③ habituate	↔	
④ continue	↔	
⑤ worthless	↔	

153

2022 9월 모평

다음 글의 밑줄 친 부분 중, 문맥상 낱말의 쓰임이 적절하지 <u>않은</u> 것은?

In economic systems what takes place in one sector has impacts on another; demand for a good or service in one sector is derived from another. For instance, a consumer buying a good in a store will likely trigger the replacement of this product, which will generate ① <u>demands</u> for activities such as manufacturing, resource extraction and, of course, transport. What is different about transport is that it cannot exist alone and a movement cannot be ② <u>stored</u>. An unsold product can remain on the shelf of a store until bought (often with discount incentives), but an unsold seat on a flight or unused cargo capacity in the same flight remains unsold and cannot be brought back as additional capacity ③ <u>later</u>. In this case an opportunity has been ④ <u>seized</u>, since the amount of transport being offered has exceeded the demand for it. The derived demand of transportation is often very difficult to reconcile with an equivalent supply, and actually transport companies would prefer to have some additional capacity to accommodate ⑤ <u>unforeseen</u> demand (often at much higher prices).

*reconcile 조화시키다

154

(A), (B), (C)의 각 네모 안에서 문맥에 맞는 낱말로 가장 적절한 것은?

Fast food has proven to be a revolutionary force in American life. I am interested in it both as a commodity and as a metaphor. What people eat has always been (A) ⃞determined / disregarded⃞ by a complex interplay of social, economic, and technological forces. A nation's diet can be more revealing than its art or literature. On any given day in the United States about one quarter of the adult population visits a fast food restaurant. During a relatively brief period of time, the fast food industry has (B) ⃞transformed / suspended⃞ not only the American diet, but also their landscape, economy, workforce, and popular culture. Fast food and its consequences have become (C) ⃞escapable / inescapable⃞, regardless of whether you eat it twice a day, try to avoid it, or have never taken a single bite.

	(A)	(B)	(C)
①	determined	transformed	escapable
②	determined	transformed	inescapable
③	determined	suspended	inescapable
④	disregarded	transformed	inescapable
⑤	disregarded	suspended	escapable

출제 어휘 확인하기

① demand	↔	
② store	↔	
③ later	↔	
④ seize	↔	
⑤ unforeseen	↔	

출제 어휘 확인하기

(A) determine	/ disregard
(B) transform	/ suspend
(C) escapable	/ inescapable

155

다음 글의 밑줄 친 부분 중, 문맥상 낱말의 쓰임이 적절하지 <u>않은</u> 것은?

One of the most common claims made by those who do not like some particular scientific result is that the scientists who found it were biased. After all, if one suspects that all science is biased, it may not seem so egregious to consider a theory that might be ① <u>contaminated</u> by one's own ideological beliefs. No matter how good the evidence, a scientific theory can never be proven true. Because of the way that scientific evidence is gathered, it is always theoretically possible that some future piece of data might come along and ② <u>disprove</u> a theory. It does mean that at some point scientists must admit that even their strongest explanations cannot be offered as truth, but only strongly warranted ③ <u>belief</u> based on justification given the evidence. This alleged ④ <u>strength</u> of scientific reasoning is often exploited by those who would claim that they are the real scientists. If science is an open process, then it should not be in the business of ⑤ <u>excluding</u> alternative theories. Until a theory is absolutely proven, they believe, a competing theory could always be true.

*egregious 말도 안 되는, 어처구니없는

156

2021 10월 학평

다음 글의 밑줄 친 부분 중, 문맥상 낱말의 쓰임이 적절하지 <u>않은</u> 것은?

How people behave often depends on what others do. If other car drivers or subway users leave for work at 8 a.m., it may be to my ① <u>advantage</u> to leave at 6 a.m., even if that is really too early from my point of view. In equilibrium, flows ② <u>stabilize</u> so that each person makes the best trade-off between their ideal schedule and the congestion they will suffer on their commute. In making such choices, agents seek to ③ <u>differentiate</u> their behavior from that of others. On other occasions, agents have a problem with coordination. They would like to choose to behave the same way as others. For example, if most of my fellow citizens did not pay their parking tickets, there would be (unfortunately) strong pressure for an amnesty for such offenders, which would ④ <u>increase</u> my incentive to pay my parking tickets too. There may be multiple equilibria, so that two otherwise identical societies may ⑤ <u>adopt</u> different behavioral patterns.

*equilibrium 균형(상태) **amnesty 사면

<table>
<tr><td colspan="3">출제 어휘 확인하기</td></tr>
<tr><td>① contaminate</td><td>↔</td><td></td></tr>
<tr><td>② disprove</td><td>↔</td><td></td></tr>
<tr><td>③ belief</td><td>↔</td><td></td></tr>
<tr><td>④ strength</td><td>↔</td><td></td></tr>
<tr><td>⑤ exclude</td><td>↔</td><td></td></tr>
</table>

<table>
<tr><td colspan="3">출제 어휘 확인하기</td></tr>
<tr><td>① advantage</td><td>↔</td><td></td></tr>
<tr><td>② stabilize</td><td>↔</td><td></td></tr>
<tr><td>③ differentiate</td><td>↔</td><td></td></tr>
<tr><td>④ increase</td><td>↔</td><td></td></tr>
<tr><td>⑤ adopt</td><td>↔</td><td></td></tr>
</table>

157

다음 글의 밑줄 친 부분 중, 문맥상 낱말의 쓰임이 적절하지 <u>않은</u> 것은?

We're biologically wired to have biases, and they aren't inherently negative. The problem arises when we refuse to recognize our biases, sort through them, and then overcome the ones that are based on beliefs that are untrue, unhelpful, or unfair to others. ① <u>Ignorance</u> of biases isn't bliss, as they do exist in *all* of us and, unchecked, can lead to stereotyping and bigotry. Biologically, we're all naturally biased toward the things we like, the things we grew up with, the things familiar to us. Our brains readily identify with things that ② <u>reflect</u> situations in our own lives because those are typically the things that also mean safety, security, and ease. From an evolutionary standpoint, this affinity bias, or the desire to be around people like us, ③ <u>disappeared</u> because people in our tribe or group or cave tended to look like us. People who didn't could be dangerous marauders. Again, like many of our ④ <u>inherent</u> systems for sorting the world around us, identifying someone we recognized as safe was automatic and done without thought. In today's multicultural, almost borderless world, the same safety rules do not apply, and we must overcome our natural affinity bias to avoid ⑤ <u>excluding</u> valuable "others."

*bigotry 편협함　**affinity 친밀감　***marauder 약탈자

출제 어휘 | 확인하기

① ignorance	↔	
② reflect	↔	
③ disappear	↔	
④ inherent	↔	
⑤ exclude	↔	

158

밑줄 친 (a)~(e) 중에서 문맥상 낱말의 쓰임이 적절하지 <u>않은</u> 것은?

Aristotle did not think that all human beings should be allowed to engage in political activity: in his system, women, slaves, and foreigners were explicitly (a) <u>excluded</u> from the right to rule themselves and others. Nevertheless, his basic idea that politics is a unique collective activity that is directed at certain (b) <u>common</u> goals and ends still resonates today. But which ends? Many thinkers and political figures since the ancient world have developed different ideas about the goals that politics can or should achieve. This approach is known as political moralism.

For moralists, political life is a branch of ethics—or moral philosophy—so it is (c) <u>unsurprising</u> that there are many philosophers in the group of moralistic political thinkers. Political moralists argue that politics should be directed toward achieving substantial goals, or that political arrangements should be organized to (d) <u>protect</u> certain things. Among these things are political values such as justice, equality, liberty, happiness, fraternity, or national self-determination. At its most radical, moralism produces descriptions of ideal political societies known as Utopias, named after English statesman and philosopher Thomas More's book *Utopia*, published in 1516, which imagined an ideal nation. Utopian political thinking dates back to the ancient Greek philosopher Plato's book the *Republic*, but it is still used by modern thinkers such as Robert Nozick to explore ideas. Some theorists consider Utopian political thinking to be a (e) <u>promising</u> undertaking, since it has led in the past to justifications of totalitarian violence. However, at its best, Utopian thinking is part of a process of striving toward a better society, and many thinkers use it to suggest values to be pursued or protected.

*resonate 공명하다, 울리다　**fraternity 동포애, 우애

① (a)　② (b)　③ (c)　④ (d)　⑤ (e)

출제 어휘 | 확인하기

① exclude	↔	
② common	↔	
③ unsurprising	↔	
④ protect	↔	
⑤ promising	↔	

159

다음 글의 밑줄 친 부분 중, 문맥상 낱말의 쓰임이 적절하지 <u>않은</u> 것은?

　Brands are used as symbolic devices, because of their ability to help users express something about themselves to their peer groups, with users taking for granted functional capabilities. Consumers ① personify brands and when looking at the symbol values of brands, they seek brands which have very clear personalities and select brands that best match their actual or desired self-concept. For example, in the beer market there are only ② marginal product differences between brands. Comparative consumer trials of competing beer brands without brand names present showed no significant preferences or differences. Yet, when consumers repeated the test with brand names present, significant brand preferences ③ emerged. On the first comparative trial, consumers focused on functional (rational) aspects of the beers and were ④ unable to notice much difference. On repeating the trials with brand names present, consumers used the brand names to recall distinct brand personalities and the symbolic (emotional) aspect of the brands ⑤ kept preference.

160

다음 글의 밑줄 친 부분 중, 문맥상 낱말의 쓰임이 적절하지 <u>않은</u> 것은?

　If you pour water onto a rigid surface it will spread out over that surface. The more water you pour the ① bigger the pool gets. But if instead of being rigid the surface consists of a thin rubber sheet which is supported only at the ② edges, then a curious thing happens. The pool of water does not go on spreading but reaches a limited size. No matter how much more water is poured onto the sheet the pool does not increase in diameter. What happens is that the weight of the water depresses the sheet. More water only depresses the sheet ③ further. As the centre of the sheet is depressed, the walls of the depression get steeper and steeper and so ④ prevent the water from spreading. In effect one has a stabilized system with the thin rubber sheet. The difficulty of spread (steepness of walls) is ⑤ disproportionate to the amount of water, so no matter how much more water one puts onto the sheet it cannot spread. This is in sharp contrast to the unstabilized system, in which a greater amount of water means greater spread.

출제 어휘 확인하기	
① personify	↔
② marginal	↔
③ emerge	↔
④ unable	↔
⑤ keep	↔

출제 어휘 확인하기	
① bigger	↔
② edge	↔
③ further	↔
④ prevent	↔
⑤ disproportionate	↔

161

다음 글의 밑줄 친 부분 중, 문맥상 낱말의 쓰임이 적절하지 <u>않은</u> 것은?

Those who limit themselves to Western scientific research have virtually ① <u>ignored</u> anything that cannot be perceived by the five senses and repeatedly measured or quantified. Research is dismissed as superstitious and invalid if it cannot be scientifically explained by cause and effect. Many continue to ② <u>object</u> with an almost religious passion to this cultural paradigm about the power of science—more specifically, the power that science gives them. By dismissing non-Western scientific paradigms as inferior at best and inaccurate at worst, the most rigid members of the conventional medical research community try to ③ <u>counter</u> the threat that alternative therapies and research pose to their work, their well-being, and their worldviews. And yet, biomedical research cannot explain many of the phenomena that ④ <u>concern</u> alternative practitioners regarding caring-healing processes. When therapies such as acupuncture or homeopathy are observed to result in a physiological or clinical response that cannot be explained by the biomedical model, many have tried to ⑤ <u>deny</u> the results rather than modify the scientific model.

*acupuncture 침술 **homeopathy 동종 요법

162

다음 글의 밑줄 친 부분 중, 문맥상 낱말의 쓰임이 적절하지 <u>않은</u> 것은?

Early human societies were nomadic, based on hunting and gathering, and, in a shifting pattern of life in search of new sources of food, qualities such as lightness, portability, and adaptability were dominant criteria. With the evolution of more settled rural societies based on agriculture, other characteristics, other traditions of form appropriate to the new patterns of life, rapidly ① <u>emerged</u>. It must be emphasized, however, that tradition was not static, but constantly subject to minute ② <u>variations</u> appropriate to people and their circumstances. Although traditional forms reflected the experience of social groups, specific ③ <u>manifestations</u> could be adapted in various minute and subtle ways to suit individual users' needs. A chair could keep its ④ <u>basic</u>, accepted characteristics while still being closely shaped in detail to the physique and proportions of a specific person. This basic principle of customization allowed a constant stream of incremental modifications to be ⑤ <u>refused</u>, which, if demonstrated by experience to be advantageous, could be integrated back into the mainstream of tradition.

*physique 체격 **incremental (점진적으로) 증가하는

출제 어휘 확인하기

① ignore	↔	
② object	↔	
③ counter	↔	
④ concern	↔	
⑤ deny	↔	

출제 어휘 확인하기

① emerge	↔	
② variation	↔	
③ manifestation	↔	
④ basic	↔	
⑤ refuse	↔	

163

2020 수능

다음 글의 밑줄 친 부분 중, 문맥상 낱말의 쓰임이 적절하지 <u>않은</u> 것은?

Suppose we know that Paula suffers from a severe phobia. If we reason that Paula is afraid either of snakes or spiders, and then ① <u>establish</u> that she is not afraid of snakes, we will conclude that Paula is afraid of spiders. However, our conclusion is reasonable only if Paula's fear really does concern either snakes or spiders. If we know only that Paula has a phobia, then the fact that she's not afraid of snakes is entirely ② <u>consistent</u> with her being afraid of heights, water, dogs or the number thirteen. More generally, when we are presented with a list of alternative explanations for some phenomenon, and are then persuaded that all but one of those explanations are ③ <u>unsatisfactory</u>, we should pause to reflect. Before ④ <u>denying</u> that the remaining explanation is the correct one, consider whether other plausible options are being ignored or overlooked. The fallacy of false choice misleads when we're insufficiently attentive to an important hidden assumption, that the choices which have been made explicit exhaust the ⑤ <u>sensible</u> alternatives.

*plausible 그럴듯한 **fallacy 오류

164

(A), (B), (C)의 각 네모 안에서 문맥에 맞는 낱말로 가장 적절한 것은?

Childhood and old age are very similar. In both cases, for different reasons, there is an element of (A) defenselessness / effectiveness ; we are either not yet, or we have ceased to be, part of the active world, and our responses can be spontaneous, open. During adolescence an invisible shell begins to harden around our bodies, and gets thicker and thicker throughout our adult life. It grows rather like the way a pearl grows: the bigger and deeper the wound, the (B) smoother / stronger the crust becomes. However, like a dress we wear too often, with the passage of time it begins to get thin in some places until, quite unexpectedly, as the result of a sudden movement, it splits. At first, (C) confident / insecure in the protection of your shell, you notice nothing; then something quite banal happens and, without knowing why, you find yourself crying like a baby.

*banal 평범한, 진부한

	(A)	(B)	(C)
①	defenselessness	smoother	confident
②	defenselessness	stronger	confident
③	defenselessness	stronger	insecure
④	effectiveness	smoother	confident
⑤	effectiveness	stronger	insecure

출제 어휘 확인하기

① establish	↔
② consistent	↔
③ unsatisfactory	↔
④ deny	↔
⑤ sensible	↔

출제 어휘 확인하기

(A) defenselessness	/ effectiveness
(B) smoother	/ stronger
(C) confident	/ insecure

165

다음 글의 밑줄 친 부분 중, 문맥상 낱말의 쓰임이 적절하지 <u>않은</u> 것은?

Physical activity—whether through exercise, exploration, competition, or celebration—makes us happier because it stimulates these instincts. Movement is intertwined with some of the most basic human ① joys, including self-expression, social connection, and mastery. When we are ② active, we access innate pleasures, from the satisfaction of synchronizing to the beat of music to the sensory thrill of moving with speed, grace, or power. Movement can also ③ fulfill core human needs, such as the desires to connect with nature or to feel a part of something bigger than yourself. The physical pastimes we are most drawn to seem uniquely devised to harness our individual strengths—the abilities to persist, endure, learn, and grow—while simultaneously ④ suppressing our instincts to work together. When physical activity is most psychologically fulfilling, it's because our participation both reveals the good in us and lets us witness the good in others. This is one reason every culture puts movement at the ⑤ heart of its most joyous and meaningful traditions.

*harness 활용[이용]하다

166

밑줄 친 (a)~(e) 중에서 문맥상 쓰임이 적절하지 <u>않은</u> 것은?

In studies examining the effectiveness of vitamin C, researchers typically divide the subjects into two groups. One group (the experimental group) receives a vitamin C supplement, and the other (the control group) does not. Researchers observe both groups to determine whether one group has fewer or shorter colds than the other. The following discussion describes some of the pitfalls inherent in an experiment of this kind and ways to (a) avoid them. In sorting subjects into two groups, researchers must ensure that each person has an (b) equal chance of being assigned to either the experimental group or the control group. This is accomplished by randomization; that is, the subjects are chosen randomly from the same population by flipping a coin or some other method involving chance. Randomization helps to ensure that results reflect the treatment and not factors that might influence the grouping of subjects. Importantly, the two groups of people must be similar and must have the same track record with respect to colds to (c) rule out the possibility that observed differences in the rate, severity, or duration of colds might have occurred anyway. If, for example, the control group would normally catch twice as many colds as the experimental group, then the findings prove (d) nothing. In experiments involving a nutrient, the diets of both groups must also be (e) different, especially with respect to the nutrient being studied. If those in the experimental group were receiving less vitamin C from their usual diet, then any effects of the supplement may not be apparent.

*pitfall 함정

① (a)　　② (b)　　③ (c)　　④ (d)　　⑤ (e)

출제 어휘 확인하기	
① joy	↔
② active	↔
③ fulfill	↔
④ suppress	↔
⑤ heart	↔

출제 어휘 확인하기	
① avoid	↔
② equal	↔
③ rule out	↔
④ nothing	↔
⑤ different	↔

167

2021 7월 학평

다음 글의 밑줄 친 부분 중, 문맥상 낱말의 쓰임이 적절하지 <u>않은</u> 것은?

Prior to the Industrial Revolution, the ① <u>quantity</u> of freight transported between nations was negligible by contemporary standards. For instance, during the Middle Ages, the totality of French imports via the Saint-Gothard Passage would not fill a freight train. The amount of freight transported by the Venetian fleet, which dominated Mediterranean trade, would not fill a ② <u>modern</u> container ship. The volume, but not the speed, of trade improved under mercantilism, notably for maritime transportation. In spite of all, distribution capacities were very limited and speeds ③ <u>slow</u>. For example, a stagecoach going through the English countryside in the sixteenth century had an average speed of 2 miles per hour; moving one ton of cargo 30 miles inland in the United States by the late eighteenth century was as costly as moving it across the Atlantic. The inland transportation system was thus very ④ <u>limited</u>. By the late eighteenth century, canal systems started to emerge in Europe. They permitted the large movements of bulk freight inland and expanded regional trade. Maritime and riverine transportation were consequently the ⑤ <u>outdated</u> modes of the pre-industrial era.

*fleet 선단, 배의 무리   **mercantilism 중상주의

168

다음 글의 밑줄 친 부분 중, 문맥상 낱말의 쓰임이 적절하지 <u>않은</u> 것은?

Because people often have their own personal beliefs about the effectiveness of various treatments, it is desirable to conduct experiments in such a way that subjects do not ① <u>grasp</u> what treatment they are receiving. For example, in an experiment comparing four different doses of a medication for relief of headache pain, someone who knows that he is receiving the medication at its highest dose may be ② <u>deliberately</u> influenced to report a greater degree of headache pain reduction. By ensuring that subjects are not aware of which treatment they receive, we can ③ <u>prevent</u> the subjects' personal perceptions from influencing the response. An experiment in which subjects do not know what treatment they have received is described as single-blind. Of course, not all experiments can be made single-blind. For example, in an experiment to compare the effect of two different types of exercise on blood pressure, it is not possible for participants to be ④ <u>unaware</u> of whether they are in the swimming group or the jogging group! However, when it is possible, "blinding" the subjects in an experiment is generally a ⑤ <u>good</u> strategy.

출제 어휘 확인하기	
① quantity	↔
② modern	↔
③ slow	↔
④ limited	↔
⑤ outdated	↔

출제 어휘 확인하기	
① grasp	↔
② deliberately	↔
③ prevent	↔
④ unaware	↔
⑤ good	↔

169

다음 글의 밑줄 친 부분 중, 문맥상 낱말의 쓰임이 적절하지 <u>않은</u> 것은?

There are good theoretical reasons to expect that humans should possess a capacity to assess the trustworthiness of others. Yet there has been very little evidence to ① <u>confirm</u> it. For decades, scientists have searched for the clues without much ② <u>success</u>. I realize that there are many books that promise to teach you how to read everything from intelligence to deceptiveness from body language. With respect to trust, these books are of ③ <u>questionable</u> value at best. Scientific understanding of how nonverbal cues and physiological markers might be used to identify feelings and motives is being rapidly ④ <u>redefined</u>. Traditional methods for using cues to assess emotions, trust, and deception have been shown to be virtually ⑤ <u>useful</u>. Even current programs developed by the government to identify possible threats using nonverbal behavior possess no strong empirical validity.

170

(A), (B), (C)의 각 네모 안에서 문맥에 맞는 낱말로 가장 적절한 것은?

Obesity is no longer just a problem confined to the West. Rising (A) affluence / application in Asia means many people now have more food on their plate than they need. At the same time, physical activity in the region's cities is increasingly (B) expanding / shrinking. The result: more and more Asians are overweight. The health risks for extremely overweight people are enormous, and include heart diseases and arthritis. But for many, exercise and diets no longer seem to be enough. An increasing number of severely obese Asians are turning to a surgery, in which doctors seal off most of the stomach to (C) limit / stimulate food intake. Antiobesity surgery is a growing trend in Asian countries.

*arthritis 관절염

	(A)		(B)		(C)
①	affluence	········	expanding	········	limit
②	affluence	········	shrinking	········	stimulate
③	affluence	········	shrinking	········	limit
④	application	········	shrinking	········	limit
⑤	application	········	expanding	········	stimulate

171

다음 글의 밑줄 친 부분 중, 문맥상 낱말의 쓰임이 적절하지 <u>않은</u> 것은?

One misconception that often appears in the writings of physical scientists who are looking at biology from the outside is that the environment appears to them to be a static entity, which cannot contribute new bits of information as evolution progresses. This, however, is by no means the case. Far from being static, the environment is constantly changing and offering new ① challenges to evolving populations. For higher organisms, the most significant changes in the environment are those produced by the contemporaneous evolution of other organisms. The evolution of a horse's hoof from a five-toed foot has ② enabled the horse to gallop rapidly over open plains. But such galloping is of no ③ advantage to a horse unless it is being chased by a predator. The horse's efficient mechanism for running would never have evolved except for the fact that meat-eating predators were at the same time evolving more efficient methods of ④ attack. Consequently, laws based upon ecological relationships among different kinds of organisms are ⑤ optional for understanding evolution and the diversity of life to which it has given rise.

*hoof 발굽   **gallop 질주하다   ***predator 포식자

172

다음 글의 밑줄 친 부분 중, 문맥상 낱말의 쓰임이 적절하지 <u>않은</u> 것은?

Movies may be said to support the dominant culture and to serve as a means for its reproduction over time. But one may ask why audiences would find such movies enjoyable if all they do is give cultural directives and ① prescriptions for proper living. Most of us would likely grow ② tired of such didactic movies and would probably come to see them as propaganda, similar to the cultural artwork that was common in the Soviet Union and other autocratic societies. The simple answer to this question is that movies do ③ more than present two-hour civics lessons or editorials on responsible behavior. They also tell stories that, in the end, we find ④ satisfying. The bad guys are usually punished; the romantic couple almost always find each other despite the obstacles and difficulties they encounter on the path to true love; and the way we wish the world to be is how, in the movies, it more often than not winds up being. No doubt it is this ⑤ educational aspect of movies that accounts for why we enjoy them so much.

*didactic 교훈적인   **autocratic 독재적인

173

2020 수능 응용

다음 글의 밑줄 친 부분 중, 문맥상 낱말의 쓰임이 적절하지 <u>않은</u> 것은?

The future of our high-tech goods may lie not in the limitations of our minds, but in our ability to secure the ingredients to produce them. In previous eras, such as the Iron Age and the Bronze Age, the ① <u>discovery</u> of new elements brought forth seemingly unending numbers of new inventions. Now the combinations may truly be unending. We are now witnessing a fundamental ② <u>shift</u> in our resource demands. At no point in human history have we used *more* elements, in *more* combinations, and in increasingly refined amounts. Our ingenuity will soon ③ <u>outpace</u> our material supplies. This situation comes at a defining moment when the world is struggling to reduce its reliance on fossil fuels. Fortunately, rare metals are key ingredients in ④ <u>green</u> technologies such as electric cars, wind turbines, and solar panels. They help to convert free natural resources like the sun and wind into the power that fuels our lives. But without ⑤ <u>decreasing</u> today's limited supplies, we have no chance of developing the alternative green technologies we need to slow climate change.

*ingenuity 창의력

출제 어휘 확인하기

① discovery ↔
② shift ↔
③ outpace ↔
④ green ↔
⑤ decrease ↔

174

2022 수능

밑줄 친 (a)~(e) 중에서 문맥상 낱말의 쓰임이 적절하지 <u>않은</u> 것은?

Classifying things together into groups is something we do all the time, and it isn't hard to see why. Imagine trying to shop in a supermarket where the food was arranged in random order on the shelves: tomato soup next to the white bread in one aisle, chicken soup in the back next to the 60-watt light bulbs, one brand of cream cheese in front and another in aisle 8 near the cookies. The task of finding what you want would be (a) <u>time-consuming</u> and extremely difficult, if not impossible.

In the case of a supermarket, someone had to (b) <u>design</u> the system of classification. But there is also a ready-made system of classification embodied in our language. The word "dog," for example, groups together a certain class of animals and distinguishes them from other animals. Such a grouping may seem too (c) <u>abstract</u> to be called a classification, but this is only because you have already mastered the word. As a child learning to speak, you had to work hard to (d) <u>learn</u> the system of classification your parents were trying to teach you. Before you got the hang of it, you probably made mistakes, like calling the cat a dog. If you hadn't learned to speak, the whole world would seem like the (e) <u>unorganized</u> supermarket; you would be in the position of an infant, for whom every object is new and unfamiliar. In learning the principles of classification, therefore, we'll be learning about the structure that lies at the core of our language.

① (a) ② (b) ③ (c) ④ (d) ⑤ (e)

출제 어휘 확인하기

① time-consuming ↔
② design ↔
③ abstract ↔
④ learn ↔
⑤ unorganized ↔

175

다음 글의 밑줄 친 부분 중, 문맥상 낱말의 쓰임이 적절하지 <u>않은</u> 것은?

   When it comes to learning, putting children on the fast track often does more harm than good. Researchers warn that specializing in a sport at too young of an age can lead to physical and psychological ① <u>damage</u>. The same goes for education. A growing body of evidence suggests that children learn better when they learn at a ② <u>slower</u> pace. Some experts recently tested 120 preschool kids. Half went to nursery schools that stressed social interaction and a ③ <u>playful</u> approach to learning: the rest attended nursery schools that rushed them towards ④ <u>academic</u> achievement. They found that the children from the more ⑤ <u>stressful</u>, slower environment turned out to be less anxious, more eager to learn, and better able to think independently.

176

다음 글의 밑줄 친 부분 중, 문맥상 낱말의 쓰임이 적절하지 <u>않은</u> 것은?

   It's likely that for a very long time people managed to survive with draped animal pelts and then began roughly sewing these together. Ultimately, though, the ① <u>advantages</u> of using woven fabric for clothing would have become obvious. A fur pelt offers ② <u>inadequate</u> thermal protection if someone is sitting still, but once on the move or in strong winds, this is less true, because pelts aren't shaped close to the body. The more air gets between the body and the clothing, the less effective it is at trapping an insulating layer of air close to the skin. In fact, the insulating properties of clothing ③ <u>decrease</u> very much when walking quickly. Clothing also needs to be breathable, because damp clothes are bad at keeping the wearer warm and become very heavy. Woven fabrics are more breathable than fur and, when specifically tailored to the body, make excellent internal layers, ④ <u>preventing</u> cold air from getting direct access to the skin's surface. Thus the ability to create woven clothing would have offered material advantages to our early ancestors once they had left Africa for ⑤ <u>cooler</u> areas.

*drape 걸치다   **thermal 열의   ***insulate 단열하다

출제 어휘 확인하기	
① damage	↔
② slower	↔
③ playful	↔
④ academic	↔
⑤ stressful	↔

출제 어휘 확인하기	
① advantage	↔
② inadequate	↔
③ decrease	↔
④ prevent	↔
⑤ cooler	↔

177

다음 글의 밑줄 친 부분 중, 문맥상 낱말의 쓰임이 적절하지 <u>않은</u> 것은?

The printing press boosted the power of ideas to copy themselves. Prior to low-cost printing, ideas could and did spread by word of mouth. While this was tremendously powerful, it limited the ① <u>complexity</u> of the ideas that could be propagated to those that a single person could remember. It also added a certain amount of guaranteed ② <u>error</u>. The spread of ideas by word of mouth was equivalent to a game of telephone on a global scale. The advent of literacy and the creation of handwritten scrolls and, eventually, handwritten books ③ <u>weakened</u> the ability of large and complex ideas to spread with high fidelity. But the incredible amount of time required to copy a scroll or book by hand ④ <u>limited</u> the speed with which information could spread this way. A well-trained monk could transcribe around four pages of text per day. A printing press could copy information thousands of times faster, ⑤ <u>allowing</u> knowledge to spread far more quickly, with full fidelity, than ever before.

*propagate 전파하다 **fidelity 충실

출제 어휘	확인하기		
① complexity		↔	
② error		↔	
③ weaken		↔	
④ limit		↔	
⑤ allow		↔	

178

다음 글의 밑줄 친 부분 중, 문맥상 낱말의 쓰임이 적절하지 <u>않은</u> 것은?

There are some obvious consequences to maintaining competent interpersonal relationships in an intercultural world. Such relationships will inevitably introduce doubt about others' expectations and will reduce the ① <u>certainty</u> that specific behaviors, routines, and rituals mean the same things to everyone. Cultural mixing implies that people will not always feel completely comfortable as they attempt to communicate in another language or as they try to talk with individuals who are not ② <u>proficient</u> in theirs. Many people will need to live in two or more cultures concurrently, shifting from one to another as they go from home to school, from work to play, and from the neighborhood to the shopping mall. The ③ <u>improvements</u> inherent in creating successful intercultural communities are obvious as well. Examples abound that underscore how ④ <u>difficult</u> it is for groups of culturally different individuals to live, work, play, and communicate harmoniously. The consequences of ⑤ <u>failing</u> to create a harmonious intercultural society are also obvious—human suffering, hatred passed on from one generation to another, disruptions in people's lives, and unnecessary conflicts that undermine people's creative talents and energies.

출제 어휘	확인하기		
① certainty		↔	
② proficient		↔	
③ improvement		↔	
④ difficult		↔	
⑤ fail		↔	

179

2020 10월 학평

다음 글의 밑줄 친 부분 중, 문맥상 낱말의 쓰임이 적절하지 <u>않은</u> 것은?

In collectivist groups, there is considerable emphasis on relationships, the maintenance of harmony, and "sticking with" the group. Members of collectivist groups are socialized to avoid conflict, to ① <u>empathize</u> with others, and to avoid drawing attention to themselves. In contrast, members of individualist cultures tend to define themselves in terms of their independence from groups and autonomy and are socialized to ② <u>value</u> individual freedoms and individual expressions. In individualist cultures, standing out and being different is often seen as a sign of ③ <u>weakness</u>. Implicit in the characterization of collectivist and individualist groups is the assumption that deviance will be ④ <u>downgraded</u> more in groups that prescribe collectivism than in groups that prescribe individualism. Indeed, empirical research shows that individualist group norms broaden the latitude of ⑤ <u>acceptable</u> group member behavior and non-normative characteristics.

*deviance 일탈, 표준에서 벗어남

180

다음 글의 밑줄 친 부분 중, 문맥상 낱말의 쓰임이 적절하지 <u>않은</u> 것은?

Why is Jackie Robinson the only player whose number was retired by every baseball team? Find out in this movie on an amazing athlete and pioneer for social justice! It will introduce you to baseball's "color ① <u>barrier</u>," which kept people with dark skin out of the majors for more than 50 years. You'll find out how a man named Branch Rickey teamed up with Robinson to ② <u>shatter</u> this obstacle, and why Robinson's athletic talent wasn't the only reason he was signed! You'll also learn about the ③ <u>abuse</u> Robinson was forced to endure during his rookie season, and how he rose above it, carving out a brilliant career and ④ <u>paving</u> the way for African-American athletes. Finally, you'll learn how his base-running ability ⑤ <u>pleased</u> opposing pitchers and helped his team win pennant after pennant!

*pennant 우승기

출제 어휘 확인하기

① empathize	↔
② value	↔
③ weakness	↔
④ downgrade	↔
⑤ acceptable	↔

출제 어휘 확인하기

① barrier	↔
② shatter	↔
③ abuse	↔
④ pave	↔
⑤ please	↔

181

(A), (B), (C)의 각 네모 안에서 문맥에 맞는 낱말로 가장 적절한 것은?

Science is subject to human bias. This is especially true for social scientists. Since human behavior is their area of study, they are actually part of the subject matter. Furthermore, human behavior patterns vary from one place to another and from one group to another. This is in (A) contrast / agreement to the subject matter of the natural sciences. When a chemist studies hydrogen, he can assume that one hydrogen atom is very much like another, wherever it is found, and that the conditions surrounding it can be quite accurately (B) controlled / unrestrained . The same is true when a physicist measures a metal bar; he can be quite sure that it will not stretch or shrink in length as long as natural conditions are the same. This is why Earl Barbie quotes economist Daniel Suits, who calls the natural sciences the 'easy sciences' because of the (C) predictable / unpredictable nature of their subject matter.

	(A)	(B)	(C)
①	contrast	controlled	predictable
②	contrast	unrestrained	predictable
③	contrast	unrestrained	unpredictable
④	agreement	controlled	predictable
⑤	agreement	controlled	unpredictable

182

2021 수능

밑줄 친 (a)~(e) 중에서 문맥상 낱말의 쓰임이 적절하지 않은 것은?

Our irresistible tendency to see things in human terms—that we are often mistaken in attributing complex human motives and processing abilities to other species—does not mean that an animal's behavior is not, in fact, complex. Rather, it means that the complexity of the animal's behavior is not purely a (a) product of its internal complexity. Herbert Simon's "parable of the ant" makes this point very clearly. Imagine an ant walking along a beach, and (b) visualize tracking the trajectory of the ant as it moves. The trajectory would show a lot of twists and turns, and would be very irregular and complicated. One could then suppose that the ant had equally complicated (c) internal navigational abilities, and work out what these were likely to be by analyzing the trajectory to infer the rules and mechanisms that could produce such a complex navigational path. The complexity of the trajectory, however, "is really a complexity in the surface of the beach, not a complexity in the ant." In reality, the ant may be using a set of very (d) complex rules: it is the interaction of these rules with the environment that actually produces the complex trajectory, not the ant alone. Put more generally, the parable of the ant illustrates that there is no necessary correlation between the complexity of an (e) observed behavior and the complexity of the mechanism that produces it.

*parable 우화 **trajectory 이동 경로

① (a)　② (b)　③ (c)　④ (d)　⑤ (e)

01 필수 어휘

01 flexible *a* _____

02 enduring *a* _____

03 absolute *a* _____

04 confront *v* _____

05 diversity *n* _____

06 evolutionary *a* _____

07 struggle *v* _____

08 cope *v* _____

09 incorporate *v* _____

10 subsequent *a* _____

11 disregard *n* _____

12 ingredient *n* _____

13 특징으로 하다 *v* _____

14 moderate *a* _____

15 outgrow *v* _____

02 필수 어휘

01 remote *a* _____

02 absorption *n* _____

03 declare *v* _____

04 alternative *n* _____

05 strive *v* _____

06 consequence *n* _____

07 exaggerate *v* _____

08 exploit *v* _____

09 foresee *v* _____

10 인공의 *a* _____

11 relative *a* _____

12 definite *a* _____

13 temporary *a* _____

14 exceed *v* _____

15 tolerate *v* _____

03 필수 어휘

01 refer to _____

02 prone to _____

03 assess *v* _____

04 differentiate *v* _____

05 frustrate *v* _____

06 conventional *a* _____

07 generate *v* _____

08 반박하다 *v* _____

09 anticipate *v* _____

10 toxic *a* _____

11	address	v	
12	potential	n	
13	underestimate	v	
14	persuasive	a	
15	conclude	v	

⑭ 필수 어휘

01	extensive	a	
02	sensible	a	
03	sustainability	n	
04	alter	v	
05	constraint	n	
06	suitable	a	
07	흡수하다	v	
08	insight	n	
09	subjective	a	
10	perspective	n	
11	respectively	ad	
12	represent	v	
13	extraordinary	a	
14	accumulate	v	
15	significant	a	

⑮ 필수 어휘

01	variation	n	
02	inspiring	a	
03	reinforce	v	
04	공격적인	a	
05	scarcity	n	
06	intensify	v	
07	nutrition	n	
08	drawback	n	
09	distress	n	
10	correspond to		
11	inappropriate	a	
12	multiple	a	
13	inform	v	
14	recognition	n	
15	controversy	n	

⑯ 필수 어휘

01	adjust	v	
02	characteristic	n	
03	facilitate	v	
04	outcome	n	

05	tangible	*a*
06	authority	*n*
07	enforce	*v*
08	fundamental	*a*
09	sympathy	*n*
10	discipline	*n*
11	impulse	*n*
12	이성적인	*a*
13	alert	*a*
14	derive	*v*
15	imply	*v*

⑦ 필수 어휘

01	dictate	*v*
02	remarkable	*a*
03	trigger	*v*
04	passionate	*a*
05	강렬함, 강도	*n*
06	project	*v*
07	complementary	*a*
08	distribute	*v*
09	futile	*a*

10	susceptible	*a*
11	thrive	*v*
12	commit	*v*
13	candidate	*n*
14	irrelevant	*a*
15	crucial	*a*

⑧ 필수 어휘

01	seemingly	*ad*
02	abstract	*a*
03	optimum	*a*
04	territory	*n*
05	extreme	*a*
06	vital	*a*
07	intact	*a*
08	estimate	*v*
09	outweigh	*v*
10	literally	*ad*
11	해석하다	*v*
12	credible	*a*
13	assume	*v*
14	integrative	*a*

15 settlement   *n* _____

① 어휘 모의고사

01 determine   *v* _____

02 intentional   *a* _____

03 prompt   *v* _____

04 ultimately   *ad* _____

05 pursuit   *n* _____

06 reference   *n* _____

07 activate   *v* _____

08 concern   *n* _____

09 diminish   *v* _____

10 assertion   *n* _____

11 domestic   *a* _____

12 distinctive   *a* _____

13 endure   *v* _____

14 engage in _____

15 상호작용하다   *v* _____

② 어휘 모의고사

01 foster   *v* _____

02 ensure   *n* _____

03 persist in _____

04 움츠리다, 물러나다   *v* _____

05 equivalent   *a* _____

06 accommodate   *v* _____

07 commodity   *n* _____

08 contaminate   *v* _____

09 justification   *n* _____

10 coordination   *n* _____

11 identical   *a* _____

12 arise   *v* _____

13 standpoint   *n* _____

14 explicitly   *ad* _____

15 radical   *a* _____

③ 어휘 모의고사

01 emerge   *v* _____

02 consist of _____

03 depress   *v* _____

04 superstitious   *a* _____

05 modify   *v* _____

06 subtle   *a* _____

07 통합하다   *v* _____

08 consistent   *a* _____

09 mislead   *v* _____

10 spontaneous   *a* _____

11 invisible   *a* _____

12 innate   *a* _____

13 fulfill   *v* _____

14 assign   *v* _____

15 apparent   *a* _____

04 어휘 모의고사

01 transport   *v* _____

02 contemporary   *a* _____

03 grasp   *v* _____

04 confirm   *v* _____

05 empirical   *a* _____

06 obesity   *n* _____

07 shrink   *n* _____

08 static   *a* _____

09 contribute   *v* _____

10 dominant   *a* _____

11 account for   _____

12 reliance   *n* _____

13 전환하다   *v* _____

14 classify   *v* _____

15 distinguish   *v* _____

05 어휘 모의고사

01 turn out   _____

02 property   *n* _____

03 boost   *v* _____

04 advent   *n* _____

05 proficient   *a* _____

06 abound   *v* _____

07 undermine   *v* _____

08 emphasis   *n* _____

09 공감하다   *v* _____

10 implicit   *a* _____

11 shatter   *v* _____

12 quote   *v* _____

13 visualize   *v* _____

14 analyze   *v* _____

15 correlation   *n* _____

III 어법·어휘 모의고사

183

2019 4월 학평

다음 글의 밑줄 친 부분 중, 어법상 **틀린** 것은?

The present moment feels special. It is real. However much you may remember the past or anticipate the future, you live in the present. Of course, the moment ① during which you read that sentence is no longer happening. This one is. In other words, it feels as though time flows, in the sense that the present is constantly updating ② itself. We have a deep intuition that the future is open until it becomes present and ③ that the past is fixed. As time flows, this structure of fixed past, immediate present and open future gets carried forward in time. Yet as ④ naturally as this way of thinking is, you will not find it reflected in science. The equations of physics do not tell us which events are occurring right now—they are like a map without the "you are here" symbol. The present moment does not exist in them, and therefore neither ⑤ does the flow of time.

184

2019 7월 학평

(A), (B), (C)의 각 네모 안에서 문맥에 맞는 낱말로 가장 적절한 것은?

One factor contributing to students' difficulty in making accurate judgments of their own knowledge is hindsight bias: the tendency to assume once something happens that one knew all along that it was going to happen. When students receive feedback suggesting that their knowledge is incomplete, such as getting an exam item (A) incorrect / right , they may respond by telling themselves that they actually did know the information. Although they do not have a strong grasp of the material, they feel as if they do because they recognize something about the item content. Looking back, once they know the answer, the solution seems obvious. This feeling of (B) familiarity / novelty can lead students to have an exaggerated sense of what they know. Hindsight bias therefore (C) diminishes / reinforces the feeling that their failure was due to the nature of the assessment rather than the nature of their knowledge—which makes it more difficult for them to learn from feedback.

*hindsight bias 사후 과잉 확신 편향

	(A)	(B)	(C)
①	incorrect	familiarity	diminishes
②	incorrect	novelty	diminishes
③	incorrect	familiarity	reinforces
④	right	novelty	reinforces
⑤	right	familiarity	diminishes

185

다음 글의 밑줄 친 부분 중, 어법상 틀린 것은?

Who discovered gunpowder for the first time? The English, Arabs, Hindus, and Greeks say they ① did. We know that the ancient Greeks made Greek fire—a sticky mixture that terrorized their enemies when thrown at ② themselves, not only because it stuck, but its flames were hard to put out. Perhaps this was the beginning of gunpowder. Gunpowder is mainly potassium nitrate ③ which burns fiercely when blended with about equal amounts of charcoal and sulfur. If confined in a container of sorts, there is an explosion. Perhaps in this way 600 to 700 years ago gunpowder became something ④ to use to blow things up. Some historians think the advent of gunpowder ⑤ signaled the end of the large castles of the Middle Ages because the walls could be blown apart. Without a doubt, gunpowder changed not only warfare, but also human history.

*potassium nitrate 질산칼륨 **sulfur 황

186

다음 글의 밑줄 친 부분 중, 문맥상 낱말의 쓰임이 적절하지 않은 것은?

Visual systems that allow people to work ① remotely already exist. Without ever putting their hands inside a patient, surgeons can use robotic devices to remove tumors or repair wounds that are deep in the body. Cameras are put on the robotic tools to help doctors move them ② skillfully inside patients' bodies. On video screens, they can see what they are doing with their tools. But these visual systems have ③ flaws. For one thing, doctors can't always tell if they're pulling too hard or not pushing hard enough. In other words, they ④ retain the sense of touch. To fill the gap, researchers are adding a sense of touch to a robotic surgical device called the da Vinci System. They've developed sensors that ⑤ measure how much pressure the robot is applying to the body.

출제 의도 파악하기

❶ ....
❷ ....
❸ ....
❹ ....
❺ ....

출제 어휘 확인하기

① remotely   ↔
② skillfully   ↔
③ flaw   ↔
④ retain   ↔
⑤ measure   ↔

187

다음 글의 밑줄 친 부분 중, 어법상 틀린 것은?

Everyone has their own individual style. There is not one good style of debating ① that you should adopt. Part of ② what makes debates interesting is the different styles that debaters use to persuade audiences. Furthermore, ③ adopting a different style that doesn't really suit your personality will only come across as insincere. Insincerity is the enemy of persuasion. Therefore, while it is okay (even recommended) ④ to experiment with different styles and learn from the styles of debaters you admire, you should always seek to be true to your personality. The search for a "good style" starts from not-so-good styles or very fundamental elements of public speaking. These are basically the things you should avoid doing or ⑤ ensuring that you do, as they strongly affect the chances of persuading your audience. These are also very fundamental elements that all judges will be able to identify.

188

다음 글의 밑줄 친 부분 중, 문맥상 낱말의 쓰임이 적절하지 않은 것은?

The cost of producing a $100 note is around ten cents, but in terms of the goods it can buy its value is much ① higher. From an economic point of view, the value of money usually means the quantity and quality of merchandise that can be bought with a unit amount of money. Modern economies function only if people trust the social meaning of factually ② priceless bits of paper. In other words, coins and banknotes are valuable because we trust that they will be accepted by others in the market—they do not have any real (intrinsic) value but are valuable only because people ③ agree that they do. However, when a society decides, for example, to switch from one currency system to another—as in German marks to the euro or money redenomination—the original currency ④ loses its value. In this sense, the value of money might ⑤ change over time depending on various situational factors. Moreover, the way people value money might depend on various individual factors, like income, money attitudes or social comparisons.

*redomination 화폐 단위 변경

출제 의도 파악하기
1
2
3
4
5

출제 어휘 확인하기
① higher   ↔
② priceless   ↔
③ agree   ↔
④ lose   ↔
⑤ change   ↔

189

다음 글의 밑줄 친 부분 중, 어법상 틀린 것은?

　　Chicago seems to have a meaning more clearly ① established than usual. A French explorer who visited the region in 1688 ② saying the natives called it Chicagou because of the abundance of wild onions
5 growing there. Students have thought it was the disagreeable odor of the pink blossoms of the little wild onions ③ that inspired the Indian name, and that "place of the bad smell" or "place of the skunk" might be more accurate interpretations of the name. On the
10 other hand, ④ those anxious to defend the name of the city insist that its name as the Indians thought of it meant merely "strong" and that "strong-town" is much nearer the proper sense. Thus research and jest and imagination play upon many Indian terms, and it soon
15 becomes impossible to sift out of the result the grain of truth, if any, ⑤ from which it all began.

*jest 농담　**sift out 걸러내다, 가려내다

190

밑줄 친 (a)~(e) 중에서 문맥상 쓰임이 적절하지 <u>않은</u> 것은?

　　In many mountain regions, rights of access to water are associated with the possession of land—until recently in the Andes, for example, land and water rights were (a) combined so water rights were
5 transferred with the land. However, through state land reforms and the development of additional sources of supply, water rights have become separated from land, and may be sold at auction. This therefore (b) favours those who can pay, rather than ensuring access to all in
10 the community. The situation arises, therefore, where individuals may hold land with no water. In Peru, the government grants water to communities separately from land, and it is up to the community to allocate it. Likewise in Yemen, the traditional allocation was one
15 measure (tasah) of water to one hundred 'libnah' of land. This applied only to traditional irrigation supplies—from runoff, wells, etc., where a supply was (c) guaranteed. Water derived from the capture of flash floods is not subject to Islamic law as this constitutes
20 an uncertain source, and is therefore free for those able to collect and use it. However, this traditional allocation per unit of land has been bypassed, partly by the development of new supplies, but also by the (d) decrease in cultivation of a crop of substantial
25 economic importance. This crop is harvested throughout the year and thus requires more than its fair share of water. The economic status of the crop (e) ensures that water rights can be bought or bribed away from subsistence crops.

*irrigation 관개(灌漑)　**bribe 매수하다　***subsistence crop 생계용 작물

① (a)　　② (b)　　③ (c)　　④ (d)　　⑤ (e)

출제 의도 파악하기

❶ _____
❷ _____
❸ _____
❹ _____
❺ _____

출제 어휘 확인하기

① combine　　↔
② favour　　↔
③ guarantee　　↔
④ decrease　　↔
⑤ ensure　　↔

191

2020 6월 모평

다음 글의 밑줄 친 부분 중, 어법상 틀린 것은?

An interesting aspect of human psychology is that we tend to like things more and find them more ① appealing if everything about those things is not obvious the first time we experience them. This is certainly true in music. For example, we might hear a song on the radio for the first time that catches our interest and ② decide we like it. Then the next time we hear it, we hear a lyric we didn't catch the first time, or we might notice ③ what the piano or drums are doing in the background. A special harmony ④ emerges that we missed before. We hear more and more and understand more and more with each listening. Sometimes, the longer ⑤ that takes for a work of art to reveal all of its subtleties to us, the more fond of that thing—whether it's music, art, dance, or architecture— we become.

*subtleties 중요한 세부 요소[사항]들

192

다음 글의 밑줄 친 부분 중, 문맥상 낱말의 쓰임이 적절하지 않은 것은?

Art has been called a visual dialogue, for it expresses its creator's imagination just as surely as if he were speaking to us, though the object itself is ① mute. Even the most private artistic statements can be ② understood on some level, even if only on an intuitive one. For there to be a dialogue, however, requires our active participation. If we cannot ③ literally talk to a work of art, we can at least learn how to respond to it. The process is similar to learning a foreign language. We must learn the style and outlook of a country, period, and artist if we are to understand the work properly. Taste is conditioned solely by culture, which is so varied that it is ④ possible to reduce art to any one set of precepts. It would seem, therefore, that we cannot but view works of art in the ⑤ context of time and circumstances.

출제 의도 **파악하기**

❶ ....

❷ ....

❸ ....

❹ ....

❺ ....

출제 어휘 **확인하기**

① mute	↔
② understand	↔
③ literally	↔
④ possible	↔
⑤ context	↔

193

다음 글의 밑줄 친 부분 중, 어법상 틀린 것은?

The causes of the various kinds of unhappiness ① lie partly in the social system, partly in individual psychology—which, of course, is itself to a considerable extent a product of the social system. I have written before about the changes in the social system ② required to promote happiness. Concerning the abolition of war, of economic exploitation, of education in cruelty and fear, it is not my intention to speak in this volume. ③ To discover a system for the avoidance of war is a vital need of our civilization. But no such system has a chance while men are so unhappy that mutual extermination seems to them less ④ dreadfully than continued endurance of the light of day. Education in cruelty and fear is bad, but no other kind can ⑤ be given by those who are themselves the slaves of these passions.

*extermination 전멸, 근절

194

다음 글의 밑줄 친 부분 중, 문맥상 낱말의 쓰임이 적절하지 않은 것은?

Not everything we do, want to do, and praise is done for ① reasons. A lifeguard who leaps into the sea to save a drowning person does not first formulate beliefs and make these the cause of his action. A mother who ② nurtures her brain-damaged infant may not even be able to supply rational motives for the action for doing so. When we admire the character of the lifeguard and the mother, character is not the possession of a set of rationally justified beliefs in the lifeguard or the mother, but healthy impulses and sound instincts. It is certainly not true that what we do ③ self-consciously we do more effectively. Conscious attentiveness to our moves can at best be one of the means to eliminate a bad habit. It must be ④ maintained when we have learned to swim and swim like a fish, and when we have learned to type. Thought itself is not produced by ⑤ deliberation about how to form concepts and how to connect them; insights come as gifts from a contact with things.

195

다음 글의 밑줄 친 부분 중, 어법상 틀린 것은?

There is a strong social aspect to the way people respond to humor. If you watch your favorite comedy in the presence of people remaining straight-faced, it can stop you from finding ① it so funny. Because it's important ② to sense other people responding to humor, 'canned laughter' is used for television or radio comedy. The same joke can work brilliantly in one context and die in another, as many comedians find, ③ travelling from one venue to another. Like other aspects of language, humor is a way ④ which people show their allegiance to a group. If someone signals his or her intention to say something humorous, the listeners are immediately ready to laugh. People often laugh when ⑤ given this sort of cue, regardless of whether they even get the joke.

*canned 녹음된

196

(A), (B), (C)의 각 네모 안에서 문맥에 맞는 낱말로 가장 적절한 것은?

Even if we don't want to admit it, the ability to overcome most obstacles is within our hands. We can't blame family, society, or history if our work is meaningless, dull, or stressful. Admittedly, there are few options when we realize that our job is useless or actually harmful. Perhaps the only choice is to (A) advance / quit as quickly as possible, even at the cost of severe financial hardship. In terms of the bottom line of one's life, it is always better to do something one feels good about than something that may make us materially comfortable but emotionally miserable. Such decisions are notoriously difficult and require great (B) falsehood / honesty with oneself. As Hannah Arendt, a German-born American political theorist, has shown with regard to Adolf Eichmann and the other employees of the Nazi extermination camps, it is easy to (C) disguise / reveal the responsibility for even the cold-blooded murder of thousands with the excuse: "I only work here."

	(A)		(B)		(C)
①	advance	········	falsehood	········	disguise
②	advance	········	honesty	········	reveal
③	quit	········	falsehood	········	disguise
④	quit	········	honesty	········	disguise
⑤	quit	········	honesty	········	reveal

출제 의도 파악하기

❶ _____
❷ _____
❸ _____
❹ _____
❺ _____

출제 어휘 확인하기

(A) advance	/ quit
(B) falsehood	/ honesty
(C) disguise	/ reveal

197

다음 글의 밑줄 친 부분 중, 어법상 틀린 것은?

Not long ago, economist Michael Housman was leading a project to figure out why some customer service agents stayed in their jobs longer than others. He thought that people with a history of job-hopping would quit sooner, but they ① didn't. Employees who had held five jobs in the past five years weren't any more likely to leave their positions than those who had stayed in the same job for five years. Hunting for other hints, he noticed that his team had captured information about which Internet browser employees had used when they logged in ② to apply for their jobs. On a whim, he tested ③ whether that choice might be related to quitting. He didn't expect to find any correlation, ④ assuming that browser preference was purely a matter of taste. But when he looked at the results, he was stunned: Employees who used Firefox or Chrome to browse the Web ⑤ remaining in their jobs 15 percent longer than those who used Internet Explorer or Safari.

198

밑줄 친 (a)~(e) 중에서 문맥상 낱말의 쓰임이 적절하지 않은 것은?

To the extent that sufficient context has been provided, the reader can come to a well-crafted text with no expert knowledge and come away with a good approximation of what has been intended by the author. The text has become a public document and the reader can read it with a (a) minimum of effort and struggle; his experience comes close to what Freud has described as the deployment of "evenly-hovering attention." He puts himself in the author's hands (some have had this experience with great novelists such as Dickens or Tolstoy) and he (b) follows where the author leads. The real world has vanished and the fictive world has taken its place. Now consider the other extreme. When we come to a badly crafted text in which context and content are not happily joined, we must struggle to understand, and our sense of what the author intended probably bears (c) close correspondence to his original intention. An out-of-date translation will give us this experience; as we read, we must bring the language up to date, and understanding comes only at the price of a fairly intense struggle with the text. Badly presented content with no frame of reference can provide (d) the same experience; we see the words but have no sense of how they are to be taken. The author who fails to provide the context has (e) mistakenly assumed that his picture of the world is shared by all his readers and fails to realize that supplying the right frame of reference is a critical part of the task of writing.

*deployment (전략적) 배치

**evenly-hovering attention 고르게 주의를 기울이는 것

① (a)　　② (b)　　③ (c)　　④ (d)　　⑤ (e)

199

2018 6월

다음 글의 밑줄 친 부분 중, 어법상 **틀린** 것은?

Though most bees fill their days visiting flowers and collecting pollen, some bees take advantage of the hard work of others. These thieving bees sneak into the nest of an ① <u>unsuspecting</u> "normal" bee (known as the host), lay an egg near the pollen mass being gathered by the host bee for her own offspring, and then sneak back out. When the egg of the thief hatches, it kills the host's offspring and then eats the pollen meant for ② <u>its</u> victim. Sometimes called brood parasites, these bees are also referred to as cuckoo bees, because they are similar to cuckoo birds, which lay an egg in the nest of another bird and ③ <u>leaves</u> it for that bird to raise. They are more ④ <u>technically</u> called cleptoparasites. *Clepto* means "thief" in Greek, and the term *cleptoparasite* refers specifically to an organism ⑤ <u>that</u> lives off another by stealing its food. In this case the cleptoparasite feeds on the host's hard-earned pollen stores.

*brood parasite (알을 대신 기르도록 하는) 탁란 동물

200

2020 6월 모평

다음 글의 밑줄 친 부분 중, 문맥상 낱말의 쓰임이 적절하지 **않은** 것은?

Sometimes the awareness that one is distrusted can provide the necessary incentive for self-reflection. An employee who ① <u>realizes</u> she isn't being trusted by her co-workers with shared responsibilities at work might, upon reflection, identify areas where she has consistently let others down or failed to follow through on previous commitments. Others' distrust of her might then ② <u>forbid</u> her to perform her share of the duties in a way that makes her more worthy of their trust. But distrust of one who is ③ <u>sincere</u> in her efforts to be a trustworthy and dependable person can be disorienting and might cause her to doubt her own perceptions and to distrust herself. Consider, for instance, a teenager whose parents are ④ <u>suspicious</u> and distrustful when she goes out at night; even if she has been forthright about her plans and is not ⑤ <u>breaking</u> any agreed-upon rules, her identity as a respectable moral subject is undermined by a pervasive parental attitude that expects deceit and betrayal.

*forthright 솔직한, 거리낌 없는 **pervasive 널리 스며 있는

출제 의도 파악하기

❶
❷
❸
❹
❺

출제 어휘 확인하기

① realize ↔
② forbid ↔
③ sincere ↔
④ suspicious ↔
⑤ break ↔

201

다음 글의 밑줄 친 부분 중, 어법상 <u>틀린</u> 것은?

Body monitoring is most accurate when ① <u>done</u> with full skin contact. This is a clear benefit for body-worn devices, especially in cases ② <u>where</u> long-term monitoring is required. Health services are a big business around the world. Public health care is naturally more tempting, with often instant large-quantity orders, but ③ <u>is</u> strictly regulated in most countries. Doctors are reluctant to adopt either new devices or procedures for the amount of administrative work involved in getting them approved by officials. ④ <u>Change</u> anything in the procedures of hospitals and public health centers would only add to the stress of the often over-worked staff. On the other hand, if personal, body-worn instruments could be read and analyzed ⑤ <u>remotely</u>, both doctors and their patients could save time and money with less routine visits. The private sector is maybe more viable, but any new technology used there needs to be approved by officials, just as in the public sector.

*viable 실행 가능한, 실용적인

202

2019 수능

다음 글의 밑줄 친 부분 중, 문맥상 낱말의 쓰임이 적절하지 <u>않은</u> 것은?

Europe's first *Homo sapiens* lived primarily on large game, particularly reindeer. Even under ideal circumstances, hunting these fast animals with spear or bow and arrow is an ① <u>uncertain</u> task. The reindeer, however, had a ② <u>weakness</u> that mankind would mercilessly exploit: it swam poorly. While afloat, it is uniquely ③ <u>vulnerable</u>, moving slowly with its antlers held high as it struggles to keep its nose above water. At some point, a Stone Age genius realized the enormous hunting ④ <u>advantage</u> he would gain by being able to glide over the water's surface, and built the first boat. Once the ⑤ <u>laboriously</u> overtaken and killed prey had been hauled aboard, getting its body back to the tribal camp would have been far easier by boat than on land. It would not have taken long for mankind to apply this advantage to other goods.

*exploit 이용하다   **haul 끌어당기다

출제 의도 파악하기	
❶	
❷	
❸	
❹	
❺	

출제 어휘 확인하기		
① uncertain	↔	
② weakness	↔	
③ vulnerable	↔	
④ advantage	↔	
⑤ laboriously	↔	

203

다음 글의 밑줄 친 부분 중, 어법상 틀린 것은?

In our daily life we can observe people drawing ① whatever conclusions they wish from their own experiences. There is the man who makes the same mistake over and over again. If you succeed in convincing him of his mistake, he will react in one of several ways. He may say: 'You're right—I'll know better next time'. This is not a common reaction. He is more likely to protest that he has been making the same mistake for so long ② that it would be impossible to break the habit. Or he will blame his parents, or his education, for his mistake. He may complain that nobody ever cared for him, or that he was overindulged as a child. No matter what excuse he makes, he reveals one thing, and that is a desire ③ to be relieved of further responsibility. In this way he justifies his behaviour and puts ④ himself above criticism. He himself is never to blame. It's always someone else's fault if he did not achieve what he set out to do. What such individuals overlook is the fact that they themselves have made very few efforts to overcome their faults or ⑤ avoided repeating their mistakes.

*overindulged 응석받이로 자란

204

2020 4월 학평

(A), (B), (C)의 각 네모 안에서 문맥에 맞는 낱말로 가장 적절한 것은?

Play can be costly because it takes energy and time which could be spent foraging. While playing, the young animal may be at great (A) comfort / risk . For example, 86 percent of young Southern fur seals eaten by sea lions were play-swimming with others when they were caught. Against these costs many functions have been proposed for play, including practice for adult behaviours such as hunting or fighting, and for developing motor and social interaction skills. However, for these theories, there is (B) much / little experimental evidence in animals. For example, detailed studies which tracked juvenile play and adult behaviour of meerkats couldn't prove that play-fighting influenced fighting ability as an adult. Therefore, the persistence of play across so many animal species (C) remains / resolves a mystery. The answers are likely to involve diverse and multiple factors, which may be quite different in different species, as might what we call *play* itself.

*forage 먹이를 찾아 다니다 **juvenile 성장기의

	(A)	(B)	(C)
①	comfort	little	remains
②	comfort	much	resolves
③	risk	little	remains
④	risk	much	remains
⑤	risk	little	resolves

205

다음 글의 밑줄 친 부분 중, 어법상 틀린 것은?

A long time ago you learned how to write a high school theme or essay. You were taught ① that you need a good introduction, a well-organized body and a conclusion. Unfortunately, you may have applied the same logic to your life, and come to see the whole business of living as a theme. The introduction was your childhood ② which you were preparing to be a person. The body is your adult life, which is organized and planned out in preparation for your conclusion, which is the retirement and happy ending. All of this organized thinking keeps you from ③ living your present moments. Living according to this plan implies a guarantee ④ that everything will be okay forever. Security means no excitement, no risks, no challenge. Besides, security is a myth. As long as you are a person on earth, and the system stays the same, you can never have security. And even if it ⑤ weren't a myth, it would be a horrible way to live. Certainty eliminates excitement and growth.

*theme (학교 과제물로 내는) 리포트[작문]

출제 의도 파악하기

❶ _____
❷ _____
❸ _____
❹ _____
❺ _____

206

밑줄 친 (a)~(e) 중에서 문맥상 낱말의 쓰임이 적절하지 <u>않은</u> 것은?

While the world is filled with limitless information and stimulation, our brain cannot, and should not, process everything we see. If it did, we would be (a) overwhelmed with data. Imagine standing in Times Square. If our eyes are wide open, they are encountering thousands of physical things all at once—dozens of flashing billboards, garishly lit buildings, taxis, shops, and some of the 330,000 people who pass through the same spot daily—but we do not "see" it all. Our brain automatically filters our surroundings and allows only a small percentage of information to pass through to protect us from an information overload that might otherwise (b) paralyze us.

Consider what the modern brain manages as we walk down a street talking on the phone. Our body is navigating the pavement and potential obstacles; we are noticing people and landmarks as we pass them, possibly interacting with them or making a mental note of something; we are carrying on a conversation with the person on the other end of the phone, talking, listening, responding; and we do it all (c) effortlessly. We are only able because our brain has filtered out the (d) unnecessary: the ants on the sidewalk, the breeze in the branches, the crumbs on the mustache of the man who just passed us. If we paid attention to every piece of information in our path, we wouldn't get far past our front door.

Dr. Barbara Tversky, professor of psychology and education at Columbia University explains, "The world is terribly confusing; there's too much happening at the same time—visually, auditorily, everything—and the way we cope is by categorizing. We process the (e) maximum we need in order to behave properly."

*garishly 화려하게

① (a)　② (b)　③ (c)　④ (d)　⑤ (e)

출제 어휘 확인하기

① overwhelm　↔
② paralyze　↔
③ effortlessly　↔
④ unnecessary　↔
⑤ maximum　↔

207

2018 9월 모평

다음 글의 밑줄 친 부분 중, 어법상 틀린 것은?

The lack of real, direct experience in and with nature has caused many children to regard the natural world as mere abstraction, that fantastic, beautifully filmed place ① filled with endangered rainforests and polar bears in peril. This overstated, often fictionalized version of nature is no more real—and yet no less real— to them than the everyday nature right outside their doors, ② waits to be discovered in a child's way, at a child's pace. Consider the University of Cambridge study which found that a group of eight-year-old children was able to identify ③ substantially more characters from animations than common wildlife species. One wonders whether our children's inherent capacity to recognize, classify, and order information about their environment—abilities once essential to our very survival—is slowly devolving to facilitate life in ④ their increasingly virtualized world. It's all part of ⑤ what Robert Pyle first called "the extinction of experience."

*peril 위험 **devolve 퇴화하다

208

다음 글의 밑줄 친 부분 중, 문맥상 낱말의 쓰임이 적절하지 않은 것은?

An important part of children's social reality is their role as consumers. Television has an obvious impact on children as consumers in countries like the United States, where television is an almost purely ① commercial venture and television advertising is an important part of children's exposure to the medium. However, television also affects the child as consumer even when there is no advertising at all. In the 1950s it was found that British children who had access only to the BBC, which carries no advertising, had more materialistic ② ambitions than those without television. Adolescent boys who watched television, for example, were ③ more focused on what they would *have* in the future; adolescent boys without television were more focused on what they would be *doing*. The longer the child's experience with television, the more this materialistic outlook ④ decreased. Apparently, the visual images of television create an emphasis on visible and ⑤ tangible objects, hence on consumption, in defining one's identity and life style.

209

다음 글의 밑줄 친 부분 중, 어법상 틀린 것은?

In the 16th century, the Irish discovered that a few acres of marginal land could produce enough potatoes ① to feed a large family and its livestock. The Irish also found ② that they could grow these potatoes with a
5 bare minimum of labor or tools, in something called a "lazy bed." The potatoes were simply laid out in a rectangle on the ground; then, with a spade, the farmer would dig a drainage trench on either side of his potato bed, covering the potatoes with ③ whatever soil or
10 plant materials came out of the drainage trench. No plowed earth, no rows, and certainly no beautiful crops. Potato growing looked nothing like agriculture and ④ providing none of the satisfactions of an orderly laid-out field of grain, no golden wheat ripening in the
15 sun. Wheat pointed up, to the sun and civilization; the potato pointed down. Potatoes formed their plain-looking brown tubers ⑤ unseen beneath the ground, throwing a bunch of untidy vines above.

*drainage trench 배수 도랑 **tuber 구근

출제 의도 파악하기

❶ ....
❷ ....
❸ ....
❹ ....
❺ ....

210

밑줄 친 (a)~(e) 중에서 문맥상 낱말의 쓰임이 적절하지 않은 것은?

Much of our knowledge of the biology of the oceans is derived from "blind" sampling. We use instruments to measure bulk properties of the environment, such as salinity and temperature, and we use bottle or net samples to (a) extract knowledge about the organisms 5 living in the ocean. This kind of approach has contributed important knowledge but has also influenced the way we view marine life. It leads us to focus on abundances, production rates, and distribution patterns. Such a perspective is very 10 (b) relevant in the context of the ocean as a resource for fisheries. It is also helpful in developing an understanding of biogeochemical issues such as ocean carbon fluxes. But on its own, this approach is (c) insufficient, even for those purposes. The kind of 15 intuition that we develop about marine life is, of course, influenced by the way we (d) observe it. Because the ocean is inaccessible to us and most planktonic organisms are microscopic, our intuition is elementary compared, for example, to the intuitive 20 understanding we have about (macroscopic) terrestrial life. Our understanding of the biology of planktonic organisms is still based mainly on examinations of (dead) individuals, field samples, and incubation experiments, and even our sampling may be severely 25 biased toward those organisms that are not destroyed by our harsh sampling methods. Similarly, experimental observations are (e) extended to those organisms that we can collect live and keep and cultivate in the laboratory. 30

*salinity 염도 **flux 흐름 *** terrestrial 육지의

① (a)　　② (b)　　③ (c)　　④ (d)　　⑤ (e)

출제 어휘 확인하기

① extract　　　　　　↔
② relevant　　　　　↔
③ insufficient　　　　↔
④ observe　　　　　↔
⑤ extend　　　　　　↔

211

2019 9월 모평 응용

다음 글의 밑줄 친 부분 중, 어법상 틀린 것은?

Although most people, including Europe's Muslims, have numerous identities, few of these are ① politically salient at any moment. It is only when a political issue affects the welfare of those in a particular group ② that identity assumes importance. For instance, when issues arise that touch on women's rights, women start to think of gender as their principal identity. Whether such women are American or Iranian or whether they are Catholic or Protestant ③ matters less than the fact that they are women. Similarly, when famine and civil war threaten people in sub-Saharan Africa, many African-Americans are reminded of their kinship with the continent ④ which their ancestors originated centuries earlier, and they lobby their leaders to provide humanitarian relief. In other words, each issue calls forth somewhat different identities that ⑤ help explain the political preferences people have regarding those issues.

*salient 두드러진

212

다음 글의 밑줄 친 부분 중, 문맥상 낱말의 쓰임이 적절하지 않은 것은?

Perhaps the most striking quality of satiric literature is its freshness, its originality of perspective. Satire rarely offers ① original ideas. What they do is look at familiar conditions from a perspective that makes these conditions seem foolish or harmful. Satire startles us into a pleasantly shocked realization that many of the values we unquestioningly accept are ② false. *Don Quixote* makes chivalry seem absurd; *Brave New World* ridicules the pretensions of science; *A Modest Proposal* dramatizes starvation by advocating cannibalism. However, none of these ideas is original. Chivalry was ③ suspected before Cervantes. Humanists ④ objected to the claims of pure science before Aldous Huxley. And people were ⑤ ignorant of famine before Swift. It was not the originality of the idea that made these literary works popular. It was the manner of expression, the satiric method, that made them interesting and entertaining.

*satire 풍자 **chivalry 기사도 ***cannibalism 식인 풍습

출제 의도 파악하기

① _____
② _____
③ _____
④ _____
⑤ _____

출제 어휘 확인하기

① original	↔
② false	↔
③ suspect	↔
④ object	↔
⑤ ignorant	↔

213

다음 글의 밑줄 친 부분 중, 어법상 틀린 것은?

At almost the precise midpoint of the 20th century, George Orwell published *1984*. The book pictured a government in total control of the mass media. Orwell correctly envisioned such technologies as two-way television screens that could be used to deliver the state's propaganda to viewers while simultaneously ① spying on them. His warnings about potential invasions of privacy are, if anything, ② understated. But he did not foresee—nor ③ was anyone else at the time—the most important revolution of the era: the shift from an economy based on muscle to one dependent on mind. He did not, therefore, anticipate today's ④ astonishing proliferation of new communication tools. The number and variety of these technologies is now so great, and changing so greatly, ⑤ that even experts are bewildered. But look at things from a distance, and the basic outlines of tomorrow's media become clear. They are interactivity, mobility, convertibility, connectivity, ubiquity, and globalization.

*proliferation 확산, 증식

214

2021 7월 학평

밑줄 친 (a)~(e) 중에서 문맥상 낱말의 쓰임이 적절하지 않은 것은?

There is something about a printed photograph or newspaper headline that makes the event it describes more real than in any other form of news reporting. Perhaps this is because there is an undeniable reality to the newspaper itself: it is a real material object. That (a) authenticity rubs off on the news. It can be pointed to, underlined, cut out, pinned on notice boards, stuck in a scrap-book, or archived in libraries. The news becomes an artifact, (b) frozen in time; the event may be long gone, but it lives on as an indisputable fact because of its material presence—even if it is untrue.

In contrast, news websites seem short-lived. Although they too are archived, there is no unique physical component to point to as (c) evidence of the information they convey. For this reason, there is a sense in which they can be more easily manipulated, and that history itself could be altered. At the same time, it is precisely this immediacy and (d) rigidity of content that makes the digital media so exciting. The news website is in tune with an age that sees history as much less monolithic than previous eras once did. Digital news websites are potentially much more (e) democratic, too, for while a physical newspaper requires huge printing presses and a distribution network linking trains, planes, trucks, shops, and ultimately newspaper sellers, in the digital world a single person can communicate with the whole world with the aid of a single computer and without requiring a single tree to be cut down.

*archive 보관하다

① (a)　　② (b)　　③ (c)　　④ (d)　　⑤ (e)

출제 의도 파악하기

❶ _____
❷ _____
❸ _____
❹ _____
❺ _____

출제 어휘 확인하기

① authenticity　　↔
② frozen　　↔
③ evidence　　↔
④ rigidity　　↔
⑤ democratic　　↔

215

2018 7월 학평

다음 글의 밑줄 친 부분 중, 어법상 틀린 것은?

When it comes to medical treatment, patients see choice as both a blessing and a burden. And the burden falls primarily on women, who are ① typically the guardians not only of their own health, but that of their husbands and children. "It is an overwhelming task for women, and consumers in general, ② to be able to sort through the information they find and make decisions," says Amy Allina, program director of the National Women's Health Network. And what makes it overwhelming is not only that the decision is ours, but that the number of sources of information ③ which we are to make the decisions has exploded. It's not just a matter of listening to your doctor lay out the options and ④ making a choice. We now have encyclopedic lay-people's guides to health, "better health" magazines, and the Internet. So now the prospect of medical decisions ⑤ has become everyone's worst nightmare of a term paper assignment, with stakes infinitely higher than a grade in a course.

*lay-people 비전문가

216

다음 글의 밑줄 친 부분 중, 문맥상 낱말의 쓰임이 적절하지 <u>않은</u> 것은?

Competence is similar to power in that it implies control over environmental factors. At a very early age, children begin illustrating their need for competence by touching and handling objects to become ① familiar with them. Later on, they begin trying to take things apart and put them back together again. As a result, children learn ② tasks at which they are competent. On the job, the competence motive ③ reveals itself in the form of a desire for job mastery and professional growth. An individual begins matching his or her abilities and skills against the environment in a contest that is ④ challenging but that can be won. Organizations that provide meaningful work help their people meet the need for competence. In some companies, such as those using assembly lines, such jobs are not in abundance, and the competence motive often goes ⑤ gratified.

출제 의도 파악하기

❶ _____
❷ _____
❸ _____
❹ _____
❺ _____

출제 어휘 확인하기

① familiar ⟷
② task ⟷
③ reveal ⟷
④ challenging ⟷
⑤ gratified ⟷

217

2017 6 모평 응용

다음 글의 밑줄 친 부분 중, 어법상 틀린 것은?

What story could be harsher than that of the Great Auk, the large black-and-white seabird that in northern oceans took the ecological place of a penguin? Its tale rises and falls like a Greek tragedy, with island populations ① savagely destroyed by humans until almost all were gone. Then the very last colony found safety on a special island, one ② protected from the destruction of humankind by vicious and unpredictable ocean currents. These waters presented no problem to perfectly adapted seagoing birds, but they prevented humans from making any kind of safe landing. After enjoying a few years of comparative safety, disaster of a different kind struck the Great Auk. Volcanic activity caused the island refuge ③ to sink completely beneath the waves, and surviving individuals were forced to find shelter elsewhere. The new island home they chose ④ lacking the benefits of the old in one terrible way. Humans could access it with comparative ease, and they ⑤ did! Within just a few years the last of this once-plentiful species was entirely eliminated.

*Great Auk 큰바다쇠오리

218

다음 글의 밑줄 친 부분 중, 문맥상 낱말의 쓰임이 적절하지 않은 것은?

The word "consumption" implies an almost mechanical efficiency, suggesting that all traces of whatever we consume magically ① vanish after we use it. In fact, when we consume something, it doesn't go away at all. Rather, it is ② transformed into two very different kinds of things: something "useful" and the material left over, which we call "waste." Moreover, anything we think of as useful becomes waste as soon as we are finished with it, so our ③ perception of the things we consume must be considered when deciding what is and isn't waste. Until recently, ④ most of these issues has seemed important. Indeed, a high rate of consumption has often been mentioned as an ⑤ inevitable characteristic of an advanced society. Now, however, this attitude can no longer be considered in any way healthy, desirable, or acceptable.

출제 의도 파악하기

❶ _____
❷ _____
❸ _____
❹ _____
❺ _____

출제 어휘 확인하기

① vanish ↔
② transform ↔
③ perception ↔
④ most ↔
⑤ inevitable ↔

219

다음 글의 밑줄 친 부분 중, 어법상 틀린 것은?

Although ① <u>unfocused</u>, this work demonstrates that an essay about an otherwise insignificant topic can in fact be insightful and even touching. By establishing a strong sense of tension at the beginning of the essay, this essay succeeds ② <u>where</u> other personal reflections often falter. The author does not begin with a topic sentence or other device ③ <u>that</u> states the essay's point right away. To do so in this sort of essay would be to make the piece too much like a "what-I-did-last-summer" narrative. Instead, the reader is kept in suspense until the second paragraph of the piece about ④ <u>what</u> is causing the author's angst. Only then ⑤ <u>do</u> the author spell out that it is his impending wrist surgery—and not a shot or test results—which has caused such great anxiety. Overall, the writing is clear and unpretentious.

*falter 영향력이 없어지다

220

(A), (B), (C)의 각 네모 안에서 문맥에 맞는 낱말로 가장 적절한 것은?

Children learn that adults are (A) reluctant / willing to reprimand them in the homes of others. Trusting geography, they choose these locations to misbehave. But, this strategy can be counteracted best by letting the hosts set the rules of their own house and carry out their enforcement. When a child jumps on the sofa in Aunt Mary's house, let Aunt Mary decide whether or not the sofa is for jumping, and let her invoke the limit. The mother, relieved of (B) complimentary / disciplinary obligation, can help the child by voicing understanding of the child's wishes and feelings: "You really enjoy jumping on her sofa, but this is Aunt Mary's home and we have to respect her wishes." If the child (C) consents / dissents, saying "But you let me jump on our sofa," we can respond with "These are Aunt Mary's rules; we have different rules in our home."

*reprimand 꾸짖다, 훈계하다

	(A)		(B)		(C)
①	reluctant	⋯⋯	complimentary	⋯⋯	consents
②	reluctant	⋯⋯	disciplinary	⋯⋯	consents
③	reluctant	⋯⋯	disciplinary	⋯⋯	dissents
④	willing	⋯⋯	complimentary	⋯⋯	consents
⑤	willing	⋯⋯	disciplinary	⋯⋯	dissents

출제 의도 파악하기

❶ _____
❷ _____
❸ _____
❹ _____
❺ _____

출제 어휘 확인하기

(A) reluctant / willing
(B) complimentary / disciplinary
(C) consent / dissent

221

다음 글의 밑줄 친 부분 중, 어법상 틀린 것은?

It is often the case that students worry more about transcribing everything from the PowerPoint slides than ① whether they understand those notes. Likewise, instructors may rush through lectures in order to get
5 through the material, without attending to ② what students are learning. McKeachie, a retired American psychologist and former chair of the Department of Psychology at the University of Michigan, discussed one way of checking for and ③ encouraging student
10 understanding of material—*summary writing*. Writing summaries of lectures or reading material ④ requires increased cognitive activity on the part of students, who must reorganize and synthesize information. It also provides the opportunity for students to put
15 information into their own words, ⑤ for which they will likely remember better than the instructor's words. Research shows that such summary writing can have a substantial impact on learning.

222

밑줄 친 (a)~(e) 중에서 문맥상 낱말의 쓰임이 적절하지 <u>않은</u> 것은?

The right to privacy may extend only to the point where it does not restrict someone else's right to freedom of expression or right to information. The scope of the right to privacy is (a) <u>similarly</u> restricted by the general interest in preventing crime or in 5 promoting public health. However, when we move away from the property-based notion of a right (where the right to privacy would protect, for example, images and personality), to modern notions of private and family life, we find it (b) <u>easier</u> to establish the limits of 10 the right. This is, of course, the strength of the notion of privacy, in that it can adapt to meet changing expectations and technological advances.

In sum, *what* is privacy today? The concept includes a claim that we should be unobserved, and that certain 15 information and images about us should not be (c) <u>circulated</u> without our permission. *Why* did these privacy claims arise? They arose because powerful people took offence at such observation. Furthermore, privacy incorporated the need to protect the family, 20 home, and correspondence from arbitrary (d) <u>interference</u> and, in addition, there has been a determination to protect honour and reputation. *How* is privacy protected? Historically, privacy was protected by restricting circulation of the damaging 25 material. But if the concept of privacy first became interesting legally as a response to reproductions of images through photography and newspapers, more recent technological advances, such as data storage, digital images, and the Internet, (e) <u>pose</u> new threats 30 to privacy. The right to privacy is now being reinterpreted to meet those challenges.

*arbitrary 임의의

① (a)　　② (b)　　③ (c)　　④ (d)　　⑤ (e)

출제 의도 파악하기

❶ ....
❷ ....
❸ ....
❹ ....
❺ ....

출제 어휘 확인하기

① similarly	↔
② easier	↔
③ circulate	↔
④ interference	↔
⑤ pose	↔

01 어법 · 어휘 모의고사

01   anticipate   *v*   _____

02   intuition   *n*   _____

03   equation   *n*   _____

04   contribute to   _____

05   accurate   *a*   _____

06   새로움, 참신함   *n*   _____

07   exaggerated   *a*   _____

08   assessment   *n*   _____

09   put out   _____

10   blend   *v*   _____

11   confine   *v*   _____

12   explosion   *n*   _____

13   advent   *n*   _____

14   signal   *v*   _____

15   device   *n*   _____

16   flaw   *n*   _____

17   retain   *v*   _____

18   surgical   *a*   _____

19   debate   *v*   _____

20   adopt   *v*   _____

21   ensure   *v*   _____

22   fundamental   *a*   _____

23   identify   *v*   _____

24   function   *v*   _____

25   intrinsic   *a*   _____

26   income   *n*   _____

27   attitude   *n*   _____

28   comparison   *n*   _____

29   region   *n*   _____

30   abundance   *n*   _____

31   disagreeable   *a*   _____

32   영감을 주다   *v*   _____

33   interpretation   *n*   _____

34   transfer   *v*   _____

35   grant   *v*   _____

36   allocate   *v*   _____

37   be subject to   _____

38   bypass   *v*   _____

39   cultivation   *n*   _____

40   substantial   *a*   _____

41   share   *n*   _____

02 어법 · 어휘 모의고사

01	appealing	*a*	
02	obvious	*a*	
03	emerge	*v*	
04	fond of		
05	architecture	*n*	
06	mute	*a*	
07	statement	*n*	
08	직관적인	*a*	
09	participation	*n*	
10	literally	*ad*	
11	outlook	*n*	
12	considerable	*a*	
13	promote	*v*	
14	abolition	*n*	
15	exploitation	*n*	
16	intention	*n*	
17	mutual	*a*	
18	endurance	*n*	
19	supply	*v*	
20	impulse	*n*	

21	instinct	*n*	
22	의식적인, 의도적인	*a*	
23	eliminate	*v*	
24	insight	*n*	
25	context	*n*	
26	regardless of		
27	overcome	*v*	
28	obstacle	*n*	
29	financial	*a*	
30	hardship	*n*	
31	notoriously	*ad*	
32	responsibility	*n*	
33	figure out		
34	apply for		
35	correlation	*n*	
36	preference	*n*	
37	vanish	*v*	
38	translation	*n*	
39	reference	*n*	
40	critical	*a*	
41	up to date		

03 어법·어휘 모의고사

01	take advantage of	_____
02	offspring	*n* _____
03	specifically	*ad* _____
04	awareness	*n* _____
05	동기, 혜택	*n* _____
06	consistently	*ad* _____
07	commitment	*n* _____
08	perception	*n* _____
09	suspicious	*a* _____
10	undermine	*v* _____
11	deceit	*n* _____
12	tempting	*a* _____
13	instant	*a* _____
14	regulate	*v* _____
15	reluctant	*a* _____
16	procedure	*n* _____
17	analyze	*v* _____
18	routine	*a* _____
19	live on	_____
20	ideal	*a* _____

21	vulnerable	*a* _____
22	overtake	*v* _____
23	tribal	*a* _____
24	convince	*v* _____
25	정당화하다	*v* _____
26	costly	*a* _____
27	propose	*v* _____
28	interaction	*n* _____
29	track	*v* _____
30	diverse	*a* _____
31	multiple	*a* _____
32	imply	*v* _____
33	guarantee	*n* _____
34	stimulation	*n* _____
35	overwhelm	*v* _____
36	encounter	*v* _____
37	overload	*n* _____
38	paralyze	*v* _____
39	confusing	*a* _____
40	categorize	*v* _____
41	filter	*v* _____

01	endangered	*a*	
02	overstate	*v*	
03	inherent	*a*	
04	classify	*v*	
05	facilitate	*v*	
06	소멸, 사멸, 멸종	*n*	
07	commercial	*a*	
08	exposure	*n*	
09	livestock	*n*	
10	lay out		
11	orderly	*ad*	
12	derive	*v*	
13	property	*n*	
14	extract	*v*	
15	distribution	*n*	
16	inaccessible	*a*	
17	biased	*a*	
18	harsh	*a*	
19	laboratory	*n*	
20	numerous	*a*	
21	assume	*v*	
22	principal	*a*	
23	famine	*n*	
24	originate	*v*	
25	original	*a*	
26	absurd	*a*	
27	ridicule	*v*	
28	starvation	*n*	
29	advocate	*v*	
30	의심하다	*v*	
31	object	*v*	
32	precise	*a*	
33	envision	*v*	
34	simultaneously		
35	foresee	*v*	
36	ubiquity	*n*	
37	artifact	*n*	
38	convey	*v*	
39	manipulate	*v*	
40	alter	*v*	
41	era	*n*	

05 어법 · 어휘 모의고사

01 overwhelming   *a* _____

02 explode   *v* _____

03 prospect   *n* _____

04 infinitely   *ad* _____

05 역량, 능력   *n* _____

06 illustrate   *v* _____

07 assembly   *n* _____

08 ecological   *a* _____

09 tragedy   *n* _____

10 vicious   *a* _____

11 disaster   *n* _____

12 comparative   *a* _____

13 efficiency   *n* _____

14 transform   *v* _____

15 mention   *v* _____

16 desirable   *a* _____

17 acceptable   *a* _____

18 insignificant   *a* _____

19 tension   *n* _____

20 impending   *a* _____

21 counteract   *v* _____

22 carry out   _____

23 enforcement   *n* _____

24 relieve   *v* _____

25 obligation   *n* _____

26 transcribe   *v* _____

27 get through   _____

28 인지의, 인지적인   *a* _____

29 restrict   *v* _____

30 scope   *n* _____

31 circulate   *v* _____

32 arise   *v* _____

33 incorporate   *v* _____

34 interference   *n* _____

35 determination   *n* _____

36 reputation   *n* _____

37 pose   *v* _____

38 threat   *n* _____

39 reinterpret   *v* _____

40 challenge   *n* _____

41 lecture   *n* _____

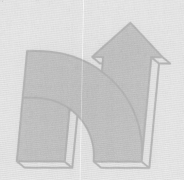

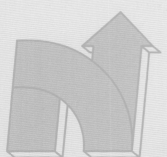

메가스터디 N제

영어영역 어법·어휘

수능 완벽 대비 예상 문제집

정답 및 해설

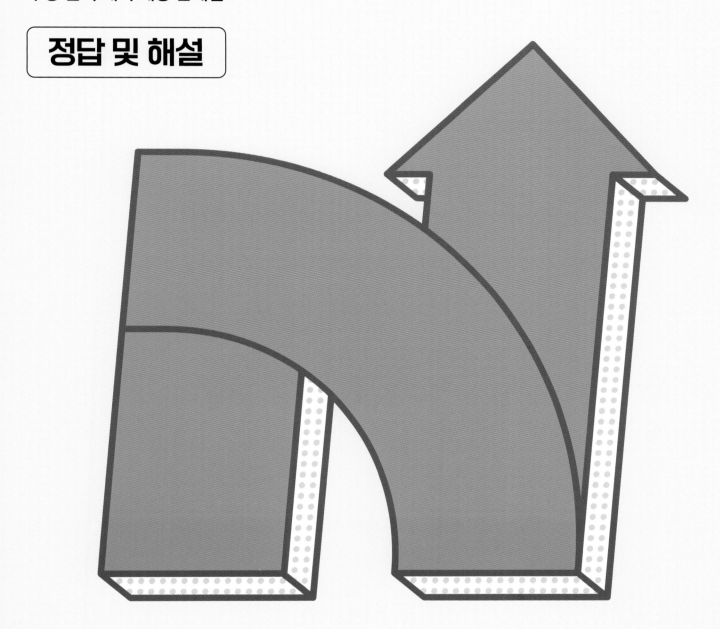

222제

메가스터디 BOOKS

메가스터디 N제

영어영역 어법·어휘

222제

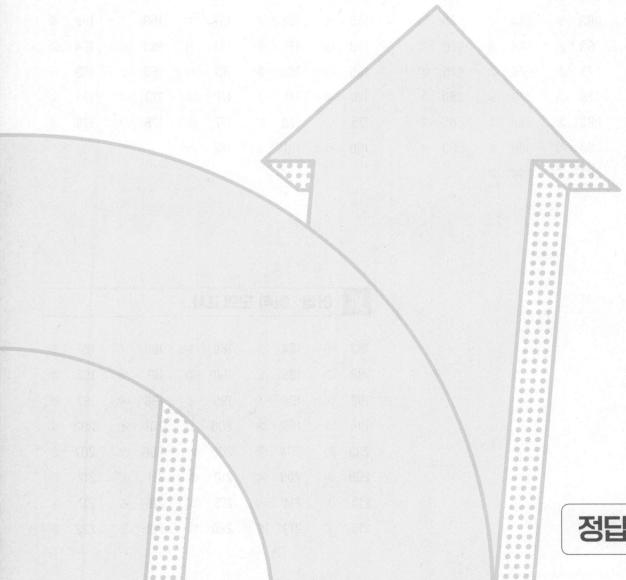

정답 및 해설

I 어법

001	⑤	002	③	003	①	004	③	005	①
006	③	007	②	008	④	009	⑤	010	③
011	③	012	①	013	④	014	②	015	④
016	④	017	③	018	④	019	⑤	020	④
021	④	022	⑤	023	②	024	③	025	⑤
026	③	027	④	028	②	029	③	030	③
031	②	032	②	033	④	034	⑤	035	⑤
036	④	037	⑤	038	③	039	④	040	④
041	⑤	042	⑤	043	④	044	③	045	②
046	④	047	⑤	048	④	049	②	050	③
051	③	052	⑤	053	①	054	④	055	③
056	②	057	④	058	④	059	⑤	060	②
061	③	062	②	063	⑤	064	⑤	065	⑤
066	④	067	⑤	068	④	069	⑤	070	②
071	⑤	072	⑤	073	④	074	②	075	④
076	④	077	④	078	③	079	④	080	③
081	②	082	④	083	②	084	③	085	②
086	②	087	③	088	④	089	⑤	090	③
091	②	092	⑤	093	③	094	③		

II 어휘

095	④	096	③	097	③	098	④	099	③
100	⑤	101	⑤	102	④	103	⑤	104	④
105	⑤	106	②	107	⑤	108	⑤	109	⑤
110	④	111	④	112	⑤	113	③	114	③
115	①	116	⑤	117	④	118	③	119	④
120	④	121	③	122	④	123	⑤	124	⑤
125	⑤	126	⑤	127	⑤	128	①	129	④
130	③	131	③	132	④	133	⑤	134	⑤
135	⑤	136	④	137	③	138	④	139	④
140	④	141	③	142	④	143	④	144	④
145	③	146	⑤	147	⑤	148	④	149	⑤
150	④	151	③	152	⑤	153	④	154	②
155	④	156	④	157	④	158	⑤	159	⑤
160	⑤	161	②	162	⑤	163	④	164	②
165	④	166	⑤	167	⑤	168	②	169	⑤
170	③	171	⑤	172	⑤	173	⑤	174	③
175	⑤	176	②	177	③	178	③	179	③
180	⑤	181	①	182	④				

III 어법·어휘 모의고사

183	④	184	③	185	②	186	④	187	⑤
188	②	189	②	190	④	191	⑤	192	④
193	④	194	④	195	④	196	④	197	⑤
198	③	199	③	200	②	201	④	202	⑤
203	⑤	204	③	205	②	206	⑤	207	②
208	④	209	④	210	⑤	211	④	212	⑤
213	③	214	④	215	⑤	216	⑤	217	④
218	④	219	⑤	220	③	221	⑤	222	②

01 주어와 동사

본문 pp.008~011

Q1

1 <u>How you do it during meetings</u> can affect your promotion.

2 <u>The question whether to confess or not</u> troubled the girl.

3 <u>The news that he was to lose his job</u> came as a rude shock.

4 <u>The number of restaurants</u> has increased where fusion food is served.

5 <u>The book I happened to find on the shelf</u> was an unexpected treasure.

6 <u>To create obstacles to the realization of potential</u> is to limit personal growth.

Q2 **1** was **2** to go **3** have **4** that **5** show **6** means

---

001 ⑤　　**002** ③　　**003** ①　　**004** ③　　**005** ①

006 ③

Q1

1. [풀이] 의문사 How가 이끄는 명사절이 주어이다.
[해석] 여러분이 회의 동안에 그 일을 어떻게 하는지가 여러분의 승진에 영향을 줄 수 있다.

2. [풀이] 핵심 주어인 The question 뒤에 접속사 whether가 이끄는 동격어구가 왔다.
[해석] 고백을 할 것인지 말 것인지의 문제가 그 소녀를 힘들게 했다.

3. [풀이] 핵심 주어인 The news 뒤에 접속사 that이 이끄는 동격절이 왔다.
[해석] 그가 직장을 잃게 되었다는 소식은 갑작스런 충격으로 다가왔다.

4. [풀이] The number가 핵심 주어이고 of restaurants가 이를 수식한다.
[해석] 퓨전 음식이 제공되는 식당의 수가 증가해 왔다.

5. [풀이] 핵심 주어인 The book을 목적격 관계대명사가 생략된 관계절이 수식한다.
[해석] 내가 우연히 서가에서 발견한 책은 뜻밖의 보물이었다.

6. [풀이] to부정사인 To create가 주어를 이끈다.
[해석] 잠재력을 실현하는 데 장애물을 만드는 것은 개인의 성장을 제한하는 것이다.

Q2

1. [풀이] 주어의 핵이 단수인 One이고 lessons는 주어의 수식어구 중 일부이므로 단수 동사 was가 알맞다.
[해석] 선수들이 배운 가장 중요한 교훈 중 하나는 절대 포기하지 말라는 것이었다.

2. [풀이] 문맥상 It은 형식상의 주어이므로 내용상의 주어를 이끄는 to부정사 to go가 알맞다.

[해석] 자동차 경주 대회에 가는 것은 통상적인 가족 외출이었다.

3. [풀이] 주어의 핵인 복수 명사 concerns에 이어지는 동사가 필요하므로 have가 알맞다.
[해석] 도시 오염에 대한 높아져가는 우려가 정부로 하여금 전기 자동차에 주의를 재집중하게 했다.

4. [풀이] 문맥상 It은 형식상의 주어이므로 내용상의 주어인 that절이 되도록 that이 오는 것이 알맞다.
[해석] 출생 순서가 성인기의 성격과 성취에 직접적으로 영향을 미친다고 여겨져 왔다.

5. [풀이] 전치사구 from cities all over the world의 수식을 받는 핵심 주어 Studies에 이어지는 동사가 필요하므로 show가 알맞다.
[해석] 전 세계의 도시에서 행해진 연구들은 도시의 매력으로서의 생활과 활동의 중요성을 보여 준다.

6. [풀이] 주어로 쓰인 동명사구 Having a personality에 이어지는 동사가 필요하므로 means가 알맞다.
[해석] 습성을 갖는다는 것은 시간이 흐르면서 일관된 행동 양식을 보여 준다는 것을 의미한다.

---

001 답 ⑤

출제 의도 파악하기

① 대명사의 수 일치　　② 접속사 that의 쓰임
③ to부정사의 쓰임　　④ 부사의 쓰임
⑤ 형식상의 주어와 내용상의 주어

정답풀이

⑤ 바로 앞의 and에 의해 두 개의 절이 병렬로 연결된 구조이다. 문맥상 and 뒤의 절에서 주어는 that the final ~ to be said이므로, 앞에 이를 대신하는 형식상의 주어 it이 필요하다. 따라서 what을 형식상의 주어 it으로 바꿔 써야 한다.

오답풀이

① it은 Modern-day science를 가리키는 주격 대명사로 적절하게 쓰였다.
② 뒤에 완전한 구조의 절이 이어지고, 문맥상 and 앞의 that절과 병렬구조를 이루며 동사 argued의 목적어 역할을 하는 명사절을 이끄는 접속사 that의 쓰임은 적절하다.
③ don't know의 목적어 역할을 하는 「의문사+to부정사」를 이루는 to reconcile은 어법상 적절하다.
④ 형용사 emerging이 new evidence를 수식하는 구조에서 emerging을 수식하는 부사 constantly는 알맞다.

전문해석

현대 과학은 가장 중요한 질문들과 관련해 집단적인 무지를 공개적으로 인정한다는 점을 고려하면 지식의 독특한 전통이다. 다윈은 결코 자신이 '생물학자들의 보증'이라고 주장하지 않았고, 생명의 수수께끼를 최종적으로 풀었다고 주장하지 않았다. 여러 세기에 걸친 광범위한 과학적 연구 후에도 생물학자들은 뇌가 어떻게 의식을 만들어 내는지에 대한 좋은 설명이 아직 없다는 것을 인정한다. 물리학자들은 무엇이 빅뱅을 일으켰는지 또는 양자역학과 일반상대성이론을 어떻게 조화시켜야 할지 모른다는 점을 인정한다. 다른 경우, 경쟁하는 과학 이론들은 끊임없이 새로이 떠오르는 증거들을 근거로 시끄럽게 논의된다. 가장 중요한 사례는 경제를 어떻게 가장 잘 운영할 것인지에 대한 논쟁이다. 비록 개별 경제학자들은 그들의 방법이 최고의 방법이라고 주장할지 모르지만, 금융 위기와 증권 거래의 거품 때마다 정설은 변화하며, 경제학에 관한 최종적인 발언이 아직 나오지 않았다는 점이 널리 인정되고 있다.

구문풀이

6행 [After centuries of extensive scientific research], biologists admit [that they still don't have any good explanation for {how brains produce consciousness}].

: 첫 번째 [ ]는 시간을 나타내는 부사구이다. 두 번째 [ ]는 admit의 목적어로 쓰인 명사절이며 그 안의 { }는 전치사 for의 목적어로 쓰인 의문사절이다.

어휘풀이

- inasmuch as ~인 점을 고려하면, ~이므로
- ignorance *n* 무지
- seal *n* 보증해 주는 것, 인장, 봉인
- once and for all 최종적으로
- consciousness *n* 의식
- quantum mechanics 양자역학
- the theory of general relativity 일반상대성이론
- emerging *a* 신흥의, 떠오르는
- crisis *n* 위기
- argue *v* 주장하다
- riddle *n* 수수께끼
- extensive *a* 광범위한
- reconcile *v* 조화시키다, 일치시키다
- prime *a* 가장 중요한

002 답 ③

출제 의도 파악하기

①	주어와 동사의 수 일치	②	대명사의 수 일치
③	관계대명사 which의 쓰임	④	형용사의 쓰임
⑤	분사의 태		

정답풀이

③ 뒤에 완전한 구조의 절이 이어지므로 관계대명사 which는 쓸 수 없다. 문맥상 those ~ it의 절이 strong guarantees와 동격 관계를 이루므로 which를 동격 접속사 that으로 바꿔 써야 한다.

오답풀이

① 주어의 핵은 commonality로 단수이므로 단수형 동사 is는 적절하다.
② it은 A prey를 가리키는 목적격 대명사로 적절하게 쓰였다.
④ 「keep+목적어+목적격보어(형용사)」를 수동태로 전환한 형태이므로 형용사 honest는 어법상 적절하다.
⑤ 수식을 받는 information이 '전달되는' 대상이므로 과거분사 communicated는 올바르게 쓰였다.

전문해석

다른 이들이 전달하고 있는 것이 무엇이든지 그것을 받아들이는 것은 그들의 관심사가 우리의 관심사와 일치하는 경우에만 성공하는데, 몸속의 세포, 벌집 속의 벌을 생각해 보라. 인간 간의 의사소통에 관한 한, 관심사의 그러한 공통성은 좀처럼 성취되지 않는데, 심지어 임산부조차도 자신의 태아가 보내는 화학적 신호를 믿지 못할 이유가 있다. 다행스럽게도, 가장 적대적인 관계에서조차도 의사소통이 이루어지게 할 방법들이 있다. 먹잇감은 포식자에게 자신을 쫓지 않도록 설득할 수 있다. 그러나 그러한 의사소통이 일어나기 위해서는 신호를 받는 자들이 그것을 믿는 것이 더 나을 것이라는 강력한 보장이 있어야 한다. 메시지는 전반적으로 정직한 상태로 유지되어야 한다. 인간의 경우에 정직성은 전달된 정보를 평가하는 일련의 인지 기제에 의해 유지된다. 이러한 기제는 우리가 가장 유익한 메시지를 받아들이며(개방적이면서), 반면에 가장 해로운 메시지를 거부할(경계할) 수 있게 해 준다.

구문풀이

10행 But [for such communication to occur], there must be strong guarantees [that those {who receive the signal} will be better off

believing it].

: 첫 번째 [ ]는 목적을 나타내는 to부정사로, for such communication은 to부정사구의 의미상 주어이다. 두 번째 [ ]는 strong guarantees와 동격 관계를 이루는 절로, 그 안의 { }는 those를 수식하는 관계절이다.

어휘풀이

- communicate *v* 전달하다
- correspond to ~와 일치하다, ~에 상응하다
- commonality *n* 공통성
- prey *n* 먹잇감
- predator *n* 포식자
- be better off *doing* ~하는 것이 더 낫다
- on the whole 전반적으로, 대체로
- cognitive *a* 인지의
- evaluate *v* 평가하다
- reject *v* 거부하다
- pay off 성공하다
- pregnant *a* 임신한
- convince *v* 설득하다
- guarantee *n* 보장
- maintain *v* 유지하다
- mechanism *n* 기제
- beneficial *a* 유익한, 이로운

003 답 ①

출제 의도 파악하기

①	문장의 구조 파악	②	to부정사의 쓰임
③	동사의 태	④	부사의 쓰임
⑤	분사의 태		

정답풀이

① 문장의 주어인 the age distribution에 이어지는 본동사가 없는 상태이므로, being ~ changing이 본동사 역할을 하도록 being을 is로 바꿔 써야 한다.

오답풀이

② '~하기에'의 의미로 형용사 insufficient를 수식하는 to부정사구를 이끄는 to maintain은 적절하다.
③ 주어인 Italy's population이 '전망되는' 대상이므로, 수동태 동사 is forecast는 어법상 적절하다.
④ 형용사구 fitter and more active를 수식하므로 부사 generally의 쓰임은 적절하다.
⑤ 수식을 받는 명사 wealth는 '축적되는' 대상이므로 과거분사 accumulated는 적절하게 쓰였다.

전문해석

몇몇 국가들에서 더 짧은 주당 근무 시간, 더 유연한 근무 관행 그리고 더 이른 은퇴 쪽으로의 경향이 있다. 그러나 이것과 결부되어 가처분 소득(세금을 뺀 실질 소득) 증가의 많은 부분을 누리는 국가들에서 연령 분포가 점차 변화하고 있다. 이런 국가들의 인구는 점차 노령화되며, 정말로 많은 국가들에서 재생산 비율이 인구 수준을 유지하는 데 불충분하다. 예를 들어, 이탈리아의 인구는 2050년까지 30퍼센트 감소할 것으로 전망된다. 이 더 노령화된 인구는 은퇴에 도달함에 따라 더 많은 자유 시간을 가지며 이전 세대보다 전반적으로 건강이 더 좋고 더 활동적이다. 이런 특성은 더 많아진 축적된 부와 결합되어 더 많은 관광과 다른 여가 활동을 허용한다. 이것 가운데 일부는 외식하러 이동하거나 스포츠클럽과 같은 지역 휴양지로 이동한다는 면에서 상당히 지방색이 부여되어 있다.

구문풀이

10행 This older population [has more leisure time {as it reaches retirement}] and [is generally fitter and more active than previous generations].

: 두 개의 [ ]는 and로 연결되어 문장의 술어를 이룬다. { }는 시간 부사절로, as는 '~함에 따라'의 의미이다.

어휘풀이

- workweek *n* 주당 근무 시간
- flexible *a* 유연한, 탄력성 있는
- retirement *n* 은퇴
- distribution *n* 분포, 배포
- disposable income 가처분 소득
- indeed *ad* 정말로, 사실은
- reproduction *n* 재생산
- insufficient *a* 불충분한
- forecast *v* 전망하다
- decline *v* 감소하다
- leisure *n* 여가
- previous *a* 이전의
- accumulate *v* 축적하다
- localize *v* 지방색을 부여하다, 한 지방에 한정시키다
- in terms of ~의 측면[관점]에서
- recreational *a* 휴양의

어휘풀이

- resource *n* 자원
- transform *v* 바꾸다
- biology *n* 생명 작용
- courage *n* 용기
- anxiety *n* 불안감
- confidence *n* 자신감
- willingness *n* 기꺼이 하는 마음
- take action 행동에 옮기다
- quicken *v* 빨라지다
- tension *n* 긴장감
- access *n* 이용할 기회, 접근 방법

004 답 ③

출제 의도 파악하기

❶	help의 목적격보어	❷	대명사의 수 일치
❸	문장의 구조 파악	❹	접속사 that의 쓰임
❺	형식상의 주어와 내용상의 주어		

정답풀이

③ When이 이끄는 부사절 다음에 이어지는 주절에서 realizing 뒤에 다른 술어 동사가 없는 상태이다. 따라서 주절이 명령문이 되도록 realizing을 동사원형 realize로 고쳐 써야 한다.

오답풀이

① 동사 help는 목적격보어로 to부정사나 원형부정사를 취하므로 원형부정사 do는 어법상 적절하다.

② 앞에 나온 the stress를 가리키는 목적격 대명사 it은 어법상 적절하다.

④ 뒤에 완전한 구조의 절이 이어지고, remind의 직접목적어 역할을 하는 명사절을 이끌므로 접속사 that은 어법상 적절하다.

⑤ 앞의 it은 형식상의 주어이고 to go on your first date가 내용상의 주어에 해당하므로, to부정사구를 유도하는 to go는 어법상 적절하다.

전문해석

스트레스 반응을 자원으로 보는 것은 두려움이라는 생리 기능을 용기라는 생명 작용으로 바꿀 수 있다. 그것은 위협을 도전으로 바꿀 수 있고 여러분이 압박감 속에서도 최선을 다하도록 도울 수 있다. 불안감의 경우에서처럼 스트레스가 도움이 되지 않는다고 느껴질 때조차 그것을 기꺼이 받아들이는 것은 그것을 도움이 되는 어떤 것, 즉 더 많은 에너지, 더 많은 자신감 그리고 더 기꺼이 행동을 취하려는 마음으로 바꿀 수 있다. 여러분이 스트레스의 징후를 감지할 때마다 이 전략을 여러분 자신의 삶에 적용할 수 있다. 여러분이 심장 박동이나 호흡이 빨라지는 것을 느낄 때 그것은 여러분에게 더 많은 에너지를 주려고 노력하는 여러분 몸의 방식이라는 것을 깨달으라. 여러분의 몸에서 긴장을 감지한다면, 스트레스 반응이 여러분에게 자신의 힘을 이용할 기회를 준다는 것을 상기하라. 손바닥에 땀이 나는가? 여러분이 첫 데이트에 나갔을 때 어떤 기분이었는지를 기억하라. 즉, 여러분이 원하는 어떤 것에 가까이 있을 때 손바닥에 땀이 난다.

구문풀이

4행 Even when the stress doesn't feel helpful—as in the case of anxiety—welcoming it can transform it into something [that is helpful]: more energy, more confidence, and a greater willingness [to take action].

: 첫 번째 [ ]는 something을 수식하는 관계절이며, 두 번째 [ ]는 a greater willingness를 수식하는 to부정사구이다.

005 답 ①

출제 의도 파악하기

❶	주어와 동사의 수 일치	❷	형식상의 주어와 내용상의 주어
❸	접속사 that의 쓰임	❹	동사의 태
❺	부사의 쓰임		

정답풀이

① that major or ~ that they do는 The fact와 동격 관계를 이루는 명사절로, 동사의 수는 핵심 주어 The fact에 일치시켜야 한다. 따라서 form을 단수형 동사 forms로 바꿔 써야 한다.

오답풀이

② because 뒤에 나온 형식상의 주어 it에 대한 내용상의 주어를 이끄는 to부정사 to prevent는 적절하다.

③ 뒤에 완전한 구조의 절이 이어지고, make sure의 목적어 역할을 하는 명사절을 이끌므로 접속사 that은 적절하게 쓰였다.

④ when이 이끄는 부사절에서 주어인 different institutions는 '고려되는' 대상이므로 「take ~ into consideration(~을 고려하다)」을 수동태로 쓴 are taken은 옳다.

⑤ 부사 similarly는 동사 perform을 수식하므로 적절하다.

전문해석

산업체는 조직과 같은 일부 또는 다른 기관 내에서 각각 특정 과업이나 노동을 수행하는 서로 다른 개인들로 구성된다. 개인들 사이에 그리고 그들이 하는 다양한 일들 사이에 주요한 또는 작은 차이가 존재한다는 사실은 그러한 조직이나 기관의 효율적인 기능의 기초를 형성한다. 그것은 또한 '부적임자'의 발생을 방지하는 것이 인사과의 명시적인 과업이기 때문에 그처럼 인사 관리 기능과 밀접하게 연관되어 있다. 다시 말해서, 인사 관리자는 개인의 차이를 염두에 두어야 하며, 모든 개인 또는 직원이 자신의 업무에 적합하고 행복한 것을 보장하기 위해 사람들 사이의 차이점을 충분히 알고 있어야 한다. 여러 다양한 기관들을 고려할 때, 이 과업은 대단히 복잡해진다. 비슷한 유형의 개인들은 동일한 과업을 하면서 비슷하게 수행할 수 있겠지만 그들의 수행은 다른 기관이나 작업 그룹 내에서 다를 것이다.

구문풀이

3행 [The fact {that major or small differences exist between individuals and between the various jobs <that **they** do>}], forms the basis of the efficient functioning of such organizations or institutions.

: [ ]는 문장의 주어이고, 그 안의 { }는 The fact와 동격 관계를 이루는 절이다. < >는 the various jobs를 수식하는 관계절이며, they는 앞에 나온 individuals를 가리킨다.

어휘풀이

- be composed of ~로 구성되다
- institution *n* 기관
- efficient *a* 효율적인
- personnel management 인사 관리
- explicit *a* 명시적인, 뚜렷한
- be mindful of ~을 염두에 두다
- sufficient *a* 충분한
- complicated *a* 복잡한
- take ~ into consideration ~을 고려하다

❶	대명사의 쓰임과 수 일치	❷	to부정사의 쓰임
❸	문장의 구조 파악	❹	전치사+관계대명사
❺	분사의 태		

정답풀이

③ 문장의 주어는 The courage ~, the intelligence ..., and the emotions ~ of이고, 이와 연결되는 술어 동사가 필요하다. 따라서 준동사 being을 본동사 are로 고쳐 써야 한다. the Lion wants, the Scarecrow longs for, the Tin Man dreams of는 각각 앞에 있는 The courage, the intelligence, the emotions를 수식하는 관계절이다.

오답풀이

① to give의 의미상 주어는 the Wizard이고 목적어는 Dorothy and her three friends로 서로 다르므로 to give의 목적어로 them을 쓴 것은 어법상 적절하다.
② the power를 수식하는 to부정사구를 이끄는 to fulfill은 어법상 적절하다.
④ 선행사가 positive ways이고 뒤에 완전한 구조의 절이 이어지고 있으므로, 「전치사+관계대명사」 형태의 in which는 적절하게 쓰였다.
⑤ 수식을 받는 a journey가 '동기가 부여된' 대상이므로 과거분사 motivated는 어법상 적절하다.

전문해석

〈오즈의 마법사〉를 동기 부여에 관한 심리학적 연구로 생각해 보라. Dorothy와 그녀의 세 친구들은 Emerald 시로 가기 위해 열심히 노력하면서 장애물을 극복하고, 모든 적들에게 끈질기게 맞선다. 그들은 마법사가 그들에게 없는 것을 줄 것이라고 기대하기 때문에 그렇게 한다. 대신에, 그 멋진 (그리고 현명한) 마법사는 자신이 아니라 그들이 항상 자신들의 소원을 실현할 힘을 가지고 있었음을 그들이 깨닫도록 한다. Dorothy에게 '집'은 장소가 아니라 그녀가 사랑하는 사람들과 함께하는 안락함, 즉 안전함의 느낌이고, 그녀의 마음이 있는 곳이면 어디든 집인 것이다. 사자가 원하는 용기, 허수아비가 바라는 지성, 그리고 양철 인간이 꿈꾸는 감정은 그들이 이미 가지고 있는 속성들이다. 그들은 이러한 속성들에 대해 내적인 조건이 아니라 이미 자신들이 다른 사람들과 관계를 맺는 긍정적인 방식으로 생각할 필요가 있다. 결국, 그들은 자신들이 원하는 무언가를 얻을 수 있을 것이라는 미래의 가능성에 관한 생각, 즉 어떤 '기대'에 지나지 않는 것에 의해 동기가 부여된 여행인 오즈로 가는 여정에서 그러한 자질들을 보여 주지 않았는가?

구문풀이

2행 Dorothy and her three friends work hard [to get to the Emerald City], [overcoming barriers], [persisting against all adversaries].

: 첫 번째 [ ]는 목적을 나타내는 to부정사구이고, 두 번째와 세 번째 [ ]는 Dorothy and her three friends를 의미상의 주어로 하는 분사구문이다.

어휘풀이

- motivation *n* 동기 부여
- barrier *n* 장벽, 장애(물)
- fulfill *v* 실현하다, 성취하다
- scarecrow *n* 허수아비
- possess *v* 가지고 있다, 소유하다
- relate *v* 관계를 맺다
- little more than ~에 지나지 않는
- overcome *v* 극복하다
- persist *v* 끈질기게 계속하다
- security *n* 안전, 안정
- attribute *n* 속성
- internal *a* 내적인
- demonstrate *v* 보여 주다
- likelihood *n* 가능성

---

02 동사의 활용

본문 pp.014 ~ 017

Q1 **1** should have paid **2** try **3** was asked **4** was
   5 to cancel

Q2 **1** must have painted **2** monitored
   3 was referred to as **4** criticized

---

007 ②　　**008** ④　　**009** ⑤　　**010** ③　　**011** ③

012 ①

Q1

1. 풀이 문맥상 과거의 일에 대한 후회나 유감을 나타내므로 「should have p.p.」가 알맞다.

　해석 나는 그에게 거의 주의를 기울이지 않았던 것을 후회한다. 다시 말해서, 나는 그에게 더 많은 주의를 기울였어야 했다.

2. 풀이 주장을 뜻하는 동사 insisted가 쓰였으며, 당위의 의미를 나타내므로 that 절의 동사로는 (should) try가 알맞다.

　해석 Tara는 내게 자신의 안경을 써 보라고 고집했다. 그래서 나는 안경을 썼고, 세상이 흐릿한 모양으로 변해 버렸다.

3. 풀이 주어인 I가 '요청받는' 대상이므로 수동태인 was asked가 알맞다.

　해석 우리 학급에서 가장 총명한 일원이어서, 나는 학교 행사를 위해 꽤 긴 시를 암송해 달라는 요청을 받았다.

4. 풀이 suggested가 '제안했다'라는 당위의 뜻이 아니라 '암시했다'라는 뜻으로 쓰였으므로 that절의 동사는 that절 주어의 수와 시제가 반영된 was가 알맞다.

　해석 Emily의 소지품은 그녀가 내과의사임을 암시했다.

5. 풀이 사역동사 made의 목적격보어였던 원형부정사 cancel은 수동태 문장에서 to부정사가 되어야 하므로 to cancel이 알맞다.

　해석 정부는 여론 때문에 그 계획을 취소하게 되었다.

Q2

1. 풀이 과거 사실에 대한 확신을 나타내므로 「must have p.p.」 형태로 고쳐 써야 한다.

　해석 Henry의 아버지는 주택 도장공이었다. 평생 동안 그는 수백 채의 집 안팎을 칠했음에 틀림없다.

2. 풀이 뇌 활동은 '추적 관찰되는' 대상이므로 수동태가 되어야 한다.

　해석 지원자들이 고전 작품들을 읽을 때 그들의 뇌 활동이 추적 관찰될 것이다.

3. 풀이 「refer to ~ as ...(~을 ...라고 부르다)」의 수동태 문장이므로 be referred to as의 어순으로 써야 한다.

　해석 그 프로젝트는 그 업계에서 획기적인 성과로 불렸다.

4. 풀이 선행사 A child를 수식하는 주격 관계대명사절 동사의 태를 묻는 것으로, 문맥상 A child가 '비판받는' 대상이므로 수동태가 되어야 한다.

　해석 수학에서 부진한 (학업) 성취로 반복해서 비판을 받아 온 아이는 더 이상의 처벌을 피하기 위해 어려운 수학 문제를 이리저리 피하는 방법을 배우게 될 수도 있다.

007 답 ②

출제 의도 파악하기

❶ 동사의 태	❷ 문장의 구조 파악
❸ 병렬구조	❹ 관계대명사 that의 쓰임
❺ 접속사 whether의 쓰임	

정답풀이

② 문맥상 문장의 술어 동사는 requires이므로 Learn ~ a decision은 주어 역할을 해야 한다. Learn은 주어부를 이끌 수 없으므로 동명사 Learning이나 to부정사 To Learn으로 고쳐 써야 한다.

오답풀이

① 주격 관계대명사 that의 선행사는 several actions이고, 이는 '평가되는' 대상이므로 수동태 동사 be evaluated는 어법상 적절하다.
③ rely on과 or로 연결되어 to에 이어져서 「의문사+to부정사」 구문을 이루므로 have는 어법상 적절하다.
④ 이어지는 절에서 create의 주어 역할을 하면서 앞에 있는 명사구 gray areas를 수식하는 관계절을 유도하는 주격 관계대명사 that은 알맞다.
⑤ 「whether+to부정사」는 '~할 것인지 (아닌지)'라는 뜻으로 decide의 목적어로 적절하게 쓰였다.

전문해석

윤리적 문제를 인식하는 것은 비즈니스 윤리를 이해하는 데 있어 가장 중요한 단계이다. 윤리적 문제는 옳거나 그르다고, 윤리적이거나 비윤리적이라고 평가될 수 있는 여러 가지 행동들 중에서 한 사람이 선택해야 하는 식별 가능한 문제, 상황 또는 기회이다. 대안들로부터 선택하고 결정을 내리는 방법을 배우는 것은 훌륭한 개인적 가치관뿐만 아니라 관련된 비즈니스 분야에서의 지식 역량도 필요하다. 직원들은 또한 언제 자신이 속한 조직의 정책과 윤리 강령에 의존해야 할지 또는 언제 적절한 행동에 관해 동료나 관리자와 논의해야 할지를 알 필요가 있다. 윤리적 의사 결정이 항상 쉬운 것은 아닌데, 왜냐하면 결정이 어떻게 내려지든 딜레마를 만드는 애매한 부분이 항상 있기 때문이다. 예를 들어, 직원은 시간 훔치기(일하지 않은 시간에 대해 보상을 받는 행위)를 하는 동료에 대해 보고해야 하는가? 판매원은 고객에게 (상품을) 제시할 때 어떤 제품의 안전 상태가 좋지 않다는 기록에 대한 사실을 생략해야 하는가? 그러한 질문들은 의사 결정자가 자신이 한 선택의 윤리를 평가하여 지침을 요청할 것인지 결정할 것을 요구한다.

구문풀이

2행 An ethical issue is an identifiable problem, situation, or opportunity [that requires a person to choose from among several actions {that may be evaluated as right or wrong, ethical or unethical}].

: [ ]는 an identifiable problem, situation, or opportunity를 수식하는 관계절이고, 그 안의 { }는 several actions를 수식하는 관계절이다.

19행 Such questions require the decision maker [to {evaluate the ethics of his or her choice} and {decide whether to ask for guidance}].

: [ ]는 require의 목적격보어 역할을 하는 to부정사구이고, 그 안의 두 개의 { }가 and로 연결되어 to에 이어진다.

어휘풀이

- ethical *a* 윤리적인
- ethics *n* 윤리
- identifiable *a* 식별 가능한
- evaluate *v* 평가하다
- alternative *n* 대안
- competence *n* 역량
- policy *n* 정책
- dilemma *n* 딜레마, 진퇴양난
- engage in ~을 하다, ~에 관여하다

- time theft 시간 훔치기(일하지 않은 시간에 대해 보상을 받는 행위)
- guidance *n* 지도, 안내

008 답 ④

출제 의도 파악하기

❶ to부정사의 쓰임	❷ 부사의 쓰임
❸ 관계대명사 which의 쓰임	❹ 수동태 문장에 쓰인 지각동사의 목적격보어
❺ 접속사 that의 쓰임	

정답풀이

④ 「지각동사+목적어+목적격보어(원형부정사)」가 수동태로 전환되면, 목적격보어로 쓰인 원형부정사는 to부정사로 바뀐다. 따라서 능동태 have seen chimpanzees take care of ~가 수동태로 전환된 형태이므로 take를 to take로 바꿔 써야 한다.

오답풀이

① assume의 목적어로 쓰인 명사절에서 동사 is에 대한 주어 역할을 하는 to부정사구를 이끄는 to be는 알맞다.
② to ensure를 수식하는 부사 successfully는 적절하다.
③ 앞 절의 내용을 부연 설명하는 관계절을 이끄는 계속적 용법의 주격 관계대명사 which는 적절하게 쓰였다.
⑤ 「given that ~」은 '~을 고려하면'의 의미로, that은 접속사로서 뒤에 완전한 구조의 절이 이어진다. 여기서도 뒤에 주어(chimpanzees)와 동사(live)를 갖춘 완전한 구조의 절이 이어지므로 접속사 that은 적절하다.

전문해석

사람들이나 집단이 서로에게 잔인하게 보일 때마다 널리 퍼져 있는 부적당한 관점은 이것이 '적자생존'에 대한 하나의 예라는 것이다. 많은 사람들은 자연에서뿐만 아니라 사회에서도 강하고 공격적인 것이 생존을 위한 유일한 조건이라고 잘못 가정하고 있다. 그러나 사실 진화는 생물들이 그들의 생존을 성공적으로 보장하기 위해서 단지 잔인함만이 아닌 모든 종류의 다른 행동을 보여 줄 것을 요구한다. 침팬지나 보노보와 같은 우리의 가장 가까운 종족들을 포함한 많은 동물들은 생존을 위해서 서로에게 의존하는데, 이것은 배려해 주고 동정적인 행동이 그들의 진화에서 핵심적인 요소 중 하나라는 것을 의미한다. 예를 들어, Ivory Coast의 Tai 국립공원에서 침팬지들이 피와 먼지를 조심스럽게 제거하고 상처 근처에 모이는 파리를 손을 흔들어 쫓음으로써 표범에 의해 상처를 입은 집단의 동료들을 돌보는 것이 목격되었다. 그것들은 부상당한 동료들을 보호하고, 그것들이 (무리를) 따라오지 못하면 천천히 이동한다. 침팬지가 늑대, 돌고래, 인간처럼 집단 속에서 생활한다는 점을 감안하면 이 모든 것은 완벽히 이치에 들어맞는다.

구문풀이

3행 Many people wrongly assume [that, {in society **as well as** in nature}, {to be strong and aggressive} is the only condition for survival].

: [ ]는 동사 assume의 목적어로 쓰인 명사절이다. 첫 번째 { }는 명사절 안에 삽입된 부사구로, 「A as well as B(B뿐만 아니라 A도)」 구문이 쓰였다. to부정사구인 두 번째 { }가 that절의 주어이며 is가 that절의 동사이다.

어휘풀이

- cruel *a* 잔인한
- inadequate *a* 부적당한
- survival of the fittest 적자생존
- assume *v* 가정하다
- aggressive *a* 공격적인
- evolution *n* 진화, 발전
- a whole range of 모든 종류의
- cruelty *n* 잔인함

- ensure ⓥ 보장하다
- sympathetic ⓐ 동정의
- leopard ⓝ 표범
- relative ⓝ 동족, 친척
- wound ⓥ 부상을 입히다 ⓝ 상처
- make sense 이치에 맞다

- regulate ⓥ 규제하다
- astronomy ⓝ 천문학
- passage ⓝ 흐름, 지나감, 통과
- predictability ⓝ 예측 가능성
- solstice ⓝ [천문] 지점(至點)(태양이 적도로부터 북쪽 또는 남쪽으로 가장 치우쳤을 때)
- equinox ⓝ [천문] 분점(分點)
- agricultural ⓐ 농업의
- formal ⓐ 공식적인
- regularity ⓝ 규칙성
- inhabit ⓥ 살다, 서식하다
- immediate ⓐ 즉각적인, 눈앞에 있는

009 답 ⑤

출제 의도 파악하기

①	대명사의 수 일치	②	주어와 동사의 수 일치
③	관계부사 where의 쓰임	④	동사의 태
⑤	병렬구조		

정답풀이

⑤ the ability of the human mind를 수식하는 to부정사구 to see ~ appearances와 and에 의해 병렬구조를 이루는 자리이다. 따라서 discovers는 적절하지 않으며, to부정사의 to가 생략된 discover로 바꿔 써야 한다. to 부정사(구)가 병렬구조를 이룰 때 뒤에 오는 to는 생략할 수 있다.

오답풀이

① 복수 명사인 humans를 가리키므로 소유격 대명사 their는 알맞다.
② 주어인 Stonehenge에 연결되는 동사 is는 알맞다. the 4,000-year-old ring of stones in southern Britain은 주어인 Stonehenge를 부연 설명하는 동격어구이다.
③ 뒤에 「주어(the sun)+동사(rises)+부사구(at the solstices and equinoxes)」를 갖춘 완전한 구조의 절이 왔으므로, the spots on the horizon을 수식하는 관계절을 이끄는 관계부사 where는 알맞다.
④ 주어인 The stones가 '사용되는' 대상이므로, 완료형 「have p.p.」와 결합된 수동태 been used는 알맞다.

전문해석

대부분의 과학 역사가들은 별과 행성에 대한 연구, 즉 우리가 현재 천문학이라 부르는 것에 관해 배우려는 동기로 농업 활동을 규제하기 위한 믿을 만한 달력의 필요성을 지적한다. 초기 천문학은 언제 작물을 심을지에 관한 정보를 제공했으며 인간에게 시간의 흐름을 기록하는 그들 최초의 공식적인 방법을 제공했다. 영국 남부에 있는 4,000년 된 고리 모양을 하고 있는 돌들인 Stonehenge(스톤헨지)는 아마도 우리가 사는 세계에서 규칙성과 예측 가능성 발견에 있어 가장 잘 알려진 기념비일 것이다. Stonehenge의 커다란 표식은 우리가 계절의 시작을 표시하기 위해 여전히 사용하는 날짜인 지점(至點)과 분점(分點)에서 태양이 뜨는 지평선의 지점을 가리킨다. 그 돌들은 심지어 (해·달의) 식(蝕)을 예측하는 데 사용되었을 수도 있다. 글자가 없었던 사람들에 의해 세워진 Stonehenge의 존재는 자연의 규칙성뿐만 아니라 즉각적인 겉모습의 이면을 보고 사건에서 더 깊은 의미를 발견할 수 있는 인간의 정신적 능력 또한 말없이 증언한다.

구문풀이

1행 Most historians of science point to the need for a reliable calendar [to regulate agricultural activity as the motivation for {learning about what we now call astronomy, <the study of stars and planets>}].

: [ ]는 a reliable calendar를 수식하는 to부정사구이며, 그 안의 { }는 전치사 for의 목적어로 쓰인 동명사구이다. 〈 〉는 astronomy와 동격 관계를 이루는 어구이다.

4행 Early astronomy [provided information about {when to plant crops}] and [gave humans {their first formal method of recording the passage of time}].

: 문장의 주어인 Early astronomy에 두 개의 동사구 [ ]가 병렬구조로 연결되었다. 첫 번째 { }는 전치사 about의 목적어로 쓰인 명사구(의문사+to부정사)이고, 두 번째 { }는 동사 gave의 직접목적어로 쓰인 명사구이다.

010 답 ③

출제 의도 파악하기

①	전치사+관계대명사	②	의문사 what의 쓰임
③	대동사	④	접속사 that의 쓰임
⑤	동사의 태		

정답풀이

③ 반복되는 일반동사 gives in을 대신하는 대동사 자리이므로, be동사가 아니라 do동사를 써야 한다. 따라서 is를 does로 바꿔 써야 한다.

오답풀이

① 뒤에 완전한 구조의 절이 이어지고 있고, the formal institution을 선행사로 하는 관계대명사 which가 전치사 through의 목적어로 쓰여 관계절에서 부사구 역할을 하고 있으므로 「전치사+관계대명사」 형태의 through which는 어법상 적절하게 쓰였다.
② 전치사 of의 목적어 역할을 하는 절을 이끌며 이어지는 절에서 주어 역할을 하는 의문사 what은 적절하다.
④ 뒤에 완전한 구조의 절이 이어지며, 문맥상 앞의 명사 trust와 동격을 이루는 명사절을 이끌므로 접속사 that의 쓰임은 적절하다.
⑤ if절의 핵심 주어인 the interests and perspectives가 '맞춰지는' 대상이므로 be동사 are와 함께 수동태를 이루는 과거분사 aligned는 적절하다.

전문해석

나는 국가의 문제가 해결되려면 국가가 어떻게 함께, 협력하여 행동해야 할지 강조해 왔다. 정부는 국가의 문제를 해결하기 위해 우리가 함께, 공동으로 행동하는 공식적인 기관이다. 불가피하게, 개인들마다 무엇이 이뤄져야 하는지에 대한 견해가 다르기 마련이다. 그것이 집단적인 행동이 매우 어려운 이유 중 하나이다. 거기에는 타협이 필요하며 타협은 신뢰에 근거해야 한다. 즉, 그것은 다른 집단이 다른 해에는 양보할 것이라는 이해 속에서 한 집단이 오늘 양보한다는 신뢰이다. 모든 것이 공정하게 처리될 것이라는 신뢰가 있어야 하며, 만약 어떤 정책의 지지자들이 나타날 것이라고 주장하는 방식과 다르게 일들이 나타난다면 그 예상치 못한 상황에 맞추기 위한 변화가 있게 된다. 하지만 집단의 구성원들이 가진 이해와 견해가 최소한 느슨하게라도 맞추어져 있다면, 말하자면 모두가 같은 배를 탔다면, 함께 행동하는 것은 더 쉽다.

구문풀이

11행 There must be trust [that all will be treated fairly], and if matters turn out differently from [how the proponents of a measure claim it **will**], there will be change [to accommodate the unexpected circumstances].

: 첫 번째 [ ]는 trust와 동격 관계를 이루는 절이다. 두 번째 [ ]는 전치사 from의 목적어이며, will 다음에는 turn out이 생략되었다. 세 번째 [ ]는 change를 수식하는 to부정사구이다.

어휘풀이

- cooperatively ⓐⓓ 협력하여
- inevitably ⓐⓓ 불가피하게
- institution ⓝ 기관
- compromise ⓝ 타협, 절충

- give in (마지못해) 동의하다[받아들이다], 양보하다
- proponent *n* 지지자, 찬성자
- accommodate *v* (환경 등에) 맞추다, 수용하다
- align *v* 맞추다, 협력[제휴]하다
- measure *n* 조치, 정책
- as it were 말하자면, 이를테면

011 답 ③

출제 의도 파악하기
❶ 주어와 동사의 수 일치	❷ 부사의 쓰임
❸ 문장의 구조 파악	❹ 의문사 how의 쓰임
❺ 동사의 태	

정답풀이

③ to assume의 목적어 역할을 하는 that절에서 주어 anyone who sees an object에 연결되는 술어 동사가 없는 상태이다. 따라서 준동사인 seeing을 본동사인 sees로 고쳐 써야 한다.

오답풀이

① 주어의 핵은 parts이므로 복수형 동사 get의 쓰임은 적절하다.
② 형용사인 sensitive를 수식하므로 부사 extremely를 쓴 것은 적절하다.
④ 이어지는 절이 완전한 구조를 이루고 있고, to imagine의 목적어 역할을 하는 의문사절을 이끌고 있으므로 의문사 how는 적절하게 쓰였다.
⑤ 주어인 it(= an object)이 '움직이는' 주체이므로 is와 함께 능동태를 이루는 현재분사 moving은 적절하다.

전문해석

뇌 시각 체계의 다양한 부분들은 꼭 필요한 때 꼭 필요한 것만 알려주는 방식으로 정보를 얻는다. 여러분의 손 근육이 어떤 물체에 닿을 수 있도록 돕는 세포들은 그 물체의 크기와 위치를 알아야 하지만 색깔에 대해서는 알 필요가 없다. 그 세포들은 모양에 대해 약간 알아야 하지만 매우 자세히는 아니다. 여러분이 사람들의 얼굴을 인식하도록 돕는 세포들은 모양의 세부 사항에 극도로 예민해야 할 필요가 있지만, 위치에는 신경을 덜 쓸 수 있다. 어떤 물체를 보는 사람은 누구나 모양, 색깔, 위치, 움직임 같이 그것에 관한 모든 것을 보고 있다고 추정하는 것은 당연하다. 하지만 여러분 뇌의 한 부분은 그것의 모양을 보고, 다른 한 부분은 색깔을 보며, 다른 한 부분은 위치를 감지하고, 또 다른 한 부분은 움직임을 인식한다. 따라서 국부적 뇌 손상 후에 물체의 특정한 측면들은 볼 수 있으면서 다른 측면들은 볼 수 없는 것이 가능하다. 수 세기 전에 사람들은 어떻게 누군가가 어떤 색깔인지 보지 못하면서 그 물체를 볼 수 있는지 상상하기가 어려웠다. 심지어 오늘날에도, 여러분은 물체가 어디에 있는지 보지 못하면서 그것을 보거나 그것이 움직이고 있는지 보지 못하면서 그것을 보는 사람들에 대해 알게 되면 놀라워할지도 모른다.

구문풀이

18행 Even today, you might find **it** surprising [to learn about people {who see an object without seeing <where it is>, or see it without seeing <whether it is moving>}].

: it은 find의 형식상의 목적어이며 to부정사구인 [ ]가 내용상의 목적어이다. { }는 people을 수식하는 관계절이고, 두 개의 < >는 모두 명사절로, 각각 앞에 있는 seeing의 목적어 역할을 한다.

어휘풀이

- visual *a* 시각의
- on a need-to-know basis 꼭 필요한 때 꼭 필요한 것만 알려주는 방식으로
- cell *n* 세포
- in detail 상세하게
- sensitive *a* 예민한
- detect *v* 감지하다
- localized *a* 국부적인
- muscle *n* 근육
- extremely *ad* 극도로
- assume *v* 추정하다
- consequently *ad* 따라서
- aspect *n* 측면

012 답 ①

출제 의도 파악하기
❶ 관계대명사 which의 쓰임	❷ 주어와 동사의 수 일치
❸ 부사의 쓰임	❹ 동명사의 쓰임
❺ 대동사	

정답풀이

① 이어지는 절을 보면 완전한 구조를 이루는 두 개의 등위절이 and로 연결되어 있다. 따라서 관계대명사 which는 적절하지 않고, performance showcases를 선행사로 하는 관계부사 where를 써야 한다.

오답풀이

② 핵심 주어는 The provision이므로 단수형 동사 is의 쓰임은 적절하다.
③ not necessarily는 '반드시 ~은 아닌'이라는 부분 부정을 나타내고, not necessarily와 excellence 사이에 demonstrating이 생략된 것으로 볼 수 있다. 따라서 동명사 demonstrating을 수식하는 부사 necessarily는 적절하다.
④ 「see A as B(A를 B로 간주하다)」 구문에서 전치사 as의 목적어 역할을 하는 동명사구를 이끄는 fostering은 적절하다.
⑤ 바로 앞에 나온 일반동사구 win or place를 대신하는 대동사를 써야 하는데, 주격 관계대명사절의 동사는 선행사에 수를 일치시키므로 복수형 those에 수를 일치시킨 do는 적절하다.

전문해석

경쟁을 벌이는 활동은, 최고는 인정받고 나머지는 무시되는, 단지 수행 기량을 보여 주는 공개 행사 그 이상일 수 있다. 참가자들에게 수행 기량에 대한 시기적절하고 건설적인 피드백을 제공하는 것은 일부 대회와 경연이 제공하는 자산이다. 어떤 의미에서는 모든 대회가 피드백을 제공한다. 많은 경우에 이것은 참가자가 수상자인지에 대한 정보에 제한된다. 그런 유형의 피드백을 제공하는 것은 반드시 탁월함은 아닌, 보다 뛰어난 수행 기량을 보여 주는 것으로 강조점을 이동하는 것으로 해석될 수 있다. 최고의 대회는 단지 이기는 것이나 다른 사람을 '패배시키는 것'만이 아니라 탁월함을 장려한다. 우월함에 대한 강조는 우리가 일반적으로 유해한 경쟁 효과를 조장하는 것이라고 간주하는 것이다. 수행 기량에 대한 피드백은 프로그램이 '이기거나 입상하거나 보여 주는' 수준의 피드백을 넘어설 것을 요구한다. 수행 기량에 관한 정보는 이기지 못하거나 입상하지 못하는 참가자에게뿐만 아니라 이기거나 입상하는 참가자에게도 매우 유용할 수 있다.

구문풀이

15행 Performance feedback **requires** [that the program **go** beyond the "win, place, or show" level of feedback].

: 요구를 나타내는 동사(requires)가 이끄는 that절에 당위성이 나타나 있으면 동사로 「(should)+동사원형」을 쓴다. 여기서도 that절에 should가 생략된 동사원형 go가 쓰였다.

어휘풀이

- showcase *n* (사람의 재능·사물의 장점 등을 알리는) 공개 행사
- overlook *v* 무시하다, 간과하다
- provision *n* 제공, 공급
- timely *a* 시기적절한
- constructive *a* 건설적인
- asset *n* 자산, 재산
- restrict *v* 제한[한정]하다
- interpret *v* 해석하다, 이해하다
- emphasis *n* 강조(점), 중점
- demonstrate *v* 분명히 보여 주다, 입증하다
- promote *v* 촉진하다, 증진시키다
- superiority *n* 우월, 월등

Q1 **1** Giving **2** being **3** have been built **4** playing **5** to stop

Q2 **1** to participate **2** choosing **3** keeping **4** to hatch

013 ④　　**014** ②　　**015** ④　　**016** ④　　**017** ③

018 ④

Q1

1. 풀이 ┃ 문장의 동사인 accelerates와 목적어인 progress가 있고, 이에 대한 주어를 묻는 것이므로 주어 역할을 할 수 있는 동명사 Giving이 알맞다. 주어부에 「give+간접목적어(people)+직접목적어(the latitude ~ talents)」 구조가 쓰인 것이다.

해석 ┃ 사람들에게 그들의 판단력을 사용하고 그들의 재능을 적용할 수 있는 자유와 융통성을 주는 것은 발전을 빠르게 가속화시킨다.

2. 풀이 ┃ 문장에 본동사 is가 있으므로 접속사 없이 are는 올 수 없으며 전치사 about의 목적어 역할을 하는 동명사 being이 와야 한다. 여기서 their children은 동명사의 의미상 주어이다.

해석 ┃ 더 중요한 것은 자녀들이 이기는 팀에 속하는 것에 대한 부모들의 관심의 엄청난 증가이다.

3. 풀이 ┃ to부정사가 본동사보다 앞선 일을 나타내므로 to부정사의 시제는 완료형인 「to have p.p.」가 되어야 한다.

해석 ┃ 거의 알려진 바가 없는 이 교회는 이미 15세기 말에 지어졌다고 몇몇 사람들에 의해 믿어진다.

4. 풀이 ┃ 「when it comes to ~」는 '~에 관해 말하자면'의 뜻이다. 여기서 to는 전치사이므로 뒤에 명사(구) 또는 동명사(구)가 온다.

해석 ┃ 이 기타를 치는 것으로 말하자면 그가 최고다.

5. 풀이 ┃ advise는 목적격보어로 to부정사를 취하는 동사이다.

해석 ┃ Taylor는 내게 그러한 계획을 수행하는 것에 대해 생각하는 것을 멈추라고 충고했다.

Q2

1. 풀이 ┃ it은 make의 형식상의 목적어이고 for teachers 이하가 내용상의 목적어에 해당한다. 따라서 for teachers를 의미상의 주어로 하는 to부정사 형태인 to participate로 고쳐 써야 한다.

해석 ┃ 저희는 선생님들께서 귀교의 일정에 맞추어 편리한 시간에 심폐 소생술 교육에 참여하기 쉽게 해드립니다.

2. 풀이 ┃ 전치사 by의 목적어 역할을 하는 동시에 뒤에 이어지는 only ~ courses를 목적어로 취해야 하므로 동명사 choosing으로 고쳐 써야 한다.

해석 ┃ 각 참가자는 다음의 코스 중 하나만 선택하여 기부 목표를 정해야 한다.

3. 풀이 ┃ 「objection to ~」는 '~에 대한 반대'라는 뜻으로, 이때 to는 전치사이므로 목적어로 쓰이기 위해서는 동명사 keeping으로 고쳐 써야 한다.

해석 ┃ 자녀를 집에서 있게 하는 것을 반대하는 한 가지 이유는 자녀들이 다른 아이들과 어울리는 것을 배우지 못할 것이라는 점이다.

4. 풀이 ┃ 문맥상 '부화하기 위해서'라는 목적의 의미를 나타내야 하므로 to부정사인 to hatch로 고쳐 써야 한다.

해석 ┃ 그 사실들 중 하나는 알을 부화하기 위해서는 공룡의 체온이 공기보다 높아야 했다는 것이다.

013　답 ④

출제 의도 │ 파악하기
❶ 접속사 whether의 쓰임　　❷ 분사구문의 태
❸ 재귀대명사　　❹ 관계대명사 which의 쓰임
❺ 형식상의 주어와 내용상의 주어

정답풀이

④ 뒤에 완전한 구조의 절이 이어지고 있으므로 관계대명사 which는 쓸 수 없으며, 문맥상 앞에 있는 the signs와 동격 관계를 이루는 절을 이끌도록 접속사 that으로 바꿔 써야 한다.

오답풀이

① 뒤에 완전한 구조의 절이 이어지고 있고, 목적어로 쓰인 세 개의 to부정사구(to have seen ~, to have heard ~, to have been ~)가 or로 연결되어 「Whether A, B or C(A이든 B이든 C이든)」 구문을 이루고 있으므로 접속사 Whether는 적절하다.
② 문장의 주어인 some people을 의미상의 주어로 하는 분사구문으로, 주어가 '~하는 척하는' 주체이므로 능동의 의미를 나타내는 현재분사 pretending은 알맞게 쓰였다.
③ 문맥상 '스스로에게 납득시킨다'는 의미로, convince의 주어와 목적어가 Narcissists로 동일하다. 따라서 재귀대명사 themselves는 알맞다.
⑤ 앞에 있는 it이 형식상의 주어이고 to pull 이하가 내용상의 주어인 to부정사구로, to pull은 적절하게 쓰였다.

전문해석

사람들은 때때로 긍정적인 시각으로 그들 자신을 그리려고 정말로 노력한다. 그들이 가상의 텔레비전 쇼에서 우주 아기를 보았거나 존재하지 않는 사람들에 대해 들어본 척을 했든, 또는 자신이 더 중요해 보이도록 하기 위해 바쁜 척을 했든, 사람들은 여러분이 그들을 어떻게 생각하는지에 대해 엉망으로 만들려고 할 것이다. 게다가, 어떤 사람들은 중요한 척하며 다른 사람들보다 이런 행동을 더 하기 쉽다. 나르시시스트들은 심지어 자신들의 변명이 사실이라고 스스로를 어떻게든 납득시키곤 한다. 하지만 희망은 있다. 여러분은 쉽게 속일 수 있는 정체성에 대한 주장과 속이기 어려운 행동 잔여물 간의 불일치와 같은, 누군가가 여러분을 속이려고 한다는 표시에 주의를 기울일 수 있다. 덧붙여, 연구는 사람들이 대개 자신을 거짓된 시각으로 묘사하기를 원하지 않는다는 것을 보여 준다. 그들은 약간 과장할 수도 있지만, 과장할 여지는 많지 않고, 큰 속임수를 부리기는 매우 어렵다.

구문풀이

2행 [**Whether** they are pretending {to have seen the space baby on a fictitious television show}, {to have heard of nonexistent people}, **or** {to have been busy to make themselves appear more important}], people are going to try to mess with [how you think of them].

: 첫 번째 [ ]는 「Whether A, B or C」 구문으로, 'A이든 B이든 C이든'의 의미를 나타낸다. 세 개의 to부정사구 { }가 or로 병렬 연결되어 동사 are pretending에 이어진다. 두 번째 [ ]는 전치사 with의 목적어로 쓰인 명사절이다.

- **light** *n* 관점, 시각
- **mess** *v* 엉망으로 만들다
- **manage to** *do* 간신히 ~하다
- **at hand** 가까운, 머지않아
- **fake** *v* 위조하다, ~인 척하다
- **behavioral** *a* 행동의, 행동에 관한
- **portray** *v* 묘사하다
- **pull off** ~을 성사시키다
- **fictitious** *a* 허구의, 지어낸
- **be prone to** ~하기 쉽다
- **convince** *v* 확신[납득]시키다
- **discrepancy** *n* 불일치, 모순
- **identity** *n* 정체성
- **fool** *v* 속이다, 기만하다
- **exaggerate** *v* 과장하다
- **deception** *n* 속임수, 기만

014 답 ②

출제 의도 파악하기

① 분사구문	② 관계대명사 which의 쓰임
③ 강조의 do	④ 지시대명사 that
⑤ judge의 목적격보어	

정답풀이

② 뒤에 주어(they), 동사(have), 목적어(some difficulty)를 모두 갖춘 완전한 구조의 절이 이어지고 있으므로 관계대명사 which는 쓸 수 없다. 문맥상 관계절에서 with gestures의 전치사구 역할을 하도록 「전치사+관계대명사」 형태의 with which로 고쳐 써야 한다.

오답풀이

① 완전한 구조의 절 다음에 접속사나 관계사 없이 이어지는 것으로 보아, seeming 이하는 분사구문임을 알 수 있다. infants를 의미상의 주어로 하면서 이를 부가적으로 설명하는 분사구문을 이끄는 seeming은 알맞게 쓰였다.
③ 일반동사 succeed의 의미를 강조하는 조동사 do는 어법상 적절하다.
④ bodily movements를 대신하는 지시대명사 those는 어법상 적절하다.
⑤ 동사 judge는 목적격보어로 to부정사를 취하므로 to부정사 to be는 어법상 적절하다.

전문해석

많은 연구들이 사회적 자극에 차별적으로 반응하는 타고난 인간의 성향에 대한 상당한 증거를 제공한다. 태어날 때부터 아기들은 사람의 얼굴과 목소리 쪽으로 우선하여 향하게 되는데, 이러한 자극이 특히 그들에게 의미가 있다는 것을 알고 있는 것 같다. 게다가, 그들은 혀 내밀기, 입술 다물기, 입 벌리기와 같이 그들에게 보여지는 다양한 얼굴 제스처를 모방하면서 이러한 연결을 적극적으로 마음속에 새긴다. 심지어 그들은 자신들이 다소 어려워하는 제스처에 맞추려고 노력할 것이고, 성공할 때까지 자기 자신의 얼굴로 실험할 것이다. 정말로 성공하면 그들은 눈을 반짝이면서 기쁨을 보여 주고, 실패하면 괴로움을 보여 준다. 다시 말해, 그들은 운동감각적으로 경험한 그들 자신의 신체적 움직임과 시각적으로 지각되는 다른 사람들의 신체적 움직임을 일치시키는 타고난 능력을 가지고 있을 뿐만 아니라, 그렇게 하려는 타고난 욕구도 가지고 있다. 즉, 그들은 자신들이 '나와 비슷하다'라고 판단하는 다른 사람들을 모방하려는 타고난 욕구가 있는 것 같다.

구문풀이

14행 In other words, they **not only** have an innate capacity [for **matching** their own kinaesthetically experienced bodily movements **with those** of others {that are visually perceived}]; they have an innate drive [to do so].

: 「not only A but also B(A뿐만 아니라 B도)」 구문이 쓰였는데, 여기서는 세미콜론(;)이 but also를 대신하고 있다. 첫 번째 [ ]는 an innate capacity를 수식하는 전치사구이고, 그 안의 { }는 those of others를 수식하는 관계절이다. 「match A with B(A와 B를 일치시키다)」 구문이 쓰였으며, those는 bodily movements를 대신한다. 두 번째 [ ]는 an innate drive를 수식하는 to부정사구이다.

18행 That is, they seem to have an innate drive [to imitate others {whom they judge to be 'like me'}].

: [ ]는 an innate drive를 수식하는 to부정사구이고, 그 안의 { }는 others를 수식하는 관계절이다.

- **substantial** *a* 상당한
- **differentially** *ad* 차별적으로
- **orient** *v* 향하다
- **register** *v* 마음속에 새기다, 명심하다
- **imitate** *v* 모방하다
- **protrusion** *n* 내밀기
- **distress** *n* 고통, 괴로움
- **visually** *ad* 시각적으로
- **drive** *n* 욕구
- **evidence** *n* 증거
- **stimulus** *n* 자극 (*pl.* stimuli)
- **preferentially** *ad* 우선적으로
- **actively** *ad* 적극적으로
- **a variety of** 다양한
- **experiment** *v* 실험하다
- **capacity** *n* 능력
- **perceive** *v* 지각[인지]하다
- **judge** *v* 판단하다

015 답 ④

출제 의도 파악하기

① 관계대명사 who의 쓰임	② 대명사의 수 일치
③ to부정사의 쓰임	④ 문장의 구조 파악
⑤ 주어와 동사의 수 일치	

정답풀이

④ 뒤에 주어(contested elections of directors), 동사(are), 보어(rare)로 이루어진 완전한 구조의 절이 이어지므로 관계대명사나 의문사로 쓰이는 what은 적절하지 않다. 문맥상 대시(—)로 묶인 부분 앞의 so numerous와 함께 「so ~ that ....」 구문을 이루어 '매우 ~해서 …하다'의 의미를 나타내도록 접속사 that으로 고쳐 써야 한다.

오답풀이

① boards of directors를 선행사로 하는 관계절을 이끌며 관계절에서 주어 역할을 하는 주격 관계대명사 who의 쓰임은 적절하다.
② 앞에 나온 board elections를 가리키는 목적격 대명사로 them은 적절하게 쓰였다.
③ 능동태 designed corporate law and governance to function이 수동태로 전환되면서 designed의 목적격보어였던 to부정사 to function이 그대로 남은 형태로 어법상 적절하다.
⑤ 문장의 주어는 large public companies ~ century이며, 주어의 핵은 companies이므로 복수형 동사 were는 어법상 적절하다.

전문해석

상장 기업은 이사회에 의해 법적으로 감독되는데, 그들은 주주들에 의해 공식적으로 선출된다. 더 작은 기업에서는 이러한 형식이 현실에 적용되어 소수의 주주들이 이사 선거를 그리고 그것을 통해 기업을 효과적으로 통제한다. 이것이 법인 법과 기업 지배구조가 작동하도록 고안된 방식이다. 그러나 초대형 상장 기업에는 오랫동안 주주들이 너무나 많아서, 즉 회사 주식을 1% 넘게 소유하는 사람이 한 명도 없어서, 이사를 선출하는 경쟁적인 선거가 드물다. 이사회 구성원은 대체로 독립적이고 비상근으로 근무하기 때문에 경영진을 지휘하는 데 제한된 힘을 가진다. 20세기 말에 이사회의 권한이 커졌지만, 그들은 여전히 경영진에게 가벼운 제약만 가한다. 그 결과, 20세기 대부분의 기간 동안 대형 상장 기업은 소유주가 아닌 경영진에 의해 통제되었다. 이 사실은 Adolf Berle와 Gardiner Means의 〈The Modern Corporation and Private Property〉라는 1932년의 책에서 처음 강조되었다.

구문풀이
15행 As a result, large public companies for most of the twentieth century were controlled [**not** by their owners **but** by their executives].

: [ ]는 「not A but B(A가 아니라 B)」가 사용된 전치사구이다.

어휘풀이
- public company 상장 기업
- board of directors 이사회
- formality *n* 형식
- corporate *a* 기업의, 법인의
- contested *a* 경쟁적인, 경합하는
- mild *a* 가벼운, 약한
- executives *n* 경영진, 실무자
- oversee *v* 감독하다
- shareholder *n* 주주
- map onto ~에 적용되다
- numerous *a* 수없이 많은
- impose *v* 부과하다, 지우다
- constraint *n* 제약

016 답 ④

출제 의도 파악하기
❶	tempt의 목적격보어	❷	도치구문
❸	재귀대명사	❹	문장의 구조 파악
❺	관계대명사 whose의 쓰임		

정답풀이
④ that feeling of superiority를 선행사로 하는 주격 관계대명사 that이 이끄는 관계절의 동사가 필요하므로, 준동사 actualizing을 본동사 actualizes로 고쳐야 한다. 관계대명사 that과 fully actualizes 사이에 so to say(독립부정사)와 lately contained in the secret(분사구문)이 삽입된 구조이다.

오답풀이
① 「tempt+목적어+목적격보어(to부정사)」(~가 …하도록 부추기다) 구문으로 tempt의 목적격보어로 to repeat는 적절하게 쓰였다.
② 한정적인 의미를 갖는 only의 수식을 받는 부사절(Only when ~ repeated)이 문두로 나와 주어 its possessor와 조동사 can이 도치되었다. 따라서 조동사 can에 이어지는 동사원형 turn은 적절하다.
③ 「keep ~ to oneself」는 '~을 혼자만 알다'라는 뜻으로, 주어인 he와 같은 대상을 나타내는 재귀대명사 himself는 적절하다.
⑤ 관계절 속의 "friend"를 한정하며 the subject of gossip을 부연 설명하는 관계절을 이끌고 있으므로, 소유격 관계대명사 whose는 적절하다. 이 관계절은 and he presents himself as the subject's friend로 이해할 수 있다.

전문해석
심리적인 이유부터 시작하자면, 다른 사람의 개인적인 일에 대해 아는 것은 이 정보를 가진 사람이 그것을 뒷공론으로 반복하도록 부추길 수 있는데, 왜냐하면 숨겨진 정보로서 그것은 사회적으로 비활동적인 상태이기 때문이다. 그 정보를 소유한 사람은 그것이 반복될 때에만 자신이 무언가를 알고 있다는 사실을 사회적 인정, 명성 그리고 악명과 같은 사회적으로 가치 있는 무언가로 바꿀 수 있다. 자신의 정보를 자기 혼자만 아는 동안은 자신이 그것을 알지 못하는 사람들보다 우월하다고 느낄 수도 있다. 그러나 알면서 말하지 않는 것은 '말하자면 그 비밀 속에 보이지 않게 들어 있다가 폭로의 순간에만 완전히 실현되는 우월감'이라는 그 기분을 그에게 주지 못한다. 이것이 잘 알려진 인물과 윗사람에 대해 뒷공론을 하는 주요 동기이다. 뒷공론을 만들어 내는 사람은 자신을 그의 '친구'라고 소개하는 그 뒷공론 대상의 '명성' 일부가 자신에게 옮겨질 것이라고 생각한다.

구문풀이
5행 [Only when the information is repeated] **can its possessor** turn the fact [that he knows something] into something [socially valuable like social recognition, prestige, and notoriety].

: Only의 수식을 받는 부사절인 첫 번째 [ ]가 문두로 나와 주어(its possessor)와 조동사(can)가 도치되었다. 두 번째 [ ]는 the fact와 동격 관계를 이루는 절이다. 세 번째 [ ]는 something을 수식하는 형용사구이다.

어휘풀이
- psychological *a* 정신적인, 심리적인
- possessor *n* 소유자
- gossip *n* 남의 뒷말, 뒷공론 *v* 험담[남의 이야기]을 하다
- inactive *a* 활동하지 않는, 비활동성의
- superior *a* 우월한 *n* 윗사람, 우월한 사람 (*cf.* superiority *n* 우월, 탁월)
- so to say 말하자면
- disclosure *n* 폭로, 발각, 드러남
- figure *n* 인물
- rub off on ~으로 옮겨지다, ~에 영향을 주다
- affair *n* 개인적인 문제[관심사]
- recognition *n* 인지, 인식, 인정
- actualize *v* 현실화하다, 실현하다
- motive *n* 동기, 이유
- assume *v* 가정[추정]하다

017 답 ③

출제 의도 파악하기
❶	주어와 동사의 수 일치	❷	분사구문의 태
❸	문장의 구조 파악	❹	to부정사의 쓰임
❺	동명사의 쓰임		

정답풀이
③ 문장의 주어인 What is not universal에 이어지는 술어 동사가 없는 상태이므로 준동사 형태인 being을 본동사 is로 바꿔 써야 한다.

오답풀이
① 주어는 Rational behavior이므로 단수형 동사 tends는 적절하다. behavior resulting ~ response는 Rational behavior와 동격 관계를 이루는 명사구이다.
② 주어 It(= Rational behavior)을 부연 설명하는 분사구문을 유도하는 분사로, It이 '의도되는' 대상이므로 수동의 의미를 나타내는 과거분사 intended는 적절하다.
④ to satisfy는 '~하기 위해서'라는 의미의 목적을 나타내는 부사적 용법으로 적절하게 쓰였다.
⑤ 뒤에 목적어 the processes를 취하며 전치사 to의 목적어로 쓰인 동명사 advancing은 적절하다.

전문해석
이성적인 행동, 즉 의식적인 생각과 결정에서 비롯되며, 생각이 없는 감정적 반응에서 비롯되는 것이 아닌 행동은 목표 지향적인 경향이 있다. 그것은 목적이 있으며, 무언가를 성취하려는 의도를 가진다. 그 '무언가'는 어떤 욕구를 충족시키는 것과 관련 있다. 예를 들어, 생존, 안전, 애정, 존경 또는 성취에 대한 인간의 욕구는 보편적이다. 보편적이지 않은 것은 우리가 우리의 욕구를 충족시키기 위한 다양한 수단에 두는 가치이다. 문화적 차이의 한 가지는 우리 모두에게 잘 알려진 것, 바로 음식이다. 나는 나의 배고픔을 만족시키기 위해 치킨 수프에 더 많은 가치를 둘 수 있지만, 여러분은 상어 지느러미 수프나 크림 수프를 선호할지도 모른다. 다른, 문화에 기반한 가치의 차이는 여기서 우리에게 더 많은 관심사가 된다. 예를 들어, 한 가지 욕구인 자아실현은 한 문화에서 부, 찬사 또는 다른 형태의 개인적인 인정을 축적함으로써 충족될 수 있는 반면, 다른 문화에서는 그것(자아실현)이 자신의 작업 집단에서의 (업무) 처리를 진전시키는 데 가치 있는 공헌을 하는 것을 의미할 수도 있다.

1행 Rational behavior, that is, [behavior {resulting from conscious thought and decision and not from an unthinking emotional response}], tends to be goal-directed.

: [ ]는 Rational behavior와 동격 관계를 이루는 명사구이고, 그 안의 { }는 behavior를 수식하는 분사구이다.

어휘풀이
- rational *a* 이성적인, 합리적인
- unthinking *a* 생각이 없는
- satisfy *v* 충족시키다, 만족시키다
- affection *n* 애정
- universal *a* 보편적인
- shark fin 상어 지느러미
- praise *n* 칭찬, 찬사
- worthy *a* 가치 있는
- advance *v* 전진시키다, 진전시키다
- conscious *a* 의식적인
- purposeful *a* 목적을 가진, 의도적인
- security *n* 안전
- esteem *n* 존중, 존경
- means *n* 수단, 방법
- self-actualization *n* 자아실현
- recognition *n* 인정, 인식
- contribution *n* 공헌, 기여

018 답 ④

출제 의도 파악하기
❶ 관계대명사 what의 쓰임 ❷ 접속사 that의 쓰임
❸ 형식상의 주어와 내용상의 주어 ❹ 주어와 동사의 수 일치
❺ 동명사의 쓰임

정답풀이
④ 주어가 동명사구인 Using ~ about이고, 동명사구 주어는 단수 취급하므로 are를 단수형 동사 is로 바꿔 써야 한다.

오답풀이
① have의 목적어 역할을 하는 절을 이끄는 동시에 그 절에서 describe의 목적어 역할을 해야 하므로, 선행사를 포함하는 관계대명사 what은 적절하다.
② 뒤에 주어(one), 동사(draw), 목적어(more inferences ~)를 갖춘 완전한 구조의 절이 이어지므로 requiring의 목적어 역할을 하는 명사절을 이끄는 접속사 that은 적절하다.
③ 문맥상 It은 형식상의 주어이고 to identify 이하의 to부정사구가 내용상의 주어로, to identify는 적절하게 쓰였다.
⑤ 뒤에 목적어 interpretations ~를 취하며 「from A to B」 구문에서 전치사 to의 목적어로 쓰인 동명사 making은 적절하다.

전문해석
인류 문화의 고고학 기록을 살펴볼 때, 우리는 그것이 엄청나게 불완전하다는 점을 고려해야 한다. 인류 문화의 많은 측면들은 고고학자들이 낮은 고고학적 가시성이라고 말하는 것을 지니고 있고, 이는 그것들이 고고학적으로 식별하기 어렵다는 것을 의미한다. 고고학자들은 문화의 유형적 (또는 물질적) 측면, 즉 도구, 음식, 구조물처럼 다루고 사진 찍을 수 있는 것들에 집중하는 경향이 있다. 문화의 무형적 측면을 재구성하는 것은 더 어려워서, 우리는 유형적인 것에서 더 많은 추론을 도출해야 한다. 예를 들면, 고고학자들이 석기와 음식 유물로부터 기술과 식습관을 식별하고 그것에 관한 추론을 도출하기는 비교적 쉽다. 같은 종류의 물질적 유물을 사용하여 사회 체계와 사람들이 무엇을 생각하고 있었는지에 관한 추론을 이끌어 내는 것은 더 어렵다. 고고학자들은 그것을 하지만, 쓰레기(쓸모없는 것)로 인식되는 물리적 유물로부터 신념 체계에 관한 해석에 이르는 데는 어쩔 수 없이 더 많은 추론이 수반된다.

구문풀이
3행 Many aspects of human culture have [what archaeologists describe as low archaeological visibility], [meaning {they are difficult to identify archaeologically}].

: 첫 번째 [ ]는 have의 목적어로 쓰인 명사절로, 선행사를 포함한 관계사 what이 이끌고 있다. 두 번째 [ ]는 앞의 절을 부연 설명하는 분사구문이며, 그 안의 { }는 meaning의 목적어로 쓰인 명사절이다.

16행 Archaeologists do it, but there are necessarily more inferences [involved in getting **from** {physical remains <recognized as trash>} **to** {making interpretations about belief systems}].

: [ ]는 more inferences를 수식하는 과거분사구이다. 두 개의 { }는 「from A to B」 구조로 연결된 명사구와 동명사구이고, 〈 〉는 physical remains를 수식하는 과거분사구이다.

어휘풀이
- vastly *ad* 엄청나게, 거대하게
- describe *v* 말하다, 묘사하다
- identify *v* 식별하다, 확인하다
- intangible *a* 무형의
- remains *n* 유물, 유적
- recognize *v* 인식하다, 알아보다
- aspect *n* 측면
- visibility *n* 가시성
- tangible *a* 유형의
- inference *n* 추론
- involved in ~에 수반되는
- interpretation *n* 해석

Q1 1 living 2 depressed 3 Amazed 4 Situated
 5 watching

Q2 1 ○ 2 ×, employed 3 ○ 4 ×, called

019 ⑤ **020** ④ **021** ④ **022** ③ **023** ②

024 ③

Q1

1. 풀이 앞에 있는 cats를 수식하는 분사의 자리로, cats가 '사는' 주체이므로 능동의 의미를 나타내는 현재분사가 알맞다.
해석 파라오 시대에는 세계의 다른 어떤 지역보다 이집트에 사는 고양이가 많았다.

2. 풀이 감정 표현의 타동사는 주어가 느끼는 감정을 표현할 때 과거분사를 쓴다. 따라서 여기서도 '낙담시키다, 울적하게 하다'라는 뜻의 감정동사 depress를 과거분사로 쓰는 것이 알맞다.
해석 나는 내 앞에 놓여 있는 힘든 일을 생각하면서 마음이 아주 울적했다.

3. 풀이 감정동사가 쓰인 분사구문에서 의미상 주어인 I가 '놀란' 것이므로 과거분사가 알맞다.
해석 그녀에게 쏟아지고 있는 그 모든 관심에 놀라서 나는 그녀가 그 항공사에 근무하는지 물어보았다.

4. 풀이 Katmandu(카트만두) 시가 위치를 정하는 주체가 아니라, '위치가 정해진' 대상이므로 수동의 의미를 나타내는 과거분사가 알맞다. situate는 '위치하게 하다'라는 의미의 타동사이다.
해석 1,350m의 고도에 위치하여, Katmandu(카트만두) 시에서는 이곳 생활을 쾌적하게 해 주는 연중 따뜻한 기후를 누릴 수 있다.

5. 풀이 「with+명사(구)+분사」 구문으로, you와 watch는 의미상 능동의 관계이므로 현재분사가 알맞다.
해석 네가 나를 보고 있어서, 나는 공부하는 데 집중할 수 없었다.

Q2

1. 풀이 분사구문의 의미상 주어인 they(= schools)가 '양성하는' 주체이므로 능동을 나타내는 현재분사 producing은 알맞다.
해석 학교가 단지 지식만을 제공한다면, 학교는 창의성을 파괴하여 그저 평범한 사람들만을 양성할지도 모른다.

2. 풀이 수식받는 명사구 an extremely slippery synthetic substance가 '사용되는' 대상이므로 수동을 나타내는 과거분사 employed로 고쳐 써야 한다. 여기서 an extremely slippery synthetic substance ~ utensils는 앞에 있는 Teflon과 동격이다.
해석 조리 기구의 코팅 막으로 사용되는 매우 미끈거리는 합성 물질인 Teflon은 1938년에 발명되었다.

3. 풀이 분사구문의 의미상 주어가 문장의 주어인 we와 달라 분사 앞에 의미상 주어인 The sun을 그대로 써 준 것이므로 알맞다. rise의 시점이 문장의 시제인 과거(started)보다 더 앞선 시점임을 나타내기 위해 「having p.p.」 형태가 쓰인 것이다.

해석 해가 뜨고 나서 우리는 그 마을을 향해 출발했다.

4. 풀이 수식받는 a book이 〈The Art of Travel〉이라고 '불리는' 대상이므로 수동임을 나타내는 과거분사로 고쳐 써야 한다.
해석 그것은 〈여행의 기술〉이라는 책에서 Francis Galton이 하는 충고였다.

---

019 답 ⑤

출제 의도	파악하기
❶ 전치사+관계대명사	❷ 주어와 동사의 수 일치
❸ 부사의 쓰임	❹ 분사구문의 태
❺ with+명사(구)+분사	

정답풀이

⑤ 「with+명사(구)+분사」 구문으로, their upper branches는 '형성되는' 대상이므로 forming을 수동의 의미를 나타내는 과거분사 formed로 고쳐 써야 한다.

오답풀이

① The various shapes를 수식하는 관계절을 유도하며, 뒤에 완전한 구조의 절이 이어지므로 「전치사+관계대명사」 형태의 into which는 어법상 적절하다.
② 주어인 The manipulation of this canopy, or canopy management에 이어지는 술어 동사로, 단수 주어에 수를 일치시킨 is는 어법상 적절하다.
③ 「both A and B」에 의해 부사구 from the reflected heat ~ 'pudding stones'와 병렬로 연결되어 동사구 traps ~ rays를 부가적으로 수식하므로 부사 directly는 어법상 적절하다.
④ 분사구문의 의미상 주어인 the stones가 '감싸는' 주체이므로 능동의 의미를 나타내는 현재분사 enveloping은 적절하다.

전문해석

포도나무가 가꿔질 수 있는 다양한 형태는 열이 포도의 숙성에 미치는 영향을 제어할 또 다른 방법을 제공한다. 잎의 배열은 포도나무의 캐노피라고 알려진 것을 형성한다. 이 캐노피의 조작, 즉 캐노피 관리는 태양 광선의 영향을 최대화하거나 최소화하기 위해 다양한 양식의 가꾸기가 사용될 수 있는 한계 기후에서 특히 중요하다. Châteauneuf-du-Pape와 같은 포도밭에서는 포도나무의 (포도) 생산 부분이 땅에 가깝도록 줄기가 짧은 덤불 양식으로 포도나무를 가꿈으로써 태양의 영향이 의도적으로 강조된다. 이는 태양 광선으로부터, 직접적으로뿐만 아니라 '갈레(프랑스어로 자갈)', 즉 '역암'에서 반사되는 열로부터도 최대한의 온기를 가둔다. 이 영향은 밤까지 지속되는데, 그때 돌은 거대한 축열기 역할을 하여 포도나무를 따뜻한 공기로 감싼다. 더 가볍고 산뜻한 와인이 선호될 수 있는 더운 기후에서는 위쪽 가지가 퍼걸러 형태로 만들어진 상태로 포도나무가 높이 가꿔진다. 이 형태에서 포도는 잎사귀 아래에 매달려 있고 상대적으로 시원한 그늘에 있게 된다.

구문풀이

18행 In hot climates [where a lighter, crisper wine might be desired], the vines are trained high, [**with** their upper branches **formed** into a pergola].

: 첫 번째 [ ]는 hot climates를 수식하는 관계절이고, 두 번째 [ ]는 「with+명사구+과거분사」 구문으로 '~가 …된 상태로'의 의미를 나타낸다.

어휘풀이

- vine *n* 포도나무
- arrangement *n* 배열
- marginal *a* 한계의
- ripening *n* 숙성, 성숙
- manipulation *n* 조작
- ray *n* 광선

- vineyard *n* 포도밭
- bush *n* 덤불
- gigantic *a* 거대한
- crisp *a* 산뜻한, 상쾌한
- underneath *prep* ~의 아래에
- deliberately *ad* 의도적으로
- trap *v* 가두다, 붙잡다
- envelop *v* 감싸다, 뒤덮다
- branch *n* 가지
- comparative *a* 비교적인, 상대적인

- emphasize *v* 강조하다
- organic *a* 생물의, 유기체의 (↔ inorganic 무생물의)
- sphere *n* 범위, 영역
- animated *a* 생명이 있는, 살아 있는
- dual *a* 둘의, 이중의
- anthropomorphism *n* 의인화
- visual *a* 시각의, 시각적인
- conceptualize *v* 개념화하다
- light *n* 견해, 관점
- inhabit *v* ~에 살다[거주하다]
- unlettered *a* 읽고 쓸 줄 모르는, 문맹의
- integrated *a* 통합된
- totality *n* 총체, 전체
- tendency *n* 경향
- regard A as B A를 B로 간주하다
- mythology *n* 신화
- in terms of ~의 관점[면]에서
- preoccupation *n* 몰두
- profoundly *ad* 대단히, 크게

020 답 ④

정답풀이

④ becomes가 문장의 동사이므로, inhabited their world는 앞에 있는 명사구 the nonhuman creatures를 수식하는 분사구이다. 수식을 받는 the nonhuman creatures(인간이 아닌 생명체들)가 인간 세계에 '살고 있는' 주체이므로, 과거분사 inhabited를 능동의 의미를 나타내는 현재분사 inhabiting으로 고쳐 써야 한다.

오답풀이

① Speculations about the meaning and purpose of prehistoric art가 문장의 주어부이고, 복수 명사인 Speculations가 주어의 핵이므로 이에 수를 맞춘 복수형 동사 rely는 어법상 알맞다.
② 주어(Such primitive societies)와 동사(tend) 사이에 삽입되어 '~처럼, ~듯이'라는 의미의 부사절을 이끄는 접속사 as는 어법상 알맞다.
③ 콤마(,) 앞뒤의 절을 연결하는 접속사의 역할을 하면서 동시에 *anthropomorphism* (the practice of regarding animals as humans) and *totemism* (the practice of regarding humans as animals)를 대신하는 대명사의 역할을 하는 관계대명사 which는 어법상 알맞다.
⑤ 동사 broods upon의 목적어가 주어인 an unlettered humanity와 동일한 대상이므로 재귀대명사 itself는 어법상 알맞다.

전문해석

선사 시대 예술의 의미와 목적에 대한 고찰은 현대의 수렵 채집 사회와의 사이에서 이끌어 낸 유사점에 크게 의존한다. Steven Mithen이 〈The Prehistory of the Modern Mind〉에서 강조하듯이, 그러한 원시 사회는 인간과 짐승, 동물과 식물, 생물체의 영역과 무생물체의 영역을 통합적이고 살아 있는 총체에 대한 참여자로 여기는 경향이 있다. 이런 경향이 표현된 두 가지가 '의인화(동물을 인간으로 간주하는 관행)'와 '토테미즘(인간을 동물로 간주하는 관행)'인데, 이 두 가지는 원시 문화의 시각 예술과 신화에 널리 퍼져 있다. 따라서 자연의 세계는 인간의 사회적 관계 측면에서 개념화된다. 이런 측면에서 고려될 때, 초기 인류가 자신들의 세계에 살고 있는 인간 이외의 생명체들에 대하여 시각적으로 집착한 것은 깊은 의미를 띠게 된다. Claude Lévi-Strauss가 말했듯이, 수렵 채집인들에게 동물은 먹기 좋은 대상일 뿐만 아니라 '생각해 보기에도 좋은' 대상이기도 하다. 토테미즘의 풍습에서 문맹의 인류는 '자연 속에서의 자신과 자신의 위치에 대해 곰곰이 생각한다'고 그는 말했다.

구문풀이

1행 [Speculations about the meaning and purpose of prehistoric art] rely heavily on analogies [drawn with modern-day hunter-gatherer societies].

: 첫 번째 [ ]는 문장의 주어 역할을 하는 명사구이고, 두 번째 [ ]는 analogies를 수식하는 과거분사구이다.

어휘풀이

- prehistoric *a* 선사 시대의
- primitive *a* 원시의, 원시 시대의

021 답 ④

정답풀이

④ 주어인 positive comments는 학생들에게 '동기를 부여하는' 주체이므로 과거분사 motivated를 능동의 의미를 나타내는 현재분사 motivating으로 바꿔 써야 한다.

오답풀이

① 주어는 developing music students이고, 주어의 핵은 students이다. 따라서 복수형 동사 rely는 적절하다. developing은 동명사가 아니라 music students를 수식하는 현재분사임에 주의해야 한다.
② the feedback을 대신하는 지시대명사 that을 수식하는 주격 관계대명사절을 이끄는 관계대명사 which는 적절하다.
③ 뒤에 완전한 구조의 절이 이어지고 있고, 문맥상 '~인지'라는 의미로 explored의 목적절을 이끌므로 접속사 whether는 적절하다.
⑤ '아마도'라는 뜻으로 more helpful이라는 형용사구를 수식하고 있으므로 부사 likely는 적절하다.

전문해석

학생들에게 피드백을 제공하는 것은 교사들에게 중요한 과제이다. 일반 심리학은 결과에 대해 아는 것이 기술을 향상시키는 데 있어 필요하다는 것을 보여 주었다. 숙련된 음악가들은 자신의 연주를 스스로 비판할 수 있지만, 성장하고 있는 음악 전공 학생들은 평가적 피드백을 제공하는 교사들에 의존한다. 가장 건설적인 피드백은 음악 한 곡에 대한 학생의 연주와 최적의 버전 사이의 차이를 표현하는 것이다. 숙련된 교사들은 일반적인 평가보다 더 상세한 피드백을 주고, 음악 교육자들은 더 구체적인 교사 피드백이 학생의 연주 향상을 촉진한다고 일반적으로 인정한다. 연구자들은 또한 유능한 교사의 피드백이 더 자주 긍정적으로 또는 부정적으로 표현되는지, 즉 칭찬 또는 비판을 이루는지 탐구했다. 사람들은 긍정적인 의견이 학생들에게 더욱 동기를 부여하고, 결과적으로 효과적인 가르침과 더욱 연관되어 있다고 직관적으로 생각할 수도 있다. 그러나 그 연구는 다소 다른 그림을 그린다. 긍정적인 피드백이 어린 학습자들과 일대일 교수에서는 아마도 더욱 도움이 되겠지만, 더 숙련된 음악 전공 학생들은 수업에서 더 높은 수준의 비평을 받아들이고 그것으로부터 이점을 얻는 것처럼 보인다.

구문풀이

9행 Expert teachers give **more** detailed feedback **than** general appraisals, and music educators generally recognize [that more specific teacher feedback facilitates student performance improvement].

: 「more ~ than ....」의 비교구문이 쓰였으며, [ ]는 recognize의 목적어로 쓰인 명사절이다.

어휘풀이

- critical *a* 매우 중요한
- advanced *a* 숙련된
- evaluative *a* 평가적인
- discrepancy *n* 차이, 불일치
- detailed *a* 상세한
- specific *a* 구체적인
- explore *v* 탐구하다
- criticism *n* 비판
- motivated *a* 동기가 부여된
- likely *ad* 아마도
- improve *v* 향상시키다
- self-critique *v* 스스로 비판하다
- constructive *a* 건설적인
- optimal *a* 최적의
- appraisal *n* 평가, 판단
- facilitate *v* 촉진하다
- constitute *v* 이루다, 구성하다
- intuitively *ad* 직관적으로
- be associated with ~와 연관되다
- instruction *n* 교수, 가르침

022 답 ③

정답풀이

③ 콤마(,) and 앞의 절은 주어인 water에 두 개의 동사구 is absorbed through the roots와 (is) transferred to the leaves by the xylem이 연결된 구조이다. 따라서 and 뒤에도 문법상 대등한 절의 형태가 와야 하므로 준동사 형태인 being은 적절하지 않다. 주어인 carbon dioxide에 이어지는 동사구를 이루도록 being을 is로 바꿔 써야 한다. 이때 is obtained ~ leaves와 (is) dispersed to chlorophyll은 and 다음에 오는 절의 술어가 된다.

오답풀이

① a chemical process가 선행사이고, 뒤에 주어(green plants), 동사(produce), 목적어(carbohydrates)를 갖춘 완전한 구조의 절이 이어지므로 관계절 안에서 in the chemical process의 부사구 역할을 하는 「전치사+관계대명사」 형태의 in which가 쓰인 것은 적절하다.

② chlorophyll과 의미상 동격인 a green pigment를 수식하는 형용사구를 이끄는 capable은 적절하다. capable 앞에 「주격 관계대명사+be동사(which is)」가 생략되었다고 볼 수 있다.

④ 동사 lack은 '~이 없다[부족하다]'의 의미를 갖는 타동사로 뒤에 바로 목적어를 취할 수 있다.

⑤ 수식을 받는 a process가 '불리는' 대상이므로 과거분사 called는 적절하다.

전문해석

광합성은 녹색식물이 태양의 빛 에너지를 이용하여 이산화탄소와 물로 탄수화물을 생성해 내는 화학적 과정이다. 이 과정은 빛 에너지를 저장되어 필요할 때 사용될 잠재 에너지 형태로 전환할 수 있는 녹색 색소인 엽록소를 사용하여 식물 세포에서 일어난다. 이들 식물에서 물은 뿌리를 통해서 흡수되어 물관부에 의하여 잎으로 전달되고, 이산화탄소는 잎에 있는 기공들을 통해 공기로부터 얻고 엽록소로 분산된다. 그러나 인디언 파이프와 같은 몇몇 식물은 이 엽록소가 없다. 그러므로 그 식물들은 유기물질로부터 탄수화물을 얻는 반면에, 몇몇 박테리아는 화학 합성이라 불리는 과정으로 수소와 무기 화합물에서 얻는 에너지를 이용하여 스스로 탄수화물을 만들어낸다.

구문풀이

3행 The process takes place in the plant cells [using chlorophyll], [a green pigment {capable of **converting** light energy **into** a latent form of energy <which then will be stored and used when needed>}].

: 첫 번째 [ ]는 분사구문이고, 두 번째 [ ]는 chlorophyll과 의미상 동격을 이룬다. { }는 a green pigment를 수식하는 형용사구이다. 「convert *A* into *B*」는 '*A*를 *B*로 전환하다'의 의미이다. < >는 a latent form of energy를 수식하는 관계절이다.

어휘풀이

- photosynthesis *n* 광합성
- pigment *n* 색소, 색소제
- latent *a* 잠재적인
- secure *v* 확보하다
- inorganic *a* 무기의, 무기성의
- carbohydrate *n* 탄수화물
- convert *v* 전환시키다, 변형시키다
- disperse *v* 분산시키다
- organic material 유기물질
- compound *n* 화합물

023 답 ②

출제 의도 파악하기

① 관계부사 where의 쓰임	② 분사의 태
③ 주어와 동사의 수 일치	④ 접속사 as의 쓰임
⑤ to부정사의 쓰임	

정답풀이

② 수식을 받는 something은 '근접하는' 주체이므로 과거분사 approached를 능동의 의미를 나타내는 현재분사 approaching으로 바꿔 써야 한다.

오답풀이

① 뒤에 완전한 구조의 절이 이어지고, 그 절이 선행사 a number of examples를 수식하므로 관계부사 where는 적절하다.

③ 주어부 A strong element of the appeal of such sports songs에서 주어의 핵은 element이므로 이에 수를 맞춘 단수형 동사 is는 적절하다.

④ 뒤에 완전한 구조의 절을 이끌며 문맥상 그 절이 이유를 나타내므로 부사절을 이끄는 접속사 as는 적절하다.

⑤ '~이 …라고들 한다'라는 의미의 「주어+be said+to부정사」 구문을 이루는 to display는 어법상 적절하다.

전문해석

사전적 정의에 따르면, 찬가(讚歌)는 흔히 국가에 대한 충성의 노래이자 한 곡의 '성스러운 음악'인데, 둘 다 스포츠 상황에 적용이 가능한 정의들이다. 이 장르는 독점적이지는 않을지라도 축구에서 두드러지게 나타나며, 인기 있는 노래들이 구단과 밀접한 연관을 갖게 되고 팬들에 의해 열광적으로 받아들여지는 많은 사례를 만들어 냈다. 이에 더하여, 그것들은 흔히 충성과 정체성의 자발적인 표현이며, Desmond Morris에 따르면, '지역 예술 형태에 근접하는 어떤 것의 수준에 도달했다'. 그러한 스포츠 노래들의 강력한 매력 요소는 그것들이 '팬들이 참여할 수 있는 외우기 쉽고 부르기 쉬운 합창'을 특징으로 한다는 것이다. 이는 팬들의 존재를 더 확실히 하기 때문에 팀의 수행에 매우 중요한 부분이다. 이러한 형태의 대중문화는 '품위 있는 미적 거리와 통제'를 유지하는 경향이 있는 지배적인 문화와는 대조적으로, 즐거움과 감정적 과잉을 보여 준다고 말할 수 있다.

구문풀이

4행 This genre is dominated, [although not exclusively], by football and has produced a number of examples [where popular songs {become synonymous with the club} and {are enthusiastically adopted by the fans}].

: 첫 번째 [ ]는 삽입된 양보의 부사절로 although it is not exclusively dominated에서 반복된 요소가 생략된 표현이다. 두 번째 [ ]는 a number of examples를 수식하는 관계절이며, 그 안에서 두 개의 { }는 popular songs의 술어로 병렬구조를 이룬다.

16행 This form of popular culture can **be said to display** pleasure and emotional excess in contrast to the dominant culture [which tends to maintain 'respectable aesthetic distance and control'].

: We can say that this form of popular culture displays pleasure ~.가 수동태로 전환된 It can be said that this form of popular culture displays pleasure ~.에서 형식상의 주어 It 대신 that절의 주어 this form of popular culture가 문두에 오면서 that절의 동사 displays가 to display로 바뀐 형태이다. [ ]는 the dominant culture를 수식하는 관계절이다.

어휘풀이

- definition *n* 정의
- loyalty *n* 충성(심)
- applicable *a* 적용 가능한
- dominate *v* 두드러지게 하다, 지배하다
- exclusively *ad* 독점적으로, 배타적으로
- enthusiastically *ad* 열광적으로
- identity *n* 정체성
- feature *v* ~을 특징으로 하다
- presence *n* 존재, 참석
- excess *n* 과잉, 초과
- maintain *v* 유지하다
- respectable *a* 품위 있는, 존경할 만한
- aesthetic *a* 미적인
- anthem *n* 찬가(讚歌)
- sacred *a* 성스러운
- spontaneous *a* 자발적인
- appeal *n* 매력, 호소
- chorus *n* 합창
- display *v* 보이다, 나타내다
- in contrast to ~와는 대조적으로

024 답 ③

출제 의도 파악하기

❶	to부정사의 쓰임	❷	분사구문의 태
❸	재귀대명사	❹	부사의 쓰임
❺	접속사 that의 쓰임		

정답풀이

③ 문맥상 protect의 동작 주체는 Maasai spears이고 대상은 they(= cattle)이므로 의미상 주어와 목적어가 다르다. 따라서 재귀대명사 themselves를 them으로 바꿔 써야 한다.

오답풀이

① 문맥상 '~하기 위해'라는 목적의 의미로 쓰인 to부정사 to eat은 알맞다.
② Left on their own은 they(= cattle)를 의미상 주어로 하는 분사구문이며, 문맥상 they는 leave의 주체가 아닌 대상이므로 수동의 의미를 나타내는 과거분사 Left는 알맞다.
④ 동사구인 take out grass를 수식하므로 원급 비교구문에 쓰인 부사의 원급 effectively는 알맞다.
⑤ say의 목적어인 명사절을 유도하며, 뒤에 이어지는 절이 완전한 구조를 갖추고 있으므로 접속사 that은 알맞다.

전문해석

만일 아프리카에 사람들이 하나도 없다면, 그 대륙은 몇 가지 중대한 변화를 겪을 것이다. 한때, 북아프리카의 소는 야생이었다. 그러나 수천 년 동안 인간과 지낸 다음, 그것들은 밤에는 풀을 뜯을 수 없으므로 낮 동안 엄청난 양의 먹이를 먹기 위해 거대한 발효통과 같은 창자를 갖도록 선택되었다. 그러므로 현재 그것들은 그리 빠르지 않다. 그것들만 남겨지면 그것들은 오히려 취약한 1등급 소고기가 될 것이다. 소는 현재 아프리카 사바나의 생태계의 생물 무게의 절반 이상을 차지한다. 그것들을 지키는 마사이 족의 창이 없다면, 그것들은 사자와 하이에나에게 진수성찬을 제공할 것이다. 일단 소가 사라지면, 다른 모든 동물들의 먹이가 두 배 이상 있게 될 것이다.

150만 마리의 누가 소와 똑같이 효과적으로 풀을 먹을 것이다. 그러면 세계는 그것들과 코끼리 사이의 훨씬 더 긴밀한 상관관계를 볼 수 있을 것이다. 그것들은 마사이 족이 '소는 나무를 키우고, 코끼리는 풀을 키운다(소는 풀을 뜯어먹어 나무가 자랄 환경을 만들고 코끼리는 나무를 뽑아 내어 풀이 자랄 환경을 만든다)'라고 말할 때 언급하는 역할을 할 것이다.

구문풀이

1행 **If** there **were** no people in Africa, the continent **would undergo** some key changes.

: if절에 과거 동사인 were가 쓰이고, 주절에 「would+동사원형」이 쓰인 가정법 과거 문장으로, 현재 상황과 반대되거나 일어나기 힘든 일에 대한 가정을 나타낸다.

어휘풀이

- undergo *v* 겪다
- cattle *n* 소
- graze *v* 풀을 뜯다
- prime beef 1등급 소고기
- spear *n* 창
- refer to ~라고 말하다, ~라고 부르다
- key *a* 중요한, 중대한
- oversized *a* 아주 큰
- vulnerable *a* 취약한
- account for ~을 차지하다
- feast *n* 진수성찬, 잔치

Q1 **1** those **2** its **3** that **4** them **5** the other

Q2 **1** ○ **2** ×, that **3** ×, them **4** ×, those

025 ⑤ **026** ③ **027** ④ **028** ② **029** ③

030 ③

Q1

1. 풀이 대명사가 대신하는 것이 복수 명사구인 The results이므로 those가 알맞다.

해석 실험 A의 결과는 실험 B의 결과보다 더 신뢰할 만하다.

2. 풀이 대명사가 가리키는 것이 단수 명사인 Korea이므로 its가 알맞다.

해석 그러나 한국은 이러한 국가들과 인접해 있음에도 불구하고 그 치명적인 질병으로부터 시달리지 않는 상태를 유지해 왔다.

3. 풀이 대명사가 대신하는 것이 단수 명사구인 the grass이므로 that이 알맞다.

해석 이 정원에 들어와서 내가 첫 번째로 알아차린 것은 발목 높이의 풀이 울타리 반대편의 풀보다 더 푸르다는 것이다.

4. 풀이 문맥상 함께 있는 것을 즐기는 주체는 The sea lions이고 함께 있는 대상은 those humans로 서로 다르므로 재귀대명사가 아닌 them이 알맞다.

해석 바다사자들은 자기들이 알고 있는 그 사람들에게 우호적이었으며 심지어 그들과 함께 있기를 즐겼다.

5. 풀이 정해진 두 개 중에서 하나는 one이고 나머지 하나를 말하는 것이므로 the other가 알맞다.

해석 나는 두 대의 개인용 컴퓨터를 갖고 있는데, 하나는 데스크톱이고 나머지 하나는 랩톱이다.

Q2

1. 풀이 동사원형으로 시작하는 명령문에서 생략된 주어는 you이고 목적어가 you와 동일하므로 Promise의 목적어로 쓰인 재귀대명사 yourself는 알맞다.

해석 아무리 할 일이 많더라도 항상 하루 저녁은 푹 쉬겠다고 자신에게 약속하라.

2. 풀이 대명사가 대신하는 것은 단수 명사구인 The percentage of people ~ sites이므로 that으로 고쳐 써야 한다.

해석 프랑스에서 주로 뉴스 사이트를 통해 뉴스 영상을 시청하는 사람들의 비율은 독일에서의 비율보다 더 높다.

3. 풀이 대명사가 가리키는 것은 복수 명사구인 strong negative feelings이므로 단수 대명사 it을 them으로 고쳐 써야 한다.

해석 강한 부정적인 감정에 대처하는 데 도움이 되는 방법은 그 감정을 있는 그대로 받아들이는 것이다.

4. 풀이 대명사가 대신하는 것은 복수 명사인 sounds이므로 복수 대명사 those로 고쳐 써야 한다.

해석 음악적 소리는 고정된 음 높이의 사용을 수반한다는 사실에 의해 자연의 소리와 구별될 수 있다.

---

025 답 ⑤

출제 의도 파악하기

❶ 부사의 쓰임 ❷ 대명사의 쓰임과 수 일치
❸ 분사의 태 ❹ 주어와 동사의 수 일치
❺ 관계대명사 that의 쓰임

정답풀이

⑤ 접속사 before가 이끄는 절에서 동사는 appeared이고 that ~ as science가 이에 대한 주어에 해당한다. 즉, that은 명사절을 이끄는 동시에 그 절에서 recognize의 목적어 역할을 해야 하므로 어법상 적절하지 않다. that을 선행사를 포함한 관계대명사인 what으로 바꿔 써야 한다.

오답풀이

① 전치사구 in the Islamic world를 수식하는 부사 exclusively는 적절하다.

② but 다음에 이어지는 주어 it과 전치사 to의 목적어로 쓰인 it은 각각 앞에 나온 This science와 our science today를 가리키는 말로, 서로 다른 대상을 지칭한다.

③ 수식을 받는 all the cities는 cover(~에 걸치다)의 주체에 해당하므로 현재분사 covering은 적절하다.

④ 문장의 주어는 Almost every word in the modern scientific lexicon that begins with the prefix "al"이고, that begins with the prefix "al"은 Almost every word in the modern scientific lexicon을 수식하는 관계절이다. 주어의 핵은 word이므로 단수형 동사 owes는 적절하다.

전문해석

서기 8세기부터 12세기까지, 유럽이 아마도 지나치게 극적인 이름이 붙여진 '암흑시대'를 겪고 있던 시기에, 지구상의 과학은 거의 오로지 이슬람 세계에서만 발견될 수 있었다. 이 과학은 오늘날 우리의 과학과 똑같지는 않았지만, 그것(이 과학)은 확실히 그것(우리의 과학)에 선행했고 그럼에도 불구하고 세상에 대해 아는 것을 목표로 한 활동이었다. 무슬림 통치자들은 엄청난 자원을 도서관, 천문대, 병원과 같은 과학 기관에 주었다. 근동 아랍과 북아프리카(그리고 심지어 스페인까지)에 걸친 모든 도시의 훌륭한 학교들은 여러 세대의 학자들을 양성했다. 접두사 'al'로 시작하는 현대 과학 어휘 목록의 거의 모든 단어, 즉 알고리즘, 연금술, 알코올, 알칼리, 대수학은 이슬람 과학에 그 기원을 두고 있다. 그리고 그것이 시작된 지 막 400년이 넘었던 그때, 그것은 서서히 멈춘 것 같았고, 얼추 몇 백 년 후에 우리가 오늘날 과학이라고 확실히 인식하게 될 것이 갈릴레오, 케플러 그리고 조금 후에 뉴턴과 함께 유럽에서 출현했다.

구문풀이

4행 This science was not exactly like our science today, but **it** [was surely antecedent to **it**] and [was nonetheless an activity {aimed at knowing about the world}].

: 두 개의 [ ]는 첫 번째 it에 이어지는 술어로 병렬구조로 연결되었다. 첫 번째 it은 This science를, 두 번째 it은 our science today를 가리키는 대명사이다. { }는 an activity를 수식하는 과거분사구이다.

15행 And then, just over 400 years after it started, it ground to an apparent halt, and [**it would be** a few hundred years, give or take, **before** {what we would today unmistakably recognize as science} appeared in Europe—with Galileo, Kepler, and, a bit later, Newton].

: [ ]는 「it is+시간+before+주어+동사」 구문으로, 시간의 경과(~가 …하기까지 (시간)이 걸리다)를 표현하고 있다. before절에서 주어는 { }로 표시된 명사절이고, 동사는 appeared이다.

어휘풀이

- exclusively *ad* 오로지, 배타적으로
- institution *n* 기관
- observatory *n* 천문대
- alchemy *n* 연금술
- grind to a halt 서서히 멈추다
- apparent *a* ~인 것 같은, ~인 것으로 보이는
- unmistakably *ad* 확실히
- grant *v* 주다, 수여하다
- tremendous *a* 엄청난
- prefix *n* 접두사
- algebra *n* 대수학

026 답 ③

출제 의도 파악하기

❶ to부정사의 쓰임		❷ 동사의 discuss의 쓰임	
❸ 부정대명사 one		❹ 의문사 what의 쓰임	
❺ help의 목적격보어			

정답풀이

③「turn *A* into *B*(*A*를 *B*로 바꾸다)」구문이 쓰인 문장으로, 여기서 *A*와 *B*는 어법상 대등한 구조를 이루어야 한다. one은 앞에 있는 복수 명사 conversations를 대신하여 쓰인 부정대명사이므로, 복수형인 ones로 바꿔 써야 한다.

오답풀이

① proceeded 뒤에 to부정사가 와서 '계속해서 ~하다'라는 의미를 나타내므로 to carry는 적절하다.
② discuss는 타동사로 전치사 없이 바로 목적어를 취할 수 있으므로, 목적어 cell phone manners가 바로 뒤에 오도록 쓰인 discuss는 알맞다. discuss는 타동사이므로 전치사(about)와 함께 쓰지 않는다는 것에 유의해야 한다.
④ can't imagine의 목적어를 이루는 자리로, 의문사 what이 휴대폰 없이 자라는 것은 '어떤 것'이었는지의 의미를 나타내는 의문사절을 이끌도록 쓰인 것은 적절하다.
⑤ 동사 help는 목적격보어로 원형부정사나 to부정사를 취한다. 따라서 원형부정사 understand는 알맞게 쓰였다.

전문해석

내 아들 James의 휴대폰이 울렸을 때 나는 그와 함께 가게에서 줄을 서 있었다. 그는 계산원이 그가 구입한 물건을 입력하는 동안 대화를 계속했다. 가게를 나선 후 나는 James에게 응대를 받는 동안 통화를 하는 것은 무례하다고 말했다. 그가 "모두가 그렇게 해요."라고 말했을 때, 나는 지금이 휴대폰 예절에 대해 논의하기에 좋은 시기라는 것을 알았다. 나는 사람들이 전화로 크게 말하는 경향이 있어서 다른 사람들을 방해하고 사적인 대화를 공개적인 대화로 바꾼다고 말했다. James는 그것에 대해 그렇게 생각하지 않았다고 말했다. 그는 우리가 외출할 때 휴대폰을 진동으로 해놓고 나중에 다시 전화하기로 동의했다. 내 아들은 휴대폰 없이 자라는 것이 어떤 것이었는지 상상할 수 없다. 하지만 나는 우리가 그것들을 그저 가지고 있다고 해서 우리가 항상 그것들을 사용할 필요는 없다는 것을 그가 알도록 도우려고 하고 있다. 그리고 그 좋은 매너는 여전히 적용되고 있다.

구문풀이

7행 I said [people tend to talk loudly on their phones, {disturbing others and **turning** private conversations **into** public **ones**}].

: [ ]는 said의 목적어 역할을 하는 명사절이다. { }는 people ~ phones의 내용을 의미상 주어로 하는 분사구문이다.「turn *A* into *B*」는 '*A*를 *B*로 바꾸다'의 의미를 나타낸다. 부정대명사 ones는 conversations를 대신한다.

어휘풀이

- proceed to *do* 계속해서 ~하다
- carry on ~을 계속하다

- ring up (상품 가격 등)을 입력하다
- vibrate *n* 진동
- disturb *v* 방해하다

027 답 ④

출제 의도 파악하기

❶ 접속사 in that의 쓰임		❷ 생략구문	
❸ 주어와 동사의 수 일치		❹ 지시대명사 that	
❺ 부사의 쓰임			

정답풀이

④ 문맥상 앞에 나온 단수 명사구 Color vision을 대신해야 하므로, 복수 대명사 those는 적절하지 않으며 단수형인 that으로 바꿔 써야 한다.

오답풀이

① 뒤에 주어(they), 동사(will make), 목적어(discriminations)를 갖춘 완전한 구조의 절이 이어지므로, '~라는 점에서'라는 접속사 역할을 하는 in that은 적절하다.
②「as+형용사+as」의 원급 비교구문으로, is 다음에 반복되는 relevant가 생략된 형태이다.
③ 동명사구 teaching ~ colors가 주어이고, 동명사구 주어는 단수 취급하므로 단수형 동사 is의 쓰임은 적절하다.
⑤ 부사 carefully는 과거분사 conducted를 수식하므로 적절하게 쓰였다.

전문해석

행동주의 심리학자들에게 자주 던져지는 질문은 동물들이 색각을 가지고 있는가이다. 가축의 모든 종들은 그것들이 색상에 근거한 구별을 할 것이라는 점에서 색각을 가지고 있다는 것이 드러났다. 그러나 색상이 새, 물고기 그리고 영장류와 관련된 것만큼 이러한 동물들과 관련이 있는 것은 아니다. 예를 들어, 고양이는 쉽게 다른 시각적 구별을 배우고 초록과 파랑을 흡수하는 두 종류의 원뿔체를 가지고 있지만, 고양이에게 색상들을 구별하도록 가르치는 것은 아주 어렵다. 그럼에도 불구하고 고양이, 개, 말, 소, 돼지, 염소, 그리고 양은 모두 단지 색상에만 근거하여 구별을 할 수 있다. 가축에게 색각은 인간의 그것(색각)과 동일하지 않다. 대부분의 세심하게 수행된 연구에서 개는 회색의 색조가 아니라 오히려 보라, 파랑, 노랑의 색조로 세상을 보는 것처럼 보인다.

구문풀이

6행 For example, [teaching cats to discriminate between colors] **is** very difficult, [although **they** {learn other visual discriminations with ease} and {have two types of cones <that absorb green and blue>}].

: 첫 번째 [ ]는 동명사구로 된 주어이고, 동명사구 주어는 단수 취급하므로 단수형 동사 is가 쓰였다. 두 번째 [ ]는 양보의 부사절이며, 주어 they는 cats를 가리키고 두 개의 { }가 술어로 연결되어 있다. < >는 two types of cones를 수식하는 관계절이다.

어휘풀이

- behaviorist *n* 행동주의 심리학자
- discrimination *n* 구별, 차별
- cone *n* 원뿔체, 추상체
- conduct *v* 수행하다
- domestic animal 가축
- be relevant to ~와 관련 있다
- identical *a* 동일한
- shade *n* 색조

028 답 ②

출제 의도 파악하기

❶ 접속사 that의 쓰임		❷ 대명사의 쓰임과 수 일치	
❸ 분사의 태		❹ 부사의 쓰임	
❺ 분사구문의 태			

② how가 이끄는 의문사절에서 동사 present의 목적어는 주어와 동일한 people이므로 them을 재귀대명사인 themselves로 바꿔 써야 한다.

오답풀이

① 뒤에 완전한 구조의 절이 이어지고, is의 보어 역할을 하는 명사절을 이끌 므로 접속사 that은 적절하다.

③ 수식을 받는 the meanings는 '연관되는' 대상이므로 수동의 의미를 지닌 과거분사 associated는 적절하다.

④ 수동태를 이루는 과거분사 purchased를 수식하는 역할을 하는 부사 inexpensively는 적절하게 쓰였다.

⑤ 앞 절 내용의 결과를 나타내는 능동의 분사구문을 이끄는 현재분사 opening은 적절하다.

전문해석

유행은 사람들이 자신을 재조정할 새로운 기회를 끊임없이 제시하며 변화의 때를 나타낸다. 어떻게 유행이 궁극적으로 사람들에게 힘과 자유를 줄 수 있는지를 이해하기 위해서는 먼저 변화를 위한 기반으로서의 패션의 중요성에 대해 논의해야 한다. 패션이 왜 그렇게 매력적인지에 대해 나의 정보 제공자들이 해 준 가장 흔한 설명은 그것이 일종의 연극적인 의상을 구성한다는 것이다. 옷은 사람들이 자신을 세상에 보여 주는 방식의 일부이고, 패션은 사회에서 일어나고 있는 일 그리고 패션 자체의 역사와 관련하여 그들을 현재에 위치시킨다. 표현의 한 형태로서 패션은 많은 모호함을 담고 있어서 사람들이 특정한 옷과 연관된 의미를 재창조할 수 있게 해 준다. 패션은 자기표현의 가장 단순하고 저렴한 방법 중 하나로, 옷은 저렴하게 구매할 수 있으며, 부, 지적 능력, 휴식 또는 환경 의식에 대한 개념을, 비록 이것들 중 어느 것도 사실이 아니라고 해도, 전달하기 쉽게 해 줄 수 있다. 패션은 또한 다양한 방법으로 발동력을 강화하여 행동을 위한 공간을 열어 줄 수 있다.

구문풀이

[6행] [The most common **explanation** {offered by my informants as to <why fashion is so appealing>}] **is** [that it constitutes a kind of theatrical costumery].

: 첫 번째 [ ]가 주어이며, 주어의 핵인 explanation에 수를 맞추어 단수형 동사 is가 쓰였다. { }는 The most common explanation을 수식하는 과거분사구이고, < >는 전치사 as to의 목적어로 쓰인 의문사절이다. 두 번째 [ ]는 is의 보어로 쓰인 명사절이다.

[15행] Fashion is among the simplest and cheapest methods of self-expression: clothes can be inexpensively purchased [while making **it** easy {to convey notions of wealth, intellectual stature, relaxation or environmental consciousness}], [even if none of these is true].

: 첫 번째 [ ]는 접속사 while을 생략하지 않은 분사구문이고, 두 번째 [ ]는 even if가 이끄는 부사절이다. 첫 번째 [ ]에서 it은 형식상의 목적어이고, { }가 내용상의 목적어이다.

어휘풀이

- trend *n* 유행, 경향, 추세
- suggest *v* 제시하다, 제안하다
- represent *v* 나타내다
- ultimately *ad* 궁극적으로
- appealing *a* 매력적인
- theatrical *a* 연극적인
- locate *v* 위치시키다
- a host of 다수의, 많은
- convey *v* 전달하다
- intellectual *a* 지적인
- consciousness *n* 의식
- agency *n* 힘, 발동력, 작용
- constantly *ad* 끊임없이
- restage *v* 재조정하다
- occasion *n* 때, 경우
- informant *n* 정보 제공자
- constitute *v* 구성하다
- costumery *n* 의상, 복장
- relative to ~와 관련하여
- ambiguity *n* 모호함, 불분명함
- notion *n* 개념, 관념
- relaxation *n* 휴식
- strengthen *v* 강화하다

---

029 답 ③

출제 의도 파악하기

❶ 문장의 구조 파악		❷ 동사의 태	
❸ 재귀대명사		❹ 동명사의 쓰임	
❺ 접속사 that의 쓰임			

정답풀이

③ the belief와 동격 관계를 이루는 that절에 「it is[was] ~ that ....」 강조 구문이 쓰여 주어인 personal satisfaction을 강조하는 구조이다. kept의 목적어는 successful artists로 주어와 다른 대상이므로 재귀대명사 themselves를 them으로 고쳐 써야 한다.

오답풀이

① 문장의 주어는 The picture people have of the art world로, people have of the art world는 The picture를 수식하는 관계절이다. 따라서 문장의 술어 동사 역할을 하는 depends는 어법상 적절하다.

② 주어인 Their success(그들의 성공)가 '여겨지는' 대상이므로 수동태 동사 be viewed는 어법상 적절하다.

④ 동사 avoid는 동명사를 목적어로 취하므로 동명사 exhibiting은 어법상 적절하다.

⑤ conclude의 목적어 역할을 하는 명사절을 유도하는 접속사 that은 뒤에 완전한 구조의 절을 이끌며 적절하게 쓰였다.

전문해석

사람들이 예술계에 대해 갖는 이미지는 그들이 우연히 알게 되는 예술가들에 따라 달라진다. 성공한 예술가들은 당면한 문제에 대해 사실상 자신이 완전히 잘 알고 있다는 일반적인 메시지를 전달한다. 그들의 성공은 그들의 노력과 헌신의 결과로 여겨질 수 있다. 그들은 성공하기 전에 낮은 수입에 대한 보상으로 자신들을 견디게 한 것은 바로 개인적 만족감이었다는 믿음을 존속시킨다. 그러나 실패한 예술가들은 다른 신호를 보내지만 기이하게도 같은 통념을 고수한다. 이 '실패자들'이 자신의 쓰라림을 드러내는 것을 피할 수는 없지만, 자신의 실패에 대해 예술계를 탓하는 경우는 거의 없다. 그들은 예술가가 너무 많지도 모른다는 결론을 내리지 않는다. 대신 그들은 헌신적인 노력이 부족하다고 스스로를 탓한다.

구문풀이

[1행] The picture [people have of the art world] depends on the artists [they happen to know].

: 두 개의 [ ]는 각각 The picture와 the artists를 수식하는 관계절이다.

[6행] They perpetuate the belief [that before their success, **it was** personal satisfaction **that** kept them going as compensation for their low incomes].

: [ ]는 the belief와 동격 관계를 이루는 절이고, 그 안에 personal satisfaction을 강조하는 「it is[was] ~ that ....」 강조구문이 쓰였다.

어휘풀이

- general *a* 일반적인
- well-informed *a* 잘 알고 있는, 박식한
- at hand 당면한
- perpetuate *v* 지속시키다, 영속시키다
- compensation *n* 보상
- myth *n* (잘못된) 통념, 신화
- bitterness *n* 쓰라림
- conclude *v* 결론을 내리다
- dedication *n* 헌신
- stick to ~을 고수하다
- exhibit *v* 드러내다
- blame *v* 비난하다

030 답 ③

출제 의도 파악하기

❶	지시대명사 that	❷	분사의 태
❸	문장의 구조 파악	❹	전치사+관계대명사
❺	부사의 쓰임		

정답풀이

③ 주어는 An individual neuron이고 동사는 uses이다. 따라서 주어와 동사 사이에 삽입되어 주어를 수식하는 분사구를 이끌도록 sends를 현재분사 sending으로 고쳐야 한다.

오답풀이

① those는 앞에 나온 running costs를 대신하는 지시대명사로 적절하게 쓰였다.

② 수식을 받는 명사구 brain cells가 '분화된' 대상이므로 과거분사 specialized의 쓰임은 적절하다.

④ 이어지는 절이 완전한 구조를 이루므로, 관계절에서 at the efficiency의 부사구 역할을 하는 「전치사+관계대명사」 형태의 at which는 적절하다.

⑤ 「as+형용사[부사]의 원급+as」의 원급 비교구문으로, 동명사구 recognizing and picking up one of the chess pieces를 수식하므로 부사의 원급 easily의 쓰임은 적절하다.

전문해석

현대 성인의 뇌는 무게가 전체 체중의 50분의 1에 불과하지만, 총 에너지 필요량의 5분의 1까지 사용한다. 단위 질량당 뇌의 유지비용은 신체 근육의 유지비용의 8배에서 10배 정도이다. 그리고 그 에너지의 약 4분의 3은 우리의 생각과 행동을 만들어 내기 위해 광대한 연결망에서 소통하는 분화된 뇌세포인 뉴런에 사용된다. 뇌에서 신호를 보내는 개개의 뉴런은 마라톤을 하고 있는 다리 근육 세포만큼 많은 에너지를 사용한다. 물론, 전반적으로는 달리고 있을 때 더 많은 에너지를 사용하지만, 우리가 항상 움직이고 있는 것은 아닌 반면에 우리의 뇌는 절대 꺼지지 않는다. 비록 뇌가 신진대사 작용에서 탐욕스럽기는 해도, 수행할 수 있는 계산과 이를 수행하는 효율성 두 가지 면 모두에서 그것은 여전히 어떠한 데스크톱 컴퓨터보다도 훨씬 뛰어나다. 우리가 최고의 그랜드 마스터 체스 선수들을 이길 수 있는 컴퓨터를 만들었을지는 모르지만, 일반적인 세 살배기 아이가 할 수 있는 것만큼 쉽게 체스의 말 중 하나를 인식하고 그것을 집어들 수 있는 컴퓨터를 만드는 것과는 아직도 거리가 멀다.

구문풀이

16행 We may have built computers [that can beat our top Grand Master chess players], but we are still far away from designing one [that is capable of recognizing and picking up one of the chess pieces as easily as a typical three-year-old child **can**].

: 두 개의 [ ]는 각각 computers와 one(= a computer)을 수식하는 관계절이다. can 다음에는 반복되는 동사구 recognize and pick up ~ pieces가 생략되었다.

어휘풀이

- running costs 유지비, 운영비
- unit mass 단위 질량
- expend *v* (시간·노력·에너지 등을) 들이다[소비하다]
- neuron *n* 뉴런, 신경 단위
- specialize *v* 분화시키다
- generate *v* 일으키다, 발생시키다
- be on the move 움직이고 있다
- switch off (기계 등을) 끄다
- metabolically *ad* 신진대사로, 대사 작용으로
- greedy *a* 게걸스러운, 탐욕스러운
- outclass *v* ~보다 훨씬 뛰어나다
- calculation *n* 계산
- efficiency *n* 효율(성)
- be capable of *doing* ~할 수 있다
- typical *a* 전형적인, 일반적인

---

06 형용사 부사
본문 pp.038 ~ 041

Q1 1 fully 2 nervous 3 specific 4 unfortunate 5 like

Q2 1 ✕, full 2 ✕, tightly 3 ○ 4 ✕, significantly

031 ②	032 ②	033 ④	034 ⑤	035 ⑤
036 ④				

Q1

1. 풀이 앞에 있는 are의 보어가 아니라 뒤에 있는 과거분사 prepared를 수식하는 것이므로 부사가 알맞다.
해석 지나친 자신감은 학생들로 하여금 자신들이 시험에 충분히 준비되어 있고 더 이상 공부할 필요가 없다는 잘못된 생각을 하도록 둘 수 있다.

2. 풀이 made의 목적어인 him에 대한 목적격보어 자리이므로 형용사가 알맞다. 비교급 강조 부사 even이 more nervous를 강조하고 있다.
해석 그녀의 명백한 무관심이 그를 훨씬 더 초조하게 만들었다.

3. 풀이 불완전자동사 Be의 보어 자리이므로 형용사가 알맞다.
해석 여러분의 경력을 계획할 때 가능한 한 구체적으로 하라.

4. 풀이 be동사 was의 주격보어 자리이므로 형용사가 알맞다. It이 형식상의 주어이고 that 이하가 내용상의 주어인 구조이다.
해석 그 환자가 나날이 악화되는 것은 불행한 일이었다.

5. 풀이 뒤에 동명사구 목적어를 취할 수 있는 전치사 like가 알맞다. alike는 형용사나 부사로 쓰인다.
해석 사랑에 빠지는 것은 마법의 구름에 둘러싸이는 것과 같다.

Q2

1. 풀이 명사구 her victory를 뒤에서 수식하는 형용사구를 이끄는 자리이므로 형용사인 full로 고쳐 써야 한다.
해석 환호하는 친구들에게 둘러싸여 그녀는 기쁨으로 가득 찬 승리를 즐겼다.

2. 풀이 how 이하는 동명사 assessing의 목적어 역할을 하는 의문사절이고, 의문사절 동사인 are rolled를 수식하는 자리이므로 부사인 tightly로 고쳐 써야 한다.
해석 홍차의 품질을 평가하는 특징 가운데 하나는 잎이 얼마나 단단히 말려 있는지를 평가하는 것이다.

3. 풀이 make의 목적어인 himself or herself에 대한 목적격보어는 형용사인 available이고, readily는 이를 수식하는 부사이므로 알맞다.
해석 사람은 장기적인 관계를 목표로 하고 있는 사람에게 자기 자신을 항상 쉽게 만날 수 있게 해서는 안 된다.

4. 풀이 문맥상 불완전자동사 feels의 보어는 비교급 형용사인 less이며 이를 수식해야 하므로 부사인 significantly로 고쳐 써야 한다.
해석 숫자 799가 800보다 현저히 작게 느껴지는 것은 우리가 전자(799)를 7인 어떤 것으로, 후자(800)를 8인 어떤 것으로 보기 때문이다.

031 답 ②

출제 의도	파악하기
(A)	형용사와 부사
(B)	대동사
(C)	관계대명사 that과 what

정답풀이

(A) 의문사 how가 이끄는 절의 주어(your speech), 동사(may or may not be)에 이어지는 주격보어가 빠져 있으므로, 주격보어로 쓰일 수 있는 형용사 successful이 알맞다.

(B) 문맥상 앞에 나온 일반동사구 attend events를 대신하는 대동사가 와야 하므로 do가 알맞다.

(C) 뒤에 온 you feel은 삽입절이므로 이를 떼어놓고 문장을 보면, 동사 is와 연결되는 주어가 없는 불완전한 구조이다. 바로 앞의 전치사 to의 목적어를 이루는 절을 이끄는 동시에 그 절에서 is의 주어 역할을 하는 선행사를 포함하는 관계대명사 what이 알맞다.

전문해석

연설자가 고려해야 할 한 가지 요점은 청중이 그곳에 있는 동기인데, 이는 여러분의 연설이 얼마나 성공적일지 그렇지 않을지에 큰 차이를 만들 수 있기 때문이다. 많은 사람들이 개인적 또는 사업상의 관심사로 대중 연설 행사에 참석하며, 공유되는 정보를 열심히 듣고 싶어 한다. 그러나 때때로 사람들은 자신들이 원해서라기보다는 그렇게 해야 하기 때문에 행사에 참석한다. 예를 들어, 어떤 직원은 회사를 대신하여 회의에 참석해야 하거나 어떤 학생은 공부하는 과목의 학점 인정 요건으로 참석해야 할 수 있다. 이러한 상황에서 청중 구성원들은 여러분이 제공할 연설에 대해 덜 열의를 보일 가능성이 있다. 여러분이 이러한 사람들을 인식하지 못한다면, 여러분이 생각하기에 좋고 가치 있는 토론이라는 것에 그들이 반응하지 않는다는 것을 알게 될 때 여러분의 자신감은 심각하게 손상을 입을 수 있다.

구문풀이

1행 One point [to consider for a speaker] is the motivation of the audience in being there, [since this can make a big difference to {how successful your speech may or may not be}].

: 첫 번째 [ ]는 One point를 수식하는 to부정사구이다. 두 번째 [ ]는 '~이기 때문에'라는 의미로 쓰인 접속사 since가 이끄는 이유 부사절이다. { }는 전치사 to의 목적어로 쓰인 의문사절이다.

15행 If you are not cognizant of these people, your confidence may be severely compromised [when you find {that they are not responding to what <you feel> is a good and valuable discussion>}].

: [ ]는 접속사 when이 이끄는 시간 부사절이며, { }는 find의 목적어 역할을 하는 명사절이다. < >는 what절에 삽입된 삽입절이다.

어휘풀이

- motivation *n* 동기
- audience *n* 청중
- make a difference 차이를 만들다, 중요하다
- be eager to *do* 열심히 ~하고 싶어 하다
- be required to *do* ~해야 하다
- conference *n* 회의, 회담
- on behalf of ~을 대신하여
- a credit requirement 학점 요구 사항
- enthusiastic *a* 열정적인, 열광하는
- severely *ad* 심하게
- compromise *v* 손상을 입히다

032 답 ②

출제 의도	파악하기		
❶	형식상의 목적어와 내용상의 목적어	❷	부사의 쓰임
❸	분사의 태	❹	관계대명사 what의 쓰임
❺	접속사 that의 쓰임		

정답풀이

② how가 이끄는 의문사절에서 dominantly는 become의 보어에 해당한다. 부사는 보어로 쓰일 수 없으므로 dominantly를 형용사 dominant로 바꿔 써야 한다.

오답풀이

① 「making+it(형식상의 목적어)+목적격보어(harder)+의미상의 주어(for new players)+내용상의 목적어(to compete with them)」의 구조로, 내용상의 목적어를 이끄는 to부정사 to compete는 적절하다.

③ 뒤에 anybody를 목적어로 취하고 있고, 수식을 받는 regulations가 '유리하게 하는' 주체이므로 현재분사 favoring은 적절하다.

④ 전치사 at의 목적어 역할을 하는 절을 이끄는 동시에 그 절에서 doing의 목적어 역할을 하므로 선행사를 포함한 관계대명사 what은 어법상 적절하다.

⑤ 뒤에 완전한 구조의 절이 이어지고, 그 절이 문맥상 a sign과 동격의 관계를 이루므로 동격절을 이끄는 접속사 that은 적절하다.

전문해석

독점과 관련한 실제 문제들은 자본주의가 아니라 국가 통제주의에 의해 초래된다. 국가 통제주의 사회 체제하에서는 세금, 보조금, 관세 그리고 규제가 흔히 시장에서 기존의 대기업들을 보호하는 역할을 한다. 그러한 기업들은 외국과의 경쟁을 방지하는 새로운 관세, 신규 기업들이 그들과 경쟁하는 것을 더 어렵게 만드는 보조금, 또는 대기업이 자산을 가지고 있어 준수할 수 있는 규제 조치와 같은 보호책들을 유지하거나 확대하기 위해 정실 전략을 자주 사용한다. 반면에, 자본주의 사회 체제하에서 정부는 기업이 자신의 산업에서 얼마나 우위를 점하게 될지 또는 어떻게 기업들이 서로 인수하고 합병하는지에 전혀 관여할 수 없다. 게다가, 자본주의 사회는 권리를 침해하는 세금, 관세, 보조금 또는 누군가에게 유리한 규제가 없고, 그것은 독점 금지법도 없다. 자본주의하에서 우위는 여러분이 하고 있는 일에 정말로 능숙해짐으로써만 얻어질 수 있다. 그리고 우위를 유지하기 위해서 여러분은 계속해서 경쟁자에 앞서 있어야 하는데, 경쟁자도 또한 여러분의 우위와 이익을 다른 사람들이 벌 수 있는 돈이 있다는 신호로 여기기 때문이다.

구문풀이

14행 Furthermore, a capitalist society doesn't have rights-violating taxes, tariffs, subsidies, or regulations favoring anybody [**nor does it** have antitrust laws].

: [ ]는 부정어 nor가 앞에 나와서 주어(it)와 조동사(does)가 도치된 구문으로, and it does not have antitrust laws로 풀어 쓸 수 있다.

18행 And to maintain dominance, you have to continue to stay ahead of the competition, [which sees your dominance and profits as a sign {that there is money <**to be made** by others>} as well].

: [ ]는 the competition을 부연 설명하는 관계절이며, 그 안의 { }는 a sign과 동격 관계를 이루는 절이다. < >는 money를 수식하는 to부정사구로, money와 make가 수동의 관계이므로 수동형 to be made가 쓰였다.

어휘풀이

- monopoly *n* 독점, 전매
- capitalism *n* 자본주의
- subsidy *n* 보조금
- tariff *n* 관세
- regulation *n* 규제, 규정
- tactic *n* 전략, 전술
- retain *v* 유지하다, 보유하다
- regulatory measure 규제 조치

- comply with ~을 준수하다
- take over ~을 인수하다
- rights-violating *a* 권리를 침해하는
- dominance *n* 우위, 지배
- stay ahead of ~에 앞선 상태에 있다
- competition *n* (집합적) 경쟁자
- have no say 전혀 관여할 수 없다
- merge *v* 합병하다
- favor *v* 유리하게 하다, 특혜를 주다

- in terms of ~의 관점[측면]에서
- relaxation *n* 이완, 휴식
- objectify *v* 객관화하다, 구체화하다
- recurrent *a* 되풀이되는
- resolution *n* 해소
- exertion *n* 힘쓰기, 노력, 힘의 발휘
- enduring *a* 오래 지속되는
- pitch *n* 음의 높이
- construct *v* 구성하다
- frequency *n* 주파수
- tension *n* 긴장
- interval *n* 간격
- similarity *n* 유사성
- partial *a* 부분적인
- resemble *v* 닮다, 비슷하다
- temporary *a* 일시적인
- hierarchical *a* 계층적인
- scale *n* 음계
- count as ~로 간주되다
- ratio *n* 비율

033 답 ④

출제 의도 파악하기
❶	재귀대명사	❷	접속사 for의 쓰임
❸	부사의 쓰임	❹	관계대명사 which의 쓰임
❺	동사 count의 쓰임		

정답풀이
④ the system을 수식하는 관계절을 이끄는 자리인데, 뒤에 이어지는 절이 주어(the scale), 수동태 동사(is constructed)를 갖춘 완전한 구조이므로, 관계대명사 which는 쓸 수 없다. 「전치사+관계대명사」가 되어야 하는데, 문맥상 '체계를 통해'라는 뜻이 적절하므로 through which 정도로 바꿔 써야 한다.

오답풀이
① 주어인 We를 강조하는 재귀대명사 ourselves의 쓰임은 적절하다. 재귀대명사 ourselves는 문장에 빠진 요소가 없으므로 목적어 자리에 온 것이 아닌 강조 용법으로 쓰인 것이다.
② 이유를 나타내는 부사절을 이끄는 접속사로 쓰인 for는 적절하다.
③ '지속하는'의 의미를 갖는 형용사 enduring을 수식하는 부사 relatively는 알맞다.
⑤ should note의 목적어로 쓰인 that절에서 주어부를 구성하는 what절의 동사로 쓰인 자동사 counts는 어법상 적절하다.

전문해석
우리는 긴장과 이완의 관점에서 불협화음과 화음의 패턴을 경험하는 경향이 있다. 우리는 간격 사이의 긴장 정도에 대응하여 스스로 긴장과 이완을 느끼고, 또한 음악의 특징으로서 긴장과 이완을 객관화하는 경향이 있다. 우리는 음악의 행동과 우리의 활동 사이의 유사성을 쉽게 감지하는데, 음악에서 되풀이되는 긴장과 이에 이어지는 그러한 긴장의 부분적이거나 혹은 완전한 해소를 우리가 알아차리기 때문이다. 이러한 것들은 우리가 힘을 발휘하고 이완하는 패턴과 닮았다. 예를 들어, 우리는 힘을 쓴 시간 다음에는 쉬는 시간을 가진다. 이것들은 일시적일 수도 있고 상대적으로 오래 지속될 수도 있다. 그러나 간격 사이의 상대적 긴장감은 음계 내의 음 높이의 계층적 구조에 따라 달라지는데, 이는 그것을 통해 음계가 구성되는 체계에 익숙하지 않은 청취자에게는 즉각 명확하지 않을 수 있다는 점에 우리는 주목해야 한다. 또한 우리는 화음이라고 간주하는 것이 비록 간단한 주파수 비율에 근거하기는 하지만 음악적인 체계에서 상대적인 것이라는 점도 주목해야 한다.

구문풀이
13행 We should note, however, [that a sense of relative tension among intervals depends upon the hierarchical organization of pitches within a scale, {which may not be immediately obvious to the listener <who is unfamiliar with the system (through which the scale is constructed)>}].

: [ ]는 should note의 목적어로 쓰인 명사절이며, { }는 the hierarchical organization of pitches within a scale을 부연 설명하는 관계절이다. < >는 the listener를, ( )는 the system을 수식하는 관계절이다.

034 답 ⑤

출제 의도 파악하기
❶	지시대명사 that	❷	분사구문의 태
❸	재귀대명사	❹	to부정사의 쓰임
❺	부사의 쓰임		

정답풀이
⑤ 「so ~ that ...」 구문에서 so ~ 부분이 문두로 나와 주어와 be동사가 도치된 구조로, uniformly는 is의 보어에 해당한다. 그런데 부사는 보어로 쓰일 수 없으므로 형용사인 uniform으로 바꿔 써야 한다.

오답풀이
① 「from *A* to *B*(*A*에서 *B*로)」 구문이 쓰인 구조로, the depiction of objects가 *A*에 해당하며, that of abstract notions가 *B*에 해당한다. 여기서 that은 앞에 나온 the depiction을 받아서 의미상 the depiction of abstract notions(추상적 개념의 묘사)를 나타내므로 어법상 적절하다.
② 앞에 주어(Sumerian cuneiform), 동사(was), 보어(a linear writing system)를 갖춘 완전한 구조의 절이 왔고, 또 다른 접속사나 관계사가 없으므로 its symbols usually set 이하의 분사구문임을 알 수 있다. 의미상의 주어인 its symbols가 '놓인' 대상이므로 수동의 의미를 나타내는 과거분사 set은 적절하다.
③ do not organize의 주어는 objects이고 문맥상 목적어도 동일한 대상이므로 목적어 자리에 쓰인 재귀대명사 themselves는 알맞다.
④ 앞에 주어(Early rock paintings)와 동사(were shaped and organized)를 갖춘 완전한 구조의 절이 왔고, to부정사구인 to follow 이하가 부사적 용법으로 목적을 나타내고 있으므로 to follow는 알맞다.

전문해석
세계 최초의 복잡한 쓰기 형태인 수메르 쐐기 문자는 기원전 3500년 즈음에 그림 문자에서 표의 문자적 표현으로, 즉 사물의 묘사에서 추상적 개념의 묘사로 나아가며 진화적 경로를 따랐다. 수메르 쐐기 문자는 선형의 쓰기 체계였는데, 보통은 그것의 기호가 세로 단에 놓인 채로 위에서 아래로 그리고 왼쪽에서 오른쪽으로 읽혔다. 이 조직화는 일종의 추상 개념이었는데, 세계가 선형 공간이 아니고 사물은 실제 삶에서 수평적으로 또는 수직적으로 스스로를 구조화하지 않는다는 것이었다. 의례적 목적을 위해 만들어졌다고 여겨지는 초기의 암각화들은 아마도 동굴의 벽이나 화가의 바람을 따르도록 형상화되고 구조화됐을 것이고, 그들은 상징적으로, 예술적으로, 심지어 무작위로 그것들(암각화)을 구조화했을지도 모른다. 그렇지만 쐐기 문자 이후에는 등장한 사실상 모든 형태의 문자는 분명한 시작과 종료 지점이 있는 줄로 나열되어 왔다. 정말로 이러한 예상은 너무나도 획일적이어서 특이한 예외는 주목할 만하고 일반적으로 특정한 목적을 위해 설정된다.

11행 Early rock paintings, [thought **to have been created** for ritual purposes], were possibly shaped and organized [to follow {the walls of the cave}, or {the desires of the painters}, {who may have organized them symbolically, or artistically, or even randomly}].

: 첫 번째 [ ]는 주어와 동사 사이에 삽입된 분사구이며, 그 안의 to have been created는 본동사 were의 시제인 과거보다 앞서므로 「to have p.p.」 형태로 쓰인 것이다. 두 번째 [ ]는 목적을 나타내는 to부정사구이며, or로 연결된 첫 번째와 두 번째 { }가 follow의 목적어를 이루고 있다. 세 번째 { }는 the painters를 부연 설명하는 관계절이다.

어휘풀이

- complex *a* 복잡한
- path *n* 길, 경로
- ideographic *a* 표의 문자의
- depiction *n* 묘사
- notion *n* 개념
- column *n* 세로 단
- organize *v* 구성하다, 조직하다
- vertically *ad* 수직으로
- desire *n* 욕망
- virtually *ad* 사실상, 거의
- uniformly *ad* 획일적으로, 동일하게
- noteworthy *a* 주목할 만한
- evolutionary *a* 진화적인, 진화의
- pictographic *a* 그림 문자의
- representation *n* 표현
- abstract *a* 추상적인
- linear *a* 선형의, 직선형의
- abstraction *n* 추상
- horizontally *ad* 수평으로
- ritual *n* 의례
- randomly *ad* 무작위로, 임의로
- emerge *v* 등장하다, 출현하다
- odd *a* 특이한

035 답 ⑤

① 주어와 동사의 수 일치	② 분사의 태
③ so ~ that ... 구문	④ 지각동사의 목적격보어
⑤ 부사의 쓰임	

정답풀이

⑤ has made의 목적격보어 자리인데, 부사는 보어로 쓰일 수 없으므로 resistantly를 형용사 resistant로 고쳐야 한다.

오답풀이

① to부정사구(To pass judgment ~ angry) 주어는 단수 취급하므로 단수형 동사 is는 적절하게 쓰였다.
② happiness는 '진가를 인정받는' 대상이므로 목적격보어로 과거분사 appreciated를 쓴 것은 어법상 적절하다.
③ '매우 ~해서 …하다'라는 의미를 나타내는 「so ~ that ...」 구문으로, 결과의 부사절을 이끄는 that은 어법상 적절하다.
④ 지각동사 have heard의 목적어 someone이 expel의 주체이므로 목적격보어로 쓰인 원형부정사 expel은 어법상 적절하다.

전문해석

화는 정상적인 감정이다. 화는 좋은 것도 나쁜 것도 아니며, 그것에 대해 어떤 판단도 결부될 필요가 없다. 어떤 사람들은 화를 내면 문제가 생긴다고 믿는다. 이런 생각은 사실이 아니다. 화에 대해 판단을 내리면서 화가 난 것을 인정하는 사람들을 비난하는 것은 사람들에게서 사람됨을 빼앗는 것과 동등한 것이다. 슬픔은 행복의 진가를 더 알게 만드는 기준점을 제공한다. 긴장은 긴장의 완화와 비교될 때 더 잘 이해될 수 있다. 화에 대해 가치 판단을 하는 것을 이제 멈출 때가 되었다. 여러분은 바로 지금 몹시 화가 날 수 있지만 여러분이 화와 관련된 어떤 행동을 보이지 않는 한 아무도 그것을 알지 못할 것이다. 화는 나쁜 것이라는 믿음이 아주 강하게 몸에 배어

있어서 화가 도처에서 넘쳐흐르고 있을 때조차도 사람들은 때때로 그것의 존재를 부인할 것이다. 우리 모두는 얼굴이 빨개진 어떤 사람이 화난 말을 내뱉은 다음 "나는 화나지 않았어!"라고 말하는 것을 들어보았다. 화가 받아 온 비난은 그것이 연구되는 것을 더욱더 저항력 있게(힘들게) 만들었다.

4행 [To {pass judgment on anger} and {condemn those <who admit to becoming angry>}] is the equivalent of [robbing people of their humanness].

: 첫 번째 [ ]가 문장의 주어이고, 문장의 동사는 is이다. To에 이어지는 두 개의 { }가 병렬구조로 연결되어 있고, < >는 those를 수식하는 관계절이다. 두 번째 [ ]는 전치사 of의 목적어 역할을 하는 동명사구이다.

어휘풀이

- attach *v* 붙이다, 결부시키다
- equivalent *n* 동등한 것
- reference point 기준점
- tension *n* 긴장
- furious *a* 몹시 화난, 격노한
- deny *v* 부인하다
- expel *v* 분출하다
- condemn *v* 비난하다
- humanness *n* 사람됨, 인간성
- appreciate *v* 진가를 알다
- relaxation *n* 긴장의 완화
- demonstrate *v* 보여 주다, 입증하다
- spill out 넘쳐흐르다
- examination *n* 연구, 조사

036 답 ④

① 주어와 동사의 수 일치	② 의문사 what의 쓰임
③ 분사구문의 태	④ 부사의 쓰임
⑤ 관계대명사 that의 쓰임	

정답풀이

④ 동사 are의 보어에 해당하므로 형용사 close로 써야 한다. 부사는 보어로 쓸 수 없다.

오답풀이

① 「some of+명사」와 같이 부분을 나타내는 표현이 주어로 쓰이면 of 뒤의 명사에 동사의 수를 일치시키므로 evidence에 수를 맞춘 단수형 동사 comes의 쓰임은 적절하다.
② have examined의 목적절을 이끌며 이어지는 절에서 주어 역할을 하는 의문사 what은 적절하다.
③ 분사구문의 의미상 주어인 advanced musicians가 '연습하는' 주체이므로 능동의 의미를 나타내는 현재분사 practicing은 적절하다.
⑤ crude ~ of the music을 선행사로 하며 이어지는 관계절에서 동사 allow의 주어 역할을 하는 관계대명사 that은 적절하다.

전문해석

심적 표상은 감각에 실제로 존재하지 않는 것들에 대한 심상이다. 일반적으로, 심적 표상은 우리가 학습하는 데 도움을 줄 수 있다. 이에 대한 최고의 증거 중 몇몇은 음악 연주 분야에서 온다. 여러 연구자들은 무엇이 최고의 음악가들과 실력이 더 낮은 음악가들을 구분 짓는가를 조사해 왔으며, 주요한 차이점들 중 하나가 최고의 음악가들이 만들어 내는 심적 표상의 질에 있다. 새로운 작품을 연습할 때 상급 음악가들은 작품에 대한 자신의 연습 그리고 궁극적으로 자신의 연주를 이끌기 위해 자신이 사용하는 음악에 대한 매우 상세한 심적 표상을 가지고 있다. 특히, 그들은 자신이 그 작품을 제대로 이해하는 것에 얼마나 근접했는지와 그들이 향상하기 위해 무엇을 다르게 할 필요가 있는지를 알기 위해 심적 표상을 자기 자신의 피드백을 제공하는 데 사용한다. 초급 및 중급 학생들은 가령 자신이 언제 틀린 음을 쳤는지 알게 해 주는 음악에 대한 투박한 표상을 가질 수도 있겠으나, 더 미세한 실수와 약점을 알아내

기 위해서는 선생님의 피드백에 의존해야 한다.

구문풀이

5행 Several researchers have examined [what differentiates the best musicians from lesser ones], and one of the major differences lies in the quality of the mental representations [the best ones create].

: 첫 번째 [ ]는 have examined의 목적어 역할을 하는 의문사절이고, 두 번째 [ ]는 the mental representations를 수식하는 관계절이다.

어휘풀이

- representation *n* 표현, 표상
- differentiate *v* 구별하다
- in particular 특히
- intermediate *a* 중급의
- subtle *a* 미세한, 미묘한
- imagery *n* 심상, 표상
- ultimately *ad* 궁극적으로
- get ~ right ~을 올바르게 하다
- identify *v* 밝혀내다

---

07 관계사

본문 pp.044 ~ 047

Q1 **1** that **2** that **3** where **4** at which **5** which

Q2 **1** ×, that 또는 which **2** ×, where 또는 in which
3 ○ **4** ×, what

037 ⑤   **038** ③   **039** ④   **040** ④   **041** ⑤

042 ⑤

Q1

1. 풀이 선행사는 special events이고 이어지는 절이 동사 need의 주어가 빠진 불완전한 구조이므로 주격 관계대명사 that이 알맞다.

해석 기념일과 밸런타인데이는 아름답고 신중하게 고른 꽃이 필요한 특별한 행사들이다.

2. 풀이 선행사 a word가 있고, 뒤에 don't know의 목적어가 빠진 불완전한 구조의 절이 이어지므로 목적격 관계대명사 that이 알맞다.

해석 (의미를) 모르는 단어를 만날 때마다 사전을 참조하라.

3. 풀이 관계사 이하의 절이 완전한 구조이므로 선행사 a small house를 부연 설명하는 절을 이끄는 관계부사 where가 알맞다.

해석 그녀는 작은 집에서 살았으므로, 그곳에서 그녀는 다른 가족들을 방해하지 않고는 연습을 할 수 없었고, 주로 밖에서 고음을 연습했다.

4. 풀이 선행사는 a point이고, 뒤에 완전한 구조의 절이 이어지므로 「전치사+관계대명사」 형태의 at which가 알맞다.

해석 많은 사람들이 우리가 결국 자원의 유한한 특성과의 갈등이 불가피한 지점에 도달하게 될 것이라고 믿는다.

5. 풀이 선행사 air가 있고, 콤마(,) 뒤에서 air를 부연 설명하므로 계속적 용법의 관계대명사 which가 알맞다.

해석 건물은 공기로 둘러싸여 있는데, 그것이 떨어지는 구슬에 마찰을 가하며 속도를 떨어뜨린다.

Q2

1. 풀이 선행사 chemical compounds가 있으므로 선행사를 포함하는 관계대명사 what은 적절하지 않으며, 뒤에 오는 동사 nourish, heal, delight의 주어 역할을 하는 관계대명사 that 또는 which로 고쳐 써야 한다.

해석 영양분을 공급하고 치료하고 감각을 즐겁게 하는 화학 합성물들이 식물들로부터 나온다.

2. 풀이 뒤에 완전한 구조의 절이 이어지므로 관계대명사 which는 적절하지 않으며, one big contest를 선행사로 하는 관계부사 where 또는 「전치사+관계대명사」 형태의 in which로 고쳐 써야 한다.

해석 여러분은 세상을 모든 사람이 다른 모든 사람과 경쟁하고 있는 하나의 큰 경기로 여긴다.

3. 풀이 선행사 the yellow and white lights가 있고, 뒤에 주어가 빠진 불완전한 구조의 절이 이어지므로 주격 관계대명사 that은 알맞다.

해석 파란색 불빛은 밤에 도시의 상당 부분을 밝히는 노란색과 흰색 불빛보다 더 매력적이고 차분하다.

4. 풀이 the message 뒤의 that은 동격의 접속사이고, 이 동격절에서 관계사 앞에 선행사가 없으므로 which는 적절하지 않다. 동격절의 주어가 되는 명사절을 이끌도록 선행사를 포함하는 관계대명사 what으로 고쳐 써야 한다.

해석 여러분은 화자가 말하고 있는 것이 여러분에게 중요하다는 메시지를 보내고 싶어 한다.

---

037 답 ⑤

출제 의도 파악하기	
❶ 동사의 수와 태	❷ 복합관계대명사 whatever의 쓰임
❸ 전치사+관계대명사	❹ 접속사 that의 쓰임
❺ 문장의 구조 파악	

정답풀이
⑤ 문장의 주어는 Dinners이고 동사는 dragged이다. 따라서 접속사 없이 또 다른 동사 put은 올 수 없으며, 문맥상 앞 절의 내용을 의미상의 주어로 하는 능동의 분사구문을 이끌도록 put을 현재분사 putting으로 바꿔 써야 한다.

오답풀이
① 주어인 nearly all the dishes of the meal이 식탁에 '놓여 있는' 대상이고, 주어의 핵은 dishes이므로 이에 수를 일치시킨 수동태 동사 were placed는 적절하게 쓰였다.
② 전치사 to의 목적어 역할을 하는 명사절을 이끄는 자리로, 그 절이 주어가 빠진 불완전한 구조이므로 anything that(~하는 것은 무엇이든지)의 의미를 갖는 복합관계대명사 whatever는 적절하다.
③ 뒤에 주어(food)와 동사(was delivered)를 갖춘 완전한 구조의 절이 이어지고, 선행사인 *service à la russe* (Russian service)가 의미상 전치사 in의 목적어로 쓰였으므로 「전치사+관계대명사」 형태인 in which는 적절하다.
④ 뒤에 완전한 구조의 절이 이어지므로 동사 meant의 목적절을 이끄는 접속사 that은 적절하게 쓰였다.

전문해석
19세기는 음식이 제공되는 방식에 있어서 변화의 시기를 나타냈다. 1850년대 이전에, 식사의 거의 모든 요리는 처음부터 식탁 위에 놓여 있었다. 손님들은 도착하면 음식이 기다리고[준비되어] 있는 것을 발견하곤 했다. 그들은 근처에 있는 것은 무엇이든 맘껏 먹고, 다른 요리가 전달되도록 요청하거나 요리를 가지고 오라고 하인을 부르곤 했다. 이런 스타일의 식사는 'service à la française'(프랑스식 접대)로 알려졌으나, 이제는 음식이 코스로 식탁으로 배달되는 'service à la russe'(러시아식 접대)로 알려진 새로운 방식이 도입되었다. 많은 사람들이 이 새로운 방식을 싫어했는데, 왜냐하면 그것은 모든 사람들이 같은 순서와 속도로 모든 것을 먹어야 한다는 것을 의미했기 때문이다. 만약 한 사람이 느리면, 그것은 다른 모든 사람들을 위한 다음 코스를 지연시켰고, 그것은 음식이 식는다는 것을 의미했다. 이제 디너는 종종 몇 시간 동안 계속되었고, 이는 거의 모든 사람들의 방광에 심한 부담을 주었다.

구문풀이
14행 If one person was slow, it [held up the next course for everyone else], and [meant {that food lost heat}].

: and로 연결된 두 개의 [ ]는 주절의 술어를 이룬다. { }는 meant의 목적어로 쓰인 명사절이다.

어휘풀이
- at the outset 처음부터, 처음에
- nearby *a* 근처의, 가까운
- servant *n* 하인, 종
- fetch *v* 가지고[데리고] 오다
- pace *n* 속도
- hold up ~을 지연시키다
- drag on (너무 오랫동안) 질질 끌다[계속되다]
- strain *n* 부담, 압박

---

038 답 ③

출제 의도 파악하기	
❶ 지시대명사 that	❷ 분사의 태
❸ 관계대명사 which의 쓰임	❹ 분사구문
❺ enable의 목적격보어	

정답풀이
③ 뒤에 있는 명사구 rhythmic time을 한정하면서 선행사인 others를 수식하는 관계절을 이끌어야 하므로 관계대명사 which를 소유격 관계대명사 whose로 고쳐 써야 한다.

오답풀이
① those는 앞에 나온 the communities and interactions of organisms를 대신하므로 어법상 적절하다.
② 문장의 주어는 The processes이고 동사는 differ이다. 따라서 The processes를 능동의 의미로 수식하는 분사구를 이끄는 현재분사 governing은 적절하다.
④ 완전한 구조의 절 다음에 접속사나 관계사 없이 이어지는 것으로 보아, other things 이하는 분사구문임을 알 수 있다. 따라서 being은 other things를 의미상의 주어로 하면서 조건의 의미를 나타내는 분사구문을 이루는 현재분사로 알맞게 쓰였다.
⑤ 동사 enable은 목적격보어로 to부정사를 취하므로 to survive는 어법상 적절하다.

전문해석
생태계들은 구성과 범위 면에서 차이가 있다. 그것들은 여러분의 입안에 있는 유기체들의 군집과 상호작용 혹은 열대 우림의 덮개 안에 있는 그것(유기체들의 군집과 상호작용)들에서부터 지구의 바다에 있는 모든 그것(유기체들의 군집과 상호작용)들까지의 범위에 이르는 것으로 정의될 수 있다. 그것들을 지배하는 과정들은 복잡성과 속도의 면에서 차이가 있다. 몇 분 안에 바뀌는 시스템도 있고, 규칙적으로 순환하는 시간이 수백 년까지 연장되는 시스템도 있다. 어떤 생태계는 광범위하고(아프리카 사바나 같은 '생물군계'), 어떤 생태계는 지역들에 걸쳐 있으며(강의 유역), 많은 생태계가 마을 군집을 포함하고(작은 분수령들), 다른 생태계들은 단 하나의 마을 차원으로 국한된다(마을 연못). 각각의 사례에는 불가분성이라는 요소가 있다. 어떤 생태계를 장벽을 만들어 부분들로 나누면, 그 부분들의 생산성의 총합은 일반적으로, 다른 것들이 동일하다면, 전체의 생산성보다 더 낮다는 것이 발견될 것이다. 생물학적 개체군의 이동성이 한 가지 이유이다. 예를 들어, 안전한 통행은 이동하는 생물 종들을 생존할 수 있게 한다.

구문풀이
14행 **Divide** an ecosystem into parts by creating barriers, **and** the sum of the productivity of the parts will typically be found to be lower than the productivity of the whole, [other things being equal].

: 「명령문 ~, and ....」 구문이 쓰였다. [ ]는 조건을 나타내는 분사구문이며 other things는 분사구문의 의미상 주어이다.

어휘풀이
- composition *n* 구성
- extent *n* 범위
- community *n* 군집
- organism *n* 유기체
- govern *v* 지배하다, 관리하다
- complexity *n* 복잡성

- turn over 바뀌다
- extend *v* 연장되다
- biome *n* (숲·사막 같은 특정 환경 내의) 생물군계
- cluster *n* 무리
- confine *v* 제한하다
- barrier *n* 장벽
- mobility *n* 이동성
- rhythmic *a* 규칙적으로 순환하는
- extensive *a* 광범위한
- watershed *n* 분수령
- indivisibility *n* 불가분성
- productivity *n* 생산성
- migratory *a* 이동[이주]하는

- spur *v* 촉진하다
- address *v* 다루다
- concentration *n* 집중, 집약
- variation *n* 변화, 변동
- taxing *a* 과중한, 부담이 큰
- routinely *ad* 일상적으로
- abundance *n* 많음, 풍부함
- decline *v* 감소하다
- land clearing 토지 개간
- demonstrate *v* 보여 주다, 논증하다
- peasant *n* 농부, 소작농
- composition *n* 구성
- peak *n* 절정, 최고조
- undertake *v* 떠맡다
- emigration *n* 이민, 이주

039 답 ④

출제 의도 파악하기
❶ 의문사 how의 쓰임		❷ 동사의 태
❸ 주어와 동사의 수 일치		❹ 전치사+관계대명사
❺ 주어와 동사의 수 일치, 동사 decline의 쓰임		

정답풀이

④ physically taxing work를 수식하는 관계절을 유도하는 관계사를 묻는 것으로, 이어지는 절이 술어 동사인 will undertake의 목적어가 없는 불완전한 구조이다. 따라서 in which를 관계대명사 which 또는 that으로 바꿔 써야 한다.

오답풀이

① 뒤에 완전한 구조의 절이 이어지고, 전치사 about의 목적어 역할을 하는 의문사절을 이끌고 있으므로 의문사 how는 적절하다.
② 주어인 This weakness가 '다루어져 온' 대상이므로, 현재완료 수동태를 이루는 과거분사 addressed는 적절하게 쓰였다.
③ 주어의 핵이 Variations이므로 복수형 동사 influence는 어법상 적절하다.
⑤ 주절에서 핵심 주어는 the likelihood로 단수이고, decline은 자동사로도 쓰일 수 있으므로 declines는 어법상 적절하다.

전문해석

최근까지, 인구 증가와 열대 삼림 벌채 사이의 인과관계에 대해 찬성 의견을 말해 온 대부분의 연구는 인구 증가가 어떻게 토지 개간을 촉진했는지에 대한 상세하고 경험적인 설명을 제공하지 않았다. 이 약점은 지난 10년 동안 여러 가지 다른 방식으로 다루어져 왔다. 1970년대와 1980년대 동안 코스타리카의 숲 분포율 변화에 관한 한 연구는 토지가 없는 농민의 집중과 인근 삼림의 파괴 사이에 양의 상관성을 보여 주었다. 가구 구성의 변화 역시 토지 개간률에 영향을 미친다. 땅에서 1차 열대우림(인간에 의한 생태학적 과정의 방해가 없는 열대우림)을 개간하는 것은 육체적인 힘이 최고조에 있는 젊은이들만이 일상적으로 떠맡는, 육체적으로 과중한 일이다. 이 때문에 젊은 노동자가 많은 가정과 지역 사회만이 많은 땅을 개간하게 마련이다. 이민이나 출생률 저하가 한 가정의 젊은 노동자의 수를 감소시킬 경우, 그 가구의 토지에 대한 삼림 개간 가능성 또한 낮아진다.

구문풀이

`1행` Until recently, most studies [that have argued for a causal connection between population growth and tropical deforestation] have not provided detailed, empirical accounts about [how population growth has spurred land clearing].

: 첫 번째 [ ]는 most studies를 수식하는 관계절이고, 두 번째 [ ]는 전치사 about의 목적어 역할을 하는 의문사절이다.

어휘풀이

- argue for ~에 찬성 의견을 말하다
- connection *n* 관계, 연결
- empirical *a* 경험적인
- causal *a* 인과관계의
- deforestation *n* 삼림 벌채
- account *n* 설명

040 답 ④

출제 의도 파악하기
❶ 형용사의 쓰임		❷ 병렬구조
❸ 재귀대명사		❹ 문장의 구조 파악
❺ 관계대명사 that의 쓰임		

정답풀이

④ explain의 목적어이며 why로 시작되는 절의 주어 orangutans에 이어지는 술어 동사가 필요하므로 준동사인 being을 are로 바꿔 써야 한다. who ~ neighbors는 주어인 orangutans를 부연 설명하는 관계절이다.

오답풀이

① '두 배만큼 ~한'의 의미를 나타내는 「twice as+원급(+as)」의 배수 표현으로, are의 보어 역할을 하는 형용사 large는 어법상 적절하다.
② 문맥상 and 앞의 communicate와 병렬로 연결되어 help의 목적격보어 역할을 하는 원형부정사 manipulate는 어법상 적절하다.
③ recognize의 주어와 목적어가 they(= the apes)로 같으므로 목적어로 재귀대명사 themselves를 쓴 것은 적절하다.
⑤ some other factor를 수식하는 관계절을 유도하며, 그 관계절에서 주어 역할을 하는 주격 관계대명사 that은 어법상 적절하다.

전문해석

원숭이의 지능은 우리의 가장 가까운 친척인 오랑우탄, 고릴라, 침팬지, 보노보와 같은 대형 유인원들의 지능에 비해 떨어지는데, 그것들의 뇌는 그것들의 몸무게에 비하여 두 배 더 크다. 대부분의 영장류 동물학자들은 유인원들이 더 큰 뇌를 얻어서 자신의 동료와 소통하고 그들을 조종하는 것을 돕게 되었다고 생각한다. 그리고 그것들은 분명히 자신의 집단 안에서 복잡한 사회적 상호작용을 보여 준다. 그것들은 공감을 느낄 수 있는 것처럼 보이고, 자아상을 가지고 있으며, 거울에서 자신을 인식할 수 있는 것처럼 어느 정도의 지각을 보인다. 하지만 이 '사회적 가설'은 그렇게 영리해진 것이 원숭이나 육상 포유류 집단이기보다는 왜 대형 유인원이었는지를 설명하지 못한다. 또한 왜 자신의 이웃과 거의 만나지 않는 오랑우탄이 그렇게 똑똑한지도 설명하지 못한다. 애초에 유인원이 더 똑똑해지도록 하고, 그 이후로 그 집단의 일부 구성원이 높은 수준의 사회성을 개발할 수 있게 한 어떤 다른 요인이 작용했음이 틀림없는 것 같아 보인다.

구문풀이

`14행` **Nor does it** explain [why orangutans, {who seldom encounter their neighbors}, are so intelligent].

: 부정어 Nor가 문두에 쓰여 주어 it과 조동사 does가 도치되었다. [ ]는 explain의 목적어 역할을 하는 의문사절이고, 그 안의 { }는 주어와 동사 사이에 삽입된 관계절로, 주어인 orangutans를 부연 설명한다.

`16행` **It** seems likely [that some other factor must have been in play {that caused apes to become more intelligent in the first place}, and {which could subsequently have enabled some members of the group to develop high-level sociality}].

: It은 형식상의 주어이며 [ ]가 내용상의 주어이다. 두 개의 { }는 some other factor를 수식하는 관계절이다.

어휘풀이

- pale in comparison with ~에 비해 떨어지다
- relative *n* 친척
- bonobo *n* 보노보(유인원의 일종)
- acquire *v* 얻다, 획득하다
- peer *n* 동료
- empathy *n* 공감
- consciousness *n* 지각, 의식
- encounter *v* 만나다
- subsequently *ad* 그 이후로
- ape *n* 유인원
- relative to ~에 비하여
- manipulate *v* 조종하다
- exhibit *v* 보여 주다
- self-image *n* 자아상
- hypothesis *n* 가설
- in the first place 애초에
- sociality *n* 사회성

041 답 ⑤

출제 의도	파악하기
❶ 동명사의 쓰임	❷ 주어와 동사의 수 일치
❸ 부사의 쓰임	❹ 도치구문의 수 일치
❺ 관계대명사 what의 쓰임	

정답풀이

⑤ 선행사 majors를 수식하는 관계절을 이끄는 자리로, 선행사를 포함하는 관계대명사 what은 쓸 수 없다. 뒤에 오는 관계절의 동사 have tended의 주어 역할을 할 수 있도록 주격 관계대명사 that 또는 which로 바꿔 써야 한다.

오답풀이

① your를 의미상의 주어로 하며 전치사 toward의 목적어를 이루고 있으므로 동명사 achieving의 쓰임은 적절하다.
② 주어는 The primary focus of ~ fields이며 주어의 핵은 focus이므로 단수형 동사 is는 알맞다.
③ 형용사구인 more career-oriented를 수식하므로 부사인 generally는 어법상 적절하다.
④ 부정어인 nor가 절의 앞에 쓰였으므로 「조동사+주어+동사원형」 어순으로 도치되어 does가 it 앞에 온 것은 적절하다.

전문해석

매우 일반적인 규칙으로서 (예외는 풍부하지만) 인문학, 사회과학, 자연과학은 근본적으로 여러분이 지적 성장과 발전을 이루는 데 더 맞춰져 있다. 이러한 '문과' 분야의 주요 초점은 졸업과 동시에 직접 연관된 분야에서 직업을 얻는 데 있지 않다. 반면 사업 경영, 교육, 공학, 건축, 간호, 약학, 언론학, 사회복지, 보건 관련 등의 분야는 대체로 더 직업 중심적인 분야이다. 이러한 연구 분야는 졸업 후 직접 관련된 직업의 형태로 (학비를) 더 지불할 수 있는 경우가 많다. 이것은 여러분이 문과 과목을 전공하기로 결정하면 직업을 구할 수 없을 것임을 의미하지도 않고, 더 직업 중심적인 분야를 전공함으로써 지적 성장과 발전을 얻을 수 없다는 것을 암시하지도 않는다. 오히려 그것은 역사적으로 더 직업 지향적인 경향이 있어 온 전공에 대한 여러분의 관심을 환기시킨다.

구문풀이

12행 This does not mean [you will not be able to find employment {if you decide to major in the liberal arts}]; nor does it imply [that you cannot gain intellectual growth and development by majoring in more career-oriented fields].

: 첫 번째 [ ]는 mean의 목적어로 쓰인 명사절이고, 그 안의 { }는 명사절 내의 조건 부사절이다. 두 번째 [ ]는 imply의 목적어로 쓰인 명사절이다.

어휘풀이

- exception *n* 예외
- humanity *n* 인문학
- geared toward ~에 맞춰진
- liberal art 문과 과목, (인문학, 자연과학, 사회과학, 어학 등의) 교양 과목
- administration *n* 경영, 관리
- pharmacy *n* 약학
- payable *a* (학비를) 지불할 수 있는
- plenty *a* 풍부한, 많은
- fundamentally *ad* 근본적으로
- primary *a* 주요한
- architecture *n* 건축
- journalism *n* 언론학, 언론계
- imply *v* 암시하다

042 답 ⑤

출제 의도	파악하기
❶ 주어와 동사의 수 일치, 동사 pay의 쓰임	
❷ 병렬구조	❸ 전치사+관계대명사
❹ 형식상의 목적어와 내용상의 목적어	❺ 관계절 동사의 수 일치

정답풀이

⑤ 주격 관계대명사절 동사의 수는 선행사에 일치시키는데, 여기서 주격 관계대명사 which의 선행사는 money, interest, and middlemen이다. 따라서 단수형 동사 allows를 복수형 allow로 고쳐 써야 한다.

오답풀이

① 핵심 주어는 an exchange이며, 여기서 pays는 '이득이 되다, 이롭다'는 뜻의 자동사로 적절하게 쓰였다.
② 전치사 in의 목적어로 쓰인 동명사 giving과 병렬구조를 이루는 receiving은 어법상 적절하다. one farmer는 동명사구의 의미상 주어이다.
③ 뒤에 주어, 동사, 목적어를 갖춘 완전한 구조의 절이 이어지고, 문맥상 and in a division of labor의 의미를 나타내므로 「전치사+관계대명사」 형태의 in which는 적절하다.
④ which가 이끄는 관계절에서 형식상의 목적어 it에 대한 내용상의 목적어를 이끄는 to부정사 to trade는 적절하다. for producers는 이 to부정사구의 의미상 주어에 해당한다.

전문해석

경제생활에서 전형적인 포지티브섬 게임은 잉여물의 거래이다. 농부가 자신이 먹을 수 있는 것보다 더 많은 곡식을 가지고 있고, 목축업자가 자신이 마실 수 있는 것보다 더 많은 우유를 가지고 있을 경우에, 그들이 약간의 밀과 약간의 우유를 교환한다면 그들은 둘 다 결국 이득을 본다. 사람들이 말하듯, 모든 사람이 이긴다. 물론, 한 시점에서의 교환은 분업이 있을 때에만 이득이 된다. 한 농부가 다른 농부에게 1부셸의 밀을 주고 그 대가로 1부셸의 밀을 받는 것은 아무런 의미가 없을 것이다. 현대 경제학의 근본적인 통찰은 부 창출의 핵심은 분업이고, 그 안에서 전문가들은 비용 효율성을 늘리면서 상품을 생산하는 법을 배우고 자신의 특화된 상품을 효율적으로 교환할 수 있는 수단을 갖는다는 것이다. 효율적인 교환을 가능하게 하는 한 가지 기반 시설은 운송이며, 이는 생산자들이 거리상 떨어져 있을 때에도 자신들의 잉여물을 교환하는 것을 가능하게 한다. 또 다른 하나는 돈, 이자, 중간 상인인데, 이는 생산자들이 여러 시점에서 많은 다른 생산자들과 많은 종류의 잉여물들을 교환할 수 있게 해 준다.

구문풀이

10행 A fundamental insight of modern economics is [that the key to the creation of wealth is a division of labor], [in which specialists {learn to produce a commodity with increasing cost-effectiveness} and {have the means to exchange their specialized products efficiently}].

: 첫 번째 [ ]는 is의 보어로 쓰인 명사절이다. 두 번째 [ ]는 a division of labor를 부연

설명하는 관계절이며, 두 개의 { }는 and로 연결되어 관계절의 술어를 이룬다.

15행 One infrastructure [that allows efficient exchange] is transportation, [which makes **it** possible {for producers to trade their surpluses even when they are separated by distance}].

: 첫 번째 [ ]는 One infrastructure를 수식하는 관계절이고, 두 번째 [ ]는 transportation을 부연 설명하는 관계절이다. it은 형식상의 목적어이고, { }가 내용상의 목적어이다.

어휘풀이

- classic *a* 전형적인
- positive-sum game 포지티브섬 게임(개별적으로 자신의 이득을 추구하는 합리적 참여자 간에 상호적인 협력이 발생할 가능성이 높은 게임)
- surplus *n* 잉여물
- herder *n* 목축업자
- come out ahead 결국 이득을 보다
- division of labor 분업
- bushel *n* 부셸(곡물이나 과일의 중량 단위)
- in return 대가로
- fundamental *a* 근본적인
- insight *n* 통찰
- commodity *n* 상품
- cost-effectiveness *n* 비용 효율성
- efficiently *ad* 효율적으로
- infrastructure *n* 사회 기반 시설
- transportation *n* 운송, 수송
- middleman *n* 중간 상인

---

08 전치사와 접속사
본문 pp.050~053

Q1 **1** being **2** because of **3** Although **4** during **5** that

Q2 **1** ○ **2** ×, or **3** ×, if 또는 whether **4** ×, because of

043 ④ **044** ③ **045** ② **046** ④ **047** ⑤

048 ④

Q1

1. 풀이 「object to(~에 반대하다)」에서 to는 전치사이므로 뒤에는 동명사가 오는 것이 알맞다.

해석 나는 내 신용카드 사용에 대해 수수료를 부과받는 것에 강력히 반대한다.

2. 풀이 명사구 the mental skills가 이어지므로 구전치사인 because of가 알맞다. it helps to develop은 the mental skills를 수식하는 목적격 관계대명사절로, 관계대명사 that[which]이 생략된 형태이다.

해석 우리는 그것(철학)이 발달시키도록 도움을 주는 정신적 능력 때문에 철학을 공부한다.

3. 풀이 뒤에 주어(a person's good look)와 동사(may get), 목적어(our attention)를 갖춘 절이 이어지므로 접속사가 알맞다.

해석 비록 사람의 멋진 외모가 우리의 이목을 끌 수 있겠지만 그것이 반드시 지속되는 인상은 아니다.

4. 풀이 뒤에 명사구 a conversation이 이어지므로 전치사가 알맞다.

해석 기술 사용이 능숙한 오늘날의 세상에서도 대화 중에 전화를 받는 것은 무례한 일이다.

5. 풀이 뒤에 주어(our ability ~ creative), 동사(is), 보어(unrivaled)를 갖춘 절이 이어지고 있고, 이 절이 the possibility와 의미상 동격 관계를 이루므로 접속사 that이 알맞다.

해석 갑자기 우리는 우리의 창의적인 능력에 경쟁할 상대가 없지 않게 되는 가능성에 직면할 것임에 틀림없다.

Q2

1. 풀이 명령문 주절에 이어지는 부사절을 이끌면서 문맥상 이유를 나타내므로 접속사 as는 알맞다.

해석 대부분의 사람들은 한쪽 발이 다른 한쪽보다 약간 더 크므로 양쪽 신발 모두를 신어 보라.

2. 풀이 'A 또는 B 둘 중 하나'라는 의미의 상관접속사 「either A or B」 구문이므로 nor를 or로 고쳐 써야 한다.

해석 모든 상품은 소비재 또는 생산재로 구분될 수 있다.

3. 풀이 뒤에 주어(anything), 동사(could save), 목적어(his company)를 갖춘 절이 이어지고 있고, 이 절이 wondering의 목적어인 명사절을 이루면서 문맥상 '~인지'의 의미를 나타내야 하므로 접속사 if 또는 whether로 고쳐 써야 한다.

해석 어느 날, 그는 자신의 회사를 파산으로부터 구할 무언가가 있을지를 궁리하며 공원 벤치에 앉아 있었다.

4. **풀이** 문장의 주어는 to부정사구인 To argue ~ conflicts이고 동사는 misses인 구조이다. 뒤에 명사구인 the African or Middle Eastern conflicts가 이어지므로 접속사 because를 구전치사인 because of로 고쳐 써야 한다.

해석 아프리카나 중동의 갈등 때문에 지식이 진보하지 않는다고 주장하는 것은 요점에서 벗어난다.

---

043 답 ④

출제 의도 파악하기

❶ 주어와 동사의 수 일치		❷ 대명사의 쓰임과 수 일치	
❸ 접속사 that의 쓰임		❹ 동사의 태	
❺ 접속사 whether의 쓰임			

정답풀이

④ 관계대명사 what이 이끄는 명사절에서 주어 역할을 하는 what은 '~라고 불리는' 대상이므로, referred를 수동태 was referred로 고쳐 써야 한다.

오답풀이

① that leaders ~ nonleaders는 The idea와 동격 관계를 이루는 절이므로, 핵심 주어 The idea에 수를 일치시킨 단수형 동사 was는 적절하다.
② 관계절의 동사 allow의 의미상 주어와 목적어는 각각 the traits와 some individuals로 서로 다른 대상이다. 따라서 some individuals를 대신하는 목적격 대명사 them의 쓰임은 적절하다.
③ 뒤에 완전한 구조의 절이 이어지고, 문맥상 앞의 the widely stated argument와 동격 관계를 이루는 절을 이끌므로 접속사 that은 적절하다.
⑤ whether가 이끄는 부사절에서 주어가 주절의 주어와 같고 동사가 be동사일 때 「주어+be동사」는 생략이 가능하다. 여기서도 원래의 whether they are innate or learned에서 「주어+be동사」인 they are가 생략된 형태로 접속사 whether의 쓰임은 적절하다.

전문해석

지도자들이 그들을 지도자가 아닌 사람들과 구별해 주는 특정한 신체적, 지적 혹은 성격적 특성을 '선천적으로' 가지고 있다는 생각은 리더십에 대한 특성 기반 접근법의 기초적인 믿음이었다. 이 접근법은 1800년대 후반부터 1940년대 중반까지 리더십 연구를 지배했고 지난 몇 십 년 동안 관심이 되살아나는 것을 경험했다. 초기 특성 이론가들은 어떤 사람들의 경우 위대한 지도자가 되게 해 주는 특성을 가지고 태어난다고 믿었다. 따라서 이 분야의 초기 연구는 '지도자는 만들어지는 것이 아니라 태어나는 것'이라는 널리 언급되는 주장을 자주 제시했다. 또한, 초기 리더십 연구 중 일부는 '위인' 이론이라 불리는 것에 기반을 두었는데, 이는 그 당시 연구자들이 일반적으로 남성이면서 귀족이거나 정치나 군대의 리더십과 관련이 있는 역사에서 매우 눈에 띄는 지도자들의 특성을 확인하는 데 초점을 맞췄기 때문이다. 더 최근의 역사에서 수많은 저자들은 타고난 것이든 학습된 것이든 리더십 잠재력에 기여하는 많은 지속되는 자질이 있다는 것을 인정했다. 이러한 특성에는 '추진력', '자신감', '인지 능력', '성실성', '결단력', '지능' 그리고 '청렴'과 같은 것들이 포함된다.

구문풀이

12행 Also, some of the earliest leadership studies were grounded in [what was referred to as the "great man" theory] because researchers at the time focused on identifying traits of highly visible leaders in history [who were typically male and associated with the aristocracy or political or military leadership].

: 첫 번째 [ ]는 전치사 in의 목적어 역할을 하는 명사절이고, 두 번째 [ ]는 highly visible leaders in history를 수식하는 관계절이다.

어휘풀이

- inherently *ad* 선천적으로
- distinguish *A* from *B A*를 *B*와 구별하다
- foundational *a* 기본의, 기초적인
- ground *v* ~의 기초[근거]를 …에 두다
- identify *v* 확인하다, 알아보다
- typically *ad* 보통, 일반적으로
- innate *a* 타고난
- drive *n* 추진력
- cognitive *a* 인지의
- determination *n* 결심, 결단력
- possess *v* 지니다, 갖추고 있다
- dominate *v* 지배하다, 우세하다
- refer to *A* as *B A*를 *B*라고 부르다
- visible *a* 눈에 보이는
- enduring *a* 오래가는, 지속되는
- contribute to ~에 기여하다
- self-confidence *n* 자신감
- conscientiousness *n* 성실성
- integrity *n* 청렴

044 답 ③

출제 의도 파악하기

❶ 대동사		❷ 구전치사 because of	
❸ 문장의 구조 파악		❹ 병렬구조	
❺ 분사의 태			

정답풀이

③ 문장의 주어 The honey bees I kept에 호응하는 동사가 와야 하므로, visiting을 문맥상 시제에 맞게 과거 동사 visited로 바꿔 써야 한다. 핵심 주어인 The honey bees가 목적격 관계대명사 that 또는 which가 생략된 관계절 I kept의 수식을 받는 구조이다.

오답풀이

① 반복되는 일반동사 inspire를 대신하므로 대동사 do는 적절하다.
② 뒤에 명사구인 the sustaining role이 이어지고 있으므로 구전치사 because of는 적절하다. they ~ our hominid ancestors는 the sustaining role을 수식하는 관계절이다.
④ and 앞의 동사 fed upon과 병렬로 연결되어 주어 The bees의 술어 역할을 하는 converted는 적절하게 쓰였다.
⑤ the way를 수식하는 분사구를 유도하는 현재분사 leading은 적절하다.

전문해석

꽃들은 오늘날 길모퉁이, 꽃가게, 농산물 직판장, 책, 그림, 조각, 상업 광고에서 그러는 것처럼 최초의 예술가, 작가, 사진작가, 과학자들에게 영감을 주었다. 그것들은 쉽게 온라인으로 이동했다. 그것들이 우리 인간 조상들의 삶에서 의심할 여지없이 수행한 지속적인 역할 때문에, 거의 틀림없이, 꽃에 대한 애호가 없었다면 우리는 여기에 없을지도 모른다. 한번은 꽃들에게 매료된 적이 있었는데, 나는 소년 시절의 우리 집 근처 정원의 꽃과 야생화들로 이루어진 자연의 무한한 색조를 관찰했다. 내가 기르던 꿀벌들은 꽃의 꿀과 꽃가루라는 보상을 위해 꽃을 방문했다. 벌들은 꽃가루를 먹었으며, 꽃의 꿀을 내가 아침식사의 뜨거운 토스트 조각 위에 뿌린 맛있는 금빛의 걸쭉한 꿀로 변환시켰다. 어렸을 때, 야생화 위에 있는 모든 종류의 벌들을 발견하고 관찰하는 것이 캘리포니아의 야생지대를 가로지르는 나의 열정과 탐구가 되었다. 벌들은 내게 꽃을 피우는 식물에 대한 평생의 헌신으로 이어지는 길을 보여 주었다.

구문풀이

12행 The bees [fed upon the pollen] and [converted the nectar into delicious, golden, thick honey {I drizzled atop slices of hot toast at breakfast}].

: and로 연결된 두 개의 [ ]는 The bees에 이어지는 술어이다. { }는 delicious, golden, thick honey를 수식하는 관계절이다.

어휘풀이

- inspire *v* 영감을 주다, 고무시키다
- commercial advertising 상업 광고
- sculpture *n* 조각(품)
- with ease 쉽게

- arguably *ad* 거의 틀림없이
- fondness *n* 애호, 좋아함
- infinite *a* 무한한
- nectar *n* 꽃의 꿀, 화밀
- feed upon ~을 먹고 살다
- drizzle *v* 조금씩 뿌리다[붓다]
- quest *n* 탐구, 추구
- lifelong *a* 평생의
- sustaining *a* 지속적인, 유지시키는
- captivate *v* 매료시키다, 매혹하다
- palette *n* 색상, 색조, 팔레트
- pollen *n* 꽃가루
- convert *v* 변환시키다
- atop *prep* 맨 위에
- wildlands *n* 야생지대, 황무지
- dedication *n* 헌신, 전념

045 답 ②

출제 의도	파악하기		
❶	접속사 as의 쓰임	❷	문장의 구조 파악
❸	동사의 태	❹	접속사 that의 쓰임
❺	관계대명사 who의 쓰임		

정답풀이

② the belief와 동격 관계를 이루는 that절에서 주어인 individual successes에 이어지는 동사가 없으므로 depending을 depend로 바꿔 써야 한다.

오답풀이

① 문맥상 이유를 나타내는 절이 적절히 이어지고 있으므로 접속사 as는 알맞다.
③ 주어인 The independent self가 '유도되는' 대상이므로 may 뒤에 be와 함께 수동태를 이루는 과거분사 driven은 알맞다.
④ has shown의 목적절을 이끄는 접속사 that은 알맞다.
⑤ people을 수식하는 관계절에서 주어 역할을 하는 주격 관계대명사 who는 알맞다.

전문해석

더 개인주의적인 문화 환경에서 온 사람들은 자신에게 초점을 맞춘 주체성이나 통제력을 유지하도록 동기 부여를 받는 경향이 있는데, 이러한 것들이 자아 존중감의 토대 역할을 하기 때문이다. 이러한 형태의 주체성으로부터 개인의 성공은 주로 자신의 능력과 행동에 달려 있다는 신념이 나타나며, 따라서 환경에 영향을 미치는 것에 의해서든, 자신의 상황을 받아들이려고 노력하는 것에 의해서든, 통제력의 사용은 궁극적으로 개인에게 집중된다. 독립적인 자기는 주체 의식 또는 통제 의식에 호소함으로써 대처하도록 더욱 유도될 수도 있다. 그러나 더욱 상호 의존적인 문화 환경에서 온 사람들은 개인의 성공과 발동력의 문제에 덜 집중하고 집단의 목표나 화합을 향한 방향에 더욱 동기 부여를 받는 경향이 있다. 연구에 따르면 동아시아인들은 어떤 경우에 개인적인 통제를 추구하기보다는 더 많은 사회적 지원을, 추구하진 않지만, 받는 것을 선호한다고 한다. 그러므로 더 상호 의존적인 자기 구성을 지닌 사람들은 관계 속에서 화합을 증진시키는 방법으로 대처하는 것을 선호할 수도 있다.

구문풀이

11행 However, people [from more interdependent cultural contexts] tend to be [less focused on issues of individual success and agency] and [more motivated towards group goals and harmony].

: 문장의 주어는 people, 동사는 tend이며, 첫 번째 [ ]는 people을 수식하는 전치사구이다. and로 연결된 두 번째와 세 번째 [ ]는 병렬구조를 이루며 to be에 이어진다.

어휘풀이

- individualistic *a* 개인주의적인
- agency *n* 주체성, 발동력
- primarily *ad* 주로
- cope *v* 대처하다
- motivate *v* 동기를 부여하다
- self-worth *n* 자아 존중감
- ultimately *ad* 궁극적으로
- interdependent *a* 상호 의존적인

046 답 ④

출제 의도	파악하기		
❶	관계대명사 what의 쓰임	❷	부사의 쓰임
❸	분사구문의 태	❹	be used to+-ing
❺	접속사 that의 쓰임		

정답풀이

④ 문맥상 엑스레이 광선이 머리를 통과하며 얻어진 정보를 뇌의 수평 단면을 보여 주는 이미지로 전환하기 위해서 컴퓨터가 사용된다는 내용이므로, '~하기 위해서 사용되다'라는 의미를 나타내는 「be used+to부정사」 형태가 되어야 한다. 따라서 converting을 동사원형 convert로 고쳐야 한다. 「be used to+-ing」는 '~하는 데 익숙하다'라는 의미를 나타낸다는 점에 유의한다.

오답풀이

① 주절의 동사 is의 주어 역할을 하는 절을 이끌면서 comes의 주어 역할을 해야 하므로 선행사를 포함하는 관계대명사 what의 쓰임은 적절하다.
② 동사의 과거분사형인 seen을 수식하므로 부사 previously는 적절하다.
③ 의미상 주어인 this new technology가 '설계된' 대상이므로 수동의 의미를 나타내는 과거분사 Designed의 쓰임은 적절하다.
⑤ 뒤에 완전한 구조의 절이 이어지므로 the fact와 동격 관계를 이루는 절을 이끄는 접속사 that의 쓰임은 적절하다.

전문해석

사람들이 첨단 기술의 경이로움에 관해 생각할 때, 마음에 떠오르는 것은 통신위성과 멀리 떨어진 은하계를 관찰할 수 있는 거대한 크기의 망원경이다. 하지만 기술에서의 최근의 발전은 또한 우리가 과학의 눈을 우리 자신에게, 이전에 본 적이 없는 인간 뇌의 내면으로 돌리는 것을 가능하게 했다. 우리가 수술용 칼을 들 필요 없이 살아있는 인간 뇌의 시각적 이미지를 제공하기 위해서 설계된 이 새로운 기술은 수천 장의 스틸 '스냅 사진'을 활동 중인 뇌의 모델로 결합하기 위해서 컴퓨터를 사용한다. 몇 가지 영상 기술의 기본적인 유형들이 있는데, 그중 하나는 컴퓨터 단층 촬영(CT)이다. 이 기술에서 엑스레이 광선이 180도에 걸쳐서 1도 간격으로 머리를 통과하며, 컴퓨터가 이 정보를 뇌의 수평 단면을 보여 주는 이미지로 전환하기 위해서 사용된다. 이 기술은 고도로 초점이 맞춰진 엑스레이 광선이 신체 내부를 통과할 때, 그것이 통과하는 조직의 상대 밀도에 영향을 받는다는 사실을 이용한다.

구문풀이

1행 [When people think about the wonders of high technology], [what comes to mind] is global communication satellites and giant-size telescopes [that can spy on the distant galaxies of the universe].

: 첫 번째 [ ]는 부사절이고 what 이하가 주절이다. 두 번째 [ ]는 주절의 주어 역할을 하는 명사절이고, 세 번째 [ ]는 giant-size telescopes를 수식하는 관계절이다.

18행 This technique takes advantage of the fact [that {when a highly focused beam of X-rays is passed through the body}, the beam is affected by the relative density of the tissue {through which it passes}].

: [ ]는 the fact와 동격 관계를 이루는 명사절로, when이 이끄는 부사절과 주절로 이루어져 있다. 두 번째 { }는 the tissue를 수식하는 관계절이다.

어휘풀이

- wonder *n* 놀라움, 경이
- telescope *n* 망원경
- galaxy *n* 은하계
- visual *a* 시각의
- snapshot *n* 스냅 사진(순간 촬영 사진)
- satellite *n* 위성
- spy *v* 염탐하다, 몰래 조사하다
- advance *n* 발전, 진보
- combine *v* 결합하다
- tomography *n* 단층 촬영

- beam *n* 광선
- arc *n* 호(弧)
- horizontal *a* 수평의
- relative *a* 상대적인
- tissue *n* (신체의) 조직
- interval *n* 간격
- depict *v* 묘사하다
- take advantage of ~을 이용하다
- density *n* 밀도

- electricity *n* 전기
- trip *v* (스위치 등을) 잘못 작동시키다
- blow *v* (퓨즈를) 끊어지게 하다
- home center 주택[건축] 자재점, 건재상
- hand over ~을 넘겨주다
- circuit breaker 회로 차단기
- appliance *n* 가전제품
- troubleshooting *n* 고장의 수리

047 답 ⑤

출제 의도 파악하기

❶	형용사의 쓰임	❷	접속사 whether의 쓰임
❸	분사의 태	❹	미래완료 시제
❺	혼합 가정법의 if 생략		

정답풀이

⑤ 문맥상 '(과거에) ~했더라면, (지금) … 할 것이다'라는 뜻을 나타내고 있으므로 혼합 가정법을 쓰는 것이 알맞다. 혼합 가정법은 조건절에 가정법 과거완료(had p.p.)가 오고, 주절에 가정법 과거(조동사의 과거형+동사원형)가 와야 하는데, 조건절의 if가 생략되면 주어와 조동사가 도치된다. 따라서 여기서는 가정법 과거완료에 쓰인 had가 주어 앞으로 도치된 형태여야 하므로 Have를 Had로 바꿔 써야 한다.

오답풀이

① be동사 are (not)의 주격보어로 쓰인 형용사 likely는 알맞다.
② whether가 「주어(the outlet)+동사(is supplying)+목적어(electricity)」의 완전한 구조의 절을 이끌고, 이 절이 동사 check의 목적어로 쓰여 '~인지를 확인하다'라는 의미를 나타내고 있으므로 접속사 whether는 알맞다.
③ 수식을 받는 명사 light bulb가 '(퓨즈가) 끊어진' 대상이므로, 수동의 의미를 나타내는 과거분사 blown은 알맞다.
④ 문맥상 미래의 어느 시점이면 '문제를 해결했을 것이다'라는 의미를 나타내므로 미래완료 시제 will have solved는 알맞다. 미래완료 시제(will have p.p.)는 어떤 일이 미래의 어느 시점에 완료되었을 것임을 나타낸다.

전문해석

램프 스위치를 켰는데 불이 안 들어온다. 램프의 스위치가 고장 났거나 램프의 배선이 합선되었다고 즉시 말하겠는가? 아니다. 그것은 곧이곧대로 생각하고 있는 것일 것이다. 지금까지 램프가 완벽하게 작동해 왔다면 그런 이유들은 전혀 그럴듯하지 않다. 하지만 여러분은 램프 코드가 자주 콘센트에서 뽑힌다는 것을 알고 있어서 여러분은 그것을 먼저 확인할 것이다. 만약 그것이 문제가 아니라면, 여러분은 콘센트가 전기를 공급하고 있는지를 (아마 회로 차단기가 잘못 작동되었을 수도 있다) 확인할 것이고, 그래서 그 콘센트를 시험하기 위해 다른 가전제품을 그 콘센트에 꽂을 것이다. 만약 콘센트가 원인이 아니라면, 또 다른 흔한 원인인 퓨즈가 끊긴 전구가 있다. 그래서 여러분은 그것을 확인해 보려 할 것이다. 고장 수리에 있어 이쯤이면, 그 경우의 99.9%는 여러분이 그 문제를 해결했을 것이다. 짧은 시간에 (새 전구를 제외하면) 비용 없이 말이다. 만약 여러분이 곧이곧대로 생각했다면, 여러분은 새 램프용으로 많은 돈을 건네려고 건재상에 반쯤 가 있을 것이다.

구문풀이

1행 Do you immediately declare [that the lamp's switch is broken] or [that the lamp's wiring has shorted out]?

: or로 연결된 두 개의 [ ]는 declare의 목적어 역할을 하는 명사절이다.

어휘풀이

- declare *v* 말하다, 선언하다
- short out (전기 회로가) 합선되다
- outlet *n* 콘센트
- wiring *n* 배선, 전선
- pull out ~을 뽑다
- supply *v* 공급하다

048 답 ④

출제 의도 파악하기

❶	so ~ that … 구문	❷	관계대명사 what의 쓰임
❸	형식상의 주어와 내용상의 주어	❹	병렬구조
❺	분사구문의 태		

정답풀이

④ 문맥상 조동사 can 뒤의 동사원형 take와 등위접속사 or에 의해 병렬구조로 연결되는 자리이므로, refused를 동사원형 refuse로 고쳐 써야 한다.

오답풀이

① 뒤에 주어(they), 동사(respond), 부사구(in ways ~)를 갖춘 완전한 구조의 절이 이어지고 있고, 또한 앞에 있는 so averse와 함께 「so ~ that … (너무 ~해서 …하다)」 구문을 이루므로 접속사 that은 알맞다.
② 관계대명사 who가 이끄는 절에서 동사 study의 목적어를 이루는 자리로, 뒤에 이어지는 절이 do의 목적어가 빠진 불완전한 구조이므로 선행사를 포함하는 관계대명사 what은 알맞다.
③ 문맥상 뒤에 있는 to부정사구 to do so가 내용상의 주어이고, 이에 대한 형식상의 주어로 쓰인 것이므로 it은 알맞다.
⑤ 앞에 나온 절의 내용을 의미상의 주어로 하는 분사구문으로, 앞 내용이 leave의 주체이므로 능동의 의미를 나타내는 현재분사 leaving은 알맞다.

전문해석

인간은 속고 있다고 느끼는 것을 매우 싫어해서 흔히 겉보기에는 거의 말이 되지 않는 방식으로 반응한다. 인간의 마음이 계산기처럼 작동한다고 단순히 가정하는 부류의 사람들과는 대조적으로 사람들이 하는 것을 실제로 연구하는 경제학자들인 행동경제학자들은, 사람들은 그렇게 하는 것(불공정한 제안을 거부하는 것)이 자신에게 돈을 들게 한다고 해도 불공정한 제안을 거부한다는 것을 반복해서 보여 주었다. 대표적인 실험은 최후통첩 게임이라고 불리는 과업을 이용한다. 그것은 매우 간단하다. 짝을 이루는 두 사람 중 한 사람이 얼마간의 돈, 가령 10달러를 받는다. 그러고 나서 그 사람은 자기 짝에게 그 돈의 일부를 주는 기회를 가진다. 그 짝에게는 두 가지의 선택권만 있다. 그는 주어지는 것을 받거나, 아무것도 받지 않겠다고 거절할 수 있다. 협상의 여지는 없고, 그런 이유로 그것은 최후통첩 게임이라 불린다. 대체로 어떤 일이 일어나는가? 많은 사람들이 짝에게 똑같이 나눈 몫을 제안하며, 그것은 두 사람을 모두 행복하게 하고 장차 서로를 기꺼이 신뢰하게 한다.

구문풀이

16행 Many people offer an equal split to the partner, [leaving both individuals {happy and willing to trust each other in the future}].

: [ ]는 앞 절의 내용을 의미상의 주어로 하는 분사구문이며, and it leaves ~로 바꿔 쓸 수 있다. { }는 leaving의 목적격보어 역할을 하는 형용사구이다.

어휘풀이

- seemingly *ad* 겉보기에, 외견상으로
- assume *v* 가정하다, 생각하다
- straightforward *a* 간단한
- make sense 말이 되다, 이치에 맞다
- reject *v* 거부하다, 거절하다
- negotiation *n* 협상, 교섭

09 병렬구조 및 특수구문

본문 pp.056 ~ 059

Q1 1 was he 2 dusted 3 helping 4 prevent
5 put them up
Q2 1 ✕, write 2 ✕, happen 3 ○ 4 ✕, do

049 ②   **050** ③   **051** ③   **052** ⑤   **053** ①

054 ④

Q1

1. 풀이 부정어구 Not only가 문두에 왔으므로 주어와 동사가 도치된다.
해석 그는 유명한 작가였을 뿐만 아니라 재능 있는 연설가였다.

2. 풀이 과거 동사 made, straightened, did와 병렬구조를 이루므로 과거 동사가 알맞다.
해석 나는 침대를 정리했고 방을 정돈했으며 바닥의 먼지를 털었고 그리고 그 밖에 마음속에 떠오르는 일이라면 모두 했다.

3. 풀이 비교구문에서 비교되는 요소들은 문법적으로 서로 대등해야 하므로, 전치사구 to giving ~ else와 병렬구조를 이루도록 전치사 to에 이어지는 동명사 helping이 알맞다.
해석 아이들은 누군가 다른 사람을 돕는 것보다는 무언가를 주는 것에 훨씬 더 저항한다.

4. 풀이 drugs를 수식하는 주격 관계대명사절의 동사 block과 등위접속사 or에 의해 병렬구조를 이루는 자리이므로 prevent가 알맞다.
해석 오늘날 가장 활발한 의학 연구 분야 중의 하나는 발열원의 생성을 차단하거나 예방하는 약을 만들어 내는 것을 목표로 한다.

5. 풀이 「타동사+부사」의 목적어가 대명사인 them이므로 동사와 부사 사이에 오는 것이 알맞다.
해석 나는 크리스마스에 쓸 장식들을 샀고, 토요일 파티가 열리기 전에 그것들을 장식할 것이다.

Q2

1. 풀이 문맥상 read, think와 병렬로 연결되어 Assigning의 목적격보어 역할을 하는 to부정사구를 이루어야 하므로 write로 고쳐 써야 한다.
해석 학생에게 어려운 텍스트를 혼자 읽고 그것에 관해 생각해 보고 그것에 관한 글을 쓰도록 과제를 주는 것은 충분하지 않다.

2. 풀이 일반동사를 강조하는 조동사 do(does) 뒤에는 동사원형이 온다.
해석 모든 일은 이유가 있기에 일어나는데, 즉 사건에는 원인이 있고, 원인은 항상 사건 이전에 옴을 말하는 것이다.

3. 풀이 위치를 나타내는 부사구 Right in front of his eyes가 문두에 왔으므로 주어와 be동사가 도치된 것이며, 주어의 핵이 복수 명사인 rows이므로 were는 알맞다.
해석 바로 그의 눈앞에 손대주기를 기다리는 맛있어 보이는 초코바들의 줄이 있었다.

4. 풀이 but 이하는 「so+조동사/be동사+주어(~ 또한 그러하다)」 구문이며, 주어가 복수 명사구인 other things이므로 조동사 does를 do로 고쳐 써야 한다.

앞에 있는 not only does it become easier는 부정어구 not only가 절 앞에 와서 조동사 does가 주어 앞으로 도치되고 주어 뒤에 동사원형이 온 구조이다.

해석 계속하여 하나의 습관을 충분히 오래 들이려고 노력하라, 그러면 그 습관이 더 쉬워질 뿐만 아니라 다른 일들 또한 더 쉬워진다.

---

049 답 ②

출제 의도 파악하기
① 도치구문   ② 비교구문
③ 분사구문의 태   ④ consider의 목적격보어
⑤ 부사의 쓰임

정답풀이
② 앞에 more가 있고, 문맥상 with writing ~ exercise와 with providing ~ practice를 비교하고 있으므로 비교급 비교구문을 이루도록 as를 than으로 바꿔 써야 한다.

오답풀이
① 부정어 nor가 절의 맨 앞으로 나오면서 주어 it과 조동사 has가 도치된 구조로 has it은 어법상 적절하다.
③ consisting은 완전한 구조의 절 다음에 이어지는 분사구문을 이끄는 분사로, 의미상 주어인 Greek music과 능동 관계를 이루므로 현재분사 형태로 쓴 것은 어법상 적절하다.
④ 동사 consider는 목적격보어로 to부정사를 취하므로 to be는 적절하게 쓰였다.
⑤ 동사 span을 수식하므로 부사 generally는 알맞다.

전문해석
우리는 고대 그리스 음악이 어떤 소리를 냈는지 알지 못하는데, 그것이 기록되거나 악보에 적힌 형태로 되어 있는 사례가 없고 구전으로도 살아남지 못했기 때문이다. 어쨌든 그것의 많은 부분은 아마도 특정 규칙과 관례 내에서 즉흥적으로 연주되었을 것이다. 그래서 우리는 주로 플라톤과 아리스토텔레스 같은 저술가들의 설명으로부터 그것의 토대를 추측할 수밖에 없는데, 그들은 그것의 실제에 대한 기술적인 입문서를 제공하는 것보다 철학적이고 윤리적인 실천으로서의 음악에 대해 글을 쓰는 것에 대체로 더 관심이 있었다. 그리스 음악은 대개 성악 형식이었고, 수금(竪琴)이나 퉁기는 키타라('기타'의 뿌리)와 같은 악기의 반주에 노래되는 운문으로 구성되었던 것처럼 보인다. 사실, 플라톤은 춤이나 노래의 반주로서가 아닌 수금(竪琴)과 피리만 연주되는 음악을 '매우 조잡하고 무미건조한' 것으로 여겼다. 그 선율은 매우 제한된 음역을 가지고 있었던 것처럼 보이는데, 그 악기들은 일반적으로 (우리가 그것을 현재 정의하는 대로) 한 E에서 다음 E까지 단지 한 옥타브에만 걸쳐 있기 때문이다.

구문풀이
5행 So we are forced largely to guess at its basis from the accounts of writers such as Plato and Aristotle, [who were generally **more** concerned {with writing about music as a philosophical and ethical exercise} **than** {with providing a technical primer on its practice}].

: [ ]는 Plato and Aristotle을 부연 설명하는 관계절이고, 그 안에 more ~ than의 비교구문이 쓰여 두 개의 { }를 비교하고 있다.

13행 In fact, Plato **considered** music [in which the lyre and flute played alone and not as the accompaniment of dance or song] **to be** 'exceedingly coarse and tasteless'.

: 「consider+목적어+목적격보어(to부정사)」 구문으로, [ ]는 목적어 music을 수식하는 관계절이다.

어휘풀이

- notate *v* 악보에 적다
- improvise *v* 즉흥 연주를 하다
- account *n* 설명
- philosophical *a* 철학의
- predominantly *ad* 대개
- verse *n* 운문
- pluck *v* (현악기를) 퉁기다
- exceedingly *ad* 매우
- pitch *n* 음의 높이
- oral tradition 구전(口傳)
- convention *n* 관례, 관행, 약속
- be concerned with ~에 관심이 있다
- ethical *a* 윤리적인, 도덕적인
- consist of ~로 구성되다
- accompany *v* 반주해 주다
- accompaniment *n* 반주
- tasteless *a* 무미건조한, 멋없는
- span *v* 걸치다

050 답 ③

출제 의도 파악하기

❶	비교구문	❷	형식상의 목적어와 내용상의 목적어
❸	병렬구조	❹	관계대명사 which의 쓰임
❺	to부정사의 쓰임		

정답풀이

③ 문맥상 '통계와 다른 정보를 수집하고 의사결정을 위한 기술을 개발하는 업무'라는 내용으로, the tasks of에 연결되는 collecting과 병렬구조를 이루어야 하므로 develop을 동명사 developing으로 고쳐야 한다.

오답풀이

① 「as much on *A* as on *B*」 형태의 원급 비교구문이므로 as는 적절하게 쓰였다.

② 「동사+형식상의 목적어(it)+목적격보어(necessary)+내용상의 목적어(to부정사구)」의 구조로, 뒤에 있는 내용상의 목적어 to take 이하를 대신하는 형식상의 목적어 it은 적절하다.

④ 뒤에 있는 동사 led의 주어 역할을 하면서 앞에 나오는 the development of techniques ~ systems analysis를 부연 설명하는 절을 이끄는 계속적 용법의 주격 관계대명사 which는 적절하게 쓰였다.

⑤ to provide 이하는 the theory of systems를 수식하는 형용사적 용법의 to부정사구로 적절하게 쓰였다.

전문해석

제2차 세계 대전은 경영자의 정체성에 큰 영향을 미치게 되어 있었다. 조직의 관리는 군사적 대립을 지시하는 능력만큼이나 보급품의 제조와 운송을 조직하는 능력에 달려 있었던 전쟁에서 승리하는 데 핵심적인 측면이 되었다. 따라서 전쟁 동안에 정부는 관리와 행정의 기술을 심각하게 받아들일 필요가 있다는 것을 알게 되었다. 미국에서 정부는 통계와 다른 정보를 수집하고 많은 다른 조직들에 걸쳐 조정된 의사결정을 위한 기술을 개발하는 업무를 포함하여 전쟁 경제를 관리하는 어려움을 해결하기 위해 경영대학원에 의지했다. 이것은 선형 프로그래밍과 시스템 분석 같은 기술의 개발로 이어졌고, 이것은 나중에 컴퓨터 시뮬레이션, 네트워크 분석 그리고 비용 계산 시스템으로 이어졌다. 무기의 품질 보장에 대한 압박하에 조사 방법 및 관심 집단에서뿐만 아니라 통계 및 통계 표본 추출에서도 진전이 있었다. 엔지니어들은 자기 조절 제어의 형태를 제공하는 시스템 이론을 개발했다.

구문풀이

2행 The management of organizations became a key aspect of winning a war [that depended **as** much on the ability {to organize the manufacture and transport of supplies} **as** on the ability {to direct military confrontations}].

: [ ]는 a key aspect of winning a war를 수식하는 관계절이며, 「as+원급+as」의 비교 구문이 사용되었다. 두 개의 { }는 각각 앞에 있는 the ability를 수식하는 형용사적 용법의 to부정사구이다.

어휘풀이

- identity *n* 정체성
- manufacture *n* 제조
- supplies *n* 보급품
- administration *n* 행정
- address *v* (문제 등을) 해결하다, 다루다
- administer *v* 관리하다
- coordinate *v* 조정하다
- analysis *n* 분석
- sampling *n* 표본 추출
- armament *n* 무기, 장비
- management *n* 관리, 경영
- transport *n* 운송
- confrontation *n* 대립, 대항
- turn to ~에 의지하다
- statistics *n* 통계(학), 통계 자료
- linear *a* 선형의, 직선의
- cost-accounting *a* 비용 계산의
- assure *v* 보장하다
- self-regulating *a* 자기 조절의

051 답 ③

출제 의도 파악하기

❶	병렬구조	❷	도치구문의 수 일치
❸	사역동사의 목적격보어	❹	접속사 unless의 쓰임
❺	to부정사의 쓰임		

정답풀이

③ 사역동사 having의 목적어 its privileges(그것의 특권)는 '빼앗기는' 대상으로 take와 수동의 관계를 이룬다. 따라서 목적격보어 자리에는 원형부정사 take가 아니라 과거분사 taken이 와야 한다.

오답풀이

① 접속사 before 뒤의 절에서 주어인 we에 이어지는 동사의 자리로, punish와 병렬구조를 이루는 동사 look은 알맞다.

② 문두에 only의 수식을 받는 부사구가 와서 「조동사 do+주어+동사원형」으로 도치된 구조로, 단수 주어 a dog에 수를 일치시킨 does는 적절하다.

④ 문맥상 '주인이 개의 자연스런 반응을 이해하지 못한다면'이라는 의미가 자연스러우므로 '~하지 않는다면'이라는 의미로 부사절을 이끄는 접속사 unless는 적절하다. 주절의 주어 it은 형식상의 주어가 아니라 the punishment를 가리키는 대명사이다.

⑤ to부정사구 to love, (to) honor, (to) obey ~가 앞의 명사구 a potential inclination을 수식하는 형용사적 용법으로 쓰인 구조로 to love는 알맞다.

전문해석

개를 훈련시킬 때, 개에게 벌을 주거나 실망감이나 혐오감으로 바라보기 전에 모든 것을 고려해야만 한다. 개는 아주 어릴 때 단지 반복에 의해서만 어떤 것이 옳은 것인지 잘못된 것인지를 안다. 개는 이것을 경험으로부터, 즉 주인의 화난 어조의 목소리, 개줄을 갑자기 잡아당기는 것, 또는 버릇이 없을 때 자신의 특권을 빼앗기는 것으로부터 배운다. 다시 말해서, 개의 정신은 옳고 그름에 대한 추론을 할 수 없다는 것이다. 그러나 개가 받거나 곧 받게 될 대우에 대한 그 개의 자연스런 반응을 주인이 이해하지 못한다면 어떤 벌을 주더라도 효과적이지 못하다. 개의 행동을 바꾸는 것에 대한 핵심은 개가 아니라 주인의 마음에 달려 있다. 나쁜 개는 한 마리도 없으며, 단지 그들의 개가 정말로 그들을 사랑하고 존경하며 복종할 잠재적인 성향을 가지고 있다는 것을 알아차리지 못하는 경험 없는 주인들만 있을 뿐이다.

구문풀이

3행 [Only by repetition] **does a dog** know [what is right or wrong] [when very tiny].

: Only를 포함한 부사구인 첫 번째 [ ]가 문두에 나가 주어(a dog)와 조동사(does)가 도치되었다. 두 번째 [ ]는 know의 목적어로 쓰인 명사절이다. 세 번째 [ ]에서 when 다음에는 「주어+be동사」인 it(= a dog) is가 생략되었다.

어휘풀이

- disgust *n* 싫증, 혐오
- privilege *n* 특권, 특전
- treatment *n* 취급, 대우
- notice *v* 알아차리다
- inclination *n* 경향, 성향
- obey *v* 복종하다
- leash *n* 가죽 끈, 개줄
- naughty *a* 버릇없는, 말을 듣지 않는
- lie in ~에 달려 있다
- potential *a* 잠재적인
- honor *v* 존경하다, 경의를 표하다

052 답 ⑤

출제 의도 파악하기

❶	강조의 do	❷	주어와 동사의 수 일치
❸	사역동사의 목적격보어	❹	형용사의 쓰임
❺	문장의 구조 파악		

정답풀이

⑤ 콤마(,) 앞뒤의 절을 연결하는 접속사가 없으므로 it 대신 접속사의 역할을 하면서 앞 절의 내용을 대신하는 관계대명사 which를 써야 한다.

오답풀이

① 이어지는 일반동사 have를 강조하는 조동사 do의 쓰임은 적절하다.
② 문장의 핵심 주어는 One wise friend이므로 단수형 동사 advises는 적절하게 쓰였다.
③ 사역동사 Have의 목적어 them(= children)은 '지우는' 주체이므로 목적격보어로 원형부정사 cross를 쓴 것은 적절하다.
④ wherever와 possible 사이에 it is가 생략된 형태로 형용사 possible의 쓰임은 적절하다.

전문해석

아이들이 어릴 때 일의 많은 부분은 그들이 정말로 통제권을 가지고 있음을 그들에게 보여 주는 것이다. 20년간 부모 교육자였던 우리의 현명한 친구 한 명은 취학 전 연령의 아이들에게 달력을 주고 아이들 생활에서 중요한 모든 일들을 적어 보라고 조언하는데, 이는 부분적으로 아이들이 시간의 흐름을 더 잘 이해하도록 그리고 자신들의 하루하루가 어떻게 펼쳐질지 이해하도록 도움을 주기 때문이다. 아이들이 자신의 하루를 통제하고 있다고 느끼도록 돕는 데 있어서 달력이라는 도구의 중요성은 아무리 과장해도 지나치지 않다. 요일들에 다가가면서 아이들에게 그 요일들을 지우게 하라. 가능한 경우마다 그 일정에 대해 아이들에게 선택권을 주면서 그날의 일정을 검토하는 데 시간을 보내라. 이러한 의사소통은 존중을 보여 주어서 아이들이 자신들이 그저 여러분의 하루와 여러분의 계획에 붙어서 따라다니는 사람이 아니라는 것을 알게 되고, 어떤 일이 언제, 왜 일어나게 될지 이해하게 된다. 나이가 더 들어감에 따라 아이들은 그 다음에 스스로 중요한 일들을 적어 넣기 시작할 것이며, 그것은 나아가 그들이 자신의 통제감을 발달시키는 데 도움을 준다.

구문풀이

3행 One wise friend of ours [who was a parent educator for twenty years] advises [giving calendars to preschool-age children] and [writing down all the important events in their life], in part because it **helps** children **understand** [the passage of time] better, and [how their days will unfold].

: 첫 번째 [ ]는 One wise friend of ours를 수식하는 관계절이다. and로 연결된 두 번째와 세 번째 [ ]는 advises의 목적어이다. understand는 동사 helps의 목적격보어로 쓰인 원형부정사이며, 네 번째와 다섯 번째 [ ]는 understand의 목적어 역할을 하는 명

사구와 명사절이다.

어휘풀이

- demonstrate *v* (실례를 통해) 보여 주다
- preschool-age *a* 취학 전 연령의
- unfold *v* 펼쳐지다, 전개되다
- cross off (선을 그어) ~을 삭제하다
- tagalong *n* 항상 붙어 다니는 사람
- passage *n* 흐름, 경과, 추이
- overstate *v* 과장해서 말하다
- go over ~을 자세히 검토하다
- sense of control 통제감

053 답 ①

출제 의도 파악하기

❶	도치구문의 수 일치	❷	부사의 쓰임
❸	병렬구조	❹	동사의 태
❺	의문사 which의 쓰임		

정답풀이

① 문맥상 문장의 주어는 the parenting and child-care philosophies and methods이고, Critical to crime rates in any culture는 보어로, 보어가 문두로 나와 동사가 주어 앞으로 도치된 구조이다. 따라서 주어가 복수이므로 is를 are로 바꿔 써야 한다.

오답풀이

② 이어지는 형용사 responsible을 수식하는 부사 primarily는 적절하다.
③ 문맥상 and 앞의 동사 assures와 병렬로 연결되어 주어 The first type of society에 대한 술어를 이루어야 하므로 단수형 동사 provides는 올바르게 쓰였다.
④ nothing이 주어이며 '아무것도 요구되지 않는다'는 뜻으로 수동의 의미를 나타내므로 is와 함께 수동태를 이루는 과거분사 required는 적절하다.
⑤ 의문사 which가 system을 한정하면서 determine의 목적어 역할을 하는 의문사절을 이끌고 있으므로 어법상 적절하다. which는 의문대명사 및 의문형용사로도 쓰이므로 정확한 해석을 통해 which의 어법적 기능을 판단해야 한다.

전문해석

어떤 문화에서든 범죄율에 있어 결정적인 것은 육아 및 보육의 철학과 방법이다. 모든 사회에서 강도와 약탈 같은 대부분의 노상 범죄들은 청소년과 젊은이들 사이에서 발생한다. 어떤 사회에서는 자녀에 대한 책임이 주로 부모에게 있다고 여기지만, 모든 시민들이 그 책임을 공유한다. 다른 사회에서는 자녀가 소유물, 즉 부모의 재산으로 취급된다. 첫 번째 유형의 사회는 부모가 유아 보육에 대한 준비를 받도록 보장하면서 (동시에) 자녀들을 돌보는 데 있어 부모에게 지원을 제공한다. 두 번째 유형의 사회는 그런 지원 제도가 존재하지 않는다. 이런 사회에서는 부모가 되는 데에 아무것도, 즉 지식도, 기술도, 수입도 요구되지 않으며 자녀를 보살피는 것이 전적으로 부모에게 맡겨져 있다. 어떤 체제가 법을 잘 지키는 젊은이를 배출할 가능성이 더 큰지 결정하기란 어렵지 않다.

구문풀이

15행 **It** is not difficult [to determine {which system is more likely to produce a law-abiding young adult}].

: It은 형식상의 주어이고, [ ]가 내용상의 주어로 쓰인 to부정사구이다. 그 안의 { }는 to determine의 목적어 역할을 하는 의문사절이다.

어휘풀이

- critical *a* 중요한, 결정적인
- burglary *n* 강도
- adolescent *n* 청소년
- philosophy *n* 철학
- robbery *n* 약탈, 강도
- property *n* 소유물, 재산

- assure **v** 확실하게 하다, 보장하다
- income **n** 수입, 소득
- infant **n** 갓난아기, 유아

- disaster **n** 재난
- hardship **n** 고난, 역경
- catastrophe **n** 큰 재해, 참사
- heatwave **n** 폭염
- aftermath **n** (전쟁·재해 등의) 직후 시기, 여파
- mobilise **v** 동원하다
- affect **v** 해치다, 침범하다
- overwhelm **v** 압도하다
- foreign aid agencies 해외 원조 단체
- criticise **v** 비판하다
- association **n** 협회
- scarce **a** 부족한
- harsh **a** 가혹한, 척박한
- landslide **n** 산사태
- strike action 파업
- assistance **n** 원조, 도움, 지원
- indigenous **a** 토착의
- influx **n** 유입
- undermine **v** 악화시키다
- shattered **a** 산산조각 난

054 답 ④

출제 의도 파악하기

❶	분사의 태	❷	주어와 동사의 수 일치
❸	to부정사의 쓰임	❹	문장의 구조 파악
❺	강조구문		

정답풀이

④ some of ~ 앞에 문장을 연결하는 접속사가 없으므로, 문장을 연결하는 접속사와 소유격 대명사 their의 역할을 동시에 하는 소유격 관계대명사 whose를 써야 한다.

오답풀이

① 앞에 있는 명사 communities를 수식하는 분사로, communities가 live의 주체이므로 현재분사 living은 적절하게 쓰였다.
② 문장의 핵심 주어는 Studies로 복수형 동사 suggest는 적절하게 쓰였다.
③ 문맥상 '(도움을) 제공하기 위해'라는 의미이므로 목적을 나타내는 부사적 용법의 to부정사 to provide는 적절하게 쓰였다.
⑤ 「it is[was] ~ that ...」 강조구문으로 were의 주어인 the informal neighbourhood associations를 강조하고 있다.

전문해석

비공식 네트워크는 어려움과 재난에 대처할 수 있는 사람들의 능력을 향상시킨다. 고난의 시기에 부족한 자원을 공유하는 것은 가난이나 가혹한 환경에서 살아가는 공동체들 사이에서 흔하며, 일부 공동체 구성원의 생존에 결정적일 수 있다. 산사태나 폭염, 장기 파업과 같은 큰 재난이 덮친 지역 사회에 관한 연구는 네트워크가 없어지거나 존재하지 않는 지역 사회보다 강력한 사회 네트워크를 가진 지역 사회가 회복될 가능성이 더 높다는 것을 시사한다. 2004년 쓰나미 피해 직후 스리랑카에서는 현지 네트워크가 해안가에서 피해를 입은 사람들에게 원조를 제공하기 위해 동원되었다. 이러한 토착의 노력은 곧 선의의 외국 원조 단체들의 유입에 압도되었는데, 그들의 활동 중 일부는 살아남은 공동체의 역량을 약화시킨다는 비판을 받아 왔다. 마찬가지로, 허리케인 카트리나가 뉴올리언스에 광범위한 홍수를 일으킨 후 몇 달 동안 주정부 기관이나 비정부 기구보다는 지역 사회가 산산조각 난 삶을 재건할 수 있도록 돕는 데 가장 효과적인 것은 비공식적인 이웃 협회였다.

구문풀이

2행 [Sharing scarce resources during times of hardship] **is** common among communities [living in poverty or harsh environments], and **can be** crucial to the survival of some community members.

: 첫 번째 [ ]가 문장의 주어 역할을 하는 동명사구이고, 이에 이어지는 동사 is와 can be가 and로 연결되었다. 두 번째 [ ]는 communities를 수식하는 현재분사구이다.

6행 Studies of communities [hit by catastrophe, such as a landslide, heatwave or long strike action], suggest [that those {with strong social networks} are more likely to recover than those {where networks are obliterated or non-existent}].

: 첫 번째 [ ]는 communities를 수식하는 과거분사구이다. 두 번째 [ ]는 suggest의 목적어로 쓰인 명사절이고, 그 안의 두 개의 { }는 각각 앞에 있는 those(= communities)를 수식하는 전치사구와 관계절이다.

어휘풀이

- enhance **v** 향상시키다, 강화하다
- cope with ~에 대처하다

055 ③	**056** ②	**057** ④	**058** ④	**059** ⑤
060 ②	**061** ③	**062** ②		

055 답 ③

출제 의도 파악하기

❶ 관계부사 where의 쓰임	❷ 형용사의 쓰임
❸ 문장의 구조 파악	❹ 관계대명사 that의 쓰임
❺ to부정사의 쓰임	

정답풀이

③ propose의 목적어 역할을 하는 that절에서 주어는 incorporating ~ mastery이고 동사는 must enhance이다. 문맥상 that promoting learning and mastery는 nonacademic factors를 수식하는 관계절이며, that은 주격 관계대명사로 쓰였으므로 promoting은 관계절의 술어 동사 역할을 해야 한다. 따라서 준동사 promoting을 본동사 promote로 고쳐 써야 한다.

오답풀이

① cultural contexts, student interests, and real-life situations를 수식하는 관계절을 유도해야 하는데, 이어지는 절이 주어(all students), 동사(develop), 목적어(positive identities as mathematics learners)를 모두 갖춘 완전한 구조이므로 관계부사 where는 어법상 알맞다.
② 동사 renders의 목적격보어로 쓰인 형용사 helpless는 어법상 알맞다.
④ 선행사 environments를 수식하는 관계절을 유도하면서 관계절에서 주어 역할을 하는 주격 관계대명사 that은 어법상 알맞다.
⑤ to foster는 결과의 의미를 나타내는 to부정사로 적절하게 쓰였다.

전문해석

수학 연습과 담화는 모든 학생들이 수학 학습자로서 긍정적인 정체성을 발달시키는 문화적 맥락, 학생 관심사 그리고 실생활 상황 안에 위치해야 한다. 수학 기술을 따로 그리고 학생의 이해와 정체성이 결여된 채로 지도하는 것은 그들이 명시적 교수로부터 이익을 얻는 데 무력하게 만든다. 따라서 우리는 명시적 교수가 학생들에게 유익하다는 데에는 동의하지만, 문화적으로 적합한 교수법과 학습 및 숙달을 촉진하는 비학습 요소들에 대한 고려를 포함하는 것이 수학 교수에서 명시적 교수를 틀림없이 강화할 것이라고 제안한다. 나아가 교사는 교실에서의 담화와 연습을 통해 학생의 정체성, 주체성 그리고 독립심을 장려하는 환경을 개발하는 데 매우 중요한 역할을 한다. 맥락화된 학습 과정에 적극적으로 참여하는 학생들은 학습 과정을 통제하고 있고 과거 학습 경험과 연계를 맺어 더 깊고 더 의미 있는 학습을 촉진할 수 있다.

구문풀이

[4행] Instruction in mathematics skills [in isolation] and [devoid of student understandings and identities] renders them helpless to benefit from explicit instruction.

: 두 개의 [ ]는 and에 의해 대등하게 연결되어 Instruction in mathematics skills를 수식한다.

[7행] Thus, we [agree {that explicit instruction benefits students}] but [propose {that incorporating culturally relevant pedagogy and consideration of nonacademic factors <that promote learning and mastery> must enhance explicit instruction in mathematics instruction}].

: 두 개의 [ ]는 but에 의해 대등하게 연결되어 we의 술어 역할을 한다. 두 개의 { }는 각각 agree와 propose의 목적어 역할을 하는 명사절이며, < >는 nonacademic factors를 수식하는 관계절이다.

어휘풀이

• discourse *n* 담화, 이야기	• context *n* 맥락, 환경
• instruction *n* 지도, 교수	• in isolation 별개로, 따로, 고립되어
• devoid of ~이 결여된 채로	• helpless *a* 무기력한
• explicit *a* 명시적인	• propose *v* 제안하다
• incorporate *v* 포함하다, 통합하다	• relevant *a* 적합한, 관련 있는
• consideration *n* 고려 (사항)	• enhance *v* 강화하다, 높이다
• encourage *v* 장려하다	• agency *n* 주체성
• independence *n* 독립(심)	• be engaged in ~에 참여하다
• contextualized *a* 맥락화된	• foster *v* 촉진하다

056 답 ②

출제 의도 파악하기

❶ 감정동사의 분사형	❷ 대동사
❸ to부정사의 쓰임	❹ 병렬구조
❺ 의문사 what의 쓰임	

정답풀이

② 비교구문에서 앞에 나온 술어의 반복을 피하기 위해 사용된 대동사 자리인데, has ~ neurons가 술어에 해당하므로 was를 일반동사를 대신하는 did로 고쳐 써야 한다.

오답풀이

① 감정을 나타내는 동사 depress(우울하게 하다)의 분사형 형용사가 사물의 특성을 나타낼 때는 현재분사형을 쓰므로 depressing은 어법상 적절하다. depressed는 '우울해하는(사람이 느끼는 일시적 감정)'을 뜻한다.
③ 문맥상 '~하기 위해'라는 목적의 의미를 나타내는 to부정사 to replace는 적절하게 쓰였다.
④ 문장의 주어 thousands of new cells에 이어지는 술어 동사 originate, move와 and로 병렬 연결된 형태이므로 link는 어법상 적절하다.
⑤ figure out의 목적어 역할을 하는 명사절에 동사 do의 목적어가 없으므로 의문대명사 what을 쓴 것은 어법상 적절하다.

전문해석

단 몇 년 전까지만 해도, 우리가 내내 갖게 될 모든 뇌세포를 지니고 태어난다고 널리 여겨졌다. 이것은 뇌가 날마다 수천 개의 뉴런을 잃으면서 우리 모두 서서히 내리막을 걷는다는 우울한 생각으로 이어졌다. 우리는 이제 지속적인 쇠락에 직면하는 것이 아니라, 건강한 75세의 뇌가 25세의 신체로 삶을 질주하고 있을 때 갖고 있던 바로 그만큼 많은 뉴런을 갖고 있다는 것을 안다. 뇌가 매일 세포를 잃는 것이 사실이긴 하지만, 그것은 동시에 그것들을 대체하기 위해 새로운 뉴런을 기른다. 이 과정은 신경 생성이라 불리는데, 새로운 뇌세포의 생산이다. 날마다 수천 개의 새로운 세포가 뇌 안 깊숙이에서 생겨나, 표면으로 이동하고, 다른 뉴런과 연결되어 뇌 회로의 일부가 된다. 이것은 뇌 과학자들에게 깜짝 놀랄 뉴스였는데, 그들은 이제 그 새로운 세포가 무엇을 하는지 알아내야 한다. 필시 그것들은 학습, 기억 그리고 변화하는 상황에 대한 우리의 적응 능력과 관련이 있을 것이다.

구문풀이

[1행] Until only a few years ago, **it** was widely believed [that we are born with all the brain cells {we will ever have}].

: it은 형식상의 주어이고 [ ]가 내용상의 주어이며, { }는 all the brain cells를 수식하는 관계절이다.

5행 Rather than facing a steady decline, we now know [that a healthy 75-year-old brain has **just as** many neurons **as** it **did** {when it was careening through life in the body of a 25-year-old}].

: [ ]는 know의 목적어로 쓰인 명사절이다. 명사절에 「just as+원급+as+주어+대동사 (did)」가 쓰여 '바로 ~한 그만큼 …'이라는 뜻을 나타내고 있다. did는 대동사로 had many neurons를 대신하며, 결국 부사절 { }를 포함하여 '~할 때 뇌가 갖고 있던 바로 그만큼 많은 뉴런'이라는 뜻을 나타낸다.

어휘풀이

- depressing *a* 우울한
- decline *n* 쇠락, 쇠퇴
- replace *v* 대체하다
- originate *v* 생기다
- stunning *a* 깜짝 놀랄
- adapt to ~에 적응하다

- steady *a* 지속적인, 꾸준한
- simultaneously *ad* 동시에
- neurogenesis *n* 신경 생성
- circuitry *n* 회로
- figure out ~을 알아내다, ~을 파악하다
- circumstance *n* 상황

057 답 ④

출제 의도 파악하기

❶	부사의 쓰임	❷	관계부사 where의 쓰임
❸	분사의 태	❹	감정동사의 분사형
❺	형식상의 목적어와 내용상의 목적어		

정답풀이

④ humiliate의 의미상 주어는 it(= This data)이고, it이 '창피함을 주는' 것이므로 능동임을 나타내는 현재분사 humiliating으로 바꿔 써야 한다. 과거분사가 되면 의미상 주어가 창피함을 느낀다는 의미가 된다.

오답풀이

① to부정사구에 쓰인 동사 flow를 수식하는 부사 freely는 알맞다.
② 뒤에 주어(an extensive ~ about us)와 동사(will be ~)를 갖춘 완전한 구조의 절이 이어지고 있고, 앞에 장소의 선행사 a world가 있으므로 관계부사 where는 알맞다.
③ 앞에 있는 명사구 a detailed record를 수식하는 자리로, 어린 시절부터 '시작하는' 상세한 기록이라는 능동의 의미이므로 현재분사 beginning은 알맞다.
⑤ 「find+목적어+목적격보어」 구조에서 find 뒤에 형식상의 목적어 it이 쓰였고, 그 뒤에 to부정사구 to engage in self-exploration이 내용상의 목적어로 쓰인 것이므로 it은 알맞다.

전문해석

인터넷은 정보가 이전의 그 어느 때보다 더 자유롭게 흐르도록 한다. 우리는 전례없는 방식으로 의사소통하고 아이디어를 공유할 수 있다. 이러한 발전은 우리의 자기표현을 혁신하고 우리의 자유를 증진하고 있다. 하지만 한 가지 문제가 있다. 우리는 우리에 관한 단편적인 정보의 광범위한 흔적이 인터넷상에 영원히 보존되어 검색 결과에서 즉각 보이게 될 세상을 향해 나아가고 있다. 우리는 전 세계 어느 곳에서나 검색할 수 있고 접근할 수 있는, 우리가 어디에 가든 평생 우리와 함께 할, 어린 시절부터 시작하는 상세한 기록을 지니고 살 수 밖에 없을 것이다. 이러한 정보는 자주 신뢰성이 의심스러울 수 있거나 틀릴 수 있거나 혹은 사실이지만 매우 굴욕적일 수도 있다. 새 출발을 하거나 다시 한 번 기회를 갖는 것이 점점 더 어려워질 수 있다. 만약 모든 실수와 어리석은 행동이 영구적인 기록으로 영원히 보존된다면, 우리는 자아를 탐구하기가 더 어렵다는 것을 알게 될지도 모른다.

구문풀이

5행 We're heading toward a world [where {an extensive trail of information fragments about us} will be forever preserved on the Internet, {displayed instantly in a search result}].

: [ ]는 a world를 수식하는 관계절이다. 첫 번째 { }는 관계절 내의 주어부이며, 관계절의 동사는 will be preserved이다. 두 번째 { }는 분사구문이다.

8행 We will be forced to live with a detailed record [beginning with childhood] [that will stay with us for life wherever we go], [searchable and accessible from anywhere in the world].

: 첫 번째 [ ]는 a detailed record를 수식하는 현재분사구이고, 두 번째 [ ]는 a detailed record ~ childhood를 수식하는 관계절이다. 세 번째 [ ]는 a detailed record ~ wherever we go를 부가적으로 수식하는 형용사구이다.

어휘풀이

- unprecedented *a* 전례 없는
- trail *n* 자국, 흔적, 자취
- preserve *v* 보존[관리]하다, 지키다, 보호하다
- detailed *a* 상세한
- humiliate *v* 창피를 주다
- self-exploration *n* 자기 탐색

- extensive *a* 광범위한, 대규모의
- fragment *n* 조각, 파편
- reliability *n* 신뢰할 수 있음, 신뢰도
- engage in ~에 관여[참여]하다
- permanent *a* 영구[영속]적인

058 답 ④

출제 의도 파악하기

❶	동명사의 쓰임	❷	동사의 태
❸	to부정사의 쓰임	❹	관계대명사 which의 쓰임
❺	분사구문		

정답풀이

④ which 이하는 when이 이끄는 부사절 다음에 이어지는 주절에 해당한다. 관계대명사 which는 문장에서 「접속사+대명사」 역할을 하는데, 여기서는 접속사가 필요없으므로 which를 앞 절의 내용을 대신하는 this 또는 it으로 바꿔야 어법상 적절하다.

오답풀이

① 전치사 on의 목적어로 쓰인 동명사구를 이끄는 being은 어법상 적절하다. the external air temperature는 이 동명사구의 의미상 주어이다.
② 주어인 natural convection은 '이용되는' 대상이므로 수동태 동사 be used는 적절하다.
③ 「형용사+enough+to부정사(~할 정도로 충분히 …한)」 구문을 이루는 to bring은 어법상 적절하다.
⑤ the perception of thermal comfort를 의미상의 주어로 하는 분사구문 While being generally applicable에서 being이 생략된 형태로 applicable의 쓰임은 적절하다.

전문해석

모든 점유된 건물은 신선한 공기의 공급을 필요로 하며, 이는 기후의 하루 동안 및 계절적 변동에 따라 세계 대부분의 지역에서 자연 대류에 의해 얻어질 수 있다. 내부의 증가된 열을 제거하기 위한 자연 대류의 이용은 외부 공기 온도가 내부적으로 요구되는 것보다 더 낮은 것에 달려 있다. 북유럽에서 외부 공기 온도는 일반적으로 원하는 내부 온도 이하이므로, 1년 중 많은 시간에 걸쳐 원하지 않는 열을 제거하기 위해 낮 동안 자연 대류를 이용할 수 있다. 남유럽에서 여름의 외부 공기 온도는 건물의 사용 및 시공 특성에 따라 낮 동안 그리고 밤에 건물로 유입될 수 있을 정도로 충분히 낮을 수 있다. 그러나 외부 공기 온도가 원하는 내부 공기 온도 이상일 때, 이는 (가정용이 아닌 건물에서) 공급된 공기가 자연적으로 또는 기계적으로 사전 냉각되어야 하며, 환풍기가 적절하게 제어되어야 함을 의미한다. 일반적으로 적용 가능하지만, 열 쾌적성의 인식은 내부 표면 온도 및 내부의 (축적된) 열용량에 의해 영향을 받을 것이다.

구문풀이

4행 [**The use** of natural convection to remove internal heat gains] **is** dependent on [the external air temperature being lower than that {required internally}].

: 첫 번째 [ ]가 주어부이고, 핵심 주어는 The use이므로 단수형 동사 is가 쓰였다. 두 번째 [ ]는 전치사 on의 목적어로 쓰인 동명사구이며, { }는 that(= the air temperature)을 수식하는 과거분사구이다.

15행 However, when the external air temperature is above the desired internal air temperature, this implies [that (in non-domestic buildings) the air **supplied** must be pre-cooled either naturally or mechanically], and [that ventilators must be controlled appropriately].

: 두 개의 [ ]는 동사 implies의 목적어로 쓰인 명사절이며 and에 의해 병렬구조로 연결되었다. supplied는 the air를 수식하는 과거분사이다.

어휘풀이

- occupied *a* 점유된, 점령된
- internal *a* 내부의
- be dependent on ~에 달려 있다, ~에 의지하다
- desired *a* 원하는, 바라는
- non-domestic *a* 가정용이 아닌
- ventilator *n* 환풍기
- applicable *a* 적용 가능한
- thermal *a* 열의
- interior *n* 내부
- variation *n* 변동, 변화
- gain *n* 증가, 이익
- imply *v* 의미하다, 시사하다
- mechanically *ad* 기계적으로
- appropriately *ad* 적절하게
- perception *n* 인식, 지각
- comfort *n* 쾌적성, 편안함

059 답 ⑤

출제 의도 | 파악하기

❶	분사의 태	❷	대명사의 수 일치
❸	부사의 쓰임	❹	주어와 동사의 수 일치
❺	관계대명사 what의 쓰임		

정답풀이

⑤ to know의 목적어 역할을 하는 명사절을 이끄는 자리로, 뒤에 주어(the subject's responses), 동사(are), 보어(typical or atypical ~)를 갖춘 완전한 구조의 절이 이어지므로 관계대명사 what은 쓸 수 없다. 뒤의 or와 함께 「whether A or B」의 형태로 쓰여 'A인지 또는 B인지'의 의미를 나타내도록 명사절을 이끄는 접속사 whether를 써야 한다.

오답풀이

① 수식을 받는 the restrictions는 associate(~을 연관시키다)의 대상이므로 과거분사 associated는 적절하다.
② 앞에 나온 명사 an experiment를 가리키는 대명사로 it은 적절하게 쓰였다.
③ 동사 remains의 보어로 쓰인 형용사 problematic을 수식하므로 부사 deeply는 알맞다.
④ 주어는 동명사구인 knowing ~ exists이며 동명사구 주어는 단수 취급하므로 단수형 동사 does는 알맞다.

전문해석

인간 피험자에 관한 과학 실험을 다루는 규정은 엄격하다. 피험자는 충분한 설명에 입각한 서면으로 된 동의를 해야 하며, 실험자는 자신들의 계획된 실험을 제출하여 감독 기관에 의한 철저한 심사를 받아야 한다. 자신을 실험하는 과학자들은, 법률적으로는 아니라고 해도 기능상으로는 다른 사람들을 실험하는 것과 관련된 규제를 피

할 수 있다. 그들은 또한 관련된 대부분의 윤리적인 문제도 피할 수 있는데, 실험을 고안한 과학자보다 그것의 잠재적인 위험을 더 잘 알고 있는 사람은 아마 없을 것이다. 그럼에도 불구하고, 자신을 실험하는 것은 여전히 매우 문제가 많다. 한 가지 명백한 문제점은 (실험에) 수반되는 위험인데, 위험이 존재한다는 것을 아는 것이 위험을 줄이는 데 있어 무언가를 하는 것은 결코 아니다. 덜 명백한 문제점은 실험이 만들어 낼 수 있는 제한된 범위의 데이터이다. 인체의 해부학적 구조와 생리는 성별, 나이, 생활 방식 그리고 기타 요인에 따라 사소하지만 의미 있는 방식으로 다양하다. 따라서 단 한 명의 피험자로부터 얻어진 실험 결과는 가치가 제한적이며, 피험자의 반응이 집단으로서의 인간 반응의 전형적인 것인지 또는 이례적인 것인지 알 방법이 없다.

구문풀이

5행 Scientists [who experiment on themselves] can, [functionally if not legally], avoid the restrictions [associated with experimenting on other people].

: 첫 번째 [ ]는 주어인 Scientists를 수식하는 관계절이고, 두 번째 [ ]는 술어 동사인 can avoid 사이에 삽입된 부사구이다. 세 번째 [ ]는 the restrictions를 수식하는 과거분사구이다.

18행 Experimental results [derived from a single subject] are, therefore, **of** limited **value**; there is no way [to know {whether the subject's responses are typical or atypical of the response of humans as a group}].

: 첫 번째 [ ]는 주어인 Experimental results를 수식하는 과거분사구이다. 「of+추상명사」는 형용사(구)처럼 쓰일 수 있으므로, 여기서 are의 보어로 of limited value가 왔다. 두 번째 [ ]는 way를 수식하는 to부정사구이며, 그 안의 { }는 to know의 목적어로 쓰인 명사절이다.

어휘풀이

- regulation *n* 규정, 규제
- informed *a* 충분한 설명에 입각한
- submit *v* 제출하다
- thorough *a* 철저한
- restriction *n* 규제, 제한
- ethical *a* 윤리적인
- presumably *ad* 아마, 짐작건대
- hazard *n* 위험
- problematic *a* 문제가 많은
- do nothing 아무 영향도 미치지 않다
- derive *v* 얻다, 이끌어 내다
- atypical *a* 이례적인, 전형적이지 않은
- subject *n* 피험자, 실험 대상
- consent *n* 동의
- proposed *a* 계획된, 제안된
- oversee *v* 감독하다
- sidestep *v* 비켜 피하다, 회피하다
- involved *a* 수반되는
- potential *a* 잠재적인
- devise *v* 고안하다
- drawback *n* 결점, 문제점
- generate *v* 일으키다, 발생시키다
- of value 가치 있는, 유용한

060 답 ②

출제 의도 | 파악하기

❶	의문사 what의 쓰임	❷	부사의 쓰임
❸	지시대명사 that	❹	병렬구조
❺	동명사의 쓰임		

정답풀이

② 5형식 문장에서 동사 consider의 목적어로 "laws"가 왔고, 이에 대한 목적격보어 자리이므로 부사인 differently를 형용사 different로 바꿔 써야 한다.

오답풀이

① 앞에 있는 전치사 of의 목적어로 쓰인 의문사절을 이끄는 what은 알맞다.
③ 문맥상 지시대명사가 대신하는 것은 앞에 나온 these three이므로 복수형

those는 알맞다.

④ 등위접속사 but 앞에 주어인 an action의 동사로 may be considered가 왔고, 같은 주어에 대한 두 번째 동사가 오는 자리이다. 따라서 조동사 may에 이어지는 동사원형 be와 병렬구조를 이루는 be는 알맞다.

⑤ 전치사 without의 목적어로 쓰인 동명사 asking은 알맞다. 별도의 의미상의 주어가 없는 동명사는 그 의미상의 주어가 주절의 주어와 같다. 여기에서의 주어는 물건을 집어간 어떤 사람, 즉 Someone인데, 그 Someone이 '물어보지도 않고' 물건을 집어갔다고 보는 것이 타당하므로 능동형 동명사 asking이 온 것이다. ask는 자동사, 타동사로 모두 쓰일 수 있는 동사이며 이 문장에서는 뒤에 목적어를 동반하지 않는 자동사로 쓰였다.

전문해석
정의에 대한 개념의 차이는 법이란 무엇인가에 대해 여러 사회들이 갖고 있는 관념에 있다. 서양에서는 사람들이 '법'은 '관습'과 아주 다르다고 생각한다. 또한 '(도덕적) 죄'와 '(법적) 범죄' 사이에도 큰 차이가 있다. 그러나 많은 비서양 문화에서는 관습과 법, 종교적 믿음에 대한 구별이 거의 없다. 다른 문화들에서는 이 세 가지가 서로 잘 구별될 수도 있겠지만 여전히 서양에서의 그것들과는 매우 다르다. 이런 이유들 때문에 어떤 행동이 한 나라에서는 범죄라고 생각될지 모르나 다른 문화에서는 사회적으로 받아들여질 수도 있는 것이다. 예를 들어, 도둑은 대부분의 세계에서 범죄자로 여겨지지만 물건들에 대해 상당한 공유 의식이 있는 어떤 작은 마을에서는 '도둑'이라는 단어가 별 의미가 없을 수도 있다. 물어보지도 않고 무언가를 집어가는 누군가는 단지 예의 없는 사람으로 생각될 뿐인 것이다.

구문풀이
11행 For instance, although a thief **is viewed as** a criminal in much of the world, in a small village [where there is considerable sharing of objects], the word "thief" may have little meaning.

: 「view *A* as *B*(*A*를 *B*로 보다[여기다])」 구문이 수동태로 전환된 문장이다. [ ]는 a small village를 수식하는 관계절이다.

어휘풀이
- concept *n* 개념
- contrast *n* 대조, 차이
- criminal *n* 범죄자
- justice *n* 정의, 공정
- separation *n* 구분, 분리
- considerable *a* 상당한

---

061 답 ③

정답풀이
③ 문장의 주어는 An example of this이고 동사는 is seen이며 접속사가 없으므로, 또 다른 동사는 필요하지 않다. 문맥상 a range of subjects를 수식하는 분사구를 유도하는 분사 형태가 되어야 하는데, a range of subjects가 '가르쳐지는' 대상이므로 have taught를 과거분사 taught로 고쳐 써야 한다.

오답풀이
① a chart를 수식하는 관계절을 유도하며, 관계절에서 주어 역할을 하므로 주격 관계대명사 that은 어법상 적절하다.
② 능동의 의미로 앞 절 내용에 대한 결과를 나타내는 분사구문을 유도하는 현재분사 creating은 어법상 적절하다.
④ and 앞의 동사 takes와 병렬로 연결되어 주어 The researcher에 이어지

는 현재형 동사 calculates는 어법상 적절하다.
⑤ 목적의 의미를 나타내는 to부정사구를 유도하는 to elicit는 어법상 적절하다.

전문해석
방사형 차트라고도 불리는 스파이더 차트는 선 그래프의 한 형태이다. 그것은 연구자가 상호 연관된 변수들에 대해 하나의 척도에서 응답의 상대적인 크기를 보여 주는 차트로 그들의 데이터를 나타내도록 도와준다. 막대그래프와 마찬가지로, 데이터는 모든 변수들에 공통인 하나의 척도를 가져야 한다. 스파이더 차트는 변수들이 차트에 걸치면서 그려져 거미줄을 만든다. 이것의 한 예는 중등학교에서 첫 학기에 가르쳐진 다양한 과목들에 걸쳐 7학년 학생들의 자가 보고된 자신감을 살펴보는 조사 연구에서 보여진다. 연구자는 표본 집단으로부터 응답들을 가져와서 스파이더 차트에 나타낼 평균치를 계산한다. 스파이더 차트는 연구자가 표본 집단의 여러 다른 과목들에서의 자신감 정도를 쉽게 비교하고 대조할 수 있도록 한다. 파이 차트와 마찬가지로, 이 차트는 이후에 연구 결과의 추가 분석을 도출하기 위해 연구 내의 다른 학생 집단들로 세분화될 수 있다.

구문풀이
6행 The spider chart is drawn [**with** the variables **spanning** the chart], [creating a spider web].

: 첫 번째 [ ]는 「with+명사(구)+분사」 구문으로 is drawn과 동시에 일어나는 상황을 나타내며, 두 번째 [ ]는 결과를 나타내는 분사구문이다.

13행 The spider chart allows the researcher [to easily compare and contrast {the confidence level in different subjects for the sample group}].

: [ ]는 allows의 목적격보어로 쓰인 to부정사구이며, { }는 to compare와 (to) contrast의 공통 목적어이다.

어휘풀이
- represent *v* 나타내다
- scale *n* 척도
- variable *n* 변수
- confidence *n* 자신(감)
- plot *v* (그래프 등으로) 나타내다[기입하다]
- elicit *v* 도출하다
- relative *a* 상대적인
- interrelated *a* 상호 연관된
- span *v* 걸치다
- mean *n* 평균치
- analysis *n* 분석

---

062 답 ②

정답풀이
② 문장의 주어는 The attitude toward time and environment이고 동사는 does not represent이다. 따라서 knows as "multitasking"은 주어와 동사 사이에 삽입되어 주어를 수식하는 분사구가 되어야 하는데, The attitude는 '알려진' 대상이므로 knows를 과거분사 known으로 고쳐야 한다.

오답풀이
① 문맥상 it은 makes의 형식상의 목적어이고, to부정사구인 to adopt 이하가 내용상의 목적어로 to adopt는 적절하게 쓰였다.
③ 앞에 나온 Human beings를 대신하는 부정대명사 ones는 적절하다.
④ 앞에 있는 명사구 an attentive technique을 수식하는 형용사구를 이끄

는 indispensable은 어법상 적절하다.

⑤ 「lest+주어+(should) 동사원형(~가 …하지 않도록)」 구문으로, 주어인 it(= an animal)이 '잡아먹히는' 대상이므로 수동태 동사 be eaten은 올바르게 쓰였다.

전문해석

과도한 긍정성은 자극, 정보, 충동의 과잉으로 표출된다. 그것은 주의 구조와 경제를 근본적으로 바꾼다. 지각은 파편화되고 분산된다. 게다가, 업무 부담의 증가는 시간과 주의를 향한 특별한 배치를 채택하는 것을 필수적으로 만드는데, 이것은 결과적으로 주의와 인식의 구조에 영향을 미친다. '멀티태스킹'이라고 알려진, 시간 및 환경에 대한 태도는 문명의 진보를 의미하지 않는다. 근대 후기의 노동 및 정보 사회에 사는 인간만이 멀티태스킹 능력이 있는 것은 아니다. 멀티태스킹은 야생의 동물들 사이에서도 흔한 일이다. 멀티태스킹은 야생에서의 생존을 위해 필수적인 주의 관리 기법이다. 예를 들면, 먹느라 분주한 동물은 경쟁자를 먹이로부터 멀리 있도록 해야 한다. 그 동물은 먹는 중에 (자기가) 잡아먹히지 않도록 끊임없이 경계해야 한다. 동시에 그 동물은 자신의 새끼를 보호해야 하며, 짝짓기 상대를 주시해야 한다. 야생에서 동물은 다양한 활동 사이에 주의를 분배할 수밖에 없다.

구문풀이

8행 The attitude toward time and environment [known as "multitasking"] does not represent civilizational progress.

: [ ]는 주어인 The attitude toward time and environment를 수식하는 과거분사구이다.

어휘풀이

- excessive *a* 지나친, 과도한
- stimulus *n* 자극
- radically *ad* 근본적으로, 급진적으로
- scattered *a* 흩뿌려진, 분산된
- burden *n* 부담
- dispositions *n* 준비, 작전 계획
- cognition *n* 인식
- multitasking *n* 멀티태스킹, 여러 일을 동시에 하는 것
- represent *v* 의미하다, 나타내다, 대표하다
- commonplace *a* 아주 흔한
- attentive *a* 주의를 기울이는, 신경을 쓰는
- indispensable *a* 필수적인, 없어서는 안 될
- prey *n* 먹이, 사냥감
- young *n* (동물의) 새끼
- positivity *n* 긍정성
- impulse *n* 충동
- fragmented *a* 분열된, 파편이 된
- mounting *a* 증가하는, 커져가는
- adopt *v* 채택하다
- in turn 결과적으로
- be on the lookout 경계하다
- keep an eye on ~을 계속 지켜보다

어법 모의고사 2회

본문 pp.064 ~ 067

063 ⑤	**064** ⑤	**065** ⑤	**066** ④	**067** ⑤
068 ④	**069** ⑤	**070** ②		

063 답 ⑤

출제 의도 | 파악하기

❶ 분사의 태	❷ 도치구문의 수 일치
❸ 접속사 where의 쓰임	❹ 동사의 태
❺ 문장의 구조 파악	

정답풀이

⑤ 앞에 주어(Human settlements), 동사(show), 목적어(similar variety)를 갖춘 완전한 구조의 절이 왔으므로 접속사 없이 동사인 arise가 또 올 수 없다. 따라서 전치사 with 이하가 부대상황을 표현하는 「with+명사(구)+분사(~가 …하면서)」 구문이 되도록 현재분사 arising으로 바꿔 써야 한다. differences in size가 분사의 의미상의 주어인 구조이다.

오답풀이

① crossing이 수식하는 millions of locusts가 cross의 동작 주체이므로, 능동의 의미를 나타내는 현재분사 crossing은 알맞다.

② Not only가 문장 앞으로 이동하면서 주어와 조동사가 도치된 구조이다. 주어 the sizes of groups가 복수 명사구이고 동사는 일반동사 vary이므로, 수와 시제를 일치시킨 조동사 do가 온 것은 적절하다.

③ 뒤에 완전한 구조의 절이 왔고, 앞에 있는 동사 originate는 자동사로 쓰여 목적어가 필요 없는 구조이다. 즉, to originate where ~ distributed는 「자동사+부사절」의 구조가 된다. 따라서 '~하는 곳에서'라는 의미로 부사절을 이끄는 접속사 where는 적절하다.

④ 핵심 주어 individuals가 '발견되는' 대상이므로 수동태 동사 are found는 어법상 알맞다.

전문해석

동물의 집단은 나뭇가지에 앉아 있는 두 마리의 까치부터 사막을 가로지르는 수백만 마리의 메뚜기 떼의 이상 번식까지 크기가 다양하다. 집단의 크기는 종마다 다를 뿐만 아니라 종 안에서 극적으로 변할 수도 있다. 어떤 경우에는, 집단 크기의 변화는 환경의 변화에 달려 있다. 예를 들어, 메뚜기 떼의 발생은 자원이 군데군데 분포되어 있는 곳에서 발생하는 것으로 여겨지는데, 이것이 메뚜기 떼들을 이러한 한정된 자원을 향해 이동하게 만들기 때문이다. 다른 경우에는 유사한 환경의 개체들이 매우 다른 크기의 집단으로 발견된다. 어부들은 물고기 떼의 크기에 있어서 이러한 본질적인 변화에 익숙하다. 어떤 날은 그물에 세 마리의 물고기가 있고, 반면에 그 다음 날에는 그물에 수만 마리의 물고기가 있다. 인간의 정착지는 원래 정착지가 세워졌던 환경에 큰 차이가 없이 규모에서 차이가 생기면서 작은 마을에서 대도시까지 규모 면에서 비슷한 다양함을 또한 보여 준다.

구문풀이

14행 Human settlements also show similar variety in size, [from tiny villages to massive cities], [**with** differences in size **arising** without large differences in the environments {in which **they** were originally founded}].

: 첫 번째 [ ]는 삽입구이고, 두 번째 [ ]는 「with+명사(구)+분사」 구문이다. { }는 the environments를 수식하는 관계절로, they는 문장의 주어 Human settlements를 가리킨다.

어휘풀이
- vary *v* 다양하다, 변화하다
- plague *n* (유해 동물의) 이상 번식, 대량 발생
- locust *n* 메뚜기
- distribute *v* 분포시키다, 분배하다
- intrinsic *a* 본질적인, 내재한
- massive *a* 거대한
- magpie *n* 까치
- outbreak *n* 발생, 발발
- individual *n* 개체, 개인
- variation *n* 변화, 차이
- found *v* 세우다, 설립하다

064 답 ⑤

출제 의도 파악하기		
❶ 전치사+관계대명사	❷ 재귀대명사	
❸ to부정사의 쓰임	❹ 형용사의 쓰임	
❺ 관계대명사 what의 쓰임		

정답풀이

⑤ 뒤에 주어(some organisms)와 동사(must starve)를 갖춘 완전한 구조의 절이 이어지고 있으므로 관계대명사 What은 쓸 수 없으며, 문장의 주어를 이루는 명사절을 이끌도록 접속사 That으로 바꿔 써야 한다.

오답풀이

① 뒤에 주어(biological evolution)와 완전자동사(functions)를 갖춘 완전한 구조의 절이 이어지고 있고, 이 관계절이 전치사 by(~에 의해)를 수반하여 의미상 biological evolution functions by the process of selection을 나타내므로 「전치사+관계대명사」 형태의 by which는 알맞다.

② finding(찾는)의 동작 주체가 those less resourceful(수완이 모자란 것들)이고 for의 목적어 역시 those less resourceful로 동일한 대상이므로, 재귀대명사 themselves는 알맞다.

③ the way를 수식하는 to부정사구를 이끄는 to take는 알맞다. for genetic variants는 to take hold의 의미상 주어이다.

④ 「make+목적어+목적격보어」 구조에서 목적어가 길 경우, 목적어를 뒤로 보내고 목적격보어를 앞으로 도치시킬 수 있다. 여기서도 목적어 the good of greater diversity와 목적격보어 possible이 도치된 형태이므로, 목적격보어로 쓰인 형용사 possible이 make 뒤에 바로 이어진 것은 알맞다.

전문해석

모든 유기체가 생존에 충분한 먹이를 구할 수 있는 것은 아니어서, 기아는 자연에서 흔히 발견되는 일종의 반(反)가치이다. 그것은 또한 생물학적 진화가 기능하는 선택 과정의 일부이기도 하다. 기아는 살아남기에 덜 적합한 것들, 즉 자신과 자신의 새끼들을 위한 먹이를 찾는 것에 수완이 모자란 것들을 걸러 내는 데 도움을 준다. 몇몇 상황에서 그것(기아)은 유전적 변형체가 종의 개체군을 장악하는 길을 열어 주고 결국에는 이전의 종을 대신하여 새로운 종이 출현하도록 해 줄지도 모른다. 따라서 기아는 더 큰 다양성이라는 선(善)이 가능하도록 도울 수 있는 반가치이다. 기아는 내재적 반가치인 동시에 유용하거나 도구적인 가치를 지닐 수 있다. 몇몇 유기체들이 자연에서 기아를 겪어야 한다는 것은 매우 유감스럽고 슬픈 것이다. 기아가 때로는 좋은 목적에 공헌할 수도 있기는 하지만, 그 말은 여전히 확고히 진실이다.

구문풀이

1행 **Not all** organisms are able to find sufficient food to survive, so starvation is a kind of disvalue [often found in nature].

: 문장의 맨 앞에 Not all이 와서 '모든 ~이 …인 것은 아니다'라는 부분 부정의 의미를 나타내고 있다. [ ]는 a kind of disvalue를 수식하는 과거분사구이다.

어휘풀이
- organism *n* 유기체
- starvation *n* 기아, 굶주림
- sufficient *a* 충분한
- disvalue *n* 반(反)가치, (가치의) 부인

- filter out ~을 걸러 내다
- pave the way 길을 열어 주다, 상황을 조성하다
- variant *n* 변형
- emergence *n* 출현
- good *n* 선(善)
- even as ~임과 동시에
- resourceful *a* 수완이 있는
- take hold 장악하다
- in place of ~을 대신하여
- instrumental *a* 도구적인, 도움이 되는
- regrettable *a* 유감스러운

065 답 ⑤

출제 의도 파악하기		
❶ 지시대명사 that	❷ 주어와 동사의 수 일치	
❸ 관계대명사 that의 쓰임	❹ to부정사의 쓰임과 태	
❺ 동사의 태		

정답풀이

⑤ he or she 이하는 monthly retirement income을 수식하는 관계절로, he or she 앞에 관계대명사 that[which]이 생략된 형태이다. 즉, 주어인 he or she가 '의지하는' 주체이고 의지 대상이 선행사인 monthly retirement income이므로 be counted를 능동태 count로 고쳐 써야 한다.

오답풀이

① 반복되는 명사구 the idea를 대신하므로 지시대명사 that은 적절하다.

② 두 개의 절 The funds ~ the government와 the funds ~ recipients가 and로 연결된 구조로, 앞 절의 주어 The funds ~ insurance에 이어지는 동사 자리이다. 핵심 주어가 The funds이므로 복수형 동사 come을 쓴 것은 알맞다.

③ 선행사 benefits가 있고 뒤에 주어가 없는 불완전한 구조의 절이 이어지고 있으므로 관계대명사 that은 적절하다.

④ to be paid는 the benefits를 수식하는 to부정사로, the benefits는 '지급되는' 대상이므로 수동형 to부정사로 적절하게 쓰였다.

전문해석

사회보험은 19세기에 명확한 형태로 생겨난, 비교적 현대적인 개념이다. 사회보험의 개념은 정부와 국민 사이의 관계를 포함한다는 점에서 공공 지원의 개념과 비슷하다. 공공지원금과 사회보험에 드는 자금은 국민이 정부에 내는 세금에서 나오고, 그 자금은 정부가 수령인에게 지급한다. 그러나 아주 근본적인 차이점은 사회보험의 수혜자들은 자신들의 일이나 그들을 대신해서 다른 누군가가 한 일에 의해 얻은 보조금을 받고 있다는 것이다. 다양한 사회보험 프로그램에 따라 지급되는 보조금의 액수는 이론적으로 예측 가능한 정부의 의무이다. 따라서 이를테면 35세인 사람은 사회보장국에 편지를 써서 62세, 65세 또는 70세 때의 은퇴 직후에 자신이 의지할 수 있는 월 퇴직 소득의 금액을 알아낼 수 있다.

구문풀이

15행 Thus a person [who is, say, age thirty-five], can write to the Social Security Administration and find out [the amount of monthly retirement income {he or she can count on **upon retirement** at age sixty-two or sixty-five or seventy}].

: 첫 번째 [ ]는 주어 a person을 수식하는 관계절이다. 두 번째 [ ]는 find out의 목적어이며, 그 안의 { }는 monthly retirement income을 수식하는 관계절이다. 「upon+명사」는 '~하자마자, ~할 때'를 뜻한다.

어휘풀이
- social insurance 사회보험
- public assistance 공적 지원
- benefit *n* (정부 등에서 주는) 수당[보조금]
- obligation *n* 의무, 책무
- arise *v* 발생하다
- recipient *n* 수혜자

- Social Security Administration 사회보장국
- retirement *n* 은퇴

066 답 ④

출제 의도 파악하기

❶	주어와 동사의 수 일치	❷	접속사 whether의 쓰임
❸	관계부사 where의 쓰임	❹	병렬구조, 분사의 태
❺	형식상의 주어와 내용상의 주어		

정답풀이

④ 문장의 동사 watched와 병렬구조를 이룬다고 생각할 수 있지만, 문맥상 aggressively knocking과 as well as로 병렬 연결되어 지각동사 watched의 목적격보어를 이루는 자리이다. 뒤에 목적어 the doll이 있고 의미상의 주어인 the adult가 인형을 '학대하는' 주체이므로, abused를 현재분사 abusing으로 바꿔 써야 한다.

오답풀이

① 문장의 핵심 주어는 관계절 that involved ~ Bobo doll의 수식을 받는 A famous experiment in social psychology이므로, 단수형 동사 was의 쓰임은 적절하다.
② 뒤에 주어(kids), 동사(can learn), 목적어(aggressive behavior)를 갖춘 완전한 구조의 절이 이어지고, to find out의 목적절을 이끌며 '~인지 (아닌지)'를 알아보다'라는 의미를 나타내므로 접속사 whether는 적절하다.
③ 뒤에 주어(they), 동사(found), 목적어(an adult ~)를 갖춘 완전한 구조의 절이 이어지고, 콤마(,) 앞에 장소 명사구 the room이 있으므로 the room을 선행사로 하는 계속적 용법의 관계부사 where의 쓰임은 적절하다.
⑤ 문맥상 문장 맨 앞의 It이 형식상의 주어이고 that 이하가 내용상의 주어인 구조이므로 접속사 that은 적절하다.

전문해석

어린이, 성인, 부풀게 할 수 있는 Bobo 인형을 포함하는 유명한 사회 심리학 실험은 거의 반세기 전에 스탠포드 대학의 심리학자 Albert Bandura에 의해 실시되었다. Bandura와 그의 연구팀은 아이들이 성인을 보면서 공격적인 행동을 배울 수 있는지 알아보기를 원했다. 비디오 카메라와 양방향 거울이 설치되었고, 아이들은 방으로 들여보내졌는데, 그곳에서 그들은 어른과 Bobo라고 이름 붙여진 (여러분이 쓰러뜨리면 다시 튀어 오르는 종류의) 부풀린 큰 비닐 인형을 발견했다. 거기서 그들은 어른들이 공격적으로 Bobo를 두드리며 때로는 말로 인형을 학대하는 것을 지켜보았다. 잠시 후, 아이들은 Bobo와 함께 노는 것이 허용되었다. 아이들이 Bobo를 흥분하면서 발로 차고, 손바닥으로 때리면서 어른들을 모방했을 뿐만 아니라, 그 인형에 대해 자신들만의 창의적인 형태의 공격을 만들어 냈다는 것은 아마도 그리 놀라운 일이 아닐 것이다.

구문풀이

14행 **It** probably comes as little surprise [that the kids **not only** {copied the adult—excitedly knocking and smacking Bobo}—**but also** {developed their own creative forms of aggression toward the doll}].

: It은 형식상의 주어이고 [ ]가 내용상의 주어인 구조로, that절에서 「not only A but also B(A뿐만 아니라 B도)」 구문이 두 개의 { }를 병렬로 연결하고 있다.

어휘풀이

- inflatable *a* 부풀릴 수 있는
- bounce back 다시 튀어 오르다
- abuse *v* 학대하다, 남용하다
- aggressive *a* 공격적인
- verbally *ad* 말로, 구두로
- smack *v* 손으로 세게 때리다

067 답 ⑤

출제 의도 파악하기

❶	접속사 whether의 쓰임	❷	spend+시간+-ing
❸	주어와 동사의 수 일치	❹	the+비교급 ~, the+비교급 …
❺	문장의 구조 파악		

정답풀이

⑤ figure의 목적어로 쓰인 that절에서 주어인 writing down future tasks에 이어지는 술어 동사가 없다. 동명사구 주어는 단수 취급하므로 unloading을 단수형 동사 unloads로 고쳐 써야 한다.

오답풀이

① 동사 investigated의 목적어 역할을 하는 명사절을 이끄는 접속사로 whether(~인지)는 적절하게 쓰였다.
② '~하면서 (시간을) 보내다'라는 의미의 「spend+시간+-ing」 구문을 이루는 writing은 적절하게 쓰였다.
③ 핵심 주어는 관계절 who made to-do lists before bed의 수식을 받는 Those이므로 복수형 동사 were는 적절하다.
④ 「the+비교급 ~, the+비교급 …(~할수록 더욱 …하다)」 구문에서 more specific은 이어지는 동사 were의 보어에 해당하므로 형용사의 비교급으로서 적절하게 쓰였다.

전문해석

Baylor 대학의 연구자들은 다양한 종류의 글쓰기가 사람들을 편하게 하여 잠들게 할 수 있는지를 조사했다. 알아보기 위해서, 그들은 57명의 젊은 성인들에게 잠자리에 들기 전 5분간 앞으로 며칠 동안 해야 할 일의 목록 또는 지난 며칠 동안 그들이 끝낸 일들의 목록 중 하나를 쓰도록 했다. 그 결과는 모든 잠들기 전 글쓰기가 똑같이 이루어지지는 않는다는 것을 확인해 준다. 잠자리에 들기 전에 해야 할 일의 목록을 만든 사람들은 지나간 일에 관해 쓴 사람들보다 9분 더 빨리 잠들 수 있었다. 목록의 질 또한 중요했는데, 과업이 많을수록 그리고 해야 할 일의 목록이 구체적일수록, 작성자들은 더 빨리 잠들었다. 그 연구의 저자들은, 미래의 과업을 적으면 생각을 내려놓게 되어서 여러분이 그것을 곰곰이 생각하는 것을 멈출 수 있다고 결론짓는다. 여러분은 자신의 뇌에게 그 과업이 처리될 것인데 단지 지금 당장은 아니라고 말하고 있는 것이다.

구문풀이

3행 To find out, they had 57 young adults [spend five minutes before bed writing **either** a to-do list for the days ahead **or** a list of tasks {they'd finished over the past few days}].

: [ ]는 원형부정사인 spend가 이끄는 사역동사 had의 목적격보어이다. 「either A or B」는 'A와 B 둘 중 하나'라는 의미이다. { }는 tasks를 수식하는 관계절이다.

7행 [Those {who made to-do lists before bed}] **were** able to fall asleep nine minutes **faster than** [those {who wrote about past events}].

: 첫 번째 [ ]는 문장의 주어이며, 주어의 핵이 Those이므로 수 일치를 이루는 복수형 동사 were가 쓰였다. 비교구문이 쓰여 두 개의 [ ]를 비교하고 있고, 두 개의 { }는 각각 앞에 있는 Those와 those를 수식하는 관계절이다.

어휘풀이

- investigate *v* 조사하다
- confirm *v* 확인해 주다
- matter *v* 중요하다
- figure *v* 결론짓다, 생각하다, 이해하다
- unload *v* 짐을 내려놓다, 부담을 덜다
- turn ~ over in one's mind ~을 곰곰이 생각하다
- ease *v* 편안하게 만들다
- pre-sleep *a* 잠들기 전의
- specific *a* 구체적인, 상세한

068 답 ④

❶	주어와 동사의 수 일치	❷	cause의 목적격보어
❸	nor+조동사/be동사+주어	❹	문장의 구조 파악
❺	분사의 태		

정답풀이

④ 동사 determined의 목적어 역할을 하는 that절에서 핵심 주어는 현재분사구 striking the earth의 수식을 받는 a huge asteroid인데, 이에 연결되는 술어 동사가 없는 상태이다. 따라서 leading을 문맥상 시제를 반영한 과거 동사 led로 바꿔 써야 한다.

오답풀이

① 문장의 주어는 A glance at some of history's greatest discoveries and inventions이고, 주어의 핵이 단수 명사 glance이므로 단수형 동사 demonstrates는 알맞다.

② 「cause+목적어+목적격보어(to부정사)」(~에게 …하도록 야기하다) 구문에서 had caused의 목적격보어로 쓰인 to부정사 to be는 알맞다.

③ 부정어(not, no, never 등)를 포함한 문장 뒤에서 부정문이 연속됨을 나타내는 「Nor+조동사/be동사+주어」 구문으로, '~도 (또한) …하지 않다'의 의미이다. 즉, 문맥상 앞 문장의 부정 표현 wasn't burdened를 대신하는 동사로 쓰인 be동사 was는 적절하다. Nor에 이미 부정의 의미가 포함되어 있으므로 was만 온 것임에 유의한다.

⑤ 수식을 받는 explanations가 '~와 관련되는' 주체이므로 현재분사 relating의 쓰임은 적절하다.

전문해석

역사상 가장 위대한 발견과 발명 중 몇몇을 얼핏 보면 비전문인의 힘이 입증된다. Michael Ventris는 유럽에서 가장 오래된 글로, 수 세기 동안 고전학자들을 어쩔 줄 모르게 했던 언어인 선형문자 B를 여가시간에 해독한 직업 건축가였다. Ventris는 고전학의 전문지식이 부족함에도 불구하고가 아니라 그것 때문에 성공했다. 그는 틀린 지식의 부담이 없었다. Luis Alvarez 또한 마찬가지였다. 전공으로 고생물학자가 아니라 핵물리학자였던 그는 지구에 부딪힌 거대한 소행성이 공룡의 멸종을 야기했다는 것을 알아냈다. 고생물학자들은 지구에서 발생한 일과 관련된 설명, 즉 기후 변화나 어쩌면 있었을 초기 포유동물들과의 먹이 경쟁에 집착했다. Alvarez는 답을 찾아 하늘 쪽을 보았고, 그것이 그가 한 가지 답을 찾은 곳이다.

구문풀이

6행 Ventris succeeded **not** despite his lack of expertise in the classics **but** because of it.

: 「not A but B(A가 아니라 B)」 구문이 쓰였다. it은 his lack of expertise in the classics를 가리킨다.

어휘풀이

- glance *n* 얼핏 봄
- demonstrate *v* 입증하다
- classicist *n* 고전학자, 고대 그리스 · 로마 전문연구가
- at a loss 어쩔 줄 모르는
- expertise *n* 전문지식
- burden *v* 부담을 주다
- by training 전공으로
- determine *v* 알아내다
- asteroid *n* 소행성
- extinction *n* 멸종
- mammal *n* 포유류
- skyward *ad* 하늘을 향하여, 하늘 쪽으로

069 답 ⑤

❶	분사구문의 태	❷	동사의 태
❸	지시대명사 that	❹	형식상의 주어와 내용상의 주어
❺	관계대명사 which의 쓰임		

정답풀이

⑤ 뒤에 주어(opportunity)와 자동사(abounds)로 이루어진 완전한 구조의 절이 이어지므로, 관계대명사 which는 쓸 수 없다. 장소를 나타내는 a nation을 수식하는 관계부사 where로 바꿔 써야 한다.

오답풀이

① exploiting 이하는 Leaders를 의미상의 주어로 하는 분사구문으로, 의미상의 주어와 exploit가 능동의 관계이므로 현재분사 exploiting은 적절하다.

② 주어인 the underclass and downtrodden이 '갇혀 있는' 대상이므로, 수동태 동사 are kept는 적절하다.

③ that은 앞에 나온 reaction to life를 대신하는 지시대명사로 알맞게 쓰였다.

④ became convinced에 이어지는 that절 내에서 뒤에 오는 내용상의 주어 to grow ~ happiness에 대한 형식상의 주어 it은 적절하다.

전문해석

수많은 사람들이 부자들은 운이 좋았고 가난한 사람들은 소외되었다고 믿었기 때문에 너무나 많은 인생들이 낭비되었다. 모든 피부색과 민족적 배경을 가진 지도자들이 약자에게서 권력을 빼앗았고, 이 거짓말을 그들 자신의 이익을 위해 이용하고, 인종, 형제자매 그리고 계급 간에 경쟁을 붙여 왔다. 거저 주는 것을 구하도록 장려되어, 하층민들과 짓밟힌 사람들은 어디를 두드려야 할지 몰라 정신적인 어둠 속에 갇혀 있다. 인생에 대한 그들의 반응은 "왜 노력하는가? 부자는 더 부유해지고 가난한 사람은 더 가난해진다."라고 말한 누군가의 그것과 거의 같다. 그들은 인간으로서의 힘과 우리의 위대한 행성의 거주자로서의 가능성에 훨씬 못 미치게 생활한다. 위대한 철학자들이 사회에 대해 심사숙고하고 추측했을 때, 그들은 성장하고, 발전하고, 성공하고, 번영하고, 우리 몫의 행복을 찾는 것이 우리의 자연스러운 운명이라고 깊이 확신하게 되었다. 기회가 풍요로운 국가에서 우리 각자는 자신의 인생에서 개인의 부를 포함해 존재하는 최고의 것을 개인적으로 실현하라는 임무를 받은 것이다.

구문풀이

13행 As the great philosophers pondered and speculated upon society, they **became** deeply **convinced that it** is our natural destiny [to grow, to develop, to succeed, to prosper, and to find our portion of happiness].

: be convinced that ~은 '~을 확신하다'라는 의미이다. it은 형식상의 주어이며, [ ]가 내용상의 주어이다.

어휘풀이

- underprivileged *a* 가난한, 권리를 박탈당한
- ethnic *a* 민족의
- wrestle *v* (지배력 등을) 빼앗다
- exploit *v* 이용하다
- underclass *n* 최하층, 하층 계급
- downtrodden *a* 짓밟힌
- tap *v* 두드리다
- beneath *prep* ~에 미치지 못하는, ~보다 못하여
- inhabitant *n* 거주자, 주민
- ponder *v* 숙고하다
- speculate *v* 추측하다, 사색하다
- convinced *a* 납득하는, 설득된
- destiny *n* 운명
- prosper *v* 번영[번성]하다
- portion *n* 몫
- abound *v* 많이 있다, 풍부하다
- commission *v* 위임하다, 의뢰[주문]하다
- realization *n* 실현

070 답 ②

❶	접속사 whether의 쓰임	❷	문장의 구조 파악
❸	to부정사의 쓰임	❹	형용사의 쓰임
❺	전치사+관계대명사		

정답풀이

② 「전치사+관계대명사」인 through which가 이끄는 관계절에서 주어인 a car에 이어지는 본동사가 없는 상태이다. 따라서 준동사 alerting을 본동사 alerts로 고쳐 써야 한다.

오답풀이

① 문맥상 '~인지'라는 의미로 is의 보어절을 이끄는 접속사 whether의 쓰임은 적절하다.
③ the decision을 수식하는 to부정사구를 이끄는 to include는 알맞다.
④ made의 목적격보어 자리이므로 형용사 mandatory는 적절하다.
⑤ 뒤에 완전한 구조의 절이 이어지고, the 'golden hour' after a traffic accident를 선행사로 하여 관계절에서 in the 'golden hour' after a traffic accident의 부사구 역할을 하므로 「전치사+관계대명사」 형태의 in which는 적절하게 쓰였다.

전문해석

빅데이터에 수많은 잠재적인 응용 프로그램이 있다는 것은 분명하다. 그러나 그것들이 얼마나 의미가 있는지에 대해서는 회의적인 시각도 있다. 이 점에 있어서 일반적인 질문은 빅데이터가 실제로 상당한 진보를 제공하는지 여부이다. 그 질문에 대답하기 위해 다음 예를 살펴보자. eCall은 자동차 자체가 사고가 발생하면 인간의 개입 없이 응급 서비스에 위험을 알리는 시스템이다. 그것은 위치를 전달하고 자동차와 응급 서비스 사이의 오디오 연결을 개통한다. 독일에 기반을 둔 한 자동차 회사는 네덜란드에서 판매되는 모든 새로운 자동차에 이미 이 시스템을 포함하기로 하는 결정을 내렸다. 게다가, 유럽 연합은 2018년 3월 31일부터 팔리는 모든 새로운 자동차에 이 시스템이 의무화되도록 했다. 그것은 그 정책이 매년 2,500명 이상의 인간의 생명을 구할 것이라고 주장한다. 그 의무 설치는 구조 작업자들이 교통사고가 난 다음의 '골든타임'이라고 알려진, 빠르고 적절한 처치가 삶과 죽음의 차이를 의미하는 그 시간을 더 잘 활용하도록 도울 것이다.

구문풀이

17행 The mandatory installation will **help** rescue workers **make** better use of the period [known as the 'golden hour' after a traffic accident, {in which rapid and appropriate action means the difference between life and death}].

: make는 help의 목적격보어로 쓰인 원형부정사이다. [ ]는 the period를 수식하는 과거분사구이고, 그 안의 { }는 the 'golden hour' after a traffic accident를 부연 설명하는 관계절이다.

어휘풀이

- potential *a* 잠재적인
- skepticism *n* 회의론, 회의적 태도
- respect *n* 점, 사항
- go through ~을 살펴보다, ~을 검토하다
- alert *v* 위험을 알리다
- manufacturer *n* 제조업체, 제조업자
- claim *v* 주장하다
- annually *ad* 매년, 해마다
- rescue *n* 구조
- appropriate *a* 적절한
- application *n* 응용 프로그램
- regarding *prep* ~에 대하여
- significant *a* 중요한, 상당한
- intervention *n* 개입
- communicate *v* 전달하다
- mandatory *a* 의무적인
- policy *n* 정책
- installation *n* 설치
- make use of ~을 이용하다[활용하다]

---

071 ⑤	**072** ⑤	**073** ④	**074** ②	**075** ④
076 ④	**077** ④	**078** ③		

071 답 ⑤

❶	부사의 쓰임	❷	병렬구조
❸	분사의 태	❹	관계대명사 that의 쓰임
❺	문장의 구조 파악		

정답풀이

⑤ 문장의 주어는 This이고 술어 동사는 leads로, 별도의 접속사 없이 또 다른 술어 동사 believes는 쓸 수 없다. 문맥상 with 이하는 「with+명사(구)+분사」 구문이 되어야 하는데, believes 뒤에 명사절이 목적어로 왔고 의미상의 주어인 each가 believe의 주체에 해당하므로 believes를 현재분사 believing으로 고쳐 써야 한다.

오답풀이

① 동사 expose를 수식하는 부사 selectively는 어법상 적절하다.
② 문맥상 '사람들은 자신의 기존 신념 체계에 부합하는 정보를 찾고 그러한 신념에 도전하는 정보를 피한다'는 의미가 자연스러우므로, avoid는 and 앞의 seek out과 병렬로 연결되어 people에 이어지는 술어 동사로 적절하게 쓰였다.
③ 수식을 받는 명사 beliefs는 '표현되는' 대상이므로 수동의 의미를 표현하는 과거분사 expressed는 적절하다.
④ a source of news를 수식하는 관계절을 유도하며 관계절에서 주어 역할을 하는 관계대명사 that은 어법상 적절하다.

전문해석

사람들이 선택적으로 뉴스 콘텐츠에 자신을 노출시킨다는 생각은 오랫동안 있어 왔지만, 구독자의 분열과 선택의 급증으로 그것은 오늘날 훨씬 더 중요하다. 선택적 노출은 사람들이 자신의 기존 신념 체계에 부합하는 정보를 찾아내고 그러한 신념에 도전하는 정보를 피한다고 하는 심리학적 개념이다. 뉴스의 공급처가 얼마 없었던 과거에는, 사람들이 그들 자신의 신념과 상반되게 표현된 신념을 보게 될 수도 있는 주류 뉴스에 자신을 노출시키거나 뉴스를 전적으로 피할 수 있었다. 이제 아주 많은 유형의 뉴스들이 매우 다양한 틈새 구독자들에게 끊임없이 이용 가능해지면서 사람들은 자신의 개인적 신념들을 지속적으로 확인해 주는 뉴스의 공급처를 쉽게 찾을 수 있다. 이는 각자가 세상이 어떻게 돌아가는지에 대해 자신들이 옳고 다른 모든 사람들이 그르다고 강하게 믿는 사람들의 많은 다양한 소집단들을 만들 수 있는 가능성으로 이어진다.

구문풀이

4행 Selective exposure is a psychological concept [that says {people <seek out information that conforms to their existing belief systems> and <avoid information that challenges those beliefs>}].

: [ ]는 a psychological concept를 수식하는 관계절이고, { }는 says의 목적어 역할을 하는 명사절이다. 두 개의 < >는 and에 의해 대등하게 연결되어 people의 술어를 이룬다.

어휘풀이

- selectively *ad* 선택적으로
- expose *v* 노출시키다
- psychological *a* 심리학적인, 심리적인

- concept *n* 개념
- existing *a* 기존의
- mainstream *a* 주류의
- consistently *ad* 끊임없이, 지속적으로
- confirm *v* 확인하다
- conform to ~에 부합하다
- challenge *v* 도전하다
- possibility *n* 가능성

072 답 ⑤

출제 의도 파악하기

❶ 동명사의 쓰임	❷ 접속사 that의 쓰임
❸ to부정사의 시제	❹ 부사의 쓰임
❺ 문장의 구조 파악	

정답풀이

⑤ that help humans cope with such environments는 핵심 주어인 The cultural innovations를 수식하는 관계절로, 주어에 이어지는 동사가 없는 상태이다. 따라서 준동사 including을 본동사인 include로 바꿔 써야 한다.

오답풀이

① adapt to(~에 적응하다)에서 to는 전치사이므로 목적어로 동명사 형태인 surviving이 온 것은 적절하다.

② 뒤에 주어(high altitude), 동사(may have been), 보어(a source of natural selection)를 모두 갖춘 완전한 구조의 절이 이어지고 있고, 이 절이 동사 reveal의 목적어 역할을 하므로 접속사 that은 적절하다.

③ 주절의 시제인 현재(seem)보다 앞선 일을 표현하고 있으므로 완료형 부정사 to have arrived는 적절하다.

④ 뒤에 있는 과거분사 transmitted를 수식하는 부사 culturally는 적절하다.

전문해석

문화와 자연 선택의 상호작용에 대한 한 가지 흥미로운 실례는 사람들이 높은 고도에서 생존하는 데 적응해 온 방식에서 볼 수 있다. 높은 고도에서 사는 사람들을 낮은 고도에서 사는 사람들과 비교하는 문화 간 비교는 높은 고도가 일부 사람들에게서 자연 선택의 원천이었을 수 있다는 것을 보여 준다. 전 세계적으로, 인간 무리들은 산악 지역에 군락을 이루면서 생존했다. 예를 들어, 인간은 약 25,000년 전에 히말라야 산맥의 티베트 고원에 도착한 것으로 보인다. 훨씬 후인 약 10,000년 전에, 인간들은 또한 남아메리카의 안데스 산맥에 군락을 이루었다. 의심할 여지없이, 문화적으로 전달되는 정보는 이 사람들의 높은 고도에서의 성공에 결정적이었다. 인간이 이러한 환경에 대처할 수 있도록 돕는 문화 혁신에는 따뜻하고 단열된 의복과 은신처의 건설, 히말라야 야크와 같은 지역 동물 종의 가축화, 그리고 안데스 산맥에서의 고산병의 영향을 완화하기 위한 코카 잎의 사용 등이 포함된다.

구문풀이

1행 [One interesting illustrative example of the interaction of culture and natural selection] can be seen in the ways [that human populations have adapted to {surviving at high altitudes}].

: 첫 번째 [ ]가 문장의 주어이며, 동사는 can be seen이다. 두 번째 [ ]는 the ways를 수식하는 관계절이고, 그 안의 { }는 전치사 to의 목적어 역할을 하는 동명사구이다.

4행 Cross-cultural comparisons, [**comparing** {people <who live at high altitudes>} **to** {low altitude populations}], reveal [that high altitude may have been a source of natural selection in some human populations].

: 첫 번째 [ ]는 Cross-cultural comparisons를 부연 설명하는 분사구문이다. 그 안에

서 두 개의 { }가 「compare *A* to *B*(*A*를 *B*와 비교하다)」 구문으로 연결되어 있다. < >는 people을 수식하는 관계절이다. 두 번째 [ ]는 reveal의 목적어 역할을 하는 명사절이다.

어휘풀이

- illustrative *a* 실례가 되는, 예증이 되는
- interaction *n* 상호작용
- cross-cultural *a* 문화 간의
- altitude *n* 고도
- colonize *v* 군락을 이루다, 식민지를 건설하다
- transmit *v* 전달하다
- innovation *n* 혁신
- construction *n* 건설
- shelter *n* 은신처, 거처
- altitude sickness 고산병
- population *n* 사람들, 인구
- comparison *n* 비교
- reveal *v* 보여 주다, 드러내다
- crucial *a* 결정적인
- cope with ~에 대처하다
- insulate *v* 단열하다
- domestication *n* 가축화

073 답 ④

출제 의도 파악하기

❶ 분사구문의 태	❷ 생략구문
❸ 병렬구조	❹ 관계대명사 what의 쓰임
❺ 분사구문	

정답풀이

④ What ~ complex의 명사절이 but 앞 절의 주어이며 동사는 would not be이다. What이 이끄는 절은 주어(cell metabolism and structure), 동사(should be), 보어(complex)를 갖춘 완전한 구조를 이루므로, 선행사를 포함하는 관계대명사 What을 명사절을 이끄는 접속사 That으로 고쳐야 한다.

오답풀이

① 의미상의 주어인 its mother cell이 '생산하는' 주체이고, 뒤에 목적어 two daughter cells가 있으므로 능동의 분사구문을 이끄는 현재분사 producing은 어법상 적절하다.

② 원래 as the mother cell was large에서 보어인 large가 생략된 형태이다.

③ as절의 동사가 「either *A* or *B*」로 연결된 형태이므로, prepares와 병렬구조를 이루는 matures and differentiates의 쓰임은 어법상 적절하다.

⑤ each를 의미상의 주어로 하는 분사구문 each being responsible ~에서 being이 생략된 형태로 responsible의 쓰임은 어법상 적절하다.

전문해석

온전한 개체와 마찬가지로, 세포도 수명을 갖고 있다. 그것들의 생명 주기(세포 주기) 동안, 세포 크기, 모양, 물질대사 활동이 극적으로 변할 수 있다. 세포는 모세포가 분열하여 두 개의 딸세포를 만들어 낼 때 쌍둥이로 태어난다. 각각의 딸세포는 모세포보다 더 작으며, 특이한 경우를 제외하고는 각각 모세포가 그랬던 것만큼 커질 때까지 자란다. 이 기간 동안, 세포는 물, 당, 아미노산 그리고 다른 영양소를 흡수하고 그것들을 조합하여 새로운 살아 있는 원형질로 만든다. 세포가 적절한 크기로 자란 후, 그것이 분열할 준비를 하거나 또는 성숙하여 특화된 세포로 분화하면서 그것의 물질대사가 변화한다. 성장과 발달 둘 다 모든 세포 부분을 포함하는 일련의 복잡하고 역동적인 상호작용을 필요로 한다. 세포의 물질대사와 구조가 복잡할 것임은 놀라운 일이 아니겠지만, 실제로 그것들은 꽤 단순하며 논리적이다. 가장 복잡한 세포조차도 그저 몇몇 부분만을 가지고 있는데, 각각은 세포 생명의 뚜렷이 다르고, 명확한 측면을 담당하고 있다.

구문풀이

8행 During this time, the cell [absorbs water, sugars, amino acids, and other nutrients] and [assembles **them** into new, living protoplasm].

: and로 연결된 두 개의 [ ]가 문장의 술어이고, them은 water ~ other nutrients를 가리킨다.

어휘풀이

- life span 수명
- except for ~을 제외하고
- amino acid 아미노산(단백질의 기본 구성단위)
- nutrient *n* 영양소, 영양분
- assemble *A* into *B* A를 조합하여 B를 만들다
- mature *v* 다 자라다
- dynamic *a* 역동적인
- responsible *a* ~을 담당하고 있는
- well-defined *a* 명확하게 규정된
- dramatically *ad* 극적으로, 급격하게
- absorb *v* 흡수하다
- differentiate *v* 분화하다
- logical *a* 논리적인
- distinct *a* 전혀 다른, 뚜렷이 구별되는

074 답 ②

❶	관계대명사 that의 쓰임	❷	의문사 where의 쓰임
❸	문장의 구조 파악	❹	주어와 동사의 수 일치
❺	재귀대명사		

정답풀이

② 동사 argued 다음에 나온 in a book ~ the world는 부사구이고, where 뒤에 주어(dance), 동사(owes), 목적어(its origin ~)를 갖춘 완전한 구조의 절이 이어지므로 이 절은 argued의 목적어에 해당하는데, 문맥상 where가 이끄는 의문사절은 어색하다. where를 명사절을 이끄는 접속사 that으로 바꿔 써야 한다.

오답풀이

① the other animals를 수식하는 관계절을 이끌면서 관계절의 주어 역할을 하는 주격 관계대명사 that의 쓰임은 적절하다.
③ from ~ history는 삽입된 부사구이고, Our species를 주어로 하는 동사 자리이므로 gained는 적절하게 쓰였다.
④ because절에서 주어는 humans이므로 복수형 동사 were는 적절하다.
⑤ 문맥상 to think about의 의미상 주어와 목적어가 humans로 같으므로 재귀대명사 themselves는 적절하다.

전문해석

인간은 지구상에 결코 혼자 있지 않았다. 인간의 생활, 즉 문화, 기술 그리고 예술은 그들이 자신들과 땅과 바다를 공유한 다른 동물들을 보고, 듣고, 모방하는 것을 배웠기 때문에 헤아릴 수 없을 정도로 풍부해졌다. Steven Lonsdale은 세계 곳곳에서 나온 사례들로 가득 찬 책에서, 춤은 그 기원과 정교함이 인간이 포유류, 파충류, 어류, 조류 등의 다양한 움직임을 모방한 덕택이라고 주장했다. 아주 옛날부터 역사 기간 동안 우리 인간은 나머지 종으로부터 적잖은 기술을 획득했다. 인간 종과 인간의 문화는 하나의 종으로서 인간이 그들의 역사 동안에 다른 종류의 동식물과의 상호작용이 그들이 생존할지와 번식할지의 여부를 결정했던 생물군집의 일부였기 때문에 생겨난 자연 선택을 통하여 진화했다. 오늘날 인간이 저지르는 가장 큰 실수 중 하나는 자기 자신이 다른 형태의 생물과 관계없이 존재하고 행동한다고 생각하는 것이다. 어떤 종도 완전히 고립되어 존재하지 않는다. 즉, 모든 종은 생물 체계 내에서 다른 것들과 관련을 맺는다.

구문풀이

5행 Steven Lonsdale argued [in a book {filled with examples from every part of the world}] [that dance owes its origin and

elaboration to human imitation of the varied movements of mammals, reptiles, fish, birds, etc].

: 첫 번째 [ ]는 부사구이며, 그 안의 { }는 a book을 수식하는 과거분사구이다. 두 번째 [ ]는 문장의 동사인 argued의 목적어로 쓰인 명사절이다.

11행 The human species and human culture evolved through natural selection [that took place because humans during their history as a species were part of biotic communities {where their interactions with other kinds of animals and plants decided <whether or not they survived and reproduced>}].

: [ ]는 natural selection을, 그 안의 { }는 biotic communities를 수식하는 관계절이다. 〈 〉는 decided의 목적어로 쓰인 명사절이다.

어휘풀이

- immeasurably *ad* 헤아릴 수 없을 정도로
- enriched *a* 풍부한
- owe *A* to *B* A는 B의 덕분이다, A는 B에 기인하다
- elaboration *n* 정교(함), 공들임
- reptile *n* 파충류
- craft *n* 기술, 기교, (수)공예
- natural selection 자연 선택
- reproduce *v* 번식하다, 재생하다
- isolation *n* 고립
- argue *v* 주장하다, 논쟁하다
- mammal *n* 포유류
- evolve *v* 진화하다, 발달하다
- biotic community 생물군집
- without reference to ~에 상관없이

075 답 ④

❶	병렬구조	❷	접속사 because의 쓰임
❸	재귀대명사	❹	문장의 구조 파악
❺	관계대명사 what의 쓰임		

정답풀이

④ indicates의 목적어로 쓰인 that절에서 주어 our closest cousins, the chimpanzees에 이어지는 동사가 없는 상태이다. 따라서 준동사 lacking을 본동사 lack으로 바꿔 써야 한다.

오답풀이

① and 앞의 to stand와 병렬로 연결되어 Our ability를 수식하는 형용사적 용법의 to부정사구를 이루는 (to) evaluate는 알맞다.
② 접속사 because 뒤에 주어 the most recently developed part of the human brain과 동사 enables가 있는 절이 왔고, 이 절은 문맥상 이유를 나타내고 있으므로 부사절을 이끄는 접속사 because는 알맞다.
③ as if가 이끄는 절에서 전치사 of의 목적어가 주어인 we와 동일하므로 재귀대명사 ourselves는 알맞다. 주어와 목적어가 동일한 대상일 때, 목적어 자리에 오는 대명사는 재귀대명사로 쓴다.
⑤ 앞에 있는 are thinking의 목적절을 이끌며 관계절에서 목적어 역할을 하는 관계대명사 what은 알맞다.

전문해석

메타인지는 단순히 '생각에 대해 생각하는 것'을 의미하며, 그것은 인간의 두뇌와 다른 종의 두뇌 간의 주요 차이점 중 하나이다. 우리의 통상적인 사고 과정 위에 있는 사다리에 높이 서서 왜 우리가 지금 생각하고 있는 것처럼 생각하고 있는지를 평가할 수 있는 우리의 능력은 진화론적으로 경이로운 일이다. 인간 두뇌의 가장 최근에 발달한 부분인 전두엽 피질이 자기 성찰적이고 추상적인 사고를 가능하게 하기 때문에 우리는 이 능력을 가진다. 우리는 우리가 우리 자신의 일부가 아닌 것처럼 우리 자신에 대해 생각할 수 있다. 영장류의 행동에 대한 연구는 우리의 가장 가까운 사촌

인 침팬지조차도 (거울에 비친 모습을 다른 침팬지라고 생각하지 않고 거울 속의 자기 자신을 알아볼 수 있는 것과 같이, 그것들이 약간의 자기 성찰적인 능력을 가지고 있기는 하지만) 이 능력이 결여되어 있음을 보여 준다. 그 능력은 양날의 칼인데, 왜냐하면 그것은 우리로 하여금 우리가 생각하고 있는 것을 왜 생각하고 있는지 평가하도록 하는 한편, 또한 우리로 하여금 쉽게 강박 관념이 될 수 있는 어려운 실존적 질문들과 접하게 하기 때문이다.

구문풀이

16행 The ability is a double-edged sword, because [while it allows us to evaluate {why we are thinking <what we are thinking>}], it also puts us in touch with difficult existential questions [that can easily become obsessions].

: 첫 번째 [ ]는 '~하는 한편'이라는 의미의 접속사 while이 이끄는 부사절이다. 그 안의 { }는 to evaluate의 목적어로 쓰인 명사절이며, ⟨ ⟩는 are thinking의 목적어로 쓰인 명사절이다. 두 번째 [ ]는 difficult existential questions를 수식하는 관계절이다.

어휘풀이

- metacognition *n* 메타인지
- normal *a* 보통의, 정상적인
- evolutionary *a* 진화의
- prefrontal cortex 전두엽 피질
- abstract *a* 추상적인
- instead of *doing* ~하는 대신에, ~하지 않고
- reflection *n* (거울 등에) 비친 그림자
- obsession *n* 집착, 강박 관념
- distinction *n* 차이, 구별
- evaluate *v* 평가하다
- marvel *n* 경이, 기적
- reflective *a* 반성하는, 숙고하는
- primate *n* 영장류
- double-edged *a* 양날의, 양면적인
- existential *a* 실존주의의

076 답 ④

| 출제 의도 | 파악하기 |

① 관계대명사 what의 쓰임 ② to부정사의 쓰임
③ 주어와 동사의 수 일치 ④ 문장의 구조 파악
⑤ 도치구문

정답풀이

④ if가 이끄는 부사절에 이어 주절이 시작되는 부분이다. 절을 이루기 위해서는 주어와 동사가 있어야 하는데, 주어 역할을 할 수 있는 말이 없는 상태이다. 따라서 '암송해 보라'는 의미의 명령문이 되도록 reciting을 동사원형 recite로 고쳐 써야 한다.

오답풀이

① commemorate의 목적어 역할을 하는 명사절을 이끌면서 동시에 관계절의 주어 역할을 해야 하므로, 선행사를 포함하는 관계대명사 what의 쓰임은 적절하다.
② to get은 '~하기 위해서'라는 의미의 목적을 나타내는 부사적 용법으로 적절하게 쓰였다.
③ 핵심 주어는 Printed words이므로 복수형 동사 communicate는 적절하게 쓰였다.
⑤ 한정적인 의미를 갖는 only의 수식을 받는 부사가 문두에 쓰여 문장의 주어 you와 조동사 will이 도치된 형태로, will you는 어법상 적절하다.

전문해석

1863년에 워싱턴 DC에서 펜실베이니아로 가는 기차에서 Abraham Lincoln은 미국 역사상 당시에도 그랬고 여전히 가장 피비린내 나는 전투로 남아 있는 것을 기념하기 위해 뭔가 말할 수 있도록 Gettysburg 연설문을 썼다. 현재 미국의 초등학생들은 Lincoln과 그의 시대를 더 잘 이해하기 위해 그 남자의 짧은 연설문을 암기하

고 암송한다. 종이에 인쇄된 말이 그의 메시지의 의미와 힘의 일부를 전달해 준다. 그러나 만일 Lincoln의 말에 담긴 그 힘을 모두 느끼고자 한다면 그 연설을 큰 소리로 암송해 보라. 그래야만 그의 말과 연설이 1863년 그날 모인 군중에게 미친 영향을 느낄 것이다. 나는 만일 Lincoln의 연설문이 몇몇 신문에 실리기만 하고 대중에게 연설되지 않았더라면, 미국의 초등학생들이 그것을 매년 기억하고 암송하고 있을지 의문이다.

구문풀이

13행 **Had** Lincoln's address **been printed** in a few newspapers and not declaimed to an audience, I doubt American schoolchildren **would be memorizing** and **reciting** it each year.

: 혼합 가정법으로 조건절에는 과거 사실에 반대되는 가정법 과거완료의 형태가 쓰였다. 조건절에서 If가 생략되어 Had가 주어인 Lincoln's address 앞으로 도치되었다. 주절은 현재 사실에 반대되는 추측을 나타내므로 가정법 과거 동사 would be memorizing and reciting이 쓰였다.

어휘풀이

- commemorate *v* 기념하다
- recite *v* 암송하다
- declaim *v* 연설하다
- bloody *a* 유혈의, 피비린내 나는
- delivery *n* 연설, 강연
- doubt *v* ~이 아닐까 생각하다

077 답 ④

| 출제 의도 | 파악하기 |

① 부정대명사 one ② 동명사의 쓰임
③ 형용사의 쓰임 ④ 관계부사 where의 쓰임
⑤ 관계부사 how의 쓰임

정답풀이

④ the part of philosophy를 수식하는 관계절에서 appears의 주어가 빠져 있으므로 관계부사 where는 쓸 수 없다. where를 주격 관계대명사 that 또는 which로 고쳐 써야 한다.

오답풀이

① 앞에 나온 명사구 a field를 대신하는 부정대명사 one은 어법상 적절하다.
② 뒤에 목적어 ideas를 취하면서 전치사 for의 목적어 역할을 하는 동명사 expressing의 쓰임은 적절하다.
③ 「make+목적어+목적격보어」 구문으로 German philosophers such as Immanuel Kant가 목적어이고 형용사 difficult가 목적격보어로 적절하게 쓰였다.
⑤ 뒤에 완전한 구조의 절이 이어지고, '~하는 방법'이라는 의미로 전치사 at의 목적어 역할을 하는 명사절을 이끄는 how는 어법상 적절하다.

전문해석

철학은 어떤 면에서는 수학과 같은데, 이는 그것이 위조되거나 왜곡될 수 있는 경험적 자료보다 많은 철학과의 전문 분야 중 하나인 논리에 더 많이 의존하기 때문이다. 원칙적으로 철학자는 무엇이든 논의할 수 있다. 철학은 자료를 수집하고 분석하는 표준적인 방법이라는 일반적인 의미에서 방법론적 선호가 있는 분야가 아니라, 체계적이고 명확하게 사고하는 방법을 강하게 강조하는 분야이다. 언어는 사상을 표현하는 주요한 도구이기 때문에 언어는 철학 저술에서 특히 중요한 역할을 한다. 일부 언어는 추상화 수준에 더 잘 적용된다. 예를 들어, 독일어에서는 동사를 추상명사로 바꾸는 것이 쉬운데, 이는 Immanuel Kant와 같은 독일 철학자들을 번역하기 어렵게 만든다. 윤리학은 진실성의 문제에 대한 논의에서 가장 자주 나타나며 다른 학문들의 심의에서도 자주 나타나는 철학의 한 부분이다. 전문 철학자들은 때때로 훈련되지 않은 철학자들이 자신들 분야의 개념을 사용하는 방식에 대해 절망하지만, 어떤

면에서 그것은 또한 그것의 중요성에 대한 표시이기도 하다.

구문풀이

1행 Philosophy is in some sense like mathematics [because it relies **more** on logic−{one of the specialties in many philosophy departments}−**than** on empirical data, {which can be falsified or distorted}].

: [ ]는 because가 이끄는 부사절이고, 그 안에 「more ~ than ....」의 비교구문이 쓰였다. 첫 번째 { }는 logic을 부가적으로 설명하는 동격의 명사구이고, 두 번째 { }는 empirical data를 부가적으로 설명하는 관계절이다.

13행 In German, for example, **it** is easy [to turn a verb into an abstract noun], [which makes German philosophers such as Immanuel Kant hard to translate].

: it은 형식상의 주어이고, 첫 번째 [ ]가 내용상의 주어이다. 두 번째 [ ]는 앞 절의 내용을 부연 설명하는 관계절이다.

어휘풀이
- rely on ~에 의존하다
- specialty _n_ 전문 분야, 전공
- falsify _v_ 위조하다
- in principle 원칙적으로
- preference _n_ 선호
- systematically _ad_ 체계적으로
- adapt to ~에 적용되다
- abstract noun 추상명사
- ethics _n_ 윤리(학)
- deliberations _n_ 심의, 토의, 협의
- despair at ~에 절망하다
- logic _n_ 논리
- empirical _a_ 경험적인
- distort _v_ 왜곡하다
- methodological _a_ 방법론적인
- analyse _v_ 분석하다
- primary _a_ 주요한, 근원적인
- abstraction _n_ 추상화
- translate _v_ 번역하다
- integrity _n_ 진실성, 온전함, 정직
- discipline _n_ 학문 (분야)

078 답 ③

출제 의도 파악하기
❶ 의문사 what의 쓰임		❷ 상관접속사 구문의 수 일치	
❸ 도치구문의 수 일치		❹ 부사의 쓰임	
❺ 관계대명사 that의 쓰임			

정답풀이
③ 관계부사 where가 이끄는 절에서 위치의 부사구 just beneath your single footprint가 앞으로 나오면서 「자동사+주어」로 도치가 일어난 형태이다. 주어가 hundreds of seeds이므로 sits를 복수형 동사 sit으로 바꿔 써야 한다.

오답풀이
① is known의 주어가 되는 절을 이끌며 그 절에서 is waiting for의 목적어 역할을 하는 의문사 What은 적절하다.
② 상관접속사 「neither _A_ nor _B_」로 연결되는 주어는 _B_에 동사의 수를 일치시키므로 the old oak에 수를 일치시킨 단수형 동사 is의 쓰임은 적절하다.
④ 뒤에 있는 현재분사 wishing을 수식하므로 부사 fervently는 적절하다.
⑤ 선행사 a seed를 수식하는 관계절에서 동사 waited의 주어 역할을 하는 주격 관계대명사 that은 적절하다.

전문해석
씨앗은 어떻게 기다려야 하는지 알고 있다. 대부분의 씨앗은 자라기 시작하기 전 적어도 1년은 기다린다. 각각의 씨앗이 정확히 무엇을 기다리는지는 그 씨앗만이 안다. 기다리는 동안에도 씨앗은 살아 있다. 씨앗도, 나이 든 떡갈나무도 자라지 않고 있다. 둘 다 그저 기다리고 있다. 그러나 그 둘의 기다림은, 나무는 죽기만을 기다리지만, 씨앗은 번성하기를 기다린다는 점에서 다르다. 숲에 갈 때, 여러분은 아마 여러분이 도달할 수 있는 것보다 훨씬 더 높이 자란 나무들을 올려다보려 할 것이다. 아마 밑은 내려다보지 않을 텐데, 그곳에서는 여러분의 발자국 하나하나 아래에 수백 개의 씨앗이 있으며 각각이 살아서 기다리고 있다. 그것들은 절대 오지 않을지도 모르는 기회를 가망이 없는데도 기다린다. 숲에 있을 때 눈에 보이는 나무 한 그루마다 땅속에서 살아서 나무가 되기를 열렬히 바라며 기다리고 있는 적어도 수백 그루의 나무가 있다. 모든 시작은 기다림의 끝이다. 우리에게는 각각 정확하게 한 번의 기회가 주어진다. 우리 각자는 불가능하면서도 필연적이다. 모든 무성한 나무는 처음에는 기다리던 씨앗이었다.

구문풀이

7행 [When you go into a forest], you probably tend to look up at the plants [that have grown so much taller than you ever **could**].

: 첫 번째 [ ]는 접속사 When이 이끄는 부사절이다. 두 번째 [ ]는 the plants를 수식하는 관계절이다. could 다음에는 grow tall이 생략되었다.

어휘풀이
- seed _n_ 씨앗
- flourish _v_ 잘 자라다, 번성하다
- footprint _n_ 발자국
- hope against hope 가망이 없는데도 희망을 계속 가지다
- soil _n_ 땅, 흙
- oak _n_ 떡갈나무
- beneath _prep_ ~의 바로 밑에

079 ④	**080** ③	**081** ②	**082** ④	**083** ②
084 ③	**085** ②	**086** ②		

- encompass *v* 망라하다, 포함하다
- occasional *a* 이따금씩의, 가끔의
- suggestive *a* 연상시키는
- inland *a* 내륙의
- net bag 망태기
- conduct *v* 운영하다, 관리하다
- barter *n* 물물교환
- spectrum *n* 전 범위, 영역
- band *n* 무리
- flea market 벼룩시장
- in rows 줄지어
- equivalent *a* 같은, 동등한
- utilitarian *a* 실용적인

079 답 ④

출제 의도 파악하기

❶ 도치구문의 수 일치	❷ 도치구문
❸ 문장의 구조 파악	❹ 분사의 태
❺ 관계대명사 that의 쓰임	

정답풀이

④ 수식을 받는 명사구 a number of pots and coconuts가 '판단되는' 대상이므로 judging을 수동의 의미를 나타내는 과거분사 judged로 고쳐 써야 한다.

오답풀이

① 위치를 나타내는 부사구인 At the simplest level이 문두에 와서 주어와 be동사가 도치된 구문이다. 주어는 the occasional trips이므로 이에 수를 맞춘 be동사 are는 어법상 적절하다.

② the occasional markets가 주어, were가 동사인 문장에서 Suggestive of our open-air markets and flea markets는 문두로 도치된 보어 역할을 하는 형용사구이다. 따라서 Suggestive는 어법상 적절하다.

③ Up to a few dozen people from each side가 문장의 주어이고 이에 이어지는 다른 동사가 없으므로 문장의 술어 역할을 하는 sat은 어법상 적절하다.

⑤ 뒤에 visited의 목적어가 없는 불완전한 구조의 절이 이어지고, 이 절이 the islands를 수식하므로 목적격 관계대명사 that은 어법상 적절하다.

전문해석

전통적인 거래의 형식과 빈도는 전 범위를 망라한다. 가장 단순한 단계에서 !Kung 족과 Dani 족 일원이 다른 무리나 마을에 있는 그들 각각의 거래 상대를 방문하기 위해 이따금 이루어지는 왕래가 있다. 뉴기니 북동쪽 해안에 사는 Sio 마을 사람들이 내륙 마을에서 온 뉴기니 사람들을 만나는 이따금 서는 시장은 우리의 노천 시장과 벼룩시장을 연상시켰다. 각각의 편에서 온 수십 명에 이르는 사람들이 서로 마주 보고 줄지어 앉았다. 한 내륙인이 10에서 35파운드 사이의 타로토란과 고구마가 든 망태기를 앞으로 내밀면, 맞은편에 앉은 Sio 마을 사람은 그 망태기에 든 음식과 가치가 같다고 판단되는 몇 개의 단지와 코코넛을 내놓아 응했다. Trobriand 섬의 카누 상인들은 자신들이 방문하는 섬들에서 비슷한 시장을 운영하며, 물물교환으로 실용품(음식, 단지, 그릇)을 교환했고, 동시에 그들과 그들의 개별 거래 상대는 서로에게 사치품(조개목걸이와 팔찌)을 답례품으로 주었다.

구문풀이

5행 [Suggestive of our open-air markets and flea markets] were the occasional markets [at which Sio villagers {living on the coast of northeast New Guinea} met New Guineans from inland villages].

: 문장의 보어인 첫 번째 [ ]가 문두로 나가 주어와 be동사가 도치된 형태이다. 두 번째 [ ]는 the occasional markets를 수식하는 관계절이고, 그 안의 { }는 Sio villagers를 수식하는 현재분사구이다.

어휘풀이

- format *n* 형식
- frequency *n* 빈도(수)

080 답 ③

출제 의도 파악하기

❶ 부정대명사 one	❷ 주어와 동사의 수 일치
❸ 문장의 구조 파악	❹ to부정사의 쓰임
❺ 접속사 that의 쓰임	

정답풀이

③ 문장의 주어는 students who had succeeded on the test이고, who had succeeded on the test는 students를 수식하는 관계절로, 주어에 이어지는 술어 동사가 없는 상태이다. 따라서 준동사 engaging을 본동사 engaged로 고쳐 써야 한다.

오답풀이

① 문맥상 an experience를 대신하는 부정대명사 one은 어법상 적절하다.

② 문장의 주어는 students informed that they had performed poorly on a test of social sensitivity이고, 주어의 핵은 과거분사구 informed that they had performed poorly on a test of social sensitivity의 수식을 받는 students이다. 따라서 이에 수를 일치시킨 복수형 동사 were는 적절하다.

④ to appear competent는 The desire를 수식하는 형용사적 용법의 to부정사구로 적절하게 쓰였다.

⑤ 뒤에 완전한 구조의 절이 이어지고, 이 절이 the chance와 문맥상 동격 관계를 이루므로 동격절을 이끄는 접속사 that은 적절하다.

전문해석

실패, 즉 임박한 실패에 대한 두려움은 유능해 보이는 것에 대한 우려를 증폭시킨다. 만약 여러분이 똑똑하다고 다른 사람들이 생각하기를 원한다면, 시험에 떨어지는 것은 여러분에게 매우 해로운 경험이 될 것이며, 이는 여러분으로 하여금 자기 홍보를 위한 온갖 수단에 손을 뻗게 할 수 있는 경험이다. 한 실험에 따르면, 자신이 사회적 민감성 테스트에서 낮은 점수를 받았다는 사실을 알게 된 학생들은 이후에 적응이 잘 된 것처럼 자신을 표현할 가능성이 특히 높았다. 이에 비해, 테스트에서 잘한 학생들은 더 겸손하게 자기 자신을 표현했는데, 이는 그들이 테스트를 통해 자신의 사회적 역량을 검증받았기에 대신에 호감을 얻는 데 집중할 수 있었기 때문이다. 유능해 보이고자 하는 욕구는 압박감으로 가득 찬 경쟁적인 상황에서 특히 강해질 수 있다. 역설적이게도, 그러한 상황은 또한 수행자가 '긴장해서 실수하거나' 잠재력에 훨씬 못 미치는 성과를 낼 가능성을 높인다.

구문풀이

5행 In one experiment, students [informed {that they had performed poorly on a test of social sensitivity}] were especially likely to present themselves afterward as well adjusted.

: 첫 번째 [ ]는 students를 수식하는 과거분사구이고, 그 안의 { }는 목적어 역할을 하는 명사절로 informed의 대상을 나타낸다.

어휘풀이

- amplify *v* 증폭시키다
- self-promotional *a* 자기 홍보의
- competent *a* 유능한

- **bag of tricks** 온갖 수단, 특별한 기술이나 방법을 모은 것
- **sensitivity** *n* 민감성
- **in comparison** 비교해 보면
- **modest** *a* 겸손한
- **pressure-filled** *a* 압박감으로 가득 찬
- **choke** *v* 질식하다, 긴장해서 실수하다[망치다]
- **potential** *n* 잠재력
- **adjusted** *a* 적응한
- **engage in** ~을 하다, ~에 참여하다
- **validate** *v* 검증하다
- **competitive** *a* 경쟁적인

081 답 ②

출제 의도 파악하기
1. 관계부사 where의 쓰임
2. 도치구문
3. 감정동사의 분사형
4. 주어와 동사의 수 일치
5. 병렬구조

정답풀이

② 부정어구인 not only가 문장의 앞으로 이동하여 주어와 동사가 도치된 문장이다. 동사가 일반동사인 matter이므로, 주어 앞에 be동사 are가 온 것은 적절하지 않다. are를 조동사 do로 바꿔 써야 한다.

오답풀이

① 뒤에 주어(they), 동사(need), 목적어(only some intelligence ~)를 갖춘 완전한 구조의 절이 이어지고 있고, 콤마(,) 앞에 장소를 나타내는 명사구 the world of computer agents가 있으므로, 이를 부연 설명하는 관계절을 이끄는 관계부사 where는 적절하다.
③ 의미상의 주어인 a well-executed failure가 '만족감을 주는' 주체이므로 능동의 의미를 나타내는 현재분사 satisfying은 적절하다.
④ 관계절 that rely on statistical inference의 수식을 받는 복수 명사 Tools가 주어의 핵이므로 복수형 동사 are는 적절하다.
⑤ 문맥상 전치사 by의 목적어 역할을 하는 동명사 finding과 and에 의해 병렬구조를 이루는 자리이므로 동명사 recommending은 적절하다.

전문해석

지능형 장치는 자동차, 비행기, 배의 조종에 있어 큰 진전을 보였다. 그것들은 정해진 작업을 하는 기계에 적합하다. 그것들은 단지 약간의 지능과 화면에 표시할 이미지만을 필요로 하는 컴퓨터 에이전트의 세계에서 잘 작동하는데, 실제적이고 물리적인 본체는 필요치 않다. 그것들은 게임과 오락에서 성공적인데, 인형, 로봇 애완동물 그리고 컴퓨터 게임의 캐릭터를 조종한다. 이런 환경에서는, 가끔 일어나는 착오와 실패가 중요하지 않을 뿐만 아니라, 그것들이 재미를 더해 줄 수도 있다. 오락의 세계에서는, 잘 수행된 실패가 성공보다 훨씬 더 만족스러울 수 있다. 통계 추론에 의존하는 도구가 또한 폭넓게 인기가 있고 성공적이다. 몇몇 온라인 상점들은 여러분과 취향이 비슷한 사람들이 좋아하는 것처럼 보이는 제품을 찾아 그러한 제품들을 여러분에게 추천하는 것으로 책, 영화, 음악, 심지어 주방 용품까지도 추천한다. 그 시스템은 상당히 잘 작동한다.

구문풀이

3행 They work well in the world of computer agents, [where they need only some intelligence and an image {to display on the screen}]; real, physical bodies are not needed.

: [ ]는 the world of computer agents를 부연 설명하는 관계절이고, 그 안의 { }는 an image를 수식하는 형용사적 용법의 to부정사구이다.

14행 Some online stores recommend books, movies, music, or even kitchen appliances by [finding products {that people <similar to you in taste> seem to like}] and then [recommending those items to you].

: 두 개의 [ ]는 전치사 by의 목적어로, 두 개의 동명사구가 and에 의해 병렬로 연결된 구조이다. { }는 products를 수식하는 관계절이며, 〈 〉는 people을 수식하는 형용사구이다.

어휘풀이

- **intelligent** *a* 지능형의, 지능적인
- **progress** *n* 진전, 발전
- **fixed** *a* 고정된, 정해진
- **occasional** *a* 가끔 일어나는, 가끔의
- **inference** *n* 추론
- **reasonably** *ad* 상당히, 꽤
- **device** *n* 장치, 기구
- **make sense** 통하다, 이해가 되다
- **physical** *a* 물리적인, 신체적인
- **statistical** *a* 통계의, 통계적인
- **appliance** *n* 기기

082 답 ④

출제 의도 파악하기
1. 주어와 동사의 수 일치
2. 동사의 태
3. 대명사의 it의 쓰임
4. 관계부사 where의 쓰임
5. 관계절 동사의 수 일치

정답풀이

④ 뒤에 동사 impacts의 주어가 없는 불완전한 구조의 절이 이어지고 있으므로 관계부사 where는 쓸 수 없다. 선행사 a situation을 수식하는 관계절을 이끄는 주격 관계대명사 that이나 which로 고쳐 써야 한다.

오답풀이

① Official definitions of sport가 주어이고, 주어의 핵이 definitions이므로 복수형 동사 have는 적절하다.
② 주어인 many people이 '피하는' 주체이므로 능동형 동사 avoid는 적절하게 쓰였다.
③ 문맥상 앞에 나온 to play in the local league의 내용을 가리키므로 대명사 it을 쓴 것은 옳다.
⑤ 주격 관계대명사절의 동사는 선행사에 수를 일치시키는데, 선행사가 a wide range of physical activities이므로 이에 수를 일치시킨 복수 동사 are는 적절하다.

전문해석

스포츠의 공식적인 정의는 중요한 함의를 갖는다. 정의가 규칙, 경쟁, 높은 기량을 강조할 때 많은 사람들이 참여에서 배제되고 또는 '이류'로 정의되는 다른 신체 활동을 피하게 될 것이다. 예를 들면, 12세의 선수가 상위 클럽 축구팀에서 제외되면 그 선수는 지역 리그에서 뛰고 싶어 하지 않을지도 모르는데, 그것은 그 선수가 그것을 진정한 스포츠가 아닌, '레크리에이션 활동'으로 보기 때문이다. 이는 소수의 사람들이 많은 수의 팬들을 위해 상대적으로 높은 수준의 시합을 하는 것과 동시에 대부분의 사람들이 신체적으로 활동적이지 않은 상황, 즉 건강에 부정적인 영향을 미치고 사회나 지역 사회에 의료비를 증가시키는 상황을 만들 수 있다. 스포츠가 즐거움을 위해 행해지는 폭넓은 신체 활동을 포함하도록 정의되고 사회생활의 지역적인 표현들로 통합될 때 신체 활동 비율이 높을 것이고 전반적인 건강상의 이점이 있을 수 있다.

구문풀이

9행 This can create a situation [in which most people are physically inactive] at the same time [that a small number of people perform at relatively high levels for large numbers of fans] —a situation [that {negatively impacts health} and {increases health-care costs in a society or community}].

: 첫 번째와 두 번째 [ ]는 a situation을 수식하는 관계대명사절과 관계부사절로, 이와 같이 상황을 나타내는 표현(a situation)이 선행사로 올 경우 관계부사 where나 that,

「전치사+관계대명사」를 쓸 수 있다. 반면, 세 번째 [ ]는 a situation을 수식하는 주격 관계대명사절이며 그 안에 두 개의 { }는 관계절의 술어이다.

어휘풀이

- definition *n* 정의
- exclude *v* 배제하다
- inactive *a* 활동적이지 않은
- negatively *ad* 부정적으로
- overall *a* 전반적인
- implication *n* 함의, 내포된 뜻
- exclusive *a* 상위의, 상류의, 고급의
- relatively *ad* 상대적으로
- integrate *v* 융합하다, 통합하다
- benefit *n* 이점

---

083 답 ②

출제 의도 파악하기

① 동명사의 쓰임   ② 대동사
③ 지시대명사 that   ④ 관계대명사 that의 쓰임
⑤ 동사의 태

정답풀이

② it은 the quality of monumentality를 지칭하며 문맥상 기념비성이라는 특성이 '달성되었다'는 의미가 적절하다. 따라서 did가 아니라 앞에 나온 동사 achieve의 과거 시제 수동형인 was achieved를 대신하는 was를 써야 한다.

오답풀이

① 전치사 to의 목적어 역할을 하면서 the basic characteristic of Egyptian art를 목적어로 취하는 동명사 expressing은 적절하다.
③ those는 앞에 나온 structures를 대신하는 지시대명사로 적절하게 쓰였다.
④ that gigantic pile of stones를 선행사로 하며 관계절에서 주어 역할을 하는 관계대명사로 that은 적절하게 쓰였다.
⑤ 양보 부사절의 주어인 it은 everything in it(= Egyptian art)을 가리키고, 예술 작품은 나무에 '새겨지는' 것이므로 or 앞의 is에 연결되어 수동태를 이루는 과거분사 carved는 적절하다.

전문해석

'기념비적'이라는 말은 이집트 예술의 기본적인 특징을 표현하는 데 매우 근접하는 단어이다. 그 전에도 그 이후에도, 기념비성이라는 특성이 이집트에서처럼 완전히 달성된 적은 한 번도 없었다. 이에 대한 이유는, 비록 이집트인들이 이 점에 있어서 몇 가지 대단한 업적을 달성했다는 것이 인정되지만, 그들 작품의 외적 크기와 거대함이 아니다. 많은 현대 구조물이 순전히 물리적인 크기의 면에서는 이집트의 그것들을 능가한다. 그러나 거대함은 기념비성과는 아무 관련이 없다. 예를 들어, 사람 손 크기만 한 이집트 조각물이 Leipzig(라이프치히, 독일 동부의 도시)의 전쟁 기념비를 구성하는 그 거대한 돌무더기보다 더 기념비적이다. 기념비성은 외적 무게의 문제가 아니라 '내적 무게'의 문제이다. 이 내적 무게는 이집트 예술이 지닌 특성인데, 이집트 예술은 그 안의 모든 것이 단지 폭이 몇 인치에 불과하거나 나무에 새겨져 있을지라도, 마치 산맥처럼 원시 시대의 돌로 만들어진 것처럼 보일 정도이다.

구문풀이

10행 An Egyptian sculpture [no bigger than a person's hand] is more monumental than that gigantic pile of stones [that constitutes the war memorial in Leipzig], for instance.

: 첫 번째 [ ]는 An Egyptian sculpture를 수식하는 형용사구이고, 두 번째 [ ]는 that gigantic pile of stones를 수식하는 관계절이다.

어휘풀이

- monumental *a* 기념비[기념물]의
- characteristic *n* 특성, 특징

- monumentality *n* 기념비성
- massiveness *n* 거대함
- respect *n* (측)면, 점, 사항
- purely *ad* 순전히, 전적으로
- have nothing to do with ~와 아무 관련이 없다
- sculpture *n* 조각(물)
- memorial *n* 기념물[상·비]
- possess *v* 가지다, 소유하다
- carve *v* 새기다, 조각하다
- external *a* 외적인
- admittedly *ad* 인정하건대, 명백히
- in terms of ~의 면에서
- physical *a* 물리적인
- constitute *v* 구성하다
- inner *a* 내부의, 내적인
- mountain range 산맥

---

084 답 ③

출제 의도 파악하기

① 문장의 구조 파악   ② 형용사의 쓰임
③ 병렬구조   ④ 주어와 동사의 수 일치
⑤ 형용사의 쓰임

정답풀이

③ 문맥상 동명사구 주어 cooking some mustard leaves quickly에 이어지는 술어 동사 minimizes와 but으로 병렬 연결되므로 preserving을 단수형 동사 preserves로 바꿔 써야 한다.

오답풀이

① the temperature rise within the tissue를 주어로 하는 술어 동사 speeds는 적절하다.
② ~ will leave many of the flavor molecules unharmed가 수동태로 전환된 문장으로, 능동태 문장에서 will leave의 목적격보어였던 unharmed가 수동태에 그대로 쓰인 것이므로 어법상 적절하다.
④ 관계절 that are ~ cabbage가 핵심 주어인 the compounds를 수식하는 구조이며, the compounds의 술어 동사로 복수형 동사 are가 쓰인 것은 옳다.
⑤ 동사 makes의 목적격보어로 쓰인 형용사 sweet은 적절하다.

전문해석

양배추와 그것의 친구들을 가열하는 것은 두 가지 다른 효과를 가진다. 처음에 조직 내의 온도 상승은 효소 활성과 향미 생성을 촉진하며, 약 섭씨 60도에서 최대의 활동을 한다. 만약 채소들을 끓는 물에 넣음으로써 효소가 빨리 비활성화된다면, 많은 맛 분자들은 손상되지 않은 채로 남게 될 것이다. 이것은 종종 바람직하다. 예를 들어, 약간의 겨자 잎을 재빨리 요리하는 것은 그것의 매운 맛은 최소화하지만 맛있는 쓴맛은 보존한다. 끓는 물에 넣는 것은 맛 분자를 물로 끌어 내고, 튀기거나 찌는 것보다 더 부드러운 맛을 만들어 낸다. 하지만 조리 시간이 길어진다면, 열은 점차적으로 맛 분자를 변화시킨다. 결국 너무 익힌 양배추의 강한 냄새의 주범이 되는 화합물이 생성된다. 오랫동안 조리하는 것은 양파 가족 구성원들을 달콤하게 만들지만, 양배추 가족은 맛이 좋지 않게 된다.

구문풀이

14행 Eventually [the compounds {that are mainly responsible for the strong smell of overcooked cabbage}] are formed.

: [ ]는 문장의 주어이며 그 안의 { }는 the compounds를 수식하는 관계절이다.

어휘풀이

- tissue *n* 조직
- generation *n* 발생, 생성
- molecule *n* 분자
- compound *n* 화합물
- responsible for ~에 책임[원인]이 있는
- enzyme *n* 효소
- inactivate *v* 비활성화시키다
- prolong *v* 연장하다

085 답 ②

❶ 관계부사 where의 쓰임	❷ 관계대명사 that의 쓰임
❸ 강조구문	❹ 문장의 구조 파악
❺ 부사의 쓰임	

정답풀이

② 문맥상 that ~ known은 the artists를 수식하는 관계절이 되어야 하는데, that 뒤에 완전한 구조의 절이 이어지고 있어서 어색하다. the artists를 수식하는 절을 이끄는 동시에 관계절에서 names를 한정하는 소유격 관계대명사 whose로 고쳐 써야 한다.

오답풀이

① 뒤에 완전한 구조의 절이 이어지므로, 선행사인 ancient Greece를 부연하는 계속적 용법의 관계부사 where는 적절하다.
③ 「It is not until ~ that ...(~하고 나서야 비로소 …하다)」 구문으로, A large number of female artists were not recognized and their works were not duly ~ arts until the 20th century.에서 not과 until the 20th century를 합쳐 「It is[was] ~ that ....」 강조구문으로 강조한 형태이다.
④ that절의 주어인 the Brontë sisters에 이어지는 동사 published는 적절하다. talented ~ century는 the Brontë sisters와 동격 관계를 이루는 삽입구이다.
⑤ '거의 ~ 않다'의 부정의 의미를 갖는 부사 hardly가 동사 existed를 수식하는 것으로 문맥상으로도 어법상으로도 적절하다.

전문해석

예술가들이 대단히 존경받았으며 그들의 독특한 재능이나 스타일로 유명했던 고대 그리스를 제외하고, 르네상스 시대가 되기 전까지 일반 대중들은 예술가들이 누구이며 어떤 종류의 사람들인지 거의 알지 못했다. 게다가, 이름이 알려진 예술가들 중에도 여성은 거의 없었다. 20세기가 되어서야 비로소 아주 많은 수의 여성 예술가들이 인정을 받고 그들의 작품이 예술의 모든 분야에서 정당하게 평가되었다. 19세기 초 재능 있는 시인이자 소설가였던 Brontë(브론테) 자매가 그들의 최초 시집을 남성의 필명으로 출판했다는 것은 잘 알려져 있다. 여성들이 예술작품을 창작하는 것을 가능하게 하는 사회적, 교육적, 경제적 상황이 과거에는 거의 존재하지 않았다.

구문풀이

1행 Except for ancient Greece, [where artists were highly respected and known for their unique talents and styles], before the Renaissance the public was seldom aware of [who or what kind of people artists were].

: 첫 번째 [ ]는 ancient Greece를 부연 설명하는 관계절이다. 두 번째 [ ]는 전치사 of의 목적어로 쓰인 의문사절이다.

어휘풀이

- except for ~을 제외하고
- public *n* 일반 대중
- seldom *ad* 좀처럼 ~ 않는
- be aware of ~을 알다
- recognize *v* 인정하다
- duly *ad* 정당하게, 충분히
- appreciate *v* 높이 평가하다, 진가를 알다
- novelist *n* 소설가
- publish *v* 출판하다
- collection *n* 수집품, 모음집

086 답 ②

❶ 강조구문	❷ 문장의 구조 파악
❸ 관계대명사 which의 쓰임	❹ 형식상의 주어와 내용상의 주어
❺ 관계대명사 what의 쓰임	

정답풀이

② 동사 argue의 목적어로 쓰인 that절에서 관계절 that sets ~ imitation이 핵심 주어 the one asset을 수식하는 구조이다. 따라서 주어에 연결되는 동사가 필요하므로 being은 적절하지 않으며 is로 바꿔 써야 한다.

오답풀이

① 동사 ask의 직접목적어 자리에 의문사 what이 이끄는 명사절이 왔고, 그 절에 「it is ~ that ...」 강조구문이 쓰인 것이므로 that은 적절하다. 여기서 의문사 what은 that절에 있는 전치사 of의 목적어로 쓰였다.
③ 뒤에 주어가 빠진 불완전한 구조의 절이 이어지고 있으므로, the power of influence를 선행사로 하여 부연 설명하는 관계절을 이끄는 관계대명사 which는 적절하다.
④ to share it ~을 내용상의 주어로 하는 형식상의 주어 it의 쓰임은 적절하다.
⑤ 뒤에 have given의 직접목적어가 빠진 불완전한 구조의 절이 이어지고 있고, 앞에는 선행사가 될 수 있는 명사(구)가 없으므로, 선행사를 포함하는 관계대명사 what은 적절하게 쓰였다.

전문해석

우리는 진정한 지도자가 무엇을 풍부하게 가지고 있는지 자문해 보아야 한다. 지도자는 더 나은 지식과 풍부한 에너지를 지녔을 수도 있지만, 나는 값싼 모방품과 다른 진정한 지도자를 구분하는 한 가지 자산은 힘[세력]이라고 주장한다. 진정한 지도자는 힘을 가지고 있다. 이것은 지위나 부나 직위의 힘이 아니다. 그것은 오히려 영향력이며, 그 영향력은 추종자가 되기로 선택한 사람들에 의해서만 부여될 수 있다. 그리고 진정한 지도자는 이러한 힘을 가지고 있기 때문에 그것을 공유하는 것은, 다시 말해서, 추종자들에게 권한을 부여하는 것은 그 사람의 책임이다. 그리고 아이러니하게도, 사람들이 여러분에게 그렇게 할 수 있는 힘을 부여하지 않는 한, 여러분은 사람들에게 권한을 부여할 수 없다. 이것은 사람들에게 동기를 부여하는 비결이다. 여러분은 그들이 여러분에게 준 것을 그들에게 돌려주고, 그리하여 그 결과는 상승한다[커진다]. 그것은 단지 여러분이 그들의 주인이라기보다는 그들의 종이 됨으로써 얻은 풍부한 힘을 나누는 것에 지나지 않는다.

구문풀이

15행 It is simply sharing the abundance of power [that you have earned by {being their servant rather than their master}].

: [ ]는 the abundance of power를 수식하는 관계절이고, 그 안의 { }는 전치사 by의 목적어로 쓰인 동명사구이다.

어휘풀이

- abundance *n* 풍부
- superior *a* 우수한, 더 나은
- asset *n* 자산, 재산
- set *A* apart from *B A*를 *B*와 구별되게 하다
- genuine *a* 진정한
- imitation *n* 모방
- grant *v* 주다, 부여하다
- follower *n* 추종자, 지지자
- empower *v* 권한[능력]을 부여하다
- ironically *ad* 아이러니하게, 반어적으로

087 ③	**088** ④	**089** ⑤	**090** ③	**091** ②
092 ⑤	**093** ③	**094** ③		

087 답 ③

출제 의도 파악하기

❶	전치사+관계대명사	❷	대동사
❸	강조구문 동사의 수 일치	❹	접속사 whether의 쓰임
❺	가정법 과거 구문		

정답풀이

③ 「it is[was] ~ that …」 강조구문으로 주어인 people's beliefs ~ hypnosis를 강조하고 있다. 주어의 핵이 복수 명사인 beliefs이므로 leads를 복수형 동사 lead로 바꿔 써야 한다.

오답풀이

① 뒤에 주어(the powers of memory), 동사(are), 보어(greater than normal)를 갖춘 완전한 구조의 절이 이어지고 있으므로, 선행사 a special state를 부연 설명하는 관계절을 이끄는 「전치사+관계대명사」 형태의 in which는 알맞다.

② 비교구문에서 반복되는 일반동사구 generate memories를 대신하는 대동사 do는 알맞다.

④ 뒤에 주어(the memories ~ retrieve), 동사(are), 보어(true or not)를 갖춘 완전한 구조의 절이 이어지고 있고, 이 절이 to know의 목적어 역할을 하면서 「whether A or B」 구문을 이루고 있으므로, 명사절을 이끄는 접속사 whether는 알맞다.

⑤ 현재 사실과 반대인 상황을 가정하는 것이므로, 가정법 과거 구문(if+주어+동사의 과거형 ~, 주어+조동사의 과거형+동사원형 …)을 이루는 과거 동사 knew는 알맞다.

전문해석

최면이 뇌를 기억력이 보통보다 훨씬 더 좋은 특별한 상태로 만들 수 있다는 생각은 쉽게 이끌어 내어지는 잠재력의 한 형태에 대한 믿음을 반영한다. 그렇지만 그것은 거짓이다. 최면에 걸린 사람들이 보통의 상태에서 기억을 해 내는 것보다 더 많은 '기억'을 해 내지만, 이 기억들은 사실일 만큼이나 거짓일 가능성이 있다. 최면은 사람들에게 더 많은 정보를 생각해 내게 하지만, 반드시 더 정확한 정보를 생각해 내게 하는 것은 아니다. 사실, 실제로 그들에게 더 많은 것들을 기억해 내게 하는 것은 바로 최면의 힘에 대한 사람들의 믿음일지도 모르며, 만약 사람들이 그들이 최면 상태에서 더 잘 기억해 내야 한다고 믿으면, 그들은 최면에 빠졌을 때 더 많은 기억을 상기해 내기 위해 더 열심히 노력할 것이다. 안타깝게도, 최면에 걸린 사람들이 상기해 내는 기억이 사실인지 아닌지를 알 방법은 없다. 물론 우리가 그 사람이 무엇을 기억해 낼 수 있어야만 하는지를 정확히 알지 못한다면 말이다. 하지만 만약 우리가 그것을 안다면, 그러면 애초에 최면을 사용할 필요가 없을 것이다!

구문풀이

[1행] The idea [that hypnosis can put the brain into a special state, {in which the powers of memory are dramatically greater than normal}], reflects a belief in a form of easily unlocked potential.

: [ ]는 문장의 핵심 주어인 The idea와 동격 관계를 이루는 명사절이며, 문장의 동사는 reflects이다. { }는 a special state를 부연 설명하는 관계절이다.

[9행] In fact, **it** might actually **be** people's beliefs in the power of hypnosis **that** lead them to recall more things: If people believe [that they should have better memory under hypnosis], they will try harder [to retrieve more memories **when hypnotized**].

: 「it is[was] ~ that …」 강조구문으로 주어인 people's beliefs in the power of hypnosis를 강조하고 있다. 첫 번째 [ ]는 believe의 목적어로 쓰인 명사절이다. 두 번째 [ ]는 목적의 의미를 나타내는 to부정사구이고, 접속사 when과 과거분사 hypnotized 사이에 「주어+be동사」인 they are가 생략되었다.

어휘풀이

- dramatically *ad* 훨씬, 극적으로
- normal *a* 보통의, 정상적인
- unlock *v* (재능·잠재력 등을) 이끌어 내다
- potential *n* 잠재력
- generate *v* 일으키다, 창출하다
- recollection *n* 상기하는 것, 기억
- come up with ~을 생각해 내다
- accurate *a* 정확한
- lead A to do A가 ~하도록 이끌다
- recall *v* 기억해 내다
- retrieve *v* 상기하다, 되찾다
- hypnotize *v* 최면을 걸다
- in the first place 애초에

088 답 ④

출제 의도 파악하기

❶	주어와 동사의 수 일치	❷	접속사 that의 쓰임
❸	동명사의 쓰임	❹	문장의 구조 파악
❺	관계대명사 which의 쓰임		

정답풀이

④ 문장의 주어 역할을 하는 명사절 What they find worth telling에 이어지는 술어 동사 자리이므로, being을 are로 바꿔 써야 한다. 보어로 복수 명사 facts가 왔으므로 동사의 수는 이에 일치시킨다.

오답풀이

① 문장의 주어 Men and women's assumptions to what is interesting에 이어지는 동사 자리로, 주어의 핵은 assumptions이므로 복수형 동사 are는 알맞다.

② that 이하는 involvement와 동격 관계에 있는 절로, 앞에 있는 that you care about each other와 병렬구조를 이룬다. 따라서 동격절을 이끄는 접속사 that은 적절하다.

③ 뒤에 나오는 makes가 문장의 동사이므로 주어 역할을 하는 동명사구를 이끄는 Knowing은 적절하다.

⑤ lecturing을 선행사로 하면서 관계절 안에서 동사 seems의 주어 역할을 하는 계속적 용법의 관계대명사 which는 알맞다.

전문해석

흥미로운 것에 대한 남성과 여성의 추정은 다르다. 여성에게는 오늘 무슨 일이 있었는지, 버스 정류장에서 누구를 마주쳤는지, 누구에게 전화가 왔고 그녀가 무슨 이야기를 했는지에 관해 이야기를 하고 듣는 것이 자연스러운 것으로 보이는데, 그것은 이 세세한 일들이 그것들 자체로 중요해서가 아니라 그런 이야기들을 하는 것이 여러분이 서로에게 마음 쓰고 있다는 그리고 가장 친한 친구가 있다는 관계를 입증하기 때문이다. 이런 이야기를 나중에 (누군가와) 할 수 있다는 것을 아는 것은 여러분이 하루의 혼자만의 길을 따라 걸어갈 때 덜 혼자라고 느끼게 해 준다. 남성들에게는 이런 방식으로 대화를 이용하는 것이 자연스럽지 않기 때문에 그들은 세부적인 이야기에 내재된 무의미함에 초점을 둔다. 그들이 말할 가치가 있다고 여기는 것은 스포츠, 정치, 역사 또는 일이 진행되는 방식과 같은 주제에 관한 사실들이다. 여성들은 자주 사실에 관해 이야기하는 것을 강연하는 것처럼 여기는데, 그것은 '나는 교사이고, 너는 학생이다. 나는 아는 것이 많고 너는 무지하다'라는 생색내는 듯한 태도의 초메시지를 전달하는 것처럼 보인다.

구문풀이

2행 **It** seems natural to women [to tell and hear about what happened today, who turned up at the bus stop, who called and what she said], **not** because these details are important in themselves **but** because the telling of **them** proves involvement [that you care about each other] and [that you have a best friend].

: It은 형식상의 주어이고, to부정사구인 첫 번째 [ ]가 내용상의 주어이다. 「not A but B(A가 아니라 B인)」 구문이 쓰였으며, them은 앞에 나온 these details를 가리킨다. and로 연결된 두 번째와 세 번째 [ ]는 involvement와 동격 관계를 이루는 절이다.

어휘풀이

- assumption *n* 추정, 상정
- prove *v* 입증하다
- lone *a* 혼자의, 홀로 있는
- insignificance *n* 무의미함, 중요하지 않음
- lecture *v* 강의하다, 강연하다
- turn up 나타나다
- involvement *n* 관계, 관련, 관여
- inherent *a* 내재하는
- ignorant *a* 무지한

089 답 ⑤

출제 의도 파악하기

❶	복합관계부사 wherever의 쓰임	❷	분사의 태
❸	관계대명사 that의 쓰임	❹	대명사의 쓰임과 수 일치
❺	문장의 구조 파악		

정답풀이

⑤ three technological innovations를 주어로 하는 술어 동사 자리이므로, 준동사인 upsetting을 본동사 upset으로 바꿔 써야 한다.

오답풀이

① 뒤에 오는 절이 완전한 구조이므로 문맥상 '~한 곳은 어디든지'의 의미로 부사절을 이끄는 복합관계부사 wherever는 적절하게 쓰였다.

② The one at Barbegal in southern France를 부연 설명하는 분사구로, 수동의 의미를 나타내는 과거분사 built는 적절하다.

③ an establishment of the kind를 수식하는 관계절을 이끌면서 관계절에서 주어 역할을 하는 관계대명사 that은 적절하다.

④ 주격 관계대명사절의 동사 preceded의 의미상 주어는 선행사인 the more ~ civilizations이고, 목적어는 the great Eurasian empires이므로 목적격 대명사 them을 쓴 것은 적절하다.

전문해석

서력기원 1세기 동안, 로마인들은 하천이 있는 곳 또는 수력을 제공하는 송수로가 있는 곳 어디에나 수차를 만들었다. 프랑스 남부의 Barbegal에 있는 것 하나는 서력기원 310년에 건설되었는데, 일렬로 된 16개의 상사식 수차를 사용했다. 물은 한 개의 바퀴를 넘어 흐르고, 그것을 돌리고, 그러고 나서 다음 바퀴를 돌리고, 그렇게 계속 이어졌다. 그것은 한 시간에 3톤의 곡물을 갈 수 있었고 8만 명의 사람들을 먹이기에 충분했다. 다시 말해, 그것은 18세기 산업혁명 전까지는 세계의 그 지역에서 다시는 볼 수 없었던 종류의 시설이었다. 유라시아 대제국의 시대는 그들보다 앞서 존재했던, 보다 보수적인 강 계곡 문명으로부터의 근본적인 이탈을 나타냈다. 기원전 1500년경 이전에는 강 계곡 문명과 주변 지역에 거주하던 신석기 시대의 농민과 목축인들 사이에 대략적인 균형이 있었다. 그러나 기원전 1500년 이후, 철, 길들여진 말, 바퀴 달린 탈것이라는 세 가지 기술적 혁신이 이 평형을 뒤흔들었고, 유라시아와 북아프리카의 많은 지역에 퍼진 장기간 전쟁의 시대로 이어졌다.

구문풀이

14행 Before about 1500 BCE, there **had been** a rough balance between the river valley civilizations and the Neolithic farmers and herdsmen [who inhabited the surrounding regions].

: 과거의 어느 시점 이전까지 계속된 상황을 나타내는 과거완료 시제 had been이 쓰였다. [ ]는 the Neolithic farmers and herdsmen을 수식하는 관계절이다.

어휘풀이

- waterwheel *n* 수차, 물레방아
- overshot wheel 상사식 수차(물이 바퀴 꼭대기를 쳐서 회전하는 수차)
- in a row 한 줄로
- grind *v* 갈다
- empire *n* 제국
- departure *n* 벗어남, 떠남, 출발
- civilization *n* 문명
- Neolithic *a* 신석기 시대의
- inhabit *v* 거주하다
- innovation *n* 혁신
- equilibrium *n* 균형, 평형상태
- prolonged *a* 장기적인, 연장된
- furnish *v* 공급하다, 제공하다
- be capable of ~할 수 있다
- establishment *n* 시설
- radical *a* 근본적인, 급진적인
- conservative *a* 보수적인
- precede *v* 앞서다, 선행하다
- herdsman *n* 목축인
- BCE 기원전 (= Before Common Era)
- domesticated *a* 길들여진
- era *n* 시대
- warfare *n* 전쟁 (상태)

090 답 ③

출제 의도 파악하기

❶	동사의 태	❷	대동사
❸	지각동사의 목적격보어	❹	전치사+관계대명사
❺	분사구문의 태		

정답풀이

③ we'd like to ~ stay는 all the things를 수식하는 목적격 관계대명사절로, 지각동사 see의 목적어는 선행사인 all the things이므로 to happen은 see의 목적격보어에 해당한다. 지각동사의 목적격보어로는 원형부정사가 오므로 to happen을 happen으로 바꿔 써야 한다.

오답풀이

① 주어인 hospitals는 '등급이 매겨지는' 대상이므로 수동태 동사 be rated는 적절하다.

② 문맥상 앞에 있는 일반동사구 keep it simple and just look at death rates를 대신하므로 대동사 do는 알맞다.

④ 뒤에 완전한 구조의 절이 이어지고, 이 절이 선행사인 the extent를 수식하므로 「전치사+관계대명사」 형태의 to which는 적절하다. to the extent ~는 '~ 정도까지'를 나타낸다.

⑤ 앞 절의 내용을 의미상의 주어로 하여 결과의 의미를 나타내는 분사구문을 유도하는 현재분사 making은 적절하다.

전문해석

지역 사회에서 어느 병원이 최고의 치료를 제공하는지를 묻는 것은 꽤 간단하게 들릴 수 있다. 그러나 병원들은 입원 환자 규모, 직원의 수준, 치료비 그리고 전문 업무를 포함하여 갈피를 못 잡을 정도로 다양한 고려사항 중 어느 것에 따라서든 등급이 매겨질 수 있다. 그런데 몇몇 전문가들이 그렇게 하듯이, 우리는 이것을 단순하게 유지하고, 단지 사망률만 볼 수도 있을 것이다. 병원에 머무는 동안 발생하는 것으로 우리가 보고 싶은 모든 것들 중에서, 죽음을 피하는 것이 주로 목록의 가장 위에 있다. 그러나 사망률은 단순히 병원이 제공하는 치료의 질에 달려 있는 것이 아니다. 사망률은 또한 그 병원이 치료한 사람들이 얼마나 아픈지, 얼마나 나이가 들었는지, 혹은 얼마나 가난한지, 병원이 어느 정도의 더 힘든 환자를 맡고 있는지, 병원이 최첨단의 고위험 치료를 관리할 능력이 있는지, 그리고 심지어 병원이 환자를 조기 퇴원시켜 더 많은 환자가 다른 어떤 곳에서 사망할 경향이 있는지에 따라 달라질 수 있다. 미국의 Centers for Medicare and Medicaid Services는 이러한 요인들 중 많은 부분에 대해 자신들이 공표한 병원 사망률을 조정하려고 시도하지만, 이것

이 문제를 해결하지는 못한다. 대부분의 병원들은 결국 그저 상당히 비슷한 비율을 보이게 되며, 그 목록을 거의 소용이 없게 만든다.

구문풀이

1행 **It** might sound pretty straightforward [to ask {which hospital in a community provides the best care}].

: It은 형식상의 주어이고, to부정사구인 [ ]가 내용상의 주어이다. { }는 to ask의 목적어 역할을 하는 의문사절이다.

어휘풀이

- **straightforward** *a* 간단한, 솔직한
- **community** *n* 지역 사회, 공동체
- **rate** *v* 등급을 매기다, 평가하다 *n* 비율
- **consideration** *n* 고려 (사항)
- **inpatient** *n* 입원 환자
- **volume** *n* 양, 부피, 총계
- **treatment** *n* 치료, 처리
- **specialty** *n* 전문, 특수성
- **practice** *n* (의사·변호사 등의) 전문 업무[영업]
- **render** *v* 제공하다
- **population** *n* 사람들, 인구
- **administer** *v* 관리하다, 집행하다
- **cutting-edge** *a* 최첨단의
- **discharge** *v* 퇴원시키다, 방출하다
- **prematurely** *ad* 조기에
- **adjust** *v* 조정하다
- **publish** *v* 공개하다, 발표하다

091 답 ②

출제 의도 파악하기

❶ 주어와 동사의 수 일치	❷ what의 쓰임
❸ 문장의 구조 파악	❹ 대명사의 수 일치
❺ to부정사의 쓰임	

정답풀이

② 뒤에 주어(it), 동사(is having), 목적어(a positive impact)를 갖춘 완전한 구조의 절이 이어지고 있고, 문맥상 이 절이 '~인지'의 의미를 나타내야 하므로 what은 적절하지 않으며 접속사 whether로 바꿔 써야 한다.

오답풀이

① 주어의 핵이 관계절 who ~ behavior의 수식을 받는 복수 명사 Psychologists이므로 복수형 동사 have는 알맞다.

③ what절의 술어로 앞에 있는 be동사 are와 연결되어 현재진행형(be+ -ing)을 만드는 doing은 알맞다.

④ 문맥상 앞에 나온 they를 대신하는 자리이므로 대명사 them은 알맞다.

⑤ stopped와 함께 '곰곰이 생각하다, 생각하기 위해 멈추다'라는 의미를 나타내고 있으므로 목적의 의미로 쓰인 to부정사 to think는 알맞다.

전문해석

기부하는 행위를 연구하는 심리학자들은 어떤 사람들은 하나 또는 두 개의 자선단체에 상당한 액수를 기부하는 반면, 다른 사람들은 많은 자선단체에 적은 액수를 기부한다는 것을 알아차렸다. 한두 자선단체에 기부를 하는 사람들은 그 자선단체가 무슨 일을 하고 있는가와 그것이 실제로 긍정적인 영향을 끼치고 있는가에 관한 증거를 찾는다. 증거가 자선단체가 정말로 다른 사람들을 도와주고 있다는 것을 보여 줄 경우 그들은 상당한 기부금을 낸다. 많은 자선단체에 적은 액수를 내는 사람들은 그들이 하고 있는 일이 다른 사람들을 돕는지의 여부에는 그렇게 많은 관심을 갖지 않는다. 심리학자들은 그들을 따뜻한 불빛 기부자라고 부른다. 그들의 기부가 끼치는 영향에 관계없이, 자신들이 기부를 하고 있다는 것을 아는 것이 그들로 하여금 기분 좋게 만든다. 많은 경우 기부금은 10달러 이하의 매우 적은 금액이어서, 그들이 곰곰이 생각해 보면, 기부금을 처리하는 비용이 그것(기부금)이 자선단체에 가져다주는 모든 이득을 넘어서기 쉽다는 것을 깨달을 것이다.

구문풀이

8행 Those [who give small amounts to many charities] are not so interested in [whether {what they are doing} helps others]— psychologists call them warm glow givers.

: 첫 번째 [ ]는 Those를 수식하는 관계절이다. 두 번째 [ ]는 전치사 in의 목적어 역할을 하는 명사절이고, 그 안의 { }가 이 명사절의 주어이다.

13행 In many cases the donation is **so** small—$10 or less—**that if** they **stopped** to think, they **would realize** [that the cost of processing the donation is likely to exceed any benefit {**it** brings to the charity}].

: 「so ~ that ...」 구문은 '너무 ~해서 …하다'라는 뜻이다. 가정법 「If+주어+동사의 과거형, 주어+조동사의 과거형+동사원형」 구문이 쓰여, 현재의 사실과 반대되거나 일어날 것 같지 않은 일을 나타낸다. [ ]는 would realize의 목적어로 쓰인 명사절이며, 그 안의 { }는 any benefit을 수식하는 관계절이다. it은 the donation을 가리킨다.

어휘풀이

- **psychologist** *n* 심리학자
- **substantial** *a* 상당한
- **charity** *n* 자선단체
- **seek** *v* 찾다, 구하다
- **evidence** *n* 증거
- **impact** *n* 영향
- **indicate** *v* 나타내다, 가리키다
- **glow** *n* 불빛
- **regardless of** ~에 관계없이
- **process** *v* 처리하다
- **be likely to** *do* ~일 것 같다, ~하기 쉽다
- **exceed** *v* 넘어서다, 초과하다
- **benefit** *n* 이득, 혜택

092 답 ⑤

출제 의도 파악하기

❶ 의문사 how의 쓰임	❷ 대명사 it의 쓰임
❸ 동사의 태	❹ 접속사 that의 쓰임
❺ 문장의 구조 파악	

정답풀이

⑤ who ~ team은 핵심 주어 coaches를 수식하는 관계절로, 주어에 연결되는 동사가 없다. 따라서 communicating을 복수형 동사 communicate로 바꿔 써야 한다.

오답풀이

① 뒤에 주어(other people)와 자동사(behave)로 이루어진 완전한 구조의 절이 이어지고 있고, 동명사 observing의 목적어로 쓰인 의문사절을 이끌고 있으므로 의문사 how는 알맞다.

② 동명사인 realizing의 목적어로서 앞 문장 전체의 내용을 대신하는 대명사 it은 알맞다.

③ unless(~하지 않으면)가 이끄는 부사절의 주어 it은 cheating을 대신하는 것으로, it이 detect의 대상이므로 수동태 동사인 is detected는 알맞다.

④ 주어(the end), 동사(justifies), 목적어(the means)를 갖춘 완전한 구조의 절이 may conclude의 목적어로 쓰였으므로 명사절을 이끄는 접속사 that은 알맞다.

전문해석

젊은이들은 말로 설명하는 것, 보상과 벌을 통해서뿐만 아니라 다른 사람들이 어떻게 행동하는지를 관찰하는 것으로도 도덕적 행동을 배운다. 그들은 자신들의 부모님과 동료들을 모방하고, 자신들의 영웅들을 (행동의) 모델로 삼는다. 감독들은 보통 매우 존경받고 아이들의 삶에서 매우 중요하기 때문에, 그들은 특히 모델의 역할을 할 가능성이 높다. 그것을 깨닫지 못하면, 감독들은 도덕성을 혹은 부도덕함을 가르치는 방식으로 행동할 수 있다. 예를 들어, 규칙을 왜곡해서 '경쟁(에서의) 우위'를 얻

으려고 노력함으로써, 감독들은 부정행위가 적발되지 않는다면 그것이 실제로 잘못된 것이 아니라는 인상을 아이들에게 쉽게 줄 수 있다. 감독들이 승리를 하기 위해 규칙을 왜곡할 때, 아이들은 목적이 수단을 정당화한다고 결론을 내릴 수도 있다. 마찬가지로, 심판들에게 적대감을 보이고 다른 팀을 경멸하는 감독들은 그러한 행동들이 적절하고 바람직하다는 생각을 전달한다.

구문풀이

15행 Likewise, coaches [who display hostility toward officials and contempt for the other team] communicate the notion [that such behaviors are appropriate and desirable].

: 첫 번째 [ ]는 선행사 coaches를 수식하는 관계절이고, 두 번째 [ ]는 the notion과 동격 관계를 이루는 명사절이다.

어휘풀이

- moral *a* 도덕의, 윤리의
- imitate *v* 모방하다
- serve as ~의 역할을 하다
- competitive edge 경쟁 우위, 경쟁력
- cheating *n* 부정행위
- bend the rule 규칙을 왜곡해서 고치다, 악용하다
- conclude *v* 결론을 내리다
- means *n* 수단
- hostility *n* 적대감
- contempt *n* 경멸, 모욕, 무시
- notion *n* 생각, 개념
- verbal *a* 말로 하는, 말의
- model oneself after ~을 본받다
- morality *n* 도덕성
- stretch the rule 규칙을 왜곡하다
- detect *v* 적발하다, 감지하다
- justify *v* 정당화하다
- display *v* 보이다, 드러내다
- official *n* 심판, 관리자
- communicate *v* 전달하다, 전하다
- desirable *a* 바람직한

093 답 ③

출제 의도 파악하기

① 관계대명사 who의 쓰임
② 주어와 동사의 수 일치
③ 도치구문, 문장의 구조 파악
④ 분사구문의 태
⑤ 분사의 태

정답풀이

③ 위치의 부사구 Behind the baseball museum이 문두에 와서 주어와 동사가 도치된 문장으로, to be는 someone을 주어로 하는 술어 동사가 되어야 하므로 is로 바꿔 써야 한다.

오답풀이

① 선행사 person을 수식하는 관계절에서 주어 역할을 하는 주격 관계대명사 who는 적절하다.
② 주어인 This ~ detail을 하나의 개념으로 보아 단수 취급한 것으로, 단수형 동사 drives는 적절하게 쓰였다.
④ Fueled ~ passion은 분사구문으로, 의미상의 주어는 museum curators이다. 문맥상 큐레이터들이 '에너지를 받는' 대상이므로, 수동의 의미를 나타내는 과거분사 Fueled는 적절하다.
⑤ 앞에 있는 명사 artifacts를 수식하는 현재분사구를 이끄는 pertaining의 쓰임은 알맞다.

전문해석

여러분이 우표든, 벌레든, 야구 카드이든, 찻주전자이든 무언가를 수집해 본 적이 있다면 여러분은 박물관 큐레이터가 될 타고난 성향을 가진 것이다. 특히 여러분이 밀봉된 비닐봉지에 담긴 만화의 초판본을 보관하고 그것의 역사와 가치에 관한 메모를 기록하는 부류의 사람이라면 특히 그렇다. 세부사항에 대한 이런 종류의 열정과 관심이 대부분의 큐레이터들을 끌어간다. 야구 박물관 뒤에는 그 스포츠와 모든 통계를 정말 좋아하는 사람이 있다. 공예 미술관은 수공으로 만든 보물을 위해 살아가는

사람에 의해 관리된다. 그들의 열정에 의해 에너지(연료)를 받아, 박물관 큐레이터들은 개인 시민, 비영리 기관, 정부, 사업체, 협회와 대학들을 위해 소장품을 유지하고 만든다. 대다수의 큐레이터들은 미술 소장품을 관리하지만, 박물관들은 자연사, 미국 역사, 로큰롤, 유리, 패션이나 여러분이 추측해 본 적도 없는 물건들에 속한 문화 유물들도 소장한다.

구문풀이

14행 Most organize art collections, but museums also house artifacts [pertaining to natural history, American history, rock and roll, glass, fashion, or items {you'd never guess}].

: [ ]는 artifacts를 수식하는 현재분사구이며, 그 안의 { }는 items를 수식하는 관계절이다.

어휘풀이

- inclination *n* 성향, 체질
- seal *v* 봉하다
- passion *n* 열정
- handcrafted *a* 수공으로 만든
- nonprofit *a* 비영리의
- house *v* 소장하다, 보관하다
- pertain to ~에 속하다[관계하다]
- curator *n* 큐레이터, (박물관의) 관리자
- airtight *a* 밀폐한
- stats *n* 통계 (= statistics)
- fuel *v* 연료를 공급하다
- association *n* 협회
- artifact *n* 문화 유물

094 답 ③

출제 의도 파악하기

① 주어와 동사의 수 일치
② 분사구문의 태
③ 문장의 구조 파악
④ spend+시간+-ing
⑤ 관계대명사 that의 쓰임

정답풀이

③ Judging ~ in memory research는 분사구문이고, takes 이하의 절에서 동사는 뒤에 나오는 is이므로 이에 대한 주어가 필요하다. 그러므로 takes를 주어 역할을 할 수 있는 동명사 taking이나 to부정사 to take로 고쳐야 한다.

오답풀이

① points out의 목적어 역할을 하는 that절에서 주어는 rephrasing information in our words의 동명사구이고, 동명사구 주어는 단수 취급하므로 단수형 동사 is를 쓴 것은 적절하다.
② grouping 이하는 분사구문으로, 의미상의 주어는 Human memory이다. 의미상의 주어와 능동의 관계이고 뒤에 meaningful units를 목적어로 취하고 있으므로 현재분사 grouping은 적절하게 쓰였다.
④ '~하면서 (시간)을 보내다'라는 의미의 「spend+시간+-ing」 구문을 이루는 rewriting은 적절하게 쓰였다.
⑤ a thoughtful organization을 선행사로 하고 관계절에서 주어 역할을 하는 주격 관계대명사 that은 적절하게 쓰였다.

전문해석

여러 유형의 기억 조직화에 관한 우리의 지식은 정보를 우리 자신의 말로 바꾸는 것이 (기억의) 암호화와 회수에 아주 중요하다는 것을 알려준다. 컴퓨터 디스크와는 달리, 우리는 정보의 무작위 목록을 끊임없이 탐색할 여력이 없다. 인간의 기억은 더 쉽게 회수하기 위한 의미 있는 단위의 모둠으로 묶으면서 관련 정보를 함께 구조화하는 것을 중심으로 형성된다. 기억 연구에서 그것(정보의 구조화)의 중요성으로 미루어 볼 때, 시간을 내서 여러분이 배우려고 시도하는 정보를 구조화하는 것이 이러한 목표를 달성하는 데 핵심이다. 하나의 방법은 매 수업 시간 이후에 정보의 덩어리를 계층 그리고 관련된 목록으로 구조화하면서 여러분의 노트를 다시 적는 데 시간

을 보내는 것이다. 이것은 또한 개념 간의 어떤 누락된 연결고리를 지적해 내는 데 도움을 주고, 다음 수업 시간에 여러분이 질문을 하도록 준비시켜 준다. 강의 시간에 정신없이 노트 필기하는 동안의 여러분의 정보 처리가 여러분의 학습에 적합한 사려 깊은 구조화로 이어진다고 믿을 수는 없다.

구문풀이

8행 [Judging from its importance in memory research], [taking the time to organize the information {you are attempting to learn}] is key to [accomplishing this goal].

: 첫 번째 [ ]는 분사구문이고, 두 번째 [ ]는 문장의 주어로 쓰인 동명사구이며, 그 안의 { }는 the information을 수식하는 관계절이다. 세 번째 [ ]는 전치사 to의 목적어로 쓰인 동명사구이다.

어휘풀이

- memory organization 기억 조직화
- rephrase *v* 고쳐[바꾸어] 말하다
- encode *v* 암호화하다
- random *a* 무작위의, 임의의
- judging from ~로 미루어 보아, ~로 판단하건대
- accomplish *v* 달성하다, 성취하다
- hierarchy *n* 계층, 위계
- suit *v* ~에 적합하게 하다
- point out ~을 알려주다, ~을 지적하다
- critical *a* 매우 중요한
- can't afford ~할 여력이 없다
- cluster *n* 덩어리, 무리
- session *n* 수업 시간, 회기

PART I 어휘 REVIEW

01 주어와 동사

01 무지 **02** 광범위한 **03** 설득하다 **04** 평가하다 **05** 유연한, 탄력성 있는 **06** 축적하다 **07** 자신감 **08** 이용할 기회, 접근 방법 **09** efficient **10** 명시적인, 뚜렷한 **11** 끈질기게 계속하다 **12** 실현하다, 성취하다

02 동사의 활용

01 윤리적인 **02** 역량 **03** 부적당한 **04** 동정의 **05** regulate **06** 즉각적인, 눈앞에 있는 **07** (환경 등에) 맞추다, 수용하다 **08** 맞추다, 협력[제휴]하다 **09** 따라서 **10** 측면 **11** 건설적인 **12** 제한[한정]하다

03 to부정사와 동명사

01 묘사하다 **02** 과장하다 **03** 마음속에 새기다, 명심하다 **04** 고통, 괴로움 **05** 제약 **06** 부과하다, 지우다 **07** 정신적인, 심리적인 **08** motive **09** 이성적인, 합리적인 **10** 공헌, 기여 **11** 식별하다, 확인하다 **12** 추론 **13** 무형의

04 분사

01 한계의 **02** 비교적인, 상대적인 **03** 원시의, 원시 시대의 **04** 강조하다 **05** optimal **06** 촉진하다 **07** 분산시키다 **08** 확보하다 **09** 두드러지게 하다, 지배하다 **10** 자발적인 **11** 겪다 **12** 취약한

05 명사와 대명사

01 grant **02** ~인 것 같은, ~인 것으로 보이는 **03** 방해하다 **04** 진동 **05** 구별, 차별 **06** 동일한 **07** 구성하다 **08** 전달하다 **09** 보상 **10** 드러내다 **11** 분화시키다 **12** 효율(성)

06 형용사와 부사

01 열정적인, 열광하는 **02** 손상을 입히다 **03** 유지하다, 보유하다 **04** 합병하다 **05** 일시적인 **06** 오래 지속되는 **07** abstract **08** 등장하다, 출현하다 **09** 붙이다, 결부시키다 **10** 동등한 것 **11** 중급의 **12** 미세한, 미묘한 **13** 간격

07 관계사

01 가지고[데리고] 오다 **02** 부담, 압박 **03** 바뀌다 **04** 이동[이주]하는 **05** 집중, 집약 **06** 떠맡다 **07** 조종하다 **08** 그 이후로 **09** 주요한 **10** imply **11** 잉여물 **12** 상품

08 전치사와 접속사

01 지니다, 갖추고 있다 **02** ~에 기여하다 **03** 영감을 주다, 고무시키다 **04** infinite **05** 변환시키다 **06** 동기를 부여하다 **07** 대처하다 **08** 수평의 **09** 밀도 **10** 말하다, 선언하다 **11** ~을 뽑다 **12** 거부하다, 거절하다

09 병렬구조 및 특수구문

01 관례, 관행, 약속 **02** 매우 **03** (문제 등을) 해결하다, 다루다 **04** 조정하다 **05** 특권, 특전 **06** 알아차리다 **07** (실례를 통해) 보여 주다 **08** 과장해서 말하다 **09** critical **10** 청소년 **11** 가혹한, 척박한 **12** 압도하다 **13** 토착의

01 어법 모의고사

01 결여된 채로 **02** 쇠락, 쇠퇴 **03** 대체하다 **04** ~에 관여[참여]하다 **05** 영구[영속]적인 **06** 변동, 변화 **07** 인식, 지각 **08** submit **09** 수반되는 **10** 상당한 **11** 분석 **12** 변수 **13** 자극 **14** 주의를 기울이는, 신경을 쓰는 **15** 포함하다, 통합하다

02 어법 모의고사

01 분포시키다, 분배하다 **02** 본질적인, 내재한 **03** 충분한 **04** 반(反)가치, (가치의) 부인 **05** 의무, 책무 **06** 공격적인 **07** 학대하다, 남용하다 **08** 조사하다 **09** 구체적인, 상세한 **10** 전문지식 **11** extinction **12** 번역[번성]하다 **13** 개입 **14** 정책 **15** 위험을 알리다

03 어법 모의고사

01 기존의 **02** 확인하다 **03** 전달하다 **04** 은신처, 거처 **05** absorb **06** 전혀 다른, 뚜렷이 구별되는 **07** 진화하다, 발달하다 **08** 고립 **09** 반성하는, 숙고하는 **10** 집착, 강박 관념 **11** 잘 자라다, 번성하다 **12** 경험적인 **13** 왜곡하다 **14** 번역하다 **15** 암송하다

04 어법 모의고사

01 이따금씩의, 가끔의 **02** 연상시키는 **03** 유능한 **04** 검증하다 **05** 진전, 발전 **06** 상당히, 꽤 **07** 배제하다 **08** 활동적이지 않은 **09** 전반적인 **10** 특성, 특징 **11** external **12** 연장하다 **13** 우수한, 더 나은 **14** 진정한 **15** 권한[능력]을 부여하다

05 어법 모의고사

01 보통의, 정상적인 **02** 상기하다, 되찾다 **03** 내재하는 **04** 보수적인 **05** 앞서다, 선행하다 **06** 거주하다 **07** 간단한, 솔직한 **08** 조정하다 **09** 처리하다 **10** 넘어서다, 초과하다 **11** 적발하다, 감지하다 **12** 결론을 내리다 **13** justify **14** 문화 유물 **15** 달성하다, 성취하다

N Ⅱ 어휘

01 필수 어휘
본문 pp.087~090

Q1 1 encourages 2 determine 3 isolation
      4 accurate 5 extracted

Q2 1 ② 2 ② 3 ③

095 ④	096 ③	097 ③	098 ④	099 ③
100 ⑤				

Q1

1. 해석 가족의 결속력은 대개 가족들과 함께 더 많은 시간을 보내도록 북돋운다.
[discourage 낙담시키다, 단념시키다]

2. 해석 두 번째 단계는 여러분으로 하여금 잘못된 일에 대한 다른 사람의 사과를 받아들이고, 여러분의 신뢰와 우정을 다시금 보여 줄 것을 결심하게 한다.
[hesitate 망설이다, 주저하다]

3. 해석 이 문제를 극복하는 유일한 방법은 타인들과 더 연결되는 것이고, 이 연결은 두려움과 고립을 줄일 것이다. [collaboration 협업]

4. 해석 그와는 반대로, 과학자는 자기 자신의 생각을 검증해 보고 자연의 어떤 측면에 대해 정확한 설명을 하고 싶어 하기 때문에 논거를 구성한다.
[inaccurate 부정확한]

5. 해석 그러나 이런 분자들이 과일과 채소에서 추출되어 보조제로 만들어졌을 때 그것들은 암을 줄이지 못했다. [extend 연장하다]

Q2

1. 해석 비즈니스 세계에서 생산 비용을 절감하는 것은 끊임없는 난제일 수 있다.
① 의존 ② 보충

2. 해석 어떤 사람들은 자신의 진정한 열정을 찾기 위해 경력을 쌓는 동안 직업을 여러 번 바꾼다.
① 취미 ③ 거주지

3. 해석 한국인 화자들이 서로를 부를 때 때때로 영어 화자들보다 더 정교한 체계를 사용한다.
① 자신감 있는 ② 진심 어린, 진실한

---

095 답 ④

출제 어휘 확인하기

①	restriction	제한, 제약	↔	
②	assess	평가하다	↔	
③	necessity	필수품	↔	
④	low	낮은, 싼	↔	high(높은, 비싼)
⑤	similar	비슷한, 유사한	↔	different(다른)

정답풀이
④ 델리의 상점가를 예로 들어 상점가 경제의 탄력적인 가격 설정 메커니즘을 보여 주고 있다. 구매자와 판매자가 서로의 제약을 알고 있으므로, 필수품으로 여겨지지 않는 비디오 게임의 경우에 판매자는 구매자에게 구매 의사가 생기도록 너무 '높은' 가격을 제시하지 않게 주의해야 한다는 흐름이 되어야 한다. 따라서 low(낮은)를 high 정도로 바꿔 써야 한다. 앞에 부정어 not이 있음에 유의해야 한다.

오답풀이
① 판매자와 구매자 둘 다 서로의 '제약'에 관해 알고 있어서 가격 일치가 형성될 수 있다는 맥락이므로 restrictions는 적절하다.
② 판매자와 구매자는 상대방이 무엇을 필수품과 사치품으로 여기는지를 이해한다고 했으므로, 그들이 일상생활에서 가지는 재정적 압박을 '평가할(assess)' 수 있다고 한 것은 적절하다.
③ 비디오 게임과 같은 전자 제품은 식품과 같은 '필수품'이 아니라는 맥락이므로 necessity는 적절하다.
⑤ 판매자와 구매자가 '비슷한' 문화적·경제적 배경을 공유하여 서로의 선호와 한계를 바탕으로 가격 일치가 형성된다는 맥락이므로 similar는 적절하다.

전문해석
상점가 경제는 공유되는 문화라는 더 지속적인 유대 위에 자리 잡은, 겉으로 보기에 탄력적인 가격 설정 메커니즘을 특징으로 한다. 구매자와 판매자 둘 다 서로의 ① 제약을 알고 있다. 델리의 상점가에서 구매자와 판매자는 대체로 다른 행위자들이 그들의 일상생활에서 가지는 재정적인 압박을 ② 평가할 수 있다. 특정 경제 계층에 속하는 각 행위자는 상대방이 무엇을 필수품과 사치품으로 여기는지를 이해한다. 비디오 게임과 같은 전자 제품의 경우에, 그것들은 식품 같은 다른 가정용 구매품과 동일한 수준의 ③ 필수품이 아니다. 따라서 델리의 상점가에서 판매자는 비디오 게임에 대해 곧바로 매우 ④ 낮은(→ 높은) 가격을 요구하지 않으려고 주의하는데, 구매자가 비디오 게임의 소유를 절대 없어서는 안 되는 것으로 볼 이유가 전혀 없기 때문이다. 이러한 유형의 지식에 대한 접근은 ⑤ 비슷한 문화적이고 경제적인 세상에의 속함에서 비롯된 서로의 선호 및 한계와 관련지어 가격 일치를 형성한다.

구문풀이
7행 Each actor [belonging to a specific economic class] understands [what the other sees as a necessity and a luxury].
: 첫 번째 [ ]는 Each actor를 수식하는 현재분사구이고, 두 번째 [ ]는 understands의 목적어 역할을 하는 의문사절이다.

15행 [Access to this type of knowledge] establishes a price consensus by [relating to each other's preferences and limitations {of belonging to a similar cultural and economic universe}].
: 첫 번째 [ ]는 문장의 주어이고, 두 번째 [ ]는 전치사 by의 목적어로 쓰인 동명사구이다. { }는 each other's preferences and limitations에 의미상 연결되는 전치사구이다.

어휘풀이
● bazaar n 상점가, 시장 거리 ● feature v 특징으로 하다
● apparently ad 겉으로 보기에 ● flexible a 융통성 있는, 탄력적인

- atop *prep* 위에, 맨 꼭대기에
- restriction *n* 제한, 제약
- to a large extent 대부분은, 상당한 정도로
- financial *a* 재정적인
- luxury *n* 사치품
- at no point 어느 한순간도 ~ 않은, 절대 ~ 않은
- possession *n* 소유
- establish *v* 형성하다
- enduring *a* 오래가는, 지속되는
- assess *v* 평가하다
- necessity *n* 필수품; 불가결한 일
- absolute *a* 절대적인

096 답 ③

출제 어휘 확인하기

①	alone	혼자인	↔	
②	include	포함하다	↔	exclude(제외하다, 배제하다)
③	unreasonable	비합리적인	↔	reasonable(합리적인)
④	diverse	다양한	↔	
⑤	giant	거대한	↔	

정답풀이
③ this idea는 바로 앞 문장의 내용, 즉 공룡이 몸집이 큰 동물의 역할을 모두 채웠다는 것을 가리키고, 이어지는 문장에서 트라이아스기 말에 공룡에는 많은 대형 초식동물과 육식동물이 있었다고 했다. 따라서 이러한 생각이 '비합리적(unreasonable)'이라는 것은 적절하지 않으며 '합리적인'이라는 의미의 reasonable과 같은 낱말로 바꿔 써야 한다.

오답풀이
① 포유류도 많은 미개척 적소(適所)에 있었다는 내용이 뒤에 오므로, 초기 쥐라기 공룡 생존자 중 선택된 몇몇이 그곳에 '혼자(alone)' 있었던 것은 아니라는 문맥은 적절하다.
② 문맥상 공룡은 다양하게 진화하여 대형화된 반면에 포유류는 오랫동안 설치류의 크기에 머물렀다는 것이므로, 공룡이 큰 육상 동물을 '포함했다(include)'는 것은 적절하다.
④ 앞에서 공룡의 다양성이 폭발했다고 했으므로, 트라이아스기 말에 공룡은 생태적으로 '다양한(diverse)' 무리였다고 할 수 있다.
⑤ In contrast(대조적으로)로 보아, 앞 문장과 대조적인 내용임을 알 수 있다. 따라서 트라이아스기 말에 공룡이 대형화되었던 것과는 대조적으로 포유류는 곤충만 잡아먹는 생물이어서 '거대한(giant)' 몸집으로 진화하지 못했다는 것은 적절하다.

전문해석
트라이아스기 말엽에 한두 번의 대량 멸종이 있었다고 하더라도 그리고 초기 쥐라기 공룡 생존자 중 선택된 몇몇이 많은 미개척 적소(適所)에 직면했다고 하더라도, 그것들은 ① 혼자가 아니었다. 특히 포유류 또한 그곳에 있었다. 그래서 우리에게는 여전히 풀리지 않은 문제가 남아 있다. 쥐라기가 시작될 때 비교적 '깨끗한 생태적 석판'(또는 적어도 혼란스러운 상태)이 있었다면, 왜 공룡의 다양성은 폭발하여 역사상 가장 큰 육상 동물을 ② 포함한 반면, 포유류는 그 후 1억 5천만 년 넘게 대체로 설치류의 크기에 머물렀을까? 일반적인 견해는 공룡이 몸집이 큰 동물의 역할을 모두 채웠다는 것이다. 언뜻 보기에, 이 생각은 ③ 비합리적인(→ 합리적인) 것으로 보인다. 트라이아스기 말에 공룡은 이미 생태적으로 ④ 다양한 무리였고, 많은 대형 초식동물과 육식동물이 있었다. 이와는 대조적으로, 이 시기의 거의 모든 포유류는 곤충만 잡아먹는 생물이었으며, ⑤ 거대한 몸집으로 진화하여 뻗어나갈 토대가 거의 없었던 것으로 보인다!

구문풀이
1행 [Even if there were one or two mass extinctions around the end of the Triassic], and [even if {a select few Early Jurassic dinosaur survivors} were confronted by a sea of unexploited niches], **they** were not alone.

: 두 개의 [ ]는 모두 양보의 의미를 나타내는 부사절이고, 두 번째 [ ]에서 { }는 주어이다. they는 a select few Early Jurassic dinosaur survivors를 가리키는 대명사이다.

어휘풀이
- extinction *n* 멸종
- Triassic *a* 트라이아스기(중생대의 첫 시대, 약 2억 년 전)의
- Jurassic *a* 쥐라기(중생대의 중간 시대)의
- confront *v* 직면하게 하다
- unexploited *a* 미개척된, 개발되지 않은
- ecological *a* 생태학적인, 생태상의
- chaotic *a* 혼란스러운
- diversity *n* 다양성
- of all time 역대, 지금껏
- proportion *n* 크기
- on first blush 언뜻 보기에는
- carnivore *n* 육식동물
- evolutionary *a* 진화의
- slate *n* 석판
- affair *n* 일, 문제
- explode *v* 폭발하다
- rodent *n* 설치류
- thereafter *ad* 그 후
- bunch *n* 무리
- devoted *a* 헌신적인
- radiation *n* 뻗어나감, 방사

097 답 ③

출제 어휘 확인하기

①	relief	위안	↔	
②	dependence	의존	↔	independence(자립)
③	reduce	줄이다	↔	increase(늘리다)
④	incorporate	통합하다	↔	
⑤	component	구성 요소	↔	

정답풀이
③ 요양원에 거주하는 사람들의 독립성을 유지하도록 돕는 일에 관해 설명하는 흐름이므로, 그들의 개인적 돌봄 수행 능력을 '줄이는(Reducing)' 것은 적절하지 않다. '장려하는'이라는 의미가 되도록 Encouraging 정도로 바꿔 써야 한다.

오답풀이
① 심각한 장애나 허약함을 지닌 사람들이 가정에서 분투한 후에 요양원에서 개인적인 돌봄을 받고 요리와 집안일을 걱정하지 않아도 되는 것은 '위안'이 될 수 있으므로 relief는 적절하다.
② 지나친 돌봄을 제공하는 것은 완전한 '의존'을 초래할 수 있으므로 dependence는 적절하다.
④ 돌봄을 위한 보다 통합적인 접근 방법이 필요하다고 했으므로 활동 방법이 기본적인 개인 및 임상 치료 체제에 '통합될(incorporated)' 수 있다고 하는 것은 적절하다.
⑤ 돌봄을 위한 활동 방법과 그것의 제공이 결국 통합적으로 이루어져야 함을 말하는 흐름이므로, 그것들이 전체 돌봄 과정의 '구성 요소(component)'가 되어야 한다는 것은 적절하다.

전문해석
우리가 갑자기 일상적인 일의 대부분이나 전부, 그리고 미래의 일에 대한 기대를 박탈당한다고 상상해 보라. 이것은 요양원에 거주하는 대부분의 사람들이 직면해야 하는 상황이다. 심각한 장애나 허약함을 가진 일부 사람들에게는 가정에서 대처하려고 분투한 후에, 개인적인 돌봄을 받으며 더 이상 요리와 집안일에 대한 걱정을 하지 않는 것은 ① 위안이 될 수도 있다. 그러나 위험성은 지나친 돌봄을 제공하는 것이 완전한 ② 의존을 초래한다는 것인데, 그것(완전한 의존)이 전적으로 필요한 것은 아닐

수도 있다는 것이다. 개인적인 돌봄을 수행하는 어떤 능력이라도 유지하는 것을 ③ 줄이는(→ 장려하는) 것, 옷과 음식을 고를 때 선택을 하는 것 그리고 신체적인 문제를 극복하는 방법을 찾는 것은 독립성을 유지하도록 돕는다. 돌봄을 위한 보다 더 통합된 접근 방법이 필요하다. 활동 방법은 기본적인 개인 및 임상 치료 체제에 ④ 통합될 수 있다. 어떤 종류의 활동의 제공도 '추가적인 것', '특별한 대우' 또는 '변화된 것'으로 간주되어서는 안 된다. 즉, 그것들은 전체 돌봄 과정의 중요한 ⑤ 구성 요소가 되어야 한다.

구문풀이

4행 For some with severe disabilities or frailty **it** may be a relief [after struggling to cope at home] [to receive personal care and no longer have the worry of cooking and housework].

: it은 형식상의 주어이고, 두 번째 [ ]가 내용상의 주어이다. 첫 번째 [ ]는 삽입된 부사구이다.

10행 [Encouraging the retention of any ability to perform personal care], [making choices in selecting clothes and food], and [finding ways of overcoming physical problems], help to maintain independence.

: 세 개의 [ ]는 모두 문장의 주어를 이루는 동명사구로 and로 병렬 연결되었다. 문장의 동사는 help이다.

어휘풀이

- be deprived of ~을 박탈당하다, ~을 빼앗기다
- occupation *n* 일, 직업
- resident *n* 거주자, 주민
- care home 요양원, 보호 시설
- disability *n* 장애, 무능
- frailty *n* 허약함, 취약함
- relief *n* 위안, 안심
- struggle *v* 분투하다
- cope *v* 대처하다, 극복하다
- entirely *ad* 전적으로
- retention *n* 유지, 보유
- integrated *a* 통합된
- incorporate *v* 통합하다
- clinical *a* 임상적인
- provision *n* 공급, 제공
- treat *n* (특별한) 대우, 대접
- vital *a* 중요한, 중대한
- component *n* 구성 요소

098 답 ④

출제 어휘 확인하기

① particular	특정한	↔	
② increase	증가시키다	↔	decrease(감소시키다)
③ add	더하다, 추가하다	↔	
④ counter	저지하다	↔	
⑤ reconnect	재연결하다	↔	

정답풀이

④ 섬유와 직물이 더 이상 장소에 구애받지 않게 되자, 소비자는 그러한 섬유나 직물이 어디서, 어떻게, 누구에 의해 만들어졌는지 등에 관한 정보를 얻지 못하게 되어 자신이 사용하는 제품의 생산에 투입된 기술, 자원, 생산자의 노고 등에 대해 이해하지 못하고 경시하게 되었다는 맥락이 되어야 한다. 따라서 countered(저지하다)를 resulted in(초래하다) 정도로 바꿔 써야 한다.

오답풀이

① 이어지는 내용으로 보아, 1차 산업혁명 이전에는 직물 생산이 장소에 구애받았음을 알 수 있다. 따라서 1700년대까지 직물 생산에 '특정한(particular)' 지역 내에서 이용 가능한 섬유를 사용했다는 것은 적절하다.
② 장소에 구애받던 섬유와 직물은 지역들 간의 무역을 통해 그 이용 가능성이 '증가했을' 것이므로 increased는 적절하다.
③ 지역들 간의 무역에 '더하여' 1차 산업혁명과 제조 섬유에서의 기술 발달로

인해 섬유와 직물이 더 이상 장소에 구애받지 않게 되었다는 맥락이므로 added는 문맥상 적절하다.
⑤ 앞부분 내용의 결론에 해당하는 문장으로, 장소의 가치를 새롭게 하면 분리되었던 회사 및 소비자와 특정 장소의 사람들, 지리, 문화가 '다시 연결될(reconnects)' 것이라는 내용은 문맥상 적절하다.

전문해석

'장소'의 가치는 왜 그렇게 중요한가? 역사적 관점에서 볼 때 1700년대까지 직물 생산은 지리적으로 ① 특정한 지역 내에서 이용 가능한 섬유, 예를 들어 면, 양모, 실크, 아마 섬유를 사용하는 수작업 공정이었다. 지역들 간의 무역은 이러한 섬유들과 그 섬유들로 만들어진 관련 직물들의 이용도를 ② 증가시켰다. 1차 산업혁명과 그 뒤에 이어진 제조 섬유에서의 기술 발달은 섬유와 직물이 더 이상 '장소에 구애받지' 않게 되었다는 사실을 ③ 더했다. 패션 회사들은 제품이 어디서, 어떻게 또는 누구에 의해 만들어졌는지에 대해 거의 혹은 전혀 관련 없이 직물들과 직물들로 만들어진 제품들을 만들었고 소비자들은 그것들을 얻을 수 있었다. 이것은 소비자와 그들이 매일 사용하는 제품 간의 단절, 이러한 제품을 만드는 데 필요한 기술과 자원에 대한 이해와 평가의 상실 그리고 제품 창조에 필요한 인간 자원과 천연 자원에 대한 연관된 경시를 ④ 저지했다(→ 초래했다). 따라서 '장소'의 가치를 새롭게 하는 것은 회사와 소비자를 특정 장소의 사람들, 지리 그리고 문화와 ⑤ 다시 연결한다.

구문풀이

11행 Fashion companies created and consumers could acquire [textiles and products {made from textiles} with little or no connection to {where, how, or by whom the products were made}].

: [ ]는 created와 could acquire의 공통 목적어이다. 그 안의 첫 번째 { }는 products를 수식하는 과거분사구이고, 두 번째 { }는 전치사 to의 목적어 역할을 하는 의문사절이다.

어휘풀이

- perspective *n* 관점
- fiber *n* 섬유
- geographic *a* 지리적인
- flax *n* 아마 섬유
- availability *n* 이용 가능성
- associated *a* 관련된, 연관된
- subsequent *a* (뒤에) 이어지는
- advancement *n* 발달, 진보
- disconnect *n* 단절
- appreciation *n* 평가
- disregard *n* 경시, 무시
- renew *v* 새롭게 하다

099 답 ③

출제 어휘 확인하기

(A) prefer	선호하다	/ exclude	배제하다
(B) common	공통의, 흔한	/ unique	고유한
(C) simplicity	단순함	/ variety	다양성

정답풀이

(A) 민족 유산과 향토 음식이 사람들의 음식 선택에 가장 강력한 영향을 주어 사람들은 자신의 지역 음식을 식사에 결합한다는 전체적인 글의 흐름과 일치해야 하므로, 자라면서 먹은 음식을 '선호하는(prefer)' 경향이 있다고 하는 것이 적절하다. [exclude 배제하다]
(B) 앞에서 한 나라의 모든 지역에는 그곳만의 전형적인 음식이 있고 그것을 식사에 결합시키는 방식이 있다고 했고, 뒤에 각 지역의 재료와 요리에 관한 개별적인 사례들이 이어지므로, 지역 재료와 요리 방식의 '고유한(unique)' 조합이라고 하는 것이 적절하다. [common 공통의, 흔한]
(C) 미국 음식은 많은 민족 음식과 향토 조리법을 포함한다고 했으므로, 미국 음식에 '다양성(variety)'을 더한다고 하는 것이 적절하다. [simplicity 단순함]

전문해석

음식 선택에 가장 강력한 영향을 미치는 것 중에 민족 유산과 향토 음식이 있다. 사람들은 자라면서 먹은 음식을 (A) 선호하는 경향이 있다. 모든 나라에는, 그리고 사실상 한 나라의 모든 지역에는 그곳만의 전형적인 음식과 그것들을 식사에 결합시키는 방식들이 있다. 이런 음식은 지역에서 나는 재료와 요리 방식의 (B) 고유한 조합을 반영한다. 뉴 잉글랜드의 차우더는 조개로 만들지만, 플로리다키스 제도에서는 고둥이 주요 재료이다. 조지아가 복숭아 코블러(음료의 일종)로 유명한 것처럼 태평양 연안 북서부는 매리언베리 파이로 유명하다. 필라델피아에는 치즈 스테이크가 있고, 뉴 올리언스에는 대형 굴 샌드위치가 있다. '미국 음식'은 많은 민족 음식과 향토 조리법을 포함하는데, 모든 것이 음식에 대한 (C) 다양성을 더한다.

구문풀이

1행 [Among the strongest influences on food choices] are ethnic heritage and regional cuisines.

: 보어 역할을 하는 위치, 장소의 전치사구인 [ ]가 문장의 맨 앞에 와서 주어인 ethnic heritage and regional cuisines와 동사인 are가 도치되었다.

어휘풀이

- ethnic *a* 민족의
- cuisine *n* 요리, 조리법
- combine *v* 결합시키다
- local *a* 현지의, 지역적인
- chowder *n* 차우더(생선이나 조개류 등으로 만든 걸쭉한 수프)
- clam *n* 조개
- oyster *n* 굴
- diet *n* 음식, 식단
- heritage *n* 민족 유산
- typical *a* 전형적인
- reflect *v* 반영하다
- ingredient *n* 재료, 성분
- feature *v* 특징으로 하다
- po'boy *n* 대형 샌드위치
- variety *n* 다양성

---

100 답 ⑤

출제 어휘 | 확인하기

① build	만들다	↔	
② convey	전달하다	↔	
③ additional	추가적인	↔	
④ likely	~하기 쉬운	↔	unlikely(~할 것 같지 않은)
⑤ tired	싫증 내는	↔	

정답풀이

⑤ 부모가 아이에게 하는 칭찬의 긍정적인 영향을 설명하는 내용의 글이다. 앞에서 칭찬이 일상적인 아이들이 더 큰 성취를 보인다고 했고, 뒤에는 칭찬에 대한 우리의 욕구는 항상 크다는 내용이 나오므로, 그 대조적인 경우를 설명하며 일상적 칭찬에 '싫증 내는(tired)' 어린이들이라고 표현한 것은 적절하지 않다. 칭찬을 '받지 못한다'는 맥락에서 뒤의 전치사 of와 함께 쓰여 '박탈당한'이라는 의미를 나타내도록 deprived 정도로 바꿔 써야 한다.

오답풀이

① 뇌는 뉴런의 새로운 망을 형성함으로써 성장한다고 했고, 이후 옥시토신과 엔도르핀 혼합물을 언급하고 있으므로, 특정한 호르몬이 새로운 뇌의 회로를 '만드는(building)' 데 핵심적인 연료를 제공한다는 것은 적절하다.
② 유아의 뇌에 옥시토신과 엔도르핀이 넘쳐나게 되는 것은 유아가 부모에게 칭찬을 들어서일 것이므로, 부모의 얼굴이 유아를 향한 메시지와 함께 칭찬을 '전달한다(conveys)'는 것은 적절하다.
③ 기쁨을 주는 호르몬이 부모와 자녀 관계에 친밀함과 이해를 촉진한다고 했는데, 이는 뇌 성장에 좋은 것이라고 할 수 있으므로, 뇌에 '추가적인(additional)' 연료를 공급한다는 것은 적절하다.
④ 엔도르핀과 함께 기쁨을 주는 호르몬으로 언급된 옥시토신이 적당한 수준

에서 높은 수준으로 흐르면 좋은 영향을 줄 것이므로 다른 사람들을 신뢰하기 더 '쉽고(likely)' 실망이나 배신으로부터 더욱 회복력이 있다는 것은 적절하다.

전문해석

칭찬은 건강한 뇌의 성장에 핵심적이다. 뇌는 상호 연관된 뉴런의 새로운 망을 형성함으로써 성장하는데, 그것은 뇌의 의사소통 체계의 기본적인 요소이다. 특정한 호르몬은 새로운 뇌의 회로를 (a) 만드는 데 핵심적인 연료를 제공한다. 이러한 호르몬 중 초기 두뇌 발달에 가장 중요한 것은 가끔 '유대감 형성 호르몬'이라고 불리는 옥시토신과 우리에게 황홀감을 주는, 자연스럽게 발생하는 화학물질을 분비하는 엔도르핀 혼합물이다. 부모의 얼굴이 "나는 네가 누군지 알고 싶고, 나는 너를 칭찬한단다."라는 메시지와 함께 칭찬을 (b) 전달하면, 유아의 뇌는 옥시토신과 엔도르핀으로 넘쳐난다. 이러한 기쁨을 주는 호르몬들은 부모와 자녀 사이의 친밀함과 이해를 촉진하고 (c) 추가적인 뇌 연료를 공급하는 친근하고도 지속적인 응시를 촉진한다. 신경조절물질로서, 뇌가 기능하는 방식에 영향을 주는 화학물질인 옥시토신은 우리의 판단에 영향을 준다. 우리의 뇌에서 적당한 수준에서 높은 수준으로 옥시토신이 흐르면, 우리는 다른 사람들을 신뢰하기 더 (d) 쉬우며 실망이나 배신으로부터 더 회복력이 있다. 게다가, 칭찬이 일상적인 어린이들은 3살에 그리고 다시 10살에 더 큰 성취를 보이는 반면, 일상적인 칭찬을 (e) 싫증 내는(→ 받지 못하는) 어린이들은 뇌의 신경망에서 둔감한 반응을 보이며, 특히 학습 및 동기 부여와 연관된 것에서 그렇다. 칭찬은 건강한 뇌의 핵심적인 구성 요소이며 우리는 칭찬에 대한 우리의 욕구보다 결코 더 자랄 수 없다(칭찬에 대한 욕구는 항상 크다).

구문풀이

22행 Moreover, children [for whom praise is commonplace] show greater accomplishment at the age of three years and again at the age of ten years while children [deprived of everyday praise] show blunted responses in brain networks, particularly those [associated with learning and motivation].

: 관계절인 첫 번째 [ ]와 과거분사구인 두 번째 [ ]는 각각 앞에 있는 children을 수식한다. 세 번째 [ ]는 those(= brain networks)를 수식하는 과거분사구이다.

어휘풀이

- interconnected *a* 상호 연관된
- hormone *n* 호르몬
- circuit *n* 회로
- refer to *A* as *B* A를 B라고 부르다
- endorphin *n* 엔도르핀
- release *v* 방출하다
- infant *n* 유아
- steady *a* 지속적인
- intimacy *n* 친밀함
- resilient *a* 회복력이 있는
- commonplace *a* 일상적인, 흔한
- neuron *n* 뉴런
- fuel *n* 연료
- oxytocin *n* 옥시토신
- bonding *n* 유대감 (형성)
- compound *n* 혼합물
- high *n* 황홀감
- be awash with ~으로 넘쳐나다
- gaze *n* 응시
- moderate *a* 적당한
- betrayal *n* 배신
- outgrow *v* ~보다 더 자라다[커지다]

02 필수 어휘

본문 pp.092 ~ 095

Q1 1 expansion 2 observance 3 insufficient
4 active 5 positive

Q2 1 ① 2 ② 3 ②

101 ⑤   102 ④   103 ⑤   104 ④   105 ⑤

106 ②

Q1

1. [해석] 공장 확장은 생산 능력의 상당한 증가를 가져올 것이다. [contraction 축소]

2. [해석] 우리는 모든 선수들이 경기 규칙을 철저하게 준수할 것을 기대한다.
[violation 위반]

3. [해석] 여러분의 눈은 빛이 불충분하면 초점을 맞추기 위해 추가적인 노력을 해야
하기 때문에 피로해질 수 있다. [adequate 충분한, 적합한]

4. [해석] 멋진 공연의 일환으로 그녀는 축제에서 친구들과 함께 노래를 부르고 춤을
추었다. 그 후에 그녀는 자신감이 더 생기고 적극적이게 되었다.
[passive 소극적인, 수동적인]

5. [해석] 긍정적인 시각과 끈기를 가지면 여러분은 모든 장애물을 극복하고 이겨내는
방법을 발견할 것이다. [negative 부정적인]

Q2

1. [해석] 개발자들은 자신들의 프로젝트가 유망하지 않다는 사실에 굴복해야 했다.
② 무시하다 ③ 호소하다

2. [해석] 정부는 재생 가능한 에너지를 촉진하고 탄소 배출을 줄이기 위한 새로운 프
로그램을 시작했다.
① 일축하다 ③ 검토하다

3. [해석] 그 교수는 지구 너머 외계 생명체의 존재는 실제라고 주장했다.
① 과정 ③ 중요성

---

101 답 ⑤

출제 어휘 확인하기

① remote	외딴, 동떨어진	↔
② absorption	흡수, 동화	↔
③ affect	영향을 미치다	↔
④ adapt	적응하다	↔
⑤ maintain	유지하다	↔

정답풀이

⑤ 혁신 기술이 만들어 내는 신세계로 우리가 떠나는 것이 아니라 그것이 우
리 삶으로 들어와 우리에게 적응해야 한다는 문맥이다. 따라서 컴퓨터가 우리
를 마법 같은 신세계로 데려다줄 것이라고 계속해서 더 오래 믿을수록 컴퓨터
와 우리 삶의 자연스러운 융합이 더 오래 '유지될' 것이라는 내용은 어색하다.
maintain을 delay(지연시키다) 정도로 바꿔 써야 한다.

오답풀이

① On the contrary(그와 반대로)로 시작하는 다음 문장에서 우리는 모터를
우리 삶에 가져왔다고 했으므로, 모터와 함께 산업혁명이 도래했을 때 우리는
'외딴' 모터 공간으로 가기 위해 우리의 세상을 떠나지는 않았다는 흐름이 자
연스럽다. 따라서 remote는 적절하다.

② 우리가 모터를 자동차, 냉장고, 드릴 프레스, 연필깎이와 같은 것들로 우
리 삶에 가져온 것을 말하므로 absorption(흡수)은 적절하다.

③ 모터를 적용한 혁신품들이 주요한 사회 경제적 운동으로 이어진 것은 그것
들이 우리의 일상생활에 들어와 깊은 '영향을 미쳤기' 때문이라고 할 수 있으
므로 affected는 적절하다.

④ 앞에서 인간은 수천 년 동안 근본적으로 변하지 않았지만 기술은 끊임없이
변화한다고 했으므로, 인간 중심의 컴퓨터 사용하에서는 기술이 인간에게 '적
응해야(adapt)' 한다는 것은 적절하다.

전문해석

우리가 고개를 돌리는 곳 어디에서든 우리는 전능한 '사이버공간'에 대해 듣는다! 과
대광고는 우리가 지루한 삶을 떠나 고글과 보디 슈트를 착용하고, 어떤 금속성의, 3
차원의, 멀티미디어로 만들어진 다른 세계로 들어갈 것을 약속한다. 위대한 혁신인
모터와 함께 산업혁명이 도래했을 때 우리는 어떤 ① 외딴 모터 공간으로 가기 위해
우리의 세상을 떠나지는 않았다! 그와 반대로, 우리는 모터를 자동차, 냉장고, 드릴
프레스, 연필깎이와 같은 것들로 우리 삶에 가져왔다. 이 ② 흡수는 매우 완전해서
우리는 그것들의 '모터성'이 아니라 그것들의 쓰임새를 분명하게 밝히는 이름으로
이 모든 도구를 지칭한다. 이러한 혁신품들은 정확히 우리의 일상생활에 들어와 깊
은 ③ 영향을 미쳤기 때문에 주요한 사회 경제적 운동으로 이어졌다. 사람들은 수천
년 동안 근본적으로 변하지 않았다. 기술은 끊임없이 변화한다. 기술이 우리에게 ④
적응해야 하는 그것이다. 그것이 바로 인간 중심의 컴퓨터 사용에서 정보 기술과
그 장치들에 일어날 일이다. 컴퓨터가 우리를 마법 같은 신세계로 데려다줄 것이라
고 계속해서 더 오래 믿을수록 우리는 컴퓨터와 우리 삶의 자연스러운 융합을 더 오
래 ⑤ 유지할(→ 지연시킬) 것인데, 이는 사회 경제적 혁명이라고 불리기를 열망하는
모든 주요 운동의 특징이다.

구문풀이

[10행] This absorption has been **so** complete **that** we refer to all
these tools with names [that declare their usage, not their
"motorness."]

: '매우 ~해서 …하다'를 뜻하는 「so ~ that ....」 구문이 쓰였으며, [ ]는 names를 수식
하는 관계절이다.

[19행] **The longer** we continue to believe [that computers will take
us to a magical new world], **the longer** we will maintain their
natural fusion with our lives, [the hallmark of every major
movement {that aspires to be called a socioeconomic revolution}].

: 「The+비교급 ~, the+비교급 …(~할수록 더욱 …하다)」 구문이 쓰였다. 첫 번째 [ ]는
to believe의 목적어로 쓰인 명사절이고, 두 번째 [ ]는 their natural fusion with
our lives를 부가적으로 설명하는 동격어구이다. 그 안에 쓰인 { }는 every major
movement를 수식하는 관계절이다.

어휘풀이

- almighty *a* 전능한
- three-dimensional *a* 3차원의
- on the contrary 그와는 반대로
- pencil sharpener 연필깎이
- refer to ~을 지칭하다
- socioeconomic *a* 사회 경제적인
- profoundly *ad* 깊이, 심오하게
- fusion *n* 융합
- metallic *a* 금속성의
- remote *a* 외딴, 동떨어진
- automobile *n* 자동차
- absorption *n* 흡수, 동화
- declare *v* 분명하게 밝히다, 선언하다
- precisely *ad* 정확히, 엄밀히
- fundamentally *ad* 근본적으로
- aspire *v* 열망하다

102 답 ④

출제 어휘 | 확인하기

① subjective	주관적인	↔	objective(객관적인)	
② soon	빨리	↔		
③ opposite	반대의	↔		
④ unreal	실재하지 않는	↔	real(실재하는)	
⑤ overcome	극복하다	↔		

정답풀이

④ 무언가에 대해 확신하는 경험을 알고 있기 때문에 특정한 일에 대한 불확실성을 경험하는 것이라고 했으므로, 확실성은 '실재하지 않는' 가능성이 아니라 '실재하는' 가능성이라고 할 수 있다. 따라서 unreal은 적절하지 않고 real 정도로 바꿔 써야 한다.

오답풀이

① 불확실성은 절대적인 것이 아니고, 단지 자신이 명확한 대안을 보지 못하고 있는 상태일 뿐이라는 맥락이므로 subjective(주관적인)는 문맥상 적절하다.
② 불확실한 상태에 있는 것은 전혀 유쾌하지도 바람직하지도 않다고 하므로 그러한 상태에서 가능한 한 '빨리(soon)' 벗어나야 한다는 것은 적절하다.
③ 불확실성은 결국 그와 '반대되는' 확실성의 경험이 있기 때문에 알 수 있다는 내용이므로 opposite은 적절하다.
⑤ 바로 앞 문장에서 지금 확신하지 못하는 문제에 대해서도 확실성이 가능하다고 했으므로, 이론적으로는 특정한 문제에 대한 불확실성이 언젠가 '극복될' 수 있다고 할 수 있다. 따라서 overcoming은 적절하다.

전문해석

때때로 여러분이 명확한 대안이 전혀 보이지 않는 상황에 처해 있음을 깨달을 수도 있다는 것이 객관적으로 볼 때 명확한 대안이 전혀 없다는 것을 의미하지는 않는다. 그것은 단지 여러분이 그것들을 보지 못한다는 의미일 뿐이다. 불확실성에 대한 자신의 ① 주관적인 상태를 세상 전체에 투영하여 그것의 객관적인 지위를 주장하지 마라. 진실과 관련하여 불확실한 상태에 있는 것은 전혀 유쾌하지도 바람직하지도 않으며, 우리는 그러한 상태에서 가능한 한 ② 빨리 벗어나기 위해 항상 노력해야 한다. 하지만 지금 당장 여러분은 어떤 특정한 문제에 대해 확신이 없을 수 있지만, 그러한 경험은 오직 여러분이 ③ 반대되는 경험, 즉 무언가에 대해 확신하는 경험을 알고 있기 때문에 가능한 것이라는 점을 생각해 보라. 그러므로 여러분은 확실성이 ④ 실재하지 않는(→ 실재하는) 가능성이라는 것을 알고 있다. 만약 확실성이 정말로 가능하다면, 그것은 결국 여러분이 지금 확신하지 못하는 문제와 관련해서도 가능하다. 이론적으로, 언젠가 여러분이 지금 경험하고 있는 특정한 문제에 대한 불확실성을 ⑤ 극복하는 것을 막을 것은 아무것도 없다.

구문풀이

1행 [That you might find yourself at times in a situation {in which you see no clear alternatives}] does not mean, [objectively considered], [that there are no clear alternatives].

: 첫 번째 [ ]는 문장의 주어 역할을 하는 명사절이고, 그 안의 { }는 a situation을 수식하는 관계절이다. 두 번째 [ ]는 삽입된 분사구문이며, 세 번째 [ ]는 mean의 목적어 역할을 하는 명사절이다.

어휘풀이

- alternative *n* 대안
- uncertainty *n* 불확실성
- desirable *a* 바람직한
- eventually *ad* 결국, 궁극적으로
- preclude *v* 못하게 하다, 막다
- objectively *ad* 객관적으로
- claim *v* 주장하다
- strive *v* 노력하다
- with regard to ~에 관련해서
- theoretically *ad* 이론적으로

---

103 답 ⑤

출제 어휘 | 확인하기

① moral	도덕적인	↔		
② independent	독립적인	↔	dependent(의존적인)	
③ difficulty	어려움	↔	ease(쉬움)	
④ misuse	오용	↔		
⑤ forbid	금지하다	↔	allow(허용하다)	

정답풀이

⑤ 대부분의 과학자들이 실직의 위험을 무릅쓰고도 자신의 일이 오용되는 것에 항의할 것이라고 했으므로, 이러한 과학자를 지지하는 동료들이 경멸하는 사람은 자신의 이름이나 일이 부적절하게 이용되는 것을 '허용하는' 사람일 것이다. 따라서 forbid(금지하다)를 allow 정도로 바꿔 써야 한다.

오답풀이

① 글 전체의 내용이 기업체와 함께 연구하는 응용과학자가 염두에 두어야 할 '도덕적인' 의무와 관련이 있으므로 moral은 적절하다.
② 응용과학자가 기업체와 일하는 경우에 관한 내용이 이어지므로 '독립적인(independent)' 응용과학자가 거의 없다는 것은 적절하다.
③ 앞에서 과학자가 자신의 일이 사회적 유용성이 전혀 없거나 해로운 결과를 가져온다고 믿을 때 개인적인 딜레마가 생길 수 있다고 했으므로, 이러한 맥락에서 '어려움(difficulty)'이 생겨난다는 것은 적절하다.
④ 응용과학자가 한 일이 과장되거나 의도하지 않은 방향으로 적용되는 것은 '오용'되는 것이므로 misuses는 적절하다.

전문해석

과학자들은 새로운 문제에 착수하기 전에 ① 도덕적 요인을 고려해야 한다. 이것은 특히 응용 연구에서 그러한데, 그것의 효과는 더 쉽게 예측 가능하다. ② 독립적인 행위자인 응용과학자들이 거의 없기 때문에 과학자가 기업체를 위해 자신이 하고 있는 일이 사회적 유용성이 전혀 없거나 실제로 해로운 결과를 갖고 있다고 믿을 때 심각한 개인적 딜레마가 생길 수 있다. 흔히 ③ 어려움은 그가 한 일이 과장되거나 결코 의도하지 않은 방향으로 적용된다는 사실에서 생겨난다. 이것은 자주 그를 고용하고 있는 회사의 광고 부서에 의해 행해진다. 자신들의 일이 이렇게 ④ 오용되는 것에 항의하는 것이 과학자들의 권리와 의무인데, 대부분의 과학자들은 실직의 위험을 무릅쓰고도 그렇게 할 것이다. 이런 점에서 그들은 대다수의 동료들에게 지지를 받고 있는데, 그들은 사실 자신의 이름이나 일이 부적절하게 이용되는 것을 ⑤ 금지하는(→ 허용하는) 사람들을 경멸한다.

구문풀이

4행 Since few applied scientists are independent agents, [serious personal dilemmas can arise] when a scientist believes [that the work {he is doing for an industrial firm} has either no social usefulness or actually harmful consequences].

: Since와 when이 이끄는 부사절 사이에 있는 첫 번째 [ ]가 주절에 해당한다. 두 번째 [ ]는 believes의 목적어로 쓰인 명사절이고, 그 안의 { }는 the work를 수식하는 관계절로, 앞에 목적격 관계대명사가 생략되어 있다.

어휘풀이

- moral *a* 도덕적인
- applied *a* 응용된
- dilemma *n* 딜레마, 궁지
- consequence *n* 결과, 영향
- department *n* 부서, 부
- protest *v* 항의하다
- at the risk of ~의 위험을 무릅쓰고
- undertake *v* 착수하다, 떠맡다
- agent *n* 행위자, 요원, 대리인
- firm *n* 회사
- exaggerate *v* 과장하다
- duty *n* 의무
- misuse *n* 오용
- colleague *n* 동료
- look down upon ~을 경멸하다, ~을 경시하다

- improperly *ad* 부적절하게
- exploit *v* 이용하다, 착취하다

104 답 ④

출제 어휘 확인하기

(A) compensate	보완하다	/ prepare	준비하다
(B) purposefully	의도적으로, 목적을 갖고	/ randomly	임의로
(C) independent	독립적인	/ protective	보호하는

정답풀이

(A) 합리적인 에이전트가 설계자의 사전 지식보다 자율적으로 스스로 학습하여 지각한 것에 의존해야 하는 이유는 불완전하고 부정확한 사전 지식을 '보완하기' 위해서라고 할 수 있으므로 compensate가 적절하다. [prepare 준비하다]

(B) 에이전트에게 처음부터 완전한 자율성이 필요한 것은 아니라고 했는데, 에이전트가 경험이 거의 없고 설계자의 도움이 없다면 그 에이전트는 어떤 목적을 가지고 작동하는 것이 아니라 '임의로' 작동할 것이기 때문일 것이다. 따라서 randomly가 적절하다. [purposefully 의도적으로, 목적을 갖고]

(C) 경험이 부족하여 사전 지식에 의존하던 에이전트가 학습 능력과 약간의 초기 지식을 제공받아 환경을 충분히 경험하게 되면 사전 지식으로부터 '독립하게' 될 것이므로 independent가 적절하다. [protective 보호하는]

전문해석

에이전트가 자신이 지각한 것보다 설계자의 사전 지식에 의존하는 경우에 우리는 그 에이전트에게 자율성이 부족하다고 말한다. 합리적인 에이전트는 자율적이어야만 하는데, 그것은 불완전하거나 부정확한 사전 지식을 (A) 보완하기 위해 학습할 수 있는 것을 학습해야 한다. 예를 들어, 또 다른 먼지가 어디에서 그리고 언제 나타날지 예측하는 법을 학습하는 진공 청소 에이전트는 그렇게 하지 않는 것(에이전트)보다 더 잘할 것이다. 현실적으로는 처음부터 완전한 자율성을 거의 필요로 하지 않는데, 에이전트가 경험이 거의 없거나 전혀 없을 때 그것은 설계자가 약간의 도움을 제공하지 않는다면 (B) 임의로 작동해야 할 것이다. 따라서 진화가 동물에게 스스로 학습할 수 있을 만큼 충분히 오래 생존할 수 있도록 필요한 만큼의 타고난 반사 신경을 제공하는 것처럼, 인공 지능 에이전트에게 학습할 수 있는 능력뿐만 아니라 약간의 초기 지식을 제공하는 것이 합리적일 것이다. 환경을 충분히 경험한 후, 합리적인 에이전트의 행동은 사전 지식으로부터 사실상 (C) 독립적이 될 수 있다. 따라서 학습의 통합은 매우 다양한 환경에서 성공할 하나의 합리적인 에이전트를 설계할 수 있도록 한다.

구문풀이

6행 For example, a vacuum-cleaning agent [that learns to foresee where and when additional dirt will appear] will do better than one [that does not].

: 첫 번째 [ ]는 a vacuum-cleaning agent를, 두 번째 [ ]는 one(= a vacuum-cleaning agent)을 수식하는 관계절이다.

어휘풀이

- to the extent that ~일 경우에
- prior *a* 사전의
- autonomy *n* 자율성
- incorrect *a* 부정확한
- practical *a* 현실적인
- assistance *n* 도움, 지원
- built-in *a* 내재된, 타고난
- artificial *a* 인공의
- sufficient *a* 충분한
- rely on ~에 의존하다
- percept *n* 지각된 것, 인식 결과
- partial *a* 불완전한, 부분적인
- foresee *v* 예측하다
- complete *a* 완전한
- evolution *n* 진화
- reflex *n* 반사 능력
- initial *a* 초기의, 처음의
- incorporation *n* 통합

105 답 ⑤

출제 어휘 확인하기

① fail	~하지 않다, ~하지 못하다	↔	
② happen	일어나다	↔	
③ existence	존재	↔	
④ definite	분명한	↔	indefinite(명확하지 않은)
⑤ uncertainty	불확실성	↔	certainty(확실성)

정답풀이

⑤ 글 전체적으로 과학 법칙의 '보편성'에 대해 이야기하고 있으므로 '불확실성'이 없다면 과학이 있을 수 없다고 하는 것은 적절하지 않다. uncertainty를 universality 정도로 바꿔 써야 한다.

오답풀이

① 뒤에 이어지는 내용은 전등에 불이 들어오지 않을 경우 과학자가 할 행동을 설명하므로, 전등이 켜지지 '않는다(fails)'고 한 것은 적절하다.

② 전등이 켜지는 것은 확률의 문제가 아니라 전기 역학의 법칙에 따른 것이므로, 전등이 켜지는 것을 매번 '일어나야(happen)' 하는 일이라고 한 것은 적절하다.

③ 갈릴레오의 떨어지는 물체 법칙에는 결국 중력의 '존재'라는 근본적인 원인이 있음을 설명하는 문맥이므로 existence는 적절하다.

④ 떨어지는 물체에 대한 법칙을 이용하기 위해 끌어당기는 물체의 중력 상수를 알아야 한다고 했으며, 그러한 공식으로부터 도출되는 결과는 법칙에 의한 것이므로 확실하고 '분명한' 것으로 볼 수 있다. 따라서 definite은 적절하다.

전문해석

화학의 법칙은 모든 곳에서 똑같다. 운동의 법칙은 보편적이다. 상대성 물리학의 법칙은 상대적이지 않다. 확률의 법칙은 개연적이지 않다. 과학자가 스위치를 켰을 때 그의 책상에 있는 전등이 켜지지 ① 않으면, 그는 전기 역학의 법칙을 바꾸는 것이 아니라, 전구를 갈거나 (수력 발전이 끊긴 것인지) 나이아가라 폭포에 가서 물이 흐르는 것이 멈췄는지를 볼 것이다. 램프가 켜지는 것은 확률이 높은 것이 아니다. 그것은 예외 없이 매번 ② 일어나야 하는 일이다. 모든 과학적 법칙은 적어도 어떤 원인을 내포한다. 예를 들어, 갈릴레오의 떨어지는 물체의 법칙은, 분명히 데이터의 요약이지만, 또한 떨어지는 물체의 원인으로서 중력의 ③ 존재를 내포한다. 사실, 법칙을 사용하기 위해 우리는 끌어당기는 물체의 중력 상수를 알아야만 한다. 그리고 나서야 우리는 공식으로부터 ④ 분명한 결과를 도출할 수 있다. 요약하자면, ⑤ 불확실성(→ 보편성)이 없다면 어떤 종류의 과학도 결코 있을 수 없다.

구문풀이

11행 [Galileo's **law** of falling bodies], for instance, [although certainly a summary of the data], also **implies** the existence of gravity as the cause of falling bodies.

: 첫 번째 [ ]가 주어이며, 주어의 핵이 단수인 law이므로 단수형 동사 implies가 쓰였다. 두 번째 [ ]에서 although 다음에 it is 또는 being이 생략된 것으로 볼 수 있다.

어휘풀이

- chemistry *n* 화학
- relativity physics 상대성 물리학
- probability *n* 확률, 있음 직함
- electrodynamics *n* 전기 역학
- imply *v* 내포하다, 의미하다; 암시하다
- summary *n* 요약
- attracting body 끌어당기는 물체
- definite *a* 분명한
- to sum up 요약하자면
- universal *a* 보편적인
- relative *a* 상대적인
- go on (전등이) 켜지다
- light bulb 전구
- falling body 낙하하는 물체
- gravity *n* 중력
- derive *v* 도출하다, 이끌어 내다
- formula *n* 공식

106 답 ②

출제 어휘 ✓확인하기

① exceed	넘어서다	↔	
② reasonable	합리적인	↔	unreasonable(비합리적인)
③ blame	비난하다	↔	
④ responsible	책임이 있는	↔	irresponsible(무책임한)
⑤ hazardous	위험한	↔	safe(안전한)

정답풀이

② 자동차 충돌은 사용자 개인뿐만 아니라 시스템 전체에 초점을 둠으로써 가장 효과적으로 예방될 수 있다고 했으므로, 같은 맥락에서 공중보건을 위한 식수 위생은 수원지라는 시스템에서 이루어질 필요가 있다는 흐름이 되어야 한다. 식수를 개인이 정수하도록 하는 데 의존하는 사회는 수원지에서 정수하는 사회보다 더 높은 전염성 질병으로 고통받고 있다는 내용이 뒤에 이어지므로, 식수가 수원지에서 정수되어야 한다는 것을 알고 있는데, 모든 사람들이 식수를 마시기 전에 물을 끓이기를 기대하는 것은 '합리적'이라고 할 수 없다. reasonable을 반대 의미의 unreasonable(비합리적인) 정도로 바꿔 써야 한다.

오답풀이

① 자동차 사용자만이 아닌 시스템의 변화를 통해 충돌 사고가 예방될 수 있다고 했으며, 사고 피해자가 절대적인 측면에서 수행을 잘한 경우에는 시스템에 문제가 있는 것이므로, 시스템의 요구가 사용자 수행의 수준을 '넘어설(exceeded)' 때 사고가 발생할 수 있다는 것은 적절하다.

③ 부상을 입힐 가능성이 있는 제품이나 환경을 만들고서 사용자에게 주의하도록 경고하는 것은 불행한 일이나 사고 발생의 책임을 개인에게 돌리기 위함임을 알 수 있으므로, 불행한 일(사고)이 발생했을 때 사용자를 '비난하는(blame)' 것이 일반적이라는 것은 적절하다.

④ 콜레라균을 상수도에 들여놓고 물을 끓여 먹지 않은 사람에게 병이 난 '책임이 있다'고 주장하는 사람을 용인하지 않을 것임에도 불구하고, 도로 안전에 관한 문제를 다룰 때 비슷한 종류의 주장을 자주 사용한다는 것이므로 responsible은 적절하다.

⑤ 콜레라균을 들여놓고는 물을 끓여 먹지 않은 사람에게 병의 책임을 돌리는 것과 마찬가지로 도로 안전에 관해서도 '위험한' 도로, 차량, 운전 규칙을 설정하고는 사용자가 안전하게 행동하기를 기대하는 것을 지적하는 흐름이므로 hazardous는 적절하다.

전문해석

자동차 충돌은 개인의 수행과 그 사람이 역할을 하고 있는 시스템의 요구 사이의 일시적인 불균형의 결과이다. 그 충돌은 둘 중 하나에 변화를 줌으로써 예방될 수 있지만, 그것의 사용자만이 아닌 시스템 전체에 초점을 맞춤으로써 가장 효과적으로 예방될 수 있다. 충돌은 피해자가 실제로 절대적인 측면에서 상당히 잘 수행 중이었지만 시스템의 요구가 사용자의 현재 수행 수준을 (a) 넘어설 때 발생할 수 있다. 공중보건의 많은 분야에서 우리는 이것을 매우 잘 이해하고 있다. 우리는 식수가 수원지에서 정수되어야 한다는 것을 알고 있는데, 모든 사람들이 식수를 마시기 전에 물을 끓이기를 기대하는 것은 (b) 합리적이다(→ 비합리적이다). 자신들의 식수를 정수하는 개인들에 의존하는 그러한 사회들은 수원지에서 물을 정수하는 사회들보다 훨씬 더 높은 비율의 전염성 질병으로 고통받고 있다. 아이러니하게도, 부상을 입힐 가능성이 있는 제품이나 환경을 만들고, 사용자에게 주의하라고 경고한 다음, 불행한 일(사고)이 발생하면 사용자를 (c) 비난하는 것이 꽤 일반적이다. 우리는 도시 상수도에 콜레라균을 들여놓고 모든 시민들에게 마시기 전에 물을 끓여 달라고 요청하며, 알면서 그렇게 하지 않은 사람들이 병에 걸리는 것에 (d) 책임이 있다는 주장을 펼치는 사람을 결코 용인하지 않을 것이다. 그럼에도 불구하고, 이것은 우리 모두가 도로 안전에 관한 문제들을 다룰 때 너무 자주 사용하는 종류의 주장이다. 우리는

(e) 위험한 도로, 차량 및 운전 규칙을 설정한 다음, 도로 사용자가 이상적인 방식으로 행동함으로써 안전하기를 기대한다.

구문풀이

13행 Those societies, [which depend upon individuals to purify their own drinking water], [suffer from much **higher** rates of communicable diseases **than** those {which purify water at the source}].

: 첫 번째 [ ]는 주어인 Those societies를 부연 설명하는 관계절이다. 두 번째 [ ]는 주어에 이어지는 술어부이며, 비교급 「higher ~ than ....」이 쓰였다. { }는 those(= the societies)를 수식하는 관계절이다.

어휘풀이

- crash *n* 충돌, 추락
- alteration *n* 변화, 변경
- in absolute terms 절대적인 측면에서
- purify *v* 정수하다, 정화하다
- communicable disease 전염성 질병
- tolerate *v* 용인하다, 참다
- water supply 상수도
- hazardous *a* 위험한
- temporary *a* 일시적인
- victim *n* 피해자, 희생자
- exceed *v* 넘다, 초과하다
- reasonable *a* 합리적인
- injury *n* 부상
- germ *n* 병균
- put in place 설정하다
- vehicle *n* 차량, 탈것

03 필수 어휘

Q1 1 scarcity 2 respective 3 concrete 4 complicated
5 improper

Q2 1 ③ 2 ① 3 ①

| 107 ⑤ | 108 ⑤ | 109 ⑤ | 110 ④ | 111 ④ |

112 ⑤

Q1

1. [해석] 재고품의 부족과 예기치 않은 생산량의 감소가 주요 인구 중심지에서의 물품 부족 현상을 야기했다. [abundance 풍족, 풍부]

2. [해석] 검찰관과 피고 측 변호사 중 그 어느 누구도 자신들 각자의 입장을 약화시키는 어떤 것도 고려해야 할 의무는 없다. [respectful 존중하는]

3. [해석] 그들은 그가 자신의 아내를 죽였다고 생각하지만 구체적인 증거를 갖고 있지는 못하다. [abstract 추상적인]

4. [해석] 확인[보증] 절차는 필요 이상으로 훨씬 더 복잡했다. 불필요한 서류들이 너무 많았다. [simplistic (지나치게) 단순한, 간소한]

5. [해석] 만일 어른들이 스스로 진정으로 놀 수 있도록 허락한다면, 아마도 노는 것에 있어서 그들에게 가장 큰 장애물은 자신이 어리석거나 부적절하거나 혹은 바보같이 보일 것이라는 걱정일 것이다. [proper 적절한, 바람직한]

Q2

1. [해석] 요리사는 라이브 쿠킹쇼에서 과일 조각 기술을 보여 줄 것이다.
① 조직하다 ② 요구하다

2. [해석] 우리는 (투자를) 약속하기 전에 이 투자의 장기적인 전망을 고려해야 한다.
② 의견 ③ 잠재력

3. [해석] 여러분이 더 나은 작가가 되려면 창의력과 상상력을 키워야 한다.
② 평가하다 ③ 다양화하다

107 답 ⑤

출제 어휘 확인하기

① build	만들다	↔	
② cause	일으키다, 야기하다	↔	
③ prone	~하기 쉬운	↔	
④ helpful	도움이 되는	↔	
⑤ sufficient	충분한	↔	insufficient(불충분한)

정답풀이

⑤ 새롭거나 드문 위협들은 이용할 수 있는 역사적인 데이터가 '거의 없기' 때문에 그 위험을 평가하는 것이 인간의 추론만으로는 어렵고 인과관계를 정리하고 서로 다른 영역 주변의 불확실성의 정도를 나타낼 수 있는 인공 지능 기술이 유용할 수 있다는 맥락이다. 따라서 sufficient(충분한)는 적절하지 않고 little 정도로 바꿔 써야 한다.

오답풀이

① 어떤 일이 왜 일어나는지를 설명하는 능력은 인과적 모형을 '만드는' 능력이라고 할 수 있으므로 build는 적절하다.

② 의사는 어떤 치료가 왜 효과가 있는지 그 인과관계를 설명할 수 있다는 맥락이므로 치료가 '일으키는(causes)' 변화를 설명할 수 있다고 한 것은 적절하다.

③ 인간의 인과적 추론 능력이 인공 지능 시스템보다 뛰어나다는 내용 뒤에 역접의 연결어 However로 이어지고 있다. 따라서 인과관계의 문제가 복잡해지면 인간의 추론은 혼동하고 실수를 '하기 쉽다(prone)'고 그 결점을 언급하는 흐름은 적절하다.

④ 인간의 의사 결정을 지원하기 위한 인공 지능 기술이 탐구되고 있다는 내용이 뒤에 나오므로, 체계화된 인공 지능 기반 도구로 인간의 추론을 지원하는 것이 '도움이 된다(helpful)'는 것은 문맥상 적절하다.

전문해석

매우 간단한 알고리즘을 넘어서면서 일부 인공 지능 기반의 도구들은 복잡한 영역에서 더 나은 인과적 추론과 확률적 추론을 지원할 가능성을 보인다. 인간은 인공 지능 시스템에 여전히 많이 부족한, 세상의 인과적 모형을 ① 만드는, 즉 일들이 '왜' 일어나는지를 설명하는 타고난 능력을 가지고 있다. 예를 들어, 의사는 환자에게 어떤 치료가 왜 효과가 있는지, 그것이 몸에 ② 일으키는 변화를 언급하면서 설명할 수 있는 반면, 현대의 기계 학습 시스템은 이 치료를 받는 환자들이 평균적으로 더 나아지는 경향이 있다고 여러분에게 말해 줄 수 있을 뿐이다. 하지만 정책 개입이 사회 전반에 미치는 영향을 평가하는 경우처럼, 인과관계의 문제가 충분히 복잡해지면 인간의 추론은 혼동하고 실수하기 ③ 쉽기로 여전히 악명 높다. 이런 경우에는 더 체계화된 인공 지능 기반 도구로 인간의 추론을 지원하는 것이 ④ 도움이 될 수 있다. 연구자들은 더 정확한 위험 평가를 가능하게 하는 것과 같은 의사 결정 지원을 위해 사건 간의 인과관계를 정리하고 서로 다른 영역 주변의 불확실성의 정도를 나타내기 위해 사용될 수 있는 인공 지능 기술인 Bayesian Networks 사용을 탐구해 오고 있다. 이것들은 테러리스트 공격과 새로운 생태 재난의 위험과 같은, 이용할 수 있는 역사적 데이터가 ⑤ 충분한(→ 거의 없는) 새롭거나 드문 위협들의 위험을 평가하는 데 특히 유용할 수 있다.

구문풀이

[18행] Researchers have been exploring the use of Bayesian Networks—an AI technology [that can be used {to map out the causal relationships between events}, and {to represent degrees of uncertainty around different areas}]—for decision support, such as to enable more accurate risk assessment.

: [ ]는 an AI technology를 수식하는 관계절이며, and로 연결된 두 개의 { }는 목적을 나타내는 to부정사구이다.

어휘풀이

- hold out the promise of ~의 가능성을 보이다
- support *v* 지원하다
- causal *a* 인과관계의
- probabilistic *a* 확률적인
- reasoning *n* 추론
- domain *n* 영역
- treatment *n* 치료
- work *v* 효과가 있다
- refer to ~을 언급하다
- on average 평균적으로
- prone to ~하기 쉬운
- confusion *n* 혼동
- when it comes to ~하는 경우, ~에 관해서라면
- assess *v* 평가하다
- policy intervention 정책 개입
- structured *a* 체계화된
- map out ~을 정리하다
- represent *v* 나타내다
- accurate *a* 정확한
- risk assessment 위험 평가
- novel *a* 새로운
- ecological *a* 생태상의
- disaster *n* 재난

108 답 ⑤

①	qualification	자격	↔
②	prevent	막다	↔
③	differentiate	구별하다	↔
④	challenge	도전하다	↔
⑤	diminish	줄이다	↔ amplify(증폭시키다), increase(늘리다)

정답풀이

⑤ 누구나 인터넷상에서 의견을 말할 수 있어서 잘못된 정보가 정보로 퍼지고 그것들을 구별하기가 쉽지 않은데, 연구에 일생을 보내는 과학자가 경험이 거의 없는 사람들에게 즉석으로 도전을 받고 대중이 과학자와 도전자를 똑같이 신뢰하게 되면 과학자의 좌절감은 '줄어드는' 것이 아니라 '커질' 것이다. 따라서 diminished(줄이다)를 amplified(증폭시키다) 정도로 바꿔 써야 한다.

오답풀이

① 인터넷상에서는 원하기만 하면 누구나 어떤 주제에 대해서라도 의견을 말할 수 있다는 것은 자신의 '자격'과 상관없이 그렇게 할 수 있다는 것이므로 qualifications는 적절하다.

② 인터넷상에서는 누구나 어떤 주제에 대해서라도 의견을 말할 수 있다고 했으므로, 유치원 교사나 의사가 비전문적인 정보를 제공하는 것을 '막을(preventing)' 규정이 없다는 것은 적절하다.

③ 잘못된 정보가 정보로 퍼지면 진짜 정보와 잘못된 정보를 '구별하는' 것이 어려울 것이므로 differentiate는 적절하다.

④ 인터넷상에 비전문가들의 잘못된 정보가 정보로 퍼지고 있는데, 이는 특정 주제에 대해 일생 동안 연구해 온 과학자들이 인터넷상의 비전문가들에게 '도전을 받는(challenged)' 상황이라고 할 수 있다.

전문해석

현대 기술의 경이로움이 사람들에게 우리 조상들은 꿈에도 생각해 본 적이 없을 만큼의 기회를 제공했지만, 늘 그렇듯이 좋은 점은 부정적인 면에 의해 약화된다. 그러한 부정적인 면 중 하나는 그렇게 하기로 선택한 사람은 누구나 자신의 ① 자격에 상관없이 인터넷이라는 가상의 확성기를 집어 들고 무한히 많은 주제 중 어느 것에 대해서라도 의견을 말할 수 있다는 것이다. 결국, 인터넷에는 유치원 교사가 의학적인 조언을 제공하거나 의사가 여러분의 집에 안전하게 구조적인 변화를 줄 수 있는 방법을 제안하는 것을 ② 막는 규정이 없다. 결과적으로, 잘못된 정보가 정보로 퍼지게 되고, 그 둘을 ③ 구별하는 것이 항상 쉽지만은 않다. 이것은 과학자에게 특히 좌절감을 줄 수 있는데, 그들은 자기 주변 세상의 복잡성을 이해하는 방법을 배우느라 일생을 보내지만, 결국 그들의 연구는 그 주제에 대한 경험이 분 단위로 측정될 수 있는 사람들에게 즉석으로 ④ 도전을 받게 된다. 그러면 일반 대중들의 눈에는 과학자와 도전자 둘 다 동등한 신뢰성을 부여받는다는 사실에 의해 이 좌절감은 ⑤ 줄어든다(→ 증폭된다).

구문풀이

14행 This can be particularly frustrating for scientists, [who spend their lives learning {how to understand the intricacies of the world around them}, {only to have their work summarily challenged by people <whose experience with the topic can be measured in minutes>}].

: [ ]는 scientists를 부연 설명하는 관계절이고, 그 안의 첫 번째 { }는 learning의 목적어로 쓰인 「의문사+to부정사」이다. 두 번째 { }는 결과의 의미를 나타내는 to부정사구이고, < >는 people을 수식하는 관계절이다.

어휘풀이

- beyond the wildest dreams 꿈에도 생각해 본 적이 없을 만큼

- ancestor *n* 조상
- downside *n* 부정적인 면
- megaphone *n* 확성기
- regardless of ~에 상관없이
- differentiate *v* 구별하다
- summarily *ad* 즉석으로, 즉결로
- as usual 늘 그렇듯이
- virtual *a* 가상의
- infinite *a* 무한한
- qualification *n* 자격
- frustrate *v* 좌절감을 주다
- credibility *n* 신뢰성

109 답 ⑤

(A)	huge	거대한, 엄청난 / small	작은
(B)	contradict	모순되다 / parallel	유사하다
(C)	gloomy	암울한 / positive	긍정적인

정답풀이

(A) 앞에서 창의성에 대한 전통적 관점은 재능 있는 개인에 초점을 맞추고 묘사한다고 했고, 뒤에서 환경의 역할에 대한 생각을 반박하며 환경의 중요한 역할을 설명하고 있다. 따라서 환경은 '작은(small)' 역할을 한다고 생각한다는 것이 적절하다. [huge 거대한, 엄청난]

(B) 앞에서는 창의성이 사람들이 환경에서 마주치는 경험과 구성 요소들에서 생겨난다고 했고, 뒤에서는 어떤 사업이 만들어지는가를 결정하는 데 환경이 중요한 역할을 한다는 것을 보여 주었다고 하므로, 결국 창의성과 환경의 관계가 사업 연구와 환경의 관계와 '유사한(parallel)' 것처럼 보인다는 것이 적절하다. [contradict 모순되다]

(C) 외국 기업가들이 의료 제품 회사를 설립하기 위해 미국으로 온 것은 앞서 언급된 것처럼 의료 혁신을 상업화하기 위한 환경이 좋았기 때문일 것이므로 환경이 너무도 '긍정적(positive)'이라는 것이 적절하다. [gloomy 암울한]

전문해석

창의성에 대한 우리의 전통적인 관점은 문제를 골똘히 생각하고 창의적인 아이디어와 통찰력을 만들어 내는 재능 있는 개인에 초점을 맞추고 묘사한다. 우리는 환경이 (A) 작은 역할을 한다고 생각한다. 하지만 Yale 대학교의 Jonathan Feinstein 교수는 이를 반박한다. 그의 책 <The Nature of Creative Development>에서, Feinstein은, 창의성은 개인이 세상에 참여하는 것에서 비롯된다고 주장한다. 창의성은 사람들이 환경에서 마주치는 경험과 구성 요소들에서 생겨난다. 이 견해는 사업 연구와 (B) 유사한 것처럼 보인다. Michael Porter의 책, <The Competitive Advantage of Nation>은 국제적으로 경쟁력 있는 산업에 대한 연구에 있어서 획기적인 것이었다. 그것은 어떤 사업이 만들어지는가를 결정하는 데 환경이 아주 중요한 역할을 한다는 것을 보여 주었다. 예를 들어, 미국은 자국을 의료 혁신을 상업화하기 위한 훌륭한 환경으로 만드는 많은 특성을 가지고 있다. 사실, 이러한 사업들을 위한 환경이 너무도 (C) 긍정적이어서 많은 외국 기업가들이 그들의 의료 제품 회사를 시작하기 위해 미국으로 왔다.

구문풀이

16행 For example, the United States has many characteristics [that make **it** an excellent environment for commercializing medical innovations].

: [ ]는 many characteristics를 수식하는 관계절이며, 「make+목적어(it)+목적격보어(an excellent ~ innovations)」 구조가 쓰였다. 이때 it은 the United States를 가리킨다.

18행 In fact, **so** positive is the environment for these businesses **that** many foreign entrepreneurs have come to the United States to start their medical product companies.

: 「so+형용사+that ...(너무 ~해서 …하다)」 구문에서 「so+형용사」인 so positive가

문두로 나가 주어(the environment ~ businesses)와 동사(is)가 도치된 형태이다.

어휘풀이

- conventional *a* 전통적인
- puzzle over ~을 골똘히 생각하다
- insight *n* 통찰력
- engagement *n* 참여, 가담
- landmark *n* 획기적인 것[사건]
- commercialize *v* 상업화하다, 상품화하다
- innovation *n* 혁신, 혁신적인 생각
- depict *v* 묘사하다
- generate *v* 생성하다
- dispute *v* 반박하다
- encounter *v* 만나다, 마주치다
- crucial *a* 결정적인, 아주 중요
- entrepreneur *n* 기업가

110 답 ④

출제 어휘 확인하기

① perceive	인식하다	↔
② fuel	연료	↔
③ self-understanding	자기이해	↔
④ sensible	의식하고 있는	↔ insensible(의식하지 못하는)
⑤ anticipate	예측하다	↔

정답풀이

④ 기술 발전으로 인한 변화에 걸쳐 있는 세대는 변화의 도래를 인지할 수 있다고 했으므로, but 뒤에 이어지는 내용은 그와 반대로 애초에 변화된 체계 속에서 태어난 사람은 그 변화를 '의식하지 못한다'는 흐름이 되어야 한다. 따라서 sensible(의식하고 있는)은 적절하지 않으며 반대 의미의 insensible 정도로 바꿔 써야 한다.

오답풀이

① 기술이 그것의 작동 환경 전체를 변화시킨다고 했으므로 같은 문맥에서 우리가 세상을 '인식하는(perceive)' 방식을 변화시킨다는 것은 적절하다.
② 산업화된 문화에서 태어난 사람은 자신을 기계에 비유할 수 있다고 했으므로 음식이 '연료(fuel)'로 작용한다는 것은 적절하다.
③ 태어난 환경과 문화에 따라 달라지는 '자기이해' 방식을 설명하는 문맥이므로 self-understanding은 적절하다.
⑤ 전환에 걸쳐 있는 세대는 그 변화를 인지할 수 있다고 했으므로, 컴퓨터를 사는 변화가 생길 때 부모가 가정에 일어날 변화를 '예측할(anticipate)' 수 있다는 것은 적절하다.

전문해석

기술은 그것이 작동하고 있는 전체 환경을 변화시킨다. 그것은 우리가 세상을 ① 인식하는 방식을 변화시킨다. 그것은 우리가 스스로를 이해하는 방식을 변화시킨다. 출판 문화에서 태어난 사람은 스스로를 책으로 생각할 가능성이 있다. 면접에서 아마 그 사람은 스스로를 '펼쳐진 책'으로 언급할 것이다. 하지만 산업화된 문화에서 태어난 사람은 스스로를 기계로 생각할 가능성이 있는데, 기계를 계속 작동시키기 위한 ② 연료로서 음식을 섭취한다. ③ 자기이해에 관한 그런 변화는 흔히 원상태로 돌릴 수 없다. 게다가, 우리는 종종 이런 종류의 체계적 변화를 의식하지 못한다. 이런 기술적 전환에 걸쳐 있는 세대는 그런 변화가 일어나고 있는 것을 인지할지도 모르지만, 그 변화 속에 태어난 사람들은 그것을 ④ 의식한다(→ 의식하지 못한다). 부모는 그들이 처음 컴퓨터를 살 때 그들의 가정에 일어날 변화의 일부를 ⑤ 예측할 수 있지만, 그들의 자녀는 컴퓨터가 있는 가정에서 태어난다. 그들은 다른 방식의 삶을 알지 못한다.

구문풀이

6행 But a person [born into an industrialized culture] would likely **think of** himself **as** a machine, [consuming food as fuel to keep the machine running].

: 첫 번째 [ ]는 a person을 수식하는 과거분사구이다. 「think of *A* as *B*」는 '*A*를 *B*로 생각하다'의 의미이다. 두 번째 [ ]는 a person을 의미상의 주어로 하는 분사구문이다.

어휘풀이

- operate *v* 작동하다
- print culture 출판 문화
- industrialized *a* 산업화된
- undo *v* 원상태로 돌리다
- span *v* ~에 걸치다, ~에 미치다
- recognize *v* 인식하다
- perceive *v* 인식하다, 인지하다
- refer to *A* as *B A*를 *B*라고 지칭하다
- consume *v* 섭취하다, 소비하다
- generation *n* 세대
- transformation *n* 전환, 변화
- anticipate *v* 예측하다, 기대하다

111 답 ④

출제 어휘 확인하기

① facilitate	촉진하다	↔
② preoccupation	몰두	↔
③ address	해결하다	↔
④ increase	증가시키다	↔ decrease(감소시키다)
⑤ eliminate	없애다	↔

정답풀이

④ 글의 흐름으로 보아 스트레스의 부정적인 효과에 대한 과도한 걱정이 스트레스를 성장에 활용할 수 있는 방법에 대한 이해를 '증가시켰다(increased)'고 하는 것은 적절하지 않으며 prevented(방해하다) 정도로 바꿔 써야 한다.

오답풀이

① 직장에서의 스트레스를 해로운 경험으로 본다고 했으므로, 스트레스가 성장, 발전, 성과를 '촉진하는(facilitate)' 데 사용될 수 있음을 인식하지 못한다는 것은 적절하다.
② 연구자들은 스트레스를 거의 부정적으로만 보았다는 흐름이므로 스트레스 요인의 주요 결과로서 기력 소진(번아웃)에 '몰두(preoccupation)'했다고 하는 것은 적절하다.
③ 문맥상 직원들은 그들이 직면하는 많은 요구를 '해결하는(addressing)' 적극적인 존재보다는 스트레스를 주는 상황을 수동적으로 받는 존재로 여겨진다는 것은 적절하다.
⑤ 스트레스가 긍정적으로 활용될 수 있으므로, 업무의 요구 사항을 완전히 '없애는(eliminating)' 것이 직원들이 잠재력을 최대한 발휘하는 데 부정적인 영향을 미칠 수 있다고 하는 것은 적절하다.

전문해석

직장에서의 요구 사항을 처리하는 것에 대한 많은 접근 방식은 스트레스를 어떤 대가를 치르더라도 피해야 할 본질적으로 해로운 경험으로 보며, 스트레스가 개인적인 성장, 전문적 발전 그리고 더 높은 수준의 성과를 ① 촉진하는 데 어떻게 사용될 수 있는지를 인식하지 못한다. 또한 연구자들은 힘든 근로조건에 대한 다른 가능한 반응을 조사하지 않고, 스트레스를 주는 일의 주요 결과로서 기력 소진(번아웃)에 ② 몰두함을 보여 주었다. 직원들은 그들이 직면하는 많은 요구를 주도적으로 ③ 해결할 수 있는, 업무 환경의 능동적인 건설자라기보다는 스트레스를 주는 상황을 수동적으로 받는 사람으로 종종 여겨진다. 우리는 직장에서 받는 스트레스의 부정적인 효과에 대한 과도한 걱정이 스트레스가 어떻게 성장을 위해 활용될 수 있는지에 대한 이해를 ④ 증가시켰다(→ 방해했다)고 주장한다. 업무의 요구 사항을 완전히 ⑤ 없애는 것은 직원들이 자신의 잠재력을 최대한 발휘하는 데 부정적인 영향을 미칠 수 있다.

구문풀이

1행 [Many approaches to dealing with demands at work] **view** stress as an inherently toxic experience [that should be avoided at all costs], and **do not recognize** [how stress might be used to facilitate personal growth, professional development, and higher levels of performance].

: 첫 번째 [ ]는 문장의 주어이고, 동사는 병렬구조로 연결된 view와 do not recognize 이다. 두 번째 [ ]는 an inherently toxic experience를 수식하는 관계절이고, 세 번째 [ ]는 recognize의 목적어로 쓰인 명사절이다.

어휘풀이

- approach *n* 접근법
- toxic *a* 해로운, 유독한, 독성의
- preoccupation *n* 심취, 몰두, 집착
- outcome *n* 결과
- employee *n* 직원, 피고용인
- recipient *n* 수용자, 받는 사람
- proactively *ad* 주도적으로, 적극적으로
- encounter *v* 만나다, 직면하다
- eliminate *v* 없애다, 제거하다
- inherently *ad* 본질적으로
- facilitate *v* 촉진하다
- burnout *n* 기력 소진, 번아웃 (증후군)
- examine *v* 조사하다
- passive *a* 수동적인
- constructor *n* 건설자
- address *v* 해결하다, 다루다
- hyper-concern *n* 과도한 걱정
- potential *n* 잠재력

112 답 ⑤

출제 어휘 확인하기

① different	다른	↔	same(같은)
② where	어디에서	↔	
③ easier	더 쉬운	↔	harder(더 어려운)
④ unconvinced	납득[확신]하지 못하는	↔	convinced(납득[확신]하는)
⑤ challenging	어려운	↔	

정답풀이

⑤ 앞에서 맥락 정보는 내용보다 잊어버리기가 더 쉽고 이는 기억 착각의 근원이 된다고 했다. 따라서 지식의 출처, 즉 맥락 정보를 기억하지 못하게 되면 학교에서 배운 것, 즉 내용을 기억하지 못한다고 결론을 내리기 '쉬울' 것이므로, challenging(어려운)을 easy 정도로 바꿔 써야 한다.

오답풀이

① 뒤에서 맥락을 기억하지 않고 내용을 기억해 두는 것이 지극히 가능하다고 했으므로, 맥락은 그 내용에 대한 기억과는 '다른(different)' 기억 처리 과정으로 다루어짐을 유추할 수 있다.

② 맥락을 잊어버린다는 것은 '어디에서' 내용을 들었는지 기억할 수 없는 것이므로 where는 적절하다.

③ 계속해서 내용은 기억하지만 맥락을 잊어버리는 경우에 대해 이야기하는 흐름이므로, 맥락 정보가 흔히 내용보다 잊어버리기 '더 쉽다(easier)'고 하는 것은 적절하다.

④ 사람들은 별로 신뢰할 수 없는 사람이 쓴 설득력 있는 주장에 대해 처음에는 '납득하지 못하다가' 결국에는 그 주장의 방향으로 태도가 변화한다는 흐름이므로 unconvinced는 적절하다.

전문해석

우리가 학교에서 배운 것의 대부분을 잊어버린다고 생각하는 한 가지 이유는 우리가 실제로 기억하는 것을 과소평가하기 때문이다. 다른 때에 우리는 우리가 어떤 것을 기억한다는 것을 알지만, 우리는 그것을 학교에서 배웠다는 것을 인식하지 못한다. 여러분이 무언가를 어디에서 언제 배웠는지를 아는 것은 보통 '맥락 정보'라고 불리는데, 맥락은 그 내용에 대한 기억과는 (a) 다른 기억 처리 과정으로 다루어진다. 따라서 맥락을 기억하지 않고 내용을 기억해 두는 것이 지극히 가능하다.

예를 들어, 만약 누군가가 한 영화에 대해 언급하고 여러분은 그것이 끔찍하다고 들었지만 그것을 (b) 어디에서 들었는지 기억할 수 없다고 마음속으로 생각한다면, 그 내용은 기억하고 있지만 맥락은 잃어버린 것이다. 맥락 정보는 흔히 내용보다 잊어

버리기 (c) 더 쉬우며, 그것은 다양한 기억 착각의 근원이다. 예를 들어, 만약 어떤 설득력 있는 주장이 별로 신뢰할 수 없는 사람(예를 들면, 그 주제에 대한 확실한 금전상의 관심을 가진 사람)이 쓴 것이라면, 사람들은 그 주장에 대해 (d) 납득하지 못한다. 하지만 결국에 독자의 태도는 대체로 그 설득력 있는 주장의 방향으로 변화한다. 왜일까? 독자는 그 주장의 내용은 기억하지만, 그 출처, 즉 신뢰할 수 없는 사람은 잊어버릴 가능성이 크기 때문이다. 만약 지식의 출처를 기억하는 것이 어렵다면, 여러분이 학교에서 배운 것을 많이 기억하지 못한다고 결론을 내리기가 (e) 어려울 (→ 쉬울) 것임을 알 수 있다.

구문풀이

11행 For example, if someone mentions a movie and you think to yourself [that you heard {it was terrible} but can't remember {where you heard that}], you're recalling the content, but you've lost the context.

: [ ]는 think의, 그 안의 첫 번째 { }는 heard의, 두 번째 { }는 remember의 목적어로 쓰인 명사절이다.

24행 If remembering the source of knowledge is difficult, you can see [**how it** would be easy {to conclude <you don't remember much from school>}].

: [ ]는 see의 목적어로 쓰인 명사절로, 여기서 how는 명사절을 이끄는 접속사로 쓰였다. 그 안에서 it은 형식상의 주어이고, { }가 내용상의 주어이다. < >는 to conclude의 목적어로 쓰인 명사절이다.

어휘풀이

- underestimate *v* 과소평가하다
- context *n* 맥락, 상황
- retain *v* 기억해 두다, 잊지 않다, 보유하다
- mention *v* 언급하다
- source *n* 근원, 출처
- unconvinced *a* 납득하지 못하는, 확신하지 못하는
- persuasive *a* 설득력 있는
- credible *a* 신뢰할 수 있는
- on average 대체로, 평균적으로
- recognize *v* 인식하다
- handle *v* 다루다
- recall *v* 기억하다, 회상하다
- argument *n* 주장
- financial *a* 금전상의, 재정적인
- conclude *v* 결론을 내리다

Q1 1 horizontal, vertical 2 inferior 3 irritates
4 remain 5 exceeding

Q2 1 ① 2 ② 3 ②

113 ③   114 ③   115 ①   116 ⑤   117 ④

118 ③

Q1

1. [해석] 마루는 수평이고, 벽은 수직이다. [vertical 수직의, horizontal 수평의]

2. [해석] 사람들은 자신에 대해 더 낫다고 느끼기 위해 때때로 아래로 향하는 사회적 비교를 하는데, 즉 열등하거나 생활이 더 어려운 다른 사람들과 자신을 비교한다. [superior 우월한, 우수한]

3. [해석] 땀 속의 염분이 눈을 조금 따갑게 하여 자극하기 때문에 땀을 안 나게 하는 것이 좋다. [irrigate 물을 대다, 관개하다]

4. [해석] 더 흔한 경우에, 서식지 전체가 완전히 사라지는 것이 아니라, 그 대신에 작은 면적만 남을 때까지 점진적으로 줄어든다. [lack 부족하다, 없다]

5. [해석] 그 호수가 겪은 심한 기후 변화와 담수의 유입량을 초과한 계속된 증발은 호수를 이전 크기의 20분의 1로 축소시켰다. [depress 하락시키다]

Q2

1. [해석] 돈은 목적에 대한 수단에 불과하다. 하지만 아주 흔히 우리는 수단을 목적과 혼동하여 돈(수단)을 위해서 행복(목적)을 희생한다.
② 촉진하다 ③ 잘못 생각하다

2. [해석] 우리가 사람과 기계에 관해 협업하는 시스템으로서 생각하지 않고 자동화될 수 있는 과업이면 어떤 것이든 기계에게 할당하고 나머지는 사람에게 남겨 둘 때 어려움이 발생한다.
① 제한하다 ③ 복잡하게 하다

3. [해석] 일단 인종적, 민족적 차별이 제거되고 사람들이 화합하면, 그들은 다양한 경험과 문화적 시각에도 불구하고 서로 함께 살고 일하고 노는 법을 배워야 한다.
① 무시하다 ③ 강화하다

113 답 ③

출제 어휘 | 확인하기

①	reduce	감소시키다	↔	increase(증가시키다)
②	essential	필수적인	↔	inessential(꼭 필요한 것은 아닌)
③	benefit	이득	↔	disadvantage(불리, 손해)
④	fewer	더 적은	↔	more(더 많은)
⑤	contribution	공헌	↔	

정답풀이

③ 유기농 경작 방식의 대규모 채택에는 생산비 증가라는 단점이 있다는 내용 다음에, 화학 물질이 사용될 수 없으면 잡초 방제가 어렵거나 많은 수작업을 요구할 수 있다는 추가적인 단점이 이어지고 있다. 따라서 거름 또는 친환경적인 거름 작물로서 콩과 작물을 광범위하게 사용하는 것에 '이득(benefits)'이 있다는 것은 적절하지 않으며 constraints(제약) 정도로 바꿔 써야 한다.

오답풀이

① 유기농 방식이 생물권에 해를 덜 끼친다고 시사되어 왔다는 장점을 언급하는 앞 내용과 역접(however)으로 연결되므로 유기농 방식의 단점을 언급하는 흐름이 되어야 한다. 따라서 주요 작물의 산출량을 '감소시킨다(reduce)'는 것은 적절하다.

② 유기농 방식을 대규모로 채택할 경우 생산비가 증가하는 이유를 밝히는 문장이다. 따라서 무기질 질소 공급이 비콩과 식물의 생산성 유지에 '필수적(essential)'인데, 질소성 물질의 유기적 공급이 무기 질소 비료보다 제한적이고 더 비싸기 때문이라는 것은 적절하다.

④ 사회가 더 부유해지면 손으로 하는 일을 하려는 사람의 수가 줄어들 것이므로, 기꺼이 하려는 사람이 '더 적을(fewer)' 것이라는 흐름은 적절하다.

⑤ 이전까지 유기농 방식의 단점을 서술한 이후 역접(however)으로 전환되고 있으므로, 장점이 있다는 흐름이 되는 것이 자연스럽다. 따라서 유기농 경작 방식이 농촌 생태계의 지속 가능성에 중요한 '공헌(contributions)'을 할 수 있다는 것은 적절하다.

전문해석

오직 천연물만 투입물로 사용될 수 있는 방식이라고 정의되는 '유기농' 방식은 생물권에 해를 덜 끼친다고 시사되어 왔다. 하지만 '유기농' 경작 방식의 대규모 채택은 많은 주요 작물의 산출량을 ① 감소시키며 생산비를 증가시킨다. 무기질 질소 공급은 콩이 아닌 많은 작물 종의 생산성을 중상 수준으로 유지하는 데 ② 필수적인데, 그것은 질소성 물질의 유기적 공급이 흔히 무기 질소 비료보다 제한적이거나 더 비싸기 때문이다. 더구나, 거름 또는 '친환경적인 거름' 작물로서 콩과 식물의 광범위한 사용에는 ③ 이득(→ 제약)이 있다. 많은 경우, 화학 물질이 사용될 수 없으면 잡초 방제가 매우 어렵거나 많은 수작업을 요구할 수 있는데, 사회가 더 부유해지면서 이 작업을 기꺼이 하려는 사람이 ④ 더 적을 것이다. 그렇지만 돌려짓기의 현명한 사용 및 경작과 축산 사업의 특정한 조합과 같은 '유기농' 경작에서 쓰이는 몇몇 방식들은 농촌 생태계의 지속 가능성에 중요한 ⑤ 공헌을 할 수 있다.

구문풀이

1행 It has been suggested [that "organic" methods, defined as those {in which only natural products can be used as inputs}, would be less damaging to the biosphere].

: It은 형식상의 주어이고, [ ]가 내용상의 주어이다. { }는 those(= methods)를 수식하는 관계절이다.

어휘풀이

- organic *a* 유기(농)의, 화학 비료를 쓰지 않는
- natural product 천연물
- biosphere *n* 생물권
- adoption *n* 채택
- crop *n* 작물 *v* 경작하다
- nitrogen *n* 질소
- extensive *a* 광범위한
- hand labor 손으로 하는 일
- crop rotation 돌려짓기
- livestock *n* 축산, 가축
- contribution *n* 공헌
- rural *a* 농촌의, 시골의
- input *n* 투입(물)
- large-scale *a* 대규모의
- yield *n* 산출량, 수확물 *v* 산출하다
- inorganic *a* 무기질의
- moderate *a* 중간의, 적당한
- weed control 잡초 방제
- sensible *a* 현명한, 분별 있는
- combination *n* 조합, 결합
- enterprise *n* 사업
- sustainability *n* 지속성, 지속 가능성
- ecosystem *n* 생태계

114 답 ③

출제 어휘 확인하기

①	accurate	정확한	↔	inaccurate(부정확한)
②	artificial	인위적인	↔	natural(자연적인)
③	respect	중요시하다	↔	neglect(간과하다)
④	cheer	응원하다	↔	
⑤	hollow	공허한	↔	

정답풀이

③ 이어지는 문장에서 영웅의 능력에 이바지하는 사람들의 예를 들며 그들이 하는 역할의 중요성을 보지 못할 수도 있다고 했다. 따라서 리더십이 그저 영웅적인 사람의 모습을 취한다고 믿으면 영웅의 능력에 이바지하는 그러한 여러 행동들을 '중요시할' 수 있다고 하는 것은 어색하다. respect를 반대 의미인 neglect(간과하다) 정도로 바꿔 써야 한다.

오답풀이

① 사물이 그것의 정상적인 환경에서 동떨어져 있을 때 그 본질이 크게 변한다면, 실험실 환경 안에서 조사하는 것으로는 사물의 본질에 대해 '정확히' 설명할 수 없을 것이므로 accurate의 쓰임은 적절하다.

② 사물이 자연스럽게 발생하는 환경으로부터 동떨어진 실험실 환경 같은 곳은 '인위적인' 영역이므로 artificial은 적절하다.

④ 영웅의 능력에 이바지하는 행동 중 하나에 해당하므로 옆에서 '응원한다(cheering)'는 표현은 적절하다.

⑤ 앞에서 영웅의 능력에 이바지하는 사람들의 역할이 중요함을 언급했으므로, 영웅을 지원하는 군대가 없다면 영웅들 편에 서야 한다는 그 어떤 주장도 '공허할(hollow)' 것임을 알 수 있다.

전문해석

사물의 본질이 그것(사물)이 자연스럽게 발생하는 환경으로부터 동떨어져 있을 때 그것(사물의 본질)이 근본적으로 변하는 그러한 것이라면, 여러분은 실험실 환경 안에서 그것(사물)을 조사하는 것으로 그것(사물)에 대한 ① 정확한 설명을 찾아내지 못할 것이다. 만약 그것이 그러한 ② 인위적인 영역 안에서 작동하는 것을 보는 것에만 익숙하다면, 여러분은 그것이 그것의 정상적인 상황에서 작동하고 있을 때 그것을 인식조차 못할 수도 있다. 사실, 그러한 환경에서 그것을 발견한다고 해도 여러분은 그것이 다른 것이라고 생각할지도 모른다. 마찬가지로, 만약 리더십이 그저 은유적으로 쓰인 백마를 타고 돌진하여 궁지에서 벗어나게 하는 영웅적인 사람의 모습을 취한다고 믿는다면, 여러분은 그곳에 있도록 하는 그들의 능력에 이바지하는 많은 행동들을 ③ 중요시할(→ 간과할) 수도 있다. 말을 돌보는 마부, 위기에 주의를 기울이게 하는 전령 혹은 옆에서 ④ 응원하는 사람들이 하는 역할의 중요성을 못 볼 수도 있다. 이 영웅들의 편에 서야 한다는 그 어떤 주장도 그들을 지원하는 군대가 없으면 상당히 ⑤ 공허할 것이라는 사실을 깨닫지 못할 수도 있다.

구문풀이

1행 If the nature of a thing is such [that {when removed from the environment <in which it naturally occurs>} it alters radically], you will not glean an accurate account of it by examining it within laboratory conditions.

: [ ]는 such와 동격 관계를 이루는 명사절이다. { }는 when이 이끄는 부사절이고, 그 안의 < >는 the environment를 수식하는 관계절이다.

9행 Similarly, if you believe [that leadership only takes the form of heroic men {metaphorically charging in on white horses} to save the day], you may neglect the many acts [which contribute to their ability to be there].

: 첫 번째 [ ]는 believe의 목적어로 쓰인 명사절이며, 그 안의 { }는 heroic men을 수

식하는 현재분사구이다. 두 번째 [ ]는 the many acts를 수식하는 관계절이다.

어휘풀이

- alter *v* 변하다, 변경하다
- accurate *a* 정확한
- laboratory *n* 실험실
- artificial *a* 인위적인, 인공적인
- spot *v* 발견하다
- charge in 돌진하다
- contribute to ~에 이바지하다[기여하다]
- messenger *n* 전령, 사자(使者)
- radically *ad* 근본적으로, 급진적으로
- account *n* 설명, 기술
- accustomed *a* 익숙한
- arena *n* 영역; 경기장
- metaphorically *ad* 은유적으로
- save the day 궁지에서 벗어나다
- groom *n* 마부, 신랑
- troop *n* 군대

115 답 ①

출제 어휘 확인하기

(A)	worthless	쓸모없는	/ worthwhile	가치 있는
(B)	inflame	자극하다	/ soothe	달래다, 진정시키다
(C)	utilize	활용하다	/ neglect	무시하다

정답풀이

(A) 뒤 문장에서 학계를 넘어서 밖으로 알리는 것이 좋다고 말하고 있으므로, 캐비닛에 잠가 두고 있는 연구 결과는 '쓸모없다(worthless)'는 것이 적절하다. [worthwhile 가치 있는]

(B) 윤리적 제약이 연구의 공유를 가로막는 이유에 대해 말하는 부분이므로 그것들(연구 결과)이 여론을 '자극할(inflame)' 수 있기 때문이라는 것이 적절하다. [soothe 달래다, 진정시키다]

(C) 연구 결과물을 사회 기관에 제공하면 그 사회 기관이 그 연구 결과물을 '활용하여(utilizing)' 자신들의 대의명분을 돕도록 한다는 것이 적절하다. [neglect 무시하다]

전문해석

과학적 연구를 하는 것의 핵심은 진행 중인 담론의 일부가 되는 것인데, 그것은 우리 주변의 세상을 이해할 수 있게 해 주는 끝없는 질문과 대답의 연속이다. 여러분이 여러분의 파일 캐비닛 속에 잠가 두고 있는 연구 결과는 본질적으로 (A) 쓸모가 없다. 때로는 정보 제공자들에게 해가 되거나 어떤 식으로든 여론을 (B) 자극할 수 있기 때문에 윤리적인 제약이 연구의 공유를 가로막기도 하지만, 대부분의 경우 학계를 뛰어넘어 과학을 하는 동료들과 심지어 청중들에게 말을 퍼뜨리는 것은 좋은 일이다. 처음에, 여러분의 청중은 강사 혹은 교실의 다른 학생들보다 더 크지 않을 수 있다. 그러나 어느 시점에 여러분은 회의 논문, 학술지 기사 또는 적절한 웹 사이트의 게시물의 형태로 결과를 발표할 준비가 되어 있을 것이다. 여러분은 또한 목표를 발전시키는 데 흥미가 있는 사회 기관에 여러분의 연구 결과를 제공하기를 원할 수도 있는데, 그들은 여러분의 결과물을 (C) 활용하여 자신들의 대의명분을 돕는다.

구문풀이

6행 [Sometimes ethical constraints preclude the sharing of research {because they might harm your informants or somehow inflame public opinion}], but [for the most part **it** is a good thing {to get the word out to one's scientific peers and even to audiences beyond academe}].

: 두 개의 [ ]는 but으로 연결된 등위절로, 첫 번째 [ ]에서 { }는 이유 부사절이다. 두 번째 [ ]에서 it은 형식상의 주어이고, to부정사구인 { }가 내용상의 주어이다.

어휘풀이

- ongoing *a* 계속 진행 중인
- constraint *n* 제약
- informant *n* 정보원, 정보 제공자
- discourse *n* 담론, 담화
- preclude *v* 가로막다, 배제하다
- public opinion 여론

- academe *n* 학구적 생활, 학구(學究)
- article *n* 기사, 논문
- contribute *v* 제공하다, 기고[투고]하다
- finding *n* (연구) 결과(물)
- publish *v* 발표하다
- suitable *a* 적절한
- further *v* 발전시키다

116 답 ⑤

① force	강요하다	↔	
② allow	허락하다	↔	forbid(금지하다)
③ responsibility	책임	↔	
④ forgive	용서하다	↔	
⑤ benefit	이득	↔	disadvantage(불리, 손해)

정답풀이
⑤ 뒤에 감정을 놓아주는 것은 우리 내부의 쓰라림과 증오만을 놓아주는 것이라는 내용이 이어지므로 감정 놓아주기를 우호적으로 설명하는 말이 와야 한다. 따라서 부정어 hardly가 있으므로 benefit(이득)은 적절하지 않으며, '희생'을 뜻하는 sacrifice 정도로 바꿔 써야 한다.

오답풀이
① 우리가 어떤 상황에 어떻게 반응할지에 대한 선택권을 가지고 있다는 것은 아무도 우리가 특정한 감정을 가지도록 '강요할' 수 없다는 것이므로 force는 적절하다.
② 부정적인 것과 상처받은 것을 곰곰이 생각하면서 감정적인 스펀지가 되는 것은 다른 누군가가 우리를 지배하도록 '허락하는' 것으로 볼 수 있으므로 allowing은 적절하다.
③ 슬픔을 야기한 상황으로부터 지혜와 통찰력을 가지고 배우기로 선택하는 것은 우리가 스스로의 감정에 대한 '책임'을 주장하는 것으로 볼 수 있으므로 responsibility는 적절하다.
④ 감정 놓아주기는 우리가 '용서하지' 않은 사람들과 우리를 이은 고통의 감정적 매듭을 풀어주는 것을 의미한다는 맥락에서 부정어 not과 함께 쓰인 forgiven은 적절하다.

전문해석
우리들 각자는 우리 자신의 인식을 선택할 수 있기 때문에, 아무도 우리가 어떤 특정한 감정을 느끼도록 ① 강요할 수 없는데, 우리는 우리가 어떤 상황에 어떻게 반응하는지에 대한 선택권을 항상 가지고 있다. 만약 우리가 부정적인 것을 흡수하고 상처받은 것을 곰곰이 생각하면서 감정적인 스펀지가 되기로 선택한다면, 우리는 다른 누군가가 우리를 지배하도록 ② 허락하는 것이다. 반면에, 만약 우리가 더 큰 지혜와 통찰력을 가지고 용서하고 앞으로 나아감으로써 우리에게 슬픔을 야기한 상황으로부터 배우기로 선택한다면, 우리는 진정으로 우리 자신의 감정에 대한 ③ 책임을 주장하고 있는 것이다. 이것은 (감정을) 놓아주는 의식적인 선택을 하도록 우리를 자유롭게 한다. '놓아주기'는 우리가 경험 전체를 잊어버린다는 것을 의미하지는 않는다. 그것은 우리가 ④ 용서하지 않은 사람들과 우리를 묶은 고통의 감정적 매듭을 푸는 것을 의미한다. 이것은 거의 ⑤ 이득(→ 희생)으로 여겨지지는 않는데, 왜냐하면 우리가 놓아주는 것은 단지 우리 내부의 쓰라림과 우리가 화가 난 바로 그 사람들과 우리를 이은 증오뿐이기 때문이다.

구문풀이
15행 This can hardly be considered a sacrifice, [since the only thing {we are letting go of} is our internal bitterness and the hatred {which has bonded us to the very people <with whom we are angry>}].

: [ ]는 since가 이끄는 부사절이다. 그 안의 첫 번째 { }는 the only thing을, 두 번째 { }는 the hatred를, 〈 〉는 the very people을 수식하는 관계절이다.

어휘풀이
- perception *n* 인식
- negativity *n* 부정적인 것, 소극적인 것
- dwell on ~을 곰곰이 생각하다
- grief *n* 슬픔
- insight *n* 통찰력
- conscious *a* 의식의, 의식적인
- release *v* 풀어주다, 놓아주다
- bitterness *n* 쓰라림
- bond *v* 결속하다, 잇다
- absorb *v* 흡수하다
- have power over ~을 지배하다
- wisdom *n* 지혜
- claim *v* 주장하다
- let go 놓다, 풀어주다
- knot *n* 매듭
- hatred *n* 증오

117 답 ④

① profitable	이득이 되는	↔	unprofitable(이익이 없는)
② unfavourable	불리한, 바람직하지 못한	↔	favourable(유리한)
③ discounted	할인된	↔	
④ spend	지출하다	↔	save(절약하다)
⑤ utility	효용	↔	

정답풀이
④ 가장 크게 할인된 천을 사서 똑똑한 구매에 기뻐했다고 했고, 경제적인 관점에서 볼 때 최상의 선택을 했다고 했으므로 가장 많은 돈을 '지출했다'는 것은 적절하지 않다. spent를 saved(절약하다) 정도로 바꿔 써야 한다.

오답풀이
① 뒤에 나온 주관적인 관점에서의 잘못된 결정과 대조되는 말이 와야 하므로 경제적인 관점에서는 '이득이 된다(profitable)'고 한 것은 적절하다.
② 경제적인 관점에서 이로운 결정과 반대로(but) 특정 개인의 주관적인 관점에서의 선택을 설명하는 문맥이므로 '불리한(unfavourable)' 선택이라는 것은 적절하다.
③ 원래는 각각 200달러, 250달러, 350달러였는데, 지금은 판촉으로 각각 150달러씩이라고 했으므로 '할인된(discounted)' 천이라는 것은 적절하다.
⑤ 가장 큰 천을 사서 경제적 관점에서는 가장 많은 돈을 절약했지만 그것이 너무 커서 바닥에 질질 끌린다고 했으므로, 주관적인 '효용(utility)'의 측면에서는 최악의 선택을 했다는 것은 적절하다.

전문해석
소비자들은 때때로 어떤 것들을 구매하는데, 그것이 단지 좋은 거래이기 때문이다. 하지만 실제로 그러한 '좋은 거래'는 경제적인 관점에서는 ① 이득이 됨에도 불구하고, 주관적인 관점, 즉 그 구매를 하는 사람의 선호와 필요에서는 잘못된 결정인 경우가 많다. Thaler는, 경제적인 관점에서는 매우 유익한 결정이지만 특정 개인의 관점에서는 ② 불리한 선택을 예증하는 재미있는 일화를 들려준다. 그는 소파 위에 걸쳐 놓을 천을 사고 싶어 했던 그의 친구를 묘사한다. 한 상점에서, 그녀는 세 가지 다른 사이즈의 ③ 할인된 천을 발견했는데, 원래는 각각 200달러, 250달러, 350달러였고, 지금은 판촉으로 각각 150달러씩이다. 그녀는 가장 큰 천을 샀고 자신의 '똑똑한' 구매(가장 큰 할인)에 매우 기뻐했다. 경제적인 관점에서 보면, 그녀가 가장 많은 돈을 ④ 지출했기(→ 절약했기) 때문에 그녀의 선택은 정말 최상이었다. 하지만 주관적인 ⑤ 효용의 측면에서 보면, 그녀는 최악의 선택을 했는데, 왜냐하면 가장 큰 천이 그녀의 소파에 비해 너무 크고 바닥을 따라 질질 끌리기 때문이었다.

구문풀이
11행 In one store, she found a discounted drape in three different

sizes, [which originally cost $200, $250, and $350, respectively],
and now each cost $150 in the promotion.

: [ ]는 a discounted drape in three different sizes를 부연 설명하는 계속적 용법
의 관계절이다.

어휘풀이

- **purchase** *v* 구매하다 *n* 구매
- **deal** *n* 거래
- **in practice** 실제로
- **profitable** *a* 이득이 되는
- **subjective** *a* 주관적인
- **perspective** *n* 관점
- **preference** *n* 선호
- **anecdote** *n* 일화
- **illustrate** *v* 예증하다, 예시하다
- **beneficial** *a* 이로운, 유익한
- **unfavourable** *a* 불리한, 바람직하지 못한
- **drape** *n* (덮는) 천
- **respectively** *ad* 각각
- **promotion** *n* 판촉, 홍보, 장려
- **from the angle of** ~의 측면에서 보면
- **utility** *n* 효용(성), 유용(성)
- **trail** *v* 질질 끌리다[끌다]

118 답 ③

출제 어휘 확인하기

①	fail	~하지 않다, ~하지 못하다	↔	
②	extraordinary	놀라운	↔	ordinary(평범한)
③	rapidly	빠르게	↔	slowly(느리게)
④	visible	(눈에) 보이는	↔	invisible(보이지 않는)
⑤	highlight	강조하다	↔	

정답풀이

③ 기후 변화는 일련의 놀라운 사건들로만 드러나는 것이 아니고, 환경 변화
는 감지할 수 없을 수 있다고 했다. 따라서 환경 변화는 '빠르게' 진행되는 것
이 아니라 '점진적으로' 진행된다는 것을 추론할 수 있으므로 rapidly를
gradually 정도로 바꿔 써야 한다.

오답풀이

① 앞에서 기후 위기에 대한 대중적 상상력의 많은 부분이 소설에 의해 형성
된다고 했으므로, 인간이 기후 변화에 대응하는 데 실패한 것은 부분적으로
소설이 그것을 믿을 수 있게 표현하지 '못하기(fails)' 때문이라고 하는 것은
적절하다.

② 기후 변화는 사이클론, 홍수 그리고 다른 큰 재해 같이 일상생활에 있을 법
하지 않은 것처럼 보여서 현대 소설에 대체로 등장하지 않는다는 앞 문장과
But으로 이어지는 문장이다. 따라서 기후 변화가 '놀라운(extraordinary)'
사건들로만 드러나는 것은 아니라는 내용은 적절하다.

④ 기후 변화의 영향은 매일 관찰될 수는 없지만, 이따금 폭발적이고 극적인
사건처럼 그것들의 축적된 영향에 직면할 때 '눈에 보이게' 된다는 것으로
visible은 적절하다.

⑤ 빙하와 산호초에 미치는 기후 변화의 영향을 추적하는 다큐멘터리 영화 제
작자가 같은 장소에서 찍은 '이전과 이후의' 사진을 이용하는 이유는 점진적으
로 일어나는 변화를 '강조하기(highlight)' 위해서라고 할 수 있다.

전문해석

기후 변화 전문가들과 마찬가지로 환경 인문주의자들도 기후 위기가 그 핵심에는 상
상력의 위기이며 대중적 상상력의 많은 부분이 소설에 의해 형성된다는 데 동의한
다. 인류학자이자 소설가인 Amitav Ghosh는 자신의 2016년도 저서 〈The Great
Derangement〉에서 상상과 환경 관리 사이의 이러한 관계를 다루면서, 인간이 기
후 변화에 대응하는 데 실패한 것은 최소한 부분적으로는 소설이 그것을 믿을 수 있
게 표현하지 (a) 못하기 때문이라고 주장한다. Ghosh는, 기후 변화는 그것이 상기
시키는 사이클론, 홍수 그리고 다른 큰 재해들이 그야말로 일상생활에 관한 이야기
에 속하기에는 너무 '있을 법하지 않은' 것처럼 보이기 때문에 현대 소설에 대체로

존재하지 않는다고 설명한다. 그러나 기후 변화는 일련의 (b) 놀라운 사건들로만 자
신을 드러내는 것은 아니다. 사실, Rachel Carson에서 Rob Nixon에 이르는 환경
론자들과 생태 비평가들이 지적했듯이, 환경 변화는 '감지할 수 없을' 수 있는데, 즉
그것은 (c) 빠르게(→ 점진적으로) 진행되며, 단지 이따금 '폭발적이고 극적인' 사건
들을 만들어 낼 뿐이다. 대부분의 기후 변화의 영향은 매일 관찰될 수는 없지만, 우
리가 그것들의 축적된 영향에 직면할 때 그것들은 (d) 눈에 보이게 된다.
기후 변화는 그것이 중요한 표현상의 문제를 제기하기 때문에 우리의 상상에서 벗어
난다. 그것은 '인간의 시간' 동안에는 관찰될 수 없는데, 그것이 빙하와 산호초에 미
치는 기후 변화의 영향을 추적하는 다큐멘터리 영화 제작자 Jeff Orlowski가 점진
적으로 일어난 변화를 (e) 강조하기 위해 수개월 간격으로 같은 장소에서 찍은 '이전
과 이후의' 사진을 이용하는 이유이다.

구문풀이

10행 Ghosh explains [that climate change is largely absent from
contemporary fiction because {the cyclones, floods, and other
catastrophes <it brings to mind>} simply seem **too** "improbable"
to belong in stories about everyday life].

: [ ]는 explains의 목적어로 쓰인 명사절이다. because가 이끄는 부사절에서 주어는
{ }이며 술어 동사는 seem이다. 〈 〉는 the cyclones, floods, and other
catastrophes를 수식하는 관계절이며, it은 climate change를 대신하는 대명사이다.
「too ~ to부정사」는 '너무 ~해서 …할 수 없다'라는 의미이다.

25행 It cannot be observed in "human time," [which is {why
documentary filmmaker Jeff Orlowski, <who tracks climate
change effects on glaciers and coral reefs>, uses "before and after"
photographs <taken several months apart in the same place> **to
highlight** changes <that occurred gradually>}].

: [ ]는 앞 절의 내용을 부연 설명하는 관계절이며, { }는 is의 보어로 쓰인 명사절이다.
그 안의 첫 번째 〈 〉는 documentary filmmaker Jeff Orlowski를 부가적으로 설명
하는 관계절이고, 두 번째 〈 〉는 "before and after" photographs를 수식하는 과거
분사구이다. to highlight 이하는 목적을 나타내는 to부정사구이고, 세 번째 〈 〉는
changes를 수식하는 관계절이다.

어휘풀이

- **humanist** *n* 인문주의자
- **crisis** *n* 위기
- **core** *n* 핵심, 근원
- **fiction** *n* 소설, 허구
- **take on** ~을 다루다, ~을 떠맡다
- **respond** *v* 대응하다, 반응하다
- **represent** *v* 표현하다, 나타내다
- **largely** *ad* 대체로
- **contemporary** *a* 현대의
- **absent** *a* 존재하지 않는, 부재의
- **improbable** *a* 있을 법하지 않은
- **reveal** *v* 드러내다, 보여 주다
- **extraordinary** *a* 놀라운
- **imperceptible** *a* 감지할 수 없는
- **proceed** *v* 진행되다
- **explosive** *a* 폭발적인
- **spectacular** *a* 극적인, 장관의
- **impact** *n* 영향
- **visible** *a* 가시적인, 눈에 보이는
- **be confronted with** ~에 직면하다
- **accumulate** *v* 축적하다
- **pose** *v* (위협·문제 등을) 제기하다
- **significant** *a* 중요한
- **track** *v* 추적하다
- **glacier** *n* 빙하
- **coral reef** 산호초

05 필수 어휘

Q1 1 obligatory 2 promotions 3 abandon
   4 intangible 5 fluctuate

Q2 1 ③ 2 ① 3 ①

119 ④	120 ④	121 ③	122 ③	123 ⑤
124 ⑤				

Q1

1. [해석] 전통적인 한국식 방에 들어가기 전에 신발을 벗는 것은 의무이다.
[optional 선택의]

2. [해석] 다행히, John은 승진을 했다. 그는 New South Wales 지사의 관리자가 되었다. 마침내 그는 호주 전체를 관할하는 회사의 사장이 되었다.
[pressure 압박, 압력]

3. [해석] 재정적 지원이 없었기 때문에 음모자들은 자신들의 계획을 포기할 수밖에 없었다. [overwhelm 압도하다]

4. [해석] 그러한 자산은 물리적 자산과 반대로 실체가 없는 자산으로 알려져 있다.
[tangible 실체가 있는, 유형의]

5. [해석] 금융시장들은 점점 더 변하기 쉬워졌고, 당국은 그에 대한 통제력을 잃은 것처럼 보인다. 그 결과, 금리와 환율은 현재 어느 때보다 더 빠르게 변동하고 있다. [stabilize 안정되다]

Q2

1. [해석] 자신을 실험하는 것의 한 가지 명백한 결점은 실험이 초래할 수 있는 제한된 범위의 데이터이다.
① 이점 ② 절차

2. [해석] 친구에게 손을 컵처럼 동그랗게 모으고 손바닥을 위로 향하게 하고 눈을 감으라고 요청하라. 작고 평범한 물체, 즉 반지, 지우개, 어떤 것이든지 친구의 손바닥에 놓아두고 손의 어떠한 부분도 움직이지 말고 그것을 식별하라고 요청하라.
② 독창적인 ③ 유용한

3. [해석] 그 패턴은 누군가가 예상된 것 대신에 실제로 측정된 것을 보고할 용기가 있었을 때에서야 바뀌었다.
② 추정하다 ③ 기록하다

119 답 ④

출제 어휘 [확인하기]

① defined	정해진	↔	
② rarely	거의 ~ 않다	↔	
③ individually	개성을 발휘하여	↔	
④ worthless	가치 없는	↔	worthwhile(가치 있는)
⑤ enrich	풍부하게 하다	↔	

정답풀이

④ 같은 곡을 다른 연주자들이 연주하는 것을 들을 때 흥미를 잃지 않는 이유는 표현성 때문이라고 한 앞 문장과 같은 맥락으로 이어져야 하므로, 표현성 때문에 같은 레퍼토리를 다음 세대의 연주자들이 반복하여 연주하는 것이 '가치 있다'는 내용이 되어야 한다. 따라서 worthless(가치 없는)를 반대 개념인 worthwhile(가치 있는) 정도로 바꿔 써야 한다.

오답풀이

① 악보의 특성을 나타내는 표현으로, 뒤 문장의 printed로 미루어 보아 '정해진'이라는 의미의 defined는 적절하다.
② 빠르기, 음량, 음색 및 인토네이션에 있어 광범위한 변주의 가능성이 있다는 맥락에서 같은 방식으로 두 개의 같은 음을 연주하는 경우가 '거의 없다(rarely)'고 하는 것은 적절하다.
③ 뒤에서 같은 곡을 다른 연주자들이 연주하는 것을 들을 때 흥미를 잃지 않는 것은 표현성 때문이라고 했으므로, 표현성을 작품에 기초하지만 '개성을 발휘하여(individually)' 그것에서 갈라지는 변주라고 한 것은 적절하다.
⑤ 작품에 대한 새롭고 영감을 주는 해석이 주는 이점을 서술하는 문맥이므로, 우리의 이해의 폭을 넓혀 음악계를 '풍부하게 한다(enrich)'는 것은 적절하다.

전문해석

음악가와 심리학자뿐만 아니라 열성적인 음악 애호가와 전문가도 음악의 아름다움은 정확히 ① 정해진 악보로부터의 표현상의 벗어남에 있다는 의견을 종종 내놓는다. 콘서트 공연은 악보에 인쇄된 정보를 훨씬 뛰어넘는다는 사실에서 흥미로워지고 매력을 얻는다. 음악 연주에 관한 자신의 초기 연구에서, Carl Seashore는 음악가가 정확히 같은 방식으로 두 개의 같은 음을 연주하는 경우는 ② 거의 없다는 것을 발견했다. 같은 운율 구조 내에서 빠르기, 음량, 음색 그리고 인토네이션에 있어서 광범위한 변주의 가능성이 있다. 그러한 변주는 작품에 기초하지만, ③ 개성을 발휘하여 그것으로부터 갈라진다. 우리는 일반적으로 이것을 '표현성'이라고 부른다. 이것은 왜 우리가 같은 곡을 다른 연주자들이 연주하는 것을 들을 때 흥미를 잃지 않는지를 설명한다. 이것은 또한 왜 다음 세대들이 같은 레퍼토리를 반복하는 것이 ④ 가치 없는지(→ 가치 있는지)를 설명한다. 새롭고 영감을 주는 해석은 우리가 이해를 넓히는 데 도움을 주는데, 이는 음악계를 ⑤ 풍부하게 하고 활기 있게 하는 역할을 한다.

구문풀이

1행 [**Not only** {musicians and psychologists}, **but also** {committed music enthusiasts and experts}] often voice the opinion [that the beauty of music lies in an expressive deviation from the exactly defined score].

: 첫 번째 [ ]는 문장의 주어 역할을 하는 명사구이며, 두 개의 { }가 「not only ~ but also ....」로 연결되어 있다. 두 번째 [ ]는 the opinion과 동격 관계를 이루는 명사절이다.

16행 It also explains [why **it** is worthwhile {for following generations to repeat the same repertoire}].

: [ ]는 explains의 목적어 역할을 하는 명사절이다. 그 안의 it은 형식상의 주어이고, { }가 내용상의 주어이다. for following generations는 to부정사구의 의미상 주어를 나타낸다.

어휘풀이

- committed *a* 열성적인, 헌신적인
- enthusiast *n* 열광적인 애호가
- voice *v* (강하게) 말로 표현하다
- score *n* 악보
- gain in attraction 매력을 얻다
- note *n* (악보의) 음
- metric *a* 운율의, 운문의
- potential *n* 가능성
- variation *n* 변화, 변형
- tonal *a* 음조의
- intonation *n* 인토네이션(노래나 연주 시 의도한 음정에 정확히 도달했는지 여부)
- composition *n* (음악의) 작품
- diverge *v* 갈라지다
- repertoire *n* 레퍼토리
- inspiring *a* 영감을 주는

- interpretation *n* 해석
- enrich *v* 풍부하게 하다
- music scene 음악계
- expand *v* 넓히다, 확장하다
- animate *v* 활기를 불어넣다

120 답 ④

정답풀이

④ 자동차 여행을 더 비싸게 만들거나 행정 규정으로 제한하는 것은 자동차 수요에 '부응하는' 것이 아니라 그것을 '관리하는' 방식에 해당한다. 따라서 accommodating을 managing 정도로 바꿔 써야 한다.

오답풀이

① 도시의 물리적 제약 및 그에 상응하는 접근성, 이동성, 안전, 대기 오염, 도시 거주 적합성에 대한 요구는 도로망 확장의 '제한' 사유에 해당하므로 limit는 적절하다.
② 도로망 확장이 제한되면 도시 관리자들과 계획 설계자들은 사람들이 자동차를 사용하지 않도록 '설득해야' 할 것이므로 persuading은 적절하다.
③ 걷기, 자전거 타기, 대중교통은 자동차 사용의 '대안적인' 선택 사항에 해당하므로 alternative는 적절하다.
⑤ 자동차 여행을 더 비싸게 만들거나 행정 규정으로 제한하는 것의 정당성을 설명하는 흐름이므로, 자동차 여행이 기후 변화의 원인을 제공하는 것이 이런 조치들의 불가피성을 '강화한다'고 하는 것은 적절하다.

전문해석

최근 몇 년 간 전 세계적으로 도시 교통 전문가들은 도시의 자동차 수요에 부응하기보다는 그것을 관리해야 한다는 견해를 대체로 따랐다. 소득 증가는 필연적으로 자동차 보급의 증가로 이어진다. 기후 변화로 인한 불가피성이 없다고 해도, 인구 밀도가 높은 도시들의 물리적 제약과 그에 상응하는 접근성, 이동성, 안전, 대기 오염 그리고 도시 거주 적합성에 대한 요구 모두가 단지 이러한 증가하는 수요에 부응하기 위해 도로망을 확장하는 선택권을 ① 제한한다. 결과적으로, 도시가 발전하고 그곳의 거주자들이 더 부유해짐에 따라 사람들이 자동차를 사용하지 '않기로' 결정하도록 ② 설득하는 것이 점점 더 도시 관리자들과 계획 설계자들의 핵심 중점 사항이 된다. 걷기, 자전거 타기, 대중교통과 같은 ③ 대안적인 선택 사항의 질을 향상하는 것이 이 전략의 핵심 요소이다. 하지만 자동차 수요에 ④ 부응하는(→ (를) 관리하는) 가장 직접적인 접근 방식은 자동차 여행을 더 비싸게 만들거나 행정 규정으로 그것을 제한하는 것이다. 자동차 여행이 기후 변화의 원인을 제공하는 것이 이런 불가피성을 ⑤ 강화한다.

구문풀이

1행 In recent years urban transport professionals globally have largely acquiesced to the view [that automobile demand in cities needs to be managed rather than accommodated].

: [ ]는 the view와 동격 관계를 이루는 명사절이다.

17행 However, the most direct approach to accommodating automobile demand is [making motorized travel more expensive] or [restricting **it** with administrative rules].

: 두 개의 [ ]는 or에 의해 대등하게 연결된 동명사구이고, 대명사 it은 motorized travel을 대신한다.

어휘풀이

- urban *a* 도시의
- professional *n* 전문가
- accommodate *v* (요구 등에) 부응하다, 맞추다
- income *n* 수입
- motorization *n* 자동차 보급, 전동화
- corresponding *a* 상응하는
- mobility *n* 이동성
- option *n* 선택권, 선택 사항
- purely *ad* 단지, 다만
- prosperous *a* 번영하는
- strategy *n* 전략
- restrict *v* 제한하다
- contribution *n* 원인 제공, 기여
- transport *n* 교통, 수송
- demand *n* 수요, 요구
- inevitably *ad* 불가피하게
- densely inhabited 인구 밀도가 높은
- accessibility *n* 접근성
- livability *n* 거주 적합성, 살기 좋음
- expand *v* 확장하다
- resident *n* 거주자
- alternative *a* 대안적인, 대체의
- direct *a* 직접적인
- administrative *a* 행정의
- reinforce *v* 강화하다

121 답 ③

정답풀이

③ 동물들이 공격적인 행동을 하는 이유를 말하는 부분이므로 경쟁자를 제거하여 긴장된 상태를 '강화시키기' 위해서라는 것은 적절하지 않다. intensify를 relieve(완화시키다) 정도로 바꿔 써야 한다.

오답풀이

① 동물들의 싸움이 그것들의 이익을 보호하기 위해 행해진다는 전제와 관련 지어 볼 때, 그것들의 공격적인 행동이 자원의 '부족(scarcity)'으로 인해 생긴다는 것은 적절하다.
② 개체수가 늘어나는 데 비해 이용 가능한 자원은 한정되어 있다는 것이므로 경쟁이 '증가한다(rises)'는 것은 적절하다.
④ 동물의 수가 증가하면 생기는 현상을 설명한 앞 내용에 이어 In contrast를 사용하여 반대되는 상황을 설명하고 있으므로 개체수가 '감소하는 (decreases)' 내용이 나오는 것은 적절하다.
⑤ 동물들이 먹이나 서식처 확보를 위해 경쟁할 필요가 없는 것은 '풍부'한 자원 때문이므로 abundance는 적절하다.

전문해석

기본적으로 동물들 사이에서 싸움은 그 자체를 위해서 추구되거나 가치 있다고 여겨지지는 않는다. 싸움은 오히려 환영하는 것은 아니지만 필요한 것, 즉 그들의 이익을 보호하는 수단으로 사용된다. 특히, 동물의 공격적인 행동들은 대개 먹이나 서식처와 같은 자원의 ① 부족으로 생긴다. 특정한 동물의 개체수가 증가함에 따라 이용 가능한 먹이, 짝, 영역에 대한 경쟁이 ② 증가한다. 동물들은 보다 힘이 약한 개체 구성원들을 강제로 다른 곳으로 옮겨가게 하거나 즉각 죽이는 것과 같은 방법으로 경쟁자들을 제거함으로써 증가하는 이러한 긴장을 ③ 강화시키기(→ 완화시키기) 위하여 공격적인 행동을 벌인다. 대조적으로, 개체 밀도가 ④ 감소함에 따라 공격적인 행동의 필요성 또한 그렇게 된다. ⑤ 풍부한 자원이나 낮은 개체 밀도 때문에 먹이나 서식처를 확보하기 위해 경쟁을 거의 하지 않는 동물 종들은 좀처럼 공격적인 성향을 드러내지 않는다.

구문풀이

14행 Animal species [that seldom compete for food or shelter, {**either** due to an abundance of resources **or** to a small population density}], rarely exhibit aggressive tendencies.

: 문장의 핵심 주어는 Animal species이고 동사는 exhibit이다. [ ]는 Animal species를 수식하는 관계절이고, 그 안의 { }는 「either A or B」로 연결된 전치사구이다.

어휘풀이

- **fundamentally** *ad* 기본적으로
- **resort to** ~을 사용하다, ~에 의존하다
- **scarcity** *n* 부족, 결핍
- **territory** *n* 영역
- **relocate** *v* 이전하다, 재배치하다
- **density** *n* 밀도
- **sake** *n* 목적, 이익
- **aggressive** *a* 공격적인
- **shelter** *n* 서식처, 은신처
- **intensify** *v* 강화시키다
- **outright** *ad* 즉각
- **tendency** *n* 성향

122 답 ③

출제 어휘 | 확인하기

(A)	benefit	이익, 이로움	/ drawback	단점, 결점
(B)	arise	발생하다	/ subside	가라앉다, 진정되다
(C)	clear	명확한, 확실히 알고 있는	/ unclear	불명확한, 잘 모르는

정답풀이

(A) 이어지는 문장이 역접의 But으로 시작하며 잠재적 연명 치료와 관련된 부정적인 측면을 서술하고 있으므로, 앞 문장은 반대로 긍정적인 내용이 되어야 함을 알 수 있다. 따라서 기저 질환으로 인해 죽을 수도 있는 환자의 수명을 연장하는 것을 포함해 잠재적인 '이로움(benefits)'을 가진다는 것이 적절하다. [drawback 단점, 결점]
(B) 치료의 이로움, 부담, 위험성 등이 잘 이해되지 않거나 치료 효과에 대한 불확실성이 있는 것은 부정적인 측면이므로 우려가 '발생한다(arise)'는 것이 적절하다. [subside 가라앉다, 진정되다]
(C) 잠재적 연명 치료에 대한 부정적인 내용이 추가로 이어지는 맥락이므로, 의사나 다른 관련자들 역시 법적으로 그리고 윤리적으로 허용되는 것이 무엇인지에 관해 '잘 모른다(unclear)'는 것이 적절하다. [clear 명확한, 확실히 알고 있는]

전문해석

생애말기 돌봄에서 가장 어렵고 민감한 결정은 흔히 심폐소생술(CPR), 인공 영양 및 수화(水和) 그리고 기계적 환기와 같은 잠재적 연명 치료를 시작하는 것 또는 중지하는 것과 관련된 결정이다. 이러한 치료법들은 그렇지 않으면 그들의 기저 질환으로 인해 죽을 수도 있는 환자의 수명을 연장하는 것을 포함해 많은 잠재적인 (A) 이로움이 있다. 그러나 어떤 상황에서는, 그것들은 단지 죽어가는 과정을 연장하거나 환자에게 불필요한 고통을 초래할 수 있다. 이러한 치료의 이로움, 부담 및 위험성이 언제나 잘 이해되는 것은 아니며, 특히 개별 환자에 대한 치료의 임상적 효과에 대한 불확실성이 있을 경우에 과잉 치료 혹은 치료 부족에 대한 우려, 또는 그 환자에 대한 이로움과 부담이 어떻게 평가되고 있는지에 대한 우려가 (B) 발생할 수 있다. 의사들과 의사 결정 과정에 관련된 다른 사람들은 또한 특히 잠재적 연명 치료를 중단하는 결정과 관련하여 법적으로 그리고 윤리적으로 허용되는 것이 무엇인지에 관해 (C) 잘 모를지도 모른다.

구문풀이

11행 The benefits, burdens and risks of these treatments are **not always** well understood and concerns can arise [about over- or under-treatment, {particularly where there is uncertainty about the clinical effect of a treatment on the individual patient}], or

[about how the benefits and burdens for that patient are being assessed].

: 「not always ~」는 부분 부정의 의미로 '항상 ~한 것은 아니다'라는 뜻이다. 두 개의 [ ]는 or로 연결되어 병렬구조를 이루며 앞에 있는 concerns를 부연 설명한다. { }는 '~할 경우'라는 뜻의 where가 이끄는 부사절이다.

어휘풀이

- **sensitive** *a* 민감한, 예민한
- **life-prolonging** *a* 연명의, 생명을 연장하는
- **treatment** *n* 치료, 처리
- **nutrition** *n* 영양
- **ventilation** *n* 환기(폐와 외기(外氣) 간의 가스 교환), 통풍
- **drawback** *n* 단점, 결점
- **underlying condition** 기저 질환
- **burden** *n* 부담(감)
- **subside** *v* 가라앉다, 진정되다
- **assess** *v* 평가하다, 측정하다
- **permissible** *a* 허용되는
- **artificial** *a* 인공의, 인공적인
- **hydration** *n* 수화(水和)
- **extend** *v* 연장하다
- **distress** *n* 고통
- **concern** *n* 우려, 염려
- **clinical effect** 임상 효과
- **ethically** *ad* 윤리적으로

123 답 ⑤

출제 어휘 | 확인하기

①	correspond	부합하다	↔	
②	uphold	유지시키다, 지지하다	↔	
③	match	들어맞다	↔	
④	inappropriate	부적절한	↔	appropriate(적절한)
⑤	complement	보완하다	↔	

정답풀이

⑤ 역할 갈등이 발생하는 경우에 대해 설명하는 문맥이며, 서로 양립하기 어렵거나 서로 '모순되는' 여러 가지 역할을 수행하도록 요구될 때 역할 갈등이 발생하는 것이므로 여러 역할이 서로 '보완한다'는 것은 적절하지 않다. complement를 contradict(모순되다) 정도로 바꿔 써야 한다.

오답풀이

① 이상적으로는 사람들의 행동이 특정 역할에 맞게 이루어진다는 문맥이므로 행위가 특정 역할에 '부합한다(corresponds)'는 것은 적절하다.
② 역할 기대에 대한 예로 경찰의 경우를 설명하는 부분이므로 '유지시키다, 지지하다'의 뜻인 uphold가 와서 법을 '유지시킬' 것으로 기대된다는 흐름이 되는 것은 적절하다.
③ 실제와 역할 기대 사이의 괴리를 나타내는 내용이므로 '들어맞는다'는 의미의 match가 와서 앞의 부정어 does not과 함께 이 둘이 항상 '들어맞는' 것은 아니라는 흐름이 되는 것은 적절하다.
④ 역할 기대와 실제 역할 수행이 불일치하는 이유를 설명하기 위해 사회의 특정 부분에서는 적절할 수도 있는 역할 행동이 사회 전체의 관점에서는 '부적절할' 수도 있다는 내용이 나온 것이므로 inappropriate는 적절하다.

전문해석

이상적으로는, 사람들이 서로 상호작용할 때 그들의 행위는 그들이 수행하고 있는 특정한 역할과 ① 부합한다. 어떤 역할을 수행하는 사람에게 기대되는 사회적으로 정해진 행동들을 역할 기대라고 한다. 예를 들면, 의사들은 자신의 환자를 솜씨 있고 조심스럽게 치료하도록 기대된다. 부모들은 자신의 아이들에게 정서적, 신체적 안전을 제공하도록 기대된다. 경찰은 법을 ② 유지시키도록 기대된다. 현실적으로는, 사람들의 실제 역할 행동이 사회가 기대하는 행동과 항상 ③ 들어맞는 것은 아니다. 어떤 의사들은 자신의 환자들에게 가능한 한 최고의 돌봄을 제공하지 않는다. 어떤 부모들은 자신의 아이들을 학대한다. 때때로, 사회의 어떤 특정 부분에 의해서는 적절

하다고 간주되는 역할 행동이 전체 사회에 의해서는 ④ 부적절한 것으로 보일 수 있기 때문에 이런 문제가 일어난다. 또한 이런 역할 갈등은 우리가 서로 ⑤ 보완해 주는(→ 모순되는) 여러 가지 역할을 수행하도록 요구받을 때 발생하기도 한다.

구문풀이

13행 Occasionally, this problem arises because role behaviors [considered **proper** by a certain segment of society] can be seen as inappropriate by society as a whole.

: [ ]는 role behaviors를 수식하는 과거분사구이다. 능동태인 A certain segment of society considers role behaviors proper.가 수동태로 전환되어 과거분사구로 쓰인 형태이며, 능동태일 때의 목적격보어인 형용사 proper가 수동태에서도 considered 뒤에 그대로 쓰였다.

어휘풀이

- interact *v* 상호작용하다
- correspond to ~에 부합하다, ~와 일치하다
- role expectation 역할 기대
- treat *v* 치료하다
- security *n* 안전
- uphold *v* 유지시키다, 지지하다
- actual *a* 실제의
- mistreat *v* 학대하다
- arise *v* 발생하다
- segment *n* 부분
- inappropriate *a* 부적절한
- as a whole 전체로서
- conflict *n* 갈등
- multiple *a* 많은, 여러 가지의

124 답 ⑤

출제 어휘 확인하기			
① advantage	장점	↔	disadvantage(단점)
② unusual	드문	↔	usual(보통의, 통상의)
③ criticize	비난하다	↔	
④ enjoy	즐기다	↔	
⑤ run	무릅쓰다	↔	

정답풀이

⑤ 과거와 달리 지금은 많은 과학자들이 언론과 접하고 있지만, 다른 과학자들은 기자들과의 대화를 계속해서 거부하며 자신의 과학을 위해 더 많은 시간을 지켜 내어 잘못 인용되거나 언론 보도와 관련하여 불쾌한 상황을 '피한다'는 맥락이 되어야 자연스럽다. 따라서 running(무릅쓰다)을 avoiding 정도로 바꿔 써야 한다.

오답풀이

① 언론과의 대화를 통해 메시지를 알리고 호의적인 인정을 받을 수 있다는 것은 언론과의 접촉이 가진 '장점'이라고 할 수 있으므로 advantages는 적절하다.

② 수십 년 전에 지구과학자가 언론과 접촉하는 것이 예상되거나 권장되는 일이 거의 없었던 것은 그들이 언론의 흥미를 끄는 연구 결과를 얻는 일이 '드물었기' 때문이라고 볼 수 있으므로 unusual은 적절하다.

③ 과학자들이 기후 문제에 대해 공개적으로 의견을 발표할 책임이 있다고 생각하는 지금의 상황과 대조되는 과거의 상황을 말하므로, 언론과 대화하는 과학자들이 동료들로부터 '비판을 받았다(criticized)'는 것은 적절하다.

④ 과거와 달리 지금은 과학자들이 언론과 접촉하는 것이 긍정적으로 여겨지고 있다고 했고, 같은 맥락에서 과학자들이 언론의 주목과 대중의 인정을 '즐기고 있다(enjoy)'는 것은 적절하다.

전문해석

이야기를 과대광고하는 것의 원인이 되는 것을 피하는 한 가지 방법은 아무 말도 하지 않는 것일 것이다. 그러나 그것은 대중과 정책 입안자들에게 정보를 전하고/전하

거나 제안을 제공해야 한다는 강한 책임감을 느끼는 과학자들에게는 현실적인 선택 사항이 아니다. 언론 관계자들과 이야기를 나누는 것은 메시지를 알리고 아마도 호의적인 인정을 받는 것에 있어서 (a) 장점이 있지만, 오해를 일으키고 반복적인 해명이 필요하며 끝없는 논란에 얽힐 위험이 있다. 따라서 언론과 대화할지 여부에 대한 결정은 매우 개별화되는 경향이 있다. 수십 년 전에 지구과학자들이 언론의 흥미를 끄는 (연구) 결과를 얻는 것은 (b) 드문 일이었고, 따라서 언론과의 접촉이 예상되거나 권장되는 일은 거의 없었다. 1970년대에는, 언론과 자주 대화하는 소수의 과학자들은 흔히 그렇게 한 것에 대해 동료 과학자들로부터 (c) 비난을 받았다. 지금은 상황이 아주 다른데, 많은 과학자들이 지구 온난화와 관련 문제의 중요성 때문에 공개적으로 말해야 한다는 책임감을 느끼고 있으며, 많은 기자들이 이러한 감정들을 공유하고 있기 때문이다. 게다가, 많은 과학자들은 자신이 언론의 주목과 그에 따른 대중의 인정을 (d) 즐기고 있다는 것을 알아 가고 있다. 동시에, 다른 과학자들은 기자들과 대화하기를 계속해서 거부하며, 그렇게 함으로써 자신의 과학을 위해 더 많은 시간을 지켜 내고, 잘못 인용되는 위험과 언론 보도와 관련하여 다른 불쾌한 상황을 (e) 무릅쓴다(→ 피한다).

구문풀이

2행 However, that is not a realistic option for scientists [who feel a strong sense of responsibility {to inform the public and policymakers} and/or {to offer suggestions}].

: [ ]는 scientists를 수식하는 관계절이고, 두 개의 { }는 형용사적 용법의 to부정사구로 병렬로 연결되어 a strong sense of responsibility를 수식하고 있다.

12행 Decades ago, **it** was unusual [for Earth scientists to have results {that were of interest to the media}], and consequently few media contacts were expected or encouraged.

: it은 형식상의 주어이고 [ ]가 내용상의 주어로, for Earth scientists는 to부정사구의 의미상의 주어이다. { }는 results를 수식하는 관계절이다.

어휘풀이

- contribute to ~에 기여하다
- responsibility *n* 책임
- inform *v* 알리다
- policymaker *n* 정책 입안자
- suggestion *n* 제안
- get out ~을 알려지게 하다, ~을 말하다
- favorable *a* 호의적인, 우호적인
- recognition *n* 인정
- run the risk of ~의 위험이 있다, ~의 위험을 무릅쓰다
- misinterpretation *n* 오해
- clarification *n* 해명
- controversy *n* 논란, 논쟁
- consequently *ad* 그 결과, 따라서
- resist *v* 물리치다
- preserve *v* 지키다, 보존하다
- misquote *v* (말이나 글을) 잘못 인용하다
- unpleasantry *n* 불쾌한 상황[사건]
- coverage *n* (신문·방송의) 보도

Q1 1 convict 2 infection 3 elaborate 4 Ineffective
5 temporary

Q2 1 ① 2 ② 3 ①

125 ⑤	126 ⑤	127 ⑤	128 ①	129 ④
130 ③				

Q1

1. 해석 법정은 AIDS 바이러스인 HIV를 고의적으로 퍼뜨리는 사람들에게 엄격한 형벌을 부과하여 유죄를 선고할 것이다. [convince 확신시키다, 납득시키다]

2. 해석 박테리아 감염의 가능성을 줄이기 위한 조치들이 취해져야 한다.
[inspection 검사]

3. 해석 컴퓨터 바이러스에 관한 당신의 지식을 세부적으로 상세히 말씀해 주시겠습니까? [collaborate 협업하다, 합작하다]

4. 해석 중요하지 않은 것으로부터 중요한 것을 분리하는 것이 우선순위를 결정하는 것이다. 무능한 코치는 그 중대한 과제를 일순위로 두지 못한다.
[skilled 숙련된, 노련한]

5. 해석 그것은 단지 일시적인 조치일 뿐 그 갈등에 대한 근본적인 해결책은 아니다.
[permanent 영구적인]

Q2

1. 해석 방사능 폐기물 처리는 원자력의 미래를 두고 다투어 온 핵심적인 환경 (문제의) 전쟁터 중의 하나가 되었다.
② 생성 ③ 보존

2. 해석 과학은 현대 작가에게 필수 불가결한 정보의 원천이다. 게다가, 그것은 작가의 고도로 기술적인 환경의 필수적인 부분이다.
① 끝이 없는 ③ 독립된

3. 해석 음식의 감각적 특성의 작은 변화라도 음식의 섭취를 증가시키기에 충분하다.
② 평가 ③ 구성 요소

125 답 ⑤

출제 어휘 확인하기			
① quantity	물리량	↔	
② opposite	반대	↔	
③ match	일치하다	↔	
④ influence	영향을 주다	↔	
⑤ lack	~이 없다[부족하다]	↔	have(가지다, ~이 있다)

정답풀이
⑤ 빛의 속도를 측정하는 실험에서 나타난 편승 효과를 설명하면서 실험 결과를 예상값에 부합하면 취하고, 부합하지 않으면 버리는 방식으로 조정했을 것

이라고 했다. 따라서 그러한 패턴이 바뀐 것은 예상값 대신 실제로 측정된 것을 보고할 용기가 '없었을(lacked)' 때라는 것은 적절하지 않다. 용기가 '있었을' 때라는 흐름이 되도록 had 정도로 바꿔 써야 한다.

오답풀이
① 빛의 속도를 측정해서 그 결과값을 다루는 실험에 관한 글이므로, 빛의 속도를 측정 가능한 '물리량(quantities)'이라고 한 것은 적절하다.
② 1870년부터 1900년까지의 실험에서 측정한 빛의 속도가 너무 빨랐다는 앞 문장의 내용과 '반대'로, 1900년에서 1950년의 실험에서 측정한 빛의 속도는 너무 느렸다고 했으므로 opposite은 적절하다.
③ 이어지는 내용에서 과학자들은 실험 결과가 자신이 예상한 것과 부합하면 유지하고, 부합하지 않으면 버렸다고 했으므로, 과학자들이 자신의 예상과 '일치하도록' 결과를 조정했다는 의미에서 match는 적절하다.
④ 과학자들이 다른 과학자들과 비슷한 예상값을 가설로 세우고 빛의 속도 측정 결과값을 그에 맞도록 조정했기 때문에 너무 빠르거나 또는 너무 느린 결과만 얻게 되는 편향이 발생했음을 추론할 수 있다. 따라서 과학자들이 일반 통념에 의해 '영향을 받았다'는 의미에서 influenced는 적절하다.

전문해석
편승 효과가 어떻게 발생하는지는 빛의 속도 측정의 역사에 의해 입증된다. 이 속도는 상대성 이론의 기초가 되기 때문에, 과학에서 가장 빈번하고 면밀하게 측정되는 ① 물리량 중 하나이다. 우리가 아는 한, 그 속도(빛의 속도)는 시간이 지남에 따라 변하지 않았다. 그러나 1870년부터 1900년까지 모든 실험에서 너무 빠른 속도가 발견되었다. 그런 다음, 1900년부터 1950년까지 그 ② 반대 현상이 일어났다. 즉, 모든 실험에서 너무 느린 속도가 발견된 것이었다! 결과치가 항상 실제 값의 어느 한쪽에 있는 이런 종류의 오류를 '편향'이라고 부른다. 그것은 아마 시간이 지나면서 실험자들이 자신들이 발견할 것이라 예상한 것과 ③ 일치하도록 잠재의식적으로 결과를 조정했기 때문에 발생했을 것이다. 결과가 그들이 예상한 것에 부합하면, 그들은 그 결과를 유지했다. 결과가 부합하지 않으면, 그들은 그 결과를 버렸다. 그들은 고의적으로 부정직한 게 아니라, 그저 일반 통념에 의해 ④ 영향을 받았을 뿐이었다. 그 패턴은 누군가가 예상된 것 대신에 실제로 측정된 것을 보고할 용기가 ⑤ 없었을 (→ 있었을) 때에야 비로소 바뀌었다.

구문풀이
12행 It probably happened [because over time, experimenters subconsciously adjusted their results {to match <what they expected to find>}].

: [ ]는 이유를 나타내는 부사절이고, 그 안의 { }는 목적을 나타내는 부사적 용법의 to부정사구이다. < >는 to match의 목적어 역할을 하는 명사절이다.

어휘풀이
• demonstrate v 입증하다, 보여 주다 • measurement n 측정, 치수, 크기
• relativity n 상대성 • subconsciously ad 잠재의식적으로
• adjust v 조정하다 • match v 일치하다
• intentionally ad 고의적으로 • conventional wisdom 일반 통념

126 답 ⑤

출제 어휘 확인하기			
① respect	존중	↔	
② fairness	공정성	↔	unfairness(불공평)
③ outcome	결과	↔	
④ appreciation	인정	↔	
⑤ devalue	평가 절하하다	↔	value(높이 평가하다)

⑤ 모든 계층의 조직 구성원들은 성과와 연계된 유무형의 보상으로 개인적 인정을 실천해야 한다는 내용이 이어지므로, 자신의 재능과 기여에 대해 '평가 절하될' 필요가 있다는 것은 적절하지 않다. devalued를 반대 의미의 valued(높이 평가하다)로 바꿔 써야 한다.

오답풀이

① 신뢰할 수 있는 조직에 관한 설명이므로, 개인과 조직의 가치에 대한 '존중 (respect)'을 실천한다는 것은 적절하다.
② evenhandedness(공평성)와 같은 맥락에서 CEO의 일을 설명하고 있으므로 fairness(공정성)는 적절하다.
③ 수익과 제품은 조직이 내놓는 '결과'이므로 outcomes는 적절하다.
④ 조직 구성원들은 자신들의 재능과 조직에 대한 기여 및 성과를 인정받고 보상받을 필요가 있다는 내용이 언급되고 있으므로, 직원들이 금전보다는 '인정(appreciation)'을 그리워한다는 것은 적절하다.

전문해석

신뢰할 수 있는 조직의 한 가지 특징은 개인과 조직의 가치에 대한 ① 존중을 실천하는 리더십 팀이다. 조직의 리더와 관리자는 팀으로 작업해야 한다. CEO의 일은 조직 전체에 공평함과 ② 공정성이 있는지 확인하는 것이다. 다시 말하면, CEO는 조직의 성장과 발전을 촉진하면서 조직 내 균형을 유지한다. 수익과 제품이 조직에 대한 ③ 결과일 수 있지만, 금전은 구성원들에게 좋은 동기 부여 요소가 아니다. 연구는 직원들이 그리워하는 것은 ④ 인정이라는 것을 보여 준다. 사람들은 자신들의 재능과 자신들이 조직에 기여한 것에 대해 ⑤ 평가 절하될(→ 높이 평가될) 필요가 있다. 모든 계층의 조직 구성원들은 성과와 연계된 유무형의 보상으로 개인적 인정을 실천해야 한다. 신뢰, 자부심, 충성심은 조직에 대한 보상이다.

구문풀이

11행 Studies have shown [that {what employees miss} is appreciation].

: [ ]는 have shown의 목적어 역할을 하는 명사절이고, 그 안의 { }는 선행사를 포함하는 관계대명사 what이 이끄는 절로, 목적절의 주어 역할을 한다.

어휘풀이

- characteristic *n* 특징
- evenhandedness *n* 공평성, 공평함
- facilitate *v* 촉진하다
- appreciation *n* 인정
- contribute *v* 기여하다, 이바지하다
- intangible *a* 만질 수 없는, 무형의
- self-esteem *n* 자부심, 자존감
- organization *n* 조직, 기관
- fairness *n* 공정성
- outcome *n* 결과
- devalue *v* 평가 절하하다
- recognition *n* 인정, 인식
- tangible *a* 만질 수 있는, 유형의
- loyalty *n* 충성심

127 답 ⑤

출제 어휘	확인하기		
① positive	긍정적인	↔	negative(부정적인)
② challenging	도전하는, 도전적인	↔	
③ equal	동등한	↔	unequal(동등하지 않은)
④ frightening	두려운	↔	
⑤ relieved	편안한	↔	anxious(불안한)

정답풀이

⑤ 아이들은 부모가 규칙을 세워 그것을 시행하면 안정감을 느끼는 반면에 자신들이 상황을 전적으로 책임져야 할 때는 오히려 겁을 먹는다고 했으므로, 부모가 규칙을 적용하지 않고 뒤로 물러날 때 아이들이 '편안해진다'는 것은 적절하지 않다. relieved를 anxious(불안한) 정도로 바꿔 써야 한다.

① 부모와 아이의 친구 같은 관계는 편안한 분위기를 만들어 아이에게 스트레스를 덜 주므로 아이가 '긍정적인(positive)' 성격을 갖게 된다는 것은 적절하다.
② 뒤에 규칙을 세워 시행함으로써 아이에게 부모와 권위가 동등하지 않음을 가르쳐 준다는 내용이 이어지므로, 아이의 발달 과정에서 아이가 부모의 권위에 '도전하는(Challenging)' 것을 언급하는 것은 적절하다.
③ 도전적 행동에 대한 가르침을 줄 때 권위의 동등함이 아니라 본질적인 가치에 있어 '동등하다(equal)'는 점을 일깨워 주면 아이들이 안전함을 느끼며 자신의 위치로 돌아간다는 것은 적절하다.
④ 부모가 규칙에서 뒤로 물러나 아이들이 자신이 상황을 책임지고 있다는 것을 깨달을 경우를 말하고 있으므로, 그 상황을 아이들이 '두려운(frightening)' 일로 느낀다는 것은 적절하다.

전문해석

어떤 사람들은 부모와 자식은 '친구'라야 한다고 말한다. 그들은 이런 종류의 관계가 아이들에게 편안한 분위기를 제공하고, 그러면 아이들이 스트레스를 덜 받고 자라고, 좀 더 ① 긍정적인 성격을 가지게 될 것이라고 말한다. 사실, 많은 어머니와 아버지들은 자녀들의 친구가 되려고 노력한다. 그러나 친구 같은 관계는 다소 '위험하다.' 부모 노릇을 한다는 것은 인기 경연이 아니다. 권위에 ② 도전하는 것은 어린이의 발달 과정에서 정상적인 부분이다. 규칙을 세워서 그것을 시행하는 것은 아이에게 자신이 가치에 있어서는 ③ 동등하지만 권위에 있어 동등한 것은 아님을 가르쳐 준다. 그렇게 되면 아이는 안전하고 안정감 있음을 느끼며 다시 어린아이로 돌아갈 수 있다. 믿지 않을지 모르지만, 자신들이 상황을 책임지고 있음을 깨닫는 것은 아이들에게는 ④ 두려운 일이다. 부모가 그들이 세운 규칙에서 뒤로 물러나게 되면, 아이들은 ⑤ 편안해지고(→ 불안해지고) 통제가 불가능해진다. 그들은 부모가 자신들을 보호해 줄 것이라는 것을 믿지 못하게 된다. 부모는 이러한 상황을 피하기 위해 이 충고를 따라야 한다.

구문풀이

13행 Believe it or not, **it**'s frightening [for children to realize {they are in charge of the situation}].

: it은 형식상의 주어이고, [ ]로 표시된 to부정사구가 내용상의 주어이다. { }는 to realize의 목적어에 해당하는 명사절이다.

어휘풀이

- atmosphere *n* 분위기, 환경
- challenge *v* 도전하다, 이의를 제기하다
- authority *n* 권위
- frightening *a* 두려운
- relieved *a* 안도하는, 다행으로 여기는
- character *n* 성격, 기질
- enforce *v* 집행[시행]하다, 강요하다
- in chare of ~을 책임지는

128 답 ①

출제 어휘	확인하기		
(A) collectively	집단적으로	/ individually	개인적으로
(B) benefit	이롭게 하다	/ impair	손상시키다, 해치다
(C) barrier	장애물	/ trigger	계기, 촉발제

정답풀이

(A) 이어지는 내용으로 보아, 사람들을 집단, 부족, 조직체로 묶는 것은 인간이 혼자서보다는 '집단적으로(collectively)' 더 많은 것을 할 수 있다는 전제에 기초한다는 것이 적절하다. [individually 개인적으로]
(B) 사람들이 음식과 거처를 공유하며 가족의 안전을 위해 무리를 이룬다고 했으므로, 집단에의 가담과 연합이 개인과 사랑하는 사람들을 '이롭게 할

(benefit)' 것이라는 것이 적절하다. [impair 손상시키다, 해치다]
(C) 단지 12퍼센트의 사람들만이 조직체를 통해 삶이 더 좋아졌다고 했으므로 직원 대부분은 회사가 그들의 건강과 행복에 '장애물(barrier)'이라고 느꼈다는 것이 적절하다. [trigger 계기, 촉발제]

전문해석

사람들을 집단, 부족 혹은 조직체로 묶는 개념은 인간이 홀로 할 수 있는 것보다 (A) 집단적으로 더 많은 것을 할 수 있다는 기본적인 전제에 기초를 두고 있다. 수백 년 전에, 사람들은 음식과 거처를 공유하고 그들의 가족을 안전하게 지키기 위해 무리를 이루었다. 기본적인 가정은 집단에 가담하는 것에 의해 얻어지는 연합이 개인과 그들이 사랑하는 사람들을 (B) 이롭게 할 것이라는 것이었다. 이것이 바로 이 주제에 대해 Gallup이 수행했던 연구에 의해 내가 깜짝 놀랐던 이유이다. 미국 전역의 근로자들은 그들이 일하고 있는 조직체로 인해 그들의 삶이 더 좋아졌는지에 대해 질문을 받았을 때, 단지 12퍼센트의 사람들만이 자신들의 삶이 상당히 더 좋아졌다고 주장했다. 대부분의 직원들은 그들의 회사가 그들의 전반적인 건강과 행복에 (C) 장애물이라고 느꼈다.

구문풀이

7행 The basic assumption was [that the association {gained by joining a group} would benefit individuals and their loved ones].

: [ ]는 was의 보어로 쓰인 명사절이고, 그 안의 { }는 the association을 수식하는 과거분사구이다.

어휘풀이

- bring together 불러모으다
- organization *n* 조직체
- fundamental *a* 기본적인, 근본적인
- in isolation 홀로
- for the sake of ~을 위해
- take aback 깜짝 놀라게 하다
- better off 형편이 더 좋은, 부유한
- tribe *n* 부족
- be based on ~에 기초를 두다
- premise *n* 전제
- band together 무리를 이루다
- assumption *n* 가정
- conduct *v* 수행하다
- significantly *ad* 상당히

129 답 ④

출제 어휘 확인하기

①	prefer	우선하다, 선호하다	↔	
②	extend	확장하다, 연장하다	↔	
③	refine	정련하다, 다듬다	↔	
④	superiority	우월함	↔	inferiority(열등함)
⑤	revelation	폭로, 발현	↔	concealment(숨김, 은폐)

정답풀이

④ 사람은 개인으로서는 도덕적일 수 있지만, 집단이 되면 도덕적이기 어렵다는 내용의 글이다. 그러므로 개인의 도덕성에 대한 집단 도덕성의 '우월함(superiority)'이라는 것은 적절하지 않으며 반대 의미의 inferiority(열등함) 정도로 바꿔 써야 한다.

오답풀이

① 자신의 이익 이외의 이익을 고려할 수 있다는 앞 문장의 내용과, 타인에 대한 동정과 배려심을 선천적으로 부여받는다는 뒤 문장의 내용으로 보아, 자신의 이득보다 타인의 이득을 '우선할(preferring)' 수 있다는 것은 적절하다.
② 교육적 규율은 정의감을 정련하고 그것에서 이기적 요소를 제거할 수 있다는 내용이 이어지므로, 선천적으로 부여받은 동정심과 배려심이 사회적 교육에 의해 '확장될(extended)' 수 있을 것이라는 흐름은 적절하다.
③ 교육적 규율을 통해 이기적인 마음을 제거할 수 있는 것은 개인이 갖는 정의감을 '정련하는' 것으로 볼 수 있으므로 refine은 적절하다.

⑤ 개인이 집단을 이룰 때는 집단적 충동을 제어할 강력한 이성적 힘의 정립이 어렵다고 했으므로, 개인의 이기적 충동이 혼합되어 집단 이기주의로 '드러나는 것(revelation)'이라는 표현은 적절하다.

전문해석

개개의 사람은 행동의 문제를 결정하는 데 있어 자신의 이익 이외의 이익을 고려할 수 있고, 자신의 이득보다 다른 사람들의 이득을 ① 우선할 수 있다는 의미에서 도덕적일 수 있다. 그들은 선천적으로 같은 인간에 대한 상당한 동정심과 배려심을 부여받으며, 그 폭은 빈틈없는 사회적 교육에 의해 ② 확장될 수 있을 것이다. 그들의 이성적 능력은 그들에게 정의감을 갖게 하는데, 교육적 규율이 이 정의감을 ③ 정련하고 그것에서 이기적 요소를 제거할 수 있다. 그러나 이 모든 성취들이 인간 사회와 사회 집단의 경우에는 보다 어렵다. 개인의 도덕성에 대한 집단 도덕성의 ④ 우월함(→ 열등함)의 이유는 부분적으로는, 사회가 그 응집을 이루는 자연적 충동에 대응할 만큼 강력한 이성적인 사회적 힘을 확립하는 것이 어렵기 때문이다. 그러나 부분적으로 그것은 개인들의 이기적 충동이 혼합된 집단 이기주의의 ⑤ 발현에 불과하며, 이는 하나의 공통된 충동으로 합쳐질 때 가중된 효과를 성취하게 된다.

구문풀이

1행 Individual men may be moral in the sense [that they are able to consider interests other than **their own** in determining problems of conduct, and are capable of preferring the advantages of others to **their own**].

: [ ]는 the sense와 동격 관계를 이루는 절이다. 첫번째 their own 다음에는 interests가, 두 번째 their own 다음에는 advantages가 생략되어 있다.

어휘풀이

- endow A with B A에게 B를 부여하다
- measure *n* (꽤 많은) 양, 척도
- consideration *n* 배려, 존중
- rational *a* 이성적인
- prompt *v* 촉구하다, 불어넣다
- refine *v* 정련하다, 깨끗하게 하다
- egoistic *a* 이기주의의
- cope with ~에 대처[대응]하다
- cohesion *n* 응집력, 단결
- egoism *n* 이기심, 이기주의
- by nature 날 때부터, 본래
- sympathy *n* 동정(심)
- breadth *n* 폭, 넓이
- faculty *n* 능력
- discipline *n* 규율; 학과
- rid A of B A에서 B를 제거하다
- morality *n* 도덕성
- impulse *n* 충동
- revelation *n* 폭로, 발현
- compound *v* 혼합하다, 합성하다

130 답 ③

출제 어휘 확인하기

①	label	꼬리표를 붙이다	↔	
②	rare	드문	↔	common(흔한)
③	accurate	정확한	↔	inaccurate(부정확한)
④	unconcerned	무관심한	↔	concerned(관심이 있는)
⑤	inaction	행동을 취하지 않음, 가만히 있음	↔	action(행동, 조치)

정답풀이

③ 다른 사람들의 행동으로부터 귀중한 정보를 얻는 경우를 설명한 앞 문단과 But으로 이어지는 문장이므로, 때때로 다른 사람들의 반응이 '정확하지 않은' 정보를 제공하기도 한다는 내용이 되어야 자연스럽다. 따라서 accurate(정확한)를 false(거짓의) 정도로 바꿔 써야 한다.

오답풀이

① 대기실로 쏟아져 들어오는 연기가 화재에 의한 것일 수도, 증기 파이프의 누출일 수도 있다는 것은 비상 상황에 명확한 '꼬리표가 붙어 있지' 않다는 것이므로 labeled는 적절하다.

② 주변 사람들의 행동으로부터 새로운 상황에 대한 귀중한 정보를 얻는다고 했으므로, 식당 주차장에 다른 차들이 없다면 그곳에 차를 멈추는 여행객은 '드물(rare)' 것임을 알 수 있다.

④ 내면의 불안을 제대로 보여 주지 않는, 즉 냉정을 잃는 것을 창피한 일로 여기는 사람들을 설명하는 부분이므로, 잠재적으로 심각한 상황에서 사람들은 실제보다 더 '무관심한(unconcerned)' 것처럼 보일 것이라고 한 것은 적절하다.

⑤ 군중의 수동성을 통해 사건이 비상 상황이 아님을 암시한다면 사람들은 '가만히 있을 것'이므로 inaction은 적절하게 쓰였다.

전문해석

일단 어떤 사건이 목격되면, 구경하는 사람은 그것이 정말로 비상 상황인지를 결정해야 한다. 비상 상황은 항상 명확하게 그와 같은 것으로 (a) 꼬리표가 붙어 있는 것은 아닌데, 대기실로 쏟아져 들어오는 '연기'는 화재에 의해 야기될 수도 있고 단순히 증기 파이프의 누출을 나타낼 수도 있다. 거리에서의 비명은 공격이나 가족 간의 다툼을 나타낼 수도 있다. 출입구에 누워 있는 한 남자는 관상 동맥증을 앓고 있을 수도 있고 그저 술을 깨려고 잠을 자고 있을 수도 있다.

어떤 상황을 해석하려고 하는 사람은 자신이 어떻게 반응해야 하는지 알기 위해 흔히 주변 사람들을 본다. 만약 다른 모든 사람이 침착하고 무관심하다면, 그는 그런 상태를 유지하려는 경향이 있을 것이고, 다른 모든 사람이 강하게 반응하고 있다면, 그는 아마 경계하게 될 것이다. 이러한 경향은 단순히 맹목적인 순응이 아닌데, 보통 우리는 우리 주변의 다른 사람들이 어떻게 행동하는지로부터 새로운 상황에 대한 많은 귀중한 정보를 얻는다. 길가의 식당을 고를 때 주차장에 다른 차들이 없는 곳에서 멈추기를 선택하는 여행객은 (b) 드물다.

그러나 때때로 다른 사람들의 반응은 (c) 정확한(→ 거짓) 정보를 제공한다. 연구된 치과 병원 대기실에 있는 환자의 무관심은 그들 내면의 불안을 제대로 보여 주지 않는다. 사람들 앞에서 '냉정을 잃는' 것은 창피한 일로 여겨진다. 그렇다면 잠재적으로 심각한 상황에서 그곳에 있는 모든 사람은 실제보다 더 (d) 무관심한 것처럼 보일 것이다. 따라서 군중은 수동성을 통해 사건이 비상 상황이 아님을 암시함으로써 구성원들이 (e) 가만히 있도록 강제할 수 있다. 그런 군중 속에 있는 사람은 누구라도 그 사건이 비상 상황인 것처럼 행동하면 자신이 바보처럼 보일까 봐 두려워한다.

구문풀이

9행 A person [trying to interpret a situation] often looks at those around him [to see {how he should react}].

: 첫 번째 [ ]는 A person을 수식하는 현재분사구이다. 두 번째 [ ]는 목적의 의미를 나타내는 to부정사구이고, 그 안의 { }는 to see의 목적어 역할을 하는 의문사절이다.

16행 It's a rare traveler [who, {in picking a roadside restaurant}, chooses to stop at one {where no other cars appear in the parking lot}].

: 「It is[was] ~ that ....」의 강조구문으로 a rare traveler를 강조하고 있다. 강조되는 대상이 사람이어서 that 대신 who가 쓰였다. 첫 번째 { }는 삽입어구이고, 두 번째 { }는 one(= a roadside restaurant)을 수식하는 관계절이다.

어휘풀이

- onlooker *n* 구경하는 사람
- label *v* 꼬리표를 붙이다
- signal *v* 나타내다
- alert *a* 경계하는, 기민한
- derive *v* 얻다, 이끌어 내다
- occasionally *ad* 때때로, 이따금
- anxiety *n* 불안
- lose one's cool 냉정을 잃다
- inaction *n* 행동을 취하지 않음, 가만히 있음
- imply *v* 넌지시 비추다, 암시하다
- emergency *n* 비상 상황
- indicate *v* 나타내다, 보여 주다
- interpret *v* 해석하다
- conformity *n* 순응
- rare *a* 드문
- accurate *a* 정확한
- embarrassing *a* 창피한
- acute *a* 심각한
- passivity *n* 수동성, 소극성

---

07 필수 어휘
본문 pp.117 ~ 120

Q1 1 complimented 2 banished 3 decline 4 conventional 5 deny

Q2 1 ② 2 ① 3 ②

131 ③   132 ④   133 ⑤   134 ⑤   135 ⑤

136 ④

Q1

1. [해석] 그녀는 아홉 살 난 소년의 예의 바름을 칭찬했다. [complement 보충하다]

2. [해석] 왕은 그 살인자를 나라에서 추방했다. [vanish 사라지다]

3. [해석] 좋은 소식은 연령에 상관없이 근력을 기르기 시작하기에 너무 늦은 때는 결코 없다는 것이다. 하지만 이상적으로는 근육의 양이 심하게 감소하기 시작하는 시기인 40대 중반에 시작하는 것이 가장 좋다. [rise 증가하다]

4. [해석] 여러분은 일을 하는 기존의 방식에 이의를 제기하고 혁신할 수 있는 기회를 찾아야 한다. [complementary 상호 보완적인]

5. [해석] 우리가 분노와 우리의 부정적인 생각과 감정을 억제할 필요가 있다고 말하는 것은 우리의 감정을 부정해야 한다는 것을 반드시 의미하지는 않는다. [admit 인정하다]

Q2

1. [해석] 서로의 관심과 우려에 관한 문제에 대해 이웃과 이야기할 수 없다면 민주주의 체제를 가질 수 없다.
   ① 배타적인 ③ 정당한, 적법한

2. [해석] 다음번에 여러분이 더 잘할 수 있는 것이 무엇이라고 그들이 말하는지 정말로 들으려 하기 위해서는 여러분을 불쾌하게 하는 것들을 제쳐놓으려고 하라.
   ② 변화시키다 ③ 산만하게 하다

3. [해석] 음식은 먹는 사람들을 구분 지을 뿐만 아니라 결속하기도 하는데, 왜냐하면 사람이 먹는 것과 먹는 방식이 집단 정체성에 대한 그 사람의 정서적 유대의 많은 부분을 형성하기 때문이다.
   ① 경향성 ③ 부담

---

131 답 ③

출제 어휘	확인하기		
① govern	지배하다	↔	
② inescapably	필연적으로	↔	
③ conceal	숨기다	↔	reveal(드러내다)
④ dictate	좌우하다	↔	
⑤ development	발전	↔	

정답풀이

③ 과거의 교회나 군주제의 위상에 현재 기업들이 가지는 위상을 비유한 부분

으로, 위압적 건물과 오만한 과시 속에서 절대 옳고 전지전능하다는 태도를 취하는 것은 그들이 스스로를 '숨기는' 것이라고 볼 수 없다. 따라서 concealing 은 적절하지 않으며 glorifying(미화하다) 정도로 바꿔 써야 한다.

오답풀이
① 기업이 세계의 지배적인 경제 기관이 되었고 우리의 거의 모든 것을 결정한다는 흐름이므로 '지배한다(govern)'는 것은 적절하다.
② 기업의 영향력이 막대해졌다는 내용이므로 그들의 문화와 사상에 '필연적으로(inescapably)' 둘러싸여 있다는 것은 적절하다.
④ 기업들의 커진 영향력을 보여 주는 또 다른 내용으로, 기업이 정부 감독자의 결정을 '좌우한다(dictate)'는 것은 적절하다.
⑤ 기업의 입지가 막강해졌다는 흐름이므로, 지배를 향한 극적인 '발전(development)'이라는 표현은 적절하다.

전문해석
지난 150년 넘게 기업은 상대적으로 중요하지 않은 존재에서 상승하여 세계의 지배적인 경제 기관이 되었다. 오늘날 기업은 우리 삶을 ① 지배한다. 그들은 우리가 먹는 것, 우리가 보는 것, 우리가 입는 것, 우리가 일하는 곳, 그리고 우리가 하는 일을 결정한다. 우리는 ② 필연적으로 그들의 문화와 사상에 둘러싸여 있다. 그리고 다른 시대의 교회나 군주제와 마찬가지로, 위압적인 건물과 오만한 과시 속에서 스스로를 ③ 숨기면서(→ 미화하면서) 그들은 절대 옳고 전지전능하다는 태도를 취한다. 기업은 점점 더 정부 안에 있는 자신들의 감독자의 결정을 ④ 좌우하고, 한때 공공영역 안에 굳게 박혀 있던 사회의 영역들을 통제한다. 지배를 향한 기업의 극적인 ⑤ 발전은 현대사의 주목할 만한 사건 중 하나이다.

구문풀이
7행 And, like the church and the monarchy in other times, they posture as infallible and omnipotent, [glorifying themselves in imposing buildings and arrogant displays].

: [ ]는 주절의 they를 의미상의 주어로 하여 내용을 부연 설명하는 분사구문이다.

어휘풀이
- corporation *n* 기업, 회사
- relative *a* 상대적인
- obscurity *n* 중요하지 않은 것[사람], 무명
- dominant *a* 주도하는, 지배적인
- institution *n* 기관, 단체
- inescapably *ad* 필연적으로
- ideology *n* 사상, 이데올로기
- monarchy *n* 군주제
- posture *v* 태도를 취하다 *n* 자세, 태도
- omnipotent *a* 전지전능한
- imposing *a* 위압적인
- arrogant *a* 오만한, 거만한
- dictate *v* 좌우하다; 지시하다
- overseer *n* 감독자
- domain *n* 영역, 분야
- embed *v* 박다, 끼워 넣다
- sphere *n* 영역, 분야; 구
- dominance *n* 지배, 우세
- remarkable *a* 두드러진, 주목할 만한

132 답 ④

출제 어휘 확인하기			
① identify	동질감을 갖다	↔	
② passionate	열정적인	↔	
③ failure	실패	↔	success(성공)
④ increase	늘리다	↔	decrease(줄이다)
⑤ defeat	무산시키다	↔	

정답풀이
④ 스포츠는 다른 제품에 비해 그 팬이 훨씬 강한 충성심을 가지게 되는 특성을 지니는데, 그러한 강렬한 정서적 반응은 스포츠 조직 전통에 대한 향수와 과거에 대한 집착을 갖는 것을 의미하기도 하므로, 변화하는 시장 상황에 빠

르게 대응하기는 어렵다는 내용이다. 따라서 신속하게 대응할 필요성을 '늘릴 (increase)' 수도 있다는 것은 적절하지 않으며 '무시할' 수도 있다는 의미의 ignore 정도로 바꿔 써야 한다.

오답풀이
① 스포츠의 소비자가 갖는 충성심을 다른 제품에 적용해 설명하는 흐름에서 고객이 자동차 보험 회사에 대해 강한 '동질감을 갖는' 경우를 상상해 보라는 것이므로 identifying은 적절하다.
② 일부 스포츠 추종자들의 선수, 팀 그리고 그 스포츠에 대한 관심이 집착에 가깝다는 내용이 나오므로, 이와 같은 문맥에서 매우 '열정적(passionate)'이라는 것은 적절하다.
③ 스포츠팬의 열정, 집착, 중독이 팬을 팀과 묶어 주는 정서적 접착제를 제공한다고 했으므로, 그 팀이 '실패(failure)'하더라도 충성심이 유지된다는 것은 적절하다.
⑤ 스포츠에 대한 격렬한 열정이 향수와 과거에 대한 애착을 준다고 했으므로, 구단 색깔을 바꾸자는 제안은 전통과의 관계를 끊기 때문에 '무산될 (defeated)' 수 있다는 것은 적절하다.

전문해석
스포츠는 그것의 소비자에게 다른 제품이 거의 일으키지 못하는 종류의 정서적 반응을 촉발시킬 수 있다. 은행 고객이 그들 은행에 대한 충성심을 보여 주기 위해 기념품을 구입하거나, 고객이 그들 자동차 보험 회사에 대해 매우 강하게 ① 동질감을 가져서 그 회사 로고로 문신을 한다고 상상해 보라. 우리는 일부 스포츠 추종자들이 선수, 팀 그리고 그 스포츠 자체에 매우 ② 열정적이어서 그들의 관심이 집착에 아주 가깝다는 것을 안다. 이런 중독은 팬을 팀과 묶어 주는 정서적 접착제를 제공하고, 구장에서 일어나는 ③ 실패에 직면했을 때도 충성심을 유지하게 한다. 대부분의 관리자는 스포츠팬만큼 그들 제품에 열정적인 고객을 가지기만을 꿈꾸는 한편, 스포츠로 인해 촉발되는 감정은 또한 부정적인 영향을 미칠 수 있다. 스포츠의 정서적 격렬함은 조직이 향수 및 구단 전통을 통해 과거에 대한 강한 애착을 가지고 있다는 것을 뜻할 수 있다. 결과적으로, 그것[조직]은 효율성, 생산성 및 변화하는 시장 상황에 신속하게 대응해야 할 필요성을 ④ 늘릴(→ 무시할) 수도 있다. 예를 들면, 더 매력적인 이미지를 투사하기 위해 구단 색깔을 바꾸자는 제안은 그것이 전통과의 관계를 끊기 때문에 ⑤ 무산될 수도 있다.

구문풀이
12행 [While most managers can only dream of {having customers <that are **as** passionate about their products **as** sport fans>}], the emotion [triggered by sport] can also have a negative impact.

: 첫 번째 [ ]는 접속사 While(~하는 반면, ~이지만)이 이끄는 부사절이고, 그 안의 { }는 전치사 of의 목적어로 쓰인 동명사구이다. < >는 customers를 수식하는 관계절이며 「as ~ as ...(…만큼 ~한)」 구문이 쓰였다. 두 번째 [ ]는 주절의 핵심 주어인 the emotion을 수식하는 과거분사구이다.

어휘풀이
- trigger *v* 촉발하다, 유발하다
- bring forth ~을 일으키다
- loyalty *n* 충성(심)
- identify with ~와 동질감을 갖다, ~와 동일시하다
- insurance *n* 보험
- tattoo *n* 문신
- passionate *a* 열정적인
- border on ~에 아주 가깝다, 거의 ~와 같다
- addiction *n* 중독
- glue *n* 접착제
- bind *v* 묶다, 잇다, 엮다
- in the face of ~에 직면했을 때
- intensity *n* 강렬함, 강도
- attachment *n* 애착
- nostalgia *n* 향수, 그리움
- condition *n* 여건, 조건
- proposal *n* 제안
- project *v* 투사하다, 투영하다
- defeat *v* 무산시키다, 패하게 하다

133 답 ⑤

① cooperative	협동의	↔	
② balance	균형을 이루다	↔	
③ realistic	현실적인	↔	
④ interdependent	상호 의존적인	↔	
⑤ easy	쉬운	↔	difficult(어려운)

정답풀이

⑤ 사회 집단들의 구성원들이 자주 중복되면 지도자들이 경쟁하는 동맹들을 조직하기가 '쉽지 않을' 것이므로, easy를 반대 개념의 difficult(어려운) 정도로 바꿔 써야 한다.

오답풀이

① 부족 세계의 특징은 협력, 호혜성, 상호 보완적인 대립, 중복되는 인맥이라고 했으므로, 공동 집단 내에서 수행하는 작업의 특성을 나타내는 말로 cooperative(협동의)는 적절하다.

② 개인과 가구 간 경제 활동의 공유와 생산물의 분배가 공정할 것이라는 가정은 노력과 수익이 장기적으로 '균형을 이룰' 것이라고 생각하기 때문일 것이므로 balance는 적절하다.

③ 모든 사람이 서로 알고 있고 모두의 재산과 활동이 지속적으로 공개되는 소규모 사회에서는 공정성이 '현실적이었을' 것이므로 realistic은 적절하다.

④ 남성과 여성 또는 집단 A와 집단 B 같은 사회적 범주는 연결 집합으로 취급되어, 한쪽이 다른 한쪽 없이는 존재할 수 없는 그런 것이라고 했으므로, 두 개의 '상호 의존적인(interdependent)' 절반이라고 표현한 것은 적절하다.

전문해석

부족 세계에서 대인 관계와 집단 간 관계의 주요 특징은 협력, 호혜성, 상호 보완적인 대립 그리고 중복되는 인맥이었다. 사람들은 공동 집단 내에서 ① 협동 작업으로 대부분의 일상적인 가사를 수행했다. 노력과 수익이 장기적으로 ② 균형을 이룰 것이기 때문에 공정할 것이라는 가정하에 개인과 가구 간의 호혜성에 기초하여 경제 활동이 공유되고 생산물이 분배됐다. 공정성이라는 가정은 모든 사람이 다른 모두를 알고 있고, 모든 사람의 재산과 활동이 지속적으로 공개되는 이러한 소규모 사회에서 ③ 현실적이었다. 남성과 여성 또는 집단 A와 집단 B 같은 사회적 범주는 연결 집합으로 취급되었고, 서로 다른 부분들은 더 큰 전체의 ④ 상호 의존적인 두 개의 절반, 즉 하나의 절반이 다른 절반 없이는 존재할 수 없는 그런 것으로 문화적으로 이해되었다. 사회 집단들의 구성원들은 또한 자주 중복되었는데, 이는 야심 찬 지도자들이 경쟁하는 동맹들을 조직하는 것을 ⑤ 쉽게(→ 어렵게) 만드는 교차 인맥을 형성했다.

구문풀이

6행 Economic activities were shared and products were distributed on the basis of reciprocity between individuals and households, on the assumption [that this would be fair because effort and returns would balance out over the long run].

: [ ]는 the assumption과 동격 관계를 이루는 명사절이다.

10행 The assumption of fairness was realistic in these small societies [where {everyone knew everyone else}, and {everyone's possessions and activities were on constant public display}].

: [ ]는 these small societies를 수식하는 관계절이고, 그 안에 두 개의 { }가 and에 의해 대등하게 연결되어 where에 이어진다.

어휘풀이

- feature *n* 특성
- tribal *a* 부족의

- cooperation *n* 협동
- complementary *a* 상호 보완적인
- overlapping *a* 중복되는, 겹치는
- corporate *a* 공동의
- assumption *n* 전제, 가정
- interdependent *a* 상호 의존적인
- alliance *n* 동맹
- reciprocity *n* 호혜성
- opposition *n* 경쟁, 대립
- domestic *a* 가사의, 국내의
- distribute *v* 분배하다
- possession *n* 소유(물), 재산
- aspiring *a* 야심 찬

134 답 ⑤

출제 어휘

① vice	악덕	↔	virtue(덕, 선)
② cheat	속이다, 속여서 빼앗다	↔	
③ undone	미완성인	↔	done(완료된)
④ futile	쓸데없는, 무익한	↔	fruitful(유익한)
⑤ praise	칭찬	↔	criticism(비판, 비난)

정답풀이

⑤ 필자가 Thoreau의 생각을 이해할 수 있다는 것은 필자의 의견이 Thoreau의 의견과 일치한다는 것으로 볼 수 있으므로, Thoreau도 편지를 부치러 우체국으로 향하는 미국인들의 행동을 부정적인 관점에서 보았을 것이다. 따라서 praise(칭찬)는 적절하지 않으며 contempt(경멸) 정도로 바꿔 써야 한다.

오답풀이

① 효율성, 시간 엄수, 성취와 성공에 대한 욕구 등이 미국인들을 매우 불행하고 긴장하게 만든다고 했으므로, 이를 부정적인 관점에서 표현한 '악덕(vices)'은 적절하다.

② 앞서 말한 악덕에 속하는 것들이 미국인들에게서 빈둥거리는 권리를 앗아간다고 했으므로, 같은 문맥에서 즐겁고 한가하며 아름다운 오후를 '빼앗는다(cheat)'는 것은 적절하다.

③ 효율성과 시간 엄수 같은 것들이 불행과 긴장을 만든다고 했으므로, 일을 마무리짓는 것보다는 '미완성인(undone)' 채로 두는 것을 더 고결하다고 보는 것은 적절하다.

④ 편지를 서랍에 넣어 둔 뒤 나중에 읽어 보면 편지에 신속히 답장할 필요가 없음을 깨닫게 된다는 흐름이므로, 모든 편지에 답장하는 것이 '무익하다(futile)'는 것은 적절하다.

전문해석

미국인의 가장 큰 3대 ① 악덕은 효율성, 시간 엄수 그리고 성취와 성공에 대한 욕구인 것 같다. 그것들이 미국인들을 매우 불행하고 긴장하게 만드는 것들이다. 그것들은 미국인들에게서 양도할 수 없는 빈둥거림의 권리를 앗아가며, 많은 즐겁고 한가하며 아름다운 오후를 ② 빼앗는다. 우리는 이 세상에 대참사는 없으며, 일을 마무리짓는 고결한 기술 외에, ③ 미완성인 채로 두는 더 고결한 기술이 있다는 믿음으로 시작해야 한다. 대체로, 만약에 편지에 대한 답장을 신속히 한다면, 결과는 아예 답장하지 않는 것만큼 좋을 수도 있고 나쁠 수도 있다. 만약 편지를 석 달 동안 서랍에 넣어 둔 뒤 석 달 후에 읽어 본다면, 그 모든 편지들에 답장하는 것이 얼마나 철저히 ④ 무익하고, 시간 낭비일 수 있었는지를 깨닫게 될지도 모른다. 이런 의미에서 나는 항상 우체국으로 가는 미국인들에 대한 Thoreau의 ⑤ 칭찬(→ 경멸)을 이해할 수 있다.

구문풀이

6행 One must start out with a belief [that there are no catastrophes in this world], and [that besides the noble art of getting things done, there is nobler art of leaving things undone].

084 메가스터디 N제 영어 어법·어휘 222제

: 두 개의 [ ]는 모두 a belief와 의미상 동격 관계를 이루는 절로, and에 의해 병렬 연결되었다.

어휘풀이
- vice _n_ 악덕, 부도덕; 결함, 약점
- inalienable _a_ 양도할 수 없는, 빼앗을 수 없는
- cheat _v_ 속이다, 속여서 빼앗다
- idle _a_ 한가한, 태만한
- catastrophe _n_ 큰 재앙, 대참사
- noble _a_ 고귀한, 고결한
- promptly _ad_ 즉시, 신속히
- utterly _ad_ 완전히, 아주, 철저히
- futile _a_ 쓸데없는, 무익한

135 답 ⑤

(A) disturb	방해하다	/ help	돕다
(B) resistant	저항하는, 견디는	/ susceptible	취약한
(C) prevent	예방하다	/ worsen	악화시키다

정답풀이
(A) Alternatively(그 대신)로 연결되어, 앞에 서술된 기후 변화 과정의 부정적 영향과 반대되는 내용, 즉 더 높은 비율의 새로운 토양 형성에 기여할 수 있다는 것과 같은 긍정적인 내용이 나오고 있다. 따라서 생물 생산량 증가에 긍정적인 영향을 준다는 의미가 되도록 help(돕다)를 쓰는 것이 적절하다. [disturb 방해하다]
(B) 건조한 지역은 땅을 갈고 나면 온도 상승과 수분 증발, 토지 이용 가속화 등이 결합되면서 생기는 가뭄에 더 견디기 어려워질 것이므로 susceptible(취약한)이 적절하다. [resistant 저항하는, 견디는]
(C) 뒤 문장이 Likewise(마찬가지로)로 시작하며 기온 상승이 농업 생산성에 미치는 부정적인 영향에 대해 서술하고 있다. 따라서 앞 문장 역시 부정적인 영향에 관해 언급하는 것이 자연스러우므로 물 (부족)의 압박을 '악화시킬(worsen)' 수 있다고 하는 것이 적절하다. [prevent 예방하다]

전문해석
현재의 추세는 인구 증가가 몇몇 경제 개발도상국에서 가장 높다는 것을 보여 준다. 이러한 많은 지역에서는 영양실조가 이미 중대한 문제일 뿐만 아니라, 그 지역들 중 다수는 기후 변화 과정에 의해 더 부정적으로 영향을 받을 수 있는 중요한 열대 지역을 포함하고 있기도 하다. 그 대신, 대기 중 CO_2 수준의 증가 및 그와 관련된 질소 고정의 증가는 생물 생산량을 증가시키는 데 (A) 도움을 주고, 더 높은 비율의 새로운 토양 형성에 기여할 수 있다. 기후 변화 과정은 물 공급과 수요의 변화를 일으킬 가능성이 있다. 건조한 지역은 땅을 갈고 난 이후에 더 따뜻한 온도, 수분 증발, 토지 이용 기술이 결합되어 생기는 가뭄에 특히 (B) 취약할 수 있다. 도시화의 증가된 속도와 불균등한 인구 증가는 일부 지역에서 물 (부족)의 압박을 (C) 악화시킬 수 있다. 마찬가지로, 더 따뜻한 기온은 해충 개체수의 번성 및 농업 생산성에 미치는 부정적인 영향의 원인이 될 가능성이 높다.

구문풀이
3행 **Not only is malnutrition** already a significant issue in many of these places, **but** many of them also include significant tropical areas [which may be more negatively affected by climate change processes].

: 'A뿐만 아니라 B도'라는 뜻의 「Not only A, but (also) B」 구문이 쓰인 문장으로, 부정어구인 Not only가 문장의 앞에 위치하여 주어 malnutrition과 동사 is가 도치되었다. [ ]는 significant tropical areas를 수식하는 관계절이다.

어휘풀이
- malnutrition _n_ 영양실조
- tropical area 열대 지역

- alternatively _ad_ 대신에
- atmospheric _a_ 대기의
- productivity _n_ 생산(성)
- contribute to ~에 기여하다, ~의 원인이 되다
- formation _n_ 형성
- generate _v_ 일으키다, 만들어 내다
- susceptible _a_ 취약한
- drought _n_ 가뭄
- evaporation _n_ 증발
- urbanization _n_ 도시화
- uneven _a_ 불균등한
- thrive _v_ 번성하다
- pest _n_ 해충
- agricultural _a_ 농업의

136 답 ④

①	accurate	정확한	↔	inaccurate(부정확한)
②	better	더 잘하는	↔	worse(더 서투른)
③	irrelevant	관련 없는	↔	relevant(관련 있는)
④	relaxed	편안한	↔	
⑤	effective	효과적인	↔	ineffective(효과적이지 못한)

정답풀이
④ 어떠한 조치라도 놓치지 않기 위한 체크리스트가 필요한 상황은 많은 관련 요인들이 있고 상황이 매우 불확실한 상황, 예를 들어 집중 치료 중인 환자에게 하루에 수백 가지의 작은 조치가 필요한 상황으로, 이는 사람들이 '편안하다'고 느낄 때가 아니라 '일이 많다'고 느낄 때라고 할 수 있다. 따라서 relaxed를 overloaded 정도로 바꿔 써야 한다.

오답풀이
① 간단한 예측 문제에 대해 알고리즘이 전문가의 판단을 능가할 수 있다는 사례를 드는 문장이므로, 알고리즘의 예측이 인간의 예측보다 더 '정확하다(accurate)'는 것은 적절하다.
② 계속해서 많은 연구를 통해 알고리즘이 전문가의 판단을 능가할 수 있다는 것이 입증되었음을 이야기하고 있으므로, 알고리즘이 인간 전문가보다 중요한 예측을 '더 잘한다(better)'는 것은 적절하다.
③ 알고리즘은 가장 중요한 요소들에 초점을 맞추고 일관성을 유지하지만 인간의 판단은 그렇지 않다는 맥락이므로, 인간의 판단이 '관련이 없는(irrelevant)' 고려 사항에 쉽게 영향을 받는다고 하는 것은 적절하다.
⑤ 체크리스트를 사용하면 다양한 영역에서 전문가의 결정의 질을 향상할 수 있다는 맥락이므로 effective(효과적인)는 적절하다.

전문해석
심지어 매우 간단한 알고리즘조차도 간단한 예측 문제에 대한 전문가의 판단을 능가할 수 있다는 증거가 있다. 예를 들어, 가석방으로 풀려난 어떤 죄수가 계속해서 또 다른 범죄를 저지를 것인지를 예측하거나 잠재적인 후보자가 장차 직장에서 업무를 잘 수행할 것인지를 예측하는 데 있어 알고리즘이 인간보다 더 (a) 정확하다는 것이 입증되었다. 많은 다른 영역에 걸친 100개가 넘는 연구에서 모든 사례의 절반은 간단한 공식이 인간 전문가보다 중요한 예측을 (b) 더 잘하고 그 나머지는 (아주 적은 소수를 제외하고) 둘 사이의 무승부를 보여 준다. 관련된 많은 다른 요인들이 있고 상황이 매우 불확실할 때 가장 중요한 요소들에 초점을 맞추고 일관성을 유지함으로써 간단한 공식이 승리할 수 있는 반면, 인간의 판단은 특히 두드러지고 아마도 (c) 관련이 없는 고려 사항에 의해 너무 쉽게 영향을 받는다. '체크리스트'가 사람들이 (d) 편안하다고(→ 일이 너무 많다고) 느낄 때 중요한 조치나 고려 사항을 놓치지 않게 함으로써 다양한 영역에서 전문가의 결정의 질을 향상할 수 있다는 추가적인 증거가 비슷한 생각을 뒷받침한다. 예를 들어, 집중 치료 중인 환자를 치료하는 데 하루에 수백 가지의 작은 조치가 필요할 수 있고, 작은 실수 하나가 목숨을 잃게 할 수 있다. 어떠한 중요한 조치라도 놓치지 않기 위해서 체크리스트를 사용하는 것은 당면한 감염을 예방하는 것에서부터 폐렴을 줄이는 것에 이르기까지 다양한 의료 상황

에서 현저하게 (e) 효과적이라는 것이 입증되었다.

구문풀이

24행 [Using checklists to ensure {that no crucial steps are missed}] has proved to be remarkably effective in a range of medical contexts, [from preventing live infections to reducing pneumonia].

: 첫 번째 [ ]는 문장의 주어 역할을 하는 동명사구이고, 그 안의 { }는 to ensure의 목적어 역할을 하는 명사절이다. 두 번째 [ ]는 a range of medical contexts를 부연 설명하는 전치사구이다.

어휘풀이

- evidence *n* 증거
- expert *n* 전문가
- accurate *a* 정확한
- commit *v* (범죄 등을) 저지르다
- candidate *n* 후보
- formula *n* 공식
- handful *n* 소수
- irrelevant *a* 관련이 없는
- intensive care 집중 치료
- crucial *a* 매우 중요한
- live *a* 당면한, 생생한
- outperform *v* 능가하다
- prediction *n* 예측
- release *v* 풀어주다
- potential *a* 잠재적인
- domain *n* 영역
- remainder *n* 나머지
- consistent *a* 일관성이 있는
- step *n* 조치
- cost *v* 잃게 하다
- remarkably *ad* 현저하게
- infection *n* 감염

Q1 **1** Minorities **2** victim **3** inconsistent **4** induce **5** resistant

Q2 **1** ③ **2** ③ **3** ①

137 ③ **138** ④ **139** ④ **140** ④ **141** ③

142 ②

Q1

1. 해석 소수 집단은 큰 힘이나 지위를 갖지 않는 경향이 있으며, 심지어는 말썽꾼, 극단주의자 또는 단순히 '별난 사람들'로 일축되기도 한다. [majority 대다수]

2. 해석 기억상실증은 환자를 새로운 기억을 형성할 수 없는 상태에 있게 하는 뇌 손상으로 인해 대부분 발생하지만, 과거의 기억 대부분은 손상되지 않은 채로 있게 한다. [suspect 용의자]

3. 해석 여러분은 상당한 정서적, 심리적 혹은 신체적 스트레스를 겪고 있는 동안에 누군가를 만난 적이 있는가? 여러분은 아마도 평소에 행동하는 방식과 일치하지 않는 행동을 보였을 것이다. 극도로 스트레스를 받고 있을 때 누군가를 만나는 것은 여러분에 대한 정확하지 않은 인상을 만들어 낼 수 있다. [consistent 일치하는, 일관적인]

4. 해석 때때로 처벌이 몇 번 가해진 후에는 그것이 계속될 필요가 없는데, 왜냐하면 처벌하겠다는 단순한 위협만으로도 바라는 행동을 유도하기에 충분하기 때문이다. [deduce 추론하다, 연역하다]

5. 해석 민족과 민족적 하위 집단의 다른 뿌리 깊은 문화적인 특징은 변화시키기가 훨씬 더 어렵다. 이것들은 변화에 너무나 저항적이어서 선천적인 것처럼 보이는 문화 양상이다. [susceptible 영향을 받기 쉬운]

Q2

1. 해석 일단 인터넷이 음악을 쉽게 접근할 수 있게 만들자, 새로운 음악의 이용 가능성이 대중화되었는데, 그것은 비평가들이 더 이상 고유한 접근을 가지지 않는다는 것을 의미했다.
① 개작할 수 있는 ② 분배할 수 있는

2. 해석 다시 말하자면, 한 공동체의 운명은 그 공동체가 구성원들을 얼마나 잘 기르는지에 달려 있다.
① 사회화시키다 ② 결집시키다

3. 해석 마찬가지로, 수백만 년에 걸쳐 기후가 어떻게 변해 왔는지를 이해하는 것은 현재의 지구 온난화 추세를 적절히 평가하기 위해 매우 중요하다.
② 사소한 ③ 부적당한

137 답 ③

①	struggle	애쓰다	↔	
②	memory	기억	↔	
③	improbable	일어날 것 같지 않은	↔	probable(있음 직한, 있을 것 같은)
④	mentally	머릿속으로	↔	
⑤	start	시작	↔	end(끝)

정답풀이

③ 우리는 음악을 음의 덩어리로 인식하고 처리하므로 개별 음이 아니라 과정을 인식해서 음악을 기억한다는 내용의 글이다. 우리가 음악을 한 음씩 뇌에서 부호화하기는 힘들다는 내용이 앞에 나왔으므로 뛰어난 음악가들이 개별적인 음을 기억해서가 아니라 과정을 기억함으로써 수천 개의 음으로 된 곡을 완전히 기억으로만 연주하는 굉장한 일이 '일어날 수 있다'는 흐름이 되어야 자연스럽다. 따라서 '일어날 것 같지 않게(improbable)' 된다는 것은 적절하지 않으며 possible(가능한) 정도로 바꿔 써야 한다.

오답풀이

① 우리가 음악을 인식하는 데 있어 덩어리로 묶는 것은 필수적이라고 했으므로, 반대로 덩어리로 묶어서 기억하지 않고 한 음 한 음을 따로 기억해야 한다면 복잡한 것을 이해하는 데 '애쓰게(struggle)' 될 것이라는 흐름은 적절하다.
② 음악가들이 수천 개의 음을 포함하는 곡을 한 음도 틀리지 않고 '기억'으로만 연주할 수 있다고 한 다음, 그것을 기억의 성취라고 지칭하며 그렇게 할 수 있는 이유를 부연하고 있으므로 memory는 적절하다.
④ 피아니스트가 곡의 한 특정한 부분을 기억하고자 하는 방법을 운전해서 직장에 가는 방법에 비유하면서 그 방법은 도로 하나하나의 이름을 기억하는 것이 아니라 마음속에서 길을 되밟아 가면서 경로를 구성하는 것이라고 했으므로, 그 음이 속한 더 큰 부분을 '머릿속으로(mentally)' 되짚어가면서 기억해 낸다는 흐름은 적절하다.
⑤ 우리는 길을 기억할 때 마음속에서 그것을 되밟아 감으로써 경로를 구성한다고 했으므로, 이와 마찬가지로 음악가들은 리허설에서 실수하면 그 부분이 속한 더 큰 부분, 즉 그 음이 속한 악구의 '시작(start)'으로 되돌아간다는 것은 적절하다.

전문해석

덩어리로 나누는 것은 음악의 인식에서 필수적이다. 만일 우리가 그것(음악)을 한 음 한 음 뇌에서 부호화해야 한다면, 우리는 가장 단순한 동요보다 더 복잡한 것은 어느 것이나 이해하기 위해 ① 애쓰게 될 것이다. 물론, 대부분의 뛰어난 음악가들은 한 음도 틀리지 않고 수천 개의 음을 포함하는 곡을 완전히 ② 기억으로만 연주할 수 있다. 그렇지만 겉보기에는 굉장한 것 같은 이러한 기억의 성취는 보통 말하는 그런 개별적인 음이 아니라 음악적인 '과정'을 기억함으로써 ③ 일어날 것 같지 않게 되는 (→ 가능해지는) 것이다. 만일 여러분이 피아니스트에게 모차르트 소나타를 41번 마디부터 시작해 달라고 요청하면, 그녀는 아마도 그 마디에 이를 때까지 그 음악을 처음부터 ④ 머릿속으로 재생해야 할 것이다. 그 악보는 그저 그녀의 머릿속에 펼쳐져 있어서 어떤 임의의 지점부터 읽힐 수 있는 것이 아니다. 그것은 흡사 여러분이 운전해서 직장에 가는 방법을 설명하는 것과 같다. 여러분은 추상적인 목록으로 도로의 이름을 술술 말하는 것이 아니고 마음속에서 그것을 되밟아 감으로써 경로를 구성해야 한다. 음악가들이 리허설을 하는 동안 실수한다면, 그들은 다시 시작하기 전에 한 악구의 ⑤ 시작으로 되돌아간다('2절부터 다시 합시다').

구문풀이

15행 It's rather like describing [how you drive to work]: you [don't simply recite the names of roads as an abstract list], but [have to construct your route by mentally retracing it].

: 첫 번째 [ ]는 describing의 목적어인 의문사절이다. 두 번째와 세 번째 [ ]는 주어인 you에 공통으로 연결되는 술어이다.

어휘풀이

- vital *a* 필수적인
- accomplished *a* 기량이 뛰어난
- seemingly *ad* 겉보기에는
- score *n* 악보, 작품
- abstract *a* 추상적인
- phrase *n* 악구
- encode *v* 부호화하다
- composition *n* 작품, 곡
- as such 보통 말하는 그런
- recite *v* 나열하다
- retrace *v* 되짚어가다
- verse *n* (노래의) 절

138 답 ④

①	vary	다양하다, 다르다	↔	
②	reduce	감소시키다	↔	increase(증가시키다)
③	advantage	장점	↔	disadvantage(단점)
④	immobile	비이동성의, 움직이지 않는	↔	mobile(이동성의, 이동하기 쉬운)
⑤	predictable	예측할 수 있는	↔	unpredictable(예측할 수 없는)

정답풀이

④ 극한의 사막이나 몹시 추운 환경에서의 무리 이동성을 서술하는 문맥인데, 무리의 영역이 매우 넓어져야 한다고 했으므로 '이동성이 증가한다'는 흐름이 되어야 한다. 따라서 immobile(비이동성의, 움직이지 않는)을 반대 개념인 mobile(이동성의, 이동하기 쉬운)로 바꿔 써야 한다.

오답풀이

① 이어지는 내용에서 자연 환경에 따라 무리 영역의 크기가 '달라짐'을 보여주고 있으므로, varies는 적절하다.
② 먹이를 구하기 위해 필요 이상으로 멀리 걷기를 원하지 않는다고 했으므로 무리 이동성이 '감소한다(reduce)'는 말은 적절하다.
③ 자연이 식량 공급을 재생산하고 유지하는 일을 대신 수행한다는 것은 수렵채집 생산 체계의 '장점(advantage)'에 해당한다.
⑤ 강우량과 무리 밀도 사이의 관계를 수학적으로 설명할 수 있다고 했으므로, 매우 '예측 가능하다(predicable)'고 표현한 것은 적절하다.

전문해석

무리 크기에 대한 사회적 그리고 문화적 한계는 일정불변한 것이고, 그 한계가 일정한 최적 개체군 크기를 규정하지만, 무리 영역의 크기는 지역 생태계의 자연 환경 생산성에 따라 크게 ① 달라진다. 자연 환경이 매우 풍부하면 작은 고밀도 영역이 가능하고, 아무도 먹이를 구하기 위해 필요 이상으로 멀리 걷기를 원하지 않기 때문에 무리 이동성이 ② 감소한다. 수렵채집 생산 체계의 ③ 장점은 자연이 식량 공급을 재생산하고 유지하는 일을 수행한다는 것이다. 태양 에너지가 물 공급을 정화하고 재활용한다. 자연이 제공하는 서비스의 교환 조건은 극한의 사막이나 몹시 추운 환경에서는 무리 영역이 매우 넓어져야 하고 무리 ④ 비이동성이(→ 이동성이) 높아진다는 것이다. 물이 생물학적 생산성을 결정하는 사막 환경에서 강우량과 무리 밀도 사이의 관계는 매우 ⑤ 예측 가능하여 수학적으로 설명될 수 있다.

구문풀이

9행 The advantage of a forager production system is [that nature does the work of reproducing and maintaining {the food supply}].

: [ ]는 주격보어 역할을 하는 명사절이고, 그 안의 { }는 reproducing과 maintaining의 공통 목적어이다.

15행 In desert environments, [where water determines biological productivity], the relationship between rainfall and band density is **so** predicable **that** it can be described mathematically.

: 첫 번째 [ ]는 desert environments를 부연 설명하는 관계절이다. '매우 ~해서 …하다'라는 뜻의 「so ~ that …」 구문이 쓰였다.

어휘풀이

- constant *n* 일정불변의 것 *a* 일정한
- population *n* 개체군
- in response to ~에 응하여
- ecosystem *n* 생태계
- mobility *n* 이동성
- maintain *v* 유지하다
- recycle *v* 재활용하다
- extreme *a* 극단의
- determine *v* 결정하다
- optimum *a* 최적의
- territory *n* 영역
- productivity *n* 생산성
- high-density *a* 고밀도의
- reproduce *v* 재생산하다
- purify *v* 정화하다
- trade-off *n* 교환 (조건)
- arctic *a* 몹시 추운
- rainfall *n* 강우(량)

139 답 ④

출제 어휘	확인하기			
①	identical	동일한	↔	
②	texture	질감	↔	
③	confirm	사실임을 확인해 주다	↔	
④	more	더 많은	↔	less(더 적은)
⑤	slow-cooked	천천히 조리된	↔	

정답풀이

④ 우리가 더 씹어야 하고 덜 가공된 음식을 먹을 때 그것들을 소화하는 데 더 많은 에너지가 필요하다고 했으므로 그렇게 소모된 에너지로 인해 우리의 몸이 받아들이는 칼로리는 '더 적을' 것이다. 따라서 more는 적절하지 않으며 반대 의미의 less로 바꿔 써야 한다.

오답풀이

① 두 무리의 쥐에게 각각 딱딱한 알갱이 사료와 부드러운 알갱이 사료를 먹였고 그 둘은 영양소와 칼로리가 같다고 했으므로, 음식이 처리된 정도만 다르고 다른 모든 면은 '동일했다(identical)'는 것은 적절하다.
② 쥐 실험에서 먹이가 처리된 정도를 달리한 것이므로 체중 증가에 중요한 요소로 작용한 것이 '질감(texture)'인 것은 적절하다.
③ 먹이의 요리 방법을 달리한 비단뱀과 관련된 추가 연구에서도 먹이의 질감과 체중 증가의 연관성에 관해 쥐 실험과 비슷한 결과를 얻었을 것임을 추론할 수 있으므로 결과가 '사실임을 확인했다(confirmed)'는 것은 적절하다.
⑤ 같은 칼로리일 때 더 씹어야 해서 소화하는 데 더 많은 에너지가 드는 아삭한 생사과보다 '천천히 조리된(slow-cooked)' 사과 퓌레로부터 더 많은 에너지를 얻는다는 것은 적절하다.

전문해석

현재의 비만 위기가 부분적으로는 우리가 먹는 것에 의해서가 아니라 (물론 이것도 아주 중요하기는 하지만) 우리가 먹기 전에 음식이 처리된 정도에 의해서 야기됨을 제시하는 좋은 증거가 있다. 그것은 때때로 '칼로리 착각'이라고 불린다. 2003년 일본 규슈 대학의 과학자들은 한 무리의 쥐에게 딱딱한 알갱이 사료를 먹이고, 다른 무리에게는 부드러운 알갱이 사료를 먹였다. 다른 모든 면에서 알갱이 사료는 ① 동일했는데, 즉 같은 영양소와 같은 칼로리였다. 22주 후에, 부드러운 먹이를 식단으로 한 쥐들은 비만이 되었고, 이것은 ② 질감이 체중 증가에 중요한 요소임을 보여 주었다. 비단뱀과 관련된 (갈아서 요리된 스테이크를 먹는 것과 손대지 않은 날것을 먹는) 추가 연구는 이러한 결과가 ③ 사실임을 확인해 주었다. 우리가 더 씹어야 하고 덜 가공된 음식을 먹을 때, 그것들을 소화하는 데 더 많은 에너지가 필요해서 우리의 몸이 받아들이는 칼로리가 ④ 더 많다(→ 더 적다). 여러분은 칼로리가 동일하더라도 아삭한 생사과보다 ⑤ 천천히 조리된 사과 퓌레로부터 더 많은 에너지를 얻을 것이다.

구문풀이

1행 There is good evidence [to suggest {that the current obesity crisis is caused, in part, **not** <by what we eat (though this is of course vital, too)> **but** <by the degree (to which our food has been processed before we eat it)>}].

: [ ]는 good evidence를 수식하는 to부정사구이고, 그 안의 { }는 to suggest의 목적어 역할을 하는 명사절이다. 「not *A* but *B*(*A*가 아니라 *B*인)」로 두 개의 전치사구 < >가 연결되었다. 두 번째 ( )는 the degree를 수식하는 관계절이다.

어휘풀이

- obesity *n* 비만
- vital *a* 매우 중요한
- delusion *n* 착각, 망상, 오해
- nutrient *n* 영양분
- ground *a* 같은, 갈아서 만든
- confirm *v* 사실임을 확인해 주다
- digest *v* 소화시키다
- purée *n* 퓌레(야채·고기를 삶아 거른 진한 수프)
- crunchy *a* 아삭한
- crisis *n* 위기
- be referred to as ~로 불리다
- identical *a* 동일한
- texture *n* 질감
- intact *a* 손대지 않은, 손상되지 않은
- chewy *a* (충분히) 씹어야 하는

140 답 ④

출제 어휘	확인하기			
①	encounter	대면, 만남	↔	
②	minimize	최소화하다	↔	maximize(최대화하다)
③	distance	멀리하다	↔	
④	routine	일상	↔	
⑤	nuisance	성가신 존재	↔	

정답풀이

④ 곤충과 멀어지기 위한 구체적인 활동들이 문화적으로 인간의 삶을 너무나 많이 형성했다고 했으므로 곤충에 관한 것이라면 최대한 피하려고 했을 것임을 추론할 수 있다. 따라서 공공장소에서 곤충에 관해 토론하는 것이 '일상'이 되었다는 것은 적절하지 않으며 '금기'가 되었다는 의미의 taboo 정도로 바꿔 써야 한다. 앞에 언급된 활동들로 인해 routine을 자칫 옳은 것으로 생각할 수 있으나 그런 활동의 목적은 수많은 곤충과 최대한 멀어지기 위함이므로 공공장소에서 곤충에 관해 토론하는 것이 일상이 되었다는 것은 흐름상 어색하다.

오답풀이

① 곤충의 수가 너무나도 많아서 지구상에서 곤충과 인간이 대립하는 것은 불가피하다고 했고 곤충이 인간의 삶에 손상을 입힌다고 했으므로 인구 수가 많은 도시 지역에서 곤충과의 '대면, 만남(encounters)'은 더 심각하다고 하는 것은 적절하다.
② 곤충이 인간의 삶을 해치고 무력하게 만든다고 했으므로 인간은 곤충과 덜 접하고자 할 것이다. 따라서 사람들이 곤충 세계와의 상호작용을 '최소화하려는(minimize)' 노력을 한다는 것은 적절하다.
③ 집을 밀폐하거나 살충제를 뿌리고 몸을 청결하게 하는 것 등은 곤충을 '멀리하려고' 하는 행동이므로 distance는 적절하다.
⑤ 곤충이 인류를 죽음과 파괴로 괴롭혔다는 내용이 이어지므로 대다수의 사람들이 곤충을 단지 '성가신 존재(nuisance)'로만 생각하고 있는 것은 잘못된 것이라는 흐름은 적절하다.

전문해석

곤충과 인간의 상호작용의 역사는 문명의 시작으로 거슬러 올라간다. 추정된 수가 1,000경에 달하는 곤충은 지구상에 존재하는 모든 형태의 다세포 생물보다 수가 많고 (영향력이) 더 크다. 인간이 식량, 주거지, 자원을 위해 지구를 이용하기 때문에

곤충과 인간의 대립은 불가피하다. 게다가, 관련된 많은 곤충들이 인간의 자원을 공유할 뿐만 아니라 인간의 삶을 손상하거나 무력하게 만들고 재산에 피해를 주는 것으로 알려져 있기 때문에, 시가지나 도시와 같은 장소에서의 (곤충과의) ① 대면은 더 심각하다. 따라서 대다수의 사람들이 곤충 세계와의 상호작용을 ② 최소화하려는 노력을 하는 것은 드문 일이 아니다. 집은 밀폐되고, (살충제가) 뿌려지고, 청결하게 유지되며, 가능한 한 곤충으로부터 인간을 ③ 멀어지게 하려고 몸을 씻고, 머리를 감으며, 옷을 세탁한다. 문화적으로 이러한 활동들이 인간의 삶을 너무 많이 형성해서, 어떤 사회에서는 공공장소에서 곤충을 논하는 것이 ④ 일상(→ 금기)이 되었다. 도시 생활의 관점에서 보면, 대다수의 사람들은 곤충을 단지 ⑤ 성가신 존재인 것으로 잘못 생각하고 있다. 곤충이 과거에 죽음과 파괴로 인류를 정말로 괴롭혔다는 사실도 반드시 언급해야 한다.

구문풀이

7행 Moreover, [**encounters** in places such as urban areas or cities] **are** more serious, [as many of the insects involved are known to {injure or disable human lives} and {damage property}, as well as sharing human resources].

: 첫 번째 [ ]가 주어이며 주어의 핵인 encounters가 복수이므로 복수형 동사 are가 쓰였다. 두 번째 [ ]는 as가 이끄는 이유의 부사절이며, 그 안에서 두 개의 { }가 병렬구조를 이루어 are known to에 연결된다.

어휘풀이

- civilization *n* 문명
- outnumber *v* ~보다 수가 많다
- multicellular *a* 다세포의
- inevitable *a* 불가피한
- encounter *n* 대면, 만남, 조우
- disable *v* 무력하게 하다, 불구로 만들다
- seal *v* 밀폐[밀봉]하다
- nuisance *n* 성가신 존재, 골칫거리
- imperative *a* 반드시 해야 하는, 필수적인
- literally *ad* 정말로, 문자 그대로
- plague *v* 괴롭히다, 역병에 걸리게 하다
- estimate *v* 추정하다, 어림잡다
- outweigh *v* (영향력이) ~보다 크다
- confrontation *n* 대립, 대면, 직면
- exploit *v* 이용하다, 착취하다
- injure *v* 해를 입히다, 상처를 주다
- property *n* (건물·토지 등의) 재산
- distance *v* 멀리하다, 거리를 두다

141 답 ③

출제 어휘	확인하기			
(A) follow	따르다, 추종하다	/ worsen	악화시키다	
(B) generous	관대한	/ stubborn	고집스러운, 완고한	
(C) accuracy	정확성	/ universality	보편성	

정답풀이

(A) 주장하는 사람에게 공정하기 위해 모든 노력을 기울여야 한다고 했으므로 신뢰를 낮추는 자료를 추가하거나 신뢰를 높이는 자료를 삭제하여 주장을 '악화시켜서는(worsen)' 안 된다는 것이 적절하다. [follow 따르다, 추종하다]
(B) 자비로운 해석의 방향을 부연 설명하고 있으므로 이와 일맥상통하는 '관대한(generous)' 해석적 자비라고 하는 것이 적절하다. [stubborn 고집스러운, 완고한]
(C) 다른 사람의 말이나 글을 향상시키기 위해 우리가 너무 많은 것을 하면 원래의 글이나 생각으로부터 멀어진다고 했으므로, '정확성(accuracy)'에서 멀어지게 한다는 것이 적절하다. [universality 보편성]

전문해석

우리는 주장을 해석할 때, 주장하는 사람에게 공정하기 위해 모든 노력을 기울여야 한다. 주장을 덜 신뢰성 있게 만들 수 있는 자료를 추가하거나 그것을 더 신뢰성 있게 만들 수 있는 자료를 삭제함으로써 주장을 (A) 악화시켜서는 안 된다. 우리는 사

용된 정확한 단어에 상당히 가깝게 표준화된 견해를 유지시키도록 노력해야 한다. 그렇지 않으면 다른 사람에 의해 우리에게 주어진 주장(다른 사람이 하는 주장)을 이해하는 것이 아니라 우리 자신의 새로운 주장을 형성하기 시작할 것이다. 가끔은 말이나 글로 쓰인 구절을 가능한 한 그럴듯하고 합리적으로 해석하면서 우리가 자비로운 해석의 방향으로 더 나아가야 한다고 제안된다. 그런 (B) 관대한 해석적 자비는 화자나 저자에게 가장 공정한 일이라고 주장되어 왔다. 하지만 여기에는 약간의 위험이 있다. 다른 누군가의 말이나 글을 향상시키기 위해 너무 많은 것을 하면, 우리 자신의 생각을 너무 많이 읽어 들일 수 있고, 원래의 글이나 생각으로부터 너무 멀리 이동할 수 있다. 자비가 지나치게 취해지면 그것은 우리를 (C) 정확성으로부터 멀어지게 할 수 있다.

구문풀이

9행 Sometimes **it** is suggested [that we go further in the direction of charitable interpretation, {interpreting a speech or a written passage **so as to render** it as plausible and reasonable as possible}].

: it은 형식상의 주어이고 [ ]로 표시된 명사절이 내용상의 주어이다. { }는 앞선 절의 we를 의미상의 주어로 하는 분사구문이다. 「so as+to부정사」는 '~하기 위하여'라는 뜻으로 목적을 나타낸다.

어휘풀이

- interpret *v* 해석하다
- make an effort 노력하다
- delete *v* 삭제하다, 빼다
- version *n* 견해, 생각, 설명
- construct *v* 형성하다, 구성하다
- as opposed to ~가 아니라, ~와는 대조적으로
- direction *n* 방향, 지시
- render *v* (어떤 상태가 되게) 만들다
- generous *a* 관대한
- argument *n* 주장, 논거, 논쟁
- credible *a* 신뢰할 수 있는, 믿을 수 있는
- standardized *a* 표준화된
- reasonably *ad* 상당히, 합리적으로
- charitable *a* 자비로운, 자선의
- plausible *a* 그럴듯한, 이치에 맞는
- stubborn *a* 완고한

142 답 ②

출제 어휘	확인하기			
① suppress	억누르다	↔		
② block	막다, 방해하다	↔		
③ vary	달라지다	↔		
④ competitively	경쟁적으로	↔		
⑤ less	덜	↔	more(더)	

정답풀이

② 고용 협상에서 구직자와 고용주가 다른 가능성들, 즉 이사 비용과 시작 날짜 또한 협상하게 되면 급여 문제에서의 합의나 절충안을 도출할 수 있다는 맥락이므로, 급여 문제의 해결을 '방해할' 수 있다고 하는 것은 적절하지 않다. block을 facilitate(촉진하다) 정도로 바꿔 써야 한다.

오답풀이

① 고정된 파이를 믿는 사람들은 당사자들의 이해관계가 통합적인 합의와 상호 이익이 되는 절충안의 가능성이 없는 반대 입장에 있다고 가정한다고 했다. 따라서 그들은 통합적인 합의와 상호 이익이 되는 절충안을 찾으려는 노력을 '억누를(suppress)' 것이다.
③ 뒤에 이어지는 실험에서 참가자들에게 갈등 상황의 본질을 세 가지 다른 관점에서 보도록 했을 때 협상을 고정된 파이 관점에서 보는 경향이 '달라졌음'을 알 수 있다. 따라서 varies는 적절하다.
④ 개인적 이득에 초점을 맞춘 협상가들은 협상을 고정된 파이 관점에서 보므로 상황에 '경쟁적으로(competitively)' 접근할 것이다.

⑤ 스트레스가 많은 조건은 오해의 원인이 될 수 있으므로, 결과적으로 합의
는 '덜(less)' 통합적일 것이다.

전문해석
많은 협상가들은 모든 협상이 고정된 파이를 수반한다고 가정한다. 협상가들은 보통
통합 협상 기회를 제로섬 상황이나 승패 교환으로 접근한다. 허구의 고정된 파이를
믿는 사람들은 당사자들의 이해관계가 통합적인 합의와 상호 이익이 되는 절충안의
가능성이 없는 반대 입장에 있다고 가정하므로 그것을 찾으려는 노력을 (a) 억누른
다. 고용 협상에서 급여가 유일한 문제라고 생각하는 구직자는 고용주가 7만 달러를
제시할 때 7만 5천 달러를 요구할 수 있다. 두 당사자가 가능성에 대해 더 자세히 논
의할 때만 이사 비용과 시작 날짜 또한 협상할 수 있다는 사실을 발견하게 되는데,
이는 급여 문제의 해결을 (b) 방해할(→ 촉진할) 수 있을 것이다.
협상을 고정된 파이 관점에서 보는 경향은 사람들이 주어진 갈등 상황의 본질을 어
떻게 보느냐에 따라 (c) 달라진다. 이는 징역형에 대한 검사와 피고측 변호인 간의
모의 협상을 포함하는 Harinck, de Dreu와 Van Vianen의 기발한 실험에서 밝혀
졌다. 어떤 참가자들은 개인적 이득의 관점에서 그들의 목표를 보라는 말을 들었고
(예를 들어, 특정 징역형을 정하는 것이 당신의 경력에 도움이 될 것이다), 다른 참가
자들은 그들의 목표를 효과성의 관점에서 보라는 말을 들었으며(특정 형은 상습적
범행을 방지할 가능성이 가장 크다) 그리고 또 다른 참가자들은 가치에 초점을 맞추
라는 말을 들었다(특정 징역형은 공정하고 정당하다). 개인적 이득에 초점을 맞춘 협
상가들은 고정된 파이에 대한 믿음의 영향을 받아 상황에 (d) 경쟁적으로 접근할 가
능성이 가장 컸다. 가치에 초점을 맞춘 협상가들은 문제를 고정된 파이 관점에서 볼
가능성이 가장 낮았고 상황에 협력적으로 접근하려는 경향이 더 컸다. 시간 제약과
같은 스트레스가 많은 조건은 이러한 흔한 오해의 원인이 되며, 이는 결국 (e) 덜 통
합적인 합의로 이어질 수 있다.

구문풀이
4행 [Those {who believe in the mythical fixed pie}] assume [that
parties' interests stand in opposition, with no possibility for
{integrative settlements} and {mutually beneficial trade-offs}], so
they suppress efforts to search for them.

: 첫 번째 [ ]는 so 앞 절의 주어이고, 그 안의 { }는 Those를 수식하는 관계절이다. 두
번째 [ ]는 assume의 목적어 역할을 하는 명사절이며, 그 안의 두 개의 { }는 전치사
for의 목적어 역할을 하는 명사구이다.

어휘풀이
- negotiator *n* 협상가
- integrative *a* 통합의
- zero-sum *a* (게임 · 관계 등이) 쌍방 득실의 차가 없는
- mythical *a* 허구의, 신화적인
- settlement *n* 합의
- trade-off *n* 절충, 타협
- resolution *n* 해결
- defense lawyer 피고측 변호인
- in terms of ~의 관점에서
- competitively *ad* 경쟁적으로
- contribute to ~의 원인이 되다
- assume *v* 가정하다
- opposition *n* 반대
- mutually *ad* 상호 간에
- suppress *v* 억누르다
- simulated *a* 모의의
- jail sentence 징역형
- arrange *v* 정하다
- constraint *n* 제약
- misperception *n* 오해

143　답 ④

출제 어휘 확인하기

①	tension	긴장	↔	
②	recreate	재현하다, 다시 만들다	↔	
③	hurt	아프다	↔	
④	lower	낮추다	↔	raise(높이다)
⑤	chemical	화학적인	↔	

정답풀이
④ 앞에서 언급한 웃음의 신체적인 이득과 관련하여 웃음이 고통을 견딜 수
있게 하려면 고통의 역치를 '낮추는' 것이 아니라 '높여야' 하므로 lowered를
반대의 의미를 가진 raised로 바꿔 써야 한다.

오답풀이
① 웃음이 무해한 것으로 밝혀진, 두려운 상황에 대한 안도감의 표현으로 시
작되었다면 즐거움과 밀접한 관련이 있다고 했으므로, 웃음은 '긴장
(tension)'의 해소라고 할 수 있다.
② 완전히 인위적인 상황에서 농담을 하는 것은 이전에 겪은 긴장 해소의 느
낌을 '재현하기' 위한 것이라고 할 수 있으므로 recreate는 적절하다.
③ 우리 몸을 지배하면서 눈물이 나게 하는 웃음은 표면적으로는 '고통을 주
는' 것이라고 할 수 있으므로 hurt는 적절하다.
⑤ 엔도르핀 분비와 뇌의 옥시토신 방출은 몸에 '화학적' 반응이 일어나는 것
이므로 chemical은 적절하다.

전문해석
만약 웃음이 무해한 것으로 밝혀진, 두려운 상황에 대한 안도감의 표현으로 시작되
었다는 것이 사실이라면, 그에 따라 웃음의 감각은 즐거움과 밀접한 관련이 있다는
것이고, 그것은 ① 긴장의 해소이다. 사실, 웃음은 매우 유쾌해서 우리는 완전히 인
위적인 상황에서 농담을 함으로써 그 해소의 느낌을 ② 재현하기 위해 많은 노력을
기울인다. 그리고 그것은 여전히 재미있다. 농담에는 실제적인 위협이 전혀 없지만,
그럼에도 불구하고 우리는 약간 어지러운 기대의 전환을 즐긴다. 왜 웃는 것이 그렇
게 즐거운가? 특히 최고의 웃음 종류는 ③ 아프기 시작하는 종류인데, 즉 우리 몸을
지배하고 때로는 눈물로 변하기도 하는 것이다. 수년 동안, 과학자들은 웃음의 신체
적인 이득을 알아내기 위해 노력해 왔다. Robin Dunbar 교수의 최근 연구는 웃음
이 사람들의 고통의 역치를 ④ 낮춘다(→ 높인다)는 것을 발견했다. 그의 설명에 따
르면, 공유된 사회적 웃음은 우리가 인간의 접촉에 하는 것과 같은 ⑤ 화학적 반응인
엔도르핀 분비와 뇌의 옥시토신 방출을 유발한다는 것이다.

구문풀이
1행 If **it**'s true [that laughter originated as an expression of relief
in response to a fearful situation {that turned out to be harmless}],
it follows that the sensation of laughter is closely associated
with pleasure—it's a release of tension.

: If가 이끄는 조건절에서 it은 형식상의 주어이고, [ ]가 내용상의 주어이다. 그 안의 { }
는 a fearful situation을 수식하는 관계절이다. 주절에서 it follows that ~은 '~은
사실이다, ~라는 결론에 이르게 되다'라는 의미를 가진 관용 표현이다.

17행 His explanation is [that shared social laughter causes {an endorphin rush and the release of oxytocin in the brain}—{the same chemical reactions <that we have to human touch>}].

: [ ]는 문장의 보어로 쓰인 명사절이며, 그 안의 첫 번째 { }는 causes의 목적어로 쓰인 명사구이고, 두 번째 { }는 첫 번째 { }를 부가적으로 설명하는 동격의 명사구이다. 〈 〉는 the same chemical reactions를 수식하는 관계절이다.

어휘풀이
- originate *v* 시작하다, 기원하다
- harmless *a* 무해한
- release *n* 해소, 방출
- go to great lengths 많은 노력을 기울이다
- recreate *v* 재현하다, 다시 만들다
- circumstance *n* 상황
- slightly *ad* 약간
- determine *v* 알아내다, 결정하다
- rush *n* 분비
- oxytocin *n* 옥시토신
- relief *n* 안도(감)
- be associated with ~와 관련이 있다
- tension *n* 긴장
- artificial *a* 인위적인
- threat *n* 위협
- shift *n* 전환, 변환
- endorphin *n* 엔도르핀
- release *n* 방출
- chemical reaction 화학 반응

144 답 ④

출제 어휘 확인하기

① more	더 많이	↔	less(더 적게)	
② ironic	아이러니한	↔		
③ unrelated	관련 없는	↔	related(관련 있는)	
④ inappropriate	부적절한	↔	appropriate(적절한)	
⑤ accessible	접근하기 쉬운	↔	inaccessible(접근하기 어려운)	

정답풀이
④ 어떤 생각을 하지 않으려고 의도적으로 노력하면 그 생각이 억제되는 대신 오히려 증가할 수 있음을 설명하는 글이다. 해당 문장은 의도적인 운영 체계가 잘 작동하는지를 감시하는 과정에 관한 설명으로, 만약 의도된 생각과 일치하지 않는 생각(억제된 생각)과 마주치게 될 경우, 감시 과정은 의도적 운영 체계를 자극하여 억제된 생각을 '적절한' 생각(억제된 생각과 관련 없는 생각)으로 대체되도록 한다는 것이다. 따라서 '부적절한(inappropriate)' 생각으로 대체되도록 한다는 것은 적절하지 않으며 반대 의미의 appropriate(적절한) 정도로 바꿔 써야 한다.

오답풀이
① 백곰을 생각하지 말라고 하면 오히려 생각하지 않기가 어려운 것처럼 생각의 억제는 억누르고 싶은 생각을 가라앉히는 대신 그것을 실제로 증가시키는 효과가 있을 수 있다고 했으므로, 같은 문맥에서 음식을 생각하지 않으려고 하면 '더 많이(more)' 생각난다는 것은 적절하다.
② 특정 생각을 억제하려고 하면 반대로 더 생각하기 시작한다고 했으므로, 이러한 결과가 '아이러니하다(ironic)'는 것은 적절하다.
③ 억제하려는 생각을 하지 않기 위해 그것과 관련 없는 생각을 한다는 흐름에서 억제된 생각과 '관련 없는(unrelated)' 생각을 의식적으로 찾아내려고 한다는 것은 적절하다.
⑤ 역접의 연결어 However로 시작하고 있으므로 운영 체계가 제대로 기능할 때를 설명한 앞 문장과는 반대로 제대로 기능하지 못할 때를 설명하는 내용이 와야 한다. 즉, 피로 등의 이유로 인지 부하가 증가해서 운영 체계가 작동을 멈추면 감시 과정이 부적절한 생각(억제하려는 생각)을 의식으로 스며들게 해 그것을 떠올리게 만든다는 의미이므로, 부적절한 생각이 매우 '접근하기 쉬워진다(accessible)'는 것은 적절하다.

전문해석
내가 여러분에게 '백곰을 생각하지 말라.'라고 말하면 여러분은 백곰을 생각하지 않

는 것이 어렵다는 것을 알게 될 것이다. 이런 식으로, '생각을 억제하는 것은 억누르고 싶은 생각을 가라앉히는 대신 그것을 실제로 증가시킬 수 있다'. 이것의 한 가지 일반적인 예는 다이어트 중이라 음식에 대해 생각하지 않으려고 노력하는 사람들이 흔히 음식에 대해 훨씬 ① 더 많이 생각하기 시작한다는 것이다. 따라서 이 과정은 '반동 효과'라고도 알려져 있다. 이 ② 아이러니한 결과는 관련된 두 가지 인지 과정의 상호작용에 의해 야기되는 것 같다. 우선, 이 이중 처리 시스템은 의도적인 운영 체계를 포함하는데, 그것은 억제된 생각과 ③ 관련 없는 생각을 의식적으로 찾아내려 한다. 그 다음, 그리고 동시에, 무의식적인 감시 과정이 그 운영 체계가 효과적으로 작동하는지 여부를 검사한다. 감시 체계가 의도된 생각과 일치하지 않는 생각과 마주치는 경우, 그것은 의도적인 운영 체계를 자극하여 이러한 생각이 반드시 ④ 부적절한(→ 적절한) 생각으로 대체되도록 한다. 그러나 주장되는 바는, 의도적인 운영 체계는 피로, 스트레스 및 정서적 요인에 의해 생긴 증가된 인지 부하로 인해 작동을 멈출 수 있고, 그래서 감시 과정이 부적절한 생각을 걸러서 의식으로 스며들게 해, 그것을 매우 ⑤ 접근하기 쉽게 만든다는 것이다.

구문풀이
5행 One common example of this is [that people on a diet {who try not to think about food} often begin to think much more about food].

: [ ]는 문장의 보어 역할을 하는 명사절이고, 그 안의 { }는 that절의 핵심 주어인 people on a diet를 수식하는 관계절이다.

어휘풀이
- suppression *n* 억제, 억압
- cognitive *a* 인지의
- locate *v* 찾아내다
- unconscious *a* 무의식적인
- encounter *v* 마주치다
- prompt *v* 자극하다
- fatigue *n* 피로
- interplay *n* 상호작용
- intentional *a* 의도적인
- simultaneously *ad* 동시에
- monitor *v* 감시하다
- inconsistent with ~와 일치하지 않는
- load *n* 부하, 부담

145 답 ③

출제 어휘 확인하기

(A) blessing	축복	/ obstacle	장애물	
(B) empty	공허한	/ promising	유망한	
(C) self-esteem	자존감	/ vanity	허영(심)	

정답풀이
(A) 질병, 어려운 관계, 경제적 역경 등은 우리 자신이 배의 선장이 되어 헤쳐 나가야 할 '장애물'에 해당하는 것으로 볼 수 있으므로 obstacles가 적절하다. [blessing 축복]
(B) 앞에 외부적인 물건들을 얻으려는 어리석음이라는 말이 나왔으므로, 같은 맥락에서 '공허한' 일을 추구한다는 의미가 적절하다. 따라서 empty가 알맞다. [promising 유망한]
(C) 자신에 대해 좋게 느끼고 싶다면 외부적인 것으로는 충분하지 않다는 내용이 앞에 나왔으므로, 인생의 목표를 세우고 달성하기 위해 노력하는 것을 통해 '자존감'이 나온다는 의미가 되어야 자연스럽다. 따라서 self-esteem이 적절하다. [vanity 허영(심)]

전문해석
우리는 과거에 대한 후회와 현재의 스트레스 요인들에 의해 소모되는 시간을 너무 많이 보내서 미래에 대한 우리의 희망에 대해 거의 생각하지 않는다. 그렇다. (A) 장애물은 질병, 어려운 관계, 경제적 역경 등의 형태로 우리의 행로에 던져지지만, 우리는 결국 우리 자신의 배의 선장이다. 여러분은 여러분의 배가 여러분을 어디로 데

려가게 하고 싶은가? 만약 여러분이 자신이 특별하다고 느끼게 하기 위해 디자이너 의류와 같은 외부적인 물건들을 얻으려는 어리석음에 사로잡힌다면, 여러분의 초점을 바꾸려고 해 보라. (B) 공허한 일을 추구하는 것을 잊고 여러분 자신을 위한 이야기를 창조하는 쪽으로 열정을 돌려라. 만약 여러분이 자신에 대해 좋게 느끼고 싶다면 옷, 음식, 물건 그리고 교우관계를 갖는 것으로는 보통 충분하지 않다. 명확한 인생의 목표를 세우고 그것을 달성하려고 노력하는 것이 (C) 자존감이 나오는 곳이다. 여러분은 결코 목표를 달성하지 못할 수도 있지만, 그 과정에서 겪은 경험, 즉 노력, 도전, 재고, 방향 변화, 성장은 여러분이 자신의 가치를 발견하는 곳이다.

구문풀이

1행 We spend **so** much time [consumed by our regrets about the past and the stressors of the present] **that** we give little thought to our hopes for the future.

: 「so ~ that …(너무 ~해서 …하다)」 구문이 쓰였다. [ ]는 much time을 수식하는 과거분사구이다.

어휘풀이

- stressor *n* 스트레스 요인
- illness *n* 질병, 병
- hardship *n* 역경, 난관
- silliness *n* 어리석음
- empty *a* 공허한, 텅 빈
- pursuit *n* 일, (일의) 추구
- self-esteem *n* 자존심, 자긍심
- reconsideration *n* 재고, 재심
- obstacle *n* 장애물, 방해물
- financial *a* 재정적인, 금전적인
- ultimately *ad* 결국, 궁극적으로
- attain *v* 얻다, 획득하다
- promising *a* 유망한
- companionship *n* 교우관계
- vanity *n* 허영(심)

---

146 답 ⑤

출제 어휘 확인하기

① mental	정신적인	↔	physical(육체의, 신체의)
② jam-packed	빽빽이 찬	↔	
③ activate	활성화하다	↔	
④ color	(부정적인) 영향을 미치다	↔	
⑤ aware	인지하는	↔	unaware(인지하지 못하는)

정답풀이

⑤ 우리의 기준 틀이 우리의 일부가 되어 일반적으로 생각하는 것보다 말하는 사람의 메시지를 받아들이는 것이 어렵다는 것은 우리가 자신의 기준 틀의 영향력을 '인지하지 못하고 있다'는 것이다. 따라서 aware를 반대 의미인 unaware(인지하지 못하는) 정도로 바꿔 써야 한다.

오답풀이

① 다른 사람을 이해하는 것과 관련하여, 각자가 자신의 기준 틀을 개발하는 데 일생을 보냈다고 했으므로, 자신의 기준 틀과 같은 개념으로 '정신적인(mental)' 틀이라고 한 것은 적절하다.

② 우리는 스스로의 기준 틀에서 살아가고 있고 우리 자신의 경험, 의견, 편견, 화제, 감정, 가치관, 의제 등이 우리 머릿속에 있다는 흐름이므로 '빽빽이 차 있다(jam-packed)'는 것은 적절하다.

③ 우리의 머릿속에 우리 자신의 경험, 의견, 편견, 화제, 감정, 가치관, 의제 등이 차 있어서 다른 사람의 입장을 이해하려 할 때 그러한 것들이 영향을 미친다는 흐름이므로, 우리 자신의 관념이 '활성화된다(activated)'는 것은 적절하다.

④ 우리의 생각이 스스로의 사고방식에 의해 지배되기 쉽기 때문에 말하는 사람의 생각을 수용하기 어려워진다는 것이므로, 우리가 받아들이는 것에 대한 수용에 '부정적인 영향을 미친다(coloring)'는 것은 적절하다.

전문해석

다른 사람을 이해하는 데 있어서 우리가 직면하는 도전은 우리 각자가 자신의 기준 틀을 개발하는 데 일생을 보냈다는 것이다. 우리는 매일 대부분의 시간을 그 ① 정신적인 틀 안에서 살아간다. 우리의 정신은 우리 자신의 경험, 의견, 편견, 화제, 감정, 가치관, 의제 등으로 ② 빽빽이 차 있다. 누군가가 자신의 생각을 제시할 때, 그 주제에 대한 우리 자신의 관념이 ③ 활성화될 가능성이 높다. 다른 사람의 입장을 이해하는 데 우리의 정신 에너지를 집중하는 대신, 우리의 생각은 우리 자신의 사고방식에 의해 지배되기 쉽고, 그래서 우리가 받아들이는 것에 대한 수용에 ④ 부정적 영향을 미친다. 게다가, 우리의 기준 틀은 우리의 일부가 되어 버려서 우리는 대부분의 시간 동안 그것의 영향력을 ⑤ 인지한다(→ 인지하지 못한다). 그래서 말하는 사람의 메시지를 받아들이는 것은 일반적으로 인식되는 것보다 더 어려울 수 있다.

구문풀이

1행 The challenge [we face in understanding others] is [that each of us has spent a lifetime developing our own frame of reference].

: 첫 번째 [ ]는 The challenge를 수식하는 관계절이고, 두 번째 [ ]는 is의 주격보어로 쓰인 명사절이다.

어휘풀이

- face *v* 직면하다
- reference *n* 기준, 참고
- bias *n* 편견, 편향
- present *v* 제시하다, 발표하다
- activate *v* 활성화하다
- dominate *v* 지배하다
- reception *n* 수용, 수신
- frame *n* 틀
- jam-packed *a* 빽빽이 찬, 몹시 붐비는
- agenda *n* 의제
- notion *n* 관념, 개념
- be apt to *do* ~하기 쉽다
- color *v* (부정적인) 영향을 미치다

---

147 답 ④

출제 어휘 확인하기

① ignorance	무지	↔	awareness(알고 있음, 인식)
② interest	이익	↔	
③ household	가정	↔	
④ overvalue	과대평가하다	↔	undervalue(과소평가하다)
⑤ share	공유하다	↔	

정답풀이

④ 인구 과잉과 기근 문제를 개별 가구의 이익과 사회 이익의 불일치 측면에서 설명하는 글로, 전형적인 가정은 아이를 낳음으로써 이익을 얻고 사회는 그로 인한 식량 공급 감소 문제를 떠안게 된다는 것이다. 이러한 맥락에서 부모들은 자녀를 더 낳는 것이 가정의 행복에 어떻게 영향을 미치는지는 분명히 평가하지만 그로 인해 다른 사람들이 겪을 영향을 '과대평가한다'는 것은 알맞지 않다. overvalue를 overlook(간과하다) 정도로 바꿔 써야 한다.

오답풀이

① 1인당 식량 공급이 줄어드는 이유를 아이를 낳는 가정이 얻는 이익과 사회가 부담하게 되는 식량 공급 감소 문제의 측면에서 설명하고 있으므로, 그 탓을 인간의 '무지(ignorance)'로 돌리지 않았다는 것은 적절하다.

② 전형적인 가정은 또 다른 아이를 낳음으로써 이익을 얻는다는 내용이 이어지고 있으므로 개별 가구의 '이익(interests)'이라는 것은 적절하다.

③ 아이를 낳음으로써 가정은 행복과 같은 이익을 얻을 수 있다고 말하고 있으므로 '가정(household)' 수익이라는 것은 적절하다.

⑤ 아이를 낳는 데 대한 이익은 개별 가정이 얻지만, 사회는 1인당 식량 공급 감소와 같은 영향을 떠안게 된다는 것이므로, 번식의 대가가 개별 가구에게 떠맡겨지는 것이 아니라 '공유된다(shared)'는 것은 적절하다.

전문해석

인구 과잉과 기근에 대한 염려가 최고조에 달하고 있던 시기에 Garrett Hardin은 이러한 문제들을, 예를 들면 줄어드는 1인당 식량 공급을 주목하지 못하는 인간의 ① 무지 탓으로 돌리지 않았다. 그 대신에, 그의 설명은 개별 가구의 ② 이익과 사회 전체의 그것(이익) 간의 불일치에 초점을 두었다. 과도한 번식을 공유지의 비극(공유 자원의 이용을 개인의 자율에 맡길 경우 서로의 이익을 극대화함에 따라 자원이 남용·고갈되는 현상)으로 이해하려면, 예를 들면 아이가 ③ 가정 수익에 가져오는 순이익의 측면에서, 전형적인 가정은 또 다른 아이를 세상에 낳음으로써 이익을 얻을 것이라는 점을 유념하라. 그렇지만 부모들은 비록 그들 가정의 행복이 늘어난 자녀에 의해 어떻게 영향을 받는지 분명히 평가하겠지만, 그들은 다른 사람들의 1인당 식량 공급 감소와 같은 인구 증가의 다른 영향은 ④ 과대평가한다(→ 간과한다). 다시 말해, 번식에 드는 대가가 개별 가구에게 전적으로 떠맡겨지는 것이 아니라 대체로 ⑤ 공유된다. 그 결과로, 지나친 번식이 일어난다.

구문풀이

`8행` To understand excessive reproduction as a tragedy of the commons, bear in mind [that a typical household stands to gain from bringing another child into the world—in terms of the net contributions {he or she makes to household earnings}, for example].

: [ ]는 bear의 목적절이고, { }는 the net contributions를 수식하는 관계절이다.

어휘풀이

- concern *n* 염려, 우려
- famine *n* 기근
- ignorance *n* 무지
- discrepancy *n* 불일치
- household *n* 가구, 가정
- tragedy of the commons 공유지의 비극
- bear ~ in mind ~을 유념하다
- count on A to *do* A가 ~할 것이라고 믿다
- assess *v* 평가하다
- diminish *v* 감소하다
- overpopulation *n* 인구 과잉
- peak *n* 최고치, 꼭대기
- per capita 1인당
- interest *n* 이익, 이득
- reproduction *n* 번식
- net *a* (이익 등의) 순 ~
- offspring *n* 자식, 자녀, 새끼
- shouldered *a* 떠맡겨진, 어깨에 짊어진

148 답 ④

출제 어휘 확인하기

① assertion	주장	↔	
② remotely	원격으로	↔	
③ same	같은	↔	different(다른)
④ unstable	불안정한	↔	stable(안정적인)
⑤ subject	영향을 받는	↔	

정답풀이

④ 앞 문장에서 전 세계적으로 엄청난 임금 격차가 있다고 했고, 뒤에는 저숙련 이민 노동자들과 경쟁하는 국내 일자리들도 대개 임금이 적다는 내용이 이어지고 있다. 따라서 저임금 국가로 쉽게 외부 조달될 수 있고 임금도 덜 받는 국내 일자리들이 덜 '불안정하다'는 것은 적절하지 않으며, 바로 앞의 less와 결합해 덜 '안정적'이라는 의미가 되도록 stable 정도로 바꿔 써야 한다.

오답풀이

① 지구는 평평하다고 한 Thomas Friedman의 선언을 '주장(assertion)'이라고 표현한 것은 적절하다.

② 지구가 평평하다고 한 Friedman의 말을 반박하는 부분에 해당한다. 결국 위치는 많은 산업에서 여전히 중요하다고 했으므로, 반대로 인문 지리가 중요하지 않다면 '원격으로(remotely)' 이루어질 수 있는 비슷한 과업에 대해 국

가 간 임금 격차가 거의 없을 것이라는 가정은 적절하다.

③ 위치는 여전히 산업에서 중요하고 임금 격차를 만들어 내므로, 만일 위치가 중요하지 않다면 미국에서 일하든 인도에서 일하든 사람들의 임금은 거의 '같을(same)' 것이라는 흐름은 적절하다.

⑤ 저임금 국가로 외부 조달될 수 있는 일자리를 언급한 앞 문장에 이어, 저숙련 이민 노동자들과 경쟁하는 국내 일자리들의 임금이 낮다는 문맥에서 경쟁의 '영향을 받는다(subject)'는 표현은 적절하다.

전문해석

칼럼니스트인 Thomas Friedman은 "지구는 평평하다."라고 선언했는데, 그 말을 통해 그는 인터넷 덕분에 세계의 경쟁자들은 자신들의 위치와 관계없이 동등한 기회를 가진다고 주장했다. Friedman의 유명한 ① 주장에도 불구하고, 세계는 아직 평평하지 않으며, 위치는 많은 산업에서 여전히 중요한 문제이다. 만일 인문 지리가 중요하지 않다면, ② 원격으로 이루어질 수 있는 비슷한 과업에 대해 국가 간 임금 격차가 거의 없을 것이다. 만일 위치가 중요하지 않다면, 컴퓨터 프로그래머, 법률 서류 검토자, 공인회계사 그리고 심지어 방사선 전문의까지도 그들이 미국에서 일하든 인도에서 일하든 거의 ③ 같은 돈을 벌 것이다. 그러나 전 세계적으로 엄청난 임금 격차가 있다. 저임금 국가로 쉽게 외부 조달될 수 있는 일자리들은 국내에서 임금을 덜 주고 덜 ④ 불안정한(→ 안정적인) 경향이 있다. 또한, 저숙련 이민 노동자들과의 국내 경쟁의 ⑤ 영향을 받는 일자리들도 대개 낮은 임금을 준다.

구문풀이

`1행` The columnist Thomas Friedman declared, "The world is flat," [by which he claimed {that thanks to the Internet, global competitors have equal opportunities regardless of their location}].

: [ ]는 앞 절의 내용을 부연 설명하는 관계절이고, 그 안의 { }는 claimed의 목적어로 쓰인 명사절이다.

어휘풀이

- declare *v* 선언하다, 발표하다
- assertion *n* 주장
- income *n* 소득, 수입
- legal document 법률 서류
- certified accountant 공인회계사
- outsource *v* 외부 조달하다, 외주 제작하다
- domestically *ad* 국내에서
- immigrant *a* 이민자의 *n* 이민자
- flat *a* 평평한
- human geography 인문 지리(학)
- remotely *ad* 원격으로
- reviewer *n* 검토자
- vast *a* 엄청난
- domestic *a* 국내의
- wage *n* 임금, 급료

149 답 ⑤

출제 어휘 확인하기

① massive	거대한	↔	
② alternate	번갈아 나타나다	↔	
③ exception	예외	↔	
④ last	존속하다	↔	
⑤ extensive	광범위한	↔	confined(한정된)

정답풀이

⑤ 로마를 제외하고 유럽에서는 광범위한 제국에 의한 통합이 없었다는 내용의 글이므로, 이외의 다른 제국에 의한 통합 시도를 언급하는 흐름에서 지리적으로 '광범위했다'는 것은 적절하지 않다. extensive를 confined(한정된) 정도로 바꿔 써야 한다.

오답풀이

① 유럽과는 달리 다른 지역에서는 제국에 의한 광범위한 통합이 이루어졌다

는 내용의 글로, 동남아시아와 중국을 설명하는 문맥에서 제국에 의한 '거대한(massive)' 규모의 통일이라고 표현한 것은 적절하다.

② 제국이 짧게 재발생된 동남아시아와 중국처럼 인도에서도 제국들이 분절 시대와 '번갈아 나타나는(alternated)' 양상이 나타났다는 것은 적절하다.

③ 내적인 통합 또는 외부에 의한 정복이 없던 유럽에서 지중해 제국이었던 로마가 '예외'적으로 남유럽을 통합했을 뿐이라는 것이므로 exception은 적절하다.

④ 유럽에서의 예외로 들 수 있는 로마의 통합 역시 유럽 역사 전체로 보아서는 잠깐에 지나지 않는다는 문맥이므로 아주 짧은 기간 동안만 '존속했을(lasted)' 뿐이라는 것은 적절하다.

전문해석

유라시아의 조밀히 정착한 세 개의 다른 문명 구역, 즉 동남아시아, 인도, 중국의 것과 비교할 때 유럽 역사의 독특한 특징 중 하나는 제국의 통일성에 관한 것이다. 동남아시아와 중국에서, 제국에 의한 ① 거대한 규모의 통일은 그들 역사의 초반부에 이룩되었고 그 이후에는 규범이 되었으며 단지 (제국은) 비교적 짧게 재발생되었다. 인도에서조차 (인도) 아대륙의 대부분을 포괄했던 제국들은 분절 시대와 ② 번갈아 나타났다. 이와 대조적으로, 유럽은 내적인 무력에 의해 한 번도 통합된 적이 없었고 그것은 외부에 의해 정복당한 적도 없었다. 주장할 만한 유일한 ③ 예외인 로마는 유럽 제국이라기보다는 지중해 제국이었으며 남유럽만 통합했을 뿐이다. 게다가, 여러 세기 동안 견뎠고 굉장히 영향력이 크긴 했지만, 로마는 유럽 역사의 아주 작은 부분 동안만 ④ 존속했을 뿐이다. 카롤링거, 오토만, 합스부르크, 나폴레옹처럼 제국의 통합을 이루려고 했던 다른 시도들은 지리적으로 훨씬 더 ⑤ 광범위한(→ 한정적인) 것이었고 단명했다.

구문풀이

8행 Even in India, empires [that encompassed {most of the subcontinent}] alternated with periods of fragmentation.

: [ ]는 문장의 주어인 empires를 수식하는 관계절이고, 그 안의 { }는 encompassed의 목적어로 쓰인 명사구이다.

어휘풀이

- distinctive *a* 독특한, 구별되는
- dense *a* 조밀한
- imperial *a* 제국의
- unification *n* 통일
- norm *n* 규범
- empire *n* 제국
- subcontinent *n* 아대륙
- fragmentation *n* 분절, 단편(화)
- arguable *a* (충분한 이유를 들어) 주장할 수 있는
- Mediterranean *a* 지중해의
- endure *v* 견디다
- geographically *ad* 지리적으로
- feature *n* 특징
- civilization *n* 문명
- unity *n* 통일성
- thereafter *ad* 그 후에
- brief *a* 짧은
- encompass *v* 포괄하다
- alternate *v* 번갈아 나타나다
- conquer *v* 정복하다
- incorporate *v* 통합하다
- fraction *n* (매우 작은) 일부

150 답 ④

출제 어휘 확인하기

① manipulate	조작하다	↔	
② inherent	내재된	↔	acquired(습득한)
③ missing	누락된	↔	
④ uncertainty	불확실성	↔	certainty(확실성), clarity(명료성)
⑤ extend	넘어서다	↔	

정답풀이

④ 교육을 위한 활동 후에 선생님의 지도 아래 토론하고, 사고하고, 논쟁하고, 듣고, 평가하는 과정을 통해 학생들이 그것을 명확하게 이해할 수 있다는 맥락에서 '불확실성(Uncertainty)'은 적절하지 않고 Clarity(명료성) 또는 Certainty(확실성) 정도로 바꿔 써야 한다.

오답풀이

① 직접 해 보는 활동에 참여하여 학생들이 사물을 '조작한다(manipulating)'는 것은 적절하다.

② 교육자들이 과학적 지식이 직접 해 보는 활동 이후에 사고하는 인지 과정에서 비롯된다는 것을 알게 되었다는 내용이 뒤에 이어지므로, 직접 해 보는 활동의 자료 자체에 지식이 '내재되어(inherent)' 있는 것은 아님을 깨달았다고 하는 것은 적절하다.

③ 직접 해 보는 활동만으로 지식을 얻을 수 있다는 생각이 위험할 수 있다는 것을 깨달았다는 내용에 이어서 직접 해 보는 활동에서 '누락된(missing)' 요소가 있다고 설명하는 흐름은 적절하다.

⑤ 결국 아이들이 과학적 지식과 이론을 구축하는 데 필요한 것은 직접 해 보는 활동만이 아니라 그 활동을 훨씬 '넘어서는(extends)' 이후의 과정에 있다고 하는 흐름이므로 적절하다.

전문해석

상당 기간 동안, 과학 교육자들은 과학 관련 활동에 참여하는 것을 통해 '직접 해 보는' 활동이 아이들의 이해에 대한 해답이라고 믿었다. 많은 교사들은 단지 활동에 참여하고 사물을 (a) 조작하는 학생들이 그들이 얻게 되는 정보와 이해하게 되는 지식을 개념 이해로 체계화할 것이라고 믿었다. 교육자들은 지식이 자료 자체에 (b) 내재되어 있는 것이 아니라 학생들이 그 활동에서 한 것에 대한 생각과 초(超)인지에 있다는 것을 깨달으면서 '직접 해 보는' 탐구의 요소 쪽으로 추가 너무 많이 기울었다는 것을 알아차리기 시작했다. 이제 우리는 과학을 배우는 것에 대해 말할 때 '직접 해 보는'이 위험한 문구라는 것을 알게 되었다. (c) 누락된 요소는 교육적 경험의 '사고를 요구하는' 부분이다. 어떤 활동에서든 의도된 지식에 대한 (d) 불확실성(→ 명료성)은 각 학생의 개념 재창조에서 비롯되는데, 즉 그 활동을 한 뒤에 사려 깊은 선생님의 지도하에 자기 자신의 선입견에 대해 토론하고, 사고하고, 논쟁하고, 듣고, 평가하는 것을 통해서 이것을 가져올 수 있다. 결국, 음식물 던지기는 직접 해 보는 활동이지만, 여러분이 배워야 했던 모든 것은 으깬 감자를 날리는 공기역학에 관한 것이었다! 자연 세계에 대한 지식과 이론을 구축하기 위해 학생들이 필요로 하는 것에 대한 우리의 견해는 '직접 해 보는 활동'을 훨씬 (e) 넘어서는 것이다. 과학 수업에서 학생들이 재료를 사용하고 그것과 상호작용하는 것이 중요하기는 하지만, 학습은 학생들의 '직접 해 보는' 경험에 대해 의미를 부여하는 것으로부터 비롯된다.

구문풀이

4행 Many teachers believed [that {students merely engaging in activities and manipulating objects} would organize the information {to be gained} and the knowledge {to be understood} into concept comprehension].

: [ ]는 believed의 목적어 역할을 하는 명사절이다. 그 안의 첫 번째 { }는 that절의 주어이며, 두 번째와 세 번째 { }는 각각 바로 앞의 the information과 the knowledge를 수식하는 형용사적 용법의 to부정사구이다.

어휘풀이

- hands-on *a* 직접 해 보는
- manipulate *v* 조작하다
- swing *v* 흔들리다, 흔들다
- inquiry *n* 탐구, 연구
- phrase *n* 문구
- minds-on *a* 사고를 요하는
- preconception *n* 선입견
- bring about ~을 야기[초래]하다
- interact *v* 상호작용하다
- engage in ~에 참여[관여]하다
- comprehension *n* 이해
- component *n* 요소
- inherent *a* 내재된
- ingredient *n* 요소, 성분
- instructional *a* 교육의
- thoughtful *a* 사려 깊은
- mashed *a* 으깬
- sense-making *n* 의미 부여하기

151 답 ③

출제 어휘 확인하기

①	fraction	부분, 일부	↔	
②	unique	유일한, 특유한	↔	
③	likely	~할 것 같은	↔	unlikely(~할 것 같지 않은)
④	emergence	출현, 등장	↔	
⑤	ensure	확실하게 하다, 보장하다	↔	

정답풀이

③ 인간의 뇌가 수많은 사람들의 이름을 저장하도록 진화하지는 않았고, 인류 진화의 초기에 한 개인이 마주쳤던 사람들의 총 숫자는 꽤 낮았을 것이라고 했으므로, 서로 이름을 지어 주었더라도 수백 명 이상의 다른 사람들에게 노출되었을 것 '같지는 않다'고 해야 문맥상 자연스럽다. 따라서 likely를 unlikely로 바꿔 써야 한다.

오답풀이

① 진화론적으로 인간의 뇌가 수많은 사람들의 이름을 저장하도록 진화하지 않았다고 했으므로, 우리는 우리가 마주치는 이름과 얼굴의 '일부(fraction)'만 기억한다고 한 것은 적절하다.

② 한 사회 집단의 사람들을 알아보는 능력은 다른 포유류에게도 있지만, 이름을 사용하는 능력을 가진 포유류는 인간이 '유일하다'는 것이므로 unique는 적절하다.

④ 매우 적은 수의 사람들만 마주쳤던 인류 진화의 초기와 달라진 상황을 이야기하는 흐름이므로, 농업과 다른 기술적 혁신이 많은 사람들을 마주칠 수 있는 마을과 도시의 '출현(emergence)'을 촉진시켰다고 하는 것은 적절하다.

⑤ 오늘날의 사진, TV, 인터넷, 소셜 네트워킹을 포함한 추가적인 기술 발전으로 인해 우리가 노출되는 사람들의 수는 우리의 먼 조상들의 그것보다 상당히 더 많을 것이 '확실하므로' ensured는 적절하다.

전문해석

우리는 현재 우리가 저장할 수 있는 것보다 대단히 더 많은 정보에 노출되는 세상에 살고 있다. 예를 들어, 우리는 우리가 마주치는 이름과 얼굴의 ① 일부만 기억한다. 진화론적으로 말해서, 인간의 뇌가 수많은 사람들의 이름을 저장하도록 진화하지 않았다는 것은 결코 비밀이 아니다. 한 사회 집단의 사람들을 알아볼 수 있는 능력은 많은 우리의 동시대 포유류들이 공유하고 있는 능력이지만, 우리는 이름을 사용하는 능력에 있어서 ② 유일한 것으로 보인다. 게다가, 인류 진화의 초기에는 어떤 한 개인이 마주쳤던 다른 사람들의 총 숫자는 아마도 꽤 낮았을 것이다. 25만 년 전 우리의 조상들이 서로에게 이름을 지어 주었다고 가정하더라도, 그들이 수백 명이 넘는 다른 사람들에게 노출되었을 것 ③ 같다(→ 같지는 않다). 마침내 농업과 다른 기술적 혁신이 마을과 도시의 ④ 출현을 촉진시켰다. 오늘날 사진, TV, 인터넷과 소셜 네트워킹을 포함한 추가적인 기술 발전은 우리가 노출되는 사람들의 수가 우리의 먼 조상들이 마주쳤을 사람들의 수보다 아마도 상당히 더 많을 수 있다는 것을 ⑤ 확실하게 해 주었다.

구문풀이

[17행] Today, [further technological advances including photography, TV, the Internet and its social networking] have ensured [that **the number** of people {we are exposed to} **is** likely orders of magnitude higher than the number of people {our distant ancestors would have encountered}].

: 첫 번째 [ ]는 문장의 주어이고, 두 번째 [ ]는 have ensured의 목적어로 쓰인 명사절이다. 두 번째 [ ]에서 첫 번째 { }는 people을 수식하는 관계절이고, 핵심 주어 the number에 수를 맞추어 단수형 동사 is가 쓰였다. 두 번째 { }는 바로 앞의 people을 수식하는 관계절이다.

어휘풀이

- inhabit *v* 살다, 거주하다
- fraction *n* 부분, 일부
- evolutionarily *ad* 진화론적으로
- mammalian *a* 포유류의
- unique *a* 유일한, 특유한
- assume *v* 가정하다
- eventually *ad* 마침내, 결국
- innovation *n* 혁신
- emergence *n* 출현, 등장
- infinitely *ad* 대단히, 무한히
- encounter *v* 마주치다, 조우하다
- recognize *v* 알아보다, 인식하다
- contemporary *n* 동시대인
- fairly *ad* 꽤, 아주
- ancestor *n* 조상, 선조
- agriculture *n* 농업
- foster *v* 촉진하다, 육성하다
- ensure *v* 확실하게 하다, 보장하다

152 답 ⑤

출제 어휘 확인하기

①	avoid	피하다	↔	
②	withdraw	움츠리다	↔	
③	habituate	익숙하다	↔	
④	continue	계속하다	↔	
⑤	worthless	가치가 없는	↔	worthwhile(가치가 있는)

정답풀이

⑤ 익숙하지 않은 대상이 유용할 가능성도 있으므로, 그것이 즉각적인 위협을 주지 않는다면 그 대상을 자세히 살펴보는 것이 도움이 될 수 있다는 것이다. 따라서 '가치가 없을(worthless)' 수 있다는 것은 적절하지 않으며 반대 의미의 worthwhile(가치가 있는) 정도로 바꿔 써야 한다.

오답풀이

① 이어지는 문장에서 익숙하지 않은 대상이 위험할 수 있다고 했으므로, 대부분의 동물이 이전에 접해 보지 않은 대상을 선천적으로 '피한다(avoid)'는 것은 적절하다.

② 동물이 익숙하지 않은 것에 신중한 행동을 보임을 거북에 비유해 설명하는 문맥으로, 바람이 불거나 구름이 그림자를 드리울 때 등껍질 속으로 '움츠린다(withdraws)'는 것은 적절하다.

③ 신중한 행동의 지속이 먹이 섭취나 필요한 활동을 방해할 수 있다고 했으므로, 그러한 문제를 극복하기 위해 거의 모든 동물이 자주 발생하는 안전한 자극에 '익숙해져 있다(habituate)'는 것은 적절하다.

④ 동물들이 낯선 대상에 직면하면 얼어붙거나 숨으려고 하지만 불쾌한 일이 일어나지 않을 때는 활동을 하는 것이 유용할 것이므로 활동을 '계속할(continue)' 것이라는 흐름은 적절하다.

전문해석

동물이 해가 없는 자극 앞에서 움직일 수 있게 하는 것은 학습의 거의 보편적인 기능이다. 대부분의 동물은 선천적으로 이전에 접해 보지 않은 대상을 ① 피한다. 익숙하지 않은 대상은 위험할 수 있으므로, 그것을 조심해서 다루는 것은 생존가치를 가진다. 그러나 그러한 신중한 행동이 지속된다면, 그것은 조심해서 얻는 이익이 소실될 정도로 먹이 섭취와 다른 필요한 활동을 방해할 수도 있다. 바람이 조금 불 때마다 혹은 구름이 그림자를 드리울 때마다 등껍질 속으로 ② 움츠리는 거북은 게으른 토끼와의 경주라도 결코 이기지 못할 것이다. 이 문제를 극복하기 위해, 거의 모든 동물은 자주 발생하는 안전한 자극에 ③ 익숙해져 있다. 낯선 대상에 직면하면, 경험이 없는 동물은 얼어붙거나 숨으려고 할 수도 있지만, 불쾌한 일이 일어나지 않으면 그것은 머지않아 활동을 ④ 계속할 것이다. 익숙하지 않은 대상이 유용할 가능성도 있으므로, 그것이 즉각적인 위협을 주지 않는다면, 더 자세히 살펴보는 것이 ⑤ 가치가 없을(→ 가치가 있을) 수도 있다.

구문풀이

17행 The possibility also exists [that an unfamiliar object may be useful], so if it poses no immediate threat, a closer inspection may be worthwhile.

: [ ]는 The possibility와 동격 관계를 이루는 절로, 여기서는 동격절이 길기 때문에 술어 동사 exists 다음에 위치했다.

어휘풀이

- universal *a* 보편적인
- caution *n* 조심, 주의
- interfere with ~에 방해가 되다
- puff *n* (바람·연기 등의) 한 번 불기
- overcome *v* 극복하다
- confront *v* 직면하게 하다, 직면하다, 맞서다
- immediate *a* 즉각적인
- previously *ad* 이전에
- persist in ~을 지속하다
- withdraw *v* 움츠리다, 물러나다
- cast *v* (그림자를) 드리우다
- habituate to ~에 익숙해지다
- inspection *n* 검사, 조사

153 답 ④

출제 어휘	확인하기			
①	demand	수요	↔	supply(공급)
②	store	저장하다	↔	
③	later	나중에	↔	
④	seize	포착하다	↔	
⑤	unforeseen	예측하지 못한	↔	predictable(예측할 수 있는)

정답풀이

④ 운송에 해당하는 항공편의 좌석이나 화물 적재 용량은 상품과는 달리 안 팔렸을 경우 나중에 추가 용량으로 되돌릴 수 없기 때문에 운송량이 수요를 초과할 경우 그것을 이후에 사용할 기회가 '상실될' 것이다. 따라서 기회가 '포착되었다(seized)'는 것은 적절하지 않으며 missed(상실하다) 정도로 바꿔 써야 한다.

오답풀이

① 소비자가 상품을 구매하면 상품 보충이 촉발될 것이고, 그것이 결국 관련 활동에 대한 '수요'를 창출하는 것이므로 demands는 적절하다.
② 혼자서 존재할 수 없고 이동이 '저장될' 수 없는 것은 상품과 대조하여 운송이 지닌 다른 점으로 볼 수 있으므로 stored는 적절하다.
③ 안 팔린 상품은 남아 있을 수 있으나 항공편 좌석 혹은 화물 적재 용량은 안 팔린 상태로 남게 되어도 '나중에' 추가 용량으로 되가져 올 수 없으므로 later는 적절하다.
⑤ 운송 회사들이 추가 용량을 갖는 것을 선호하는 것은 '예측하지 못한' 수요를 수용할 수 있기 위함일 것이므로 unforeseen은 적절하다.

전문해석

경제 시스템에서는 한 부문에서 일어나는 일이 다른 부문에 영향을 미치고, 한 부문에서의 재화나 서비스에 대한 수요는 다른 부문에서 파생된다. 예를 들면, 상점에서 상품을 구매하는 소비자는 아마 이 상품의 보충을 촉발할 것이며, 이는 제조, 자원 추출, 그리고 물론 운송과 같은 활동에 대한 ① 수요를 창출할 것이다. 운송의 다른 점은 그것이 혼자서는 존재할 수 없으며 이동은 ② 저장될 수 없다는 점이다. 안 팔린 상품은 (흔히 할인 혜택으로) 구매될 때까지 매장 진열대에 남아 있을 수 있으나,

---

항공편의 안 팔린 좌석이나 동일 항공편의 미사용 화물 적재 용량은 안 팔린 상태로 남게 되고 ③ 나중에 추가 용량으로 되가져올 수 없다. 이런 경우, 제공되는 운송량이 그것에 대한 수요를 초과했기 때문에 기회가 ④ 포착되었다(→ 상실되었다). 파생된 운송 수요는 종종 그에 상응하는 공급과 조화를 이루기가 매우 어려워서, 실제로 운송 회사들은 (흔히 훨씬 더 높은 가격에) ⑤ 예측하지 못한 수요를 수용할 수 있는 얼마간의 추가 용량을 갖는 것을 선호할 것이다.

구문풀이

1행 In economic systems [what takes place in one sector] **has** impacts on another; [demand for a good or service in one sector] is derived from another.

: 첫 번째 [ ]는 세미콜론(;) 이전의 첫 번째 절의 주어로 쓰인 명사절이며, 명사절 주어는 단수 취급하므로 단수형 동사 has가 쓰였다. 두 번째 [ ]는 두 번째 절의 주어로 쓰인 명사구이다.

어휘풀이

- take place 일어나다
- derive *v* 파생시키다, 이끌어 내다
- replacement *n* 보충, 대체
- extraction *n* 추출
- cargo *n* 화물 (적재)
- exceed *v* 초과하다
- accommodate *v* 수용하다
- sector *n* 부문
- trigger *v* 촉발하다
- generate *v* 창출하다, 일으키다
- transport *n* 운송
- capacity *n* 용량, 수용량
- equivalent *a* 상응하는, 동등한
- unforeseen *a* 예측하지 못한

154 답 ②

출제 어휘	확인하기			
(A)	determine	결정하다	/ disregard	무시하다, 고려하지 않다
(B)	transform	변형시키다	/ suspend	중단시키다
(C)	escapable	피할 수 있는	/ inescapable	피할 수 없는

정답풀이

(A) 한 국가의 음식이 그 나라의 예술이나 문학보다 더 많은 것을 보여 줄 수 있다고 했으므로, 사람들이 먹는 것은 사회적, 경제적, 기술적 힘들의 상호작용에 의해 '결정된다(determined)'는 것이 적절하다. [disregard 무시하다, 고려하지 않다]
(B) 패스트푸드 산업의 영향력에 관한 문맥이므로, 그것이 미국의 전반적인 상황을 '변형시켰다(transformed)'는 것이 적절하다. [suspend 중단시키다]
(C) 패스트푸드의 영향력을 계속해서 설명하는 문맥이므로, 패스트푸드를 얼마나 먹는지에 상관없이 그 영향력을 '피할 수 없다(inescapable)'는 것이 적절하다. [escapable 피할 수 있는]

전문해석

패스트푸드가 미국 생활에서 혁명적인 영향력이 있다는 것이 입증되고 있다. 나는 그것을 하나의 상품으로뿐만 아니라 하나의 은유로도 흥미를 갖게 되었다. 사람들이 먹는 것은 언제나 사회적, 경제적 그리고 기술적인 힘들의 복잡한 상호작용에 의해 (A) 결정되어 왔다. 한 국가의 음식은 그 나라의 예술이나 문학보다 더 많은 것을 보여 줄 수 있다. 미국에서는 어떤 날에든 성인 인구의 4분의 1이 패스트푸드 식당을 찾는다. 상대적으로 짧은 기간 동안 패스트푸드 산업은 미국의 음식뿐만 아니라 풍경, 경제, 노동력 그리고 대중문화를 (B) 변형시켰다. 패스트푸드와 그것의 영향력은 여러분이 그것을 하루에 두 번을 먹든, 그것을 피하려고 하든, 또는 한 입도 먹은 적이 없든지에 상관없이 (C) 피할 수 없는 것이 되었다.

구문풀이

13행 Fast food and its consequences have become inescapable, regardless of [whether you eat it twice a day, try to avoid it, or have never taken a single bite].

: [ ]는 regardless of의 목적어로 쓰인 명사절이다.

어휘풀이

- revolutionary *a* 혁명적인
- metaphor *n* 은유, 상징
- interplay *n* 상호작용
- quarter *n* 4분의 1
- workforce *n* 노동력
- regardless of ~에 상관없이
- commodity *n* 상품, 일용품
- disregard *v* 무시하다, 고려하지 않다
- literature *n* 문학
- landscape *n* 풍경
- consequence *n* 영향(력), 중요성
- bite *n* 한 입

155 답 ④

출제 어휘	확인하기		
① contaminate	오염되다	↔	
② disprove	반증하다	↔	prove(입증하다)
③ belief	믿음	↔	
④ strength	강점	↔	weakness(약점)
⑤ exclude	배제하다	↔	include(포함하다)

정답풀이

④ 과학자의 가장 강력한 설명도 진리로 제시될 수 없다는 것은 과학 논증이 지닌 '약점'이라고 볼 수 있으므로 strength(강점)는 적절하지 않으며 weakness(약점) 정도로 바꿔 써야 한다.

오답풀이

① 과학 이론의 편향성을 주장하는 사람들의 입장에서는 이론이 개인의 주관적 이념에 의해 '오염될' 수 있음을 고려하는 것이 말도 안 되는 일은 아닐 것이므로 contaminated는 적절하다.

② 아무리 증거가 충분하다고 해도 과학 이론이 진리로 입증될 수는 없다고 했으므로 논리적으로 언제든 새로운 데이터가 나타나 기존 이론의 오류를 입증할, 즉 '반증할(disprove)' 가능성이 존재한다는 것은 적절하다.

③ 기존 이론은 미래에 새로운 데이터로 인해 반증될 수 있다고 했으므로, 과학적 설명은 진리가 아니라 단지 증거에 근거한 '믿음(belief)'에 불과하다는 것은 적절하다.

⑤ 진정 과학이 열린 과정이라면 어떤 이론이 완전히 증명되지 않는 이상 그 경쟁 이론이 참이 될 가능성이 있음을 고려해야 한다는 것이므로 대안 이론을 '배제하려고(excluding)' 해서는 안 된다는 것은 적절하다.

전문해석

어떤 특정 과학 연구 결과를 마음에 들어하지 않는 사람들에 의해 제기되는 가장 흔한 주장 중 하나는 그 결과를 발견한 과학자들이 편향되었다는 것이다. 결국, 만일 누군가 모든 과학이 편향되어 있다고 의심한다면 자신의 주관적인 이념적 믿음에 의해 ① 오염되었을지도 모를 이론을 고려하는 것이 그렇게 어처구니없는 일로 보이지 않을 수 있다. 증거가 아무리 충분하다고 해도 과학 이론이 진리라고 입증될 수는 없다. 과학적 증거가 모아지는 방식 때문에 미래의 어떤 새로운 데이터가 등장해 (기존의) 이론을 ② 반증할 수도 있는 것은 늘 이론적으로 가능하다. 그것은 과학자들이, 심지어 자신들의 가장 강력한 설명도 진리로 제시될 수는 없으며, 증거가 주어진 정당화에 근거한 강하게 보증된 ③ 믿음에 불과하다는 것을 언젠가 인정해야 함을 의미한다. 이렇게 주장되는 과학 논증의 ④ 강점(→ 약점)은 종종 자신들이 진정한 과학자라고 주장하는 사람들에 의해 이용된다. 만일 과학이 열린 과정이라면 대안 이론을 ⑤ 배제하는 일을 해서는 안 된다. 그들이 믿기엔 어떤 이론이 완전히 증명될 때까지 경쟁 이론은 언제나 참이 될 가능성이 있다는 것이다.

구문풀이

[6행] **No matter how** good the evidence, a scientific theory can

never be proven **true**.

: 「No matter how ~」는 '아무리 ~해도'의 의미를 나타내며, the evidence 뒤에 is가 생략된 것으로 볼 수 있다. true는 능동태 문장에서 목적격보어로 쓰인 형용사로, 수동태로 전환되어도 그대로 쓰인 것이다.

어휘풀이

- claim *n* (사실이라는) 주장
- suspect *v* 의심하다
- ideological *a* 이념적인
- disprove *v* 반증하다
- justification *n* 정당화
- exploit *v* 활용하다, (부당하게) 사용하다
- biased *a* 치우친, 편향된
- contaminate *v* 오염시키다, 더럽히다
- come along 나타나다
- warrant *v* 보장하다
- alleged *a* (증거 없이) 주장된
- alternative *a* 대체의, 대신하는

156 답 ④

출제 어휘	확인하기		
① advantage	유리함	↔	disadvantage(불리함)
② stabilize	안정되다	↔	
③ differentiate	차별화하다	↔	
④ increase	증가시키다	↔	decrease(감소시키다)
⑤ adopt	취하다	↔	

정답풀이

④ 다른 사람들과 똑같이 행동하는 것을 선택하려고 하는 것의 예시에 해당하므로 시민들 대부분이 주차 위반 벌금을 내지 않아 위반자들을 사면해야 한다는 압력이 강할 때는 역시 다른 사람들처럼 벌금을 내지 않으려 할 것이다. 따라서 벌금을 낼 동기를 '증가시킨다(increase)'는 것은 적절하지 않으며 반대 의미의 decrease(감소시키다)로 바꿔 써야 한다.

오답풀이

① 사람들의 행동은 다른 사람들이 하는 것에 달려 있다고 했으므로 다른 운전자들이 오전 8시에 출근할 경우 그들과 다른 시간인 오전 6시에 출발하는 것이 낫다는 흐름에서 '유리(advantage)'하다는 것은 적절하다.

② 각자의 이상적인 일정과 출퇴근할 때 겪을 혼잡 사이에서 최상의 균형을 이루는 상태는 교통 흐름이 '안정되는' 때일 것이므로 stabilize는 적절하다.

③ 첫 번째 사례에서 이상적인 일정과 혼잡을 피하는 것 사이에서 최상의 균형을 이루는 선택을 할 때 행위자는 자신의 행동을 다른 사람들과 다르게 '차별화하려고' 할 것이므로 differentiate는 적절하다.

⑤ 다양한 균형 상태가 존재할 수 있다고 했으므로 그렇지 않을 경우, 즉 다양한 균형 상태가 존재하지 않을 경우에는 동일했을 두 사회가 다른 행동 양상을 '취할(adopt)' 수 있다는 것은 적절하다.

전문해석

사람들이 어떻게 행동하는지는 흔히 다른 사람들이 하는 것에 달려 있다. 만약 다른 운전자 또는 지하철 이용자들이 오전 8시에 출근한다면, 비록 나의 관점에서는 그것이 정말로 너무 이르더라도, 오전 6시에 출발하는 것이 내게 ① 유리할 것이다. 균형 상태에서는 (교통) 흐름이 ② 안정되어 각자 자신들의 이상적인 일정과 자신들이 출퇴근할 때 겪을 혼잡 사이에서 최상의 균형을 이룬다. 그러한 선택을 하는 데 있어 행위자는 다른 행위자들의 행동과 자신의 행동을 ③ 차별화하려고 한다. 다른 경우에는 행위자에게 조정에 관한 문제가 생기기도 한다. 그들은 다른 사람들과 똑같이 행동하는 것을 선택하려고 한다. 예를 들면, 만약 내 동료 시민들 대부분이 주차 위반 벌금을 내지 않으면, (유감스럽게도) 그런 위반자들을 사면해야 한다는 강한 압력이 있을 것인데, 이는 내가 주차 위반 벌금을 낼 동기를 또한 ④ 증가시킬(→ 감소시킬) 것이다. 다양한 균형 상태가 존재할 수도 있으며, 그렇지 않다면 동일한 두 사회가 서로 다른 행동 양상을 ⑤ 취할 수도 있다.

8행 In making such choices, agents seek to differentiate their behavior from **that** of others.

: that은 앞에 나온 behavior를 대신한다.

어휘풀이

- leave for work 출근하다
- stabilize *v* 안정되다
- ideal *a* 이상적인
- commute *n* 통근
- differentiate *v* 차별화하다
- coordination *n* 조정
- offender *n* 위반자
- multiple *a* 다양한
- identical *a* 동일한
- flow *n* 흐름
- trade-off *n* 균형; 거래
- congestion *n* 교통체증
- agent *n* 행위자
- occasion *n* 경우, 때
- fellow *n* 동료
- incentive *n* 동기
- otherwise *ad* 그렇지 않으면
- adopt *v* 취하다, 채택하다

---

157 답 ③

출제 어휘 확인하기

① ignorance	무지	↔	awareness(알고 있음, 인식)
② reflect	반영하다	↔	
③ disappear	사라지다	↔	arise(생겨나다), appear(나타나다)
④ inherent	내재된	↔	acquired(습득한)
⑤ exclude	배제하다	↔	include(포함하다)

정답풀이

③ 우리에게 익숙한 것에 대한 편향은 안전, 보안, 편안함을 의미한다고 했으므로, 진화론적인 관점에서 친밀감 편향은 같은 부족, 집단 또는 동굴에 있는 사람들이 우리와 닮은 경향이 있기 때문에 '생겨난' 것이라고 하는 것이 자연스럽다. 따라서 disappeared(사라지다)는 적절하지 않으며 arose(생겨나다) 정도로 바꿔 써야 한다.

오답풀이

① 편향을 인정하지 않거나 자세히 살펴보지 않거나 불공평한 믿음에 기반을 둔 것들을 극복하지 않을 때 문제가 생긴다고 했으므로 편향에 대한 '무지(Ignorance)'가 축복이 아니라는 것은 적절하다.

② 우리는 우리에게 익숙한 것들에 편향되어 있다고 했으므로 우리 삶 속의 상황을 '반영하는(reflect)' 것들과 쉽게 일체감을 느낀다는 것은 적절하다.

④ 우리가 안전하다고 인식한 누군가를 식별하는 것이 자동적이고 생각 없이 이루어졌다고 했으므로 우리 주변 세계를 분류하는 시스템이 '내재된(inherent)' 것이라는 것은 적절하다.

⑤ 우리는 타고난 친밀감 편향으로 자동적이고 생각 없이 안전하다고 인식한 누군가를 식별했으나 오늘날의 다문화 세계에서는 그런 안전 규칙이 동일하게 적용되지 않으므로, 타고난 친밀감 편향을 극복하여 다른 문화의 귀중한 다른 사람들을 '배제하지(excluding)' 않아야 한다는 것은 적절하다.

전문해석

우리는 생물학적으로 편향을 갖게 되어 있고, 그것들[편향]이 본질적으로 부정적인 것은 아니다. 우리가 우리의 편향을 인정하지 않고, 그것들을 자세히 살펴보지 않고, 그다음에 다른 사람들에게 진실하지 않거나, 도움이 되지 않거나, 불공평한 믿음에 기반을 둔 것들을 극복하지 않을 때 문제가 발생한다. 편향에 대한 ① 무지는 축복이 아닌데, 편견이 우리 '모두'에게 정말로 존재하고 억제되지 않으면 고정관념과 편협함을 초래할 수 있기 때문이다. 생물학적으로, 우리 모두는 자연스럽게 우리가 좋아하는 것, 우리가 함께 자라온 것, 우리에게 익숙한 것들에 편향되어 있다. 우리의 뇌는 우리 삶 속의 상황을 ② 반영하는 것들과 쉽게 일체감을 느끼는데, 왜냐하면 그것

들은 전형적으로 안전, 보안 그리고 편안함을 또한 의미하는 것들이기 때문이다. 진화론적 관점에서 이 친밀감 편향, 즉 우리와 같은 사람들 주변에 있고 싶은 욕망은 우리 부족이나 집단 또는 동굴에 있는 사람들이 우리와 닮은 경향이 있기 때문에 ③ 사라졌다(→ 생겨났다). 그렇지 않은 사람들은 위험한 약탈자일 수도 있었다. 다시 말하지만, 우리 주변의 세계를 분류하기 위한 우리의 많은 ④ 내재된 시스템들처럼, 우리가 안전하다고 인식한 누군가를 식별하는 것은 자동적이고 생각 없이 이루어졌다. 국경이 거의 없는 오늘날의 다문화 세계에서는 동일한 안전 규칙이 적용되지 않으며, 우리는 귀중한 '다른 사람들'을 ⑤ 배제하지 않기 위해 우리의 타고난 친밀감 편향을 극복해야 한다.

2행 The problem arises [when we refuse to {recognize our biases}, {sort through them}, and then {overcome the ones <that are based on beliefs (that are untrue, unhelpful, or unfair to others)>}].

: [ ]는 when이 이끄는 부사절이다. 그 안의 세 개의 { }는 refuse to에 병렬구조로 연결된다. < >는 the ones를, ( )는 beliefs를 수식하는 관계절이다.

10행 Our brains readily identify with things [that reflect situations in our own lives] because those are typically the things [that also mean safety, security, and ease].

: 첫 번째 [ ]는 things를, 두 번째 [ ]는 the things를 수식하는 관계절이다.

어휘풀이

- biologically *ad* 생물학적으로
- bias *n* 편향, 편견
- arise *v* 생겨나다
- overcome *v* 극복하다
- bliss *n* 축복
- stereotyping *n* 고정관념 형성, 정형화
- identify with ~와 일체감을 갖다, ~와 동일시하다
- ease *n* 편안함
- standpoint *n* 관점
- wired to *do* ~하도록 되어 있는
- inherently *ad* 본질적으로
- sort through ~을 자세히 살펴보다
- ignorance *n* 무지
- unchecked *a* 억제되지 않은
- evolutionary *a* 진화적인
- borderless *a* 국경이 없는

---

158 답 ⑤

출제 어휘 확인하기

① exclude	배제하다	↔	include(포함하다)
② common	공동의	↔	
③ unsurprising	놀랍지 않은	↔	surprising(놀라운)
④ protect	보호하다	↔	
⑤ promising	유망한	↔	unpromising(가망 없는, 유망하지 못한)

정답풀이

⑤ 유토피아적인 정치사상이 전체주의적인 폭력의 정당화로 이어졌기 때문이라는 내용으로 보아, 유토피아적 정치사상에 대한 부정적인 견해를 반영하는 표현이 나와야 한다. 따라서 일부 이론가들은 유토피아적 정치사상을 '유망한(promising)' 것이라기보다는 '위험한' 것이나 '유망하지 않은' 것으로 여긴다는 맥락이 되어야 하므로 dangerous나 risky 또는 unpromising 정도로 바꿔 써야 한다.

오답풀이

① 아리스토텔레스는 모든 인간이 정치 활동을 하도록 허용되어야 한다고 생각하지 않았다고 했으므로, 여자, 노예, 외국인이 '배제되었다(excluded)'는 것은 적절하다.

② '집단 활동'이라는 표현과 문맥을 같이 하는 것이므로 '공동의(common)'

목표와 목적을 향한다는 것은 적절하다.

③ 도덕주의자들에게는 정치적 삶이 윤리, 즉 도덕 철학의 한 분야라고 했으므로, 도덕주의적 정치 사상가 중에 철학자가 많은 것이 당연한, 즉 '놀랍지 않은(unsurprising)' 일이라는 것은 적절하다.

④ 다음 문장에서 '어떤 것'의 예로 정의, 평등, 자유, 행동 등의 정치적 가치를 들었으므로 정치적 도적주의자들의 정치적인 처리 방식이 그런 정치적 가치들을 '보호하기(protect)' 위해 체계화되어야 한다고 주장한다는 것은 적절하다.

전문해석
아리스토텔레스는 모든 인간이 정치 활동에 참여하도록 허용되어야 한다고 생각하지 않았다. 즉, 그의 체제에서 여성, 노예 그리고 외국인은 자신과 다른 사람들을 다스릴 권리로부터 명백히 (a) 배제되었다. 그럼에도 불구하고, 정치는 어떤 (b) 공동의 목표와 목적을 향한 독특한 집단 활동이라는 그의 기본적인 생각은 오늘날에도 여전히 울려 퍼지고 있다. 하지만 어떤 목적인가? 고대 세계 이후에 많은 사상가와 정계 인사들이 정치가 이룰 수 있거나 이루어야 하는 목표에 관해 각기 다른 생각을 발달시켰다. 이런 접근법은 정치적 도덕주의라고 알려져 있다.

도덕주의자들에게 정치적 삶은 윤리, 즉 도덕 철학의 한 분야여서 도덕주의적 정치 사상가 집단에 많은 철학자가 있는 것은 (c) 놀랍지 않다. 정치적 도덕주의자들은, 정치는 실질적인 목표를 이루려는 쪽으로 향해야 한다고, 즉 정치적인 처리 방식은 어떤 것을 (d) 보호하기 위해 체계화되어야 한다고 주장한다. 이런 것들 중에는 정의, 평등, 자유, 행복, 동포애 또는 민족 자결권과 같은 정치적 가치가 있다. 가장 근본적인 입장에서 도덕주의는, 1516년에 출간되었고 이상 국가를 상상했던, 영국 정치가이자 철학자인 Thomas More의 책 〈Utopia〉에서 이름을 딴, 유토피아로 알려진 이상적인 정치 사회에 대한 묘사를 한다. 유토피아적 정치사상은 고대 그리스 철학자인 플라톤의 책 〈국가론〉으로 거슬러 올라가는데, 그것은 Robert Nozick과 같은 현대 사상가에 의해 아이디어를 탐구하기 위해 여전히 사용된다. 일부 이론가는 유토피아적 정치사상을 (e) 유망한(→ 위험한) 일이라고 여기는데, 그것이 지금까지 전체주의적인 폭력의 정당화로 이어졌기 때문이다. 그러나 최선의 상태에서 유토피아적 사상은 더 나은 사회를 향해 노력하는 과정의 일부이며, 많은 사상가들은 추구되거나 보호되어야 할 가치를 제안하기 위해 그것을 사용한다.

구문풀이
5행 Nevertheless, his basic idea [that politics is a unique collective activity {that is directed at certain common goals and ends}] still resonates today.

: [ ]는 문장의 주어인 his basic idea와 동격 관계를 이루는 명사절이고, 문장의 동사는 resonates이다. { }는 a unique collective activity를 수식하는 관계절이다.

어휘풀이
- explicitly *ad* 명백히
- end *n* 목적
- moralism *n* 도덕주의
- ethics *n* 윤리(학)
- arrangement *n* 처리 방식
- national self-determination 민족 자결권
- radical *a* 근본적인, 급진적인
- undertaking *n* 일, 사업
- totalitarian *a* 전체주의적인
- rule *v* 지배하다, 다스리다
- political figure 정계 인사
- moralist *n* 도덕주의자
- substantial *a* 실질적인
- equality *n* 평등
- statesman *n* 정치인, 정치가
- justification *n* 정당화
- strive *v* 노력하다, 애쓰다

159 답 ⑤

출제 어휘 확인하기

① personify	의인화하다	↔	
② marginal	미미한	↔	vast(막대한)
③ emerge	나타나다	↔	
④ unable	~할 수 없는	↔	able(~할 수 있는)
⑤ keep	유지하다	↔	

정답풀이
⑤ 브랜드 이름을 제시하지 않은 실험에서는 유의미한 브랜드 선호가 보이지 않았는데, 브랜드 이름이 제시된 상태로 실험을 반복했을 때 유의미한 브랜드 선호가 나타났다고 했으므로, 브랜드의 상징적 측면이 선호에 '영향을 주었음'을 알 수 있다. 따라서 kept(유지하다)를 influenced 정도로 바꿔 써야 적절하다.

오답풀이
① 브랜드는 또래 집단에게 자신에 대한 무엇인가를 표현하도록 돕고, 그래서 소비자는 실제 또는 원하는 자아 개념과 가장 잘 맞는 브랜드를 선택한다고 했다. 이러한 맥락에서 소비자가 브랜드를 '의인화한다(personify)'고 표현한 것은 적절하다.

② 브랜드 이름을 제시하지 않은 경쟁 맥주 브랜드들을 대상으로 한 소비자 비교 실험에서 유의미한 선호나 차이를 보이지 않았다고 했으므로, 브랜드 간 제품 차이는 '미미하다(marginal)'고 할 수 있다.

③ 브랜드 이름을 제시하지 않은 실험에서 유의미한 선호나 차이를 보이지 않았다고 한 앞 문장과 Yet으로 연결되는 문장이다. 따라서 브랜드를 제시한 실험을 반복했을 때 유의미한 브랜드 선호가 '나타났다(emerged)'는 것은 적절하다.

④ 앞에서 제품에는 미미한 차이만 있다고 했으므로, 브랜드를 제시하지 않은 실험에서 맥주의 기능적 측면에 초점을 맞춘 소비자는 많은 차이를 인지하지 '못했을' 것이다. 따라서 unable은 적절하다.

전문해석
브랜드는 사용자가 기능적 성능을 당연시하면서 또래 집단에게 자신에 대한 무엇인가를 표현하도록 돕는 그것의 능력 때문에 상징적인 장치로 사용된다. 소비자는 브랜드를 ① 의인화하고, 브랜드의 상징적 가치를 볼 때 매우 분명한 개성을 가진 브랜드를 찾고 그들의 실제 또는 원하는 자아 개념과 가장 잘 맞는 브랜드를 선택한다. 예를 들어, 맥주 시장에서는 브랜드 간 ② 미미한 제품 차이만 존재한다. 브랜드 이름을 제시하지 않은 경쟁 맥주 브랜드들을 대상으로 한 소비자 비교 실험에서는 유의미한 선호 또는 차이를 보이지 않았다. 그러나 소비자가 브랜드 이름을 제시한 실험을 반복했을 때 유의미한 브랜드 선호가 ③ 나타났다. 첫 번째 비교 실험에서 소비자는 맥주의 기능적(이성적) 측면에 초점을 맞추었고 많은 차이를 인지할 ④ 수 없었다. 브랜드 이름을 제시한 실험을 반복하자 소비자는 뚜렷한 브랜드 개성을 떠올리기 위해 브랜드 이름을 사용했고 브랜드의 상징적(감정적) 측면이 선호를 ⑤ 유지시켰다(→ ~에) 영향을 미쳤다).

구문풀이
1행 Brands are used as symbolic devices, [because of their ability

{to help users express something about themselves to their peer groups}], [**with** users **taking** for granted functional capabilities].

: 첫 번째 [ ]는 because of가 이끄는 전치사구이며, 그 안의 { }는 their ability를 수식하는 to부정사구이다. 두 번째 [ ]는 「with+명사+현재분사」 구문으로 '~가 …하면서'라는 의미를 나타낸다.

4행 Consumers personify brands and when looking at the symbol values of brands, they [seek brands {which have very clear personalities}] and [select brands {that best match their actual or desired self-concept}].

: 두 개의 [ ]는 and 다음 절의 주어 they에 연결되는 술어이며 and에 의해 병렬구조를 이룬다. 두 개의 { }는 각각 바로 앞의 brands를 수식하는 관계절이다.

어휘풀이
- device *n* 장치, 기구
- take for granted ~을 당연시하다
- personify *v* 의인화하다, 전형적으로 보여 주다
- personality *n* 개성, 성격
- marginal *a* 미미한, 주변적인
- trial *n* 실험, 시험
- preference *n* 선호(도)
- rational *a* 이성적인, 합리적인
- recall *v* 떠올리다, 회상하다
- peer group 또래 집단
- capability *n* 성능, 능력
- self-concept *n* 자아 개념
- comparative *a* 비교에 의한
- significant *a* 유의미한, 중요한
- emerge *v* 나타나다, 등장하다
- notice *v* 인지하다, 알아차리다
- distinct *a* 뚜렷한, 뚜렷이 다른

160 답 ⑤

출제 어휘 확인하기			
① bigger	더 큰	↔	smaller(더 작은)
② edge	가장자리	↔	
③ further	더욱	↔	
④ prevent	막다	↔	
⑤ disproportionate	불균형한	↔	proportionate, proportional(비례하는)

정답풀이
⑤ 딱딱한 표면에는 물을 부을수록 물웅덩이가 옆으로 계속 퍼져나가 웅덩이의 지름이 늘어나지만, 가장자리만 받쳐주는 얇은 고무 시트로 구성된 표면은 물을 부을수록 물의 무게가 시트를 눌러 시트가 아래로 오목해질 뿐 웅덩이의 지름은 증가하지 않는다는 내용이다. 즉, 고무 시트는 물의 양이 많을수록 오목해지므로 벽은 더 가파를 것임을 알 수 있다. 따라서 물의 양과 퍼짐의 난도(벽의 가파름)는 서로 균형을 이루는 '비례' 관계라고 해야 하므로, disproportionate(불균형한)는 적절하지 않으며 반대 의미인 proportional 또는 proportionate 정도로 바꿔 써야 한다.

오답풀이
① 딱딱한 표면에 물을 부으면 표면 위로 물이 퍼져나간다고 했으므로 물을 많이 부을수록 물웅덩이가 '더 커진다(bigger)'는 것은 적절하다.
② 물웅덩이가 계속 퍼져나가지 않고 한정된 크기에 도달한다고 했고 지름이 늘어나지 않는다고 했으므로, '가장자리(edges)'가 늘어나지 않도록 받쳐주는 형태의 고무 시트라는 것은 적절하다.
③ 고무 시트에 물을 많이 부어도 지름은 늘어나지 않으며 시트를 누르는 물의 무게가 증가할 것이므로, 시트가 아래쪽으로 '더욱(further)' 눌릴 뿐이라는 것은 적절하다.
④ 오목한 곳의 벽이 점점 더 가파르게 된다는 것은 물이 옆으로 퍼지는 것이 아니고 아래로만 깊어지는 것을 의미하므로, 퍼져나가는 것을 '막는다(prevent)'는 것은 적절하다.

전문해석
만약 딱딱한 표면에 물을 부으면 물은 그 표면 위로 퍼져나갈 것이다. 물을 많이 부을수록 웅덩이는 ① 더 커진다. 하지만 표면이 딱딱하지 않고 ② 가장자리만 받쳐주는 얇은 고무 시트로 구성된다면, 기이한 일이 벌어진다. 그 물웅덩이는 계속 퍼져나가지 않고 한정된 크기에 도달한다. 고무 시트에 물을 아무리 많이 부어도 웅덩이의 지름은 증가하지 않는다. 물의 무게가 시트를 아래로 누르는 일이 일어난다. 물이 많으면 시트를 ③ 더욱 아래로 누를 뿐이다. 시트의 중앙이 눌리면, 오목한 곳의 벽이 점점 더 가파르게 되어 물이 퍼져나가는 것을 ④ 막는다. 실제로 얇은 고무 시트를 가지고 있으면 안정화된 시스템을 갖출 수 있다. 퍼짐의 난도(벽의 가파름)는 물의 양과 ⑤ 불균형을 이루는데(→ 비례하는데), 그래서 시트에 물을 아무리 많이 부어도 그것은 퍼져 나가지 않는다. 이는 물의 양이 많을수록 더 많이 퍼져나가는 것을 의미하는 불안정한 시스템과는 뚜렷한 대조를 이룬다.

구문풀이
9행 [What happens] is [that the weight of the water depresses the sheet].

: 첫 번째 [ ]는 문장의 주어로 쓰인 명사절이고, 두 번째 [ ]는 주격보어로 쓰인 명사절이다.

어휘풀이
- rigid *a* 딱딱한, 단단한
- consist of ~으로 구성되다
- edge *n* 가장자리, 끝
- depress *v* (아래로) 누르다
- steep *a* 가파른
- contrast *n* 대조
- spread out 퍼져 나가다
- rubber *n* 고무
- diameter *n* 지름
- depression *n* 오목한[움푹한] 곳
- stabilized *a* 안정화된

161 답 ②

출제 어휘 확인하기			
① ignore	무시하다	↔	
② object	반대하다	↔	approve(찬성하다)
③ counter	반격하다	↔	
④ concern	관련되다	↔	
⑤ deny	부정하다	↔	accept(받아들이다, 인정하다)

정답풀이
② 과학적인 것이 아니면 무시하고 무효한 것으로 여기는 사람들에 대해 설명하는 흐름이므로, 과학의 힘에 관해 계속 '반대한다(object)'는 것은 적절하지 않으며 '집착한다'는 의미에서 cling 정도로 바꿔 써야 한다.

오답풀이
① 연구는 원인과 결과에 의해 과학적으로 설명될 수 없으면 미신적이고 무효한 것으로 일축된다는 내용이 이어지므로, 측정 및 정량화할 수 없는 것을 '무시해 온(ignored)' 것은 적절하다.
③ 서양 의학 연구 단체의 엄격한 구성원들 입장에서는 대체 의학이 주는 위협을 '반격하려고(counter)' 한다는 것은 적절하다.
④ 서양 의학 및 과학에 대한 완고한 집착에도 불구하고 생물 의학 연구가 돌봄 치료 과정에 있어 대체 의학 시술자들과 '관련된' 현상을 잘 설명할 수 없다는 것이므로 concern은 적절하다.
⑤ 서양 과학 연구에 집착하는 사람들의 입장에서 침술이나 동종 요법이 생물 의학적으로 설명될 수 없는 반응을 초래함이 관찰되면 과학적 모델을 수정하지 않고 대신 그 관찰된 반응을 '부정하려고(deny)' 애써 왔다는 것은 적절하다.

전문해석
서양의 과학 연구에 한정된 사람들은 오감으로 감지할 수 없고 반복적으로 측정하거

나 정량화할 수 없는 것은 무엇이든 거의 ① 무시해 왔다. 연구는, 원인과 결과에 의해 과학적으로 설명될 수 없으면, 미신적이고 무효한 것으로 일축된다. 많은 사람들이 과학의 힘, 보다 구체적으로 과학이 그들에게 주는 힘에 관한 이 문화적 패러다임에 거의 종교적 열정을 가지고 계속 ② 반대한다(→ 집착한다). 비서양의 과학적 패러다임을 기껏해야 열등하고 최악의 경우 부정확하다고 일축함으로써, 기존의 서양 의학 연구 단체의 가장 엄격한 구성원들은 대체 의학 요법과 연구가 자신들의 연구, 자신들의 행복 및 자신들의 세계관에 가하는 위협에 ③ 반격하려 한다. 그럼에도 불구하고, 생물 의학 연구는 돌봄 치료 과정과 관련하여 대체 의학 시술자들과 ④ 관련된 현상 중 많은 것에 관해서 설명할 수 없다. 침술 또는 동종 요법 같은 치료법이 생물 의학적 모델에 의해 설명될 수 없는 생리적 또는 임상적 반응을 초래하는 것이 관찰될 때, 많은 사람이 과학적인 모델을 수정하기보다는 그 결과를 ⑤ 부정하려 애써 왔다.

구문풀이

15행 And yet, biomedical research cannot explain many of the phenomena [that concern alternative practitioners {regarding caring-healing processes}].

: [ ]는 many of the phenomena를 수식하는 관계절이고, 그 안의 { }는 alternative practitioners를 수식하는 전치사구이다.

어휘풀이

- virtually *ad* 거의, 사실상
- measure *v* 측정하다
- dismiss *v* 일축하다, 묵살하다
- invalid *a* 무효한
- paradigm *n* 패러다임
- rigid *a* 엄격한, 완고한
- counter *v* 반격하다, 반박하다
- pose *v* 가하다, 제기하다
- phenomenon *n* 현상
- practitioner *n* 전문직 종사자, (특히) 의사
- physiological *a* 생리적인
- perceive *v* 감지하다, 인식하다
- quantify *v* 정량화하다
- superstitious *a* 미신적인
- religious *a* 종교적인
- inferior *a* 열등한
- conventional *a* 기존의
- alternative *a* 대체의
- biomedical *a* 생물 의학의
- modify *v* 수정하다, 고치다

162 답 ⑤

① emerge	나타나다	↔	
② variation	변화	↔	
③ manifestation	외적 형태	↔	
④ basic	기본적인	↔	
⑤ refuse	거부하다	↔	accept(받아들이다)

정답풀이

⑤ 기본적인 특징을 유지하면서 개인의 특정한 요구에 맞게 형태가 조정될 수 있음을 말하고 있으므로, 그 원리에 의해 변형이 '거부될' 수 있었다는 것은 적절하지 않다. refused를 introduced(도입하다) 정도로 바꿔 써야 한다.

오답풀이

① 수렵과 채집을 기반으로 한 유목 생활양식을 설명한 후, 정착된 농촌 사회의 발전과 함께 등장한 새로운 생활양식을 설명하고 있으므로 다른 형태의 전통이 '나타났다(emerged)'는 것은 적절하다.
② 전통이 특정한 개별적인 사람들과 그들의 환경에 맞추어 조정되었다는 맥락이므로 '변화(variations)'는 적절하다.
③ 기본적인 형태는 유지되더라도 개인의 필요에 따라 특정한 '외적 형태(manifestations)'가 사용자에 맞게 맞춰졌다는 것은 적절하다.

---

④ 전통적인 형태를 어느 정도 유지하면서도 특정 개인의 신체에 맞게 모양이 세부적으로 만들어진다는 것을 의자를 사례로 들어 설명하는 문맥에서 의자가 '기본적인(basic)' 특징을 유지했다는 것은 적절하다.

전문해석

초기 인간 사회는 수렵과 채집을 기반으로 한 유목 생활이었고, 새로운 식량원을 찾아 이동하는 생활양식에서는 경량성, 휴대성 그리고 적응성과 같은 특징이 지배적인 기준이었다. 농업을 기반으로 한 더 정착된 농촌 사회의 발전과 함께, 다른 특징, 즉 새로운 생활양식에 적합한 다른 형태의 전통이 급속하게 ① 나타났다. 그러나 전통은 정적이지 않았고 사람들과 그들의 환경에 적절한, 매우 작은 ② 변화를 끊임없이 겪었다는 것이 강조되어야 한다. 전통적 형태가 사회 집단의 경험을 반영하더라도, 개개의 사용자의 요구에 맞추기 위해 특정한 ③ 외적 형태가 각양각색의 미세하고 미묘한 방식으로 조정될 수 있었다. 의자는 여전히 특정 개인의 체격과 (신체) 비율에 맞게 세부적으로 면밀히 모양이 만들어지는 와중에도 그것의 ④ 기본적이고 일반적으로 용인되는 특징을 유지할 수 있었다. 맞춤 제작의 이러한 기본 원리는 일련의 끊임없이 증가하는 변형이 ⑤ 거부될(→ 도입될) 수 있도록 했고, 그것들이 경험에 의하여 유익하다고 입증되면 전통의 주류 속으로 다시 통합될 수 있었다.

구문풀이

17행 This basic principle of customization allowed a constant stream of incremental modifications [to be introduced], [which, if demonstrated by experience to be advantageous, could be integrated back into the mainstream of tradition].

: 첫 번째 [ ]는 allowed의 목적격보어로 쓰인 to부정사구이다. 두 번째 [ ]는 a constant stream of incremental modifications를 부연 설명하는 관계절이다.

어휘풀이

- nomadic *a* 유목의, 유목 생활의
- criterion *n* 기준, 척도
- circumstance *n* 환경, 상황
- subtle *a* 미묘한, 미세한
- modification *n* 변형, 수정
- mainstream *n* 주류
- portability *n* 휴대성
- minute *a* 아주 작은, 미세한
- manifestation *n* 외적, 형태, 표시
- proportion *n* 비율, 크기
- integrate *v* 통합하다

163 답 ④

① establish	규명하다	↔	
② consistent	일치하는, 양립하는	↔	inconsistent(일치하지 않는, 모순되는)
③ unsatisfactory	불충분한	↔	satisfactory(충분한)
④ deny	부정하다	↔	accept, concede(인정하다)
⑤ sensible	합리적인	↔	

정답풀이

④ 잘못된 선택의 오류를 피하기 위해서는 여러 가지 설명 중 한 가지 설명만 옳은 것이라고 '인정하기' 전에 다른 설명들을 무시하거나 간과하고 있지 않은지 고려해 보라는 흐름이다. 따라서 denying(부정하다)은 적절하지 않으며 conceding 또는 accepting 정도로 바꿔 써야 한다.

오답풀이

① Paula가 뱀과 거미 둘 중 하나를 두려워한다고 추론했으므로 거미를 두려워한다는 결론을 내릴 수 있는 경우는 뱀을 두려워하지 않는다고 확정하거나 '규명할' 때일 것이므로 establish는 적절하다.
② Paula에게 공포증이 있다는 것만을 알 경우에 그녀가 뱀을 두려워하지 않는다는 사실은 그녀가 다른 것을 무서워한다는 사실과 '양립할' 수 있으므로 consistent는 적절하다.

③ 어떤 현상에 관해 대안이 될 설명을 제공받고서 신중할 필요가 있음을 말하는 문맥으로, 대안적인 설명 중 한 가지를 제외하고는 모두 '불충분하다(unsatisfactory)'고 확신할 때 멈춰서 곰곰이 생각한다는 것은 적절하다.
⑤ 숨어 있는 중요한 가정에 주의를 충분히 기울이지 못할 때 잘못된 선택의 오류가 우리를 잘못 이끄는 상황을 설명하는 문맥이므로, '합리적인(sensible)' 대안을 고갈시키도록 한다는 것은 적절하다.

전문해석
우리가 Paula가 심각한 공포증을 겪는다는 점을 알고 있다고 가정해 보자. Paula가 뱀 또는 거미 둘 중에 하나를 두려워한다고 추론하고 난 다음 그녀가 뱀을 두려워하지 않는다는 것을 ① 규명한다면, 우리는 Paula가 거미를 두려워한다는 결론을 내릴 것이다. 하지만 우리의 결론은 정말로 Paula의 두려움이 뱀 또는 거미 둘 중 하나와 관련이 있을 경우에만 타당하다. 만약 우리가 Paula에게 공포증이 있다고만 알고 있다면, 그녀가 뱀을 두려워하지 않는다는 사실은 그녀가 높은 곳, 물, 개, 혹은 숫자 13을 무서워한다는 것과 전적으로 ② 양립한다. 보다 일반적으로, 우리가 어떤 현상에 관해 일련의 대안이 될 설명을 제공받고, 그러한 설명 중에서 한 가지를 제외한 모든 것이 ③ 불충분하다고 확신한다면, 우리는 멈춰서 곰곰이 생각해 보아야 한다. 그 남아 있는 설명이 옳은 것이라고 ④ 부정하기(→ 인정하기) 전에, 타당한 것 같은 다른 선택 사항들이 무시되거나 또는 간과되고 있는지를 고려하라. 숨어 있는 중요한 가정에 우리가 충분히 주의를 기울이지 못하면, 잘못된 선택의 오류는 명백한 것으로 밝혀진 선택들이 ⑤ 합리적인 대안을 고갈시키도록 잘못 이끈다.

구문풀이
2행 If we reason [that Paula is afraid either of snakes or spiders], and then establish [that she is not afraid of snakes], we will conclude [that Paula is afraid of spiders].

: 세 개의 [ ]는 각각 동사 reason과 establish, will conclude의 목적어로 쓰인 명사절이다.

어휘풀이
- phobia *n* 공포증
- establish *v* 규명하다, 확립하다
- consistent *a* 양립하는, 일치하는
- alternative *a* 대안적인 *n* 대안
- reflect *v* 심사숙고하다
- mislead *v* 오도하다, 오해하게 만들다
- exhaust *v* 고갈시키다, 소모하다
- reason *v* 추론하다
- concern *v* 관계가 있다
- height *n* 높은 곳, 높이
- pause *v* 멈추다, 중단하다
- overlook *v* 간과하다
- explicit *a* 명백한
- sensible *a* 합리적인, 분별 있는

164 답 ②

정답풀이
(A) 아동기와 노년의 공통점으로 활동적인 세상에 아직 이르지 못하거나 그러기를 중단했고, 자발적이고 개방적인 반응을 보인다는 내용이 이어지고 있으므로 아동기와 노년의 공통된 속성을 나타내는 말로는 '무방비(defenselessness)'가 적절하다. [effectiveness 효과성]
(B) 진주가 자라는 방식을 통해 인생을 표현하는 문맥으로, 청소년기 동안 우리 신체 주변의 보이지 않는 껍데기가 단단해지고 성인기를 지나면서 점점 더 두꺼워지며 상처가 크고 깊을수록 막이 '더 강해진다(stronger)'는 것이 적절하다. [smoother 더 부드러운]
(C) 껍데기로 보호받다가 이후에 약해진다는 흐름으로 이어지고 있으므로, 처음에는 '자신감이 있어서(confident)' 아무것도 알아차리지 못한다는 것이

적절하다. [insecure 불안한, 확신이 안 가는]

전문해석
아동기와 노년은 매우 유사하다. 두 경우 모두, 서로 다른 이유로 (A) 무방비의 요소가 있는데, 우리는 활동적인 세상의 일부가 아직 아니거나 아니면 그 일부가 되기를 중단했고, 우리의 반응은 자발적이고, 개방되어 있다. 청소년기 동안 우리 신체 주변의 보이지 않는 껍데기가 단단해지기 시작하고, 성인기를 지나면서 점점 더 두꺼워진다. 그것은 진주가 자라는 방식과 상당히 같은데, 상처가 더 크고 깊을수록, 막이 (B) 더 강해진다. 하지만 우리가 너무 자주 입는 옷과 마찬가지로, 매우 예상치 못하게 갑작스러운 움직임의 결과로 껍데기가 쪼개질 때까지 시간이 지나면서 몇몇 군데가 얇아지기 시작한다. 처음에는 껍데기의 보호 속에서 (C) 자신감이 있어서 아무것도 알아차리지 못하지만, 그런 다음 매우 평범한 어떤 일이 일어나고, 이유를 알지 못한 채 여러분은 아이처럼 울고 있는 자신을 발견한다.

구문풀이
1행 In both cases, for different reasons, there is an element of defenselessness; we are **either** not yet, **or** we have ceased to be, [part of the active world], and our responses can be spontaneous, open.

: 「either A or B」는 'A 또는 B 중의 하나'라는 뜻이다. [ ]는 we are not yet과 we have ceased to be에 공통으로 연결된 보어 역할을 한다.

어휘풀이
- element *n* 요소, 성분
- response *n* 반응, 응답
- adolescence *n* 청소년기
- wound *n* 상처, 고통
- passage *n* 경과, 지남
- split *v* 쪼개지다
- cease *v* 중단하다
- spontaneous *a* 자발적인
- invisible *a* 보이지 않는
- crust *n* (얇고 단단한) 막
- unexpectedly *ad* 예상치 못하게
- confident *a* 자신감 있는, 확신하는

165 답 ④

정답풀이
④ 신체적인 활동이나 오락은 개인의 여러 능력을 활용한다고 했고 참여를 통해 다른 사람들의 좋은 점을 목격하게 한다고 했으므로, 함께 일하고자 하는 본능을 '억누른다(suppressing)'고 하는 것은 적절하지 않다. 그러한 본능을 '불러일으킨다'는 의미에서 rousing 정도로 바꿔 써야 한다.

오답풀이
① 신체 활동은 본능을 자극해 우리를 더 행복하게 만든다고 했으므로 인간의 기본적인 '즐거움(joys)'과 엉켜 있다는 것은 적절하다.
② 즐거움을 주는 신체 활동에 관해 계속해서 설명하는 부분으로, 음악에 맞춰 움직이는 만족감을 말하고 있으므로 '활동하고(active)' 있을 때라는 것은 적절하다.
③ 움직임의 장점을 계속해서 설명하는 부분이므로 자연과의 교감 또는 더 큰 어떤 것의 일부를 느끼고자 하는 욕구 등 인간의 욕구를 '충족시킬(fulfill)' 수 있다는 것은 적절하다.
⑤ 신체 활동이 주는 여러 가지 장점을 설명했으므로, 모든 문화가 움직임을 가장 즐겁고도 의미 있는 전통의 '핵심(heart)'에 놓는다는 것은 적절하다.

전문해석

운동을 통해서든, 탐험을 통해서든, 경쟁을 통해서든, 축하를 통해서든, 신체 활동은 우리를 더 행복하게 만드는데, 그것이 이러한 본능을 자극하기 때문이다. 움직임은 자기 표현, 사회적인 연결, 숙달을 포함한 인간의 가장 기본적인 ① 즐거움 중 일부와 서로 엉켜 있다. 우리가 ② 활동하고 있을 때, 우리는 음악의 박자에 맞춰 동시에 움직이는 만족감에서부터 속도, 우아함 또는 힘을 가지고 움직이는 감각의 전율에 이르기까지 타고난 즐거움에 접근한다. 또한 움직임은 자연과 교감하거나 자신보다 더 큰 어떤 것의 일부를 느끼고자 하는 욕구와 같은 인간의 핵심적인 욕구를 ③ 충족시킬 수 있다. 우리가 가장 이끌리는 신체적인 오락은 독특하게도 우리의 개인적인 힘, 즉 집요하게 계속하고, 견디고, 배우고, 성장하는 능력을 활용하기 위해 고안된 것으로 보이는 한편, 동시에 함께 일하고자 하는 우리의 본능을 ④ 억누른다(→ 불러일으킨다). 신체적인 활동이 심리적으로 가장 만족감을 준다면, 그것은 우리의 참여가 우리 내면의 좋은 점을 드러내고 또한 다른 사람들의 좋은 점을 목격하도록 하기 때문이다. 이것은 모든 문화가 움직임을 그것의 가장 즐겁고도 의미 있는 전통의 ⑤ 핵심에 놓는 이유 중 하나이다.

구문풀이

9행 Movement can also fulfill core human needs, such as the desires [to connect with nature] or [to feel a part of something bigger than yourself].

: 두 개의 [ ]는 the desires를 수식하는 to부정사구이다.

어휘풀이

- exploration *n* 탐험
- instinct *n* 본능
- mastery *n* 숙달
- synchronize *v* 동시에 움직이다
- thrill *n* 전율
- core *a* 핵심적인
- devise *v* 고안하다
- endure *v* 견디다
- fulfilling *a* 만족감을 주는
- stimulate *v* 자극하다
- intertwine with ~와 서로 엉키다
- innate *a* 타고난
- sensory *a* 감각의
- fulfill *v* 충족시키다
- pastime *n* 오락
- persist *v* 집요하게[끈질기게] 계속하다
- simultaneously *ad* 동시에

166 답 ⑤

출제 어휘 확인하기

① avoid	피하다	↔	
② equal	같은, 동일한	↔	unequal(같지 않은)
③ rule out	~을 배제하다	↔	
④ nothing	아무것도 없음	↔	
⑤ different	다른	↔	similar(비슷한), same(같은)

정답풀이

⑤ 실험에서 연구 결과에 외부 요인이 영향을 미치지 않도록 실험 집단과 통제 집단을 분류해야 한다는 것이 글의 핵심이다. 영양분을 포함하는 실험에서 두 집단의 식단이 다르면 비타민 C 보충제의 효과를 분명하게 알 수 없으므로 효과를 입증하려면 두 집단의 식단이 '달라야' 한다는 것은 적절하지 않다. different를 similar(비슷한) 정도로 바꿔 써야 한다.

오답풀이

① 두 집단 모두를 관찰하는 종류의 실험에 내재한 함정 중 일부를 '피하는' 방법이 이어지고 있으므로 avoid는 적절하다.
② 실험 대상자를 분류할 때 실험 집단 또는 통제 집단 중에 배정될 확률이 '같은' 것은 임의 추출에 의해 성취될 수 있으므로 equal은 적절하다.
③ 두 집단의 사람들이 감기에 대해 비슷하고 동일한 기록을 가져야 하는 것

은 어떤 식으로든 관찰된 차이가 일어났을지도 모른다는 가능성을 '배제하기' 위해서이므로 rule out은 적절하다.
④ 두 집단의 사람들이 감기에 대해 비슷하고 동일한 기록을 가지고 있어야 한다고 했으므로, 두 집단이 감기와 관련해 두 배나 차이가 있다면 연구 결과가 입증할 수 있는 것은 '아무것도 없을 것'이다. 따라서 nothing은 적절하다.

전문해석

비타민 C의 효과를 조사하는 연구에서 연구자들은 보통 실험 대상자들을 두 집단으로 나눈다. 한 집단(실험 집단)은 비타민 C 보충제를 받고 다른 집단(통제 집단)은 비타민 C 보충제를 받지 않는다. 연구자들은 한 집단이 다른 집단보다 감기에 더 적게 혹은 더 짧게 걸리는지를 알아내기 위해 두 집단 모두를 관찰한다. 이어지는 논의는 이러한 종류의 실험에 내재한 함정 중 일부와 이를 (a) 피하는 방법을 자세히 설명한다. 실험 대상자를 두 집단으로 분류할 때, 연구자들은 반드시 각 개인이 실험 집단 또는 통제 집단 둘 중 한 곳에 배정될 확률이 (b) 같도록 해야 한다. 이는 임의 추출에 의해 성취되는데, 즉 실험 대상자는 동전 던지기나 우연이 포함된 어떤 다른 방법에 의해 동일 모집단에서 임의로 선택된다. 임의 추출은 반드시 결과에 처리가 반영되고, 실험 대상자의 분류에 영향을 줄 수 있는 요인은 반영되지 않도록 하는 데 도움이 된다. 중요한 것은, 감기의 비율, 심각성 또는 지속 기간에서 관찰된 차이가 어떤 식으로든 일어났을지도 모른다는 가능성을 (c) 배제하기 위해 감기와 관련해 두 집단의 사람들이 비슷하고 동일한 기록을 가지고 있어야 한다는 것이다. 예를 들면, 통제 집단이 보통 실험 집단보다 감기에 무려 두 배나 많이 걸리는 경우, 연구 결과는 (d) 아무것도 입증하지 못한다. 영양분을 포함하는 실험에서, 두 집단의 식단 또한 (e) 달라야(→ 비슷해야) 하며, 연구 중인 영양분에 관련해서 특히 그래야 한다. 실험 집단에 속한 사람들이 평소 식단에서 비타민 C를 적게 섭취하고 있었다면, 보충제의 어떤 효과도 명백하지 않을 수 있다.

구문풀이

9행 In sorting subjects into two groups, researchers must ensure [that each person has an equal chance of {being assigned to either the experimental group or the control group}].

: [ ]는 must ensure의 목적어로 쓰인 명사절이고, 그 안의 { }는 전치사 of의 목적어로 쓰인 동명사구이다.

어휘풀이

- subject *n* 피험자, 실험 대상자
- control group 통제 집단, 대조군
- assign *v* 배정하다, 할당하다
- randomization *n* 임의 추출, 무작위 추출
- population *n* 모집단, 개체군
- track record 기록, 실적
- rule out ~을 배제하다
- duration *n* 지속 (기간)
- nutrient *n* 영양분
- supplement *n* 보충제
- inherent *a* 내재한
- flip *v* (동전 등을) 던지다
- with respect to ~와 관련하여
- severity *n* 심각성
- finding *n* 연구 결과
- apparent *a* 명백한, 분명한

어휘풀이

- prior to ~에 앞서, ~ 이전에
- freight *n* 화물
- negligible *a* 무시해도 될 만한
- standard *n* 기준
- dominate *v* 지배하다
- volume *n* 양
- maritime *a* 바다의, 해양의
- capacity *n* 수용량
- countryside *n* 시골 지역
- inland *ad* 내륙으로
- emerge *v* 부상하다, 등장하다
- riverine *a* 강의
- outdated *a* 구식의
- the Industrial Revolution 산업혁명
- transport *v* 운송하다
- contemporary *a* 현대의, 동시대의
- via *prep* ~을 거쳐, ~을 경유하여
- Mediterranean *a* 지중해의
- notably *ad* 눈에 띄게, 특히
- distribution *n* 유통
- stagecoach *n* 역마차
- cargo *n* 화물
- canal *n* 운하
- bulk *a* 대량의
- consequently *ad* 결과적으로
- era *n* 시대

167 답 ⑤

출제 어휘 확인하기

① quantity	양	↔	
② modern	현대의	↔	
③ slow	느린	↔	fast(빠른)
④ limited	제한적인	↔	
⑤ outdated	구식의	↔	up-to-date(최신의)

정답풀이

⑤ 18세기 후반에 운하 체계가 부상하여 화물의 대규모 이동을 가능하게 하고 지역 무역을 확장시켰다고 했으므로, 해상과 강 운송이 산업화 이전 시대의 '구식의' 방식이었다는 것은 적절하지 않다. outdated를 dominant(지배적인) 정도로 바꿔 써야 한다.

오답풀이

① 뒤에 중세 시대의 프랑스 수입품의 총량에 관한 사례가 이어지므로 국가 간 운송 화물의 '양(quantity)'이라는 표현은 적절하다.
② 앞에서 산업혁명 이전에는 화물의 양이 적었음을 설명했으므로, 그 당시의 화물의 양이 '현대의(modern)' 화물선 하나를 채우지 못했을 것이라는 것은 적절하다.
③ 제한적이었던 유통량과 함께 속도가 '느렸다'는 것에 대해 영국 시골 지역 역마차의 사례가 이어지고 있으므로 slow는 적절하다.
④ 1톤의 화물을 내륙으로 30마일 이동시키는 비용은 대서양을 가로지르는 이동을 통한 비용만큼이나 많이 들었다고 했으므로 내륙 운송 체계가 '제한적(limited)'이었을 것이라는 흐름은 적절하다.

전문해석

산업혁명 이전에, 국가 간에 운송된 화물의 ① 양은 현대의 기준에 의하면 무시해도 될 정도였다. 예를 들면, 중세 시대에는 Saint-Gothard Passage를 통한 프랑스 수입품의 총량은 화물 열차 하나를 채우지 못했을 것이다. 지중해 무역을 지배했던 베네치아 선단에 의해 운송된 화물의 양은 ② 현대의 화물선 하나를 채우지 못했을 것이다. 속도는 아니지만, 특히 해상 운송에서, 무역의 양은 중상주의하에서 향상되었다. 이 모든 것에도 불구하고, 유통량은 매우 제한적이었으며 속도는 ③ 느렸다. 예를 들면, 16세기에 영국 시골 지역을 통과하는 역마차는 평균 시속 2마일이었다. 18세기 후반 무렵 미국에서 1톤의 화물을 내륙으로 30마일 이동시키는 것은 대서양을 가로질러 그것을 이동시키는 것만큼 비용이 많이 들었다. 따라서 내륙의 운송 체계는 매우 ④ 제한적이었다. 18세기 후반 무렵 운하 체계가 유럽에서 부상하기 시작했다. 그것은 내륙으로 선적 화물의 대규모 이동을 가능하게 했고 지역 무역을 확대시켰다. 해상 및 강 운송은 결과적으로 산업화 이전 시대의 ⑤ 구식의(→ 지배적인) 방식이었다.

구문풀이

6행 The amount of freight [transported by the Venetian fleet, {which dominated Mediterranean trade}], would not fill a modern container ship.

: [ ]는 freight를 수식하는 과거분사구이고, 그 안의 { }는 계속적 용법의 관계대명사 which가 이끄는 절로 the Venetian fleet를 부연 설명한다.

168 답 ②

출제 어휘 확인하기

① grasp	파악하다	↔	
② deliberately	의도적으로, 고의로	↔	subconsciously(잠재의식적으로)
③ prevent	막다	↔	
④ unaware	모르는, 알지 못하는	↔	aware(아는, 알고 있는)
⑤ good	좋은	↔	bad(안 좋은)

정답풀이

② 피험자가 자신이 어떤 치료를 받고 있는지 모르는 상태로 실험을 하는 이유는 피험자의 개인적 인식이 '자신도 모르게' 실험 결과에 영향을 주는 것을 막기 위해서일 것이다. 따라서 deliberately(의도적으로, 고의로)를 subconsciously(잠재의식적으로) 정도로 바꾸는 것이 문맥상 적절하다.

오답풀이

①, ③ 사람들은 치료법의 효과에 대한 자신들의 개인적 믿음이 있기에 피험자가 자신이 어떤 치료를 받고 있는지 '파악하고' 있으면 실험 결과에 영향을 주기 때문에 이를 '막기' 위해 피험자가 자신이 어떤 치료를 받고 있는지 모르게 한 채 실험을 하는 것이 바람직하다는 내용의 글이다. 따라서 grasp(파악하다)과 prevent(막다)의 쓰임은 문맥상 적절하다.
④ 수영이나 조깅은 그 실험 환경 때문에 피험자가 자신이 어떤 운동을 하고 있는지를 '알 수 있는데', 앞에 not possible이 있으므로 unaware(모르는)는 문맥상 적절하다.
⑤ 객관적인 연구를 위해서 가능한 경우 단일맹검법을 사용하는 것이 '좋으므로' good은 문맥상 적절하다.

전문해석

사람들은 종종 다양한 치료법의 효과에 관한 그들 자신의 개인적인 믿음을 가지고 있기 때문에, 피험자들이 어떤 치료를 받고 있는지를 ① 파악하지 못하는 방식으로 실험을 수행하는 것이 바람직하다. 예를 들어, 두통 완화를 위한 약물의 네 가지 서로 다른 복용량을 비교하는 실험에서 가장 많은 분량의 약을 받고 있다는 것을 알고 있는 사람은 더 높은 수준의 두통 감소를 보고하도록 ② 의도적으로(→ 잠재의식적으로) 영향을 받을 수도 있다. 피험자가 자신이 어떤 치료를 받고 있는지를 인식하지 못하는 것을 확실하게 함으로써 우리는 피험자의 개인적 인식이 반응에 영향을 주는 것을 ③ 막을 수 있다. 피험자들이 자신이 어떤 치료를 받았는지를 모르는 실험을 단일맹검법이라고 칭한다. 물론, 모든 실험을 단일맹검법으로 만들 수는 없다. 예를 들어, 두 개의 다른 종류의 운동이 혈압에 미치는 영향을 비교하는 실험에서 참가자들이 자신이 수영 집단에 있는지 아니면 조깅 집단에 있는지를 ④ 모르는 것은 가능

하지 않다! 하지만 가능할 때 실험에서 피험자들의 '눈을 가리는 것'은 일반적으로 ⑤ 좋은 전략이다.

구문풀이

1행 Because people often have their own personal beliefs about the effectiveness of various treatments, **it** is desirable [to conduct experiments in such a way {that subjects do not grasp <what treatment they are receiving>}].

: 주절에서 it은 형식상의 주어이고, [ ]가 내용상의 주어이다. { }는 a way를 수식하는 관계절이고, < >는 grasp의 목적어로 쓰인 의문사절로 what은 의문형용사이다.

5행 For example, [in an experiment {comparing four different doses of a medication for relief of headache pain}], someone [who knows {that he is receiving the medication at its highest dose}] may be subconsciously influenced to report a greater degree of headache pain reduction.

: 첫 번째 [ ]는 전치사 in이 이끄는 부사구이고, 그 안의 { }는 an experiment를 수식하는 현재분사구이다. 두 번째 [ ]는 문장의 핵심 주어인 someone을 수식하는 관계절이고, 그 안의 { }는 knows의 목적어로 쓰인 명사절이다.

어휘풀이

- effectiveness *n* 유효(성), 효과적임
- desirable *a* 바람직한
- subject *n* 피험자
- dose *n* (약의) 1회분
- medication *n* 약, 약물
- response *n* 반응
- treatment *n* 치료
- conduct *v* (실험 등을) 행하다
- grasp *v* 파악하다
- relief *n* 완화
- perception *n* 인식, 지각
- strategy *n* 전략

169 답 ⑤

출제 어휘 확인하기

①	confirm	확인하다	↔	
②	success	성공	↔	failure(실패)
③	questionable	의심스러운	↔	
④	redefine	재정의하다	↔	
⑤	useful	유용한	↔	useless(쓸모없는)

정답풀이

⑤ 신뢰성 평가를 위해 비언어적인 신호와 생리적인 표시가 사용될 수 있는 방법과 관련하여 정부에 의해 개발된 현재의 프로그램마저도 타당성이 전혀 없다는 문맥이므로 '유용한' 것으로 밝혀지고 있다는 것은 적절하지 않다. useful을 반대 의미의 useless(쓸모없는) 정도로 바꿔 써야 한다.

오답풀이

① 인간이 다른 사람들의 신뢰성을 평가할 능력을 가지고 있을 것이라고 추측할 충분한 이론적인 이유가 있다고 한 후, 역접의 연결어 Yet으로 이어지는 흐름이므로 '확인하는(confirm)' 증거가 거의 없었다는 것은 적절하다.
② 인간이 다른 사람들의 신뢰성을 평가할 능력을 가지고 있는지 확인할 증거가 거의 없었다고 말한 앞 내용과 같은 문맥이므로, 과학자들이 '성공(success)'하지 못한 채 실마리를 찾고자 해 왔다는 것은 적절하다.
③ 다른 사람들에 대한 신뢰성을 평가하는 능력의 보유 여부를 확인하기 어렵다는 앞 내용과 같은 문맥으로 이어져야 하므로, 다른 사람의 신체 언어의 속임까지 모든 것을 읽는 법을 가르쳐 준다는 책들이 '의심스러운(questionable)' 가치를 가지고 있다는 것은 적절하다.
④ 평가 방법이 신뢰할 만하지 않다는 내용이 계속 이어지는 흐름이므로, 감정과 동기 파악을 위해 비언어적 신호 및 생리적인 표시가 사용되는 방법에

대한 과학적 이해가 '재정의되는(redefined)' 중이라는 것은 적절하다. 이후 그런 방법이 쓸모없는 것으로 밝혀지고 있다는 흐름으로 자연스럽게 연결된다.

전문해석

인간이 다른 사람들의 신뢰성을 평가할 능력을 가지고 있을 것이라고 추측할 충분한 이론적인 이유가 있다. 그러나 그것을 ① 확인하는 증거는 거의 없었다. 수십 년 동안, 과학자들은 그리 ② 성공하지 못한 채 실마리를 찾고자 해 왔다. 나는 지성에서부터 신체 언어의 속임까지 모든 것을 읽는 법을 여러분에게 가르쳐 준다고 약속하는 많은 책이 있다는 것을 깨닫는다. 신뢰라는 면에서, 이러한 책들은 기껏해야 ③ 의심스러운 가치를 가지고 있을 뿐이다. 감정과 동기를 파악하기 위해 비언어적인 신호와 생리적인 표시가 사용될 수 있는 방법에 대한 과학적인 이해는 빠르게 ④ 재정의되는 중이다. 감정, 신뢰, 기만을 평가하기 위해 신호를 사용하는 전통적인 방법은 사실상 ⑤ 유용한(→ 쓸모없는) 것으로 밝혀지고 있다. 비언어적인 행동을 사용하여 있을 수 있는 위협을 파악하기 위해 정부에 의해 개발된 현재의 프로그램마저도 강력한 실증적인 타당성을 전혀 가지고 있지 못하다.

구문풀이

10행 [Scientific understanding of {how nonverbal cues and physiological markers might be used <to identify feelings and motives>}] is being rapidly redefined.

: [ ]는 문장의 주어이고, 동사는 is being redefined이다. { }는 전치사 of의 목적어로 쓰인 명사절이고, < >는 목적의 의미로 쓰인 to부정사구이다.

어휘풀이

- good *a* 충분한, 많은
- possess *v* 소유하다
- trustworthiness *n* 신뢰성, 신용
- decade *n* 10년
- with respect to ~와 관련하여
- nonverbal *a* 비언어적인
- physiological *a* 생리적인, 생리학적인
- deception *n* 기만, 속임
- validity *n* 타당성
- theoretical *a* 이론적인
- capacity *n* 능력, 수용력
- confirm *v* 확인하다, 확정하다
- deceptiveness *n* 속임, 현혹
- at best 기껏해야, 잘해야 ~인
- cue *n* 신호, 단서
- redefine *v* 재정의하다
- empirical *a* 실증적인

170 답 ③

출제 어휘 확인하기

(A)	affluence	풍요, 풍족	/	application	적용
(B)	expand	확대되다	/	shrink	줄어들다, 축소되다
(C)	limit	제한하다	/	stimulate	자극하다

정답풀이

(A) 비만은 더 이상 서양에 국한된 문제가 아니라고 했고 많은 사람들이 필요한 것보다 더 많은 음식을 먹는다고 했으므로 affluence(풍요로움)가 적절하다. [application 적용]
(B) 음식을 더 많이 먹은 결과 더욱 더 많은 아시아인들이 과체중이 된다고 했으므로 동시에 신체 활동은 '줄어들고(shrinking)' 있다는 것이 적절하다. [expand 확대되다]
(C) 비만이 심각한 사람들이 수술로 눈을 돌려 위를 봉합하는 것은 결국 음식 섭취를 '제한하기(limit)' 위한 것으로 볼 수 있다. [stimulate 자극하다]

전문해석

비만은 더 이상 서양에 국한된 문제가 아니다. 아시아에서 증가하는 (A) 풍요로움은 이제 많은 사람들이 필요한 것보다 접시에 더 많은 음식을 담는다(더 많은 음식을 먹는다)는 것을 의미한다. 동시에 그 지역 도시들에서 신체 활동은 점점 (B) 줄어들고 있다. 그 결과 더욱 더 많은 아시아인들이 과체중이 된다. 초고도로 과체중인 사

람들에게 건강상의 위협은 엄청나며, 또한 심장병과 관절염이 포함된다. 그러나 많은 사람들에게 운동이나 식이요법이 더는 충분한 것 같지 않다. 심각하게 비만인 점점 더 많은 아시아인들이 수술에 눈을 돌리고 있는데, 수술에서 의사들은 음식 섭취를 (C) 제한하기 위해 위의 대부분을 (축소) 봉합한다. 비만에 대항하는 수술이 아시아 국가들에서 유행하고 있다.

구문풀이

10행 An increasing number of severely obese **Asians are** turning to a surgery, [in which doctors seal off most of the stomach to limit food intake].

: a number of는 a lot of의 뜻인데, increasing이 수식하고 있으므로 '점점 더 많은'의 의미가 된다. 「a number of+복수명사」는 복수 취급하므로 복수형 동사 are가 쓰였다. [ ]는 a surgery를 부연 설명하는 관계절이다.

어휘풀이

- obesity *n* 비만
- physical activity 신체 활동
- overweight *a* 과체중의
- surgery *n* 수술
- stimulate *v* 자극하다
- confined *a* 국한된
- shrink *v* 줄어들다, 축소되다
- obese *a* 비만인
- seal off ~을 봉합하다
- intake *n* 섭취

171 답 ⑤

출제 어휘 확인하기			
① challenge	도전	↔	
② enable	가능하게 하다	↔	
③ advantage	이점	↔	disadvantage(불리한 점)
④ attack	공격	↔	
⑤ optional	선택적인	↔	essential(필수적인)

정답풀이

⑤ 어떤 생물의 진화는 계속 변화하는 환경 속에서 동시대의 다른 생물들의 진화와 상호작용하면서 이루어지게 된다는 내용이므로, 서로 다른 종류의 생물 간의 생태적 관계에 기초한 법칙은 진화와 생물의 다양성을 이해하는 데 있어 '선택적(optional)'이라는 것은 적절하지 않다. '필수적'이라는 의미의 essential 정도로 바꿔 써야 한다.

오답풀이

① 환경이 끊임없이 변하면서 진화하는 개체에게 새로운 '도전(challenges)'을 제공한다는 문맥이므로 적절하다.
② 발가락에서 말발굽으로의 진화가 말이 빠르게 질주하는 것을 '가능하게 했다(enabled)'는 것은 적절하다.
③ 포식자에게 쫓기는 경우가 아니라면 질주하는 것에 '이점'이 없을 것이므로 부정어 no와 함께 쓰인 advantage는 적절하다.
④ 달리기를 위한 말의 말발굽으로의 진화는 포식자의 효율적인 공격 방법의 발달과 함께 이루어졌다는 내용이므로 attack(공격)은 적절하다.

전문해석

외부에서 생물학을 바라보고 있는 물리 과학자들의 글에 자주 등장하는 한 가지 오해는 진화가 진행됨에 따라 환경이 그들에게는 새로운 정보를 제공할 수 없는 정적인 독립체로 보인다는 것이다. 하지만 이것은 결코 사실이 아니다. 정적이기는커녕 환경은 끊임없이 변하고 있으며 진화하는 개체군에게 새로운 ① 도전을 제공하고 있다. 고등 생물의 경우, 환경에서 가장 중요한 변화는 다른 생물의 동시대 진화에 의해 만들어진 변화이다. 발가락이 다섯 개 달린 발에서 말발굽으로의 진화는 말이 탁 트인 평야를 빠르게 질주하는 것을 ② 가능하게 했다. 그런데 그러한 질주는 포식자에게 추격당하는 것이 아니라면, 말에게 ③ 이점이 없다. 달리기를 위한 말의 효율적

인 기제는 육식성 포식자가 동시에 더 효율적인 ④ 공격 방법을 발달시켰다는 사실이 없었다면 결코 진화하지 않았을 것이다. 결과적으로, 서로 다른 종류의 생물 간의 생태적 관계에 기초한 법칙은 진화와 그것이 발생시킨 생물의 다양성을 이해하는 데 있어 ⑤ 선택적(→ 필수적)이다.

구문풀이

1행 One misconception [that often appears in the writings of physical scientists {who are looking at biology from the outside}] is [that the environment appears to them to be a static entity], [which cannot contribute new bits of information as evolution progresses].

: 첫 번째 [ ]는 핵심 주어인 One misconception을 수식하는 관계절이고, 동사는 is이다. { }는 physical scientists를 수식하는 관계절이다. 두 번째 [ ]는 문장의 주격보어로 쓰인 명사절이고, 세 번째 [ ]는 a static entity를 부연 설명하는 관계절이다.

19행 Consequently, laws [based upon ecological relationships among different kinds of organisms] are essential for understanding evolution and the diversity of life [to which **it** has given rise].

: 첫 번째 [ ]는 핵심 주어인 laws를 수식하는 과거분사구이며, 동사는 are이다. 두 번째 [ ]는 the diversity of life를 수식하는 관계절이고, it은 evolution을 가리킨다.

어휘풀이

- misconception *n* 오해
- static *a* 정적인
- contribute *v* 제공하다, 기여하다
- progress *v* 진행되다
- far from ~이기는커녕
- contemporaneous *a* 동시대의
- chase *v* 추격하다
- ecological *a* 생태적인, 생태학의
- biology *n* 생물학
- entity *n* 독립체
- evolution *n* 진화
- by no means 결코 ~이 아닌
- constantly *ad* 끊임없이
- plain *n* 평야, 평원
- mechanism *v* 기제, 구조, 장치
- diversity *n* 다양성

172 답 ⑤

출제 어휘 확인하기			
① prescription	처방	↔	
② tired	싫증을 내는	↔	
③ more	그 이상의	↔	less(그 이하의)
④ satisfying	만족스러운	↔	unsatisfying(만족스럽지 못한)
⑤ educational	교육적인	↔	

정답풀이

⑤ 우리가 영화를 즐겁다고 생각하는 것은 영화가 지시, 처방, 교훈만 전달하는 것이 아니라 우리를 만족스럽게 해 주는 이야기를 하기 때문이라고 설명했으므로, 영화를 즐기는 이유가 '교육적인(educational)' 측면 때문이라는 것은 적절하지 않다. 우리가 소망하는 세상의 모습을 보여 준다는 말과 일맥상통하도록 utopian(이상적인) 정도로 바꿔 써야 한다.

오답풀이

① 영화는 지배적인 문화를 지지한다고 했고 적절한 삶에 대한 문화적 지시를 전달한다고 했으므로, 같은 문맥에서 삶에 대한 어떤 것을 알려주고 가르쳐 준다는 의미로 '처방(prescriptions)'이라고 한 것은 적절하다.
② 영화가 지시와 처방만 할 뿐이라면 관객이 왜 영화를 즐겁다고 생각하는지 질문할 때 충분한 답이 되지 않는다는 것을 추론할 수 있으며, 교훈적인 영화에는 '싫증이 나므로' 그 이상의 이유가 있다는 흐름으로 자연스럽게 이어지므로 tired는 적절하다.

③ 영화가 즐거운 것은 교훈, 국민 윤리 교육이나 사설 같은 싫증나는 것을 넘어서는 다른 무언가가 있기 때문이라는 흐름이므로 '그 이상(more)'을 한다는 것은 적절하다.

④ 영화는 우리가 '만족스럽다고' 느끼는 이야기를 하기 때문에 우리가 영화를 즐겁게 여긴다는 것이므로 satisfying은 적절하다.

전문해석

영화는 지배적인 문화를 지지하고 시간이 지남에 따라 그것의 재생산을 위한 수단의 역할을 한다고 말할 수 있다. 그러나 영화가 하는 일의 전부가 적절한 삶에 대한 문화적 지시와 ① 처방을 전달하는 것뿐이라면 관객들이 왜 그러한 영화가 즐겁다고 생각하는지에 대해 질문할 수 있다. 우리들 대부분은 그러한 교훈적인 영화에는 ② 싫증이 나게 될 것이고, 아마도 그것들을 소련 그리고 다른 독재 사회에서 흔했던, 문화적 예술 작품과 유사한 선전용으로 보게 될 것이다. 이 질문에 대한 간단한 대답은 영화가 책임 있는 행동에 관한 두 시간짜리 국민 윤리 교육이나 사설을 제시하는 것 ③ 이상을 한다는 것이다. 그것들은 또한, 결국 우리가 ④ 만족스럽다고 느끼는 이야기를 한다. 나쁜 사람들은 대체로 벌을 받고, 낭만적인 커플은 진정한 사랑에 이르는 길에서 그들이 만나는 장애물과 어려움에도 불구하고 거의 항상 서로를 만나게 되며, 우리가 소망하는 세상의 모습이 영화 속에서는 대개 결국 그런 모습이 된다. 우리가 왜 그렇게 많이 영화를 즐기는지를 설명해 주는 것은 바로 영화의 이 ⑤ 교육적인(→ 이상적인) 측면임에 틀림없다.

구문풀이

5행 Most of us [would likely grow tired of such didactic movies] and [would probably come to see **them** as propaganda, similar to the cultural artwork {that was common in the Soviet Union and other autocratic societies}].

: 첫 번째와 두 번째 [ ]는 Most of us를 공통의 주어로 하는 술어이다. them은 앞에 나온 such didactic movies를 가리킨다. { }는 the cultural artwork를 수식하는 관계절이다.

어휘풀이

- dominant *a* 지배적인
- reproduction *n* 재생산
- prescription *n* 처방
- civics lesson 국민 윤리 교육
- punish *v* 처벌하다
- wind up *doing* 결국 ~로 끝나다
- means *n* 수단
- directive *n* 지시, 명령
- propaganda *n* 선전
- editorial *n* 사설
- more often than not 대개, 대체로
- account for ~을 설명하다

173 답 ⑤

출제 어휘 확인하기			
① discovery	발견	↔	
② shift	변화, 이동	↔	
③ outpace	앞지르다	↔	
④ green	친환경의	↔	
⑤ decrease	줄이다	↔	increase(늘리다)

정답풀이

⑤ 친환경 대체 기술을 지속적으로 개발하기 위해서는 그 기술 제품의 핵심 재료에 대한 공급이 확충되어야 한다는 내용의 글이다. 친환경 기술의 핵심 재료는 대부분 희귀한 금속이라고 했으므로, 이러한 제한된 공급을 '늘려야' 친환경 대체 개술을 개발할 가능성이 더 높아질 것이다. 따라서 without과 함께 쓰인 decreasing(줄이다)은 적절하지 않으며 반대 의미인 increasing(늘리다) 정도로 바꿔 써야 한다.

오답풀이

① 철기와 청동기 같은 이전 세대의 상황을 설명하는 흐름이므로 새로운 원소의 끝없는 '발견(discovery)'이 새로운 발명품을 낳았다는 것은 적절하다.

② 더 많은 조합으로, 더 정밀한 양으로, 더 많은 원소를 사용한다는 내용이 이어지고 있으므로 근본적인 '변화(shift)'라는 것은 적절하다.

③ 첫 문장에서 첨단 기술 제품의 미래는 우리의 재료 확보 능력에 달려 있는 것이지 우리 생각에는 제한점이 없다고 했으므로, 우리의 창의력이 우리의 물질 공급을 '앞지를(outpace)' 것이라는 흐름은 적절하다.

④ 전기 자동차, 풍력 발전용 터빈, 태양 전지판과 같은 기술을 가리키므로 '친환경(green)'이라는 것은 적절하다.

전문해석

첨단 기술 제품의 미래는 우리 생각의 제한점에 있는 것이 아니라, 그것을 생산하기 위한 재료를 확보할 수 있는 우리의 능력에 있을지도 모른다. 철기와 청동기 같은 이전 시대에, 새로운 원소의 ① 발견은 끝이 없어 보이는 수많은 새로운 발명품을 낳았다. 이제 그 조합은 정말로 끝이 없을 수도 있다. 우리는 이제 우리의 자원 수요에 있어서 근본적인 ② 변화를 목격하고 있다. 인류 역사의 어느 지점에서도, 우리는 (지금보다) '더 많은' 조합으로 그리고 점차 정밀한 양으로 '더 많은' 원소를 사용한 적은 없었다. 우리의 창의력은 곧 우리의 물질 공급을 ③ 앞지를 것이다. 이런 상황은 세계가 화석연료에 대한 의존을 줄이려 고군분투하고 있는 결정적인 순간에 온다. 다행히, 희귀한 금속들이 전기 자동차, 풍력 발전용 터빈, 태양 전지판과 같은 ④ 친환경 기술의 핵심 재료이다. 그것들은 태양과 바람 같은 무료 천연 자원을 우리의 생활에 연료를 공급하는 동력으로 전환하는 데 도움을 준다. 하지만 오늘날의 제한된 공급을 ⑤ 줄이지(→ 늘리지) 않고는, 우리는 기후 변화를 늦추기 위해 우리가 필요로 하는 친환경 대체 기술을 개발할 가능성이 없다.

구문풀이

9행 [At **no** point in human history] **have we** used *more* elements, in *more* combinations, and in increasingly refined amounts.

: 부정어 no를 포함한 부사구가 문두에 왔으므로 조동사 have가 주어 we 앞으로 도치되었다.

어휘풀이

- secure *v* 확보하다
- previous *a* 이전의
- combination *n* 조합
- shift *n* 변화, 이동
- outpace *v* 앞지르다
- reliance *n* 의존
- convert *v* 전환하다
- ingredient *n* 재료, 성분
- bring forth ~을 낳다
- witness *v* 목격하다
- refined *a* 정밀한, 정제된
- defining *a* 결정적인
- rare *a* 희귀한, 보기 드문
- alternative *a* 대체의, 대안의

174 답 ③

출제 어휘 확인하기			
① time-consuming	시간을 소모하는	↔	
② design	설계하다	↔	
③ abstract	추상적인	↔	concrete(구체적인, 실재적인)
④ learn	배우다	↔	
⑤ unorganized	정리되지 않은	↔	organized(정리된)

정답풀이

③ 우리는 '개'라는 단어로 특정 부류의 동물들을 분류하여 다른 동물들과 구별할 수 있는데, 이는 우리가 그 단어를 숙달했기 때문이라고 했다. 따라서 그러한 분류가 분류로 불리는 것이 너무 '추상적(abstract)'이라고 하는 것은 적절하지 않으며 obvious(명확한) 정도로 바꿔 써야 한다.

오답풀이

① 음식이 임의의 순서로 진열된 슈퍼마켓에서 쇼핑하는 것에 관한 예시이므로 원하는 것을 찾을 때 '시간을 소모할(time-consuming)' 것이라는 것은 적절하다.

② 음식이 임의로 진열될 경우, 원하는 것을 찾는 데 어려움이 생기므로 누군가가 슈퍼마켓의 분류 체계를 '설계해야(design)' 했다는 것은 적절하다.

④ 분류 체계를 이해하기 전에는 고양이를 개라고 부르는 것과 같은 실수를 했을지도 모른다는 내용이 뒤에 이어지므로, 부모님이 가르쳐 주려 애썼던 분류 체계를 '배우기(learn)' 위해 열심히 노력해야 했다는 것은 적절하다.

⑤ 언어에는 분류적 특성이 있으므로 말하기를 배우지 않았다면 세상이 분류되지 않은, 즉 '정리되지 않은(unorganized)' 슈퍼마켓처럼 보일 것이라는 것은 적절하다.

전문해석

사물을 묶어 집단으로 분류하는 것은 우리가 항상 하는 일이며, 그 이유를 들여다보는 것은 어렵지 않다. 음식이 진열대에 임의의 순서로 진열된 슈퍼마켓에서 쇼핑하려고 하는 것을 상상해 보라. 한 통로에는 흰 빵 옆에 토마토 수프가 있고, 치킨 수프는 뒤쪽의 60와트 전구 옆에 있으며, 어떤 크림치즈 브랜드는 앞쪽에, 또 다른 브랜드는 쿠키 근처의 8번 통로에 있다. 여러분이 원하는 것을 찾는 일은 불가능하지는 않겠지만, (a) 시간을 소모하고 극히 어려울 것이다.

슈퍼마켓의 경우에는 누군가가 분류 체계를 (b) 설계해야 했다. 그러나 또한 우리의 언어에 포함돼 있는 기성의 분류 체계도 있다. 예를 들면, '개'라는 단어는 특정 부류의 동물을 함께 분류하여 다른 동물들과 구분 짓는다. 그러한 분류는 분류라고 불리기에 너무 (c) 추상적으로(→ 명확해) 보일 수 있으나, 이는 그저 여러분이 이미 그 단어를 습득했기 때문이다. 말하기를 배우는 아이로서, 여러분은 부모님이 여러분에게 가르쳐 주려 애썼던 분류 체계를 (d) 배우기 위해 열심히 노력해야 했다. 여러분은 그것을 이해하기 전에, 어쩌면 고양이를 개라고 부르는 것과 같은 실수를 했을지도 모른다. 만약 여러분이 말하기를 배우지 않았다면 모든 세상이 (e) 정리되지 않은 슈퍼마켓처럼 보일 것인데, 여러분은 모든 물건이 새롭고 낯선 유아의 입장에 있을 것이다. 따라서 분류의 원리를 배울 때 우리는 우리 언어의 핵심에 있는 구조에 대해 배울 것이다.

구문풀이

18행 As a child [learning to speak], you had to work hard [to learn the system of classification {your parents were trying to teach you}].

: 첫 번째 [ ]는 a child를 능동의 의미로 수식하는 현재분사구이다. 두 번째 [ ]는 목적의 의미를 나타내는 to부정사구이고, 그 안의 { }는 the system of classification을 수식하는 관계절이다.

어휘풀이

- classify *v* 분류하다
- random *a* 임의의, 무작위의
- aisle *n* 통로, 복도
- time-consuming *a* 시간을 소모하는
- classification *n* 분류
- distinguish *v* 구별하다, 구분 짓다
- get the hang of ~을 이해하다[터득하다]
- unorganized *a* 정리[정돈]되지 않은
- unfamiliar *a* 익숙[친숙]하지 않은
- core *n* 핵심
- arrange *v* 배열하다, 정돈하다
- shelf *n* 진열대, 선반
- light bulb 백열전구
- design *v* 설계하다
- embody *v* 포함하다, 구체화하다
- abstract *a* 추상적인
- infant *n* 유아
- principle *n* 원리, 원칙

어휘 모의고사 5회   본문 pp.142 ~ 145

175 ⑤	176 ②	177 ③	178 ③	179 ③
180 ⑤	181 ①	182 ④		

175   답 ⑤

출제 어휘 확인하기

① damage	손상	↔	
② slower	더 느린	↔	faster(더 빠른)
③ playful	놀이의	↔	
④ academic	학업적인	↔	
⑤ stressful	압박이 심한	↔	comfortable(편안한)

정답풀이

⑤ 아이들은 어린 나이에 빠르게 학습하는 것보다는 느린 속도로 배울 때 더 잘 배운다는 내용이므로, '압박이 심한(stressful)' 환경의 아이들이 덜 불안해한다는 것은 적절하지 않다. '편안한' 환경이라는 뜻이 되도록 comfortable 정도로 바꿔 써야 한다.

오답풀이

① 아이의 조기 학습은 득보다 실이 많다고 했으므로 '손상(damage)'을 초래한다는 것은 적절하다.

② 빠르게 학습할 때가 아니라 '더 느린' 속도로 학습할 때 더 효과가 있다는 것이므로 slower는 적절하다.

③ 학업 성과를 강조하는 것과 대조되는 느린 학습, 즉 상호작용과 '놀이를 통한' 방식을 강조하는 문맥이므로 playful은 적절하다.

④ 사회적 상호작용과 놀이를 중심으로 하는 어린이집과 '학업적인' 성취에 초점을 두는 어린이집이 대조되는 흐름이므로 academic은 적절하다.

전문해석

학습에 관해 말하자면 아이들을 빠른 길에 올려놓는 것(조기 학습을 시키는 것)은 종종 득보다 실이 많다. 연구원들은 너무 어린 나이에 운동에 전념하는 것은 신체적인 그리고 심리적인 ① 손상을 초래할 수 있다고 경고한다. 교육에서도 마찬가지다. 점점 더 많은 증거가 아이들은 ② 더 느린 속도로 배울 때 더 잘 배운다는 것을 시사한다. 몇몇 연구원들이 최근에 120명의 취학 전 아동을 테스트했다. 절반은 사회적 상호작용과 ③ 놀이를 통해 학습에 접근하는 방식을 강조하는 어린이집에 다녔고, 나머지는 ④ 학업적인 성과를 내도록 재촉하는 어린이집을 다녔다. 그들은 보다 ⑤ 압박이 심하고(→ 편안하고) 느린 환경의 아이들이 덜 불안해하고 학습에 더 열의가 있으며 독립적으로 사고를 더 잘할 수 있게 된다는 것을 알아냈다.

구문풀이

12행 They found [that the children from the more comfortable, slower environment turned out to be {less anxious}, {more eager to learn}, and {better able to think independently}].

: [ ]는 found의 목적어로 쓰인 명사절이다. to be의 보어로 세 개의 비교급 형용사구 { }가 병렬로 연결되었다.

어휘풀이

- when it comes to ~에 관해 말하자면
- put ~ on the fast track ~에게 빠른 길을 가게 하다
- specialize in ~에 전념하다, ~을 전공하다
- a body of 다수의
- nursery *n* 놀이방, 탁아소
- go for ~에 적용되다
- preschool *a* 취학 전의
- interaction *n* 상호작용

- approach *n* 접근 (방식), 접근법
- academic *a* 학업적인
- eager *a* 열심인, 열망하는
- rush *v* 재촉하다, 몰아대다
- turn out ~임이 밝혀지다
- independently *ad* 독립적으로

- roughly *ad* 대충
- weave *v* 짜다, 엮다
- trap *v* 가두다
- breathable *a* 통기성의
- tailor *v* 맞추어 만들다
- sew *v* 바느질하다
- fabric *n* 직물
- property *n* 특성
- damp *a* 축축한

176 답 ②

출제 어휘 확인하기

①	advantage	이점	↔	disadvantage(단점)
②	inadequate	불충분한	↔	adequate(충분한)
③	decrease	감소하다	↔	increase(증가하다)
④	prevent	막다	↔	
⑤	cooler	더 추운	↔	warmer(더 따뜻한)

정답풀이

② but 다음에 털가죽은 이동하거나 강한 바람을 맞으면 열 보호를 덜 제공한다는 내용이 나오므로, but 앞부분은 가만히 앉아 있을 때는 열 보호를 '잘' 제공한다는 내용이 되어야 한다. 따라서 inadequate(불충분한)는 적절하지 않으며 excellent(우수한) 정도로 바꿔 써야 한다.

오답풀이

① 털가죽의 단점에 관한 내용이 이어지므로 결과적으로 옷으로 직물을 사용하는 것의 '이점(advantages)'은 명백해졌을 것이라는 흐름은 적절하다.
③ 털가죽의 단점을 계속 언급하는 흐름이므로, 빠르게 걸을 때 단열 속성이 많이 '감소한다(decrease)'는 것은 적절하다.
④ 털가죽과 대비되는 직물의 이점을 언급하는 흐름이므로, 몸에 맞게 만들어질 때 내부의 층이 생겨 차가운 공기가 직접 피부에 닿는 것을 '막아 준다(preventing)'는 것은 적절하다.
⑤ 앞에서 직물이 지니는 이점을 언급했으므로, 직물로 옷을 만드는 능력은 선조들이 '더 추운(cooler)' 지역으로 떠났을 때 실질적인 이점을 제공했을 것이라는 흐름은 적절하다.

전문해석

매우 오랜 시간 동안 사람들은 걸쳐진 짐승의 가죽으로 간신히 살아남았고 그러고 나서 이것들을 대충 꿰매어 잇기 시작했을 것 같다. 하지만 결국에는 옷으로 직물을 사용하는 것의 ① 이점이 분명해졌을 것이다. 털가죽은 누군가가 가만히 앉아 있다면 ② 불충분한(→ 우수한) 열 보호를 제공하지만, 일단 이동하거나 강한 바람을 맞으면 이것은 덜 그러한데, 그 이유는 가죽은 몸에 밀착하도록 모양이 잡히지 않기 때문이다. 더 많은 공기가 몸과 옷 사이에 들어올수록 그것은 공기의 단열층을 피부와 가까이에 있도록 가둬 둠에 있어 덜 효과적이다. 실제로는 빠르게 걸을 때 옷의 단열 속성은 매우 많이 ③ 감소한다. 옷은 또한 통기성이 있어야 하는데, 이는 축축한 옷이 착용한 사람을 따뜻하게 유지해 주지 못하며 매우 무거워지기 때문이다. 직물은 털보다 더욱 통기가 잘 되고 특히나 몸에 맞게 만들어질 때 우수한 내부의 층을 만들어 내고, 차가운 공기가 피부의 표면에 직접 닿는 것을 ④ 막아 준다. 그러므로 직물 옷을 만드는 능력은 우리의 선조들에게 그들이 아프리카에서 ⑤ 더 추운 지역으로 떠났을 때 실질적인 이점을 제공했을 것이다.

구문풀이

1행 It's likely that for a very long time people [managed to survive with draped animal pelts] and then [began roughly sewing these together].

: 「It's likely that ~」은 '~할 가능성이 높다, ~할 것 같다'의 의미로, It이 형식상의 주어이고 that 이하가 내용상의 주어라고 볼 수 있다. people을 공통의 주어로 하는 두 개의 동사구 [ ]가 and로 연결되었다.

어휘풀이

- manage to *do* 겨우[가까스로] ~하다, ~해내다

177 답 ③

출제 어휘 확인하기

①	complexity	복잡성	↔	simplicity(간단함)
②	error	오류	↔	
③	weaken	약화시키다	↔	strengthen(강화하다)
④	limit	제한하다	↔	
⑤	allow	허용하다	↔	forbid(금지하다)

정답풀이

③ 인쇄술 덕분에 생각이 전 세계적으로 전파될 수 있었다고 했으므로, 글을 읽고 쓰는 능력의 출현과 손으로 쓴 책의 탄생으로 복잡한 생각이 매우 충실하게 퍼져 나가는 능력이 '약화되었다'는 것은 적절하지 않다. weakened를 strengthened(강화하다) 정도로 바꿔 써야 한다.

오답풀이

① 인쇄술 도입 이전에 생각이 구전으로만 퍼져 나가던 방식의 한계점에 관한 설명이므로 생각의 '복잡성(complexity)'을 제한했다는 것은 적절하다.
② 생각의 복잡성을 제한하는 것에 더하여 정보가 구전되는 과정에서 생길 수 있는 문제를 설명하는 흐름이므로 '오류(error)'를 추가했다는 것은 적절하다.
④ 손으로 책을 복사하는 데 엄청난 양의 시간이 소요된다고 했으므로 정보가 퍼져 나가는 속도를 '제한했다(limited)'는 것은 적절하다.
⑤ 인쇄기는 정보를 수천 배 더 빠르게 복사할 수 있어서 이전 시대보다 지식이나 정보가 더 빠르고 정확하게 퍼져 나갈 수 '있도록 했다(allowing)'는 것은 적절하다.

전문해석

인쇄기는 생각이 스스로를 복제하는 능력을 증대시켰다. 낮은 비용의 인쇄술이 있기 전에, 생각은 구전의 방식으로 퍼져 나갈 수 있었고 실제로 그렇게 퍼져 나갔다. 이것은 엄청나게 강력했지만, 전파될 수 있는 생각의 ① 복잡성을 단 한 사람이 기억할 수 있는 정도로 제한했다. 그것은 또한 일정량의 보증된 ② 오류를 추가했다. 구전에 의한 생각의 전파는 전 세계적인 규모의 말 전하기 게임과 맞먹었다. 글을 읽고 쓸 줄 아는 능력의 출현과 손으로 쓴 두루마리와 궁극적으로 손으로 쓴 책의 탄생은 크고 복잡한 생각이 매우 충실하게 퍼져 나가는 능력을 ③ 약화시켰다(→ 강화시켰다). 하지만 손으로 두루마리나 책을 복사하는 데 요구되는 엄청난 양의 시간은 이러한 방식으로 정보가 퍼져 나갈 수 있는 속도를 ④ 제한했다. 잘 훈련된 수도승은 하루에 약 4쪽의 문서를 필사할 수 있었다. 인쇄기는 정보를 수천 배 더 빠르게 복사할 수 있었는데, 그것은 지식이 이전 어느 때보다 훨씬 더 빠르고 최대한 정확하게 퍼져 나갈 수 ⑤ 있도록 했다.

구문풀이

17행 A printing press could copy information thousands of times faster, [allowing knowledge to spread **far** more quickly, with full fidelity, than ever before].

: [ ]는 앞 절의 내용을 의미상의 주어로 하는 분사구문이다. 부사 far는 비교급을 강조하여 '훨씬'의 의미를 나타낸다.

어휘풀이

- printing press 인쇄기
- prior to ~ 이전에
- boost *v* 늘리다, 증대시키다
- word of mouth 구전

- tremendously *ad* 대단히
- guaranteed *a* 보장된, 확실한
- advent *n* 출현
- scroll *n* 두루마리
- transcribe *v* 필사하다, 글로 옮겨 쓰다
- complexity *n* 복잡성
- equivalent *a* 동등한, 맞먹는
- literacy *n* 글을 읽고 쓸 줄 아는 능력
- monk *n* 승려, 수도승

178 답 ③

출제 어휘 확인하기

① certainty	확신	↔	uncertainty(불확실성, 반신반의)
② proficient	능숙한	↔	
③ improvement	개선	↔	
④ difficult	어려운	↔	easy(쉬운)
⑤ fail	실패하다	↔	succeed(성공하다)

정답풀이

③ 다른 문화 간의 관계 유지와 이해에서 발생하는 어려움의 불가피성에 관한 글로, 앞에서는 서로 다른 문화의 사람들이 소통에 어려움을 겪을 수 있음을 말했고, 뒤에서는 다른 문화 간의 조화를 이루려고 할 때 발생하는 어려움과 갈등에 대해 말하고 있다. 따라서 성공적인 다문화 공동체를 만드는 데 내재된 '개선'이 명백하다는 것은 적절하지 않다. improvements를 tensions(긴장) 정도로 바꿔 써야 한다.

오답풀이

① 문화가 다른 사람과의 대인 관계에서 다른 사람의 기대에 대한 의심이 생기면 특정한 행동, 일상, 의식 등이 모든 사람들에게 같을 것이라는 '확신'을 감소시킬 것이므로 certainty는 적절하다.
② 문화적인 혼합에서 언제나 완전히 편안함을 느끼지는 못하는 것은 소통이 어려울 때, 즉 자신의 언어에 '능숙하지' 않은 사람과 대화를 할 때일 것이므로 부정어 not과 함께 쓰인 proficient는 적절하다.
④ 다른 문화 간의 소통에서 어려움이 발생할 수 있음을 계속해서 말하는 흐름이므로, 문화적으로 다른 개인들이 조화롭게 살고, 일하고, 놀고, 의사소통하는 것이 '어렵다(difficult)'는 것은 적절하다.
⑤ 인간의 고통, 세대 간 증오, 분열, 불필요한 갈등 등은 다른 문화 간의 조화를 이루지 못한 예로 볼 수 있으므로, 조화로운 다문화 사회를 만드는 데 '실패한(failing)' 결과라는 것은 적절하다.

전문해석

다문화 세계에서 유능한 대인 관계를 유지하는 것에는 몇 가지 분명한 결과들이 있다. 그러한 관계는 불가피하게 다른 사람들의 기대에 대한 의심을 불러일으킬 것이고 특정한 행동, 일상 그리고 의식이 모든 사람들에게 같은 것을 의미한다는 ① 확신을 감소시킬 것이다. 문화적 혼합은 사람들이 다른 언어로 의사소통을 시도하거나 그들의 언어에 ② 능숙하지 않은 사람들과 대화하려고 할 때 언제나 완전히 편안함을 느끼는 것은 아니라는 것을 암시한다. 많은 사람들은 집에서 학교로, 직장에서 놀이로, 그리고 동네에서 쇼핑몰로 갈 때 한 문화에서 다른 문화로 이동하면서 둘 이상의 문화에서 동시에 살 필요가 있을 것이다. 성공적인 다문화 공동체를 만드는 데 내재된 ③ 개선(→ 긴장) 또한 명백하다. 문화적으로 다른 개인들로 이루어진 집단이 조화롭게 살고, 일하고, 놀고, 소통하는 것이 얼마나 ④ 어려운지를 분명히 보여 주는 예가 많다. 조화로운 다문화 사회를 만드는 데 ⑤ 실패한 결과 또한 명백한데, 인간의 고통, 한 세대에서 다른 세대로 전해진 증오, 사람들의 삶에서의 분열, 사람들의 창의적인 재능과 에너지를 약화시키는 불필요한 갈등이 그것이다.

구문풀이

7행 Cultural mixing implies [that people will not always feel completely comfortable {as they attempt to communicate in another language} or {as they try to talk with individuals <who are not proficient in theirs>}].

: [ ]는 implies의 목적어로 쓰인 명사절이고, or로 연결된 두 개의 { }는 '~할 때'를 뜻하는 접속사 as가 이끄는 부사절이다. ⟨ ⟩는 individuals를 수식하는 관계절이다.

어휘풀이
- consequence *n* 결과, 중요성
- interpersonal *a* 개인 간의
- inevitably *ad* 불가피하게
- imply *v* 암시하다, 의미하다
- concurrently *ad* 동시에
- abound *v* 많이 있다
- underscore *v* 분명히 보여 주다, 강조하다
- hatred *n* 증오
- undermine *v* 약화시키다, 훼손하다
- competent *a* 유능한
- intercultural *a* 다른 문화 간의
- ritual *n* 의식, 예식
- proficient *a* 능숙한
- inherent *a* 내재된, 고유한

179 답 ③

출제 어휘 확인하기

① empathize	공감하다	↔	
② value	중시하다	↔	
③ weakness	약함	↔	strength(힘, 강함)
④ downgrade	격하시키다, 경시하다	↔	upgrade(승급시키다)
⑤ acceptable	용인할 수 있는	↔	unacceptable(용납할 수 없는)

정답풀이

③ 집단주의 집단과 대조되는 개인주의 문화에 관한 설명에 해당하는 부분이다. 개인주의 문화의 구성원은 독립과 자율의 관점에서 자신을 규정한다고 했으므로, 뛰는 것이나 남다른 것이 '약함'의 표시로 여겨진다는 것은 적절하지 않다. weakness를 courage(용기) 정도로 바꿔 써야 한다.

오답풀이

① 집단주의 집단은 집단 안에 머무는 것을 강조한다고 했고 그 구성원은 갈등을 피하도록 사회화된다고 했으므로 다른 사람들과 '공감한다(empathize)'는 것은 적절하다.
② 개인주의 문화에 대한 설명이므로 개인의 자유와 표현을 '중시하도록(value)' 사회화되어 있다는 것은 적절하다.
④ 개인주의 문화와는 달리, 집단주의를 규정하는 집단에서는 뛰는 것과 남다른 것을 좋게 여기지 않을 것이므로 일탈이 '경시될(downgraded)' 것이라는 가정은 적절하다.
⑤ 개인주의 문화에서는 구성원의 자유와 표현이 중시된다고 했으므로 개인주의 집단 규범이 '용인할 수 있는(acceptable)' 구성원의 행동과 비규범적 특징의 허용 범위를 넓힌다는 것은 적절하다.

전문해석

집단주의 집단에서는 관계, 화합 유지 그리고 그 집단 '안에 머무는 것'에 대한 상당한 강조가 있다. 집단주의 집단의 구성원은 갈등을 피하며 다른 사람들과 ① 공감하고, 자신에게로 관심을 끄는 것을 피하도록 사회화되어 있다. 대조적으로, 개인주의 문화의 구성원은 집단으로부터의 독립과 자율의 관점에서 자신을 규정하는 경향이 있으며 개인의 자유와 개인의 표현을 ② 중시하도록 사회화되어 있다. 개인주의 문화에서는 뛰는 것과 남다른 것이 종종 ③ 약함(→ 용기)의 표시로 여겨진다. 개인주의를 규정하는 집단에서보다 집단주의를 규정하는 집단에서 일탈이 더 ④ 평가 절하될 것이라는 가정은 집단주의 집단과 개인주의 집단의 특성 묘사에 내재한다. 정말로, 경험적 연구는 개인주의 집단 규범이 ⑤ 용인할 수 있는 집단 구성원의 행동과 비규범적인 특징의 허용 범위를 넓힌다는 것을 보여 준다.

구문풀이

16행 Indeed, empirical research shows [that {individualist group norms} broaden {the latitude of acceptable group member behavior and non-normative characteristics}].

: [ ]는 shows의 목적어로 쓰인 명사절이고, 그 안의 첫 번째 { }는 명사절 내의 주어이며, 동사는 broaden이다. 두 번째 { }는 broaden의 목적어로 쓰인 명사구이다.

어휘풀이

- collectivist *a* 집단주의의
- considerable *a* 상당한
- emphasis *n* 강조
- stick with 안에 머무르다, (집단) 밑에 머무르다
- socialize *v* 사회화하다
- conflict *n* 갈등, 충돌
- empathize *v* 공감하다
- draw attention to ~에게로 관심을 끌다
- individualist *a* 개인주의의
- autonomy *n* 자율(성)
- stand out 두드러지다, 눈에 띄다
- implicit *a* 내재하는, 암묵적인
- characterization *n* 특성[특징·성격] 묘사
- downgrade *v* 격하시키다, 경시하다
- prescribe *v* 규정하다, 처방하다
- empirical *a* 경험에 의한, 경험적인
- norm *n* 규범
- latitude *n* 허용 범위; 위도

180 답 ⑤

출제 어휘 확인하기

① barrier	장벽, 장애물	↔
② shatter	산산이 부수다	↔
③ abuse	학대	
④ pave	길을 닦다	↔
⑤ please	기쁘게 하다	↔

정답풀이

⑤ 팀이 연승을 하도록 도운 주루 능력은 상대팀 투수들을 '겁나게 했을' 것이므로, pleased(기쁘게 하다)는 적절하지 않으며 scared 정도로 바꿔 써야 한다.

오답풀이

① 이어지는 내용에서 50년 이상 동안 검은 피부를 가진 사람들을 메이저리그에서 몰아냈던 요인이라고 설명하고 있으므로 피부색 '장벽(barrier)'이라는 것은 적절하다.

② 글 앞부분에서 뛰어난 운동선수이자 사회 정의를 위한 개척자로 Robinson을 소개했으므로, Branch Rickey가 피부색 장벽을 '산산이 부수기(shatter)' 위해 그와 협력했다는 것은 적절하다.

③ 신인 시절에 참고 견뎌야 했던 일을 극복하고 화려한 경력을 쌓았다고 했으므로 '학대(abuse)'를 참고 견뎠다는 것은 적절하다.

④ Robinson이 학대를 이겨내고 경력을 쌓아 흑인 선수들을 위한 길을 '닦는' 역할을 했다는 의미이므로 paving은 적절하다.

전문해석

Jackie Robinson은 왜 모든 야구팀에서 그의 번호를 영구 결번시킨 유일한 선수일까요? 뛰어난 운동선수이자 사회 정의를 위한 개척자에 대한 이 영화에서 알아보십시오! 영화는 여러분에게 야구에서의 '피부색 ① 장벽'에 대해 소개해 드릴 텐데요, 이는 50년 이상 동안 검은 피부를 가진 사람들을 메이저리그에서 몰아냈던 요인입니다. 여러분은 Branch Rickey라는 이름을 가진 사람이 이 장애물을 ② 산산이 부수기 위해 Robinson과 어떻게 협력했는지, 그리고 Robinson의 스포츠 재능이 왜 그가 계약하게 된 유일한 이유가 아니었는지 알게 될 것입니다! 여러분은 또한 Robinson이 신인 시절에 참고 견뎌야 했던 ③ 학대에 대해서, 그리고 그것을 어떻게 극복해 화려한 경력을 쌓았고 미국 흑인 선수들을 위한 길을 ④ 닦아 놓았는지

알게 될 것입니다. 마지막으로, 여러분은 그의 주루 능력이 어떻게 상대팀 투수들을 ⑤ 기쁘게 했고(→ 겁나게 했고) 팀이 연승하는 데 도움을 주었는지 알게 될 것입니다!

구문풀이

1행 Why is Jackie Robinson the only player [whose number was retired by every baseball team]?

: [ ]는 the only player를 수식하는 소유격 관계대명사절이다.

어휘풀이

- retire *v* 등 번호를 영구 결번으로 하다
- amazing *a* 놀라운, 경이로운
- athlete *n* 운동선수
- pioneer *n* 개척자
- social justice 사회 정의
- barrier *n* 장벽, 장애물
- team up with ~와 협력하다
- shatter *v* 산산이 부수다
- abuse *n* 학대
- endure *v* 인내하다
- rookie *n* 신인 선수
- carve out ~을 노력하여 얻다
- pave the way for ~에 대해 길을 열어 주다
- base-running ability 주루 능력

181 답 ①

출제 어휘 확인하기

(A) contrast	대조	/ agreement	동의, 일치	
(B) controlled	통제되는	/ unrestrained	억제되지 않은	
(C) predictable	예측 가능한	/ unpredictable	예측할 수 없는	

정답풀이

(A) 사회과학은 인간의 선입견의 지배를 받으며 인간의 행동 패턴은 장소와 집단마다 다르지만, 자연과학의 연구 대상은 수소 원자의 예에서 보듯 어디서 발견되든 서로 유사하다고 했다. 따라서 사회과학의 연구 대상이 자연과학의 연구 대상과 '대조(contrast)'적이라고 하는 것이 적절하다. [agreement 동의, 일치]

(B) 하나의 수소 원자는 어디서 발견되든 다른 것과 상당히 유사하다고 했고, 이와 마찬가지로 금속 막대 측정 시에도 자연 조건이 똑같은 한 길이는 같다고 확신할 수 있다고 했다. 따라서 자연과학의 연구 대상을 에워싸는 환경은 상당히 정확히 '통제될(controlled)' 수 있다고 가정할 수 있다는 것이 적절하다. [unrestrained 억제되지 않은]

(C) 앞서 언급된 것처럼 자연과학은 연구 대상의 통제 용이성으로 인해 '손쉬운 과학'이라고 불린다는 흐름이므로 '예측 가능한(predictable)' 속성이라고 하는 것이 적절하다. [unpredictable 예측할 수 없는]

전문해석

과학은 인간의 선입견의 지배를 받는다. 이것은 특히 사회과학자들에게 그러하다. 인간 행동이 사회과학자들의 연구 영역이기 때문에 그들이 실제로 연구 대상의 일부이다. 게다가, 인간 행동 패턴은 장소마다 다르고 또한 집단마다도 다르다. 이것은 자연과학의 연구 대상과 (A) 대조적이다. 화학자가 수소를 연구할 때, 그는 하나의 수소 원자는 어디서 발견되든 다른 것과 상당히 유사하며, 또한 그것을 에워싸고 있는 환경은 상당히 정확하게 (B) 통제될 수 있다고 가정할 수 있다. 물리학자가 금속 막대를 측정할 때도 마찬가지다. 그는 자연 조건이 똑같은 한 그 금속 막대의 길이가 늘어나거나 줄어들지 않으리라고 상당히 확신할 수 있다. Earl Barbie가 경제학자 Daniel Suits(의 말)를 인용하는 것도 이 때문인데, 그는 그들의 연구 대상의 (C) 예측 가능한 속성으로 인해 자연과학을 '쉬운 과학'이라고 부른다.

구문풀이

11행 The same is true when a physicist measures a metal bar; he can **be** quite **sure** [that it will not stretch or shrink in length **as long as** natural conditions are the same].

: 「be sure ~」는 '~을 확신하다'의 의미로, sure는 형용사이지만 뒤에 목적어 역할을 하는 절을 취할 수 있다. 여기서도 be sure 뒤에 [ ]로 표시된 명사절이 왔다. 「as long as」는 '~하는 한'의 의미이다.

어휘풀이

- be subject to ~의 지배를 받다, ~의 영향하에 있다
- bias *n* 편견, 선입견
- chemist *n* 화학자
- hydrogen *n* 수소
- atom *n* 원자
- unrestrained *a* 억제되지 않은
- physicist *n* 물리학자
- measure *v* 측정하다
- shrink *v* 줄어들다
- quote *v* 인용하다

182 답 ④

출제 어휘 확인하기

①	product	산물, 상품	↔	
②	visualize	머릿속에 그리다	↔	
③	internal	내적인	↔	external(외적인)
④	complex	복잡한	↔	simple(단순한)
⑤	observed	관찰된	↔	

정답풀이

④ 개미에게 복잡한 내적 항행 능력이 있다고 가정해 볼 수 있지만 개미의 이동 경로의 복잡성은 그것의 내적 복잡성이 아니라고 하므로, 개미가 '복잡한' 규칙을 사용할 수도 있다는 표현은 적절하지 않다. 개미는 '단순한' 규칙을 사용하고 그것이 환경과 상호작용하여 복잡한 이동 경로를 만들어 낸다는 문맥이 적절하므로 complex를 simple 정도로 바꿔 써야 한다.

오답풀이

① '개미 우화'에서 복잡한 이동 경로를 만들어 내는 것은 개미 단독으로가 아니라 그것의 규칙과 환경의 상호작용이라고 했으므로, 동물 행동의 복잡성은 순전히 그것의 내적 복잡성의 '산물(product)'이 아니라는 것은 적절하다.
② 개미가 해변을 따라 걷는 장면을 상상해 보라(Imagine)고 했고, 뒤 문장에서 개미의 이동 경로의 모습을 기술하고 있으므로 개미의 이동 경로를 추적하는 것을 '머릿속으로 그려보라(visualize)'는 표현은 적절하다.
③ complicated internal navigational abilities(복잡한 내적 항행 능력)은 앞에 나온 internal complexity의 구체적인 예에 해당하는 것으로 internal은 적절하다.
⑤ 우리 눈에 보이는 동물의 행동이 복잡하다고 해서 반드시 그것의 내적 기제가 복잡한 것은 아니라는 것이므로 '관찰된'이라는 의미의 observed는 적절하다.

전문해석

인간의 관점에서 사물을 보는 우리의 억누를 수 없는 경향, 즉 복잡한 인간의 동기와 처리 능력이 다른 종들에게 있다고 우리가 흔히 잘못 생각하는 것은 동물의 행동이 사실 복잡하지 않다는 것을 의미하지는 않는다. 오히려 그것은 동물 행동의 복잡성이 순전히 그것의 내적 복잡성의 (a) 산물은 아니라는 의미이다. Herbert Simon의 '개미 우화'는 이 점을 매우 분명하게 한다. 개미 한 마리가 해변을 따라 걷는 것을 상상해 보고, 그 개미가 이동하는 것을 따라 그 이동 경로를 추적하는 것을 (b) 머릿속에 그려 보라. 그 이동 경로는 여러 차례 구부러지고 방향이 바뀔 것이고, 매우 불규칙하고 복잡할 것이다. 그렇다면 그 개미에게 똑같이 복잡한 (c) 내적 항행 능력이 있다고 가정하고, 그런 복잡한 항행 경로를 만들어 낼 수 있는 규칙과 기제를 추론하기 위해 그 이동 경로를 분석함으로써 이것(복잡한 내적 항행 능력)이 무엇일 수 있는지를 밝혀 낼 수 있을 것이다. 하지만 그 이동 경로의 복잡성은 '실제로는 해변 지면에서의 복잡성이지 그 개미의 내적 복잡성이 아니다'. 사실 그 개미는 일련의 매우

(d) 복잡한(→ 단순한) 규칙들을 사용하고 있을지도 모르는데, 그 복잡한 이동 경로를 실제로 만들어 내는 것은 바로 이 규칙들과 환경의 상호작용이지, 그 개미 혼자서가 아니다. 더 일반적으로 말하자면, 개미 우화는 (e) 관찰된 행동의 복잡성과 그것 (복잡한 행동)을 만들어 내는 기제의 복잡성 사이에 필연적인 상관관계가 없다는 것을 보여 준다.

구문풀이

1행 [Our irresistible tendency {to see things in human terms}]—[that we are often mistaken in attributing complex human motives and processing abilities to other species]—does not mean [that an animal's behavior is not, in fact, complex].

: 첫 번째 [ ]가 문장의 주어로, 두 번째 [ ]와 동격 관계를 이루고 있다. { }는 Our irresistible tendency를 수식하는 to부정사구이다. 세 번째 [ ]는 does not mean의 목적어 역할을 하는 명사절이다.

어휘풀이

- irresistible *a* 억누를 수 없는, 저항할 수 없는
- tendency *n* 경향
- mistake *v* 잘못 판단하다, 오해하다
- attribute A to B A가 B에 있다고 여기다
- complexity *n* 복잡성
- internal *a* 내부의
- visualize *v* 머릿속에 그리다, 상상하다
- track *v* 추적하다
- irregular *a* 불규칙적인
- complicated *a* 복잡한
- navigational *a* 항행의, 항해의
- analyze *v* 분석하다
- infer *v* 추론하다
- mechanism *n* (생물체 내에서 특정한 기능을 수행하는) 기제, 구조
- correlation *n* 상관관계

PART II 어휘 **REVIEW**

01 필수 어휘

01 융통성 있는, 탄력적인 02 오래가는, 지속되는 03 절대적인 04 직면하게 하다 05 다양성 06 진화의 07 분투하다 08 대처하다, 극복하다 09 통합하다 10 (뒤에) 이어지는 11 경시, 무시 12 재료, 성분 13 feature 14 적당한 15 ~보다 더 자라다[커지다]

02 필수 어휘

01 외딴, 동떨어진 02 흡수, 동화 03 분명하게 밝히다, 선언하다 04 대안 05 노력하다 06 결과, 영향 07 과장하다 08 이용하다, 착취하다 09 예측하다 10 artificial 11 상대적인 12 분명한 13 일시적인 14 넘다, 초과하다 15 용인하다, 참다

03 필수 어휘

01 ~을 언급하다 02 ~하기 쉬운 03 평가하다 04 구별하다 05 좌절감을 주다 06 전통적인 07 생성하다 08 dispute 09 예측하다, 기대하다 10 해로운, 유독한, 독성의 11 해결하다, 다루다 12 잠재력 13 과소평가하다 14 설득력 있는 15 결론을 내리다

04 필수 어휘

01 광범위한 02 현명한, 분별 있는 03 지속성, 지속 가능성 04 변하다, 변경하다 05 제약 06 적절한 07 absorb 08 통찰력 09 주관적인 10 관점 11 각각 12 표현하다, 나타내다 13 놀라운 14 축적하다 15 중요한

05 필수 어휘

01 변화, 변형 02 영감을 주는 03 강화하다 04 aggressive 05 부족, 결핍 06 강화시키다 07 영양 08 단점, 결점 09 고통 10 ~에 부합하다, ~와 일치하다 11 부적절한 12 많은, 여러 가지의 13 알리다 14 인정 15 논란, 논쟁

06 필수 어휘

01 조정하다　02 특징　03 촉진하다　04 결과　05 만질 수 있는, 유형의　06 권위　07 집행[시행]하다, 강요하다　08 기본적인, 근본적인　09 동정(심)　10 규율; 학과　11 충동　12 rational　13 경계하는, 기민한　14 얻다, 이끌어 내다　15 넌지시 비추다, 암시하다

07 필수 어휘

01 좌우하는; 지시하다　02 두드러진, 주목할 만한　03 촉발하다, 유발하다　04 열정적인　05 intensity　06 투사하다, 투영하다　07 상호 보완적인　08 분배하다　09 쓸데없는, 무익한　10 취약한　11 번성하다　12 (범죄 등을) 저지르다　13 후보　14 관련이 없는　15 매우 중요한

08 필수 어휘

01 겉보기에는　02 추상적인　03 최적의　04 영역　05 극단의　06 매우 중요한　07 손대지 않은, 손상되지 않은　08 추정하다, 어림잡다　09 (영향력이) ~보다 크다　10 정말로, 문자 그대로　11 interpret　12 신뢰할 수 있는, 믿을 수 있는　13 가정하다　14 통합의　15 합의

01 어휘 모의고사

01 알아내다, 결정하다　02 의도적인　03 자극하다　04 결국, 궁극적으로　05 일, (일의) 추구　06 기준, 참고　07 활성화하다　08 염려, 우려　09 감소하다　10 주장　11 국내의　12 독특한, 구별되는　13 견디다　14 ~에 참여[관여]하다　15 interact

02 어휘 모의고사

01 촉진하다, 육성하다　02 확실하게 하다, 보장하다　03 ~을 지속하다　04 withdraw　05 상응하는, 동등한　06 수용하다　07 상품, 일용품　08 오염시키다, 더럽히다　09 정당화하다　10 조정　11 동일한　12 생겨나다　13 관점　14 명백히　15 근본적인, 급진적인

03 어휘 모의고사

01 나타나다, 등장하다　02 ~으로 구성되다　03 (아래로) 누르다　04 미신적인　05 수정하다, 고치다　06 미묘한, 미세한　07 integrate　08 양립하는, 일치하는　09 오도하다, 오해하게 만들다　10 자발적인　11 보이지 않는　12 타고난　13 충족시키다　14 배정하다, 할당하다　15 명백한, 분명한

04 어휘 모의고사

01 운송하다　02 현대의, 동시대의　03 파악하다　04 확인하다, 확정하다　05 실증적인　06 비만　07 줄어들다, 축소되다　08 정적인　09 제공하다, 기여하다　10 지배적인　11 ~을 설명하다　12 의존　13 convert　14 분류하다　15 구별하다, 구분 짓다

05 어휘 모의고사

01 ~임이 밝혀지다　02 특성　03 늘리다, 증대시키다　04 출현　05 능숙한　06 많이 있다　07 약화시키다, 훼손하다　08 강조　09 empathize　10 내재하는, 암묵적인　11 산산이 부수다　12 인용하다　13 머릿속에 그리다, 상상하다　14 분석하다　15 상관관계

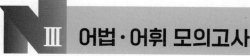

III 어법·어휘 모의고사

어법·어휘 모의고사 1회				본문 pp.152 ~ 155
183 ④	184 ③	185 ②	186 ④	187 ⑤
188 ②	189 ②	190 ④		

183　답 ④

출제 의도 파악하기

① 전치사+관계대명사　② 재귀대명사
③ 접속사 that의 쓰임, 병렬구조　④ 부사의 쓰임
⑤ 대동사

정답풀이

④ 「(as)+형용사[부사]의 원급+as+주어+동사」로 이루어진 양보 부사절에서 naturally는 이어지는 동사 is의 보어 역할을 해야 하므로 형용사 natural로 고쳐야 한다. 부사는 보어로 쓸 수 없다.

오답풀이

① the moment를 선행사로 하여 이어지는 관계절에서 during the moment의 부사구 역할을 하는 「전치사+관계대명사」 형태의 during which는 적절하게 쓰였다.

② is updating의 목적어가 주어와 같은 the present이므로 재귀대명사 itself를 쓴 것을 적절하다.

③ 뒤에 완전한 구조의 절이 이어지고, 문맥상 and 앞의 that절과 병렬구조를 이루며 a deep intuition과 동격 관계를 이루는 명사절을 이끌므로 접속사 that의 쓰임은 적절하다.

⑤ 앞의 부정문에 이어서 '~ 또한 아니다'의 의미를 나타내는 「neither+조동사[be동사]+주어」 구문이다. 앞에 일반동사 exist가 쓰였으므로 조동사 do를 주어의 수에 맞춰 쓴 does는 적절하다.

전문해석

현재 순간은 특별하게 느껴진다. 그것은 실재한다. 여러분이 아무리 많이 과거를 기억하거나 미래를 예상해도, 여러분은 현재에 살고 있다. 물론, 여러분이 그 문장을 읽은 그 순간은 더 이상 일어나고 있지 않다. 이 순간은 일어나고 있다. 다시 말해서, 현재가 지속적으로 그 자체를 갱신하고 있다는 의미에서 시간은 흐르는 것처럼 느껴진다. 우리는 미래가 그것이 현재가 될 때까지 열려 있고 과거는 고정되어 있다는 깊은 직관을 가지고 있다. 시간이 흐르면서 고정된 과거, 당면한 현재 그리고 열린 미래라는 이 구조가 시간 안에서 앞으로 흘러간다. 그러나 이러한 사고방식이 자연스러울지라도, 여러분은 이것이 과학에 반영되어 있다고 생각하지 않을 것이다. 물리학의 방정식들은 어떤 사건들이 바로 지금 발생하고 있는지 우리에게 알려주지 않는데, 그것들은 '현재 위치' 표시가 없는 지도와 같다. 현재 순간은 그것들 안에 존재하지 않으며, 그러므로 시간의 흐름도 마찬가지이다.

구문풀이

7행 We have a deep intuition [that the future is open until it becomes present] and [that the past is fixed].

: and로 연결된 두 개의 [ ]는 a deep intuition과 동격 관계를 이루는 명사절이다.

어휘풀이

- anticipate *v* 예상하다, 기대하다
- update *v* 갱신하다, 최신의 것으로 만들다
- intuition *n* 직관(력)　　　● equation *n* 방정식
- physics *n* 물리학

184 답 ③

출제 어휘 확인하기

(A) incorrect	틀린	/ right	옳은
(B) familiarity	친숙함	/ novelty	새로움, 참신함
(C) diminish	줄이다, 축소하다	/ reinforce	강화하다

정답풀이

(A) 학생들에게 그들의 지식이 불완전하다는 것을 시사하는 피드백의 예에 해당하므로, 시험 문항을 '틀린(incorrect)' 것이라는 흐름이 적절하다. [right 옳은]

(B) 시험 문항의 내용에 대해 무언가는 알고 있기 때문에 학습 내용을 파악하고 있는 것처럼 느끼는데, 이러한 '친숙함(familiarity)'의 느낌이 학생들에게 자신이 알고 있는 것을 과장되게 인식하도록 한다는 것이 적절하다. [novelty 새로움, 참신함]

(C) 학생들은 시험 문항을 틀렸을 때 문항에 대해 무언가는 알고 있기 때문에 실제로는 그렇지 않음에도 불구하고 자신이 학습 내용을 파악하고 있는 것처럼 느낀다고 했다. 따라서 이러한 사후 과잉 확신 편향은 실패가 자신이 알고 있거나 모르고 있는 것, 즉 자신이 가진 지식의 속성 때문이 아니라 평가의 속성 때문이라는 생각을 '강화한다(reinforces)'는 것이 적절하다. [diminish 줄이다, 축소하다]

전문해석

학생들이 자신의 지식에 대해 정확한 판단을 내리는 데 있어서 어려워하는 것의 원인이 되는 하나의 요인은 사후 과잉 확신 편향, 즉 어떤 일이 일어날 때 그것이 일어날 것이라는 것을 처음부터 알고 있었다고 가정하는 경향이다. 학생들이 시험 문항을 (A) 틀린 것과 같이 자신의 지식이 불완전하다는 것을 시사하는 피드백을 받을 때, 그들은 실제로는 그 정보를 정말 알고 있었다고 스스로에게 얘기함으로써 (피드백에) 반응할 수도 있다. 그들은 (학습) 내용을 완전히 파악하지 못하고 있음에도 불구하고, 그 문항의 내용에 대해 무언가를 인식하고 있기 때문에 자신들이 그 내용을 파악하고 있는 것처럼 느낀다. 되돌아보면, 일단 그들이 정답을 알면 해답은 명확해 보인다. 이러한 (B) 친숙함의 느낌은 학생들이 자기가 알고 있는 것에 대해 과장된 인식을 갖도록 이끌 수 있다. 따라서 사후 과잉 확신 편향은 실패가 그들이 가진 지식의 속성 때문이라기보다 평가의 속성 때문이라는 느낌을 (C) 강화하는데, 이는 그들이 피드백으로부터 배우는 것을 더 어렵게 만든다.

구문풀이

1행 One factor contributing to students' difficulty in making accurate judgments of their own knowledge is hindsight bias: the tendency to assume once something happens [that one knew all along {that it was going to happen}].

: 콜론(:) 이하는 hindsight bias를 구체적으로 설명하는 동격어구이다. [ ]는 to assume의 목적어로 쓰인 명사절이고, 그 안의 { }는 knew의 목적어로 쓰인 명사절이다.

15행 Hindsight bias therefore reinforces the feeling [that their failure was due to the nature of the assessment rather than the nature of their knowledge]—[which makes **it** more difficult {for them to learn from feedback}].

: 첫 번째 [ ]는 the feeling과 동격 관계를 이루는 명사절이다. 두 번째 [ ]는 앞 절의 내용을 선행사로 하는 관계절로, 그 안의 it은 makes의 형식상의 목적어이고, { }가 내용상의 목적어이다.

어휘풀이

- contribute to ~의 원인이 되다 　● accurate *a* 정확한
- all along 내내, 죽 　● have a grasp of ~을 이해[파악]하다
- novelty *n* 새로움, 참신함 　● exaggerated *a* 과장된
- nature *n* 속성, 천성 　● assessment *n* 평가

185 답 ②

출제 의도 파악하기

❶	대동사	❷	재귀대명사
❸	관계대명사 which의 쓰임	❹	to부정사의 쓰임
❺	문장의 구조 파악		

정답풀이

② when이 이끄는 시간 부사절에서 when과 과거분사 thrown 사이에 「주어+be동사」가 생략된 구조이며, 문맥상 생략된 주어는 a sticky mixture로, when a sticky mixture was thrown at their enemies ~의 의미를 나타낸다. 따라서 was thrown의 주어와 전치사 at의 목적어가 동일한 대상이 아니므로, themselves를 전치사 at의 목적어인 their enemies를 지칭하도록 대명사 them으로 바꿔 써야 한다.

오답풀이

① 문맥상 앞 문장의 일반동사구 discovered gunpowder for the first time을 대신하고 있으므로 대동사 do의 과거형인 did는 적절하다.

③ potassium nitrate를 선행사로 하는 관계절을 이끌며 관계절에서 주어 역할을 하므로 주격 관계대명사로 쓰인 which는 알맞다.

④ something을 뒤에서 수식하는 to부정사 to use는 알맞다.

⑤ 문장의 동사인 think의 목적어로 쓰인 명사절에서 주어인 the advent of gunpowder에 이어지는 동사 signaled는 적절하다.

전문해석

누가 처음으로 화약을 발견했을까? 영국인, 아랍인, 힌두인 그리고 그리스인들은 자신들이 했다고 말한다. 우리는 고대 그리스인이 그리스 화약을 만들었다는 것을 알고 있는데, 그것은 적들에게 던져졌을 때 몸에 달라붙었을 뿐만 아니라 그 불을 끄기도 힘들었기 때문에 그들을 공포에 떨게 했던 끈적거리는 혼합물이었다. 아마도 이것이 화약의 시작이었을 것이다. 화약은 주로 같은 양의 숯 그리고 유황과 섞이면 격렬하게 연소하는 질산칼륨이다. 만약 용기라고 할 수 있는 것에 넣으면, 폭발이 일어난다. 아마도 600년에서 700년 전에 이런 방식으로 화약은 무언가를 폭파하는 데 사용하는 것이 된 것 같다. 일부 역사학자들은 화약의 출현이 중세의 거대한 성의 종말을 알렸다고 생각하는데, 왜냐하면 벽이 산산조각으로 폭파될 수 있었기 때문이다. 의심할 여지없이, 화약은 전쟁뿐만 아니라 인간의 역사도 바꾸었다.

구문풀이

7행 Gunpowder is mainly potassium nitrate [which burns fiercely {when blended with about equal amounts of charcoal and sulfur}].

: [ ]는 potassium nitrate를 수식하는 관계절이다. 그 안의 { }는 부사절로, 접속사 when과 과거분사 blended 사이에 「주어+be동사」인 it(= potassium nitrate) is가 생략된 형태이다.

어휘풀이

- sticky *a* 끈적거리는, 달라붙는 　● mixture *n* 혼합물, 혼합체
- terrorize *v* 공포에 떨게 하다, 위협하다

- stick *v* 달라붙다
- put out (불·전깃불 등)을 끄다
- blend *v* 섞다
- confine *v* 넣다, 가두다
- explosion *n* 폭발
- advent *n* 도래, 출현
- warfare *n* 전투 (행위)
- flame *n* 불꽃
- fiercely *ad* 맹렬하게
- charcoal *n* 숯
- of sorts ~라고 할 수 있는
- historian *n* 역사가
- signal *v* 신호를 보내다

186 답 ④

①	remotely	원격으로	↔
②	skillfully	능숙하게	↔
③	flaw	결점	↔
④	retain	보유하다	↔ lack(~이 없다)
⑤	measure	측정하다	↔

정답풀이

④ 앞 문장에서 원격 의학 시스템의 결점에 대한 예로, 치료 과정에서 환자의 몸속에 직접 손을 넣고 하는 것이 아니라 비디오 화면으로 보면서 도구를 이용하는 것이므로 잡아당기는 강도, 누르는 세기 등을 의사들이 분간할 수 없음을 들고 있다. 따라서 촉각을 '보유하고 있다'는 것은 적절하지 않다. 강도나 세기 등을 느끼는 촉각이 '없다'는 흐름이 되도록 retain을 lack 정도로 바꿔 써야 한다.

오답풀이

① 뒤 문장에서 환자의 몸에 손을 넣지 않고도 종양을 제거할 수 있다고 하므로 '원격으로(remotely)' 작업한다는 것은 적절하다.
② 로봇으로 된 도구에 카메라가 달려 있으면 비디오 화면으로 보면서 환자의 몸속에서 도구를 '능숙하게' 움직일 수 있을 것이므로 skillfully는 적절하다.
③ 너무 세게 잡아당기고 있는지 또는 충분히 세게 누르고 있지 않은지를 항상 분간할 수 있는 것이 아닌 것은 '결점'이므로 flaws는 적절하다.
⑤ 로봇 외과 수술용 장치에 촉각을 추가하고 있다고 했으므로, 로봇이 신체에 압력을 얼마나 가하는가를 '측정하는(measure)' 센서를 개발했다는 것은 적절하다.

전문해석

사람들이 ① 원격으로 작업을 하게 해 주는 시각적 시스템은 이미 존재한다. 환자의 몸속에 손을 넣지 않고 외과 의사들은 종양을 제거하거나 몸속 깊이 있는 상처를 치료하기 위해 로봇 장치를 사용할 수 있다. 로봇으로 된 도구에 카메라가 달려 있어 의사들이 환자의 몸속에서 도구들을 ② 능숙하게 움직일 수 있게 돕는다. 비디오 화면에서 그들은 자신들이 도구를 가지고 무엇을 하는지 볼 수 있다. 그러나 이러한 시각적 시스템은 ③ 결점이 있다. 한 가지 예로, 의사들은 그들이 너무 세게 잡아당기고 있는지 또는 충분히 세게 누르고 있지 않은지를 항상 분간할 수 있는 것은 아니다. 다시 말해서, 그들은 촉각을 ④ 보유하고 있다(→ (이) 없다). 그 격차를 메우기 위해 연구원들은 da Vinci 시스템이라고 불리는 로봇 외과 수술용 장치에 촉각을 추가하고 있다. 그들은 로봇이 신체에 압력을 얼마나 가하는가를 ⑤ 측정하는 센서를 개발해 냈다.

구문풀이

2행 Without ever [putting their hands inside a patient], surgeons can use robotic devices [to remove tumors or repair wounds {that are deep in the body}].

: 첫 번째 [ ]는 전치사 Without 다음에 온 동명사구이다. 두 번째 [ ]는 목적을 나타내는 부사적 용법의 to부정사구이고, 그 안의 { }는 wounds를 수식하는 관계절이다.

- remotely *ad* 원격으로
- device *n* 장치
- wound *n* 상처
- retain *v* 보유하다
- apply *v* 힘을 가하다
- surgeon *n* 외과 의사
- tumor *n* 종양
- flaw *n* 결점
- surgical *a* 외과의, 수술의

187 답 ⑤

①	관계대명사 that의 쓰임	②	관계대명사 what의 쓰임
③	동명사의 쓰임	④	형식상의 주어와 내용상의 주어
⑤	병렬구조		

정답풀이

⑤ 문맥상 you should ~ you do는 the things를 수식하는 관계절로, 관계절 내에서 should avoid doing과 (should) ensure that you do가 병렬구조를 이루어 '여러분이 하기를 피해야 하는 또는 확실하게 해 두어야 하는'이라는 의미를 나타내야 하므로, ensuring을 동사원형인 ensure로 바꿔 써야 한다.

오답풀이

① 선행사 one good style of debating을 수식하는 관계절을 이끄는 목적격 관계대명사로 쓰인 that은 적절하다.
② 전치사 of의 목적어이자 이어지는 절의 주어 역할을 해야 하므로 선행사를 포함한 관계대명사 what은 적절하다.
③ a different style that ~ your personality를 목적어로 취하면서 문장의 주어를 이끄는 동명사 adopting은 적절하게 쓰였다.
④ 앞에 형식상의 주어 it이 왔으므로, 내용상의 주어인 to부정사구를 이루는 to experiment는 적절하다.

전문해석

모든 사람은 자신만의 개별적인 스타일을 갖고 있다. 여러분이 채택해야 할 단 한 가지의 좋은 토론 스타일은 없다. 토론을 흥미롭게 만드는 것의 일부는 청중을 설득하기 위해 토론자들이 사용하는 다양한 스타일이다. 더욱이, 여러분의 개성에 정말 잘 맞지 않는 다른 스타일을 취하는 것은 진실하지 못한 것으로 이해될 뿐이다. 정직하지 못함은 설득의 적이다. 따라서 여러 가지 스타일로 실험해 보고, 여러분이 존경하는 토론자의 스타일로부터 배우는 것이 허용되지만(심지어 권장되지만), 항상 여러분의 개성에 충실하려고 애써야 한다. '훌륭한 스타일'을 위한 탐색은 그렇게 좋지 않은 스타일 또는 대중 연설의 매우 기본적인 요소들로부터 시작된다. 이런 것들은 근본적으로 여러분이 피해야 하는 것들이거나 여러분이 확실하게 해 두어야 할 것들인데, 왜냐하면 그러한 요소들은 여러분의 청중을 설득할 가능성에 강하게 영향을 미치기 때문이다. 이러한 것들은 또한 모든 심사위원들이 식별할 수 있을 매우 중요한 요소들이다.

구문풀이

14행 These are basically the things [you should avoid doing or ensure {that you do}], [as they strongly affect the chances of persuading your audience].

: 첫 번째 [ ]는 the things를 수식하는 관계절이고, 그 안의 { }는 ensure의 목적어로 쓰인 명사절이다. 두 번째 [ ]는 '~이기 때문에'라는 의미의 접속사 as가 이끄는 부사절이다.

어휘풀이

- debate *v* 논쟁하다, 토론하다
- come across as ~라는 인상을 주다
- insincerity *n* 불성실, 부정직
- adopt *v* 채택하다
- insincere *a* 진실하지 못한, 거짓의
- seek to *do* ~하려고 노력하다

- fundamental *a* 근본적인, 중요한
- identify *v* 식별하다, 확인하다
- ensure *v* 확실하게 하다, 보장하다

- merchandise *n* 상품
- factually *ad* 사실상
- currency *n* 통화, 화폐
- income *n* 소득
- comparison *n* 비교
- function *v* 기능하다
- intrinsic *a* 본질적인, 고유의
- depending on ~에 따라
- attitude *n* 태도

188 답 ②

①	higher	더 높은	↔	lower(더 낮은)
②	priceless	대단히 귀중한	↔	worthless(무가치한)
③	agree	동의하다	↔	disagree(동의하지 않다)
④	lose	잃다	↔	get(얻다)
⑤	change	변하다	↔	

정답풀이

② 지폐는 종잇조각에 불과하므로 그 자체는 '가치가 없지만', 그 돈으로 상품을 살 수 있도록 사회적인 합의가 이루어졌기 때문에 가치가 있다는 내용이므로, priceless(대단히 귀중한)를 반대 개념인 worthless(무가치한) 정도로 바꿔야 문맥상 적절하다. 대개 -less가 붙으면 부정의 의미를 나타내지만 priceless의 경우는 예외라는 것에 유의한다.

오답풀이

① 만드는 데 10센트가 드는 100달러짜리 지폐로 100달러짜리 물건을 살 수 있으므로 그 가치가 훨씬 '더 크다(higher)'는 것은 문맥상 적절하다.
③ 돈은 본질적인 가치는 없지만 시장에서 그것이 받아들여질 것이라는 사회적인 믿음과 '합의가 있다면' 그것은 가치가 있다는 내용이므로 agree(동의하다)는 문맥상 적절하다.
④ 통화 체계를 바꾸거나 화폐 단위를 바꾸는 경우, 원래의 통화는 더 이상 사용되지 않게 되므로 그 가치를 '잃게 된다(loses)'는 것은 문맥상 적절하다.
⑤ 통화 체계와 화폐 단위의 '변경'에 대해 말하고 있으므로 change는 문맥상 적절하다.

전문해석

100달러짜리 지폐 한 장의 생산 비용은 약 10센트이지만, 그것이 구입할 수 있는 상품의 관점에서 그것의 가치는 훨씬 ① 더 크다. 경제적인 관점에서 화폐의 가치는 통상 단위 금액으로 구입될 수 있는 상품의 양과 질을 의미한다. 현대 경제는 사람들이 사실상 ② 대단히 귀중한(→ 무가치한) 종잇조각의 사회적 의미를 신뢰할 경우에만 기능을 한다. 다시 말해서, 동전과 은행권은 그것들이 시장에서 다른 사람에 의해서 받아들여질 것임을 우리가 신뢰하기 때문에 가치가 있으며, 그것들은 어떠한 실제의 (본질적인) 가치가 없지만 단지 사람들이 그것들이 그렇다고(가치가 있다고) ③ 동의하기 때문에 가치가 있다. 그러나 사회가, 예를 들어 하나의 통화 체계에서 다른 통화 체계로 전환하기로 결정할 때, 독일의 마르크화에서 유로화로의 전환 또는 화폐 단위 변경에서처럼, 원래의 통화는 그 가치를 ④ 잃는다. 이러한 의미에서 화폐의 가치는 다양한 상황적 요인들에 따라 시간이 지나면서 ⑤ 변할 수도 있다. 게다가, 사람들이 화폐를 평가하는 방식은 소득, 화폐에 대한 태도 또는 사회적 비교와 같은 다양한 개인적인 요인들에 달려 있을 것이다.

구문풀이

8행 In other words, coins and banknotes are valuable [because we trust {that they will be accepted by others in the market}] — [they do not have any real (intrinsic) value but are valuable only because people agree {that they **do**}].

: 첫 번째 [ ]는 이유를 나타내는 부사절이고, 그 안의 { }는 trust의 목적어 역할을 하는 명사절이다. 두 번째 [ ]는 앞 문장에 대한 부연 설명을 제공하며, 그 안의 { }는 agree의 목적어로 쓰인 명사절이고, do는 대동사로 have value의 의미를 나타낸다.

어휘풀이

- note *n* 지폐
- in terms of ~의 관점에서

189 답 ②

❶	분사의 태	❷	문장의 구조 파악
❸	강조구문	❹	지시대명사 those
❺	전치사+관계대명사		

정답풀이

② 문장의 핵심 주어는 A French explorer이고 관계절 who visited ~ in 1688이 이를 수식하는 구조로, 술어 동사가 없는 상태이다. 따라서 준동사 saying을 본동사 said로 바꿔 써야 한다. 여기서 the natives called 이하는 said의 목적어로 쓰인 명사절이다.

오답풀이

① 수식을 받는 명사 a meaning이 '확립되는' 대상이므로 수동의 의미를 나타내는 과거분사 established는 적절하게 쓰였다.
③ the disagreeable odor ~ wild onions를 강조하는 「it is[was] ~ that ....」강조구문이므로 that의 쓰임은 적절하다.
④ 형용사구 anxious ~ city의 수식을 받아 '~인 사람들'을 나타내는 those는 적절하다.
⑤ 관계대명사 which가 선행사인 truth를 수식하는 관계절을 이끄는데, 관계절이 주어(it)와 동사(began)를 갖춘 완전한 구조이면서 which가 전치사 from의 목적어 역할을 하므로, 「전치사+관계대명사」 형태의 from which는 적절하다.

전문해석

Chicago라고 하는 말은 보통 이상으로 훨씬 명백하게 확립된 의미를 가지고 있는 것 같다. 1688년에 그 지방을 찾아온 어떤 프랑스 탐험가는, 그 지방에 야생의 양파가 많이 자라고 있어서 토착인들이 그것(그 지역)을 Chicagou라고 불렀다고 말했다. 학자들은, 인디언의 이름에 영감을 준 것은 작은 야생 양파의 연분홍색 꽃이 가지는 고약한 냄새 때문이라고 생각했고, 그렇기에 '고약한 냄새가 나는 곳' 또는 '스컹크의 장소'가 그 이름의 좀 더 정확한 해석일 것이라고 생각하고 있다. 한편, 그 도시의 이름을 변호하고 싶어 하는 사람들은, 인디언들이 생각했던 것처럼, 그 이름이 그저 '강한'이라고 하는 뜻이었고 '강한 도시'라고 부르는 것이 본래의 의미에 훨씬 더 가깝다고 주장하고 있다. 이와 같이, 연구나 농담, 상상 따위가 많은 인디언 말을 이용하는데, 곧 그 결과물로부터 그 모든 것이 시작된 티끌만큼의 진실을 가리는 것이, 설사 있다손 치더라도, 불가능하게 된다.

구문풀이

9행 On the other hand, those [anxious to defend the name of the city] insist [that its name {as the Indians thought of it} meant merely "strong"] and [that "strong-town" is much nearer the proper sense].

: 첫 번째 [ ]는 those를 수식하는 현재분사구이다. 두 번째와 세 번째 [ ]는 문장의 동사 insist의 목적어 역할을 하는 명사절로 등위접속사 and로 연결되어 있다. 두 번째 [ ]에서 { }는 주어와 동사 사이에 삽입된 부사절이다.

어휘풀이

- explorer *n* 탐험가
- abundance *n* 풍부함
- region *n* 지역, 지방

- disagreeable *a* 불쾌한, 마음에 들지 않는
- odor *n* 냄새, 악취
- inspire *v* 영감을 주다
- interpretation *n* 해석
- play upon ~을 이용하다
- grain *n* 아주 조금, 티끌
- if any 만약에 있다면, 설사 있다손 치더라도
- blossom *n* 꽃
- accurate *a* 정확한
- anxious *a* ~하고 싶어 하는
- term *n* 말, 용어

190 답 ④

①	combine	결합하다	↔	
②	favour	유리하다	↔	
③	guarantee	보장하다	↔	
④	decrease	감소	↔	increase(증가)
⑤	ensure	보장하다	↔	

정답풀이

④ 물 권리와 토지 권리가 결합된 전통적인 분배를 회피하게 된 이유로 경제적 중요성을 갖는 작물의 재배를 언급하는 부분이다. 즉, 경제적 지위가 높은 작물의 재배는 공정한 몫 이상의 물을 필요로 하므로 생계용 작물로부터 물 권리를 매수할 수 있게 된다는 것이다. 따라서 상당한 경제적 중요성을 갖는 작물의 재배 '감소(decrease)'로 인해 전통적인 분배가 회피되었다는 것은 적절하지 않으며 반대 의미의 increase(증가)로 바꿔 써야 한다.

오답풀이

① 산악 지역에서 물 이용 권리가 토지의 소유와 연관되어 있다고 했으므로, 토지와 물 권리가 '결합되어(combined)' 함께 이전되었다는 것은 적절하다.
② 물 권리와 토지가 분리되어 경매될 수 있기 때문에 지역 사회의 모든 사람에게 이용 권리를 보장하지는 않는다는 흐름이므로, 비용을 지불할 수 있는 사람에게 '유리하다(favours)'는 것은 적절하다.
③ 전통적인 분배의 예시로 예멘에서 토지 단위당 정해진 물을 분배했다는 것을 설명하고 있으므로, 유수(流水), 우물 같은 공급이 '보장된(guaranteed)' 전통적인 관개 공급에만 적용되었다는 것은 적절하다.
⑤ 경제적 지위가 높은 작물의 재배는 물을 많이 필요로 하기 때문에 경제적 지위가 상대적으로 낮은 생계형 작물로부터 물 권리를 사들인다는 것이므로, 그 작물의 경제적인 지위가 물 권리의 매수를 '보장한다(ensures)'는 것은 적절하다.

전문해석

많은 산악 지역에서, 물을 이용할 권리는 토지의 소유와 연관되어 있는데, 예를 들어 최근까지 안데스 산맥에서는 토지와 물 권리가 (a) 결합되어 물 권리가 토지와 함께 이전되었다. 그러나 주(州) 토지 개혁과 추가적인 공급원의 개발을 통해 물 권리가 토지와 분리되었고 경매에 부쳐질 수도 있다. 그러므로 이것은 지역 사회의 모든 사람에게 이용을 보장하기보다는, 비용을 지불할 수 있는 사람에게 (b) 유리하다. 따라서 개인이 물이 없는 땅을 보유할 수도 있는 상황이 생긴다. 페루에서는, 정부가 토지와는 별도로 지역 사회에 물을 주고, 그것을 분배하는 것은 공동체에 달려 있다. 예멘에서도 마찬가지로, 전통적인 분배는 100'립나'의 토지에 1척('타사')의 물이었다. 이것은 유수(流水), 우물 등과 같이 공급이 (c) 보장된 전통적인 관개(灌漑) 공급에만 적용되었다. 갑작스럽게 불어난 물을 가둬서 얻어진 물은 불확실한 수원(水源)이 되는 것으로 여겨지기 때문에 이슬람 율법의 적용을 받지 않고, 따라서 그 물을 모아서 사용할 수 있는 사람들에게는 무료이다. 그러나 이 전통적인 토지 단위당 분배는 부분적으로는 새로운 공급의 개발에 의해서뿐만 아니라, 상당한 경제적 중요성을 갖는 작물의 재배 (d) 감소(→ 증가)에 의해서도 회피되었다. 이 작물은 일년 내내 수확되고, 따라서 공정한 몫의 물 그 이상을 필요로 한다. 그 작물의 경제적 지위는

생계용 작물로부터 물 권리를 사거나 매수할 수 있음을 (e) 보장한다.

구문풀이

18행 Water [derived from the capture of flash floods] is not subject to Islamic law [as this constitutes an uncertain source], and is therefore free for those [able to collect and use it].

: 첫 번째 [ ]는 Water를 수식하는 과거분사구이고, 두 번째 [ ]는 이유의 부사절이다. 세 번째 [ ]는 those를 수식하는 형용사구이다.

어휘풀이

- transfer *v* 이전하다
- auction *n* 경매
- grant *v* (인정하여 정식으로) 주다, 승인하다
- allocate *v* 분배하다, 할당하다
- runoff *n* (땅속으로 흡수되지 않고 흐르는) 유수(流水)
- well *n* 우물
- derived from ~에서 얻은, ~에서 끌어 낸
- flash flood 갑작스런 홍수, 갑작스럽게 불어난 물
- be subject to ~의 영향을 받다
- constitute *v* ~이 되는 것으로 여겨지다
- bypass *v* 회피하다, 무시하다, 우회하다
- cultivation *n* 재배, 경작
- share *n* 몫, 할당량
- reform *n* 개혁
- favour *v* 유리하다
- substantial *a* 상당한

191 ⑤	192 ④	193 ④	194 ④	195 ④
196 ④	197 ⑤	198 ③		

191 답 ⑤

출제 의도 파악하기

❶ 형용사의 쓰임	❷ 병렬구조
❸ 의문사 what의 쓰임	❹ 동사 emerge의 쓰임
❺ 문장의 구조 파악	

정답풀이

⑤ 'A가 ~하는 데 (시간)이 걸리다'라는 의미의 「it takes+시간+for A to do」에서 '시간'에 해당하는 표현인 long이 앞으로 나가 「the+비교급 ~, the+비교급 …」 구문을 이루는 문장이다. 따라서 that을 it으로 고쳐야 한다.

오답풀이

① 「find+목적어+목적격보어」 구문에서 목적격보어로 쓰인 형용사 appealing은 적절하다.
② 문맥상 노래를 듣고 그것이 마음에 든다고 판단할 수도 있다는 것이므로, and 앞의 동사원형 hear와 병렬구조를 이루며 조동사 might에 이어지는 동사원형 decide는 적절하다.
③ might notice의 목적절을 이끌며 그 절에서 doing의 목적어 역할을 하는 의문사 what은 적절하다.
④ A special harmony를 주어로 하는 자동사 emerges는 적절하다. that we missed before는 A special harmony를 수식하는 관계절이다.

전문해석

인간 심리의 흥미로운 한 측면은 우리가 어떤 것들을 처음 경험할 때 그런 것들에 대한 모든 것이 명확하지 않은 경우 그것들을 더 좋아하고 그것들이 더 매력적이라고 생각하는 경향이 있다는 것이다. 이것은 음악에 있어서 분명히 사실이다. 예를 들어, 우리는 라디오에서 우리의 관심을 끄는 어떤 노래를 처음 듣고, 그 노래가 마음에 든다고 판단을 내릴 수도 있다. 그러고 나서 다음에 그것을 들을 때, 우리는 처음에 알아차리지 못한 가사를 듣거나 배경에서 피아노나 드럼이 무엇을 하고 있는지 알아챌 수 있다. 우리가 이전에 놓쳤던 특별한 화음이 나타난다. 우리는 점점 더 많은 것을 듣게 되고, 매번 들을 때마다 점점 더 많이 이해하게 된다. 때때로 예술 작품이 우리에게 그것의 중요한 세부 요소들을 모두 드러내는 데 걸리는 시간이 길수록, 그것이 음악이든 미술이든 춤이든 또는 건축이든 간에 우리는 그것을 더 좋아하게 된다.

구문풀이

1행 An interesting aspect of human psychology is [that we tend to {like things more} and {find them more appealing} {if everything about those things is not obvious} {the first time we experience them}].

: [ ]는 is의 보어로 쓰인 명사절이고, and로 연결된 첫 번째와 두 번째 { }가 tend to에 이어지는 구조이다. 세 번째와 네 번째 { }는 각각 조건과 시간을 나타내는 부사절이다.

어휘풀이

- psychology *n* 심리 (상태)
- obvious *a* 분명한, 명백한
- harmony *n* 화음
- fond of ~을 좋아하는
- appealing *a* 매력적인, 마음을 끄는
- lyrics *n* (노래의) 가사
- emerge *v* 나오다, 나타나다
- architecture *n* 건축

192 답 ④

출제 어휘 확인하기

① mute	말이 없는	↔		
② understand	이해하다	↔		
③ literally	문자 그대로	↔		
④ possible	가능한	↔	impossible(불가능한)
⑤ context	맥락	↔		

정답풀이

④ 예술 작품에 반응하는 방법은 외국어를 배우는 것처럼 어떤 나라나 시대, 예술가의 스타일이나 사고방식을 배운다는 점에서 유사하다고 했고, 예술적 취향을 좌우하는 문화는 아주 다양하다고 했다. 따라서 그것을 일련의 가르침으로 한정하는 것이 '가능하다'는 것은 적절하지 않으며 반대 의미인 impossible(불가능한)로 바꿔 써야 한다. 그래야 이후 예술 작품은 시대와 상황 속에서 평가할 수밖에 없다는 내용으로 자연스럽게 연결된다.

오답풀이

① 예술은 시각적 대화로 일컬어졌고 예술의 창작자가 우리에게 말하고 있는 것처럼 상상력을 표현한다는 문맥에서 창조물인 사물 자체는 '말이 없다(mute)'고 하는 것은 적절하다.
② 창작자의 상상력을 표현하는 예술이 지극히 개인적일지라도 창작자가 우리에게 말하듯 시각적 대화가 이루어진다는 것을 설명하고 있으므로 우리에게 '이해된다(understood)'는 것은 적절하다.
③ 예술 작품과의 실제적인 대화를 의미하는 것이 아니라 창작자의 상상력과 예술적 진술을 이해한다는 것을 뜻하므로 '문자 그대로(literally)' 말을 걸 수 없다는 것은 적절하다.
⑤ 예술적 취향을 좌우하는 문화는 아주 다양하므로 예술 작품은 일련의 가르침으로 한정될 수 없으며 그 예술 작품이 속한 시대와 상황이라는 '맥락(context)'에서 평가해야 한다는 것은 적절하다.

전문해석

예술은 시각적 대화로 일컬어져 왔는데, 사물 자체는 ① 말이 없지만 마치 창작자가 우리에게 말하고 있는 것처럼 분명히 예술이 그의 상상력을 표현하기 때문이다. 지극히 개인적인 예술적 진술도 단지 직관적인 수준에서일지라도 어느 수준에서는 ② 이해될 수 있다. 그러나 거기서 대화가 이루어지는 것은 우리의 활발한 참여를 요구한다. 우리가 ③ 문자 그대로 예술 작품에 말을 걸 수는 없다 하더라도, 적어도 그것에 반응하는 방법은 배울 수 있다. 이 과정은 외국어를 배우는 것과 유사하다. 우리가 작품을 제대로 이해하기를 원한다면, 어떤 나라나 시대 그리고 예술가의 스타일이나 사고방식에 대해 배워야만 한다. (예술적) 취향은 전적으로 문화에 의해서 좌우되고, 문화는 아주 다양해서 예술을 일련의 가르침으로 한정하는 것이 ④ 가능하다(→ 불가능하다). 그러므로 우리는 예술 작품을 시대와 상황의 ⑤ 맥락에서 평가할 수밖에 없는 것 같다.

구문풀이

6행 [For there to be a dialogue], however, **requires** our active participation.

: [ ]는 명사적 용법으로 쓰인 to부정사구로, 문장의 주어이다. to부정사구 주어는 단수 취급하므로 단수형 동사 requires가 쓰였다.

어휘풀이

- mute *a* 무언의, 말 없는
- intuitive *a* 직관적인
- literally *ad* 문자 그대로
- solely *ad* 오직, 전적으로
- precept *n* 교훈, 수칙
- statement *n* 진술
- participation *n* 참여
- outlook *n* 사고방식, 예측, 전망
- reduce A to B A를 B로 한정[축소]하다
- circumstance *n* 상황

193 답 ④

정답풀이

④ 2형식 동사 seems의 주격보어 자리이므로 부사 dreadfully는 적절하지 않으며 형용사 dreadful로 바꿔 써야 한다.

오답풀이

① 문장의 핵심 주어는 The causes이고, of the various kinds of unhappiness는 이를 수식하는 어구로, 복수형 동사 lie는 적절하다. lie in은 '~에 있다'라는 뜻이다.

② 수식을 받는 the social system은 '요구되는' 대상이므로 수동의 의미를 나타내는 과거분사 required는 적절하다.

③ 동사 is에 대한 주어부를 이끄는 to부정사 To discover는 적절하다.

⑤ 주어 no other kind (of education)가 '주어지는' 대상이므로 수동태 be given은 적절하다.

전문해석

여러 종류의 불행의 원인은 부분적으로는 사회 체계에 있고 부분적으로는 개인의 심리에 있는데, 물론 그것은 그 자체로 상당 부분 사회 체계의 산물이다. 나는 전에 행복을 증진시키도록 요구되는 사회 체계의 변화에 대해 쓴 적이 있었다. 전쟁의 폐지와 경제적 착취의 폐지 그리고 혹독함과 공포 상황에서의 교육의 폐지에 대해서 이 책에서 말하고자 하는 것이 나의 의도는 아니다. 전쟁을 피하기 위한 체계를 발견하는 것은 우리 문명의 중대한 요구이다. 그러나 그런 체계는 인간이 너무 불행해서 차라리 서로를 전멸시키는 것이 하루 낮을 계속해서 참아 내는 것보다 덜 두려운 것처럼 보이는 한 기회를 갖지 못한다. 무자비함과 공포 속에서의 교육은 나쁜 것이나 그들 자신이 이런 격정의 노예인 사람들은 어떤 다른 종류의 교육도 행할 수 없다.

구문풀이

[10행] But no such system has a chance [while men are **so** unhappy **that** mutual extermination seems to them **less** dreadful **than** continued endurance of the light of day].

: [ ]는 '~하는 한'이라는 의미의 접속사 while이 이끄는 부사절이고, 그 안에 「so+형용사+that ...(너무 ~해서 ...하다)」 구문과 「less ~ than ...(...보다 덜 ~한)」의 비교구문이 쓰였다.

어휘풀이

- considerable *a* 상당한, 많은
- abolition *n* 폐지
- cruelty *n* 잔인함
- civilization *n* 문명
- endurance *n* 인내
- promote *v* 촉진시키다
- exploitation *n* 개발, 이용
- intention *n* 의도
- mutual *a* 상호의, 서로의
- passion *n* 열정

194 답 ④

출제 어휘 확인하기

①	reason	이유	↔
②	nurture	돌보다, 양육하다	↔
③	self-consciously	자기 의식적으로	
④	maintain	유지하다	↔
⑤	deliberation	숙고, 심의	↔

정답풀이

④ 의식적으로 하는 일이 더 효율적이라는 것은 옳지 않으며 행동에 대한 의식적인 주의는 나쁜 습관을 없애는 한 가지 수단일 뿐이라고 말하고 있으므로, 일단 수영하고 타이핑하는 법을 배운 후에는 의식적인 주의가 '없어져야' 한다는 내용이 되어야 자연스럽다. 따라서 maintained(유지하다)를 vanished(사라지다) 정도로 바꿔 써야 한다.

오답풀이

① 뒤 문장에 행동에 대한 신념을 세운 다음 그 신념으로 행동을 하는 게 아니라는 내용이 나오고 있다. 이는 인간의 행위가 전부 '이유'에 근거하고 있지는 않음을 의미하므로 reasons는 적절하다.

② 물에 빠진 사람을 구하기 위해 바다로 뛰어드는 구조원의 경우처럼 뇌가 손상된 아기에 대한 어머니의 건강한 충동과 건전한 본능적 행위는 그 아이를 '돌보는' 일일 것이므로 nurtures는 적절하다.

③ 뒤에 이어지는 내용에서 의식적으로 하는 일을 부정적으로 설명하고 있으므로 인간 행위의 효율성은 '자기 의식적으로(self-consciously)' 하는 일에서 오는 것이 아님을 강조하는 문맥은 적절하다.

⑤ 앞에서 언급한 사례들을 종합해 볼 때, 인간의 행동은 개념의 '숙고'에서가 아니라 사물과의 접촉에서 생기는 통찰에서 온다는 것을 강조하는 문맥이므로 부정어 not과 함께 쓰인 deliberation은 적절하다.

전문해석

우리가 하고, 하고자 원하고, 그리고 칭찬하는 모든 것이 다 ① 이유가 있는 것은 아니다. 물에 빠진 사람을 구하기 위해 바다로 뛰어드는 구조원은 먼저 신념을 세우고 나서 이 신념으로 행동을 하는 게 아니다. 뇌가 손상된 아기를 ② 돌보는 어머니는 그렇게 하는 행동의 이성적 동기를 대지조차 못할 것이다. 우리가 그 구조원과 그 어머니의 인격을 존중한다면, 그 구조원과 그 어머니에게 인격은 이성적으로 정당화된 일련의 신념을 소유하는 것이 아니라, 건강한 충동과 건전한 본능인 것이다. ③ 자기 의식적으로 하는 일을 더 효율적으로 한다는 것은 분명히 옳지 않다. 우리의 행동에 대한 의식적인 주의는 기껏해야 나쁜 습관을 없애는 한 가지 수단일 수 있을 뿐이다. 그것은 우리가 수영하는 것과 물고기처럼 헤엄치는 것을 배우면, 그리고 우리가 타이핑하는 것을 배우면 ④ 유지되어야(→ 없어져야) 한다. 생각 그 자체도 어떻게 개념들을 형성하여 연결 지을 것인가를 ⑤ 숙고함으로써 생기는 게 아니다. 통찰은 사물과의 접촉에서 생겨나는 선물로 오는 것이다.

구문풀이

[10행] It is certainly not true [that {what we do self-consciously} we do more effectively].

: It은 형식상의 주어이며, [ ]가 내용상의 주어이다. { }는 뒤에 나오는 we do의 목적어로 쓰인 명사절로 강조를 위해 앞으로 왔다.

어휘풀이

- leap into ~에 뛰어들다
- drowning *a* 물에 빠져 있는
- formulate *v* 공식화하다, 조직적으로 세우다
- nurture *v* 돌보다, 양육하다
- supply *v* 제공하다, 공급하다
- possession *n* 소유
- justify *v* 정당화하다, 옳다고 하다
- impulse *n* 충동, 추진력
- instinct *n* 본능
- conscious *a* 의식적인, 의도적인
- attentiveness *n* 주의함, 주의력
- at best 기껏해야, 잘해야
- eliminate *v* 제거하다
- deliberation *n* 숙고, 심의
- insight *n* 통찰
- infant *n* 유아
- character *n* 인격, 성격
- rationally *ad* 이성적으로
- sound *a* 건전한
- effectively *ad* 효과적으로

195 답 ④

출제 의도 파악하기

① 대명사의 수 일치 ② 형식상의 주어와 내용상의 주어
③ 분사구문의 태 ④ 관계대명사 which의 쓰임
⑤ 분사의 태

정답풀이

④ which 이하가 주어, 동사, 목적어를 모두 갖춘 완전한 구조를 이루고 있으므로 관계대명사 which는 적절하지 않다. a way를 선행사로 하여 관계절에서 부사구 역할을 하도록 in which로 고쳐야 한다.

오답풀이

① 앞에 나온 your favorite comedy를 지칭하므로 단수 대명사 it은 적절하다.
② 형식상의 주어 it에 대한 내용상의 주어로 to sense가 이끄는 to부정사구가 적절하게 쓰였다.
③ as many comedians find는 삽입절이고, travelling 이하는 The same joke를 의미상의 주어로 하는 분사구문이다. The same joke와 travel이 능동의 관계이므로 현재분사 travelling은 적절하게 쓰였다.
⑤ People ~ laugh가 주절이고 when ~ cue는 「주어+be동사」가 생략된 부사절이다. 문맥상 생략된 부사절의 주어는 주절의 주어와 같은 people이며, 사람들에게 신호가 '주어질' 때라는 수동의 의미이므로 when people are given ~에서 주어 people과 be동사 are가 생략되고 when given ~이 된 것이므로 과거분사 given은 적절하다.

전문해석

사람들이 유머에 반응하는 방식에는 강한 사회적 측면이 있다. 경직된 얼굴을 하고 있는 사람들 앞에서 여러분이 가장 좋아하는 코미디를 보게 되면, 이런 상황은 여러분으로 하여금 그 코미디가 아주 재미있다고 느끼지 못하게 할 수 있다. 다른 사람들이 유머에 반응하는 것을 느끼는 것이 중요하기 때문에 TV나 라디오 코미디에서 '녹음된 웃음'이 사용된다. 많은 코미디언들이 알게 되듯이 같은 유머라도 한 장소에서 다른 장소로 이동하면서 어떤 상황에서는 훌륭하게 전달되지만 다른 상황에서는 퇴색될 수 있다. 언어의 다른 측면들과 마찬가지로 유머도 사람들이 단체에 충성심을 보여 주는 한 가지 방법이다. 어떤 사람이 뭔가 우스운 것을 말하겠다는 의도에 대한 신호를 보내면 듣는 사람들은 즉시 웃을 준비가 되어 있다. 사람들은 심지어 자신들이 농담을 이해하는가에 상관없이 이런 종류의 신호가 주어질 때 종종 웃는다.

구문풀이

2행 If you watch your favorite comedy in the presence of people [remaining straight-faced], it can **stop** you **from finding it** so **funny**.

: [ ]는 people을 수식하는 현재분사구이다. 첫 번째 it은 앞 절의 내용을 가리키고, 두 번째 it은 your favorite comedy를 가리킨다. 「stop A from *doing*」은 'A가 ~하지 못하도록 막다'라는 의미이고, 「find+목적어+목적격보어」는 '~을 …하다고 알다[느끼다]'의 의미이다.

어휘풀이

- aspect *n* 모습, 양상, 국면
- respond *v* 반응하다
- in the presence of ~가 참석한 가운데
- straight-faced *a* 경직된 표정을 지은
- brilliantly *ad* 훌륭하게
- context *n* 상황, 문맥
- venue *n* 장소, 행위[사건]의 현장, 발생지
- allegiance *n* 충성, 성실
- intention *n* 의도
- cue *n* 신호, 실마리
- regardless of ~와 상관없이
- get the joke 농담을 이해하다

196 답 ④

출제 어휘 확인하기

(A) advance 나아가다, 전진하다 / quit 그만두다, 포기하다
(B) falsehood 기만, 거짓말 / honesty 정직
(C) disguise 숨기다, 위장하다 / reveal 드러내다, 보여 주다

정답풀이

(A) 우리의 직무가 쓸모없고 해롭다는 것을 깨달았을 때 심각한 재정적 어려움을 감수하면서 내릴 수 있는 거의 유일한 선택권이라고 했으므로 quit(그만두다)이 적절하다. [advance 나아가다, 전진하다]
(B) 앞에서 물질적으로는 편안하게 해 주지만 감정적으로는 비참하게 하는 일보다 기분이 좋다고 느끼는 일을 해야 한다고 했는데, 이어지는 나치 죽음의 수용소에서 일한 직원들의 예에서 알 수 있듯이 그러한 결정은 자신이 하는 일에 대한 자신의 감정에 '솔직'해야 이루어질 수 있다. 따라서 honesty(정직)가 적절하다. [falsehood 기만, 거짓말]
(C) 그저 일을 하는 것일 뿐이라는 변명으로 나쁜 일을 하는 것에 대한 책임을 '숨기기는' 쉽다는 것이 자연스러우므로 disguise가 적절하다. [reveal 드러내다, 보여 주다]

전문해석

우리가 인정하고 싶지 않다고 해도, 대부분의 장애물을 극복하는 능력은 우리의 수중에 있다. 우리의 일이 의미 없거나, 지루하거나, 스트레스를 준다면, 우리는 가족, 사회 혹은 역사를 탓할 수 없다. 확실히 우리의 직무가 쓸모없거나 실제로 해롭다고 깨달을 때 선택권은 거의 없다. 아마 유일한 선택은 가능한 한 빨리 (A) 그만두는 것일 텐데, 심각한 재정적 어려움의 대가를 치르고서라도 말이다. 삶의 가장 중요한 것의 측면에서, 우리를 물질적으로 편안하게 만들지만 감정적으로 비참하게 만들지도 모르는 어떤 것을 하는 것보다는 기분이 좋다고 느끼는 어떤 것을 하는 것이 언제나 더 좋다. 그런 결정은 악명 높을 정도로 어렵고 스스로에 대한 커다란 (B) 정직을 필요로 한다. 독일 태생의 미국 정치 이론가 Hannah Arendt가 Adolf Eichmann과 나치 죽음의 수용소에서 일하던 다른 사람들에 관해 보여 준 것처럼, '나는 그저 여기에서 일을 하고 있을 뿐이다.'라는 변명으로 심지어 수천 명에 대한 냉혈한 학살의 책임을 (C) 숨기기는 쉽다.

구문풀이

4행 Admittedly, there are few options [when we realize {that our job is useless or actually harmful}].

: [ ]는 접속사 when이 이끄는 부사절이며, { }는 그 안에서 realize의 목적어 역할을 하는 명사절이다.

어휘풀이

- overcome *v* 극복하다
- obstacle *n* 장애(물)
- admittedly *ad* 확실히, 틀림없이
- option *n* 선택(권)
- financial *a* 재정적인
- hardship *n* 어려움, 고난
- bottom line 가장 중요한 것
- materially *ad* 물질적으로
- miserable *a* 비참한
- notoriously *ad* 악명 높게
- extermination camp 죽음의 수용소
- responsibility *n* 책임
- cold-blooded *a* 냉혈한
- excuse *n* 변명

197 답 ⑤

출제 의도 파악하기

① 대동사 ② to부정사의 쓰임
③ 접속사 whether의 쓰임 ④ 분사구문의 태
⑤ 문장의 구조 파악

정답풀이

⑤ 관계절 who used ~ the Web의 수식을 받는 핵심 주어 Employees에 연결되는 동사가 와야 할 자리이므로 준동사 remaining을 본동사 remained 로 바꿔 써야 한다.

오답풀이

① 반복되는 동사구 didn't quit sooner를 대신하는 대동사로 didn't를 쓴 것은 적절하다.
② to apply는 '~하기 위해서'의 뜻을 나타내는 to부정사의 부사적 용법으로 적절하게 쓰였다.
③ tested의 목적어로 쓰인 명사절을 이끌면서 '~인지 어떤지'의 뜻을 나타내는 접속사 whether는 적절하다.
④ 분사구문의 의미상 주어인 He가 '생각하는' 주체이므로 능동의 의미를 나타내는 현재분사 assuming은 적절하다.

전문해석

얼마 전 경제학자 Michael Housman은 고객 상담을 하는 일부 직원들이 왜 다른 직원들보다 더 오래 근무하는지 밝히기 위한 프로젝트를 수행한 적이 있다. Housman은 과거에 이직이 잦았던 직원들이 더 빨리 그만둘 것이라고 생각했지만 그들은 그렇지 않았다. 과거 5년 동안 다섯 차례 이직을 한 직원들의 경우 5년 동안 같은 직장을 다닌 사람들보다 직장을 그만두는 확률이 더 높지 않았다. 다른 단서들을 찾다가 그는 연구팀이 그 직원들이 직장에 지원하기 위해 컴퓨터에 로그인을 할 때 어떤 인터넷 브라우저를 사용했는지에 관한 정보를 확보했다는 사실을 알게 됐다. 그는 즉흥적으로 그 선택이 사직과 연관되어 있을지 여부를 조사했다. 그는 브라우저 선택의 선호는 순전히 취향의 문제일 뿐이라고 생각했기 때문에 상관관계가 있으리라고 기대하지 않았다. 그런데 조사 결과를 본 그는 깜짝 놀랐다. 조사 결과는 웹 검색을 위해 파이어폭스나 크롬을 사용한 직원들이 인터넷 익스플로러나 사파리를 사용한 사람들보다 재직 기간이 15퍼센트 더 길었음을 보여 주었다.

구문풀이

8행 [Hunting for other hints], he noticed [that his team had captured information about {which Internet browser employees had used <when they logged in to apply for their jobs>}].

: 첫 번째 [ ]는 부대상황을 나타내는 분사구문이다. 두 번째 [ ]는 문장의 동사 noticed의 목적어 역할을 하는 명사절이고, 그 안의 { }는 전치사 about의 목적어 역할을 하는 의문사절이며, < >는 부사절이다.

어휘풀이

- figure out ~을 이해하다, ~을 알아내다
- job-hopping *n* 직업을 자주 바꾸기
- hunt *v* 찾다, 찾아 보다
- on a whim 일시적 기분으로
- preference *n* 선호
- agent *n* 직원, 대리인
- quit *v* 그만두다, 사직[퇴직]하다
- apply for ~에 지원하다
- correlation *n* 상관관계
- stunned *a* 놀란

198 답 ③

출제 어휘 확인하기

①	minimum	최소한	↔	maximum(최대한)
②	follow	따라가다	↔	
③	close	가까운	↔	distant(먼)
④	the same	똑같은	↔	different(다른)
⑤	mistakenly	잘못하여, 실수로	↔	

정답풀이

③ 앞에서는 문맥과 내용이 적절히 결합하지 않은 텍스트를 읽는 독자는 분투해야 한다고 했고, 글 끝부분에서는 문맥을 제공하지 못하는 작가는 모든 독자가 자신의 그림을 이해한다고 잘못 추정한다고 했으므로, 이런 경우에 작가의 원래 의도와 독자의 이해에는 일치하는 것이 '거의 없다'는 흐름이 되어야 한다. 따라서 원래 의도와 '가까운(close)' 일치를 지닐 것이라는 것은 적절하지 않으며 부정의 의미인 little(거의 없는) 정도로 바꿔 써야 한다.

오답풀이

① 맥락이 충분하면 독자는 전문 지식 없이도 작가의 의도에 근접할 수 있다고 했으므로, 텍스트를 읽는 노력이 '최소한(minimum)'이라는 것은 적절하다.
② 문맥이 잘 제공되는 글에 관해 설명하는 흐름이며 독자가 작가의 손에 자신을 맡긴다고 했으므로, 작가가 이끄는 곳으로 '따라간다(follows)'는 것은 적절하다.
④ 시대에 뒤떨어진 번역으로 된 텍스트를 읽을 때는 언어를 최신의 것으로 가져와야 하고 텍스트와 분투해야 한다는 내용에 이어서, 참조의 틀이 없이 잘못 제시된 내용에 관해서 말하는 부분이므로 텍스트를 이해하고자 할 때 '똑같은(the same)' 분투의 경험을 제공할 수 있다는 것은 적절하다.
⑤ 문맥을 제공하지 못하는 작가의 문제점을 지적하는 문장이므로, 작가가 자신의 그림(= 글)을 모든 독자가 공유한다고 '잘못(mistakenly)' 추정한다는 것은 적절하다.

전문해석

충분한 맥락이 제공된 경우, 독자는 전문 지식 없이도 잘 만들어진 텍스트에 다가가 작가가 의도한 것과 충분히 근접한 것을 가지고 갈 수 있다. 텍스트는 공공 문서가 되어서 독자는 (a) 최소한의 노력과 분투로 그것을 읽을 수 있으며, 독자의 경험은 프로이트가 '고르게 주의를 기울이기'의 (전략적) 배치로 묘사한 것에 가까워진다. 독자는 작가의 손에 자신을 맡기고(몇몇 사람들이 디킨스나 톨스토이 같은 위대한 소설가들과 이 경험을 했다) 작가가 이끄는 곳으로 (b) 따라간다. 현실의 세계는 사라지고 허구의 세계가 그것을 대신했다. 이제 다른 쪽 극단을 고려해 보자. 문맥과 내용이 적절하게 결합하지 않은 제대로 만들어지지 않은 텍스트의 경우, 우리는 이해하려고 분투해야 하며, 작가가 의도한 것에 대한 우리의 이해는 아마도 그의 원래 의도와 (c) 가까운(→ 거의 없는) 일치를 지닐 것이다. 시대에 뒤떨어진 번역은 우리에게 이런 경험을 줄 것인데, 우리가 읽을 때 우리는 언어를 최신의 것으로 가져와야 하고, 이해는 텍스트와의 꽤 격렬한 분투의 대가로만 오게 된다. 참조의 틀이 없이 잘못 제시된 내용은 (d) 똑같은 경험을 제공할 수 있는데, 우리는 단어를 보지만 그것들이 어떻게 받아들여져야 하는지에 대해서 이해하지 못한다. 문맥을 제공하지 못하는 작가는 세상에 대한 자신의 그림을 모든 독자가 공유한다고 (e) 잘못 추정하고, 적절한 참조의 틀을 제공하는 것이 글을 쓰는 일의 중대한 부분이라는 것을 깨닫지 못한다.

구문풀이

1행 To the extent [that sufficient context has been provided], the reader can come to a well-crafted text with no expert knowledge and come away with a good approximation of [what has been intended by the author].

: 첫 번째 [ ]는 the extent를 수식하는 관계절이다. 두 번째 [ ]는 앞에 있는 전치사 of의 목적어로 쓰인 명사절로, what은 선행사를 포함하는 관계대명사이다.

어휘풀이

- to the extent that ~할 경우에
- approximation *n* 근접(한 것)
- fictive *a* 허구의
- happily *ad* 적절하게
- out-of-date *a* 시대에 뒤떨어진, 구식의
- translation *n* 번역
- at the price of ~을 대가로, ~을 희생하여
- reference *n* 참조
- critical *a* 중대한, 결정적인
- come away with ~을 가지고 떠나다
- vanish *v* 사라지다
- extreme *n* 극단
- correspondence *n* 일치, 관련성
- up to date 최신의
- mistakenly *ad* 잘못하여

199 ③	200 ②	201 ④	202 ⑤	203 ⑤
204 ③	205 ②	206 ⑤		

199 답 ③

❶ 분사형 형용사	❷ 대명사의 수 일치
❸ 병렬구조	❹ 부사의 쓰임
❺ 관계대명사 that의 쓰임	

정답풀이

③ cuckoo birds를 선행사로 하는 which 이하의 관계절에서 leaves는 문맥상 and 앞의 동사 lay와 병렬구조를 이루며 주격 관계대명사 which에 대한 술어 역할을 해야 한다. 따라서 복수형 동사 leave로 고쳐야 한다.

오답풀이

① '의심하지 않는'이라는 의미로 이어지는 명사구 "normal" bee를 수식하는 분사형 형용사 unsuspecting의 쓰임은 적절하다.
② its는 it(= 부화한 '도둑'의 새끼 벌)을 가리키는 소유격 대명사로 적절하게 쓰였다.
④ 동사 are called를 수식하는 부사의 비교급 more technically의 쓰임은 적절하다.
⑤ an organism을 선행사로 하며 관계절에서 주어 역할을 하는 관계대명사로 that은 적절하게 쓰였다.

전문해석

대부분의 벌들은 꽃을 찾아가고 꽃가루를 모으면서 하루를 보내지만, 어떤 벌들은 다른 벌들의 힘든 노동을 이용한다. 도둑질하는 이런 벌들은 이상한 낌새를 못 챈 (숙주라고 알려진) '보통' 벌의 집으로 슬며시 들어가서 숙주 벌이 자신의 새끼를 위해 모으고 있는 꽃가루 덩어리 근처에 알을 낳은 다음 슬그머니 도로 나온다. 그 도둑의 알이 부화하면, 그것은 숙주의 새끼를 죽이고 나서 그것의 희생자를 위해 마련된 꽃가루를 먹는다. 가끔 탁란(托卵) 동물로 불리는 이 벌들은 뻐꾸기 벌이라고도 불리는데, 그것들이 다른 새의 둥지에 알을 낳고 그 알을 그 새가 기르도록 두는 뻐꾸기와 유사하기 때문이다. 그것들은 더 전문적으로는 'cleptoparasite'라고 불린다. 'clepto'는 그리스어로 '도둑'을 의미하고 'cleptoparasite'라는 말은 구체적으로 말해 먹이를 훔침으로써 다른 것에 기생하는 생물을 가리킨다. 이 경우에 그 cleptoparasite는 숙주가 애써서 얻은 꽃가루 비축물을 먹고 산다.

구문풀이

3행 These thieving bees [sneak into the nest of an unsuspecting "normal" bee (known as the host)], [lay an egg near the pollen mass {being gathered by the host bee for her own offspring}], and then [sneak back out].

: 세 개의 [ ]는 주어 These thieving bees에 연결되어 술어 역할을 한다. { }는 the pollen mass를 수식하는 과거분사구이다.

어휘풀이

- pollen *n* 꽃가루
- thieve *v* 도둑질하다
- unsuspecting *a* 이상한 낌새를 못 챈, 의심하지 않는
- host *n* (기생 동물의) 숙주
- refer to *A* as *B* *A*를 *B*라고 부르다
- take advantage of ~을 이용하다
- sneak *v* 살금살금 움직이다
- offspring *n* 새끼(들)
- cuckoo *n* 뻐꾸기

- technically *ad* 전문적으로는, 엄밀히 말해
- specifically *ad* 구체적으로 말하면, 즉
- organism *n* 생물, 유기체
- live off ~에 기생하다[얻혀살다]
- hard-earned *a* 애써서 얻은
- store *n* 비축물, 저장

200 답 ②

① realize	깨닫다	↔	
② forbid	~하지 못하게 하다	↔	allow(허용하다)
③ sincere	진실한	↔	insincere(진실되지 못한)
④ suspicious	의심스러워하는	↔	
⑤ break	어기다	↔	obey(따르다, 준수하다)

정답풀이

② 자신에 대한 타인의 불신은 자기 성찰을 하게 하여 타인의 신임을 받을 만한 자격이 더 생기도록 행동하게 한다고 했으므로, 직무의 자기 몫을 수행하지 '못하게 한다'는 것은 적절하지 않다. forbid(~하지 못하게 하다)를 motivate(~하게끔 동기를 부여하다) 정도로 바꿔 써야 한다.

오답풀이

① 공유된 책무를 동료들이 자신에게 맡기지 않는 것을 '깨달은(realizes)' 직원이 성찰을 통하여 자신이 이전에 잘못했던 분야를 알 수 있다는 것은 적절하다.
③ 불신이 가져올 수 있는 단점을 설명하는 흐름이므로, 신뢰를 받을 만한 사람이 되려는 노력을 '진실하게 하는(sincere)' 사람을 불신한다면 혼란을 줄 수 있다는 것은 적절하다.
④ 신뢰를 얻기 위해 자신의 외출 계획에 대해 솔직하게 말하는 십 대 소녀를 '의심하고' 불신하는 부모에 대한 예시를 제시하는 흐름이므로 suspicious는 적절하다.
⑤ 자신의 계획에 대해 솔직한 소녀가 규칙을 '어기고' 있지 않더라도 그녀를 불신하는 부모의 태도에 의해 그녀의 정체성이 손상된다는 흐름이 되도록 부정어 not과 함께 쓰인 breaking은 적절하다.

전문해석

신임을 얻지 못한다는 인식은 가끔 자기 성찰에 필요한 동기를 제공할 수 있다. 직장에서 동료들이 공유된 책무를 자신에게 맡기지 않고 있다는 사실을 ① 깨달은 직원은 성찰을 통하여 자신이 지속적으로 다른 사람들을 실망하게 했거나 이전의 책무들을 이행하지 못했던 분야를 발견할 수 있다. 그러면 그녀에 대한 다른 사람들의 불신은, 그녀가 그들의 신임을 받을 자격이 더 생기게 하는 쪽으로 그녀가 직무의 자기 몫을 수행하지 ② 못하게 할(→ (하게끔) 동기를 부여할) 수 있다. 하지만 신뢰할 만하고 믿을 만한 사람이 되려는 노력을 ③ 진실하게 하는 사람에 대한 불신은 혼란을 줄 수 있고, 그녀로 하여금 자신의 인식을 의심하고 자신을 불신하게 할 수 있다. 예를 들면, 밤에 외출할 때 ④ 의심스러워하며 믿지 않는 부모를 가진 십 대 소녀를 생각해 보라. 비록 그녀가 자신의 계획에 대해 솔직해 왔고 합의된 규칙은 어떤 것도 ⑤ 어기고 있지 않다고 해도, 존경할 만한 도덕적 주체로서의 그녀의 정체성은 속이는 것과 배신을 예상하는 널리 스며 있는 부모의 태도 때문에 손상된다.

구문풀이

2행 An employee [who realizes she isn't being trusted by her co-workers with shared responsibilities at work] might, upon reflection, identify areas [where she has consistently let others down or failed to follow through on previous commitments].

: 첫 번째 [ ]는 핵심 주어인 An employee를, 두 번째 [ ]는 might identify의 목적어인 areas를 수식하는 관계절이다.

10행 But [distrust of one {who is sincere in her efforts to be a trustworthy and dependable person}] can be disorienting and might **cause** her [to doubt her own perceptions] and [to distrust herself].

: 첫 번째 [ ]는 문장의 주어이고, 동사인 can be disorienting과 might cause가 주어에 공통으로 연결되어 있다. { }는 one을 수식하는 관계절이다. 「cause+목적어+to부정사(~가 …하도록 유발하다)」 구문에서 and로 연결된 두 번째와 세 번째 [ ]가 병렬구조를 이룬다.

어휘풀이

- awareness *n* 인식
- incentive *n* 동기, 혜택
- identify *v* 찾다, 발견하다
- let down ~을 실망하게 하다
- follow through on ~을 이행[완수]하다
- commitment *n* 약속, 책무
- perception *n* 인식
- agreed-upon *a* 합의된
- deceit *n* 속이는 것, 사기
- distrust *v* 신임하지 않다 *n* 불신
- self-reflection *n* 자기 성찰
- consistently *ad* 지속적으로
- disorienting *a* 혼란스럽게 만드는
- suspicious *a* 의심스러워하는
- undermine *v* 손상시키다, 훼손하다
- betrayal *n* 배신, 폭로

201 답 ④

출제 의도 파악하기

❶ 분사의 태		❷ 관계부사 where의 쓰임	
❸ 병렬구조		❹ 문장의 구조 파악	
❺ 부사의 쓰임			

정답풀이

④ would add가 문장의 술어 동사이고, 문맥상 Change ~ centers가 주어를 구성해야 한다. 따라서 이어지는 anything을 목적어로 취할 수 있도록 Change를 동명사 Changing 또는 to부정사 To change로 바꿔 써야 한다.

오답풀이

① when it is done에서 주어 it(= body monitoring)과 be동사 is가 생략된 형태이다. body monitoring은 '이루어지는' 대상에 해당하므로 수동의 의미를 나타내는 과거분사 done은 알맞다.
② cases를 수식하는 관계절을 유도하는 관계사의 자리이며, 뒤에 주어(long-term monitoring)와 동사(is required)를 갖춘 완전한 구조의 절이 이어지고 있으므로 관계부사 where는 알맞다.
③ Public health care를 공통의 주어로 하는 첫 번째 동사 is와 but으로 연결되어 병렬구조를 이루므로 is는 알맞다.
⑤ 술어 동사 could be read and analyzed를 수식하는 부사 remotely의 쓰임은 적절하다.

전문해석

신체 모니터링은 전신 피부 접촉으로 이루어질 때 가장 정확하다. 이것은 신체에 착용하는 장치에 분명한 이점인데, 특히 장기간 관찰이 필요한 경우에 그러하다. 보건 서비스는 전 세계적으로 큰 사업이다. 공공 의료는 대개 즉각적인 대량 주문이 있을 때 당연히 더 매력적이지만, 대부분의 나라에서는 엄격한 규제를 받는다. 의사들은 당국자들의 승인을 받는 데 관련된 행정 업무의 양으로 인해 새로운 장치나 절차를 채택하는 것을 꺼린다. 병원과 공공 의료 센터의 절차상 무언가를 변경하는 것은 흔히 일을 너무 많이 하는 직원들의 스트레스만 가중시킬 뿐이다. 반면 만약 개인이 신체에 착용하는 도구를 원격으로 읽고 분석할 수 있다면 의사와 환자 모두 덜 일상적인 방문으로 시간과 돈을 절약할 수 있을 것이다. 민간 부문이 아마 더 실행 가능하겠지만, 공공 부문에서와 꼭 마찬가지로 그곳에서 사용되는 어느 신기술이라도 당국자의 승인을 받아야 한다.

구문풀이

8행 Doctors are reluctant to adopt **either** new devices **or** procedures for the amount of administrative work [involved in getting them **approved** by officials].

: 'A와 B 둘 중 하나'라는 뜻의 「either A or B」 구문이 쓰였다. [ ]는 administrative work를 수식하는 분사구이다. approved는 getting의 목적격보어인데, 목적어인 them(= either new devices or procedures)이 '승인받는' 대상이므로 과거분사 형태가 쓰였다.

어휘풀이

- monitoring *n* (추적) 관찰, 모니터링
- contact *n* 접촉
- body-worn device 신체에 착용하는 장치
- tempting *a* 매력적인
- strictly *ad* 엄격하게
- reluctant *a* 꺼리는, 주저하는
- procedure *n* 절차, 방법
- approve *v* 승인하다
- analyze *v* 분석하다
- routine *a* 일상적인
- public sector 공공 부문[분야]
- accurate *a* 정확한
- instant *a* 즉각적인
- regulate *v* 규제하다
- adopt *v* 채택하다
- administrative *a* 행정의, 관리의
- official *n* 당국자, 관계자
- remotely *ad* 원격으로, 멀리서
- private sector 민간 부문[분야]

202 답 ⑤

출제 어휘 확인하기

①	uncertain	불확실한	↔	certain(확실한)
②	weakness	약점	↔	strength(강점)
③	vulnerable	취약한	↔	invulnerable(상처를 입힐 수 없는)
④	advantage	이점	↔	disadvantage(불리한 점, 약점)
⑤	laboriously	힘들게	↔	easily(쉽게)

정답풀이

⑤ 순록이 물에서 갖는 취약점이 인간에게는 사냥의 이점이 된다는 내용이 앞에 나왔으므로, 배를 이용해 '쉽게' 따라잡아 도살한 먹잇감에 대한 내용이 연결되는 것이 자연스럽다. 따라서 laboriously(힘들게)는 적절하지 않으며 easily 정도로 바꿔 써야 한다.

오답풀이

① 순록이 육지에서는 빠르게 움직이기 때문에 이상적인 상황에서조차도 사냥이 쉽지 않다는 문맥이므로 '불확실한(uncertain)' 일이라는 것은 적절하다.
② 순록이 수영을 잘하지 못하는 것을 인간이 무자비하게 이용한다는 내용이 이어지고 있으므로, 순록에게 '약점(weakness)'이 있다는 것은 적절하다.
③ 물에 떠 있는 동안 코와 뿔을 노출시키며 천천히 움직인다는 것은 공격받기 쉬운 '취약한' 대상이 되는 것이므로 vulnerable은 적절하다.
④ 물에서 천천히 움직이는 순록과 달리 인간이 배를 타고 빠르게 이동할 수 있는 것은 사냥하는 데 '이점'이 되므로 advantage는 적절하다.

전문해석

유럽 최초의 '호모 사피엔스'는 주로 큰 사냥감, 특히 순록을 먹고 살았다. 이상적인 상황에서조차도, 이런 빠른 동물을 창이나 활과 화살로 사냥하는 것은 ① 불확실한 일이다. 그러나 순록에게는 인류가 무자비하게 이용할 ② 약점이 있었는데, 그것은 순록이 수영을 잘 못했다는 것이었다. 순록은 물에 떠 있는 동안 코를 물 위로 내놓으려고 애쓰면서 가지진 뿔을 높이 쳐들고 천천히 움직이기 때문에 특히 ③ 취약하다. 어느 시점에선가, 석기 시대의 한 천재가 수면 위를 미끄러지듯이 갈 수 있게 함으로써 자신이 얻을 엄청난 사냥의 ④ 이점을 깨닫고 최초의 배를 만들었다. ⑤ 힘들게(→ 쉽게) 따라잡아서 도살한 먹잇감을 일단 배 위로 끌어 올리면, 사체를 부족이

사는 곳으로 가지고 가는 것은 육지에서보다는 배로 훨씬 더 쉬웠을 것이다. 인류가 이런 장점을 다른 물품에 적용하는 데는 긴 시간이 걸리지 않았을 것이다.

구문풀이

9행 At some point, a Stone Age genius [realized the enormous hunting advantage {he would gain by being able to glide over the water's surface}], and [built the first boat].

: and에 의해 연결된 두 개의 [ ]는 주어 a Stone Age genius에 이어지는 동사구이다. { }는 the enormous hunting advantage를 수식하는 관계절이다.

어휘풀이

- live on ~을 먹고 살다
- game *n* 사냥감
- reindeer *n* 순록
- ideal *a* 이상적인
- spear *n* 창
- bow *n* 활
- mercilessly *ad* 무자비하게, 인정사정없이
- afloat *a* (물에) 뜬
- vulnerable *a* 공격받기 쉬운, 취약한
- antler *n* (사슴의) 가지진 뿔
- glide *v* 미끄러지듯 가다
- overtake *v* 따라잡다
- tribal *a* 부족의, 종족의
- apply *v* 적용하다

203 답 ⑤

출제 의도 파악하기

❶ 복합관계형용사 whatever의 쓰임	❷ 「so ~ that ....」 구문
❸ to부정사의 쓰임	❹ 재귀대명사
❺ 병렬구조	

정답풀이

⑤ to부정사구인 to overcome과 문맥상 병렬구조를 이루어 very few efforts를 수식해야 하므로 avoided를 to avoid 또는 to가 생략된 avoid로 바꿔 써야 한다.

오답풀이

① 명사 conclusions를 수식하는 동시에 뒤에 이어지는 동사 wish의 목적어가 빠진 불완전한 절을 이끌어야 하므로 복합관계형용사로 쓰인 whatever는 적절하다. 이때 whatever는 '어떤 ~이든'이라는 뜻을 나타낸다.

② 앞에 위치한 「so+부사」 형태의 so long과 연결되어 '너무 ~하여 …하다'의 의미를 나타내는 「so ~ that ....」 구문을 이루므로 접속사 that은 적절하다.

③ 앞에 있는 명사구 a desire를 수식하여 '벗어나려는 욕구'라는 의미를 나타내고 있으므로 to부정사 to be는 알맞다.

④ 문맥상 puts의 동작 주체는 he이고, 목적어도 같은 대상이므로 목적어 자리에 쓰인 재귀대명사 himself는 적절하다.

전문해석

우리의 일상생활에서 우리는 사람들이 자신의 경험으로부터 원하는 어떤 결론이든 도출하는 것을 관찰할 수 있다. 같은 실수를 반복하는 사람이 있다. 만약 여러분이 그의 실수를 그에게 납득시키는 데 성공한다면, 그는 여러 가지 방식 중 하나로 반응할 것이다. 그는 이렇게 말할지도 모른다. "당신이 옳아요. 저는 다음에 더 잘 알게 될 거예요." 이것은 흔한 반응이 아니다. 그는 너무 오랫동안 같은 실수를 해서 그 습관을 고치는 것이 불가능할 것이라고 주장할 가능성이 더 많다. 그렇지 않으면 그는 자신의 실수에 대해 부모님이나 교육을 탓할 것이다. 그는 아무도 그를 돌보지 않았다거나, 아이처럼 응석받이로 자랐다고 불평할 수도 있다. 그가 어떤 변명을 하든, 그는 한 가지를 드러내는데, 그것은 더 이상의 책임에서 벗어나고 싶은 욕구이다. 이런 식으로 그는 자신의 행동을 정당화하고 그 자신은 비판을 모면하려 한다. 그 사람 자신은 결코 책임이 없다는 것이다. 그가 하기로 한 것을 성취하지 못한다면 그것은 항상 다른 누군가의 잘못이다. 그러한 개인들이 간과하고 있는 것은 그들 자신이 자

신들의 잘못을 극복하려거나 실수를 반복하기를 피하려는 노력을 거의 하지 않았다는 사실이다.

구문풀이

7행 He is more likely to protest [that he has been making the same mistake for **so** long **that it** would be impossible {to break the habit}].

: [ ]는 to protest의 목적어로 쓰인 명사절이다. 「so ~ that ....」은 '너무 ~해서 …하다'의 의미이다. it은 형식상의 주어이며 { }로 표시된 to부정사구가 내용상의 주어이다.

어휘풀이

- draw a conclusion 결론을 도출하다
- succeed in ~하는 데 성공하다
- convince *v* 납득시키다, 확신시키다
- protest *v* 주장하다, 항의하다
- be relieved of ~에서 벗어나다
- justify *v* 정당화하다
- above criticism 비판할 여지가 없는
- be to blame 책임이 있다, 책임을 져야 하다
- overlook *v* 간과하다

204 답 ③

출제 어휘 확인하기

(A)	comfort	편안함, 안락함	/ risk	위험
(B)	much	많은	/ little	거의 없는
(C)	remain	남아 있다	/ resolve	해결하다

정답풀이

(A) 놀이는 먹이를 찾아다니는 데 쓰일 수 있는 에너지와 시간을 앗아가므로 대가가 따를 수 있다고 했고, 이후에 물놀이를 하다가 잡아먹힌 어린 남방물개들의 예를 들고 있으므로, 어린 동물이 노는 동안 '위험(risk)'에 처할 수 있다는 것이 적절하다. [comfort 편안함, 안락함]

(B) 놀이에 따르는 대가와 대조적으로 놀이에 관한 많은 기능들이 제의되어 왔다고 했으나, 이어지는 내용에서 미어캣의 행동을 추적한 연구들이 미어캣이 다 자랐을 때 성장기 놀이의 영향을 증명할 수 없었다고 했다. 따라서 실험적 증거가 '거의 없다(little)'고 하는 것이 적절하다. [much 많은]

(C) 동물들에 있어 실험적 증거가 거의 없다고 했고 놀이의 영향에 관한 해답은 다수의 요인을 포함할 가능성이 높다고 했으므로 미스터리로 '남아 있다(remains)'고 하는 것이 적절하다. [resolve 해결하다]

전문해석

놀이는 먹이를 찾아다니는 데 쓰일 수 있는 에너지와 시간을 앗아가기 때문에 대가가 따를 수 있다. 노는 동안 어린 동물은 큰 (A) 위험에 처할 수 있다. 예를 들면, 바다사자들에게 먹힌 어린 남방물개들 중 86퍼센트가 잡힐 때 다른 물개들과 물놀이를 하는 중이었다. 이러한 대가와 대조적으로, 사냥 혹은 싸움과 같은 다 자란 동물의 행동 및 운동과 사교 기술을 발달시키기 위한 연습을 포함하여, 놀이에 있어 많은 기능들이 제의되어 왔다. 하지만 이러한 이론들에 대해 동물들에 있어 실험적 증거는 (B) 거의 없다. 예를 들어, 미어캣의 성장기 놀이와 다 자랐을 때의 행동을 추적한 상세한 연구들은 싸움 놀이가 다 자랐을 때의 싸우는 능력에 영향을 주었다는 것을 증명할 수 없었다. 그러므로 매우 많은 동물 종에 걸친 놀이의 지속은 미스터리로 (C) 남아 있다. 해답은 다양한 다수의 요인을 포함할 가능성이 높으며, 우리가 '놀이'라고 일컫는 것 자체가 그러하듯 여러 종에게 있어 꽤 다를 것이다.

구문풀이

11행 For example, detailed studies [which tracked juvenile play and adult behaviour of meerkats] couldn't prove [that play–fighting influenced fighting ability as an adult].

: 첫 번째 [ ]는 detailed studies를 수식하는 관계절이고, 두 번째 [ ]는 couldn't prove의 목적어로 쓰인 명사절이다.

어휘풀이

- costly *a* 대가가 따르는, 비용이 드는
- sea lion 바다사자
- motor *a* 운동의
- track *v* 추적하다
- persistence *n* 지속(성)
- multiple *a* 많은, 다수의
- seal *n* 물개
- propose *v* 제의하다, 제기하다
- interaction *n* 상호작용
- meerkat *n* 미어캣
- diverse *a* 다양한

205 답 ②

출제 의도 파악하기

❶ 접속사 that의 쓰임	❷ 관계대명사 which의 쓰임
❸ 동명사의 쓰임	❹ 접속사 that의 쓰임
❺ 가정법 과거 구문	

정답풀이

② 뒤에 주어(you)와 동사(were preparing)를 갖춘 완전한 구조의 절이 이어지고 있으므로 관계대명사 which는 쓸 수 없다. your childhood를 선행사로 하는 관계절을 이끌도록 「전치사+관계대명사」 형태인 in which 또는 관계부사 when이나 that으로 바꿔 써야 한다.

오답풀이

① 4형식 능동태 문장에서 taught의 간접목적어였던 You를 주어로 하여 수동태로 전환한 문장으로, 직접목적어인 that절이 수동태 동사 뒤에 이어진 구조이다. 따라서 이 목적절을 이끄는 명사절 접속사 that은 적절하다.
③ 전치사 from의 목적어 역할을 하면서 뒤에 목적어 your present moments를 취하는 동명사 living은 적절하게 쓰였다.
④ 뒤에 완전한 구조의 절이 이어지고, 그 절이 문맥상 a guarantee와 동격 관계를 이루므로 접속사 that은 적절하다.
⑤ 문맥상 현재 사실과 반대되는 가정을 나타내고 있으므로, 가정법 과거 구문에서 if절의 동사로 과거형인 weren't를 쓴 것은 적절하다.

전문해석

오래전에 여러분은 고등학교 리포트나 에세이를 쓰는 법을 배웠다. 여러분은 좋은 도입부와 잘 조직된 본문, 그리고 결론이 필요하다고 배웠다. 유감스럽게도, 여러분은 똑같은 논리를 삶에 적용했을지도 모르며, 삶이라는 일 전반을 리포트로 보게 되었는지도 모른다. 도입부는 여러분이 사람이 되기 위해 준비하던 어린 시절이었다. 본문은 어른의 삶인데, 여러분의 결론, 즉 은퇴와 해피엔딩을 준비하며 조직되고 계획되어 있다. 이 모든 조직적인 사고는 여러분이 현재의 순간을 사는 것을 막는다. 이 계획에 따라 사는 것은 모든 것이 항상 좋을 것이라는 보장을 의미한다. 보장은 흥분도, 위험도, 도전도 없다는 뜻이다. 게다가, 보장은 근거 없는 믿음이다. 여러분이 지구상에 사는 사람이고 그 체계가 그대로 유지되는 한, 여러분은 절대 보장을 가질 수 없다. 그리고 그것이 근거 없는 믿음이 아니더라도, 그것은 살기에 끔찍한 방법이 될 것이다. 확실성은 흥분과 성장을 제거한다.

구문풀이

15행 [As long as {you are a person on earth}, and {the system stays the same}], you can never have security.

: [ ]는 '~하는 한'이라는 의미의 as long as가 이끄는 조건 부사절이고, 그 안에 두 개의 절 { }가 and에 의해 병렬 연결되었다.

어휘풀이

- logic *n* 논리
- retirement *n* 퇴직
- in preparation for ~의 준비[대비]로
- imply *v* 암시하다

- guarantee *n* 보장
- myth *n* 근거 없는 믿음
- eliminate *v* 제거하다
- security *n* 보안, 보장
- certainty *n* 확실함

206 답 ⑤

출제 어휘 확인하기

①	overwhelm	압도하다	↔	
②	paralyze	마비시키다	↔	
③	effortlessly	힘들이지 않고	↔	
④	unnecessary	불필요한	↔	necessary(필요한)
⑤	maximum	최대한	↔	minimum(최소한)

정답풀이

⑤ 우리의 뇌는 불필요한 정보를 걸러낸다고 했고, 시각적, 청각적인 것을 포함한 너무 많은 일이 동시에 일어나는 혼란스러운 세상에 우리가 대처하는 방법이 분류라고 했는데, 이것은 우리에게 필요한 '최소한'만 처리할 수 있도록 뇌가 자동적으로 작용하는 것을 의미한다. 따라서 maximum(최대한)은 적절하지 않으며 반대 의미인 minimum(최소한) 정도로 바꿔 써야 한다.

오답풀이

① 세상은 무한한 정보와 자극으로 가득 차 있지만, 우리의 뇌는 우리가 보는 모든 것을 처리할 수 없다고 했으므로, 만약 그렇게 하려고 한다면 우리가 데이터에 '압도당할(overwhelmed)' 것이라는 흐름은 적절하다.
② 우리의 뇌가 자동적으로 우리 주변을 걸러내어 정보의 과부하에 걸리지 않도록 보호해 준다고 했으므로, 그렇지 않으면 정보의 과부하는 우리를 '마비시킬지도(paralyze)' 모른다는 것은 적절하다.
③ 길을 걸으면서 통화를 할 때 다른 여러 가지를 인지하고 행동할 수 있는 것은 뇌가 잠재적 장애물을 포함한 주변의 정보를 자동으로 걸러내기 때문이므로 '힘들이지 않고(effortlessly)' 할 수 있다는 것은 적절하다.
④ 개미, 미풍, 지나간 사람의 콧수염에 묻은 부스러기들은 우리가 길을 걸어가는 과정에서 걸러지는 정보들이므로 '불필요한(unnecessary)' 것들이라는 흐름은 적절하다.

전문해석

세상은 무한한 정보와 자극으로 가득 차 있지만, 우리의 뇌는 우리가 보는 모든 것을 처리할 수 없고, 처리해서도 안 된다. 만약 그렇게 한다면, 우리는 데이터에 (a) 압도당할 것이다. 타임스퀘어에 서 있다고 상상해 보라. 우리가 눈을 크게 뜨고 있다면, 눈은 동시에 수천 개의 물리적인 것, 즉 수십 개의 번쩍이는 광고판, 화려하게 불이 켜진 건물들, 택시들, 가게들 그리고 매일 같은 장소를 지나는 33만명의 사람들 중 일부와 마주하게 될 것이지만, 우리가 이 모든 것을 '보는' 것은 아니다. 우리의 뇌는 자동적으로 우리의 주변을 걸러내고, 그렇지 않으면 우리를 (b) 마비시킬지도 모르는 정보의 과부하로부터 우리를 보호하기 위해 적은 비율의 정보만 통과하도록 허락한다.

우리가 전화 통화를 하면서 길을 걸어갈 때 현대의 뇌가 무엇을 관리하는지 생각해 보라. 우리의 몸은 포장도로와 잠재적인 장애물을 지나가고 있다. 우리는 사람들이나 지표[랜드마크]를 지나칠 때 그것을 알아차리며, 아마도 그들과 상호작용하거나 어떤 것에 대한 마음속 메모를 만든다. 우리는 전화의 다른 쪽 끝에(수화기 저편에) 있는 사람과 대화하며, 말하고, 듣고, 응답한다. 그리고 (c) 힘들이지 않고 그 모든 것을 한다. 우리가 그럴 능력이 있는 것은 우리의 뇌가 보도에 있는 개미들, 나뭇가지에 부는 미풍, 방금 우리를 지나간 사람의 콧수염에 묻은 부스러기들과 같은 (d) 불필요한 것들을 걸러냈기 때문이다. 우리가 가는 길에 있는 모든 정보에 주의를 기울인다면, 우리는 우리의 현관문을 나설 수도 없을 것이다.

콜롬비아 대학의 심리학과와 교육학과 교수인 Barbara Tversky는 "세상은 매우

혼란스럽고, 너무 많은 일들이 시각적으로, 청각적으로, 모든 것이, 동시에 일어나고 있으며, 우리가 대처하는 방법은 분류에 의해서이다. 우리는 적절하게 행동하기 위해 필요한 (e) 최대한(→ 최소한)을 처리한다."라고 설명한다.

구문풀이

25행 If we **paid** attention to every piece of information in our path, we **wouldn't get** far past our front door.

: 현재 사실에 대한 가정을 나타내는 「If+주어+동사의 과거형 ~, 주어+조동사의 과거형+동사원형 …」 형태의 가정법 과거 구문이 쓰였다.

어휘풀이

- stimulation *n* 자극
- encounter *v* 마주하다, 만나다
- filter *v* 거르다, 여과하다
- paralyze *v* 마비시키다
- pavement *n* 포장도로
- effortlessly *ad* 어려움 없이, 힘들이지 않고
- breeze *n* 미풍
- mustache *n* 콧수염
- auditorily *ad* 청각적으로

- overwhelm *v* 압도하다
- billboard *n* 광고판
- overload *n* 과부하
- navigate *v* (길을) 지나가다, 항해하다
- landmark *n* 지표, 랜드마크
- crumb *n* 부스러기
- confusing *a* 혼란스러운
- categorize *v* 분류하다, 범주화하다

어법·어휘 모의고사 4회   본문 pp.164 ~ 167

207 ②	**208** ④	**209** ④	**210** ⑤	**211** ④
212 ⑤	**213** ③	**214** ④		

207 답 ②

출제 의도 파악하기

❶ 분사의 태	❷ 문장의 구조 파악
❸ 부사의 쓰임	❹ 대명사의 수 일치
❺ 관계대명사 what의 쓰임	

정답풀이

② This ~ of nature와 the everyday nature 이하를 비교하는 문장으로, 주어는 This ~ of nature이고 동사는 is이다. 또 다른 동사 waits는 필요하지 않으며, 문맥상 the everyday nature right outside their doors를 부가적으로 수식하는 분사구를 이끌도록 waits를 현재분사 waiting으로 바꾸어야 한다.

오답풀이

① filled 이하는 that fantastic, beautifully filmed place를 수식하는 분사구로, 의미상 과거분사 형태는 올바르다.
③ substantially는 비교급 more를 수식하는 부사로 올바르게 쓰였다.
④ their는 our children을 가리키는 소유격 대명사로 적절하게 쓰였다.
⑤ 전치사 of의 목적어 역할을 하는 명사절을 이끌면서 해당 절에서 called의 목적어 역할을 하는, 선행사를 포함하는 관계대명사 what의 쓰임은 적절하다.

전문해석

자연 속에서 그리고 자연과 함께하는 실제적이고 직접적인 경험의 부족은 많은 아이들이 자연 세계를 단지 추상적인 개념, 즉 멸종 위기의 열대 우림과 위험에 처한 북극곰으로 가득한, 매우 환상적이고 아름답게 영화화된 곳으로 여기게 해 왔다. 이렇게 과장되고 자주 허구화된 형태의 자연은 아이들의 방식과 속도로 발견되기를 기다리는 바로 문밖에 있는 일상의 자연보다 그들에게 더 현실적이지 않지만, 덜 현실적이지도 않다. 여덟 살 난 한 집단의 아이들이 흔한 야생의 종보다 애니메이션의 캐릭터를 상당히 더 많이 식별해 낼 수 있다는 것을 발견한 케임브리지 대학의 연구를 생각해 보라. 사람들은 자신의 환경에 대한 정보를 인식하고 분류하며 체계화하는 우리 아이들의 내재적인 능력, 즉 한때 다름 아닌 우리의 생존에 필수적이었던 능력이 서서히 퇴화하여 점점 더 가상화된 세계에서의 삶을 촉진하는지 궁금해한다. 그것은 모두 Robert Pyle이 처음으로 '경험의 소멸'이라고 부른 것의 일부이다.

구문풀이

9행 Consider the University of Cambridge study [which found {that a group of eight-year-old children was able to identify substantially more characters from animations than common wildlife species}].

: [ ]는 the University ~ study를 수식하는 관계절이고, 그 안의 { }는 found의 목적어 역할을 하는 명사절이다.

어휘풀이

- regard *A* as *B* *A*를 *B*로 간주하다[여기다]
- abstraction *n* 추상 개념
- overstate *v* 과장해서 말하다
- identify *v* 확인하다, 식별하다

- endangered *a* 멸종 위기에 처한
- fictionalize *v* 소설화[허구화]하다
- substantially *ad* 상당히

- inherent *a* 내재하는, 선천적인
- classify *v* 분류하다
- facilitate *v* 촉진[조장]하다, 용이하게 하다
- virtualize *v* 가상 현실로 바꾸다
- extinction *n* 소멸, 사멸, 멸종

208 답 ④

①	commercial	상업적인	↔	
②	ambition	야망	↔	
③	more	더	↔	less(덜)
④	decrease	감소하다	↔	increase(증가하다)
⑤	tangible	실체적인	↔	intangible(실체가 없는)

정답풀이

④ 텔레비전의 영향으로 아이들이 물질적인 것을 추구하게 된다는 것이 글의 요지이므로, 텔레비전에 대한 아이의 경험이 더 길수록, 물질적 견해가 '감소했다'는 것은 적절하지 않다. decreased를 반대 의미인 increased(증가하다)로 바꿔 써야 한다.

오답풀이

① 아이들의 사회적 현실에서 소비자로서의 역할이 중요한 부분이라고 했고, 텔레비전은 소비자로서의 아이들에게 분명한 영향을 미친다고 했으므로 아이들에게 노출되는 광고가 나오는 텔레비전을 '상업적인(commercial)' 기업이라고 한 것은 적절하다.

② 광고가 전혀 없을 때조차도 TV는 소비자로서의 아이들에게 영향을 미친다고 했으므로, 광고를 게재하지 않았던 BBC에만 접근할 수 있었던 영국 아이들이 TV가 없는 아이들보다 더 물질주의적인 '야망(ambitions)'을 가지고 있는 것으로 밝혀졌다는 것은 적절하다.

③ 텔레비전이 없는 청소년들은 그들이 무엇을 하고 있을지에 더 초점을 맞추었다고 했으므로, 이와 반대로 텔레비전을 본 아이들은 물질적인 것, 즉 무엇을 가질지에 '더(more)' 초점을 맞추었다는 것은 적절하다.

⑤ 텔레비전 광고와 같은 시각적 이미지가 물질주의적 소비로 이어진다는 문맥이므로 '실체적인(tangible)' 물건에 중점을 둔다는 것은 적절하다.

전문해석

아이들의 사회적 현실에서 중요한 부분은 소비자로서의 그들의 역할이다. 텔레비전은 미국과 같은 나라에서 소비자로서의 아이들에게 분명한 영향을 미치는데, 그곳에서 텔레비전은 거의 순전히 ① 상업적인 기업이고 텔레비전 광고는 아이들의 매체에 대한 노출의 중요한 부분이다. 그러나 텔레비전은 광고가 전혀 없을 때조차도 소비자로서의 아이들에게 영향을 미친다. 1950년대에 광고를 게재하지 않는 BBC에만 접근할 수 있었던 영국 아이들이 TV가 없는 아이들보다 더 물질주의적인 ② 야망을 가지고 있는 것으로 밝혀졌다. 예를 들어, 텔레비전을 본 청소년기의 남자아이들은 그들이 미래에 무엇을 '가질지'에 ③ 더 초점을 맞추었고, 텔레비전이 없는 청소년기 남자아이들은 그들이 무엇을 '하고 있을지'에 더 초점을 맞추었다. 텔레비전에 대한 아이의 경험이 더 길수록, 이 물질적 견해는 더 ④ 감소했다(→ 증가했다). 분명히, 텔레비전의 시각적 이미지는 우리의 정체성과 생활방식을 규정하는 데 있어 눈에 보이고 ⑤ 실체적인 물건에 대한 강조를 만들어서 결과적으로 소비에 중점을 두게 한다.

구문풀이

8행 In the 1950s **it** was found [that British children {who had access only to the BBC}, {which carries no advertising}, had more materialistic ambitions than those without television].

: it은 형식상의 주어이고, [ ]가 내용상의 주어이다. 첫 번째 { }는 that절의 핵심 주어인 British children을 수식하는 관계절이고, 두 번째 { }는 the BBC를 부연 설명하는 관계절이다.

어휘풀이

- have an impact on ~에 영향을 미치다
- commercial *a* 상업적인
- exposure *n* 접하는 것, 경험, 노출
- materialistic *a* 물질적인
- adolescent *a* 청소년기의
- tangible *a* 실체적인, 만질 수 있는
- venture *n* (투기적) 기업[사업]
- medium *n* 매체
- ambition *n* 야망
- outlook *n* 견해, 전망
- consumption *n* 소비

209 답 ④

①	to부정사의 쓰임	②	접속사 that의 쓰임
③	복합관계형용사 whatever의 쓰임	④	병렬구조
⑤	분사의 태		

정답풀이

④ 문장의 주어인 Potato growing에 이어지는 동사 looked와 and에 의해 병렬 연결되는 자리이므로 providing을 과거 동사 provided로 바꿔 써야 한다.

오답풀이

① 명사구 enough potatoes를 수식하는 to부정사구를 이끄는 to feed는 적절하다.

② 동사 found의 목적어로 쓰인 명사절을 이끄는 접속사 that은 적절하다.

③ 전치사 with의 목적어인 명사절을 이끌며 동시에 이어지는 명사구 soil or plant materials를 수식하고 있으므로 복합관계형용사로 쓰인 whatever는 알맞다.

⑤ 수식을 받는 their plain-looking brown tubers는 '보이지 않는' 대상이므로 과거분사 unseen은 적절하게 쓰였다.

전문해석

16세기에 아일랜드인들은 수익이 안 나는 몇 에이커의 땅이 대가족과 그 가축을 먹일 충분한 감자를 생산할 수 있다는 것을 알게 되었다. 아일랜드 사람들은 또한 최소한의 노동력이나 도구만으로 이 감자를 '레이지 베드(곡식을 경작하는 전통 방법)'라고 불리는 것으로 기를 수 있다는 것을 알게 되었다. 감자는 땅 위에 직사각형으로 놓였고 그런 다음 농부는 삽으로 그의 감자 이랑 양쪽에 배수 도랑을 파고는, 그 배수 도랑에서 나온 아무 흙이나 식물성 재료를 가지고 그 감자를 덮었다. 쟁기질된 땅도 없고, 줄지은 이랑도 없고, 분명 아름다운 작물도 전혀 없었다. 감자 재배는 농경과 전혀 닮지 않았고, 질서정연하게 배치된 곡물 밭이 주는 만족감도 전혀 주지 않았고, 태양에서 익어가는 황금색 밀도 주지 않았다. 밀은 태양과 문명을 향해 위를 가리키며, 감자는 아래를 가리켰다. 감자는 땅 밑에서 보이지 않는 수수한 갈색 구근을 만들었고 한 더미의 지저분한 덩굴을 땅 위로 던졌다.

구문풀이

6행 The potatoes were simply laid out in a rectangle on the ground; then, with a spade, the farmer **would** dig a drainage trench on either side of his potato bed, [covering the potatoes with whatever soil or plant materials came out of the drainage trench].

: would는 과거에 '~하곤 했다'의 의미를 나타낸다. [ ]는 the farmer를 의미상의 주어로 하는 분사구문이다.

어휘풀이

- marginal *a* (농지가) 수익이 안 나는
- a bare minimum 최소한의 것
- spade *n* 삽
- livestock *n* 가축, 축산물
- lay out ~을 배치하다
- dig *v* 파다

- plow *v* 쟁기질하다
- ripen *v* 익다
- orderly *ad* 질서정연하게
- vine *n* 덩굴

210 답 ⑤

① extract	얻다, 추출하다	↔		
② relevant	적절한	↔	irrelevant(부적절한)	
③ insufficient	불충분한	↔	sufficient(충분한)	
④ observe	관찰하다	↔		
⑤ extend	확장하다	↔	limit(제한하다)	

정답풀이

⑤ Similarly(마찬가지로)로 시작하고 있으므로 앞 내용과 유사한 문맥으로 이어져야 한다. 앞에서 표본으로 추출되는 생물도 가혹한 표집 방법에 의해 파괴되지 않은 생물로 과도하게 편향된다고 했으므로, 이와 비슷한 문맥이 되려면 산 채로 수집하여 실험실에서 기르고 배양할 수 있는 생물들로 '확장된다'는 것은 적절하지 않다. extended를 limited(제한하다) 정도로 바꿔 써야 한다.

오답풀이

① 병이나 그물을 통해 얻은 표본을 사용하는 것은 해양에 사는 생명체에 대한 지식을 '얻기' 위한 방법이므로 extract는 적절하다.
② 앞에서 우리가 사용하는 접근법이 지식을 제공해 왔다고 했고, 뒤에 생물 지구 화학적 문제에 관한 이해에 도움이 되었다는 내용이 이어지고 있다. 따라서 풍부함, 생산 비율 그리고 분포 패턴에 초점을 맞춘 관점을 긍정적으로 설명하는 흐름에서 '적절하다(relevant)'고 표현한 것은 적절하다.
③ 우리의 연구 방식에 대한 장점을 언급한 이후 But을 통해 대조적인 흐름으로 전환되었으므로 '불충분하다(insufficient)'는 것은 적절하다.
④ 이어지는 문장은 육안으로 '관찰' 가능한 육지 생물에 비해 현미경을 통해서만 '보이는' 플랑크톤과 같은 해양 생물에 대한 직관적 이해가 더 초보적이라는 내용이다. 즉, 육안으로 볼 수 있는지 아니면 현미경을 통해서만 볼 수 있는지에 따라 직관력에 차이가 난다는 내용이므로, '관찰하는(observe)' 방식에 의해 영향을 받는다는 것은 적절하다.

전문해석

해양의 생명 활동에 관한 우리 지식의 많은 부분이 '맹목적' 표집으로부터 얻어진다. 우리는 염도와 수온 같은 대량의 환경 특성을 측정하기 위해 도구를 사용하고, 해양에서 사는 생물에 관한 지식을 (a) 얻기 위해 병이나 그물을 통해 얻은 표본을 사용한다. 이런 종류의 접근법은 중요한 지식을 제공해 왔지만, 또한 우리가 해양 생물을 보는 방식에 영향을 끼치기도 했다. 그것은 우리가 풍부함, 생산 비율 그리고 분포 패턴에 초점을 맞추도록 이끈다. 그러한 관점은 어업을 위한 자원으로서의 해양이라는 맥락에서는 매우 (b) 적절하다. 그것은 또한 해양 탄소 흐름과 같은 생물 지구 화학적 문제에 관한 이해를 발전시키는 데 있어 유용하다. 하지만 단독으로는, 이러한 접근법은 심지어 그 목적을 위해서조차도 (c) 불충분하다. 물론, 우리가 해양 생물에 관해 계발하는 이런 종류의 직관력은 우리가 그것을 (d) 관찰하는 방식에 의해 영향을 받는다. 해양은 우리가 접근하기 어렵고 대부분의 플랑크톤 유기체가 현미경으로만 보일 정도로 미세하므로, 예를 들어 우리의 직관력은 (육안으로 보이는) 육지 생물에 관해 우리가 가지고 있는 직관적 이해에 비교하면 초보적이다. 플랑크톤 유기체의 생명 활동에 관한 우리의 이해는 여전히 대부분 (죽은) 개체에 대한 조사, 현장 표본, 그리고 배양 실험에 근거하고 있고, 심지어 우리의 표집조차도 우리의 가혹한 표집 방법에 의해 파괴되지 않은 그러한 생물들로 과도하게 편향적일 수 있다. 마찬가지로, 실험 관찰은 우리가 산 채로 수집하여 실험실에서 기르고 배양할 수 있는 그러한 유기체들로 (e) 확장된다(→ 제한된다).

구문풀이

15행 The kind of intuition [that we develop about marine life] is, of course, influenced by the way [we observe it].

: 첫 번째 [ ]는 문장의 핵심 주어인 The kind of intuition을 수식하는 관계대명사절이고, 두 번째 [ ]는 the way를 수식하는 관계부사절이다.

어휘풀이

- biology *n* 생명 활동, 생물학
- blind sampling 맹목적 표집
- property *n* 특성, 속성
- abundance *n* 풍부
- fishery *n* 어업, 어장
- intuition *n* 직관(력)
- planktonic *a* 플랑크톤의
- microscopic *a* (현미경으로만 보일 정도로) 미세한
- elementary *a* 초보적인, 기초의
- incubation *n* 배양
- harsh *a* 가혹한, 거친
- derive *v* 얻다, 비롯되다
- bulk *a* 대량의
- extract *v* 얻다, 추출하다
- distribution *n* 분포
- biogeochemical *a* 생물 지구 화학의
- inaccessible *a* 접근하기 어려운
- macroscopic *a* 육안으로 보이는
- biased *a* 편향된, 편견을 가진
- laboratory *n* 실험실, 연구실

211 답 ④

① 부사의 쓰임		② 강조구문	
③ 주어와 동사의 수 일치		④ 관계대명사 which의 쓰임	
⑤ 관계절 동사의 수 일치			

정답풀이

④ 뒤에 주어(their ancestors)와 자동사(originated)를 갖춘 완전한 구조의 절이 이어지고 있으므로 관계대명사 which는 쓸 수 없다. the continent를 선행사로 하여 관계절에서 in the continent의 부사구 역할을 하도록 which를 「전치사+관계대명사」 형태의 in which 또는 관계부사 where나 that으로 고쳐 써야 한다.

오답풀이

① are의 보어인 형용사 salient를 수식하므로 부사 politically는 적절하게 쓰였다.
② 「It is[was] ~ that …(…하는 것은 바로 ~이다)」 강조구문으로 부사구인 only when a political issue ~ in a particular group을 강조하고 있다.
③ 접속사 Whether가 이끄는 두 개의 명사절이 등위접속사 or에 의해 병렬 구조로 연결되어 주어 역할을 하고 있고, 명사절 주어는 단수 취급하므로 단수형 동사 matters는 적절하게 쓰였다.
⑤ 주격 관계대명사절에서 동사의 수는 선행사에 일치시킨다. 여기서 주격 관계대명사 that의 선행사는 somewhat different identities이므로 이에 수를 맞춘 관계절 동사 help는 적절하다.

전문해석

비록 유럽의 이슬람교도들을 포함하여 대부분의 사람들이 다양한 정체성을 가지기는 하지만, 이들 중에서 어떤 순간에든 정치적으로 두드러지는 정체성은 거의 없다. 정체성이 중요성을 띠는 것은 바로 어떤 정치적 문제가 특정한 집단의 사람들의 복지에 영향을 주는 경우뿐이다. 예를 들면, 여성의 권리에 관련된 문제가 발생할 때, 여성들은 성(性)을 자신들의 주된 정체성으로 생각하기 시작한다. 그러한 여성들이 미국인인지 이란인인지, 또는 그들이 가톨릭 신자인지 개신교도인지의 여부는 그들이 여성이라는 사실보다 덜 중요하다. 마찬가지로, 기근과 내전이 사하라 사막 이남의 아프리카 사람들을 위협하는 경우, 많은 아프리카계 미국인들은 수세기 이전에 자신들의 조상이 기원했던 대륙과의 혈족 관계가 떠올라서 자신들의 지도자들에게

인도주의적 구호를 제공하라는 압력을 가한다. 다시 말하면, 각각의 문제는 그 문제들에 관해 사람들이 가지는 정치적인 선호를 설명하는 데 도움을 주는 다소 서로 다른 정체성을 이끌어 낸다.

구문풀이

7행 [{Whether such women are American or Iranian} or {whether they are Catholic or Protestant}] matters less than the fact [that they are women].

: 첫 번째 [ ]는 문장의 주어로, 접속사 whether가 이끄는 두 개의 명사절 { }가 등위접속사 or에 의해 연결되었으며 matters가 동사이다. 두 번째 [ ]는 the fact와 동격 관계를 이루는 절이다.

어휘풀이

- including *prep* ~을 포함한, ~을 포함하여
- Muslim *n* 무슬림, 이슬람교도
- numerous *a* 매우 많은, 다수의
- identity *n* 정체성
- assume *v* (성질·양상 등을) 띠다[가지다]
- principal *a* 주된, 주요한
- famine *n* 기근
- civil war 내전
- sub-Saharan *a* 사하라 사막 이남의
- kinship *n* 혈족 관계, 친척 관계
- originate *v* 기원하다, 유래하다
- humanitarian *a* 인도주의의
- relief *n* (빈민·난민 등에 대한) 구제, 원조 물자
- call forth ~을 불러내다
- regarding *prep* ~에 관해

212 답 ⑤

출제 어휘	확인하기		
① original	독창적인	↔	
② false	잘못된	↔	
③ suspect	의심하다	↔	
④ object	반대하다	↔	approve(찬성하다)
⑤ ignorant	모르는	↔	aware(알고 있는)

정답풀이

⑤ 풍자문학의 특징은 아이디어의 독창성이 아니라 친숙한 상황들을 독창적인 관점을 통해 제시하는 것이라는 내용의 글이다. 즉, 글의 처음뿐만 아니라 바로 앞에서 언급한 풍자문학의 비독창성을 고려할 때 Swift 이전의 사람들이 기아 문제를 '모르고' 있었다는 것은 적절하지 않다. ignorant를 aware(알고 있는) 정도로 바꿔 써야 한다.

오답풀이

① 풍자문학이 하는 일은 친숙한 상황들을 어리석게 또는 해로워 보이도록 만드는 관점에서 그것들을 보는 것이라고 했으므로, 관점은 독창적이지만 '독창적인(original)' 아이디어를 제공하지는 않는다는 것은 적절하다.

② 우리가 아무런 의심 없이 받아들이는 친숙한 상황들을 어리석음 혹은 해로움의 관점에서 보는 것이 풍자라고 했으므로, 풍자는 우리가 의심 없이 수용하고 있는 가치가 '잘못된(false)' 것임을 깨닫게 해 준다는 것은 적절하다.

③ 〈Don Quixote〉는 기사도를 어리석어 보이도록 만든 작품인데, 그 아이디어가 독창적인 것이 아니라고 했으므로 Cervantes 이전에도 기사도가 '의심받았다(suspected)'고 한 것은 적절하다.

④ 〈Brave New World〉는 과학의 자만을 조롱하는 작품인데, 새롭거나 독창적으로 제기된 사실이 아니라는 흐름이므로 Aldous Huxley 이전에도 인본주의자들이 순수과학의 주장에 '반대했다(objected)'는 것은 적절하다.

전문해석

아마도 풍자문학의 가장 두드러진 특징은 그것의 신선함, 즉 관점의 독창성일 것이다. 풍자는 ① 독창적인 아이디어를 거의 제공하지 않는다. 그것들이 하는 일은 친숙

한 상황들을 어리석게 또는 해로워 보이도록 만드는 관점에서 그것들을 보는 것이다. 풍자는 우리를 자극하여 우리가 의심 없이 받아들이고 있는 많은 가치들이 ② 잘못된 것이라는 유쾌하게 충격적인 깨달음을 갖게 한다. 〈Don Quixote(돈 키호테)〉는 기사도를 어리석어 보이도록 만든다. 〈Brave New World(멋진 신세계)〉는 과학의 자만을 조롱한다. 〈A Modest Proposal(겸손한 제안)〉은 식인 풍습을 옹호함으로써 기아(飢餓) 문제를 극화시킨다. 그러나 이 작품들의 아이디어들은 그 어느 것도 독창적이지 않다. Cervantes 이전에도 기사도는 ③ 의심받았다. Aldous Huxley 이전에도 인본주의자들은 순수과학의 주장에 ④ 반대했다. 그리고 Swift 이전에도 사람들은 굶주림에 대해서 ⑤ 모르고(→ 깨닫고) 있었다. 이 문학 작품들을 인기 있게 만든 것은 아이디어의 독창성이 아니다. 그 작품들을 흥미 있고 재미있게 만들었던 것은 바로 그 표현 방식, 즉 풍자적인 방법이었다.

구문풀이

16행 **It was** the manner of expression, the satiric method, **that** made them interesting and entertaining.

: 「It is[was] ~ that ….」 강조구문으로 the manner ~ method가 강조되었다. 이때 the manner of expression과 the satiric method는 동격 관계를 이룬다.

어휘풀이

- striking *a* 두드러진, 강력한
- quality *n* 특성, 특징
- originality *n* 독창성
- original *a* 독창적인
- startle *A* into *B* *A*를 자극하여 *B* 시키다
- unquestioningly *ad* 의심 없이
- absurd *a* 어리석은, 황당한
- ridicule *v* 조롱하다
- pretension *n* 뽐냄, 자만
- dramatize *v* 극화하다
- starvation *n* 굶주림, 기아
- advocate *v* 옹호하다
- suspect *v* 의심하다
- object *v* 반대하다
- famine *n* 기근, 굶주림
- literary work 문학 작품

213 답 ③

출제 의도	파악하기		
①	분사의 태	②	동사의 태
③	대동사	④	분사형 형용사
⑤	「so ~ that ….」구문		

정답풀이

③ 앞에 나온 일반동사 foresee의 반복 사용을 피하기 위한 대동사 자리이므로 be동사 was는 옳지 않으며 did로 바꿔 써야 한다.

오답풀이

① spy의 의미상 주어는 two-way television screens로, 양방향 TV 화면이 시청자들(them)을 '엿보는' 주체이므로 능동의 의미를 나타내는 현재분사 spying은 적절하다.

② 그의 경고는 '약하게 말해지는' 대상이므로 are에 연결되어 수동태 동사를 이루는 과거분사 understated는 적절하다.

④ '놀라운'이라는 의미로 명사 proliferation을 수식하는 분사형 형용사 astonishing은 알맞게 쓰였다.

⑤ 「so ~ that …(너무 ~해서 …하다)」 구문에 쓰인 접속사 that은 적절하다.

전문해석

거의 정확히 20세기 중간 지점에서, 조지 오웰은 〈1984년〉을 출간했다. 그 책은 대중매체를 완전히 통제하는 정부를 그렸다. 오웰은 그러한 기술들을 정부의 선전 내용을 시청자들에게 전달하면서 동시에 그들을 엿보는 데 사용될 수 있는 양방향 TV 화면으로 정확하게 상상했다. 일어날 수 있는 사생활 침해에 대한 그의 경고는 오히려 (사실보다) 약하게 말해졌다. 그러나 그도, 그 시절의 어느 누구도 그 시대의 가장

중요한 혁명을 예상하지 못했다. 그것은 근육(힘)에 기반을 둔 경제로부터 정신에 기반을 둔 경제로의 변화였다. 따라서 그는 오늘날의 새로운 의사소통 도구의 놀라운 확산을 예측하지 못했다. 이런 기술의 수와 다양성은 이제 너무나 대단하고, 너무나 크게 변화하고 있어서 전문가들조차 어리둥절해한다. 그렇지만 멀리서 상황을 보면, 미래의 매체가 가진 기본적인 특성이 명확해진다. 그것들은 상호작용성, 이동성, 전환 가능성, 연결성, 편재성과 세계화이다.

구문풀이

3행 Orwell correctly envisioned such technologies as two-way television screens [that could be used to deliver the state's propaganda to viewers while simultaneously spying on them].

: [ ]는 two-way television screens를 수식하는 관계절이다.

어휘풀이

- precise *a* 정확한
- envision *v* 상상하다
- simultaneously *ad* 동시에
- invasion of privacy 사생활 침해
- understate *v* 작게[약하게] 말하다
- bewildered *a* 어리둥절한
- convertibility *n* 전환 가능성
- midpoint *n* 중간 지점
- propaganda *n* 선전
- spy *v* 엿보다, 몰래 감시하다
- if anything 오히려, 어느 편이냐 하면
- foresee *v* 예견하다
- interactivity *n* 상호작용성
- ubiquity *n* 어디에나 있음, 편재성

214 답 ④

정답풀이

④ 뉴스 웹 사이트에는 고유한 물리적 구성 요소가 없기 때문에 더 쉽게 조작되고 역사를 바꿀 수 있다는 인식이 있다고 했다. 즉, 뉴스 웹 사이트는 쉽게 변화될 수 있다는 의미이므로, 콘텐츠의 '경직성'이라고 하는 것은 적절하지 않으며 rigidity를 fluidity(가변성) 정도로 바꿔 써야 한다.

오답풀이

① 인쇄된 신문은 그것이 묘사하는 사건을 더 사실적으로 만드는데, 그것은 신문 자체가 실제로 있는 물체이기 때문이라는 것이므로 이를 '진정성(authenticity)'이라고 표현한 것은 적절하다.

② 신문이 유형의 물체이기 때문에 신문에 실린 뉴스는 고정되어 계속 존재할 수 있다는 흐름이므로 이를 '냉동된(frozen)' 인공물로 표현한 것은 적절하다.

③ 물리적으로 계속 존재하는 신문 뉴스와는 대조적으로(In contrast) 짧게 존재하는 뉴스 웹 사이트를 말하는 흐름이므로, 뉴스 웹 사이트가 전달하는 정보의 '증거(evidence)'라고 볼 수 있는 물리적 구성 요소가 없다는 것은 적절하다.

⑤ 뉴스 웹 사이트는 역사를 훨씬 덜 단일화된 것으로 보는 시기와 부합한다고 했고, 디지털 세계에서는 여러 유통망 없이도 한 사람이 전 세계와 소통할 수 있다고 했으므로 훨씬 더 '민주적(democratic)'이라는 것은 적절하다.

전문해석

인쇄된 사진 또는 신문 헤드라인에는 다른 어떤 뉴스 보도 형태에서보다도 그것이 묘사하는 사건을 더 사실적으로 만드는 어떤 것이 있다. 아마도 이것은 신문 자체에 부인할 수 없는 현실성이 있기 때문인데, 그것이 실제로 있는 유형의 물체라는 것이다. 그 (a) 진정성은 뉴스에 영향을 미친다. 그것은 가리킬 수 있으며, 밑줄 칠 수 있

고, 잘라낼 수 있고, 게시판에 핀으로 꽂을 수 있고, 스크랩북에 붙일 수 있으며, 또는 도서관에 보관할 수 있다. 뉴스는 시간 안에서 (b) 냉동된 인공물이 된다. 그 사건은 사라진지 오래된 것일지도 모르나, 비록 그것이 사실이 아니더라도 그것의 물질적인 존재로 인해 논쟁의 여지가 없는 사실로 계속 존재한다.

이와 대조적으로, 뉴스 웹 사이트는 짧게 존재하는 것처럼 보인다. 그것들도 물론 보관되어 있지만, 그것들이 전달하는 정보의 (c) 증거라고 가리킬 수 있는 고유한 물리적 구성 요소가 없다. 이런 이유로, 그것들은 더 쉽게 조작될 수 있고, 역사 자체가 바뀔 수 있다는 인식이 존재한다. 동시에, 디지털 미디어를 매우 흥미롭게 만드는 것은 바로 정확히 콘텐츠의 이러한 즉각성과 (d) 경직성(→ 가변성)이다. 뉴스 웹 사이트는 역사를 그 이전 시대가 한때 그랬던 것보다 훨씬 덜 단일화된 것으로 보는 시기와 부합한다. 디지털 뉴스 웹 사이트는 또한 잠재적으로 훨씬 더 (e) 민주적인데, 이는 물리적 신문이 거대한 인쇄기와 열차, 비행기, 트럭, 상점, 그리고 최종적으로 신문 판매자들을 연결하는 유통망을 필요로 하는 반면에, 디지털 세계에서는 한 사람이 컴퓨터 한 대의 도움으로 그리고 나무 한 그루도 베어질 필요 없이 전 세계와 소통할 수 있기 때문이다.

구문풀이

19행 The news website is in tune with an age [that sees history as much less monolithic than previous eras once **did**].

: [ ]는 an age를 수식하는 관계절이다. 대동사 did는 앞에 나온 sees를 대신하여 saw history as monolithic의 의미를 나타낸다.

어휘풀이

- undeniable *a* 부인[부정]할 수 없는
- rub off 영향을 미치다
- notice board 게시판
- indisputable *a* 논쟁의 여지가 없는
- manipulate *v* 조작하다
- precisely *ad* 정확히
- rigidity *n* 경직성
- era *n* 시대, 시기
- distribution *n* 유통, 배포
- authenticity *n* 진정성
- pin *v* (핀으로) 꽂다
- artifact *n* 인공물
- convey *v* 전달하다, 전하다
- alter *v* 바꾸다
- immediacy *n* 즉각성
- monolithic *a* 단일화된
- democratic *a* 민주적인
- aid *n* 도움

215 ③	**216** ⑤	**217** ④	**218** ④	**219** ⑤
220 ③	**221** ⑤	**222** ②		

215 답 ③

출제 의도	파악하기
① 부사의 쓰임	② to부정사의 쓰임
③ 관계대명사 which의 쓰임	④ 병렬구조
⑤ 주어와 동사의 수 일치	

정답풀이

③ which 이하가 주어, 동사, 보어를 모두 갖춘 완전한 구조의 절을 이루므로 관계대명사 which는 적절하지 않다. 관계절에서 from sources of information의 부사구 역할을 하도록 from which로 고쳐야 한다.

오답풀이

① 부사 typically는 동사 are를 수식하며 be동사와 명사구 보어 사이에 적절하게 쓰였다.
② for women, ~, to be … decisions는 형식상의 주어 It이 대신하는 내용상의 주어에 해당하는 to부정사구로, to be는 적절하게 쓰였다. 이때 for women, and consumers in general은 이 to부정사구의 의미상 주어를 나타낸다.
④ 문맥상 '주치의의 말을 듣고 결정하는 문제'라는 의미가 적절하므로, and 앞의 동명사 listening과 병렬구조를 이루며 전치사 of의 목적어 역할을 하는 making의 쓰임은 적절하다.
⑤ 문장의 핵심 주어는 the prospect이므로 이에 수를 맞춘 단수형 동사 has는 적절하다.

전문해석

의학 치료에 있어서 환자들은 선택을 축복이자 부담으로 여긴다. 그리고 그 부담은 주로 여성들에게 주어지는데, 그들은 일반적으로 자기 자신의 건강뿐만 아니라 남편과 아이들의 건강의 수호자이다. "여성들이, 그리고 일반적인 소비자들이, 자신이 찾는 정보를 자세히 살펴보고 결정을 내릴 수 있는 것은 매우 힘든 과업입니다."라고 National Women's Health Network의 프로그램 담당자인 Amy Allina는 말한다. 그리고 그것을 매우 힘들게 만드는 것은 그 결정이 우리 자신의 것이라는 것뿐만 아니라, 우리가 결정을 내리는 데 근거가 되는 정보 원천의 수가 폭발적으로 증가해 왔다는 것이기도 하다. 그것은 단지 여러분의 주치의가 선택 사항들을 제시하는 것을 듣고 선택을 하는 문제가 아니다. 지금 우리에게는 비전문가의 백과사전 같은 건강에 대한 안내, '더 나은 건강' 잡지들과 인터넷이 있다. 그래서 이제 의학적 결정의 가능성은 모든 이에게 학기 말 리포트 과제와 같은 최악의 악몽이 되었는데, 한 강좌에서의 성적보다 걸려 있는 것이 훨씬 더 많다.

구문풀이

`9행` And [what makes it overwhelming] is **not only** [that the decision is ours], **but** [that {**the number** of sources of information <from which we are to make the decisions>} **has exploded**].

: 첫 번째 [ ]는 문장의 주어이고, 동사는 is이며, 「not only A but (also) B」로 연결된 두 번째와 세 번째 [ ]가 보어이다. 세 번째 [ ]에서 핵심 주어는 the number이고, 이에 수를 맞춰 단수형 동사 has exploded를 썼다. 〈 〉는 sources of information을 수식하는 관계절이다.

어휘풀이

- when it comes to ~에 관한 한
- burden *n* 부담
- primarily *ad* 주로
- overwhelming *a* 저항[대응]하기 힘든
- in general (명사 뒤에서) 일반적인, 전반적인
- sort through *v* ~을 분류하다[선별하다]
- explode *v* 폭발적으로 증가하다
- encyclopedic *a* 백과사전적인, 박식한
- prospect *n* 가능성
- stake *n* (*pl.*) 내기에 건 돈
- blessing *n* 축복
- fall on (부담이) ~에게 돌아가다
- guardian *n* 보호자, 관리인
- lay out ~을 늘어놓다, ~을 제시하다
- term paper 학기말 리포트
- infinitely *ad* 무한히, 훨씬

216 답 ⑤

출제 어휘	확인하기		
① familiar	친숙한	↔	unfamiliar(생소한, 낯선)
② task	과업	↔	
③ reveal	드러내다	↔	
④ challenging	도전적인	↔	
⑤ gratified	만족한	↔	unsatisfied(만족하지 못하는)

정답풀이

⑤ 의미 있는 업무를 제공하는 조직과 조립 라인을 사용하는 기업에서의 개인의 역량 발휘를 대조하는 문맥인데, 의미 있는 업무를 제공하는 조직은 직원들의 역량에 대한 욕구를 충족시켜 준다고 했고, 조립 라인을 사용하는 기업과 같은 일부 기업에서는 그러한 일자리가 풍부하지 않다고 했으므로, 역량 동기를 '만족시킨다'는 것은 적절하지 않다. gratified를 반대 의미인 unsatisfied(만족하지 못하는) 정도로 바꿔 써야 한다.

오답풀이

① 어린아이는 사물을 만지고 다루면서 자연스럽게 그것들에 '친숙해질' 것이므로 familiar는 적절하다.
② 사물을 분해하고 다시 조립하는 시도를 하는 아이들이 역량 면에서 얻게 되는 것을 서술하는 흐름이므로, 그런 일을 통해 자신이 유능하게 할 수 있는 '과업(tasks)'을 배운다는 것은 적절하다.
③ 아이들의 역량에 관한 설명에 이어서 일터에서의 역량을 서술하는 부분으로, 역량 동기가 직무 숙달과 직업적 성장을 통해 '드러난다(reveals)'는 것은 적절하다.
④ 아이들이 사물을 분해하고 다시 조립하는 시도를 하면서 역량을 발휘할 수 있는 과업을 배우는 것처럼, 일터에서 숙달 및 성장의 열망을 충족시키고 역량을 발휘할 수 있는 경쟁이 '도전적(challenging)'이지만 이길 수 있는 경쟁이라는 것은 적절하다.

전문해석

역량은 환경적 요인에 대한 통제를 의미한다는 점에서 힘과 유사하다. 아이들은 아주 어린 나이에 사물에 ① 친숙해지기 위해 사물을 만지고 다루면서 역량에 대한 욕구를 분명히 보여 주기 시작한다. 이후에, 그들은 사물을 분해하고 다시 조립하려는 시도를 시작한다. 결과적으로, 아이들은 자신이 유능하게 할 수 있는 ② 과업을 배운다. 일터에서 역량 동기는 직무 숙달과 직업적 성장에 대한 열망의 형태로 ③ 드러난다. 개인은 ④ 도전적이지만 이길 수 있는 경쟁에서 환경에 대응하여 자신의 능력과 기술을 맞추기 시작한다. 의미 있는 업무를 제공하는 조직은 그 직원들이 역량에 대한 욕구를 충족할 수 있도록 지원한다. 조립 라인을 사용하는 기업과 같은 일부 기업에서는 그러한 일자리가 풍부하지 않고, 역량 동기를 ⑤ 만족시키는(→ 만족시키지 못하는) 경우가 많다.

10행 An individual begins matching his or her abilities and skills against the environment in a contest [that is challenging] but [that can be won].

: but으로 연결된 두 개의 [ ]는 모두 a contest를 수식하는 관계절이다.

어휘풀이
- competence *n* 역량, 능력
- imply *v* 의미하다, 암시하다
- illustrate *v* 분명히 보여 주다, 실증하다
- competent *a* 역량 있는, 유능한
- reveal oneself 나타나다, 정체를 드러내다
- assembly *n* 조립
- in abundance 풍부한; 풍부하게
- gratified *a* 만족한

217 답 ④

출제 의도	파악하기		
①	부사의 쓰임	②	분사의 태
③	cause의 목적격보어	④	문장의 구조 파악
⑤	대동사		

정답풀이
④ The new island home이 문장의 핵심 주어이고 they chose는 이를 수식하는 관계절이다. 주어에 연결되는 술어 동사가 필요하므로 lacking은 적절하지 않다. 문맥상 과거 시제 동사 lacked로 바꿔 써야 한다.

오답풀이
① 부대상황을 나타내는 「with+명사(구)+분사」 구문에서 과거분사인 destroyed를 수식하는 부사 savagely는 적절하다.
② an island를 대신하는 부정대명사 one을 수식하는 자리로, one이 '보호받는' 대상이므로 수동의 의미를 나타내는 과거분사 protected는 적절하다.
③ 동사 cause는 목적격보어로 to부정사를 취하므로 caused의 목적격보어로 쓰인 to sink는 적절하다.
⑤ 문맥상 대동사가 대신하는 것은 앞에 나온 일반동사구 access it이고, 과거 시제인 accessed it을 나타내야 하므로 대동사 did는 알맞게 쓰였다.

전문해석
어떤 이야기가 북쪽 대양에서 펭귄의 생태적 위치를 차지했던 큰 흑백 바닷새인 큰바다쇠오리에 관한 그것(이야기)보다 더 가혹할 수 있을까? 그 새의 이야기는 마치 어떤 그리스 비극과도 같이 융성하고 쇠퇴하는데, 섬의 개체군은 거의 모두가 사라질 때까지 인간에 의해 잔혹하게 파괴당했다. 그러고 나서 그 마지막 집단이 어느 특별한 섬, 즉 사납고 예측할 수 없는 해류로 인해 인간의 파괴로부터 보호되었던 한 섬에서 안전을 찾아냈다. 이런 바다는 완벽히 적응하여 항해에 알맞은 새에게는 아무 문제도 일으키지 않았지만, 그 바다는 인간이 어떠한 종류의 안전한 상륙도 하지 못하도록 막았다. 몇 년을 비교적 안전하게 누린 후, 다른 종류의 재난이 큰바다쇠오리에게 타격을 주었다. 화산 활동은 그 섬의 피난처가 완전히 바닷속에 가라앉게 했으며 살아남은 개체들은 다른 곳에서 피난처를 찾아야 했다. 그들이 선택한 새로운 섬 거처는 하나의 끔찍한 측면에 있어 옛것의 이점들이 없었다. 인간이 비교적 쉽게 그것(그 섬 거처)에 접근할 수 있었고, 인간들은 정말로 그렇게 했다! 단지 몇 년 이내에 이 한때 풍부했던 종의 마지막 개체가 완전히 없어지게 되었다.

구문풀이
1행 What story could be harsher than **that** of the Great Auk, [the large black-and-white seabird {that in northern oceans took the ecological place of a penguin}]?

: 지시대명사 that은 the story를 대신한다. [ ]는 the Great Auk와 의미상 동격 관계를 이루는 명사구이고, 그 안의 { }는 the large black-and-white seabird를 수식하는 관계절이다.

어휘풀이
- ecological *a* 생태상의, 생태학의
- tragedy *n* 비극, 참사
- population *n* 개체군, 전체 주민, 인구
- destroy *v* 죽이다, 파괴하다
- colony *n* 집단, 군체, 식민지
- vicious *a* 사나운, 악랄한, 사악한
- current *n* 해류
- present *v* (어려움 등을) 일으키다
- seagoing *a* 바다 여행에 알맞은, 항해에 알맞은
- landing *n* 상륙, 착륙
- disaster *n* 재난, 천재지변
- volcanic *a* 화산의, 화산 작용에 의한
- refuge *n* 피난처
- comparative *a* 비교적인, 상대적인
- eliminate *v* 제거하다, 없애다

218 답 ④

출제 어휘	확인하기		
① vanish	사라지다	↔	appear(나타나다)
② transform	바꾸다, 변경시키다	↔	
③ perception	인식		
④ most	대부분	↔	
⑤ inevitable	불가피한	↔	

정답풀이
④ 높은 소비율이 선진 사회의 불가피한 특징이라고 종종 언급되었으나 이제 그런 태도는 더 이상 건강하다거나 바람직하다거나 허용된다고 여겨질 수 없다는 내용이 이어지고 있다. 따라서 최근까지 이런 문제, 즉 쓰레기 문제를 고려하지 않은 소비와 관련된 문제 중 '대부분'이 중요해 보였다는 것은 적절하지 않다. 그 중 '어떤 것도 중요하지 않게' 여겨졌다는 의미를 나타내도록 most를 부정어 none(아무것도 ~ 않는 것) 정도로 바꿔 써야 한다.

오답풀이
① In fact(사실은)로 시작하며 우리가 어떤 것을 소비할 때 그것은 전혀 없어지지 않는다는 내용이 연결되므로 소비라는 단어는 우리가 소비한 흔적이 '사라진다(vanish)'는 것을 시사한다고 먼저 언급한 것은 적절하다.
② 어떤 것을 소비할 때 전혀 사라지지 않고 유용한 것과 쓰레기로 남겨진다고 했으므로 다른 두 종류로 '바뀐다(transformed)'는 것은 적절하다.
③ 우리가 소비할 때 유용한 것과 쓰레기인 것으로 물질이 남겨지며 유용하다고 생각한 것도 다 쓰자마자 쓰레기가 되어 버리기 때문에 무엇이 쓰레기인지를 결정할 때 소비에 관한 우리의 '인식(perception)'이 고려되어야 한다는 것은 적절하다.
⑤ 높은 소비율을 선진 사회의 특징이라고 언급하는 태도를 지적하는 문맥이므로 inevitable(불가피한)은 적절하다.

전문해석
'소비'라는 단어는 거의 기계적인 효율을 내포하는데, 그것은 우리가 소비하는 것은 무엇이든 우리가 그것을 사용한 후에는 모든 흔적이 마술처럼 ① 사라져 버린다는 것을 시사한다. 사실은, 우리가 어떤 것을 소비할 때 그것은 전혀 없어지지 않는다. 오히려 그것은 매우 다른 두 종류로 ② 바뀌는데, '유용한' 어떤 것과 남겨진 물질로, 우리는 그것을 '쓰레기'라 부른다. 게다가, 우리가 유용하다고 생각하는 어떤 것이든 그것을 다 쓰자마자 쓰레기가 되므로 무엇이 쓰레기이고 무엇이 쓰레기가 아닌지를 결정할 때 우리가 소비하는 것들에 대한 우리의 ③ 인식이 고려되어야 한다. 최근까지만 해도 이런 문제 중 ④ 대부분이 중요해 보였다(→ 어떤 것도 중요해 보이지 않았다). 사실 높은 소비율이 선진 사회의 ⑤ 불가피한 특징이라고 종종 언급되었다. 그러나 이제 이런 태도는 더 이상 어떤 면에서도 건강하다거나 바람직하다거나 혹은 허용될 수 있다고 여겨질 수 없다.

7행 Moreover, anything [we **think of as** useful] becomes waste [as soon as we are finished with it], so our perception of the things [we consume] must be considered [when deciding what is and isn't waste].

: 첫 번째 [ ]는 anything을 수식하는 관계절이고, 「think of A as B(A를 B로 생각하다)」 구문이 쓰였다. 두 번째 [ ]는 as soon as(~하자마자)가 이끄는 부사절이다. 세 번째 [ ]는 the things를 수식하는 관계절이고, 네 번째 [ ]는 접속사 when을 생략하지 않은 분사구문이다.

어휘풀이

- consumption *n* 소비
- efficiency *n* 효율(성)
- vanish *v* 사라지다
- transform *v* 바꾸다, 변형시키다
- mention *v* 언급하다
- acceptable *a* 허용되는
- mechanical *a* 기계적인, 자동적인
- trace *n* 흔적, 자국
- rather *ad* 오히려
- perception *n* 인식
- desirable *a* 바람직한

219 답 ⑤

출제 의도 파악하기
① 생략구문
② 접속사 where의 쓰임
③ 관계대명사 that의 쓰임
④ 관계대명사 what의 쓰임
⑤ 도치구문의 수 일치

정답풀이

⑤ 부사구 Only then이 문장의 맨 앞에 와서 「only 부사구+조동사+주어+본동사」로 도치된 형태이다. 주어가 the author이므로 do를 단수형 does로 바꿔 써야 한다.

오답풀이

① 주절의 주어와 시간, 양보, 조건을 나타내는 부사절의 주어가 일치할 때 부사절에서 「주어+be동사」는 생략이 가능하다. 여기서도 양보 접속사 Although 뒤에 it(= this work) is가 생략되어 있는 구조로 형용사 unfocused가 접속사 뒤에 바로 온 것은 적절하다.
② 뒤에 주어(other personal reflections)와 자동사(falter)를 갖춘 완전한 구조의 절이 이어지고 있고, 문맥상 '~한 상황[경우]에(서)'의 의미를 나타내므로 접속사 where는 적절하다.
③ a topic sentence or other device를 선행사로 하며, 뒤에 주어가 빠진 불완전한 절이 이어지고 있으므로 주격 관계대명사 that은 적절하게 쓰였다.
④ 이어지는 절에서 주어 역할을 하는 동시에 전치사 about의 목적어 역할을 하는 명사절을 이끌므로 선행사를 포함하는 관계대명사 what은 적절하다.

전문해석

초점이 안 맞는 점은 있지만, 이 글은 어찌 보면 하찮은 주제의 에세이가 실제로 통찰력 있고 심지어 감동적이기까지 할 수 있음을 보여 준다. 이 에세이는 첫머리에서부터 강한 긴장감을 조성함으로써, 개인 견해를 다룬 다른 글들이 흔히 영향력이 없어지는 상황에서 이 글은 성공을 거두고 있다. 글쓴이는 에세이의 핵심을 즉각 밝혀 주는 주제 문장이나 다른 장치로 글을 시작하지 않는다. 이런 종류의 에세이에서 그렇게 했다면 '지난 여름 내가 했던 일' 식의 이야기와 너무나 똑같은 글이 될 것이다. 그런데 이 작품에서는 글쓴이의 불안을 유발하는 것에 대한 요인이 나오는 둘째 문단에 이르기까지 독자는 계속해서 마음을 졸이게 된다. 이 문단에 와서야 글쓴이는 이런 큰 불안을 야기시킨 것이 주사나 검사 결과가 아니라 임박한 손목 수술이라는 것을 명쾌히 밝힌다. 전체적으로, 이 글은 명확하면서도 허세가 없다.

구문풀이

12행 **Only then does the author** spell out [that **it is** his impending wrist surgery—and not a shot or test results—**which** has caused such great anxiety].

: 부사구 Only then이 문장 맨 앞에 와서 주어와 조동사가 도치되었다. [ ]는 spell out의 목적어로 쓰인 명사절로, 그 안에 「it is[was] ~ that ...(…하는 것은 바로 ~이다)」의 강조구문이 쓰였다. 「it is[was] ~ that ...」 강조구문에서 that은 강조 대상에 따라 who, which, when 등으로 바꿔 쓸 수 있는데, 여기서는 강조 대상인 his impending wrist surgery에 따라 which가 쓰였다.

어휘풀이

- unfocused *a* 초점이 맞지 않는
- otherwise *ad* 다른 점에서는, 만약 그렇지 않으면
- insignificant *a* 하찮은, 중요하지 않은
- insightful *a* 통찰력 있는
- tension *n* 긴장감
- narrative *n* 이야기
- angst *n* 불안, 고뇌
- impending *a* 임박한, 절박한
- touching *a* 감동을 주는
- reflection *n* 생각, 감상, 의견
- suspense *n* 불안, 걱정
- spell out ~을 분명히 설명하다
- unpretentious *a* 허세가 없는

220 답 ③

출제 어휘 확인하기
(A) reluctant 꺼리는 / willing 기꺼이 ~하는
(B) complimentary 칭찬하는 / disciplinary 훈계의
(C) consent 동의하다 / dissent 동의하지 않다

정답풀이

(A) 남의 집이라서 부모가 꾸짖기를 '꺼려하기' 때문에 아이들이 못된 짓을 한다는 것이 자연스러우므로 reluctant가 적절하다. [willing 기꺼이 ~하는]
(B) 집주인인 Mary 아주머니가 결정하게 하라고 했으므로 엄마는 '훈계의(disciplinary)' 의무를 덜게 된다는 것이 적절하다. [complimentary 칭찬하는]
(C) 아이가 엄마의 말에 반론하는 내용이 이어지고 있으므로 '동의하지 않는다(dissents)'고 하는 것이 적절하다. [consent 동의하다]

전문해석

아이들은 어른들이 다른 사람들의 집에서 자신들을 꾸짖기를 (A) 꺼려한다는 것을 안다. (남의 집이라는) 지리적 특성을 신뢰하면서, 그들은 못된 짓을 하기 위해 이러한 장소들을 선택한다. 하지만 이런 전략은 집주인들에게 자기 집의 규칙을 정하고 시행을 실천에 옮기게 함으로써 가장 잘 좌절될 수 있다. 아이가 Mary 아주머니의 집 소파에서 뛸 때, 소파에서 뛰어도 되는 것인지 아닌지를 Mary 아주머니가 결정하게 하고, 그 한계를 행사하라. 엄마는 (B) 훈계의 의무를 덜면서, "너는 소파에서 뛰는 것을 정말 좋아하지만, 여기는 Mary 아주머니의 집이고 우리는 그녀의 바람을 존중해야만 해."라고 아이의 바람과 감정을 이해한다는 것을 말함으로써 아이에게 도움을 줄 수 있다. 만약 아이가 "하지만 엄마는 제게 우리 집 소파에서는 뛰게 하잖아요."라고 말하며 (C) 동의하지 않는다면, 우리는 "이것은 Mary 아주머니의 규칙이야. 우리 집에서는 그와 다른 규칙이 있단다."라고 대답할 수 있다.

구문풀이

4행 But, this strategy can be counteracted best [**by letting** the hosts {set the rules of their own house} and {carry out their enforcement}].

: 「by -ing」는 '~함으로써'라는 뜻이다. and로 연결된 두 개의 { }는 사역동사 letting의 목적격보어로 쓰인 원형부정사구이다.

어휘풀이

- reluctant *a* 꺼리는
- misbehave *v* 못된 짓을 하다
- counteract *v* 좌절시키다, 반대로 작용하다
- carry out ~을 실천에 옮기다
- invoke *v* (법 등을) 행사하다
- obligation *n* 의무
- geography *n* 지리, 지리적 특성
- enforcement *n* 시행
- relieve *v* 덜다, 경감하다
- voice *v* 말로 표현하다

- note *n* 관련 내용[정보], 필기
- rush through 서둘러 ~을 하다
- get through ~을 끝내다, ~을 마치다
- retired *a* 은퇴한
- summary *n* 요약
- synthesize *v* 합성하다
- instructor *n* 강사
- lecture *n* 강의
- attend to ~에 주의를 기울이다
- chair *n* 학장, 의장
- cognitive *a* 인지의, 인지적인
- substantial *a* 상당한

---

221 답 ⑤

출제 의도 | 파악하기

❶	접속사 whether의 쓰임	❷	관계대명사 what의 쓰임
❸	병렬구조	❹	주어와 동사의 수 일치
❺	전치사+관계대명사		

정답풀이

⑤ 관계절에서 remember는 타동사로 쓰였고, better than 다음에 오는 비교 대상인 the instructor's words와 대구를 이루는 말이 remember의 목적어로 필요하다. 즉, 관계절이 remember의 목적어가 없는 불완전한 구조를 이루므로 「전치사+관계대명사」 형태의 for which는 적절하지 않다. their own words를 선행사로 하는 목적격 관계대명사 which로 바꿔 써야 한다.

오답풀이

① 뒤에 완전한 구조의 절이 이어지고, 문맥상으로도 '~인지'의 뜻을 나타내는 접속사 whether는 적절하게 쓰였다.
② 전치사 to의 목적어 역할을 하며 이어지는 절에서 are learning의 목적어 역할을 해야 하므로 선행사를 포함하는 관계대명사 what의 쓰임은 적절하다.
③ 문맥상 and 앞의 checking for와 병렬구조를 이루며 뒤에 이어지는 student understanding 이하의 동명사구를 공통 목적어로 취하는 동명사 encouraging은 적절하다.
④ 동명사구인 Writing ~ material이 주어인데, 동명사구 주어는 단수 취급하므로 단수형 동사 requires는 적절하게 쓰였다.

전문해석

학생들이 파워포인트의 내용을 이해하는지 여부보다 그 파워포인트 슬라이드에 있는 모든 것을 기록하는 것에 대해 더 걱정하는 것은 종종 사실이다. 마찬가지로, 강사들은 학생들이 배우고 있는 것에 주의를 기울이지 않고 그 자료를 마치기 위해 서둘러 강의할 수도 있다. 은퇴한 미국 심리학자이자 전 미시간대 심리학과장인 McKeachie는 학생들의 자료 이해를 점검하고 장려하는 한 가지 방법, 즉 '요약하여 쓰기'에 대해 논의했다. 강의나 읽기 자료의 요약을 쓰는 것은 학생들의 인지 활동 증가를 필요로 하는데, 그들은 정보를 재구성하고 합성해야 한다. 그것은 또한 그들 자신의 말로 정보를 옮길 수 있는 기회를 학생들에게 제공하는데, 그들은 그것을 강사의 말보다 더 잘 기억할 가능성이 높을 것이다. 그러한 요약 글쓰기가 학습에 상당한 영향을 미칠 수 있음을 연구는 보여 준다.

구문풀이

1행 It is often the case [that students worry **more** about {transcribing everything from the PowerPoint slides} **than** {whether they understand those notes}].

: It은 형식상의 주어이고, [ ]가 내용상의 주어이다. [ ] 안에서 두 개의 { }는 각각 전치사 about의 목적어로 쓰인 동명사구와 명사절로, 「more ~ than ...」의 비교구문을 통해 비교되고 있다.

어휘풀이

- be the case that ~라는 것이 사실이다
- transcribe *v* 필기하다, 베끼다, 옮겨 적다

---

222 답 ②

출제 어휘 | 확인하기

①	similarly	비슷하게	↔	differently(다르게)
②	easier	더 쉬운	↔	harder(더 어려운)
③	circulate	유포하다	↔	
④	interference	간섭	↔	
⑤	pose	제기하다	↔	

정답풀이

② 사생활에 대한 권리의 범위와 한계에 대해 설명한 다음에 역접의 연결어 However로 이어지는 문장이므로, 사생활에 대한 권리의 개념이 속성에 기초한 권리 개념에서 사생활과 가족의 생활이라는 현대적 개념으로 이동함에 따라 그 권리의 한계를 설정하기가 '더 어려워졌을' 것이라는 흐름이 되어야 한다. 따라서 easier는 적절하지 않으며 반대 의미의 harder 정도로 바꿔 써야 한다.

오답풀이

① 앞에서 사생활에 대한 권리의 확대에 대해서 그 정도와 적정선을 언급했고, 같은 맥락에서 그 범위가 공공이익에 의해 '비슷하게' 제한될 것으로 볼 수 있으므로 similarly는 적절하다.
③ 사생활의 개념이 포함하는 것으로서 우리가 주시당하지 않아야 한다는 주장과 비슷한 맥락에서 우리의 특정 정보와 이미지가 허가 없이 '유포되지' 않을 것을 말하는 것이므로 circulated는 적절하다.
④ 사생활 주장의 발생 이유가 나열되는 문맥이므로, 추가적 이유로서 '간섭(interference)'으로부터의 보호 필요성을 말하는 것은 적절하다.
⑤ 역사적으로 사생활은 피해를 주는 자료의 유포를 제한하여 보호되었지만, 최근의 기술 발전으로 인해 새로운 문제가 생겨났다는 흐름이므로 기술 발전이 위협을 '제기한다(pose)'고 한 것은 적절하다.

전문해석

사생활에 대한 권리는 그것이 다른 사람의 표현의 자유에 대한 권리 혹은 정보에 대한 권리를 제한하지 않는 정도까지만 확대될 수 있다. 사생활에 대한 권리의 범위는 범죄 예방 또는 공중 보건 증진에서의 공공이익에 의해 (a) 비슷하게 제한된다. 그렇지만 우리가 속성에 기초한 권리 개념(예를 들면, 사생활에 대한 권리가 이미지와 인격을 보호할 개념)에서 사생활과 가족의 생활이라는 현대적 개념으로 이동할 때, 우리는 그 권리의 한계를 설정하기가 (b) 더 쉬운(→ 더 어려운) 것을 알게 된다. 이는 물론 변화하는 기대와 기술 진보에 대처하기 위해 적응할 수 있다는 점에서, 사생활 개념의 강점이다.

요약하면, 오늘날 사생활이란 '무엇'인가? 그 개념은 우리가 주시당하지 않아야 한다는 주장과 우리에 관한 특정 정보 및 이미지가 우리의 허가 없이 (c) 유포되어서는 안 된다는 주장을 포함한다. '왜' 이러한 사생활 주장들이 발생했을까? 그 주장들은 영향력 있는 사람들이 그렇게 주시당하는 것에 불쾌감을 느꼈기 때문에 발생했다. 더구나 사생활은 가족, 가정, 그리고 서신을 임의의 (d) 간섭으로부터 보호할 필요성을 포함했고, 또한 명예와 평판을 보호하고자 하는 확고한 의지가 있었다. 사생활은 '어떻게' 보호되는가? 역사적으로, 사생활은 피해를 주는 자료의 유포를 제한함으로써 보호되었다. 하지만 사생활 개념이 사진과 신문을 통한 이미지 재생산에 대한 대

응으로 처음 법적으로 관심을 끌게 되었다면, 자료 저장, 디지털 이미지, 인터넷과 같은 더 최근의 기술 발전은 사생활에 새로운 위협을 (e) 제기한다. 사생활에 대한 권리는 이제 그러한 난제들에 대처하기 위해 재해석되고 있다.

구문풀이

6행 However, when we move away **from** [the property-based notion of a right (where the right to privacy would protect, for example, images and personality)], **to** [modern notions of private and family life], we find **it** harder [to establish the limits of the right].

: 「from A to B」로 두 개의 명사구 [ ]가 연결되었다. ( )는 관계부사 where가 이끄는 절로, the property-based notion of a right을 수식한다. it은 find의 형식상의 목적어이며 to부정사구인 세 번째 [ ]가 내용상의 목적어이다.

어휘풀이

- privacy *n* 사생활
- scope *n* 범위
- property *n* 속성
- in that ~이라는 점에서
- advance *n* 진보, 발전
- unobserved *a* 주시당하지 않는, 관찰당하지 않는
- circulate *v* 유포하다
- arise *v* 발생하다
- incorporate *v* 포함하다, 통합하다
- interference *n* 간섭, 방해
- reputation *n* 평판, 명성
- storage *n* 저장
- threat *n* 위협
- challenge *n* 난제, 도전(적인 일)
- restrict *v* 제한하다, 한정하다
- general interest 공공이익
- notion *n* 개념
- meet *v* 대처하다
- permission *n* 허용, 허가, 허락
- take offence 불쾌감을 느끼다
- correspondence *n* 서신 (교환)
- determination *n* 확고한 의지, 결심
- reproduction *n* 재생산
- pose *v* (문제·의문 등을) 제기하다
- reinterpret *v* 재해석하다

01 어법·어휘 모의고사

01 예상하다, 기대하다 **02** 직관(력) **03** 방정식 **04** ~의 원인이 되다 **05** 정확한 **06** novelty **07** 과장된 **08** 평가 **09** (불·전깃불 등)을 끄다 **10** 섞다 **11** 넣다, 가두다 **12** 폭발 **13** 도래, 출현 **14** 신호를 보내다 **15** 장치 **16** 결점 **17** 보유하다 **18** 외과의, 수술의 **19** 논쟁하다, 토론하다 **20** 채택하다 **21** 확실하게 하다, 보장하다 **22** 근본적인, 중요한 **23** 식별하다, 확인하다 **24** 기능하다 **25** 본질적인, 고유의 **26** 소득 **27** 태도 **28** 비교 **29** 지역, 지방 **30** 풍부함 **31** 불쾌한, 마음에 들지 않는 **32** inspire **33** 해석 **34** 이전하다 **35** (인정하여 정식으로) 주다, 승인하다 **36** 분배하다, 할당하다 **37** ~의 영향을 받다 **38** 회피하다, 무시하다, 우회하다 **39** 재배, 경작 **40** 상당한 **41** 몫, 할당량

02 어법·어휘 모의고사

01 매력적인, 마음을 끄는 **02** 분명한, 명백한 **03** 나오다, 나타나다 **04** ~을 좋아하는 **05** 건축 **06** 무언의, 말 없는 **07** 진술 **08** intuitive **09** 참여 **10** 문자 그대로 **11** 사고방식, 예측, 전망 **12** 상당한, 많은 **13** 촉진시키다 **14** 폐지 **15** 개발, 이용 **16** 의도 **17** 상호의, 서로의 **18** 안내 **19** 제공하다, 공급하다 **20** 충동, 추진력 **21** 본능 **22** conscious **23** 제거하다 **24** 통찰 **25** 상황, 문맥 **26** ~와 상관없이 **27** 극복하다 **28** 장애(물) **29** 재정적인 **30** 어려움, 고난 **31** 악명 높게 **32** 책임 **33** ~을 이해하다, ~을 알아내다 **34** ~에 지원하다 **35** 상관관계 **36** 선호 **37** 사라지다 **38** 번역 **39** 참조 **40** 중대한, 결정적인 **41** 최신의

03 어법·어휘 모의고사

01 ~을 이용하다 **02** 새끼(들) **03** 구체적으로 말하면, 즉 **04** 인식 **05** incentive **06** 지속적으로 **07** 약속, 책무 **08** 인식 **09** 의심스러워하는 **10** 손상되다, 훼손하다 **11** 속이는 것, 사기 **12** 매력적인 **13** 즉각적인 **14** 규제하다 **15** 꺼리는, 주저하는 **16** 절차, 방법 **17** 분석하다 **18** 일상적인 **19** ~을 먹고 살다 **20** 이상적인 **21** 공격받기 쉬운, 취약한 **22** 따라잡다 **23** 부족의, 종족의 **24** 납득시키다, 확신시키다 **25** justify **26** 대가가 따르는, 비용이 드는 **27** 제의하다, 제기하다 **28** 상호작용 **29** 추적하다 **30** 다양한 **31** 많은, 다수의 **32** 암시하다 **33** 보장 **34** 자극 **35** 압도하다 **36** 마주하다, 만나다 **37** 과부하 **38** 마비시키다 **39** 혼란스러운 **40** 분류하다, 범주화하다 **41** 거르다, 여과하다

04 어법·어휘 모의고사

01 멸종 위기에 처한 **02** 과장해서 말하다 **03** 내재하는, 선천적인 **04** 분류하다 **05** 촉진[조장]하다, 용이하게 하다 **06** extinction **07** 상업적인 **08** 접하는 것, 경험, 노출 **09** 가축, 축산물 **10** ~을 배치하다 **11** 질서정연하게 **12** 얻다, 비롯되다 **13** 특성, 속성 **14** 얻다, 추출하다 **15** 분포 **16** 접근하기 어려운 **17** 편향된, 편견을 가진 **18** 가혹한, 거친 **19** 실험실, 연구실 **20** 매우 많은, 다수의 **21** (성질·양상 등을) 띠다[가지다] **22** 주된, 주요한 **23** 기근, 굶주림 **24** 기원하다, 유래하다 **25** 독창적인 **26** 어리석은, 황당한 **27** 조롱하다 **28** 굶주림, 기아 **29** 옹호하다 **30** suspect **31** 반대하다 **32** 정확한 **33** 상상하다 **34** 동시에 **35** 예견하다 **36** 어디에나 있음, 편재성 **37** 인공물 **38** 전달하다, 전하다 **39** 조작하다 **40** 바꾸다 **41** 시대, 시기

05 어법·어휘 모의고사

01 저항[대응]하기 힘든 **02** 폭발적으로 증가하다 **03** 가능성 **04** 무한히, 훨씬 **05** competence **06** 분명히 보여 주다, 실증하다 **07** 조립 **08** 생태상의, 생태학적인 **09** 비극, 참사 **10** 사나운, 악랄한, 사악한 **11** 재난, 천재지변 **12** 비교적인, 상대적인 **13** 효율(성) **14** 바꾸다, 변형시키다 **15** 언급하다 **16** 바람직한 **17** 허용되는 **18** 하찮은, 중요하지 않은 **19** 긴장감 **20** 임박한, 절박한 **21** 좌절시키다, 반대로 작용하다 **22** ~을 실천에 옮기다 **23** 시행 **24** 덜다, 경감하다 **25** 의무 **26** 필기하다, 베끼다, 옮겨 적다 **27** ~을 끝내다, ~을 마치다 **28** cognitive **29** 제한하다, 한정하다 **30** 범위 **31** 유포하다 **32** 발생하다 **33** 포함하다, 통합하다 **34** 간섭, 방해 **35** 확고한 의지, 결심 **36** 평판, 명성 **37** (문제·의문 등을) 제기하다 **38** 위협 **39** 재해석하다 **40** 난제, 도전(적인 일) **41** 강의

메가스터디 고등학습 시리즈

메가스터디 N제

영어영역 어법·어휘

정답 및 해설

메가스터디BOOKS

내용 문의 02-6984-6908 | 구입 문의 02-6984-6868,9 | www.megastudybooks.com

최신 기출 *All* × 우수 기출 *Pick*

수능 기출 올픽

수능 만점을 위한
새로운 기출 학습의 시작

수능 대비에 꼭 필요한 기출문제만 담았다!
BOOK 1 × BOOK 2 효율적인 학습 구성

BOOK 1 최신 3개년 수능·평가원 등 기출 전체 수록
BOOK 2 최신 3개년 이전 기출 중 **우수 문항** 선별 수록

국어 문학 l 독서
수학 수학 l 수학 ll l 확률과 통계 l 미적분
영어 독해

메가스터디BOOKS